THE SOC+ SOLUTION

Print

SOC+ delivers all the key terms and all the content for the **Sociology** course through a visually engaging and easy-to-review print experience.

Digital

 MINDTAP

MindTap enables you to stay organized and study efficiently by providing a single location for all your course materials and study aids. Built-in apps leverage social media and the latest learning technology to help you succeed.

1 Open the Access Card included with this text.

2 Follow the steps on the card.

3 Study.

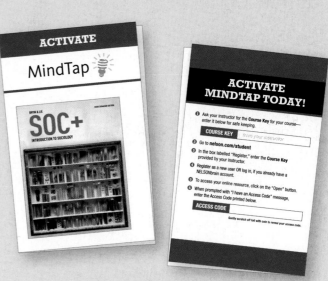

ACTIVATE
MindTap

BRYM & LIE
SOC+
INTRODUCTION TO SOCIOLOGY

ACTIVATE MINDTAP TODAY!

❶ Ask your instructor for the **Course Key** for your course—enter it below for safe keeping.

COURSE KEY *from your instructor*

❷ Go to **nelson.com/student**

❸ In the box labelled "Register," enter the **Course Key** provided by your instructor.

❹ Register as a new user OR log in, if you already have a NELSONbrain account.

❺ To access your online resource, click on the "Open" button.

❻ When prompted with "I have an Access Code" message, enter the Access Code printed below.

ACCESS CODE

Gently scratch off foil with coin to reveal your access code.

Student Resources

- Interactive eBook
- Flashcards
- Chapter Review Cards
- Matching Exercises
- Media Quizzes
- Pre-and Post-Quizzes
- Critical Thinking Questions
- Polling Questions

Students: **nelson.com/student**

Instructor Resources

- Access to All Student Resources
- Gradable Assignments
  — Social Policy
  — Sociological Imagination
  — Test Bank
- Instructor's Manual
- PowerPoint® Slides
- Image Library
- LMS Integration

Instructors: **nelson.com/instructor**

SOC+

Third Canadian Edition

ROBERT BRYM

University of Toronto

JOHN LIE

University of California, Berkeley

NELSON

NELSON

SOC+, Third Canadian Edition

by Robert Brym and John Lie

VP, Product and Partnership Solutions K–20: Anne Williams

Publisher, Digital and Print Content: Leanna MacLean

Marketing Manager: Terry Fedorkiw

Content Development Manager: Toni Chahley

Photo and Permissions Researcher: Julie Pratt

Production Project Manager: Jennifer Hare

Copy Editor: June Trusty

Proofreader: Linda Szostak

Indexer: Belle Wong

Design Director: Ken Phipps

Higher Education Design PM: Pamela Johnston

Interior Design Revisions: Sharon Lucas

Cover Design: Trinh Truong

Cover Image: © Michael Mapes; HolyCrazyLazy/ Shutterstock (cement background)

Compositor: MPS Limited

Library and Archives Canada Cataloguing in Publication Data

Brym, Robert J., 1951-, author
    SOC+ / Robert Brym, University of Toronto ; John Lie, University of California, Berkeley. — Third Canadian edition.

Includes bibliographical references and index.
ISBN 978-0-17-669999-4 (paperback).

    1. Sociology. 2. Sociology—Canada. I. Lie, John, author II. Title. III. Title: Sociology plus.

HM586.B792 2017   301
C2016-907087-5

ISBN-13: 978-0-17-669999-4
ISBN-10: 0-17-669999-6

About the Cover

Seventy-five years ago, adults rarely changed their sense of who they were, that is, their identity. Religious conversion was rare. Changing one's sex was unheard of. Married people tended to remain married. Most people voted for the same party election after election. Ethnicities tended to be singular and fixed for life.

Today, identity tends to be fluid if not fractured, as the cover photo by Michael Mapes suggests. People are freer than ever to reinvent themselves. The cover photo thus invites readers to explore one of *SOC+*'s main themes: how the Internet, multiculturalism, globalization, the erosion of authority, international migration, and other social forces have destabilized human identity.

BRIEF CONTENTS

wavebreakmedia/Shutterstock.com

CONTENTS

3 Socialization 48

Mark Makela/Corbis/Getty Image

© Tomas Loewy

4 From Social Interaction to Social Organizations 70

5 Deviance and Crime 90

Alex Milan Tracy/Sipa USA/AP Images

Steve Raymer/Corbis Documentary/Getty Images

6 Social Stratification: Canadian and Global Perspectives 110

Culture Club/Hulton Archive/Getty Images

Bruce Jenner on cereal box: Suntzulynn for LE/Splash News/Newscom

9 Families 182

Annette Shaff/Shutterstock.com

10 Religion and Education 204

Sergen Sezgin/Anadolu Agency/Getty Images

11 Health and Medicine 230

Tetra Images/Getty Images

12 The Mass Media 248

© Koren Shadmi

13 Technology, the Environment, and Social Movements 266

© Matthew Chattle/Alamy Stock Photo

© Michael Mapes

1

Introducing Sociology

LEARNING OBJECTIVES

In this chapter, you will learn to

LO¹ Define sociology.

LO² Identify the social relations that surround you, permeate you, and influence your behaviour.

LO³ Summarize the four main schools of sociological theory.

LO⁴ Describe how sociological research seeks to improve people's lives and test ideas using scientific methods.

LO⁵ Distinguish the four main methods of collecting sociological data.

LO⁶ Explain how sociology can help us deal with major challenges that society faces today.

INTRODUCTION
MY ROAD TO SOCIOLOGY

"When I started college at the age of 18," says Robert Brym, "I was bewildered by the variety of courses I could choose from. Having now taught sociology for more than 35 years and met thousands of undergraduates, I am quite sure most students today feel as I did then.

"One source of confusion for me was uncertainty about why I was in university in the first place. Like you, I knew higher education could improve my chance of finding good work. But, like most students, I also had a sense that higher education is supposed to provide something more than just the training necessary to start a career that is interesting and pays well. Several high school teachers and guidance counsellors had told me that university was also supposed to 'broaden my horizons' and teach me to 'think critically.' I wasn't sure what they meant, but they made it sound interesting enough to encourage me to know more. In my first year, I decided to take mainly 'practical' courses that might prepare me for a law degree (economics, political science, and psychology). However, I also enrolled in a couple of other courses to indulge my 'intellectual' side (philosophy, drama). One thing I knew for sure: I didn't want to study sociology.

"Sociology, I came to believe, was thin soup with uncertain ingredients. When I asked a few second- and third-year students in my dorm what sociology is, I received different answers. They variously defined sociology as the science of social inequality, the study of how to create the ideal society, the analysis of how and why people assume different roles in their lives, and a method for figuring out why people don't always do what they are supposed to do. I found all this confusing and decided to forgo sociology for what seemed to be tastier courses."

LO¹ A CHANGE OF MIND

"Despite the opinion I'd formed, I found myself taking no fewer than four sociology courses a year after starting university. That revolution in my life was partly due to the influence of an extraordinary professor I happened to meet just before I began

sociology The systematic study of human behaviour in social context.

social structures Stable patterns of social relations.

sociological imagination The quality of mind that enables one to see the connection between personal troubles and social structures.

my second year. He set me thinking in an altogether new way about what I could and should do with my life. He exploded some of my deepest beliefs. He started me thinking sociologically.

"Specifically, he first encouraged me to think about the dilemma of all thinking people. Life is finite. If we want to make the most of it, we must figure out how best to live. That is no easy task. It requires study, reflection, and the selection of values and goals. Ideally, he said, higher education is supposed to supply students with just that opportunity. Finally, I was beginning to understand what I could expect from university apart from job training.

"The professor also convinced me that sociology in particular could open up a new and superior way of comprehending my world. Specifically, he said, it could clarify my place in society, how I might best manoeuver through it, and perhaps even how I might contribute to improving it, however modestly. Before beginning my study of sociology, I had always taken for granted that things happen in the world—and to me—because physical and emotional forces cause them. Famine, I thought, is caused by drought, war by territorial greed, economic success by hard work, marriage by love, suicide by bottomless depression, rape by depraved lust. But now this professor repeatedly threw evidence in my face that contradicted my easy formulas. If drought causes famine, why have so many famines occurred in perfectly normal weather conditions or involved some groups hoarding or destroying food so others would starve? If hard work causes prosperity, why are so many hard workers poor? If love causes marriage, why does violence against women and children occur in so many families? And so the questions multiplied.

"As if it were not enough that the professor's sociological evidence upset many of my assumptions about the way the world worked, he also challenged me to understand sociology's unique way of explaining social life. He defined **sociology** as the systematic study of human behaviour in social context. He explained that social causes are distinct from physical and emotional causes. Understanding social causes can help clarify otherwise inexplicable features of famine, marriage, and so on. In public school, my teachers taught me that people are free to do what they want with their lives. However, my new professor taught me that the organization of the social world opens some opportunities and closes others, thus limiting our freedom and helping to make us what we are. By examining the operation of these powerful social forces, he said, sociology can help us to know ourselves, our capabilities, and limitations. I was hooked. And so, of course, I hope you will be, too."

When we sat down to plan this book, we figured we stood the best chance of hooking you if we drew many of our examples from aspects of social life that you enjoy and know well, such as contemporary music, fashion, sports, the Web, social networking, and other aspects of popular culture. Chances are that popular culture envelopes you and makes you feel as comfortable as a favourite piece of clothing does. Our aim is to show you that underlying the taken-for-granted fabric of your life are patterns of social relations that powerfully influence your tastes, your hopes, your actions, and your future—even though you may be only dimly aware of them now.

LO² THE SOCIOLOGICAL IMAGINATION

SOCIAL STRUCTURES

You have known for a long time that you live in a society. Until now, you may not have fully appreciated that society also lives in you. Patterns of social relations affect your innermost thoughts and feelings, influence your actions, and help shape who you are Sociologists call stable patterns of social relations **social structures**.

Nearly 60 years ago, the great American sociologist C. Wright Mills (1916–62) wrote that the sociologist's main task is to identify and explain the connections between people's personal troubles, the changing social structures in which they are embedded, and ways they can contribute to improving their lives and the state of the world. He called the ability to see these connections the **sociological imagination**. Mills wrote:

> [People] do not usually define the troubles they endure in terms of historical change. . . . Seldom aware of the intricate connection between the patterns of their own lives and the course of world history, ordinary [people] do not usually know what this connection means for the kind of [people] they are becoming and for the kind of history-making in which they might take part. . . . What they need . . . is a quality of mind that will help them to [see] . . . what is going on in the world and . . . what may be happening within themselves. It is this quality . . . that . . . may be called the sociological imagination. —C. Wright Mills (1959: 3–4)

To gain a better sense of what Mills meant by the sociological imagination, consider a story that has been repeated, with variations, many times. A 50-year-old woman loses a good job on the assembly line of a southern Ontario car plant when production moves to Mexico. After half a year of collecting employment insurance, she manages to land a job at the checkout counter of a local Walmart. She earns less than half her previous salary. She had hoped to help her son pay tuition when he started college but can no longer afford that because her income is now barely enough to pay for food, rent, and utilities. Her son is a good student but he now has to delay his plan to go to college for at least a couple years while he earns tuition money. The woman blames herself for not being able to land a better job. She becomes depressed. To cope, she starts smoking and drinking more—and taking high-interest payday loans to feed her habits. The son's resentment and anger toward his mother grow, so they argue a lot. Family life, once happy, becomes miserable.

Will the woman develop a chronic illness because of the stress, the smoking, and the drinking? Will the son get caught stealing clothes he can't afford? Will he ever make it to college? Or will they apply the sociological imagination to their situation and come to realize that their personal troubles are the result of powerful social forces that they can help to control?

Here is what the sociological imagination could teach them: Since the 1970s, many large North American corporations have been moving manufacturing industries to low-wage countries like Mexico and China so they can pay workers less and earn bigger profits. Millions of North Americans have seen their steady, relatively high-paying jobs vanish. Their quality of life has gone downhill. Yet some countries have been able to withstand the challenge of deindustrialization, which is universal. For instance, in Denmark, the government gives people who lose jobs relatively generous unemployment benefits for a couple of years, organizes programs that retrain them for skilled jobs that are in high demand, and requires that they complete such a program. Denmark therefore knows nothing like the growing unemployment and poverty that grips parts of southern Ontario, let alone the United States, where government programs are even less generous and economic inequality is higher (see the Sociology on the Tube feature in this chapter).

SOCIOLOGY ON THE TUBE

Donald Trump and Shock TV

The 2016 U.S. presidential race revealed a stark division among American workers who had been directly affected by massive job losses in the manufacturing

Donald Trump

Gino Santa Maria/Shutterstock.com

sector. A minority supported Bernie Sanders, the unsuccessful Democratic hopeful who championed the Danish model of economic restructuring. However, a disproportionately large number of white, relatively uneducated, low-income, and downwardly mobile citizens supported Donald Trump, who turned American politics into a kind of *Jerry Springer Show* (Thompson, 2016).

In 2016, Trump was already famous for his big real estate deals, his popular reality TV show, *The Apprentice*, and his widely publicized but untrue claim five years earlier that Barack Obama was ineligible to be president of the United States because he was born overseas. However, during the 2016 campaign, Trump became the world's most talked-about person. He achieved this feat by boasting unashamedly to national TV audiences about everything from his financial successes to his physical endowments, repeatedly using foul language to demean his opponents, favourably quoting Mussolini, Italy's fascist dictator during World War II, failing to disavow the support of white supremacist organizations, taking on the Pope, and making outrageous, racist promises. Among other things, Trump said that, as president, he would deport 12 million people of Mexican origin, whom he described as rapists and drug traffickers; ban Muslim immigration and carpet bomb the wives and children of Muslim terrorists; block Chinese and other foreign imports; and so on. Mainstream Republicans had previously considered it too politically dangerous to exploit simmering and usually privately expressed racist sentiment in the United States. Trump recognized that he could perhaps ride the wave of intolerance all the way to the presidency.

(Continued)

Trump's run for the presidency illustrates how much television reflects and influences the social world. Accordingly, in each chapter of this book, we analyze one or more TV shows to help you realize that even taken-for-granted aspects of your everyday life can be full of deeper meaning if you apply the sociological imagination to them.

Critical Thinking Questions

1. What *sociological* factors might have been responsible for the opposed views of Sanders and Trump supporters?
2. Are there Canadian counterparts to Sanders and Trump? If not, why not? If so, are they less extreme in their views? If so, why?

If the woman and her son—and hundreds of thousands of other like them—exercised the sociological imagination, they would realize that, collectively, they could help to elect a government that institutes similar policies in this country. They would stand a better chance of changing the course of historical forces that at first seem unstoppable, fixing a harmful aspect of Canada's social structure and improving their quality of live. That is what Mills had in mind when he introduced the idea of the sociological imagination. The Sociology at the Movies feature in this chapter will help you understand how the sociological imagination works in a very different context.

SOCIOLOGY AT THE MOVIES

12 Years a Slave

The first slaves in the Americas were Aboriginal people and white criminals brought over from England. However, they could not satisfy the demand of sugar, tobacco, and cotton plantations for cheap labour. That is why about 24 million West African blacks were rounded up like cattle and shipped across the Atlantic as slaves. In addition, free blacks in the northern United States were sometimes kidnapped and sold as slaves in the South.

One case involved Solomon Northup, an educated, economically successful, free black man with a wife and two children. Abducted from Washington, D.C., in 1841, he was taken to Louisiana and enslaved there until an itinerant Canadian carpenter helped to free him in 1853.

Northup's 1855 memoir, *Twelve Years a Slave*, became the basis for a movie of the same name. Hailed as the first realistic cinematic portrayal of slavery in the New World, it won the Oscar for best picture in 2013.

The movie is unspeakably upsetting, forcing audience members to wonder time and again how normal people could have engaged in such unrelenting cruelty toward other human beings. To the degree it provides an answer, it is this: The remorselessly brutal slave masters were anything but normal. Edwin Epps (played by Michael Fassbender) was the master of Solomon Northup (played by Chiwetel Ejiofor). He is portrayed as

a madman who rapes, beats, whips, demeans, and psychologically tortures his slaves with gusto. And of course he is a racist too, regarding blacks as more animal than human. When challenged by his Canadian carpenter to explain, "in the sight of God, what is the difference between a white man and a black man?" he replies, "You might as well ask what the difference is between a white man and a baboon. Now, I've seen one of them critters in Orleans that knowed just as much as any nigger I've got" (quoted in Northup, 1855: 266–7).

Notwithstanding the merits of *12 Years a Slave* as a movie, its explanation for slavery and the cruelties that derive from it lacks sociological imagination. It did not take sadistic madmen like Epps to enslave and brutalize other human beings. Enslavement and brutalization were normal practices among perfectly well-adjusted, church-going plantation owners in the southern United States, the Caribbean, and South America in the mid-nineteenth century. Nor was racism the cause of slavery, as is evident from the fact that white English prisoners could serve perfectly well as slaves. Rather, as Eric Williams (an historian and the first president of Trinidad and Tobago) wrote, "Slavery was not born of racism;

Chiwetel Ejiofor in *12 Years a Slave*

Regency Enterprises/The Kobal Collection at Art Resource, NY

racism was the consequence of slavery" (Williams, 1944: 8). Said differently, landowners were capitalists. They wanted to increase their profits. Yet they were constrained from doing so by a severe labour shortage. Slavery was the institutional mechanism that allowed them to realize their ambition. Thus, racism justified slavery but was not its cause. Here we have an explanation for slavery that employs the sociological imagination. It focuses on the way social relations influenced landowners' thoughts and actions.

Similarly for Epps's claim that blacks are no different from baboons. Samuel Bass, the Canadian carpenter (played by Brad Pitt), had the appropriate sociological response:

> These niggers are human beings. If they don't know as much as their masters, whose fault is it? They are not *allowed* to know anything. You have books and papers, and can go where you please, and gather intelligence in a thousand ways. But your slaves have no privileges. You'd whip one of them if caught reading a book. They are held in bondage, generation after generation, deprived of mental improvement, and who can expect them to possess much knowledge! . . . If they are baboons . . .

you and men like you will have to answer for it. —Solomon Northup (1855: 267–68)

Intuitively, Bass was employing the sociological imagination. He identified the harmful social structure underlying the plight of black slaves and suggested a program for changing it and thus improving their quality of life: End slavery and treat them as equals.

Understanding the social constraints and possibilities for freedom that envelop us requires an active sociological imagination. The sociological imagination urges us to connect biography with history and social structure just like Bass did—to make sense of our lives and the lives of others against a larger historical and social background and to act in light of our understanding. Although movies are just entertainment to many people, they often achieve by different means what the sociological imagination aims to accomplish. Therefore, in each chapter of this book, we review a movie to shed light on topics of sociological importance.

Critical Thinking Questions

1. Have you ever tried to put events in your own life into the context of history and social structure?
2. Did the exercise help you make sense of your life? If so, how?

An important step in broadening your sociological awareness involves recognizing that four levels of social structure surround and permeate us. Think of these structures as concentric circles radiating out from you (Figure 1.1):

- **Microstructures** are patterns of intimate social relations formed during face-to-face interaction. Families and friendship cliques are examples of microstructures.
- **Mesostructures** are patterns of social relations in organizations that involve people who are often not intimately acquainted and who often do not interact face to face. Social organizations such as colleges and government bureaucracies are examples of mesostructures.
- **Macrostructures** are overarching patterns of social relations that lie above and beyond mesostructures. One such macrostructure is **patriarchy**, a system of power relations and customary practices that help to ensure male dominance in economic, political, and other spheres of life.
- **Global structures** are the fourth level of society that surrounds and permeates us. Economic relations among countries and patterns of worldwide travel and communication are examples of global structures.

Personal problems are connected to social structures at the micro, meso, macro, and global levels. Whether the personal problem involves finding a job, keeping a marriage intact, or acting justly to end world poverty, considering the influence of social structures on us broadens our understanding of the problems we face and suggests appropriate courses of action.

The sociological imagination is only a couple of hundred years old. Although in ancient and medieval times some philosophers wrote about society, their thinking was not sociological. They believed that God and nature controlled society. These philosophers spent much of their time

mesostructures Patterns of social relations in organizations that involve people who are often not intimately acquainted and who often do not interact face to face.

macrostructures Overarching patterns of social relations that lie outside and above one's circle of intimates and acquaintances.

patriarchy A system of power relations and customary practices that help to ensure male dominance in economic, political, and other spheres of life.

microstructures Patterns of social relations formed during face-to-face interaction.

global structures Patterns of social relations that lie outside and above the national level.

FIGURE 1.1 **The Four Levels of Social Structure**

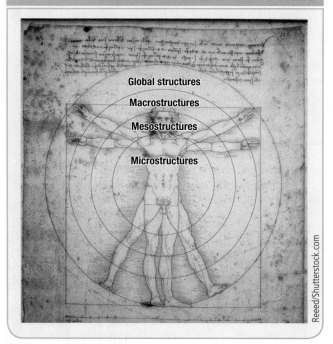

Source: *Vitruvian Man* by Leonardo Da Vinci.

Scientific Revolution
Beginning in Europe about 1550, a movement to promote the view that sound conclusions about the workings of the world must be based on solid evidence, not just speculation.

theory A conjecture about the way observed facts are related.

Democratic Revolution
The process, beginning about 1750, in which the citizens of the United States, France, and other countries broadened their participation in government, thereby suggesting that people can organize society and solve social problems.

ORIGINS OF THE SOCIOLOGICAL IMAGINATION

The sociological imagination was born when three revolutions pushed people to think about society in an entirely new way.

The Scientific Revolution

The **Scientific Revolution** began about 1550. It en-couraged the view that sound conclusions about the workings of the world must be based on evidence, not speculation. People often link the Scientific Revolution to specific ideas, such as Copernicus's theory that Earth revolves around the Sun.

sketching blueprints for the ideal society and urging people to follow those blueprints. They relied on speculation rather than evidence to reach conclusions about how society worked.

(A **theory** is a conjecture about the way observed facts are related.) However, science is less a collection of ideas than a method of inquiry. For instance, in 1609, Galileo pointed his newly invented telescope at the heavens, made some careful observations, and showed that his observations fit Copernicus's theory. This is the core of the scientific method: using evidence to make a case for a particular point of view. By the mid-1600s, some philosophers were calling for a science of society. When sociology emerged as a distinct discipline in the nineteenth century, commitment to the scientific method was one firm pillar of the sociological imagination.

The Democratic Revolution

The **Democratic Revolution** began about 1750. It suggested that people are responsible for organizing society and that human intervention can therefore solve social problems. Before the Democratic Revolution, most people thought that God ordained the social order. The American Revolution (1775–83) and the French Revolution (1789–99) helped to undermine that idea. These democratic upheavals showed that society could experience massive change quickly. They proved that people could replace unsatisfactory rulers. They suggested that *people* control society. The implications for social thought were profound, for if it was possible to change society through human intervention, a science of society could play a big role. The new science could help people find ways of overcoming social problems and improving the welfare

Liberty Leading the People. Eugene Delacroix, 1830. The democratic forces unleashed by the French Revolution suggested that people are responsible for organizing society and that human intervention can therefore solve social problems. As such, democracy was a foundation stone of sociology.

of citizens. Much of the justification for sociology as a science arose out of the democratic revolutions that shook Europe and North America.

The Industrial Revolution

The **Industrial Revolution** began about 1780. It created a host of new and serious social problems that attracted the attention of social thinkers. As a result of the growth of industry, masses of people moved from countryside to city, worked agonizingly long hours in crowded and dangerous mines and factories, lost faith in their religions, confronted faceless bureaucracies, and reacted to the filth and poverty of their existence by means of strikes, crime, revolutions, and wars. Scholars had never seen a sociological laboratory like this. The Scientific Revolution suggested that a science of society was possible. The Democratic Revolution suggested that people could intervene to improve society. The Industrial Revolution now presented social thinkers with a host of pressing social problems crying out for solution. They responded by giving birth to the sociological imagination.

 **FOUNDERS**

ÉMILE DURKHEIM AND FUNCTIONALISM

Émile Durkheim (1858–1917) is generally considered to be the first modern sociologist. Durkheim argued that human behaviour is influenced by "social facts" or the social relations in which people are embedded. He illustrated his argument in a famous study of suicide (Durkheim, 1951 [1897]). Many scholars of the day believed that psychological disorders cause suicide, but Durkheim's analysis of European government statistics and hospital records demonstrated no correlation between rates of psychological disorder and suicide rates in different categories of the population. Instead, he found that suicide rates varied with different degrees of **social solidarity** in different population categories. (A **rate** is the number of times an event happens in a given period per 100 000 members of the population.)

According to Durkheim, the greater the degree to which a group's members share beliefs and values, and the more frequently and intensely they interact, the more social solidarity exists in the group. In turn, the higher the level of social solidarity, the more firmly anchored individuals are to the social world and the less likely they are to commit suicide if adversity strikes. In other words, Durkheim found that groups with a high degree of social solidarity had lower suicide rates than groups

Émile Durkheim (1858–1917) was the first professor of sociology in France and is considered to be the first modern sociologist. In *The Rules of Sociological Method* (1938 [1895]) and *Suicide* (1951 [1897]), he argued that human behaviour is shaped by "social facts," or the social context in which people are embedded. In Durkheim's view, social facts define the constraints and opportunities within which people must act. Durkheim was also keenly interested in the conditions that promote social order in "primitive" and modern societies, and he explored this problem in depth in such works as *The Division of Labor in Society* (1997 [1893]) and *The Elementary Forms of the Religious Life* (1976 [1915/1912]).

Bettmann/Getty Images

with a low degree of solidarity—at least to a point (see Figure 1.2 and Figure 1.3). For instance, married people were half as likely as unmarried people were to commit suicide because marriage typically created social ties and a kind of moral cement that bound the individuals to society. Women were less likely to commit suicide than men were because women were generally more involved in the intimate social relations of family life. Jews were less likely to commit suicide than Christians were because centuries of

Industrial Revolution
Beginning in Britain in the 1780s, a process of rapid economic transformation that involved the large-scale application of science and technology to industrial processes, the creation of factories, and the formation of a working class.

social solidarity A property of social groups that increases with the degree to which a group's members share beliefs and values, and the frequency and intensity with which they interact.

rate The number of times an event happens in a given period per 100 000 members of the population.

FIGURE 1.2 **Durkheim's Theory of Suicide**

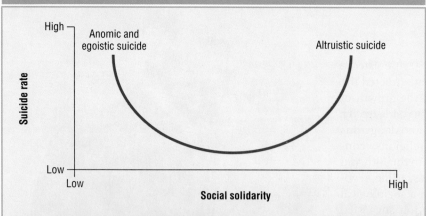

Durkheim's theory of suicide states that the suicide rate declines and then rises as social solidarity increases. Suicide in low-solidarity settings may be egoistic or anomic. **Egoistic suicide** results from the poor integration of people into society because of weak social ties to others. Someone who is unemployed and unmarried is thus more likely to commit suicide than is someone who is employed and married. **Anomic suicide** occurs when vague norms govern behaviour. The rate of anomic suicide is likely to be high among people living in a society that lacks a widely shared code of morality. Durkheim called suicides that occur in high-solidarity settings *altruistic*. **Altruistic suicide** occurs when norms tightly govern behaviour. Soldiers who knowingly give up their lives to protect comrades commit altruistic suicide out of a deep sense of patriotism and comradeship.

Source: From BRYM/LIE. *Sociology*, 1E. © 2009 Nelson Education Ltd. Reproduced by permission. www.cengage.com/permissions.

egoistic suicide The type of suicide that results from a lack of integration of the individual into society because of weak social ties to others.

anomic suicide The type of suicide that occurs when norms governing behaviour are vaguely defined.

altruistic suicide The type of suicide that occurs when norms govern behaviour so tightly that individual actions are often in the group interest.

functionalist theory Focuses on how human behaviour is governed by social structures that are based mainly on shared values and that contribute to social stability.

persecution had turned them into a group that was more defensive and tightly knit. Elderly people were more prone than young and middle-aged people were to take their own lives when faced with misfortune because they were most likely to live alone, to have lost a spouse, and to lack a job and a wide network of friends.

Durkheim's argument is an early example of functionalist theory. **Functionalist theory** focuses on how human behaviour is governed by social structures that are based mainly on shared values and that contribute to social stability. In general, functionalism incorporates the following features:

- *Social structure.* Functionalist theories stress that human behaviour is governed by stable patterns of social relations, or social structures. The social relations that Durkheim emphasized were patterns of social solidarity. Functionalists are chiefly interested in macrostructures.

- *Social stability.* Functionalist theories show how social structures maintain or fail to maintain social stability. For example, Durkheim argued that high social solidarity contributes to the maintenance of social order. He also noted that the growth of industries and cities during the Industrial Revolution caused population movements, the erosion of religious beliefs, and other rapid changes that lowered the level of social solidarity. For Durkheim, rising suicide rates were symptoms of these larger social ills.

- *Shared values.* Functionalist theories emphasize that social structures are based mainly on shared values. For example, when Durkheim wrote about social solidarity, he sometimes meant the frequency and intensity of social interaction, but more often he thought of social solidarity as a kind of moral cement that binds people together.

- *Equilibrium.* Functionalism suggests that re-establishing equilibrium can best solve most social problems. For instance, Durkheim held that social solidarity could be increased by creating new associations of employers and workers that would lower workers' expectations about what they should hope for in life. If more people could agree on wanting less, Durkheim wrote, social solidarity would rise and there would be lower suicide rates.

TALCOTT PARSONS AND ROBERT MERTON

By the 1930s, functionalism was popular in North America and it remained so until the 1960s. Talcott Parsons (1902–79) was a leading proponent of functionalism. He argued that society is well integrated and in equilibrium when the family successfully raises new generations, the military successfully defends society against external threats, schools are able to teach students the skills and values they need to function as productive

FIGURE 1.3 Suicide by Age and Sex, Canada, 2011

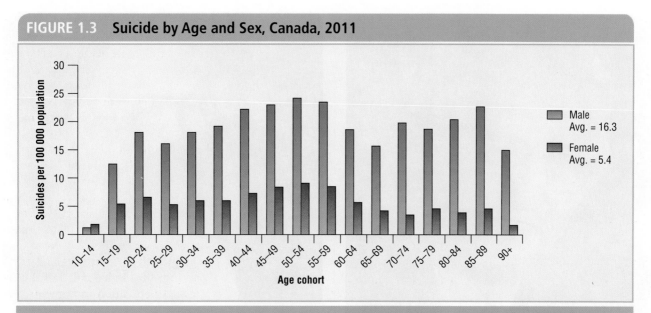

Suicide among younger age cohorts is no longer rare, as it was in Durkheim's day. Durkheim's theory helps us to understand why. In brief, shared moral principles and strong social ties have eroded since the early 1960s for Canada's younger age cohorts for the following reasons:

1. More than half of Canadians attended religious services weekly in the 1960s. Today the figure is less than one-third, and it is only one-sixth for people born after 1960.

2. While unemployment rose from around 3 percent in the 1960s to 7.0 percent in August 2016 and nearly twice as high for Canadians between the ages of 15 and 24.

3. The divorce rate has increased sixfold since the early 1960s and out-of-marriage births are more common, so children enjoy less frequent and intimate social interaction with parents and less adult supervision.

4. Since the 1960s, an increasingly large proportion of lesbians, gays, bisexuals, and transsexuals have come "out of the closet" and are prone to being bullied, terrorized, and socially excluded in school. Consequently, a high proportion of youth suicides are committed by members of sexual minorities (Carole, 2011).

5. The Canadian government and major Canadian churches did much to destroy the social fabric of Aboriginal communities in the twentieth century, resulting in extraordinarily high levels of unemployment, substance abuse, cultural disorientation, and suicide (see Chapter 7, Race and Ethnicity). Today, Aboriginal youth suffer from an extraordinarily high rate of suicide.

In sum, less firmly rooted in society and less likely to share moral standards, young people in Canada today are more likely than they were in the 1960s to take their own lives if they find themselves in the midst of a personal crisis.

Source: Statistics Canada. 2014a. "Suicides and suicide rate, by sex and age group." http://www.statcan.gc.ca/tables-tableaux/sum-som/l01/cst01/hlth66a-eng.htm (retrieved 23 June 2015).

adults, and religions create a shared moral code among people (Parsons, 1951).

However, Robert Merton (1910–2003), the other leading functionalist of the day, criticized Parsons for exaggerating the degree to which members of society share common values and social institutions contribute to social harmony. Merton proposed that social structures may have different consequences for different groups, and some of those consequences may be disruptive or have **dysfunctions** (Merton, 1968 [1949]). Moreover, said Merton, although some functions are **manifest** (intended and easily observed), others are **latent** (unintended and less obvious). For instance, a manifest function of schools is to transmit skills from one generation to the next. A latent function of schools is to encourage the development of a separate youth culture that often conflicts with parents' values (Coleman, 1961; Hersch, 1998).

KARL MARX AND CONFLICT THEORY

Karl Marx (1818–83) observed the destitution and discontent produced by the Industrial Revolution and

dysfunctions Effects of social structures that create social instability.

manifest functions Visible and intended effects of social structures.

latent functions Invisible and unintended effects of social structures.

S. D. Clark (1910–2003) received his Ph.D. from the University of Toronto. He became the first chair of the Department of Sociology at that institution. Born in Lloydminster, Alberta, he became known for his studies of Canadian social development as a process of disorganization and reorganization on a series of economic frontiers (Clark, 1968). The influence of functionalism on his work is apparent in his emphasis on the way society re-establishes equilibrium after experiencing disruptions caused by economic change.

Karl Marx (1818–83) was a revolutionary thinker whose ideas affected not just the growth of sociology but also the course of world history. He held that major socio-historical changes are the result of conflict between society's main social classes. In his major work, *Capital* (1967 [1867–94]), Marx argued that capitalism would produce such misery and collective power among workers that they would eventually take control of government and create a classless society in which production would be based on human need rather than profit.

social classes Positions people occupy in a hierarchy that is shaped by the source or amount of their income and wealth.

class conflict The struggle between classes to resist and overcome the opposition of other classes.

conflict theory Highlights the tensions underlying existing social structures and the capacity of those tensions to burst into the open and cause social change.

class consciousness Awareness of being a member of a social class.

proposed a very different argument about the way societies develop (Marx, 1904 [1859]; Marx and Engels, 1972 [1848]). He focussed on the study of **social classes**, the positions people occupy in a hierarchy that is shaped by the source or amount of their income and wealth. (Marx emphasized source of income as the determinant of a person's class position; others have emphasized amount of income.) **Class conflict**, the struggle between classes to resist and overcome the opposition of other classes, lies at the centre of Marx's ideas. In his writings lie the seeds of **conflict theory**, which highlights the tensions underlying existing social structures and the capacity of those tensions to burst into the open and cause social change.

Specifically, Marx argued that owners of industry are eager to improve the way work is organized and to adopt new tools, machines, and production methods because these innovations allow them to produce more efficiently, earn higher profits, and drive inefficient competitors out of business. However, the drive for profits also causes capitalists to concentrate workers in larger and larger establishments, keep wages as low as possible, and invest as little as possible in improving working conditions. Consequently, wrote Marx, a large and growing class of poor workers comes to oppose a small and shrinking class of wealthy owners.

Marx believed that workers would ultimately become aware of belonging to the same exploited class. He called this awareness **class consciousness**. He believed that working-class consciousness would encourage the growth of trade unions and labour parties. According to Marx, these organizations would eventually seek to put an end to private ownership of property, replacing it with a communist society, defined as a system in which there is no private property and everyone shares property and wealth according to their needs.

MAX WEBER

Although some of Marx's ideas have been usefully adapted to the study of contemporary society, his predictions about the inevitable collapse of capitalism were soon questioned. Max Weber (pronounced VAY-ber; 1864–1920), a German sociologist who wrote his major works two or three decades after Marx died, was among the first to find flaws in Marx's argument (Weber, 1946). Weber observed the rapid growth of the service sector of the economy, with its many nonmanual workers and professionals. He argued that many members of these occupational groups stabilize society because they enjoy higher status and income than do manual workers employed in the manufacturing sector. In addition, Weber showed that class conflict is not the only driving force of history. In his

Max Weber (1864–1920), Germany's greatest sociologist, profoundly influenced the development of the discipline worldwide. Engaged in a lifelong "debate with Marx's ghost," Weber held that economic circumstances alone do not explain the rise of capitalism. As he showed in *The Protestant Ethic and the Spirit of Capitalism* (1958 [1904–05]), independent developments in the religious realm had unintended, beneficial consequences for capitalist development in some parts of Europe. He also argued that capitalism would not necessarily give way to socialism. Instead, he regarded the growth of bureaucracy and the overall "rationalization" of life as the defining characteristics of the modern age. These themes were developed in *Economy and Society* (1968 [1914]).

Brown Brothers

view, politics and religion are also important sources of historical change.

Other social thinkers pointed out that Marx did not understand how investing in technology would make it possible for workers to toil fewer hours under less oppressive conditions. Nor did he foresee that higher wages, better working conditions, and welfare-state benefits would pacify manual workers.

Although Weber and others called into question the particulars of Marx's ideas, we can identify the general principles of conflict theory in his writings:

- *Macro-level structures.* Conflict theory focuses on large, macro-level structures, such as "class relations" or patterns of domination, submission, and struggle between people of high and low standing.
- *Inequality.* Conflict theory shows how major patterns of inequality in society produce social stability in some circumstances and social change in others.
- *Conflict.* Conflict theory stresses how members of privileged groups try to maintain their advantages, whereas subordinate groups struggle to increase theirs. From this point of view, social conditions at a given time are the expression of an ongoing power struggle between privileged and subordinate groups.
- *Lessening privilege.* Conflict theory typically leads to the suggestion that lessening privilege will lower the level of conflict and increase human welfare.

THE CULTURAL TURN AND POSTSTRUCTURALISM: GRAMSCI AND FOUCAULT

In the 1960s and 1970s, conflict theory took what has been called a "cultural turn." Increasingly, conflict theorists directed their attention to the ways in which language, music, literature, fashion, movies, advertising, and other elements of culture express domination by the powerful and resistance by others.

The origins of a cultural approach to the study of social conflict are found in essays written in the early twentieth century by Italian Marxist Antonio Gramsci (pronounced GRAM-shee). In Gramsci's view, ruling classes establish their dominance partly by controlling jobs, using force, and the like. However, they also exercise power in softer ways. In particular, they fund the development, transmission, and learning of ideas that seem to embody the values of everyone but are actually biased in favour of class dominance. Gramsci wrote that **cultural hegemony** exists if these values become so deeply entrenched that the great majority of people accept them as common sense

cultural hegemony Involves the control of a culture by dominant classes and other groups to the point where their values are universally accepted as common sense.

poststructuralism A school of thought that originated in mid-twentieth-century France, it denied the stability of social relations and of cultures, their capacity to always shape how people think and act, and the neat categorization of social and cultural elements as binary opposites.

Protestant ethic The sixteenth- and seventeenth-century belief that religious doubts can be reduced, and a state of grace assured, if people work diligently and live ascetically. According to Weber, the Protestant ethic had the unintended effect of increasing savings and investment, thus stimulating capitalist growth.

(Gramsci, 1957; 1971). Subordinate classes can resist cultural hegemony, Gramsci wrote, but only if they develop ideas and institutions that express and support their own cultural preferences. Later writers extended Gramsci's argument to include dominant, taken-for-granted ideas about race, ethnicity, sexuality, and so on.

The notion that culture is the site of ongoing conflict between dominant and subordinate classes and other groups was further developed in France from the 1950s to the 1980s by Michel Foucault (pronounced Foo-CŌ). Foucault made his case by studying new forms of regulation that accompany capitalist industrialization. He showed that, as the goal of maximizing economic productivity grows in importance, criminals, the physically infirm, the mentally ill, and ordinary students and workers are subjected to new structures of control in prisons, hospitals, mental institutions, workplaces, schools, and universities. According to Foucault, modern institutions sometimes use violence to regulate behaviour but they more often rely on new technologies and the *internalization* of control mechanisms. For example, modern institutions are physically, technologically, and socially designed so authorities can easily observe the behaviour of inmates, patients, workers, and students. Authorities may not always watch their "clientele," but knowing that they *may* be under the watchful eye of authorities, inmates and others usually act as if they *are* being observed. Before capitalist industrialization, control took place almost exclusively through force, but now more subtle and effective mechanisms of regulation are employed. (Michael Foucault, 1973, 1977, and 1988)

Power, Foucault held, is exercised in every social interaction, but every social interaction is also subject to resistance by subordinates. Thus, the exercise of power is unstable. Dominant groups and individuals must continuously renew power relations to maintain control but sometimes they fail, giving subordinates the opportunity to assert their interests.

Foucault was part of a movement in French social thought known as **poststructuralism**. Earlier social thinkers had argued that social relations and cultures form structures, or stable determinants of the way people think and act. These "structuralists" typically categorized elements of social relations and of culture as binary opposites: male versus female, civilized versus uncivilized people, black versus white races, and so on (Derrida, 2004: 41). In contrast, poststructuralists, Foucault among them, denied the stability of social relations and of cultures, their capacity always to shape how people think and act, and the neat categorization of social and cultural elements as binary opposites. According to the poststructuralists, the social world is a more fluid and complex place, and people are more often the agents of their own destiny, than structuralists ever imagined.

To better understand these ideas, consider that many of us casually use the term "the opposite sex" in everyday speech without giving it much thought. Yet embedded in this term is a faulty set of assumptions based on a distribution of power that favours some categories of people at the expense of others. As you will learn in Chapter 8, Sexualities and Genders, it is factually incorrect to assume that men and women are opposites in their sexual identities, preferences, and behaviours. It is more accurate to say that men and women are arrayed along one scale with respect to their sexual identities, a second scale with respect to their sexual preferences, and a third scale with respect to their sexual behaviours, and their positions on these scales can change in different circumstances.

When we think that men remain clustered on one extreme of a single scale and women on the other—when we think of women and men as fixed "opposites"—we oversimplify the complexity of real flesh-and-blood people. We also ignore that many women and men are not so neatly pigeonholed. Those who are not neatly categorized are simply defined out of existence by our casual use of language and the underlying fact that some people have more power than others to name things.

GEORGE HERBERT MEAD AND SYMBOLIC INTERACTIONISM

We noted earlier that Weber criticized Marx's interpretation of the development of capitalism. Among other things, Weber argued that early capitalist development was not caused by favourable economic circumstances alone. In addition, he said, certain *religious* beliefs encouraged robust capitalist growth. In particular, sixteenth- and seventeenth-century Protestants believed that their religious doubts could be reduced and a state of grace assured if they worked diligently and lived modestly. Weber called this belief the **Protestant ethic**. He believed it had an unintended effect: People who held to the Protestant ethic saved and invested more money than others did. Consequently, capitalism developed most vigorously where the Protestant ethic took hold. He concluded that capitalism did not develop as a result of the operation of economic forces alone, as Marx argued. Instead, it

Conflict theory became especially popular in North America in the 1960s and 1970s, a period that was rocked by major labour unrest, peace demonstrations on university campuses, the rise of the Black Power movement and the Quebec separatist movement, and the emergence of contemporary feminism. Strikes, demonstrations, and riots were almost daily occurrences in the 1960s and 1970s, and it seemed evident to many sociologists of that generation that conflict among classes, nations, races, and generations was the very essence of social life. For example, John Porter (1921–79) was Canada's premier sociologist in the 1960s and 1970s. Born in Vancouver, he received his Ph.D. from the London School of Economics. He spent his academic career at Carleton University in Ottawa, where he served as chair of the Department of Sociology and Anthropology, dean of Arts and Science, and Academic vice-president. His major work, *The Vertical Mosaic* (1965), is a study of class and power in Canada. Firmly rooted in conflict theory, it influenced a generation of Canadian sociologists in their studies of social inequality, elite groups, French–English relations, and Canadian–American relations.

depended partly on the religious meaning that individuals attached to their work (Weber, 1958 [1904–05]). In much of his research, Weber emphasized the need to understand people's motives and the meanings they attach to things to gain a clear sense of the significance of their actions.

At the University of Chicago, George Herbert Mead (1863–1931) thought along the same lines as Weber. He was the driving force behind the early study of how the individual's sense of self is formed in the course of interaction with other people (Mead, 1934). As such, he was a founder of the school of thought that came to be known as **symbolic interactionism**, which examines how various aspects of social life, including fashion, convey meaning and thereby assist or impede communication (Blumer, 1969).

symbolic interactionism
Examination of how various aspects of social life convey meaning and thereby assist or impede communication.

Mead understood that human communication involves seeing yourself from other people's points of view. For example, let's say you're standing outside talking to two classmates. One winks at you. How do you know what the wink means, that is, what your classmate wants to communicate? If the wink occurs while you are trying to pull a trick on the third classmate, it might signify that the winker knows what you're up to. If the winker has hinted earlier that she might be interested in going out on a date with you, the wink might signify that her interest has grown. If the wind is blowing, it might mean that some dust got in her eye. According to Mead, you must figure out the meaning of the wink by using your imagination to understand the social context of your interaction, take the winker's point of view for a moment and see yourself as she sees you. Only to the degree that you see yourself from her point of view—only to the extent that you succeed in "taking the role of the other," as Mead put it—will you be able to understand accurately what she means by winking at you.

All human communication depends on being able to take the role of the other, wrote Mead. And it is only by taking the role of the other and seeing ourselves as others see us hundreds of times every day that we can develop a

Erving Goffman (1922–82) was born in Mannville, Alberta. He studied sociology and anthropology at the University of Toronto. He completed his Ph.D. at the University of Chicago and pursued his academic career at the University of California, Berkeley, and the University of Pennsylvania. Goffman developed an international reputation for his approach to symbolic interactionism.

gender One's sense of being masculine or feminine as conventionally defined.

feminism A sociological school of thought claiming that male domination and female subordination are determined not by biological necessity but by structures of power and social convention.

sense of who we are. Mead concluded that our sense of self is not present from birth. It emerges only gradually as we interact with others and use symbols such as words and gestures to communicate with them.

Mead's work gave birth to symbolic interactionism, a theoretical tradition that continues to be a major force in sociology today. Symbolic interactionism incorporates the following features:

- *Micro-level communication.* It focuses on interpersonal communication in micro-level social settings, distinguishing it from both functionalist and conflict theories.
- *Subjective meanings.* Symbolic interactionism emphasizes that social life is possible only because people attach meanings to things. It follows that an adequate explanation of social behaviour requires an understanding of the subjective meanings that people associate with their social circumstances.
- *People as agents.* Symbolic interactionism stresses that people help to create their social circumstances and do not merely react to them. Functionalist and conflict theories sometimes overstate the degree to which people's behaviour is influenced by whether they are rich or poor, male or female, black or white, and so on. In contrast, symbolic interactionists emphasize human creativity—how people make choices, change their minds, and interpret social circumstances in novel ways.
- *Tolerance.* By focusing on the subjective meanings that people create, symbolic interactionists sometimes validate unpopular and nonofficial viewpoints, helping to increase our understanding and tolerance of people who may be different from us.

HARRIET MARTINEAU AND FEMINIST THEORY

Few women figured prominently in the early history of sociology. The demands placed on them by the nineteenth-century family and the lack of opportunity in the larger society prevented most of them from earning a higher education and making major contributions to the discipline. Women who made their mark on sociology in its early years tended to have unusual biographies. Some of them introduced gender issues that were ignored by Marx, Durkheim, Weber, Mead, and other early sociologists. (**Gender** is one's sense of being masculine or feminine as conventionally defined.) Appreciation for the sociological contribution of these pioneering women has grown in recent years because

concern regarding gender issues has come to form a substantial part of the modern sociological enterprise.

For example, Harriet Martineau (1802–76) is often called the first woman sociologist. Born in England to a prosperous family, she never married. She supported herself comfortably from her journalistic writings. Martineau wrote one of the first books on research methods and undertook critical studies of slavery, factory laws, and gender inequality. She was a leading advocate of voting rights and higher education for women and of gender equality in the family. As such, Martineau was one of the first feminists (Martineau, 1985).

MODERN FEMINISM

Despite its early stirrings, feminist thinking had little impact on sociology until the mid-1960s, when the rise of the modern women's movement drew attention to the many remaining inequalities between women and men. Because of feminist theory's major influence on sociology, it can fairly be regarded as sociology's fourth major theoretical tradition. Modern **feminism** has several variants (see Chapter 8, Sexualities and Genders). However, the various strands of feminist theory share the following features:

- *Patriarchy.* Feminist theory focuses on various aspects of patriarchy, the system of male domination of women. Patriarchy, feminists contend, is as important as class inequality, if not more so, in determining a person's opportunities in life.
- *Power and social convention.* Feminist theory holds that male domination and female subordination are determined not by biological necessity but by structures of power and social convention. From this point of view, women are subordinate to men only because men enjoy more legal, economic, political, and cultural rights.
- *Micro- and macro-level focus.* Feminist theory examines the operation of patriarchy in both micro- and macro-level settings.
- *Gender inequality.* Feminist theory contends that existing patterns of gender inequality can and should be changed for the benefit of all members of society. The main sources of gender inequality include differences in the way boys and girls are reared; barriers to equal opportunity in education, paid work, and politics; and the unequal division of domestic responsibilities between women and men.

Sociology's four main theoretical traditions are summarized in Concept Summary 1.1. As you will see in the following pages, sociologists have applied these traditions to all of the discipline's branches. Some sociologists work exclusively within one tradition. Others borrow from more than one tradition. Moreover, sociologists continue to elaborate and refine the ideas developed by the discipline's founders. As such, all sociologists are deeply indebted to the founders of the discipline.

CONDUCTING RESEARCH

Before we do research, we rarely see things objectively, as they are. We see them as *we* are, that is, subjectively. People's subjective experiences often lead them to ask new questions, conceive new problems, and consider new solutions to old problems. However, our conjectures may be wrong. That is why we conduct **research**—to test theories against controlled observations of the social world that other researchers can repeat to check on us. On the basis of research, we reject some theories, modify others, and are forced to invent new and better ones. Having outlined the main theoretical approaches in sociology, it is now time to discuss the research process.

LO⁴ THE RESEARCH CYCLE

Sociological research is a cyclical process that involves six steps (see Figure 1.4). The sociologist's first step is *formulating a research question.* A research question must be stated so that it can be answered by systematically collecting and analyzing sociological data.

Sociological research cannot determine whether God exists or what the best political system is. Answers to such questions require faith more than evidence. However, sociological research can determine why some people are more religious than others are and which political system creates most opportunities for higher education. Answers to such questions require evidence more than faith.

> **research** The process of systematically observing reality to assess the validity of a theory.

Courtesy of Margrit Eichler

Margrit Eichler (1942–) was born in Berlin, Germany. She took her Ph.D. at Duke University in the United States before beginning her academic career in Canada. She served as chair of the Department of Sociology at the Ontario Institute for Studies in Education (University of Toronto) and was the first director of the Institute for Women's Studies and Gender Studies at the University of Toronto. Eichler is internationally known for her work on feminist methodology (Eichler, 1987). Her work on family policy in Canada has influenced students, professional sociologists, and policy-makers for decades (Eichler, 1988).

CONCEPT SUMMARY 1.1   Four Theoretical Traditions in Society

Theoretical Tradition	Main Levels of Analysis	Main Focus	Main Question	Major Theorists
Functionalist	Macro	Values	How do the institutions of society contribute to social stability and instability?	Émile Durkheim, Talcott Parsons, Robert Merton, S.D. Clark
Conflict	Macro	Inequality	How do privileged groups seek to maintain their advantages and subordinate groups seek to increase theirs, often causing social change in the process?	Karl Marx, Max Weber, Antonio Gramsci, Michel Foucault, John Porter
Symbolic interactionist	Micro	Meaning	How do individuals communicate to make their social settings meaningful?	George Herbert Mead, Max Weber, Erving Goffman
Feminist	Macro and micro	Patriarchy	Which social structures and interaction processes maintain male dominance and female subordination?	Harriet Martineau, Margrit Eichler

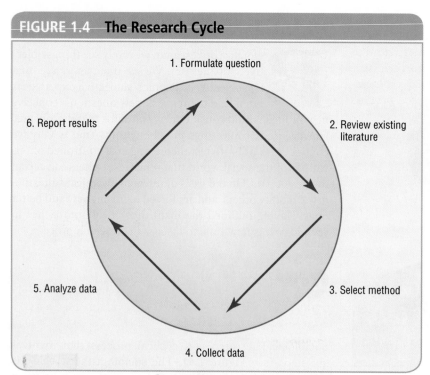

FIGURE 1.4   The Research Cycle

1. Formulate question

2. Review existing literature

3. Select method

4. Collect data

5. Analyze data

6. Report results

Source: From BRYM/LIE. *Sociology*, 1E. © 2009 Nelson Education Ltd. Reproduced by permission. www.cengage.com/permissions.

The second step involves a *review of the existing research literature*. Researchers must elaborate their research questions in the light of what other sociologists have already debated and discovered. Why? Because reading the relevant sociological literature stimulates researchers' sociological imagination, allows them to refine their initial questions, and prevents duplication of effort.

Selecting a research method is the third step in the research cycle. As we will see in detail later in this chapter, each data collection method has strengths and weaknesses. Each method is therefore best suited to studying a different kind of problem. When choosing a method, researchers must keep these strengths and weaknesses in mind.

The fourth step in the research cycle involves *collecting data* by observing subjects, interviewing them, reading documents produced by or about them, and so on. Many researchers think this is the most exciting stage of the research cycle because it brings them face to face with the puzzling sociological reality that so fascinates them.

Other researchers find the fifth step in the research cycle, when they *analyze the data*, the most challenging. During data analysis, you can learn things that nobody knew before. At this stage, data confirm some of your expectations and confound others, requiring you to think creatively about familiar issues, reconsider the relevant theoretical and research literature, and abandon pet ideas.

Research is not useful for the sociological community, the subjects of the research, or the wider society if researchers do not complete the sixth step—publish the results in a report, a scientific journal, or a book.

Publication serves another important function, too: It allows other sociologists to scrutinize and criticize the research. On that basis, errors can be corrected and new and more sophisticated research questions can be formulated for the next round of research. Science is a social activity governed by rules defined and enforced by the scientific community.

ETHICS IN SOCIOLOGICAL RESEARCH

Researchers must respect their subjects' rights throughout the research cycle. This means, first, that researchers must do their subjects no harm. This is the right to *safety*. Second, research subjects must have the right to decide whether their attitudes and behaviours may be revealed to the public and, if so, in what way. This is the right to *privacy*. Third, researchers cannot use data in a way that allows them to be traced to a particular subject. This is the subject's right to *confidentiality*. Fourth, subjects must be told how the information they supply will be used. They must also be allowed to judge the degree of personal risk involved in answering questions so that they can decide whether they may be studied and, if so, in what way. This is the right to *informed consent*.

Ethical issues arise not only in the treatment of subjects but also in the treatment of research results. For example, plagiarism is a concern in academic life, especially among students, who write research papers and submit them to professors for evaluation. One study found that 38 percent of university students admitted to committing "cut and paste" plagiarism when writing essays (Edmundson, 2003), while another found that 51 percent of high school students admitted to cheating on an exam (Josephson Institute, 2012). It's probably not news to you that you can easily buy ready-made essays.

Increased plagiarism is a consequence of the spread of the World Wide Web and the growing view that everything on it is public and therefore does not have to be cited. That view is wrong. The Code of Ethics of the American Sociological Association states that we must "explicitly identify, credit, and reference the author" when we make any use of another person's written work, "whether it is published, unpublished, or electronically available" (American Sociological Association, 1999: 16). Making such ethical standards better known can help remedy the problem of plagiarism. So can better policing. Powerful Web-based applications are now available that help college and university instructors determine whether essays are plagiarized in whole or in part (for example, visit www.turnitin.com). Perhaps the most effective remedy, however, is for instructors to ensure that what they teach really matters to their students. If they do, students won't be as inclined to plagiarize because they will regard essay writing as a process of personal discovery. You can't cut and paste or buy enlightenment (Edmundson, 2003).

Bearing in mind our thumbnail sketch of the research cycle, we devote the rest of this chapter to exploring its fourth and fifth steps—gathering and analyzing evidence. In doing so, we describe each of sociology's major research methods: field research, experiments, surveys, and the analysis of existing documents and official statistics. We turn first to field research.

LO⁵ THE MAIN SOCIOLOGICAL RESEARCH METHODS

EXPERIMENTS

In the mid-1960s, the first generation of North American children exposed to high levels of TV violence virtually from birth reached their mid-teens. At the same time, the rate of violent crime began to increase. Some commentators said that TV violence made violence in the real world seem normal and acceptable. As a result, they concluded, North American teenagers in the 1960s and subsequent decades were more likely than pre-1960s teens to commit violent acts.

Aggressive behaviour among children is common, from siblings fighting to bullying in the schoolyard. Since the inception of home TV in the 1950s, social scientists have sought to find strong research designs capable of examining the causal effects, if any, of viewing violence on television.

The increasing prevalence of violence in movies, video games, and popular music seemed to add weight to their conclusion.

Social scientists soon started investigating the connection between media and real-world violence using experimental methods. An **experiment** is a carefully controlled artificial situation that allows researchers to isolate presumed causes and measure their effects precisely (Campbell and Stanley, 1963).

Experiments use a procedure called **randomization** to create two similar groups. Randomization involves assigning individuals to two groups by chance processes. For example, researchers may ask 50 children to draw a number from 1 to 50 from a covered box. The researchers assign children who draw odd numbers to one group and those who draw even numbers to the other group. By assigning subjects to the two groups using a chance process and repeating the experiment many times, researchers ensure that each group has the same proportion of boys and girls, members of different races, children highly motivated to participate in the study, and so on.

After randomly assigning subjects to the two groups, the researchers put the groups into separate rooms and give them toys to play with. They observe the children through one-way mirrors, rating each child in terms of the aggressiveness of his or her play. This is the child's initial score on the "dependent variable," aggressive behaviour. The **dependent variable** is the presumed effect in any cause-and-effect relationship.

Then the researchers introduce the supposed (or "hypothesized") cause to one group—now called the **experimental group**. They may show children in the experimental group an hour-long TV program in which many violent acts take place. They do not show the program to children in the other group, now called the **control group**. In this case, the violent TV show is the "independent variable." The **independent variable** is the presumed cause in any cause-and-effect relationship.

Immediately after the children see the TV show, the researchers again observe the children in both groups at play. Each child's play is given a second aggressiveness score. By comparing the aggressiveness scores of the two groups before and after only one of the groups has been

experiment A carefully controlled artificial situation that allows researchers to isolate hypothesized causes and measure their effects precisely.

randomization In an experiment, assigning individuals to groups by chance processes.

dependent variable The presumed effect in a cause-and-effect relationship.

experimental group The group that is exposed to the independent variable in an experiment.

control group The group that is not exposed to the independent variable in an experiment.

independent variable The presumed cause in a cause-and-effect relationship.

TABLE 1.1 Steps in a Simple Experiment

	Time 1	Time 2	Time 3	Time 4
Control group	Randomize assignment of subjects to group	Measure dependent variable	Do not introduce independent variable	Measure dependent variable again
Experimental group	Randomize assignment of subjects to group	Measure dependent variable	Introduce independent variable	Measure dependent variable again

reliability The degree to which a measurement procedure yields consistent results.

validity The degree to which a measure actually measures what it is intended to measure.

association Relationship between two variables such that the value of one variable changes with the value of another.

exposed to the presumed cause, an experiment can determine whether the presumed cause (watching violent TV) has the predicted effect (increasing violent behaviour; see Table 1.1).

Experiments allow researchers to isolate the single cause of theoretical interest and measure its effect with high **reliability**, that is, consistently from one experiment to the next. Yet many sociologists argue that experiments are highly artificial situations. They believe that removing people from their natural social settings lowers the **validity** of experimental results, that is, the degree to which they measure what they are actually supposed to measure.

Why do experiments on the effects of media violence lack validity? First, in the real world, violent behaviour usually means attempting to harm another person physically. Shouting or kicking a toy is not the same thing. In fact, such acts may enable children to relieve frustrations in a fantasy world, lowering their chance of acting violently in the real world. Second, aggressive behaviour is not controlled in the laboratory setting as it is in the real world. If a boy watching a violent TV show stands up and delivers a karate kick to his brother, a parent or other caregiver is likely to take action to prevent a recurrence. In the lab, lack of disciplinary control may facilitate unrealistically high levels of aggression (Felson, 1996).

An **association** between two variables exists if the value of one variable changes with the value of the other. For example, if the percentage of people who approve of a man punching an adult male is *higher* among those who watch three or more hours of TV a day, a *positive* association exists between the two variables. If the percentage of people who approve of a man punching an adult male is *lower* among those who watch three or more hours of TV a day, a *negative* association exists between the two variables. The greater the percentage difference between frequent and infrequent TV viewers, the stronger the association. Table 1.2 shows that 69 percent of respondents who

TABLE 1.2 Watching TV and Approval of Punching Violence (percentage)

Approved of punching	TV Viewing: 0–2 Hours/Day (% viewers who approved)	TV Viewing: 3+ Hours/Day (% viewers who approved)	TV Viewing: Total (% viewers who approved)
Yes	69	65	67
No	31	35	33
Total	100	100	100
N	5188	5022	10 210

Source: National Opinion Research Center. 2006. *General Social Survey, 1972–2004*. Chicago: University of Chicago.

Data in this table come from the American *General Social Survey*, which regularly asks people how many hours of TV they watch every day. Until 1994, it also asked respondents if they ever approve of a man punching an adult male. This table shows the results for these two questions, combining responses from 1972 to 1994.

To interpret tables, you must pay careful attention to what adds up to 100 percent. The table says that 69 percent *of people who watched TV 0–2 hours a day* approved of a man punching an adult male. It does not say that 69 percent of all people who approved of a man punching an adult male

watched TV 0–2 hours a day. We know this because each category of the "TV viewing" variable equals 100 percent.

To test your understanding, calculate the number of respondents represented by the following percentages in the table: 69%, 65%, 31%, and 35%. Answers are given in the box below.

Answers

69% = (69/100) × 5188 = 3580 respondents; 65% = (65/100) × 5022 = 3264 respondents; 31% = (31/100) × 5188 = 1608 respondents; 35% = (35/100) × 5022 = 1758 respondents

watched TV 0–2 hours a day approved of punching, compared with 65 percent of respondents who watched TV 3 hours or more. Is this a positive or a negative association?

SURVEYS

Surveys are the most widely used sociological research method, and they also have been used to measure the effects of media violence on behaviour. Overall, the results of surveys show a weaker relationship between exposure to violent mass media and violent behaviour than do experiments, and some surveys show no relationship at all between these two variables (Anderson and Bushman, 2002; Huesmann, Moise-Titus, Podolski, and Eron, 2003; Johnson, Cohen, Smailes, Kasen, and Brook, 2002; see Table 1.2).

In a **survey**, people are asked questions about their knowledge, attitudes, or behaviour. All survey researchers aim to study part of a group—a **sample**—to learn about the whole group of interest—the **population**. To reliably generalize about the population based on findings from a sample, researchers must be sure that the characteristics of the people in the sample match those of the population. To draw a sample from which one can safely generalize, researchers must choose respondents at random, and an individual's chance of being chosen must be known and greater than zero.

When sociologists conduct a survey, they may mail a form containing questions to respondents. Respondents then mail the completed questionnaire back to the researcher. Alternatively, sociologists may conduct face-to-face interviews in which questions are presented to the respondent by the interviewer during a meeting. Sociologists may also conduct surveys by means of telephone interviews or online.

Questionnaires may contain two types of questions. A **closed-ended question** provides the respondent with a list of permitted answers. Each answer is given a numerical code so the data can later be easily input into a computer for statistical analysis. Often, the numerical results of surveys are arranged in tables like Table 1.2. An **open-ended question** allows respondents to answer in their own words. Open-ended questions are particularly useful when researchers don't have enough knowledge to create a meaningful and complete list of possible answers.

To ensure that these types of survey questions elicit valid responses, researchers must guard against four dangers:

1. The exclusion of part of the population from the sampling frame
2. The refusal of some people to participate in the survey
3. The unwillingness of some respondents to answer questions frankly
4. The asking of confusing, leading, or inflammatory questions or questions referring to several unimportant or noncurrent events

Much of the art and science of survey research involves overcoming these threats to validity (Converse and Presser, 1986; Ornstein, 1998). Recall that surveys tend to show a weaker relationship than do experiments between exposure to violent mass media and violent behaviour. That may be because survey researchers have developed more valid measures of violent behaviour.

FIELD RESEARCH

The method that comes closest to people's natural social settings is **field research**. Field research involves systematically observing people wherever they associate.

When they go into the field, researchers come prepared with strategies to ensure that their observations are accurate. One such strategy is **detached observation**, which involves classifying and counting the behaviour of interest according to a predetermined scheme. Although useful for some purposes, two main problems confound direct observation. First, the presence of the researcher may cause **reactivity**; the observed people may conceal certain things or act artificially to impress the researcher (Webb et al., 1966). Second, the meaning of the observed behaviour may remain obscure to the researcher. A wink may be an involuntary muscle contraction, an indication of a secret being kept, a sexual come-on, and so on. We can't know what a wink means just by observing it.

To avoid reactivity and understand the meaning of behaviour, we must be able to see it in its social context and from the point of view of the people we are observing. To do that, researchers must immerse themselves in their subjects' world by learning their language and their culture

survey Research method in which people are asked questions about their knowledge, attitudes, or behaviour, either in a face-to-face or telephone interview or by completion of a questionnaire.

sample The part of the population of interest that is selected for analysis.

population The entire group about which the researcher wants to generalize.

closed-ended question In a survey, a type of question that provides the respondent with a list of permitted answers. Each answer is given a numerical code so that the data can later be easily input into a computer for statistical analysis.

open-ended question In a survey, a type of question that allows respondents to answer in their own words.

field research The systematic observation of people in their natural settings.

detached observation A type of field research that involves classifying and counting the behaviour of interest according to a predetermined scheme.

reactivity The tendency of people who are observed by a researcher to react to the presence of the researcher by concealing certain things or acting artificially to impress the researcher.

members; and studied police and psychological reports and the shooters' own writings (Harding, Fox, and Mehta, 2002; Sullivan, 2002). They have concluded that only a small number of young people who are weakly connected to family, school, community, and peers are at risk of translating media violence into violent behaviour. Lack of social support allows them to magnify their personal problems, and if guns are available, they are prone to using violent media messages as models for their own behaviour. In contrast, for the great majority of young people, violence in the mass media is just a source of entertainment and a fantasy outlet for emotional issues (Anderson, 2003).

Like other research methods, participant observation has strengths and weaknesses. On the plus side, it allows researchers to develop a deep and sympathetic understanding of the way people see the world. It is especially useful in the "exploratory" stage of research, when investigators have only a vague sense of what they are looking for and little sense of what they will discover. On the minus side, because participant observation research usually involves just one researcher in one social setting, it is difficult to know if other researchers would measure things in the same way (this is the problem of reliability), and it is difficult to know how broadly findings may be generalized to other settings.

ANALYSIS OF EXISTING DOCUMENTS AND OFFICIAL STATISTICS

The fourth important sociological research method involves **analysis of existing documents and official statistics** that are created by people other than the researcher for purposes other than sociological research.

The three types of existing documents that sociologists have mined most deeply are diaries, newspapers, and published historical works. Census data, police crime reports, and records of key life events are perhaps the most frequently used sources of official statistics. Statistics Canada publishes an annual *Uniform Crime Reporting Survey* that reports the number of crimes in Canada and classifies them by the location and type of crime, the age and sex of offenders and victims, and other variables. Statistics Canada also publishes an *Annual Compendium of Vital Statistics* that reports births, deaths, marriages, and divorces by sex, age, and so on.

Census and crime data put the limited effect of media violence on violent behaviour into perspective. For example, researchers have discovered big differences in violent behaviour when they compare the United States and Canada. The homicide rate (the number of murders per 100 000 people) has historically been about four times higher in the United States. Yet TV programming, movies, and video games are nearly identical in the two countries, so exposure to media violence can't account

Researchers collect information through surveys by asking people in a representative sample an identical set of questions. People interviewed on a downtown street corner do not constitute a representative sample of Canadian adults, because the sample might not include people who live outside the urban core, it underestimates the number of older people and people with disabilities, it does not take into account regional diversity, and so on.

participant observation
Research that involves carefully observing people's face-to-face interaction and participating in their lives over a long period, thus achieving a deep and sympathetic understanding of what motivates them.

analysis of existing documents and official statistics
A nonreactive research method that involves the analysis of diaries, newspapers, published historical works, and statistics produced by government agencies, all of which are created by people other than the researcher for purposes other than sociological research.

in depth. When sociologists observe a social setting systematically *and* take part in the activities of the people they are studying, they engage in **participant observation** research (Lofland and Lofland, 1995 [1971]).

Participant observation research helps us better understand how media violence may influence youth violence. Sociologists have spent time in schools where shooting rampages have taken place; lived in the neighbourhoods where they occurred; interviewed students, teachers, neighbours, and shooters' family

Homelessness is an increasing focus of public policy. However, public support may not be adequate if the homeless are not counted properly in the census. Statistics Canada included a count of the homeless in the 2001 census. However, because the count is based on information about the use of shelters and soup kitchens, combined with an attempt at street counts, these numbers are only rough estimates.

for the difference. Researchers instead attribute the difference in homicide rates to the higher level of economic and social inequality and the wider availability of handguns in the United States (Government of Canada, 2002; Lenton, 1989; National Rifle Association, 2005; Sternheimer, 2014; see Figure 1.5).

Existing documents and official statistics have several advantages over other types of data. They can save researchers time and money because they are usually available at no cost in libraries or on the World Wide Web. Official statistics usually cover entire populations and are collected using rigorous and uniform methods, yielding highly reliable data. Existing documents and official statistics are especially useful for historical analysis. Finally, because the analysis of existing documents and official statistics does not require live subjects, reactivity is not a problem. The researchers' presence does not influence the subjects' behaviour.

Existing documents and official statistics also share one big disadvantage: They are not created with researchers' needs in mind. In a sense, researchers start at Stage 5 of the research cycle (analyze data; refer back to Figure 1.4) and then work within the limitations imposed by available data, including biases that reflect the interests of the individuals and organizations that created them. The preceding discussion should give you a pretty good idea of the basic methodological issues that confront any sociological research project. You should also know the strengths and weaknesses of some of the most widely used data collection techniques (see Concept Summary 1.2). In the remainder of this chapter, we outline what you can expect to learn from the rest of this book.

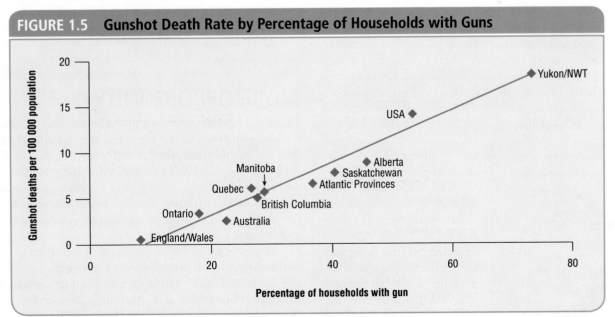

FIGURE 1.5 Gunshot Death Rate by Percentage of Households with Guns

Source: Republished with permission of Elsevier, from Ted R. Miller and Mark A. Cohen, "Costs of gunshot and cut/stab wounds in the United States, with some Canadian comparisons," *Accident Analysis and Prevention*, vol. 29, issue 3, May 1997, pp. 329–341; permission conveyed through Copyright Clearance Center, Inc.

CONCEPT SUMMARY 1.2 Strengths and Weaknesses of Four Research Methods

Method	Strengths	Weaknesses
Experiment	High reliability; excellent for establishing cause-and-effect relationships	Low validity for many sociological problems because of the unnaturalness of the experimental setting
Survey	Good reliability; useful for establishing cause-and-effect relationships	Validity problems exist unless researchers make strong efforts to deal with them
Participant observation	Allows researchers to develop a deep and sympathetic understanding of the way people see the world; especially useful in exploratory research	Low reliability and generalizability
Analysis of existing documents and official statistics	Often inexpensive and easy to obtain; provides good coverage; useful for historical analysis; nonreactive	Often contains biases reflecting the interests of their creators and not the interests of the researcher

Source: From BRYM/LIE. *Sociology*, 1E. © 2009 Nelson Education Ltd. Reproduced by permission. www.cengage.com/permissions.

LO⁶ CHALLENGES FACING US TODAY

Most of the founders of sociology developed their ideas to help solve the great sociological puzzle of their time—the causes and consequences of the Industrial Revolution. This raises two interesting questions: What are the great sociological puzzles of *our* time? How are today's sociologists responding to the challenges presented by the social settings in which *we* live? We devote the rest of this book to answering these questions in depth.

It would be wrong to suggest that just a few key issues animate the research of tens of thousands of sociologists around the world. Hundreds of debates enliven sociology today. Some focus on small issues relevant to particular fields and geographical areas, others on big issues that seek to characterize the entire historical era for humanity as a whole. Among the big issues, two stand out. The greatest sociological puzzles of ourtime are the causes and consequences of the Postindustrial Revolution and globalization.

The **Postindustrial Revolution** is the technology-driven shift from employment in factories to employment in offices, and the consequences of that shift for nearly all human activities (Bell, 1973; Toffler, 1990). For example, as a result of the Postindustrial Revolution, nonmanual occupations now outnumber manual occupations, and women have been drawn into the system of higher education and the paid labour force in large numbers. This shift has transformed the way we work and study, our standard of living, the way we form families, and much else.

Globalization is the process by which formerly separate economies, states, and cultures are becoming tied together and people are becoming increasingly aware of their growing interdependence (Giddens, 1990: 64; Guillén, 2001). Especially in recent decades, rapid increases in the volume of international trade, travel, and communication have broken down the isolation and independence of most countries and people. Also contributing to globalization is the growth of many institutions that bind corporations, companies, and cultures together. These processes have caused people to depend more than ever on people in other countries for products, services, ideas, and even a sense of identity.

MORE OPPORTUNITY?

Some sociologists think that globalization and postindustrialism will enhance the quality of life. Specifically, they forecast that postindustrialism will provide more opportunities for people to find creative, interesting, challenging, and rewarding work. They also say it will generate more equality of opportunity, that is, better chances for *all* people to get an education, influence government policy, and find good jobs.

However, as you read this book, it will become clear that although great strides have been made in providing economic and education opportunities for women, limiting discrimination, and spreading democracy, all of these seemingly happy stories have a dark underside. For example, it turns out that the number of routine jobs with low pay and few benefits is growing faster than the

Postindustrial Revolution
The technology-driven shift from manufacturing to service industries and the consequences of that shift for virtually all human activities.

globalization The process by which formerly separate economies, nation-states, and cultures are becoming tied together and people are becoming increasingly aware of their growing interdependence.

number of creative, high-paying jobs. Inequality between the wealthiest and poorest people has grown in recent decades. An enormous opportunity gulf still separates women from men. Racism and discrimination are still a part of our world. Our health care system is in trouble just as our population is aging rapidly and most in need of health care. Disasters sometimes follow technological advances—just think of the oil spill in the Gulf of Mexico in 2010 and the nuclear meltdown in Japan in 2011.

Many of the world's new democracies are only superficially democratic, while Canadians and citizens of other postindustrial societies are increasingly cynical about the ability of their political systems to respond to their needs. They are looking for alternative forms of political expression. The absolute number of desperately poor people in the world continues to grow, as does the gap between rich and poor nations. Many people attribute the world's most serious problems to globalization. They have formed organizations and movements—some of them violent—to oppose it. In short, equality of opportunity is an undeniably attractive ideal, but it is unclear whether it is the inevitable outcome of a globalized, postindustrial society.

MORE FREEDOM?

We may say the same about the ideal of freedom. In an earlier era, most people retained their religious, ethnic, racial, and sexual identities for a lifetime, even if they were not particularly comfortable with them. They often remained in social relationships that made them unhappy. One of the major themes of this book is that many people are now freer to construct their identities and form social relationships in ways that suit them. To a greater degree than ever before, it is possible to *choose* who you want to live with, who you want to associate with, and how you want to engage with them.

The postindustrial and global era frees people from traditional constraints by encouraging virtually instant global communication, international migration, greater acceptance of sexual diversity and a variety of family forms, the growth of ethnically and racially diverse cities, and so on. For instance, in the past, people often stayed in marriages even if they were dissatisfied with them. Families often involved a father working in the paid labour force and a mother keeping house and raising children without pay. Today, people are freer to end unhappy marriages and create family structures that are more suited to their individual needs.

Again, however, we must face the less rosy aspects of postindustrialism and globalization. In the following chapters, we show how increased freedom is experienced only within certain limits and how social diversity is limited by a strong push to conformity in some spheres of life. For example, we can choose a far wider variety of consumer products than ever before, but consumerism itself increasingly seems a compulsory way of life. Moreover,

it is a way of life that threatens the natural environment. Large, impersonal bureaucracies and standardized products and services dehumanize both staff and customers. The tastes and the profit motive of vast media conglomerates govern most of our diverse cultural consumption and arguably threaten the survival of distinctive national cultures. Powerful interests are trying to shore up the traditional nuclear family even though it does not suit some people. As these examples show, the push for uniformity counters the trend toward growing social diversity.

In short, postindustrialism and globalization may make us freer in some ways, but they also place new constraints on us.

WHERE DO YOU FIT IN?

Our overview of themes in this book drives home the fact that we live in an era "suspended between extraordinary opportunity . . . and global catastrophe" (Giddens, 1987: 166). A whole range of environmental issues; profound inequalities in the wealth of nations and of classes; religious, racial, and ethnic violence; and unsolved problems in the relationships between women and men continue to stare us in the face and profoundly affect the quality of our everyday lives.

Giving in to despair and apathy is one possible response to these complex issues, but it is not a response that humans often favour. If it were our nature to give up hope, we would still be sitting around half-naked in the mud outside a cave. People are more inclined to look for ways of improving their lives, and this period of human history is full of opportunities to do so. We have, for example, advanced to the point at which for the first time we have the means to feed and educate everyone in the world. Similarly, it now seems possible to erode some of the inequalities that have always been the major source of human conflict.

Sociology offers useful advice on how to achieve these goals—for sociology is more than just an intellectual exercise. It is also an applied science with practical, everyday uses. Sociologists teach at all levels, from high school to graduate school. They conduct research for local, provincial/territorial, and federal governments; colleges and universities; corporations; the criminal justice system; public opinion firms; management consulting firms; trade unions; social service agencies; international nongovernmental organizations; and private research and testing firms. They are often involved in the formulation of public policy, the creation of laws and regulations by organizations and governments. This is because sociologists are trained not just to see what is, but to see what is possible.

So please consider this book an invitation to explore your society's—and your own—possibilities. We don't provide easy answers. However, we are sure that if you try to grapple with the questions we raise, you will find that sociology can help you figure out where you fit into society and how you can make society fit you.

2

Culture

Rebecca Sapp / WireImage / Getty Images

LEARNING OBJECTIVES

In this chapter, you will learn to

LO¹ Define culture and its main functions.

LO² Explain how culture helps humans adapt and thrive in their environments.

LO³ Recognize how culture can make people freer.

LO⁴ Analyze the ways in which culture is becoming more diverse, multicultural, and globalized.

LO⁵ Recognize how culture can place limits on people's freedom.

LO¹ CULTURE AS PROBLEM SOLVING

Sidney Crosby won't sign a team jersey until he plays a regular season game in that jersey. Tiger Woods wears a red shirt on the last day of every tournament in which he competes. When Crosby and Woods started these superstitious practices, they were taking the first step toward creating one aspect of **culture**, the socially transmitted ideas, practices, and material objects that people create to deal with real-life problems. Their superstitions help to reassure them and let them play better. Research shows that, in general, superstitious practices help athletes reduce anxiety and improve

> **culture** The socially transmitted practices, languages, symbols, beliefs, values, ideologies, and material objects that people create to deal with real-life problems.

Paul Bereswill / Stringer / Getty Images

Culture can solve practical problems. Athletes (like Sidney Crosby, shown here) often develop superstitions to help them manage stress, and if such superstitions are shared, they become part of culture.

society A number of people who interact, usually in a defined territory, and share a culture.

abstraction The human capacity to create general ideas or ways of thinking that are not linked to particular instances.

symbols Things that carry particular meanings, including the components of language, mathematical notations, and signs. Symbols allow us to classify experience and generalize from it.

cooperation The human capacity to create a complex social life by sharing resources and working together.

self-confidence and performance (Damisch, Stoberock, and Mussweiler, 2010).

It is not just athletes who invent routines to help them stop worrying and focus on the job at hand. Soldiers going off to battle, university students about to write final exams, and other people in high-stress situations behave similarly. Some wear a lucky piece of jewellery or item of clothing. Others say special words or a quick prayer. Still others cross themselves. And then there are people who engage in more elaborate rituals. For example, sociologists Cheryl and Daniel Albas of the University of Manitoba interviewed 300 university students about their superstitious practices before final exams. One student felt she would do well only if she ate a sausage and two eggs sunny-side-up on the morning of each exam. The sausage had to be arranged vertically on the left side of her plate and the eggs placed to the right of the sausage so they formed the "100" percent she was aiming for (Albas and Albas, 1989). Of course, the ritual had more direct influence on her cholesterol level than on her grade. Indirectly, however, it may have had the desired effect—to the degree it helped to relieve her anxiety and relax her, she may have done better in exams. Thus, we can say that this student was beginning to create culture in the sociological sense of the term. Her practice helped her deal with the real-life problem of anxiety. Similarly, tools help people solve the problem of how to plant crops and build houses. Religion helps people give meaning to life and come to terms with death. Tools and religion are also elements of culture because they, too, help people solve real-life problems.

Note, however, that religion, technology, and many other elements of culture differ from the superstitions of athletes and undergraduates in one important respect: Superstitions are often unique to the individuals who create them. In contrast, religion and technology are widely shared. They are passed from one generation to the next. How does cultural sharing take place? Through human interaction, communication, and learning. In other words, culture becomes shared when it is socially transmitted. A **society** involves people interacting socially and sharing culture, usually in a defined geographical area. Culture, then, is the sum of the *socially transmitted* ideas, practices, and material objects that enable people to adapt to, and thrive in, their environments.

LO² THE ORIGINS AND COMPONENTS OF CULTURE

Y ou can appreciate the importance of culture for human survival by considering the predicament of early humans about 100 000 years ago. They lived in harsh natural environments. They had poor physical endowments, being slower runners and weaker fighters than many other animals. Yet, despite these disadvantages, they survived. More than that, they prospered and came to dominate nature. Domination was possible largely because humans were the smartest creatures around. Their sophisticated brains enabled them to create cultural survival kits of enormous complexity and flexibility. These cultural survival kits contained three main tools: abstraction, cooperation, and production. Each tool was a uniquely human talent, and each gave rise to a different element of culture.

ABSTRACTION: CREATING SYMBOLS

Human culture exists only because we can think abstractly. **Abstraction** is the capacity to create **symbols** or general ideas that carry particular meanings. Languages and mathematical notations are sets of symbols. They allow us to classify experience and generalize from it. For instance, we recognize that we can sit on many objects but that only some of those objects have four legs, a back, and space for one person. We distinguish the latter from other objects by giving them a name: "chairs." By the time a baby reaches the end of her first year, she has heard that word repeatedly and understands that it refers to a certain class of objects. True, a few chimpanzees have been taught to make some signs with their hands. In this way, they have learned some words and how to string together some simple phrases. However, even these extraordinarily intelligent animals cannot learn any rules of grammar, teach other chimps what they know, or advance much beyond the vocabulary of a human toddler. Abstraction at anything beyond the most rudimentary level is a uniquely human capacity. The ability to abstract enables humans to learn and transmit knowledge in a way no other animal can.

COOPERATION: CREATING NORMS AND VALUES

The ability to cooperate is a second factor that enables human culture to exist. **Cooperation** involves creating a complex social life by establishing **norms** or generally accepted ways of doing things, and **values** or ideas about what is right and wrong, good and bad, beautiful and ugly. For example, family members cooperate to raise children. In the process, they develop and apply norms and values about which child-rearing practices are appropriate and desirable. Different times and places give rise to different norms and values. In our society, parents might ground children for swearing, but in pioneer days, parents would typically "beat the devil out of them." By analyzing how people cooperate and produce norms and values, we can learn much about what distinguishes one culture from another.

Three Types of Norms: Folkways, Mores, and Taboos

If a man walks down a busy street wearing nothing on the top half of his body, he is violating a **folkway**. If he walks down the street wearing nothing on the bottom half of his body, he is violating a **more** (the Latin word for "custom," pronounced MORE-ay). Folkways are norms that specify social *preferences*. Mores are norms that specify social *requirements*. People are usually punished when they violate norms, but the punishment is usually minor if the norm is a folkway. Some onlookers will raise their eyebrows at the shirtless man. Others will shake their head in disapproval. In contrast, the punishment for walking down the street without pants is bound to be moderately harsh. Someone is bound to call the police, probably sooner than later (Sumner, 1940 [1907]). The strongest and most central norm, however, is a **taboo**. When someone violates a taboo, it causes revulsion in the community and punishment is severe. Incest is one of the most widespread taboos. (See also Sociology at the Movies.)

norms Generally accepted ways of doing things.

values Ideas about what is right and wrong, good and bad, beautiful and ugly.

folkway The least important type of norm—a norm that evokes the least severe punishment when violated.

more A core norm that most people believe is essential for the survival of their group or their society.

taboo The strongest type of norm. When someone violates a taboo, it causes revulsion in the community, and punishment is severe.

SOCIOLOGY AT THE MOVIES

Spotlight

Pedophilia is taboo. Surveys show that some regard it as more of a moral outrage than homicide (Seto, 2008: viii). Yet in at least one institution—the Catholic Church—the problem was covered up for many years. For example, in Canada, sexual abuse of minors by priests first received widespread public notice in 1975, when the Royal Newfoundland Constabulary opened an investigation into allegations of physical and sexual abuse at the Mount Cashel Orphanage, a Catholic institution. Two staff members admitted their crime, but the Department of Justice quickly ordered the investigation closed. The officer in charge of the investigation filed a report but the Chief of Police instructed him to submit a new report mentioning only physical mistreatment, deleting all references to sexual abuse. The old report was destroyed. No charges were laid (Higgins, 2012).

The Mount Cashel investigation and cover-up, and many more like it in dozens of countries since the 1970s, raise two interesting sociological questions.

The investigative reporting team in *Spotlight*.

Kerry Hayes / © Open Road Films / Courtesy Everett Collection / The Canadian Press

First, how can taboos be violated, made public, and cause widespread revulsion, yet fail to result in corrective action? Second, what kinds of people are most likely to expose the violation of taboos in such a way that they result in corrective action? The answers to both questions are suggested by *Spotlight*, the true, Oscar-winning story of how a team of *Boston Globe* reporters uncovered widespread sexual abuse of minors in the local Catholic archdiocese, breaking the story in 2002 and winning a Pulitzer Prize for their efforts.

Spotlight's answer to the first question is straightforward: Leaders of powerful institutions often have

(*Continued*)

the capacity to deflect criticism by manipulating culture in such a way as to protect those institutions. The victims of child abuse in Boston were mostly poor kids from troubled families. As one victim explained to reporter Sacha Pfeiffer (played by Rachel McAdams), when a priest asked him for a blow job he complied reluctantly but as if he had been commanded by God. When the mother of an abused child complains, a bishop—a bishop!—visits her home. How can she not be swayed by the great man's attention and compassion, made all the more real by his willingness to arrange a modest payment to compensate for the family's anguish and by his willingness to have the offender reassigned? At a charity function, *Globe* editor Robby Robinson (played by Michael Keaton) tells an influential church spokesman about his team's investigative work. The spokesman reminds Robinson that exposing the rot would hurt the church's good work in the community. The *Globe* team uncovered the horrible misdeeds of 87 priests in the Boston area; however, God, compassion, and charity are persuasive cultural ideals that are deftly employed by powerful institutional leaders to mute devout parishioners.

What kinds of people eventually overcome the silence of the lambs? They are cultural outsiders. Mitchell Garabedian (played by Stanley Tucci) is an Armenian lawyer in a city where most residents are Roman Catholic and most Roman Catholics are of Irish origin. He has been representing victims of child sexual abuse for years and provides key information to the *Globe* reporters that enable them to verify their story. Marty Baron, a Jew from Florida played by Liev Schreiber, is the new *Globe* editor. He is the persistent but soft-spoken force that pushes Robby Robinson and his team of reporters to prove that child abuse in the Catholic Church is a systemic problem.

Second, in thinking about the kinds of people who eventually forced Cardinal Bernard Law, Archbishop of

Boston, to step down in disgrace for his decades-long cover-up—and the people of Boston and beyond who demand sweeping reform in the Catholic Church—it is important to remember that the *Globe* is by far the most widely read newspaper in Boston and a newspaper with a well-deserved reputation for excellence in investigative journalism. A small local newspaper published a story about child sexual abuse in the Catholic Church years before the *Globe* did but nobody paid attention. However, when the *Globe,* a popular institution governed by the cultural principles of truth and independence, finally acted, it served as a counterweight to established interests in the church hierarchy. It is not just Mitchell Garabedian and Marty Baron who are the heroes of this story. The devotion of the *Globe* reporting staff to countervailing cultural ideals and the capacity of the *Globe* to have those ideals prevail were also responsible for the success of the newspaper's exposé.

Critical Thinking Questions

1. The best scientific estimates suggest that the prevalence of pedophilia is two to four times higher among priests than among the population as a whole (1 to 2 percent in the general population and more than 4 percent among priests; see Böhm et al., 2014: 639; Stevenson, 2014). Why do you think the prevalence is higher among priests?

2. When Archbishop Law stepped down, a *Boston Globe* editorial labelled him "the central figure in a scandal of criminal abuse, denial, payoff, and cover-up that resonates around the world" ("[The] cardinal's departure," 2002). Yet in 2004, Pope John Paul II appointed Law to a ceremonial post in Rome. Law continues to this day to serve as Cardinal Priest of Santa Susanna, the American Catholic church in Rome. Why might the church honour Law in this way?

PRODUCTION: CREATING MATERIAL CULTURE

Finally, culture can exist because humans can engage in **production**; we can make and use tools and techniques that improve our ability to take what we want from nature. Sociologists call such tools and techniques **material culture**. All animals take from nature to subsist, and an ape may sometimes use a rock to break another object or use a stick to keep its balance in a fast-flowing stream. However, only humans are sufficiently intelligent and dexterous to *make* tools and use them to produce everything from food to computers. Understood in this sense, production is a uniquely human activity.

Table 2.1 illustrates each of the basic human capacities and their cultural offshoots in the field of medicine. As in all fields of human endeavour, including medicine, abstraction, operation, and production give rise to specific kinds of ideas, norms, and elements of material culture.

production The human capacity to make and use tools. It improves our ability to take what we want from nature.

material culture The tools and techniques that enable people to accomplish tasks.

CULTURE AND SOCIAL CLASS

A society's core cultural elements are widely shared. However, culture is not homogeneous across all sectors of society. Significant variation in culture is evident in

By acquiring specialized skills, people are able to accomplish things that no person could possibly do alone.

different classes, ethnic and racial groups, genders, and regions. To illustrate this point, consider the relationship between culture and social class, remembering from Chapter 1, Introducing Sociology, that a social class is a position in a hierarchy that that is shaped by economic criteria, including wealth and income.

Sociologists distinguish **high culture** from **popular culture** or **mass culture**. High culture includes opera, ballet, classical music, fine art, and literature. Popular or mass culture includes movies, TV shows, and rock, hip hop, and country music. Popular or mass culture is consumed by many people in all social classes. In contrast, as French sociologist Pierre Bourdieu (1986) emphasized, the consumption of high culture tends to be restricted to upper classes. That is because appreciating the fine points of high culture requires a certain type of education or training that takes considerable time and money to achieve. This fact makes high culture more accessible to people in upper classes and less accessible to people in lower classes.

Sociologists who study the political effects of culture often distinguish **dominant culture** from **subordinate culture**. Dominant culture helps rich and powerful categories of people exercise control over others. Subordinate culture contests dominant culture to varying degrees.

Consider the widely held notion that anyone can become rich if he or she works hard and makes smart choices. That belief is part of our dominant culture insofar

high culture Culture consumed mainly by upper classes.

popular culture (or mass culture) Culture consumed by all classes.

dominant culture Helps rich and powerful categories of people exercise control over others.

subordinate culture Contests dominant culture to varying degrees.

TABLE 2.1 The Building Blocks of Culture

The human capacity for ...	Abstraction	Cooperation	Production
Gives rise to these elements of culture ...	Ideas	Norms and values	Material culture
In medicine, for example ...	*Theories* are developed about how a certain drug might cure a disease.	*Experiments* are conducted to test whether the drug works as expected.	*Treatments* are developed on the basis of the experimental results.

Source: Adapted from Robert Bierstedt, 1963, *The Social Order: An Introduction to Sociology*, New York: McGraw-Hill.

as it is widely shared and justifies the wealth that rich people enjoy by making it seem as if rich people became wealthy just by virtue of their cleverness and diligence. It ignores the economic and other advantages that many rich people inherit from their parents. It also plays down the fact that many people who are not rich would like to make the right choices but lack the means to do so. Some people who want to attend medical school just can't afford it. The belief that hard work and smart choices alone determine success helps to justify the transmission of valued resources from rich and powerful adults to their children while obscuring the difficulties that others may face in their effort to move up the socioeconomic hierarchy.

To the degree that members of lower classes agree that hard work and good choices alone make people rich, they accept a core idea of dominant culture. However, many members of lower classes are skeptical about this belief because they work hard but experience social constraints that prevent them and their offspring from becoming rich: diseases and accidents related to the kinds of jobs they do, insufficient money to help their children attend professional school, and so on. (See the section on Politics and the Perception of Class Inequality in Chapter 6, Social Stratification: Canadian and Global Perspectives, for survey evidence supporting this claim.) Such skepticism is part of their subordinate culture, and in certain circumstances it may boil over into outright rebellion against upper class ideas and institutions. We consider the circumstances that encourage such rebellion in Chapter 13, Technology, the Environment, and Social Movements.

Even the idea that there is a "proper" way to speak English is part of the dominant culture. After all, well-to-do people are more likely to speak proper English than others are. And even if they don't, they can most easily afford to send their children to elite schools where they can learn the right accent, a rich vocabulary, and authoritative grammatical structures. Meeting "the right sort of people" depends in part on learning how to talk to them. In this sense, proper English is a cultural tool that allows people to join useful social networks and exclude the less fortunate from them.

LANGUAGE AND THE SAPIR–WHORF THESIS

Language is in fact one of the most important parts of any culture. A **language** is a system of symbols strung together to communicate thought. Equipped with language, we can share understandings, pass experience and knowledge from one generation to the next, and make plans for the future. In short, language allows culture to develop. Consequently, sociologists commonly think of language as a cultural invention that distinguishes humans from other animals.

In the 1930s, Edward Sapir and Benjamin Lee Whorf proposed an influential argument about the connections among experience, thought, and language. It is now known as the **Sapir–Whorf thesis** (Whorf, 1956). It holds that we experience important things in our environment and form concepts about those things (path 1 to 2 in Figure 2.1). Then, we develop language to express our concepts (path 2 to 3). Finally, language itself influences how we see the world (path 3 to 1).

For example, different types of camels are important in the environment of nomadic Arabs, and different types of snow are important in the lives of the Inuit in Canada's Far North (path 1 to 2). Consequently, nomadic Arabs have developed many words for different types of camels and the Inuit have developed many words for different types of snow (path 2 to 3). Distinctions that these people see elude us because types of camels and snow are less important in our environment.

In turn, language obliges people to think in certain ways (path 3 to 1). If you are walking in a park, you will know whether a certain tree is in front of you, behind you, to the left, or to the right. When asked where the tree is, you will use such directions to describe its position. We think "egocentrically," locating objects relative to ourselves. However, egocentric directions have no meaning for speakers of Tzeltal in southern Mexico or of Guugu Yimithirr in Queensland, Australia. They lack concepts and words for "left," "right," and so on. They think geographically, and will say that the tree is to the "north," "south," "east," or "west." Trained from infancy to attend to geographic direction, Tzeltal speakers are obliged to think in those terms. If a tree to the north is

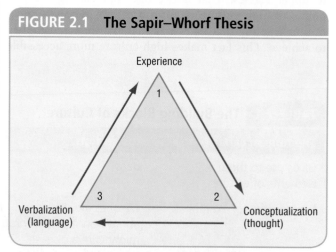

FIGURE 2.1   The Sapir–Whorf Thesis

Experience

1

3   2

Verbalization (language)   Conceptualization (thought)

Source: From BRYM/LIE. *Sociology*, 1E. © 2009 Nelson Education Ltd. Reproduced by permission. www.cengage.com/permissions.

located behind them and they are asked where the tree is, they will point to themselves, as if they don't exist. Reportedly, a Tzeltal speaker can be blindfolded, put in a dark room, and spun around 20 times until he's dizzy yet still point without hesitation to the north, south, east, and west (Boroditsky, 2010; Deutscher, 2010).

Taking an example closer to home, income and power inequality between women and men encourages some men to use terms like *fox, babe, bitch, ho,* and *doll* to refer to women. The use of such words in itself influences men to think of women simply as sexual objects. If men are ever going to think of women as equals, gender inequality will have to be reduced—but the language such men use to refer to women will also have to change.

Someone once defined language as a dialect supported by an army and a navy (Weinreich, 1945:13). The definition makes a lot of sense if we consider shifts in language use worldwide. For centuries, Great Britain, the United States, France, and Spain have gained political, cultural, and linguistic influence over much of the world by employing military violence, supporting sympathetic governments, helping to create new educational systems, and fostering the spread of the mass media. The rise of English (and, to a lesser degree, French and Spanish) has meant the elimination or endangerment of thousands of languages around the world spoken by the tribes of Papua New Guinea; the native peoples of the Americas; the national and tribal minorities of Asia, Africa, and Oceania; and marginalized European peoples, such as the Irish and the Basques. It is estimated that the 5000 to 6000 languages spoken in the world today will be reduced to 1000 to 3000 in a century.

Much of the culture of a people—its prayers, humour, conversational styles, technical vocabulary, myths, and ways of thinking—is expressed through language. Therefore, the loss of language amounts to the disappearance of tradition and perhaps even identity, and their replacement by the traditions and identity of the colonial power, with television playing an important role in the transformation (Woodbury, 2003).

CULTURE AS FREEDOM AND CONSTRAINT

A FUNCTIONALIST ANALYSIS OF CULTURE: CULTURE AND ETHNOCENTRISM

Despite its central importance in human life, culture is often invisible. That is, people tend to take their own culture for granted. It usually seems so sensible and natural that they rarely think about it. In contrast, people are often startled when confronted by cultures other than their own. The ideas, norms, values, and techniques of other cultures frequently seem odd, irrational, and even inferior.

Judging another culture exclusively by the standards of our own is known as **ethnocentrism.** Ethnocentrism impairs sociological analysis. This can be illustrated by Marvin Harris's (1974) functionalist analysis of a practice that seems bizarre to many Westerners: cow worship among Hindu peasants in India. Hindu peasants refuse to slaughter cattle and eat beef because, for them, the cow is a religious symbol of life. Pinup calendars throughout rural India portray beautiful women with the bodies of fat white cows with milk jetting out of each teat. Cows are permitted to wander the streets, defecate on the sidewalks, and stop to chew their cud in busy intersections or on railroad tracks, forcing traffic to a complete halt. In Chennai, police stations maintain fields where stray cows that have fallen ill can graze and be nursed back to health. The government even runs old-age homes for cows, where dry and decrepit cattle are kept free of

ethnocentrism The tendency to judge other cultures exclusively by the standards of your own.

© Dinodia / V.H. Mishra

Many Westerners find the Indian practice of cow worship bizarre, but it performs several useful economic functions and is, in that sense, rational. By viewing cow worship exclusively as an outsider (or, for that matter, exclusively as an insider), we fail to see its rational core.

charge. All of this special care seems mysterious to most Westerners, for it takes place amid poverty and hunger that could presumably be alleviated if only the peasants would slaughter their "useless" cattle for food instead of squandering scarce resources to feed and protect these animals.

According to Harris (1974: 3–32), however, ethnocentrism misleads many Western observers. Cow worship, it turns out, is an economically rational practice in rural India. For one thing, Indian peasants can't afford tractors, so cows are needed to give birth to oxen, which are in high demand for plowing. For another, the cows produce hundreds of millions of kilograms of recoverable manure, about half of which is used as fertilizer and half as a cooking fuel. With oil, coal, and wood in short supply, and with the peasants unable to afford chemical fertilizers, cow dung is, well, a godsend. What is more, cows in India don't cost much to maintain because they eat mostly food that is not fit for human consumption. And they represent an important source of protein as well as a livelihood for members of low-ranking castes, who have the right to dispose of the bodies of dead cattle. These "untouchables" eat beef and form the workforce of India's large leather craft industry. The protection of cows by means of cow worship is thus a sensible and efficient economic practice. It seems irrational only when judged by the standards of Western agribusiness.

Harris's (1974) analysis of cow worship in rural India is interesting for two reasons. First, it illustrates how functionalist theory can illuminate otherwise mysterious social practices. You will recall from Chapter 1 the functionalist claim that social structures have consequences that make social order possible. Some of those consequences are manifest (intended and easily observed), while others are latent (unintended and less obvious). Harris discovered that cow worship performs a range of latent functions, showing how a particular social practice has unintended consequences that make social order possible.

We can also draw an important lesson about ethnocentrism from Harris's analysis. If you refrain from judging other societies by the standards of your own, you will have taken an important first step toward developing a sociological understanding of culture.

LO³ CULTURE AS FREEDOM

Culture has two faces. First, culture provides us with an opportunity to exercise our *freedom*. We create elements of culture in our everyday life to solve practical problems and express our needs, hopes, joys, and fears.

However, creating culture is just like any other act of construction in that we need raw materials to get the job done. The raw materials for the culture we create consist of cultural elements that either existed before we were born or that other people have created since our birth. We may put these elements together in ways that produce something genuinely new, but we have no other well to drink from, so existing culture puts limits on what we can think and do. In that sense, culture *constrains* us. This is culture's second face. In the rest of this chapter, we take a close look at both faces of culture.

SYMBOLIC INTERACTIONISM AND CULTURAL PRODUCTION

Until the 1960s, many sociologists argued that culture is a "reflection" of society. Using the language introduced in Chapter 1, we can say that they regarded culture as a dependent variable. Harris's (1974) analysis of people in rural India certainly fits that mould. In Harris's view, the social necessity of protecting cows caused the cultural belief that cows are holy.

In recent decades, the symbolic interactionist tradition we discussed in Chapter 1 has influenced many sociologists of culture. Symbolic interactionists regard culture as an *independent* variable. In their view, people do not just accept culture passively—we are not empty vessels into which society pours a defined assortment of beliefs, symbols, and values. Instead, we produce and interpret culture, creatively fashioning it to suit our diverse and changing needs.

The symbolic interactionist idea that people creatively produce and interpret culture implies that, to a degree, we are at liberty to choose how culture influences us.

LO⁴ CULTURAL DIVERSIFICATION

This is a nice room tonight. When I look out, I see all kinds of different people. I see Black, White, Asian, everybody hangin' out, havin' a good time. . . . This type of thing is not going to be able to happen about 300 years from now. You realize that? . . . You realize there's not going to be any more White people? There's not going to be any more Black people? Everyone's going to be beige. . . . It's true, the whole world's mixing. There's nothing you can do about it. Eventually, we're all going to become some hybrid mix of Chinese and Indian. It's inevitable.

They're the two largest populations in the world. So you can run from us now. But sooner or later, we're going to hump you. . . . But I'm thinkin' if we're all going to mix anyway, let's start mixing people now that would never normally mix just to see what we'll get. You know, hook up a Jamaican with an Italian. They could have little Pastafarians. I'm Indian. I could hook up with a Jewish girl and we could have little Hinjews. A woman from the Philippines, a guy from Holland—little Hollapinos. A guy from Cuba, a woman from Iceland—little Ice-cubes. A French and a Greek—Freaks. A German and a Newfie— little Goofies. It's gonna happen. We might as well help it along.

—*Russell Peters (2009), Canadian comedian whose family came from India*

Part of the reason we are increasingly able to choose how culture influences us is that a greater diversity of culture is available from which to choose. Like many societies, Canada is undergoing rapid cultural diversification. Canada used to be composed almost exclusively of Christian northern

Grosse Île on the St. Lawrence River was Quebec's quarantine station and the main point of entry for immigrants coming to Canada from 1832 to 1937. In 1909, the Celtic cross memorial was erected to honour the memory of the 3000 Irish immigrants who perished from typhus between 1847 and 1848, during the Great Irish Potato Famine, and the 2000 others who died in transit from Ireland.

Europeans and an Aboriginal minority. Then, in the 1960s, Canada eliminated overt racism in its immigration policies, and the country began to diversify culturally. In the 1970s, the Canadian government continued the trend by adopting a policy of multiculturalism, which funds the maintenance of culturally diverse communities (Fleras and Elliott, 2002).

About 95 percent of immigrants who arrived in Canada before 1961 came from Europe and the United States. Now about 65 percent of immigrants come from *outside* Europe and the United States. Because of the inflow of immigrants from non-traditional sources such as China, India, Pakistan, and the Philippines (see Table 2.2), more than a fifth of the population will be non-white by 2017 (excluding Aboriginal Canadians). Nearly three-quarters of non-white Canadians will reside in Toronto, Vancouver, and Montreal, with most of the rest in Edmonton, Calgary, and Winnipeg (Cardozo and Pendakur, n.d.).

MULTICULTURALISM

Although each province and territory in Canada holds jurisdiction over education, it was common until recent decades for schools across Canada to stress the common elements of our culture, history, and society. Students learned the historical importance of the "charter groups"—the English and the French—in

Russell Peters

TABLE 2.2 Top 10 Sources of Canadian Immigrants, 2011

Country	Percentage of Total
China	13.1
India	12.8
Philippines	11.4
Pakistan	4.9
Iran	4.4
United States	3.3
United Kingdom and colonies	2.2
France	2.2
Iraq	1.9
South Korea	1.7
Other	42.1
Total	**100.0**

Source: Citizenship and Immigration Canada. 2015. "Facts and figures 2013—Immigration overview: Permanent residents." http://www.cic.gc.ca/english/resources/statistics/facts2013/permanent/10.asp (retrieved 26 June 2015).

The Canadian Press

The Canadian Charter of Rights and Freedoms forms the first part of the 1982 Constitution Act. Section 27 requires the Charter to be interpreted in a mulitnational context.

Canada's history. School curricula typically neglected the contributions of non-white, non-French, and non-English people to Canada's historical, literary, artistic, and scientific development. Moreover, students learned little about the less savoury aspects of Canadian history, including Canada's racist immigration policies that sought to preserve Canada's "English stock" by restricting or denying entry to certain groups (see Chapter 7, Race and Ethnicity). In general, history books were written from the perspective of the victors, not the vanquished.

For the past several decades, the advocates of **multiculturalism** have argued that all levels of school curricula should present a more balanced picture of Canadian history, culture, and society—one that better reflects the country's ethnic and racial diversity in the past and its growing ethnic and racial diversity today (Henry, Tator, Mattis, and Rees, 2001; James, 2003). In the words of one group of experts, "The purpose of schooling must be to 'empower' [minority groups]..., to give them the ability to participate fully in struggles, large and small, to gain respect, dignity, and power" (Gaskell, McLaren, and Novogrodsky, 1995: 105).

Advocates of multiculturalism suggest that we must bring our educational system in line with Canada's status as the world's first officially multicultural society. They point out that in launching its multiculturalism policy in 1971, the government declared that Canada, although officially bilingual, has no "official" culture—that is, none of the distinguishable cultures in Canada take precedence over the others. Moreover, with the passage of the Canadian Multiculturalism Act in 1988, the government confirmed its commitment to recognizing all Canadians "as full and equal participants in Canadian society." Multiculturalists conclude that to the extent that school curricula are culturally biased, they fail to provide students with the type of education a country devoted to multiculturalism must demand.

Some critics argue that our immigration and multiculturalist policies weaken Canada's social fabric. For one thing, they argue that multiculturalism encourages **cultural relativism**, which is the opposite of ethnocentrism. It is the idea that all cultures and cultural practices have equal value. The trouble with this view is that some cultures oppose values that most Canadians hold dear. Should we respect racist and antidemocratic cultures, such as the apartheid regime that existed in South Africa from 1948 until 1992? Or female circumcision, which is still widely practised in Somalia, Sudan, and Egypt? Critics argue that by promoting cultural relativism, multiculturalism encourages respect for practices that are abhorrent to most Canadians. (Multiculturalists reply that cultural relativism need not be taken to an extreme. *Moderate* cultural relativism encourages tolerance and should be promoted.)

multiculturalism Policy that reflects Canada's ethnic and racial diversity in the past and enhances its ethnic and racial diversity today.

cultural relativism The belief that all cultures have equal value.

Canada continues to diversify culturally.

Aaron Lynett / Toronto Star / Getty Images

A CONFLICT ANALYSIS OF CULTURE: THE RIGHTS REVOLUTION

What are the social roots of cultural diversity and multiculturalism? Conflict theory suggests where we can look for an answer. Recall from Chapter 1 the central argument of conflict theory: Social life is an ongoing struggle between more- and less-advantaged groups. Privileged groups try to maintain their advantages, while subordinate groups struggle to increase theirs. And sure enough, if we probe beneath cultural diversification and multiculturalism, we find what has been called the **rights revolution**, the process by which socially excluded groups have struggled to win equal rights under the law and in practice.

After the outburst of nationalism, racism, and genocidal behaviour among the combatants in World War II, the United Nations proclaimed the Universal Declaration of Human Rights in 1948. It recognized the "inherent dignity" and "equal and inalienable rights of all members of the human family" and held that "every organ of society"

should "strive by teaching and education to promote respect for these rights and freedoms and by progressive measures, national and international, to secure their universal and effective recognition and observance" (United Nations, 1998).

Fanned by such sentiment, the rights revolution was in full swing by the 1960s. Today, women's rights, minority rights, gay and lesbian rights, the rights of people with special needs, constitutional rights, and language rights are all part of our political discourse. Because of the rights revolution, democracy has been widened and deepened. The rights revolution is by no means finished. Many categories of people are still discriminated against socially, politically, and economically. However, in much of the world, all categories of people now participate more fully than ever before in the life of their societies (Ignatieff, 2000).

The rights revolution raises some difficult issues. For example, some members of groups that have suffered extraordinarily high levels

> **rights revolution** The process by which socially excluded groups have struggled to win equal rights under the law and in practice.

of discrimination historically, such as Aboriginal Canadians, Chinese Canadians, and others, have demanded reparation in the form of money, symbolic gestures, land, and political autonomy (see Chapter 7, Race and Ethnicity). Much controversy surrounds the extent to which today's citizens are obligated to compensate past injustices.

Such problems notwithstanding, the rights revolution is here to stay and it affects our culture profoundly. Specifically, the rights revolution fragments Canadian culture by (1) legitimizing the grievances of groups that were formerly excluded from full social participation, and (2) renewing their pride in their identity and heritage. Our history books, our literature, our music, our use of languages, and our very sense of what it means to be Canadian have diversified culturally. White, male, heterosexual property owners of northern European origin are still disproportionately influential in Canada, but our culture is no longer dominated by them in the way that it was just half a century ago.

The Coca-Cola Company was one of the first American companies to go global.

© Rob Crandall / The Image Works

proved nothing was ordained about who should rule and how they should do so. Religious dissent ensured that the Catholic Church would no longer be the supreme interpreter of God's will in the eyes of all Christians. Authority and truth became divided as never before.

Cultural fragmentation picked up steam during industrialization, as the variety of occupational roles grew and new political and intellectual movements crystallized. Its pace is quickening again today as a result of globalization. Globalization, as defined in Chapter 1, is the process by which formerly separate economies, nation-states, and cultures are becoming tied together and people are becoming increasingly aware of their growing interdependence.

Globalization has many roots. International trade and investment are expanding. Members of different ethnic and racial groups are migrating and coming into sustained contact with one another. A growing number of people from these diverse groups date, court, and marry across religious, ethnic, and racial lines. Influential "transnational" organizations have been created, such as the International Monetary Fund, the European Union, Greenpeace, Amnesty International, and *Médecins sans frontières*. Inexpensive international travel and communication make contacts between people from diverse cultures routine. The mass media make Ryan Gosling and *The*

FROM DIVERSITY TO GLOBALIZATION

The cultural diversification we witness today is not evident in preliterate or tribal societies. In such societies, cultural beliefs and practices are virtually the same for all group members. For example, many tribal societies organize **rites of passage**. These cultural ceremonies mark the transition from one stage of life to another (e.g., from childhood to adulthood) or from life to death (e.g., funerals). They involve elaborate procedures, such as body painting and carefully orchestrated chants and movements. They are conducted in public, and no variation from prescribed practice is allowed. Culture is homogeneous (Durkheim, 1976 [1915/1912]).

In contrast, pre-industrial western Europe and North America were rocked by artistic, religious, scientific, and political forces that fragmented culture. The Renaissance, the Protestant Reformation, the Scientific Revolution, the French and American revolutions—between the fourteenth and eighteenth centuries, all of these movements involved people questioning old ways of seeing and doing things. Science placed skepticism about established authority at the very heart of its method. Political revolution

rites of passage Cultural ceremonies that mark the transition from one stage of life to another (e.g., baptisms, confirmations, weddings) or from life to death (e.g., funerals).

Owen Franklin / Corbis Documentary / Getty Images

A hallmark of postmodernism is the combining of cultural elements from different times and places. Architect I. M. Pei unleashed a storm of protest when his 22-metre glass pyramid became an entrance to the Louvre in Paris. It created a postmodern nightmare in the eyes of some critics.

Vampire Diaries as well known in Warsaw as in Winnipeg, while hip-hop is as popular in Senegal and Tunisia as it is in Montreal. Globalization, in short, eliminates political, economic, and cultural isolation, bringing people together in what Canadian communications guru Marshall McLuhan (1964) called a "global village." Because of globalization, people are less obliged to accept the culture into which they are born and freer to combine elements of culture from a wide variety of historical periods and geographical settings. In 1987, nobody would have believed that in just 25 years, 2 billion people from around the world would want to view a video, "Gangnam Style," by South Korean rock star Psy and have the means to do so almost instantly, nearly without cost, and as many times as they wanted.

POSTMODERNISM

Some sociologists think that so much cultural fragmentation and reconfiguration has taken place in the last few decades that a new term is needed to characterize the culture of our times: **postmodernism**.

Scholars often characterize the last half of the nineteenth century and the first half of the twentieth century as the era of modernity. During this hundred-year period, belief in the inevitability of progress, respect for authority, and consensus around core values characterized much of Western culture. In contrast, postmodern culture involves an eclectic mix of elements from different times and places, the erosion of authority, and the decline of consensus around core values. Let us consider each of these aspects of postmodernism in turn.

Blending Cultures

A mixing of diverse elements from different times and places is the first aspect of postmodernism. In the postmodern era, it is easier to create individualized belief systems and practices by blending facets of different cultures and historical periods. Consider religion. Although most Canadians say they believe in God and continue to identify themselves as Christians, increasing numbers now identify themselves as adherents of Eastern non-Christian religions or as having "no religion" (see Chapter 10, Religion and Education). In addition, Canadians are increasingly showing a willingness to feast from a religious buffet that combines a conventional menu with a wide assortment of other supernatural beliefs and practices, including astrology, tarot, New Age mysticism, psychic phenomena, and communication with the dead (Bibby, 1987: 233, 2001: 195). Simply put, we have many more ways to worship than we used to. For example, a person can easily construct a personalized religion involving, say, belief in the divinity of Jesus *and* yoga. In the words of one journalist, "In an age when we trust ourselves to assemble our own investment portfolios and cancer therapies, why not our religious beliefs?" (Creedon, 1998).

Individuals thus draw on religions much like consumers shop in a mall. Meanwhile, churches, synagogues, and other religious institutions have diversified their menus to appeal to the spiritual, leisure, and social needs of religious consumers and retain their loyalties in the competitive market for congregants and parishioners (Finke and Stark, 1992).

postmodernism Culture characterized by an eclectic mix of cultural elements from different times and places, the erosion of authority, and the decline of consensus around core values.

Erosion of Authority

The erosion of authority is the second aspect of postmodernism. Half a century ago, Canadians were more likely than they are today to defer to authority in the family, schools, politics, and medicine. Today, we are more likely to challenge authority and hold parents, teachers, politicians, and doctors in lower regard. In the 1950s, for example, Robert Young played the firm, wise, and always-present father in the TV hit *Father Knows Best*. In the 2010s, the typical TV father is more like Homer Simpson: a fool. Another illustration of the erosion of authority concerns belief in God or a higher power. Surveys show that the percentage of Canadians saying they "definitely" believe in God or a higher power or "think so" has declined in all age cohorts between 1985 and 2015—and the decline is largest in the youngest age cohort (see Figure 2.2). Finally, consider also that voting and other forms of conventional

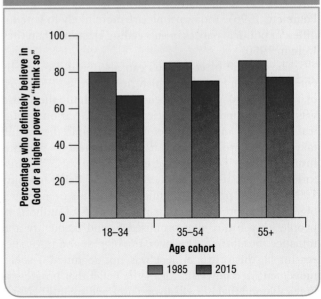

FIGURE 2.2 Belief in God or a Higher Power by Age Cohort, Canada, 1985 and 2015

Sources: Reginald Bibby, *Project Canada 1985 National Survey*; Reginald Bibby and Angus Reid, 2015 Angus Reid Institute Religion Survey.

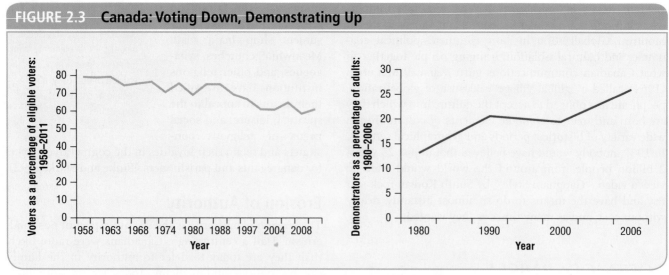

FIGURE 2.3   Canada: Voting Down, Demonstrating Up

Sources: Elections Canada, 2012, "Voter Turnout at Federal Elections and Referendums"; *World Values Survey*, 2012.

politics are less popular than they used to be, while non-conventional political action, such as participating in demonstrations, is more popular (see Figure 2.3).

Instability of Core Values

The decline of consensus around core values is the third aspect of postmodernism. Half a century ago, most people's values remained stable during their adult lives and many values were widely accepted. Today, value shifts are more rapid and consensus has broken down on many issues. For example, in the middle of the twentieth century, most adults remained loyal to one political party from one election to the next. However, specific issues and personalities have increasingly eclipsed party loyalty as the driving forces of Canadian politics (Clarke, Jenson, LeDuc, and Pammett, 1996). Today, people are more likely to vote for different political parties in succeeding elections than they were in 1950.

The decline of consensus can also be illustrated by considering the fate of "big historical projects." For most of the past 200 years, consensus throughout the world was built around big historical projects. Various political and social movements convinced people they could take history into their own hands and create a glorious future just by signing up. German Nazism was a big historical project. Its followers expected the Reich to enjoy 1000 years of power. Communism was an even bigger big historical project, mobilizing hundreds of millions of people for a future that promised to end inequality and injustice for all time. However, the biggest and most successful big historical project was not so much a social movement as a powerful idea—the belief that progress is inevitable and that life will always improve, mainly because of the spread of democracy and scientific innovation.

The twentieth century was unkind to big historical projects. Russian communism lasted 74 years. German Nazism endured a mere 12. The idea of progress fell on hard times as 100 million soldiers and civilians died in wars; the forward march of democracy took wrong turns into fascism, communism, and regimes based on religious fanaticism; and pollution from urbanization and industrialization threatened the planet. In the postmodern era,

The father figure of postmodernism?

20th Century Fox / The Kobal Collection at Art Resource, NY

people increasingly recognize that apparent progress, including scientific advances, often have negative consequences (Scott, 1998). As the poet E. E. Cummings once wrote, "Nothing recedes like progress."

IS CANADA THE FIRST POSTMODERN COUNTRY?

Until the mid-1960s, the image of Canadians among most sociologists was that of a stodgy people: peaceful, conservative, respectful of authority, and therefore unlike our American cousins.

According to conventional wisdom, the United States was born in open rebellion against the British motherland. Its western frontier was lawless. Vast opportunities for striking it rich bred a spirit of individualism. So American culture became an anti-authoritarian culture. Canada developed differently in this conventional view. It became an independent country not through a revolutionary upheaval but in a gradual, evolutionary manner. The North-West Mounted Police and two hierarchical churches (Roman Catholic and Anglican) established themselves on the western frontier *before* the era of mass settlement, allowing for the creation of an orderly society rather than a "Wild West." Beginning with the Hudson's Bay Company, large corporations quickly came to dominate the Canadian economy, hampering individualism and the entrepreneurial spirit. Consequently, Canadian culture became a culture of deference to authority. That, at least, was the common view until the 1960s (Lipset, 1963).

Although the contrast between deferential Canadian culture and anti-authoritarian American culture had validity 50 or 60 years ago, it is inaccurate today (Adams, 1997: 62–95). As we have seen, the questioning of authority spread throughout the Western world beginning in the 1960s. Nowhere, however, did it spread as quickly and thoroughly as in Canada. Canadians used to express more confidence in big business than Americans did, but surveys now show the opposite. Canadians used to be more religious than Americans were, but that is no longer the case. Fewer Canadians (in percentage terms) say they believe in God and fewer attend weekly religious services. Confidence in government has eroded more quickly in Canada than in the United States. Americans are more patriotic than Canadians, according more respect to the state. Finally, Americans are more likely than Canadians are to regard the traditional nuclear family as the ideal family form and to think of deviations from tradition—same-sex couples, single-parent families, cohabitation without marriage—as the source of a whole range of social problems. Thus, whether sociologists examine attitudes toward the family, the state, the government, religion, or big business, they now find that Americans are more deferential to traditional institutional authority than Canadians are.

Because Canadians are less deferential to traditional institutional authority than Americans are, some commentators say that Canadians lack a distinct culture. For example, American patriotism sparks awareness of great national accomplishments in art, war, sports, science, and, indeed, all fields of human endeavour. Anthems, rituals, myths, and festivities celebrate these accomplishments and give Americans a keen sense of who they are and how they differ from non-Americans. Not surprisingly, therefore, a larger percentage of Americans than of Canadians think of themselves in unhyphenated terms—as "Americans" plain and simple rather than, say, Italian-Americans. In Canada, a larger percentage of the population thinks of itself in hyphenated terms; compared with the Americans, our identity is qualified, even tentative.

Does this mean that Canadians lack a distinct national culture? Hardly. It means that although American culture is characterized by a relatively high degree of deference to dominant institutions, Canadian culture is characterized by a relatively high degree of tolerance and respect for diversity. We are more likely than Americans are to favour gender equality, accept gay and lesbian relationships, encourage bilingualism and multiculturalism, and accept the right of Aboriginals to political autonomy. Characteristically, a large international survey by a condom manufacturer found that Americans have sex more often than Canadians do, but Canadians are more likely to say that the pleasure of their partner is very important. As public opinion pollster Michael Adams writes, "Twenty-five years of public-opinion polling in Canada has taught me a seemingly paradoxical truth: Canadians feel *strongly* about their *weak* attachments to Canada, its political institutions and their fellow citizens. In other words, they feel strongly about the right to live in a society that allows its citizens to be detached from ideology and critical of organizations, and not to feel obliged to be jingoistic or sentimentally patriotic. Canadians *lack* of nationalism is, in many ways, a distinguishing feature of the country" (Adams, 1997: 171).

In short, Canadian culture *is* distinctive, and its chief distinction may be that it qualifies us as the first thoroughly postmodern society.

LO⁵ CULTURE AS CONSTRAINT

We noted above that culture has two faces. One we labelled *freedom,* the other *constraint.* Diversity, globalization, and postmodernism are all aspects of the new freedoms that culture allows us today. We now turn to an examination of two contemporary aspects of culture that act as constraining forces on our lives: rationalization and consumerism.

RATIONALIZATION

Max Weber coined the term **rationalization** to describe the application of the most efficient means to achieve given goals and the unintended, negative consequences of doing so. He claimed that rationalization has crept into all spheres of life (Figure 2.4). In Weber's view, rationalization is one of the most constraining aspects of contemporary culture, making life akin to living inside an "iron cage."

The constraining effects of rationalization are evident, for example, in the way we measure and use time. People did not always let the clock determine the pace of daily life. The first mechanical clocks were installed in public squares in Germany 700 years ago to signal the beginning of the workday, the timing of meals, and quitting time. Workers were accustomed to enjoying a flexible and vague work schedule regulated only approximately by the seasons and the rising and setting of the Sun. The strict regime imposed by the work clocks made their lives harder. They staged uprisings to silence the clocks, but to no avail. City officials sided with employers and imposed fines for ignoring the work clocks (Thompson, 1967).

Today, few people rebel against the work clock. This is especially true of urban North American couples who are employed full-time in the paid labour force and have young children. For them, life often seems an endless round of waking up at 6:30 a.m.; getting everyone washed and dressed; preparing the kids' lunches; getting them out the door in time for the school bus or the car pool; driving to work through rush-hour traffic; facing the speed-up at work resulting from the recent downsizing; driving back home through rush-hour traffic; preparing dinner; taking the kids to their soccer game; returning home to clean up the dishes and help with homework; getting the kids washed, their teeth brushed, and then into bed; and (if they have not brought some office work home) grabbing an hour of TV before collapsing, exhausted, for 6½ hours' sleep before the story repeats itself.

Life is less hectic for residents of small towns, unmarried people, couples without young children, retirees, and the unemployed. But the lives of others are typically so packed with activities that they must carefully regulate time and parcel out each moment so they can tick off one item after another from an ever-growing list of tasks that need to be completed on time (Schor, 1992). After 700 years of conditioning, allowing clocks to precisely regulate our activities seems the most natural thing in the world, although there is of course nothing natural about it.

The regulation of time ensures efficiency. It maximizes how much work you get done in a day. It enables trains to run on schedule, university classes to begin punctually, and business meetings to start on time. However, many people complain that life has become too hectic to enjoy. A popular restaurant in Japan has even installed a punch-clock for its customers. The restaurant offers all you can eat for 35 yen per minute. As a result, "the diners rush in, punch the clock, load their trays from the buffet table, and concentrate intensely on efficient chewing and swallowing, trying not to waste time talking to their companions before rushing back to punch out" (Gleick, 2000 [1999]: 244). Some upscale restaurants in New York and Los Angeles have gotten in on the act. An increasingly large number of business clients are so pressed for time, they pack in two half-hour lunches with successive guests. The restaurants oblige, making the resetting of tables "resemble the pit-stop activity at the Indianapolis 500" (Gleick, 2000 [1999]: 155). As these examples illustrate, a *rational* means (the use of the work clock) has been applied to a *given goal* (maximizing work) but has led to an *irrational end* (a too-hectic life).

> **rationalization** The application of the most efficient means to achieve given goals and the unintended, negative consequences of doing so.

FIGURE 2.4   The Rationalization of Chinese Script

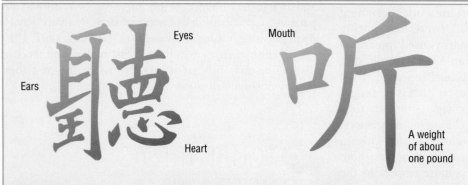

Reprinted here are the Chinese characters for "listening" (t'ing) in traditional Chinese script (left) and simplified, modern script (right). Each character is composed of several word-symbols. In traditional script, listening is depicted as a process involving the eyes, the ears, and the heart. It implies that listening demands the utmost empathy and involves the whole person. In contrast, modern script depicts listening as something that involves merely one person speaking and the other "weighing" speech. Modern Chinese script has been rationalized. Has empathy been lost in the process?

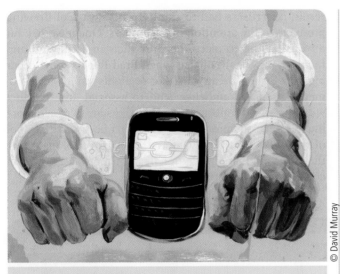

"Cuffberry" by David Murray

CONSUMERISM

The second constraining aspect of culture we will examine is consumerism. **Consumerism** is the tendency to define ourselves in terms of the goods and services we purchase. As artist Barbara Kruger once put it, "I shop, therefore I am."

The rationalization process, when applied to the production of goods and services, enables us to produce more efficiently, to have more of just about everything than previous generations did. However, it is consumerism that ensures that most of the goods we produce will be bought. Of course, we have lots of choices. We can select from dozens of styles of running shoes, cars, toothpaste, and all the rest. We can also choose to buy items that help define us as members of a particular **subculture**, adherents of a set of distinctive values, norms, and practices within a larger culture. But, individual tastes aside, we all have one thing in common. We tend to be good consumers. We are motivated by advertising, which is based on the accurate insight that people will tend to be considered cultural outcasts if they fail to conform to stylish trends. By creating those trends, advertisers push us to buy, even if doing so requires that we work more and incur large debts (Schor, 1999). That is why the

A Boxing Day sale lineup

"shop-till-you-drop" lifestyle of many North Americans prompted French sociologist Jean Baudrillard to remark pointedly that even what is best in America is compulsory (Baudrillard, 1988 [1986]; see the Sociology on the Tube feature in this chapter).

Recent innovations in advertising take advantage of our tendency to define ourselves in terms of the goods we purchase. For example, when channel surfing and the use of personal video recorders became widespread, advertisers realized they had a problem. Viewers started skipping TV ads that cost millions of dollars to produce. As a result, advertisers had to think up new ways of drawing products to the attention of consumers. One idea they hit on was paying to place their products in TV shows and movies. They realized that when Brad Pitt or some other big star drinks a can of Coke or lights up a Marlboro, members of the audience tend to associate the product with the star. Wanting to be like the star, they are more likely to buy the product. The product becomes a symbol of what many viewers wanted to be, again demonstrating that consumerism, like rationalization, acts as a powerful constraint on our lives.

SOCIOLOGY ON THE TUBE

Hoarders: Is Consumerism a Social Disease?

The *Diagnostic and Statistical Manual of Mental Disorders* (DSM-5) is the psychiatrist's "bible." It lists defining criteria for hundreds of ailments. An entire chapter is devoted to "Obsessive Compulsive and Related Disorders." According to the DSM-5, people suffer from a compulsion if they feel they have to perform repetitive behaviour to reduce stress, even though the behaviour cannot realistically neutralize it. One compulsive disorder is hoarding (American Psychiatric Association, n.d.).

Consider Debra, whom viewers met during Season 6 of the reality TV show *Hoarders*. Her kitchen is pictured here. The surfaces are not visible because, like the rest of her house, they are covered with all manner of objects that she has compulsively purchased. Her children and husband are distraught over her behaviour. Thanks to a psychologist's intervention, we learn that Debra's compulsive behaviour is likely a response to a series of bitter disappointments—having boys when she wanted girls, watching her husband have multiple affairs, and so on.

Although DSM-5 lists hoarding as a mental disorder, it fails to appreciate the sociological fact that different social settings create opportunities for expressing compulsions in different forms. In intensely spiritual sixteenth-century Spain, the compulsive behaviour of Ignatius of Loyola, a devout priest and the founder of the Jesuits, took a religious form. He was never satisfied

Scene from *Hoarders*

A&E / The Kobal Collection at Art Resource, NY

that he had confessed his sins sufficiently and could not stop himself from compulsively going to confession many times a day, although doing so tormented him (Ganss, 1991: 77–78).

The United States and Canada are consumer societies. We don't earn enough to buy all that we want, so we borrow money to feed our compulsion; on average, Canadians owed 168 percent more than they earned annually in 2016, a record high (Isfeld, 2016). Do we all, to varying degrees, suffer from a compulsive disorder?

Critical Thinking Questions

1. What are the negative consequences of shopping addiction for individuals and for society?
2. What are the positive consequences?
3. Do the positive consequences outweigh the negative consequences or vice versa?

FROM COUNTERCULTURE TO SUBCULTURE

In concluding our discussion of culture as a constraining force, we note that consumerism is remarkably effective at taming countercultures. Countercultures are subversive subcultures. They oppose dominant values and seek to replace them. The hippies of the 1960s formed a counterculture and so do environmentalists today.

Countercultures rarely pose a serious threat to social stability. Most often, the system of social control, of rewards and punishments, keeps countercultures at bay. In our society, consumerism acts as a social control mechanism that normally prevents countercultures from disrupting the social order. It does that by transforming deviations from mainstream culture into means of making money and by enticing rebels to become entrepreneurs (Frank and Weiland, 1997). The development of hip-hop helps to illustrate the point (Brym, 2015: 13–31).

Hip-hop originated in the American inner city in the 1970s. At the time, manufacturing industries were leaving the inner city for suburban or foreign locales, where land values were lower and labour was less expensive. Unemployment among black youth rose to more than 40 percent. At the same time, many middle-class blacks left the inner city for the suburbs. Their migration robbed the remaining young people of successful role models. It also eroded the taxing capacity of municipal governments, leading to a decline in public services. Meanwhile, the American public elected conservative governments at the state and federal levels. They cut school and welfare budgets, thus deepening the destitution of ghetto life (Piven and Cloward, 1977: 264–361; 1993; Wilson, 1987).

With few legitimate prospects for advancement, poor black American youth in the inner city turned increasingly to crime and, in particular, to the drug trade. In the late 1970s, cocaine was expensive and demand for the drug was flat. Consequently, in the early 1980s, Colombia's Medellin drug cartel introduced a less expensive form of cocaine called "rock" or "crack." Crack was inexpensive, it offered a quick and intense high, and it was highly addictive. It offered many people a temporary escape from hopelessness and soon became wildly popular in the inner city. Turf wars spread as gangs tried to outgun each other for control of the local traffic. The sale and use of crack became so widespread it corroded much of what was left of the inner city black American community (Davis, 1990).

The shocking conditions described above gave rise to a shocking musical form: hip-hop. Stridently at odds with the values and tastes of both whites and middle-class black Americans, hip-hop described and glorified the mean streets of the inner city while holding the police, the mass media, and other pillars of society in contempt. Furthermore, hip-hop tried to offend middle-class sensibilities, black and white, by using highly offensive language.

In 1988, more than a decade after its first stirrings, hip-hop reached its political high point with the release of the album *It Takes a Nation of Millions to Hold Us Back* by Chuck D and Public Enemy. In "Don't Believe the Hype," Chuck D accused the mass media of maliciously distributing lies. In "Black Steel in the Hour of Chaos," he charged the FBI and the CIA with assassinating the two great leaders of the black American community in the 1960s, Martin Luther King and Malcolm X. In "Party for Your Right to Fight," he blamed the federal government for organizing the fall of the Black Panthers, the radical black nationalist party of the 1960s. Here, it seemed, was an angry expression of subcultural revolt that could not be tamed.

> **countercultures** Subversive subcultures that oppose dominant values and seek to replace them.

However, the seduction of big money did much to mute the political force of hip-hop. As early as 1982, with the release of Grandmaster Flash and the Furious Five's "The Message," hip-hop began to win acclaim from mainstream rock music critics. With the success of Run-D.M.C. and Public Enemy in the late 1980s, it became clear there was a big audience for hip-hop. Significantly, much of that audience was composed of white youths. As one music critic wrote, they "relished . . . the subversive 'otherness' that the music and its purveyors represented" (Neal, 1999: 144). Sensing the opportunity for profit, major media corporations, such as Time/Warner, Sony, CBS/Columbia, and BMG Entertainment, signed distribution deals with the small independent recording labels that had formerly been the exclusive distributors of hip-hop CDs. In 1988, *Yo! MTV Raps* debuted on MTV. The program brought hip-hop to middle America.

Most hip-hop recording artists proved they were eager to forgo political relevancy for commerce. For instance, WU-Tang Clan started a line of clothing called WU-Wear, and, with the help of major hip-hop recording artists, companies as diverse as Tommy Hilfiger, Timberland, Starter, and Versace began to market clothing influenced by ghetto styles. Independent labels such as Phat Farm and Fubu also prospered. Puff Daddy reminded his audience in his 1999 CD, *Forever:* "N___ get money, that's simply the plan." According to *Forbes* magazine, he became one of the country's 40 richest men under 40. By 2005, having renamed himself Diddy, he had his own line of popular clothing.

The members of Run-D.M.C. once said that they "don't want nobody's name on my behind" but those days were long past by the early 1990s. Hip-hop was no longer just a musical form but a commodity with spinoffs. Rebellion had been turned into mass consumption. Hip-hop's radicalism had given way to the lures of commerce. A counterculture had become a subculture.

Radical political currents in hip-hop still exist. For example, in 2012, Macklemore and Lewis's first hit,

"Same Love," criticized homophobia in hip-hop and promoted gay rights. Their single, "Thrift Shop," which topped the *Billboard* "Hot 100" for six weeks and won a Grammy award for best rap song in 2014, is a critique of mindless consumerism. Nonetheless, such currents seem to be less common in English-speaking countries than elsewhere. In Senegal, the playing of hip-hop that is highly critical of the government is widely believed to have helped topple the ruling party in the 2000 election. In France, North African youth living in impoverished and segregated slums use hip-hop to express their political discontent, and some analysts say the genre helped mobilize youth for antigovernment rioting in 2005 (Akwagyiram, 2009). *Rais Lebled* [Mr. President], a song by Tunisian rapper El Général, became the anthem of young people participating in the democratic uprisings in Tunisia, Egypt, and elsewhere in the Arab world in 2011: "Mr. President, your people are dying/People are eating rubbish/Look at what is happening/Miseries everywhere, Mr. President/I talk with no fear/Although I know I will get only trouble/I see injustice everywhere" (Ghosh, 2011).

In North America, however, hip-hop has become, for the most part, an apolitical commodity that increasingly appeals to a racially heterogeneous, middle-class audience. As one of hip-hop's leading analysts and academic sympathizers writes, "the discourse of ghetto reality or 'hood authenticity remains largely devoid of political insight or progressive intent" (Forman, 2001: 121). The fate of hip-hop is testimony to the capacity of consumerism to change countercultures into mere subcultures, thus constraining dissent and rebellion.

Macklemore and Lewis

Phillip Chin / WireImage / Getty Images

READY TO STUDY?

IN THE BOOK, YOU CAN:

❏ Tear out the chapter review card at the back of the book to have a summary of the chapter and key terms handy.

ONLINE YOU CAN:

❏ Work through key concepts with a Guided Learning Question.

❏ Prepare for tests with quizzes.

❏ Review the key terms with flash cards.

❏ Explore practical examples of chapter concepts with Connect a Concept exercises.

GO TO NELSON.COM/STUDENT TO ACCESS THESE DIGITAL RESOURCES.

3
Socialization

LO¹ SOCIAL ISOLATION AND SOCIALIZATION

One day in 1800, a 10- or 11-year-old boy walked out of the woods in southern France. He was filthy, naked, and unable to speak, and he had not been toilet trained. After being taken by the police to a local orphanage, he repeatedly tried to escape and refused to wear clothes. No parent ever claimed him. He became known as "the wild boy of Aveyron." A thorough medical examination found no major abnormalities of either a physical or a mental nature. Why, then, did the boy seem more animal than human? Because, until he walked out of the woods, he had been raised in isolation from other humans for years (Shattuck, 1980).

Similar horrifying reports lead to the same conclusion. Occasionally, a child is found locked in an attic or a cellar, where he or she saw another person for only short periods each day to receive food. Like the wild boy of Aveyron, such children rarely develop normally. Typically, they remain uninterested in games. They cannot form intimate social relationships with other people. They develop only the most basic language skills.

Some of these children may suffer from congenitally low intelligence. The amount and type of social contact they had before they were discovered is unknown. Some may have been abused, so their condition may not be due to social isolation alone. However, these examples do at least suggest that the ability to learn culture and become human is only a potential. To be actualized, **socialization** must unleash this potential. Socialization is the process by which people learn their culture. They do so by (1) entering into and disengaging from a succession of roles and (2) becoming aware of themselves as they interact with others. A **role** is the behaviour expected of a person occupying a particular position in society.

Convincing evidence of the importance of socialization in unleashing human potential comes from a study conducted by René Spitz (1945, 1962). Spitz compared children who were being raised in an orphanage with children who were being raised in a

LEARNING OBJECTIVES

In this chapter, you will learn to

LO¹ Recognize that human abilities remain undeveloped unless social interaction unleashes them.

LO² Compare change over the past century in the socializing influence of the family, schools, peer groups, and the mass media.

LO³ Appreciate that people's identities change faster, more often, and more completely than they did just a couple of decades ago.

LO⁴ List the factors transforming the character of childhood and adolescence today.

> **socialization** The process by which people learn their culture. They do so by (1) entering into and disengaging from a succession of roles and (2) becoming aware of themselves as they interact with others.
>
> **role** A set of behaviours expected of a person occupying a particular position in society.

nursing home attached to a women's prison. Both institutions were hygienic and provided good food and medical care. However, the children's mothers cared for the babies in the nursing home, whereas only six nurses cared for the 45 babies in the orphanage. The orphans therefore had much less contact with other people. Moreover, from their cribs, the nursing home infants could see a slice of society. They saw other babies playing and receiving care. They saw mothers, doctors, and nurses talking, cleaning, serving food, and providing medical treatment. In contrast, the caregivers in the orphanage would hang sheets from the cribs to prevent the infants from seeing the activities of the institution. Depriving the infants of social stimuli for most of the day apparently made them less demanding.

Social deprivation had other effects too. Because of the different patterns of child care just described, by the age of 9 to 12 months the orphans were more susceptible to infections and had a higher death rate than the babies in the nursing home. By the time they were two to three years old, all of the children from the nursing home were walking and talking, compared with fewer than 8 percent of the orphans. Normal children begin to play with their own genitals by the end of their first year. Spitz found that the orphans began this sort of play only in their fourth year. He took this as a sign that they might have an impaired sexual life when they reached maturity. This outcome has been observed in rhesus monkeys raised in isolation. Spitz's natural experiment thus amounts to quite compelling evidence for the importance of childhood socialization in making us fully human. Without childhood socialization, most of our human potential remains undeveloped.

THE CRYSTALLIZATION OF SELF-IDENTITY

The formation of a sense of self continues in adolescence. Adolescence is a particularly turbulent period of self-development. Consequently, many people can remember experiences from their youth that helped crystallize their self-identity. Do you? Robert Brym clearly recalls one such defining moment (Brym, 2006).

"I can date precisely the pivot of my adolescence," says Robert. "I was in Grade 10. It was December 16. At 4 p.m. I was a nobody, and I knew it. Half an hour later, I was walking home from school, delighting in the slight sting of snowflakes melting on my upturned face, knowing I had been swept up in a sea of change.

"About 200 students had sat impatiently in the auditorium that last day of school before the winter vacation. We were waiting for Mr. Garrod, the English teacher who headed the school's drama program, to announce the cast of *West Side Story*. I was hoping for a small speaking part and was not surprised when Mr. Garrod failed to read my name as a chorus member. However, as the list of remaining characters grew shorter, I became despondent. Soon only the leads remained. I knew that an unknown kid in Grade 10 couldn't possibly be asked to play Tony, the male lead. Leads were usually reserved for more experienced Grade 12 students.

"Then came the thunderclap. 'Tony,' said Mr. Garrod, 'will be played by Robert Brym.'

"'Who's Robert Brym?' whispered a girl sitting two rows ahead of me. Her friend merely shrugged in reply. If she had asked *me* that question, I might have responded similarly. Like nearly all 15-year-olds, I was deeply involved in the process of figuring out exactly who I was. I had little idea of what I was good at. I was insecure about my social status. I wasn't sure what I believed in. In short, I was a typical teenager. I had only a vaguely defined sense of self.

In the 1960s, researchers Harry and Margaret Harlow placed baby rhesus monkeys in various conditions of isolation to study the animals' reactions. Among other things, they discovered that baby monkeys raised with an artificial mother made of wire mesh, a wooden head, and the nipple of a feeding tube for a breast were later unable to interact normally with other monkeys. However, when the artificial mother was covered with a soft terry cloth, the infant monkeys clung to it in comfort and later exhibited less emotional distress. Infant monkeys preferred the cloth mother even when it had less milk than the wire mother. The Harlows concluded that emotional development requires affectionate cradling.

Science Source/Getty Images

"A sociologist once wrote that 'the central growth process in adolescence is to define the self through the clarification of experience and to establish self-esteem' (Friedenberg, 1959: 190). From this point of view, playing Tony in *West Side Story* turned out to be the first section of a bridge that led me from adolescence to adulthood. Playing Tony raised my social status in the eyes of my classmates, made me more self-confident, taught me I could be good at something, helped me to begin discovering parts of myself I hadn't known before, and showed me that I could act rather than merely be acted upon. In short, it was through my involvement in the play (and, subsequently, in many other plays throughout high school) that I began to develop a clear sense of who I am."

The crystallization of self-identity during adolescence is just one episode in a lifelong process of socialization. To paint a picture of the socialization process in its entirety, we first review the main theories of how a sense of self develops during early childhood. We then discuss the operation and relative influence of society's main socializing institutions or "agents of socialization": families, schools, peer groups, and the mass media. In these settings, we learn, among other things, how to control our impulses, think of ourselves as members of different groups, value certain ideals, and perform various roles. You will see that these institutions do not always work hand in hand to produce happy, well-adjusted adults. They often give mixed messages. That is, they teach children and adolescents different and even contradictory lessons. You will also see that although recent developments give us more freedom to decide who we are, they can make socialization more disorienting than ever before.

Finally, in the concluding section of this chapter, we examine how decreasing supervision and guidance by adult family members, increasing assumption of adult responsibilities by youths, and declining participation in extracurricular activities are changing the nature of childhood and adolescence today. Some analysts even say that childhood and adolescence are vanishing before our eyes. So the main theme of this chapter is that the development of self-identity is often a difficult and stressful process—and it is becoming more so.

The contours of the self are formed during childhood. We therefore begin by discussing the most important social-scientific theories of how the self originates in the first years of life.

THE SYMBOLIC-INTERACTIONIST FOUNDATIONS OF CHILDHOOD SOCIALIZATION

Socialization begins soon after birth. Infants cry, driven by elemental needs, and are gratified by food, comfort, and affection. Because their needs are usually satisfied immediately, they do not at first seem able to distinguish themselves from their main caregivers, usually their mothers. However, social interaction soon enables infants to begin developing a self-image or sense of self—a set of ideas and attitudes about who they are as independent beings.

SIGMUND FREUD

Austrian psychoanalyst Sigmund Freud proposed the first social-scientific interpretation of the process by which the self emerges (Freud, 1962 [1930], 1973 [1915–17]). He noted that infants demand immediate gratification but begin to form a self-image when their demands are denied—when, for example, parents decide not to feed and comfort them every

> **self** A set of ideas and attitudes about who one is as an independent being.

Sigmund Freud (1856–1939)

© Hemis/Alamy

id Freud's term for the pleasure-seeking component of the self.

superego Freud's term for the restraining component of the self.

ego Freud's term for the mechanism that balances the id and the superego.

looking-glass self Cooley's description of the way our feelings about who we are depend largely on how we see ourselves evaluated by others.

I According to Mead, the subjective and impulsive aspect of the self that is present from birth.

me According to Mead, the objective component of the self that emerges as people communicate symbolically and learn to take the role of the other.

significant others The people who play important roles in the early socialization experiences of children.

time they wake up in the middle of the night. The parents' refusal at first incites howls of protest. However, infants soon learn to eat more before going to bed, sleep for longer periods, and go back to sleep if they wake up. Equally important, the infant begins to sense that its needs differ from those of its parents, it has an existence independent of others, and it must somehow balance its needs with the realities of life. Because of many such lessons in self-control, the child eventually develops a sense of what constitutes appropriate behaviour and a moral sense of right and wrong. Soon a personal conscience crystallizes. It is a storehouse of cultural standards. In addition, a psychological mechanism develops that normally balances the pleasure-seeking and restraining components of the self. (Freud called the pleasure-seeking component of the self the **id**, the restraining component the **superego**, and the balancing mechanism the **ego**.) Earlier thinkers believed that the self emerges naturally, the way a seed germinates. In a revolutionary departure from previous thinking on the subject, Freud argued that only social interaction can allow the self to emerge.

CHARLES HORTON COOLEY

American scholars took ideas about the emergence of the self in a still more sociological direction. Notably, sociologist Charles Horton Cooley introduced the idea of the **looking-glass self**, making him a founder of the symbolic-interactionist tradition and an early contributor to the sociological study of socialization.

Cooley observed that when we interact with others, they gesture and react to us. This allows us to imagine how we appear to them. We then judge how others evaluate us. Finally, from these judgments we develop a self-concept or a set of feelings and ideas about who we are. In other words, our feelings about who we are depend largely on how we see ourselves evaluated by others. Just as we see our physical body reflected in a mirror, so we see our social selves reflected in people's gestures and reactions to us (Cooley, 1902). When teachers evaluate students negatively, for example, students may develop a negative self-image that causes them to do poorly in school. Poor performance may have as much to do with teachers' negative evaluations as with students' innate abilities (Hamachek, 1995; see Chapter 10, Religion and Education). Here, succinctly put, we have the hallmarks of what came to be known as symbolic interactionism—the idea that in the course of face-to-face communication, people engage in a creative process of attaching meaning to things.

GEORGE HERBERT MEAD

George Herbert Mead (1934) took up and developed Cooley's idea of the looking-glass self. Like Freud, Mead noted that a subjective and impulsive aspect of the self is present from birth. Mead called it the **I**. Again like Freud, Mead argued that a storehouse of culturally approved standards emerges as part of the self during social interaction. Mead called this objective social component of the self the **me**. However, whereas Freud focused on the denial of impulses as the mechanism that generates the self's objective side, Mead drew attention to the unique human capacity to "take the role of the other" as the source of the me.

Mead understood that human communication involves seeing yourself from other people's points of view. How, for example, do you interpret your mother's smile? Does it mean "I love you," "I find you humorous," or something else entirely? According to Mead, you can find the answer by using your imagination to take your mother's point of view for a moment and see yourself as she sees you. In other words, you must see yourself objectively as a me to understand your mother's communicative act. All human communication depends on being able to take the role of the other, wrote Mead. The self thus emerges from people using symbols, such as words and gestures, to communicate. It follows that the me is not present from birth. It emerges only gradually during social interaction.

Mead's Stages of Development

Mead saw the self as developing in various stages of role-taking:

1. At first, children learn to use language and other symbols by *imitating* important people in their lives, such as their mother and father. Mead called such people **significant others**.

2. Second, children pretend to be other people. That is, they use their imaginations to role-play in games, such as "house," "school," and "doctor."

3. Third, about the time they reach the age of seven, children learn to play complex games that require

them to take the role of several other people simultaneously. In baseball, for example, the infielders have to be aware of the expectations of everyone in the infield. A shortstop may catch a line drive. If she wants to make a double play, she must almost instantly be aware that a runner is trying to reach second base and that the person playing second base expects her to throw there. If she hesitates, she probably cannot execute the double play.

4. Once a child can think in this complex way, he or she can begin the fourth stage in the development of the self, which involves taking the role of what Mead called the **generalized other**. Years of experience may teach an individual that other people, employing the cultural standards of their society, usually regard him or her as funny or temperamental or intelligent. A person's image of these cultural standards and how they are applied to him or her is what Mead meant by the generalized other.

Since Mead, some psychologists interested in the problem of childhood socialization have analyzed how the style, complexity, and abstractness of thinking (or "cognitive skills") develop in distinct stages from infancy to the late teenage years (Piaget and Inhelder, 1969). Others have analyzed how the ability to think morally develops in stages (Kohlberg, 1981). However, from a sociological point of view, it is important to emphasize that the development of cognitive and moral skills is more than just the unfolding of a person's innate characteristics. As we will now see, the structure of a person's society and his or her position in it also influences socialization (see the Sociology on the Tube feature in this chapter).

GENDER DIFFERENCES

One of the best-known examples of how social position affects socialization comes from the research of Carol Gilligan. Gilligan showed that sociological factors help explain differences in the sense of self that boys and girls usually develop. That is because parents and teachers tend to pass on different cultural standards to each gender. Such adult authorities usually define the ideal woman as eager to please and therefore not assertive. Most girls learn this lesson as they mature. The fact that girls usually encounter more male and fewer female teachers and other authority figures as they grow up reinforces the lesson. Consequently, much research shows that girls tend to develop lower self-esteem than boys do, although it seems doubtful that teenage girls in general experience the decline in self-esteem that Gilligan detected in her early work (Brown and Gilligan, 1992; Kling, Hyde, Showers, and Buswell, 1999).

CIVILIZATION DIFFERENCES

In a like manner, sociological factors help explain the development of different ways of thinking or cognitive styles of different civilizations (Cole, 1995; Vygotsky, 1987). Consider, for example, the contrast between ancient China and ancient Greece. In part because of complex irrigation needs, the rice agriculture of ancient southern China required substantial cooperation among neighbours. It had to be centrally organized in an elaborate hierarchy within a large state. Harmony and social order were therefore central to ancient Chinese life. Ancient Chinese thinking, in turn, tended to stress the importance of mutual social obligation and consensus rather than debate. Ancient Chinese philosophy focused on the way in which whole systems, not analytical categories, cause processes and events.

In contrast, the hills and seashores of ancient Greece were suited to small-scale herding and fishing. Ancient Greece was less socially complex than ancient China was. It was more politically decentralized. It gave its citizens more personal freedom. As a result, philosophies tended to be analytical, which means, among other things, that processes and events were viewed as the result of discrete categories rather than whole systems. Markedly different civilizations grew up on these different cognitive foundations. Ways of thinking depended less on people's innate characteristics than on the structure of society (Nisbett, Peng, Choi, and Norenzayan, 2001).

The Art Archive at Art Resource, NY

From *Extreme Makeover* to *Revenge Body*

It all began with *Extreme Makeover* in 2002. In a typical episode, a team comprising a plastic surgeon, a personal trainer, a hairdresser, and a wardrobe consultant refashioned a woman's exterior. The cameras recorded the woman's doubts and suffering, but also her resilience and determination. In the end, when she saw the finished product, her self-esteem skyrocketed and her family and friends waxed ecstatic over her Cinderella transformation.

As of 2016, Wikipedia listed 37 English-language makeover reality TV shows that offered fast solutions to problems of housing, career, intimate relations, wardrobe, and so on. Local variants of many of these shows were available for Canadian audiences. The latest was Khloe Kardashian's *Revenge Body*. The show featured young women who had been dumped by their husbands. After spending countless hours at the gym, dieting rigorously, allowing talented hairdressers and makeup artists to beautify them, scoring a gorgeous new wardrobe, and posting umpteen selfies on Facebook, they finally got what they wanted: a body so alluring that exes who saw the photos broke down crying and wanted desperately to rekindle the romance.

Of course, almost everyone wants to be attractive and have a good job, a long-lasting intimate relationship with another adult, and material comforts. However, makeover reality TV shows like *Revenge Body* teach viewers that all we need to be happy is the achievement of commercially manufactured ideas of what constitutes the perfect body, face, career, partner, house, and wardrobe. Said differently, their common message is that the surest path to self-awareness and self-fulfillment involves accepting images generated by others as ideals. To be happy, all you have to do is please other people, including the lout who dumped you because he was unable to appreciate your intelligence, compassion, and good humour.

Mead would say that makeover reality TV shows make it seem as if all worthwhile self-development comes from the "me"—the objectification supplied, in this case, largely by marketing experts—not from thoughtful exploration of the creative "I." The tough questions posed by ancient Greek philosophy—Who

Revenge Body, Khloe Kardashian's reality TV show, is based on the idea that happiness comes from having the perfect body, face, house, partner, career, and so on—as defined by advertisers. Do realistic alternatives to this vision exist or does the show make a valid point?

am I? What do I need to make me happy?—have no relevance in this context. Arguably, shows like *Revenge Body* turn answers to these difficult questions into instant and, for most people, unrealistic solutions focusing on the commercial images others provide. They teach us little about how to know ourselves and thus how to live happily.

Critical Thinking Questions

1. In your opinion, at what point(s) in the life cycle—childhood, adolescence, early adulthood, mature adulthood, retirement—are people most influenced by commercially generated ideals?
2. Why do you think such influence is strongest at a particular point (or particular points) in the life cycle?

H.M. HERGET/National Geographic Creative

Clearly, society plays a major role in shaping the way we think and the way we think of ourselves (refer back to the Sociology on the Tube feature in this chapter). Freud and the early symbolic interactionists discovered the fundamental process by which the self develops, and later researchers emphasized the gender, civilizational, and other social bases of diverse socialization patterns.

LO² FUNCTION, CONFLICT, SYMBOLIC INTERACTION, AND GENDER: HOW AGENTS OF SOCIALIZATION WORK

Early work on childhood socialization leaves two key questions unanswered. First, does socialization help to maintain social order or does it give rise to conflict that has the potential to change society? Second, if society socializes people, how much freedom do individuals have to choose, modify, or even reject these influences? Functionalists, conflict theorists, symbolic interactionists, and feminists answer these key questions differently:

- Functionalists emphasize how socialization helps to maintain orderly social relations. They also play down the freedom of choice that individuals enjoy in the socialization process.
- Conflict and feminist theorists typically stress the discord based on class, gender, and other divisions that

is inherent in socialization and that sometimes causes social change.

- Symbolic interactionists highlight the creativity of individuals in attaching meaning to their social surroundings. They focus on the many ways in which we often step outside of, and modify, the values and roles that authorities try to teach us.

Whether it maintains order or engenders conflict, shapes us or allows us to shape it, the socialization process operates through a variety of social institutions, including families, schools, peer groups, and, in modern times, the mass media. We now consider how these various "agents of socialization" work. As we do so, please take careful note of the functionalist, conflict, symbolic-interactionist, and feminist interpretations embedded in our discussion.

FAMILY FUNCTIONS

Few sociologists would disagree with the functionalist claim that the family is the most important agent of primary socialization, the process of mastering the basic skills required to operate in society during childhood. After all, the family is well suited to providing the kind of careful, intimate attention required for primary socialization. It is a small group, its members are in frequent face-to-face contact, and most parents love their children and are therefore highly motivated to care for them. These characteristics make most families ideal for teaching small children everything from language to their place in the world.

Note, however, that the socialization function of the family was more pronounced a century ago, partly because adult family members were more readily available for child care and supervision than they are today. As industry grew across Canada, families left farming for city work in factories and offices. Many women had to work outside the home for a wage to maintain an adequate standard of living for their families. Fathers spent less time working with children on the family farm. Fathers partly compensated by spending somewhat more time caring for their children. However, because divorce rates have increased and many fathers have less contact with their children after divorce, children probably see less of

> **primary socialization** The process of acquiring the basic skills needed to function in society during childhood. Primary socialization usually takes place in the family.

The family is still an important agent of socialization, although its importance has declined since the nineteenth century.

secondary socialization
Socialization outside the family after childhood.

hidden curriculum Teaches students what will be expected of them as conventionally good citizens once they leave school.

their fathers on average now than they did a century ago. In some countries, such as Sweden and France, the creation of state-funded child-care facilities compensated for these developments by helping teach, supervise, and discipline children (see Chapter 9, Families). In Canada, however, child care—and therefore childhood socialization—became a big social problem, leading in some cases to child neglect and abuse. Families are still the most important agent of primary socialization, but they are less important than they once were, and they sometimes function poorly.

SCHOOLS: FUNCTIONS AND CONFLICTS

For children over the age of five, the child-care problem was resolved partly by the growth of the public school system, which became increasingly responsible for **secondary socialization**, or socialization outside the family after childhood. In addition, industry needed better-trained and better-educated employees. Therefore, by the early twentieth century, every province had passed laws prescribing the ages between which a child had to attend school. Today, about 85 percent of Canadians between the ages of 25 and 65 have completed high school and about 55 percent have postsecondary qualifications (Statistics Canada, 2009c). This makes Canadians among the most highly educated people in the world.

Instructing students in academic and vocational subjects is the school's *manifest* function. One of its latent functions is to teach what sociologists call the **hidden curriculum**. The hidden curriculum instructs students in what will be expected of them in the larger society once they graduate—it teaches them to be conventionally "good citizens." Most parents approve. According to one survey conducted in several highly industrialized countries, the capacity of schools to socialize students is more important to the public than all academic subjects except math (Galper, 1998).

What is the content of the hidden curriculum? In the family, children tend to be evaluated on the basis of personal and emotional criteria. As students, however, they are led to believe that they are evaluated solely on the basis of their performance on impersonal, standardized tests. They are told that similar criteria will be used to evaluate them in the work world. The lesson is, of course, only partly true. As you will see in Chapter 7 (Race and Ethnicity), Chapter 8 (Sexualities and Genders), and Chapter 10 (Religion and Education), it is not just performance but also class, gender, sexual orientation, and racial criteria that help to determine success in school and in the work world. But the accuracy of the lesson is not the issue here. The important point is that the hidden curriculum does its job if it convinces students that they are judged on the basis of performance alone. Similarly, a successful hidden curriculum teaches students punctuality, respect for authority, the importance of competition in leading to excellent performance, and other conformist behaviours and beliefs that are expected of good citizens, conventionally defined.

The idea of the hidden curriculum was first proposed by conflict theorists, who, you will recall, see an ongoing struggle between privileged and disadvantaged groups whenever they probe beneath the surface of social life (Willis, 1984). Their research on socialization in schools highlights the way many students—especially those from working-class and racial-minority families—struggle against the hidden curriculum.

Conflict theorists acknowledge that schools teach many working-class and racial-minority students to act like conventional good citizens. However, they also note that a disproportionately large number of such students reject the hidden curriculum because their experience and that of their friends, peers, and family members make them skeptical about the ability of school to open good job opportunities for them. As a result, they rebel against the authority of the school. Expected to be polite and studious, they openly violate rules and neglect their work. Consequently, they do poorly in school and eventually enter the work world near the bottom of the socioeconomic hierarchy. Paradoxically, the rebellion of working-class and racial-minority students against the hidden curriculum typically helps to sustain the overall structure of society, with all of its privileges and disadvantages.

SYMBOLIC INTERACTIONISM AND THE SELF-FULFILLING PROPHECY

Early in the twentieth century, symbolic interactionists proposed the **Thomas theorem**, which holds that "situations we define as real become real in their consequences" (Thomas, 1966 [1931]: 301). They also developed the closely related idea of the **self-fulfilling prophecy**, an expectation that helps to cause what it predicts. Our analysis of the hidden curriculum suggests that the expectations of working-class and racial-minority students often act as self-fulfilling prophecies. Expecting to achieve little if they play by the rules, they reject the rules and so achieve little.

The self-fulfilling prophecy does not operate only among students. Teachers, too, develop expectations that help to cause what they predict. In one famous study, two researchers informed the teachers in a primary school that they were going to administer a special test to the pupils to predict intellectual "blooming." In fact, the test was just a standard IQ test. After the test, they told teachers which students they could expect to become high achievers and which students they could expect to become low achievers. In fact, the researchers assigned pupils to the two groups at random. At the end of the year, the researchers repeated the IQ test. They found that the students singled out as high achievers scored significantly higher than those singled out as low achievers. Because the only difference between the two groups of students was that teachers expected one group to do well and the other to do poorly, the researchers concluded that teachers' expectations alone influenced students' performance (Rosenthal and Jacobson, 1968).

The clear implication of this research is that if a teacher believes that poor or minority-group children are likely to do poorly in school, chances are they will. That is because students who are members of groups that are widely expected to perform poorly *internalize* social expectations. They feel anxious about their performance and anxiety lowers their performance level (Steele, 1997).

PEER GROUPS

Like schools, **peer groups** are agents of socialization whose importance grew in the twentieth century. Peer groups consist of individuals who are not necessarily friends but who are about the same age and of similar status. (**Status** refers to a recognized social position an individual can occupy.) Peer groups help children and adolescents to separate from their families and develop independent sources of identity. They particularly influence such lifestyle issues as appearance, social activities, and dating. In fact, from middle childhood through adolescence, the peer group is often the dominant socializing agent.

As you probably learned from your own experience, conflict often exists between the values promoted by parents and those promoted by the adolescent peer group. Issues such as tobacco, drug, and alcohol use; hair and dress styles; political views; musical taste; and curfew times are likely to become points of conflict between the generations. Adolescent peer groups are controlled by youth, and through them, young people begin to develop their own identities. They do this by rejecting some parental values, experimenting with new elements of culture, and engaging in various forms of rebellious behaviour (see Figure 3.1 and Figure 3.2). Such rejection is typically a group phenomenon, not just a matter of individual choice. Thus, one Canadian survey found that

Thomas theorem
"Situations we define as real become real in their consequences."

self-fulfilling prophecy
An expectation that helps bring about what it predicts.

peer groups A person's peer group comprises people who are about the same age and of similar status as that person. The peer group acts as an agent of socialization.

status A recognized social position that an individual can occupy.

© iStockphoto.com/RyanJLane

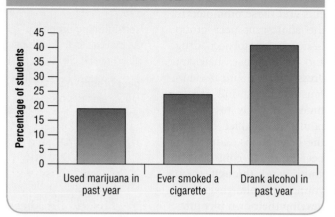

FIGURE 3.1   Marijuana, Cigarette, and Alcohol Use among Canadian Youth, Grades 7–12

Source: Health Canada, 2014a. *Summary of results of the Youth Smoking Survey, 2012–2013.* http://www.hc-sc.gc.ca/hc-ps/tobac-tabac/research-recherche/stat/_survey-sondage_2012-2013/result-eng.php (retrieved 5 July 2015).

12- and 13-year-old Canadians who identified themselves as belonging to a group that did "risky" things were up to seven times more likely than others were to report smoking, disorderly conduct, skipping school at least once, and attaching low importance to marks. They were also much more likely to report at least three instances of stealing and fighting. Of 12- and 13-year-olds who smoked, 84 percent reported having three or more friends who also smoked, while only 26 percent of their nonsmoking counterparts claimed that three or more of their friends smoked. Although parents'

smoking behaviour—especially that of mothers—was linked to a youth's decision to smoke, the influence of peers was far greater (Statistics Canada, 1999).

We don't want to overstate the significance of adolescent–parent conflict. For one thing, the conflict is usually temporary. Once adolescents mature, the family usually exerts a more enduring influence on many important issues. Research shows that, on average, families have more influence than peer groups do over the educational aspirations and the political, social, and religious preferences of adolescents and university students (Bibby, 2001: 55; Davies and Kandel, 1981; Milem, 1998).

A second reason that we should not exaggerate the extent of adolescent–parent discord is that peer groups are not just sources of conflict. They also help integrate young people into the larger society. A study of pre-adolescent children in a small North American city illustrates the point well. Over eight years, two sociologists conducted in-depth interviews at schools with children between the ages of 8 and 11 (Adler and Adler, 1998). They lived in a well-to-do community comprising about 80 000 whites and 10 000 racial-minority group members. In each school they visited, they found a system of cliques arranged in a strict hierarchy, much like the arrangement of classes and racial groups in adult society. In schools with a substantial number of visible-minority students, cliques were divided by race. Visible-minority cliques were usually less popular than white cliques were. In all schools, the most popular boys were highly successful in competitive and aggressive achievement-oriented activities, especially athletics. The most popular girls came from well-to-do and permissive families. One important

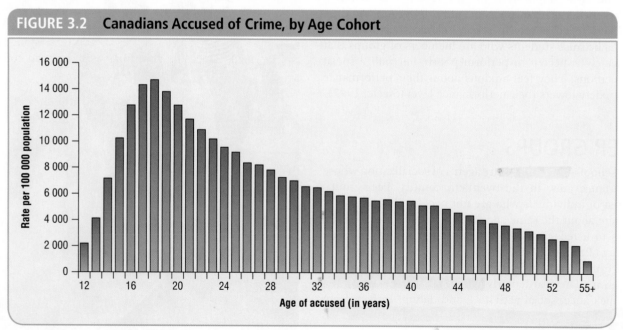

FIGURE 3.2   Canadians Accused of Crime, by Age Cohort

Source: Shannon Brennan and Mia Dauvergne. 2011. "Police-reported crime statistics in Canada, 2010." *Juristat* p. 22. http://www.statcan.gc.ca/pub/85-002-x/2011001/article/11523-eng.pdf (retrieved 5 July 2015).

basis of the students' popularity was that they had the means and the opportunity to participate in the most interesting social activities, ranging from skiing to late-night parties. Physical attractiveness was also an important basis of girls' popularity.

Elementary school peer groups thus prepared these youngsters for the class and racial inequalities of the adult world and the gender-specific criteria that would often be used to evaluate them as adults, such as competitiveness in the case of boys and attractiveness in the case of girls. (For more on gender socialization, see the discussion of the mass media below and in Chapter 8, Sexualities and Genders.) What we learn from this research is that peer groups function not only to help adolescents form an independent identity by separating them from their families, but also to teach them how to adapt to the ways of the larger society.

THE MASS MEDIA

Like the school and the peer group, the mass media became increasingly important socializing agents in the twentieth and twenty-first centuries. In fact, we now spend more hours per week interacting with the mass media than we do sleeping, working, or going to school (see Figure 3.3). The mass media constitute such an influential socializing agent today that we devote most of Chapter 12 (The Mass Media) to the subject. Here, we accomplish two tasks to introduce you to the topic. First, we describe the reach of television and the Internet, the two mass media that consume most of our time. Second, we illustrate the impact of the mass media by discussing how they help to teach people gender roles or the behaviours associated with widely shared expectations about how males and females are supposed to act.

The mass media include television, the Internet, radio, movies, videos, CDs, newspapers, magazines, and books. Television viewing still consumes more of the average Canadian's free time than any other mass medium

does. Ninety-nine percent of Canadians own at least one colour television set, and watching more hours of television is associated with having relatively few years of formal education and being more than 49 years old, among other factors (Statistics Canada, 2001; Television Bureau of Canada. 2015: 172, 174, 178; see Figure 3.4).

Despite television's wide reach, the Internet is catching up fast. Worldwide, the number of Internet users jumped from a mere 40 million in 1996 to 3.6 billion in 2016 (*Internet World Stats*, 2012; 2016). It is particularly among young people and those with more years of formal education that we witness the most startling gains in Internet use. For example, Canadians between the ages of 18 and 24 spend more than 37 hours a week on the Internet—nearly three times more than Canadians over the age of 49 (refer back to Figure 3.3). Much of this time is spent using social media, including Facebook, Twitter, Instagram, Snapchat, and so on. Seventy-five percent of Canadians between the ages of 18 and 34 have a Facebook profile, and 60 percent of them visit Facebook more than once a day (Forum Research Inc., 2015).

THE MASS MEDIA AND THE FEMINIST APPROACH TO SOCIALIZATION

Although people are free to choose socialization influences from the mass media, they choose some influences more than others. Specifically, they tend to choose influences that are more pervasive, fit existing cultural standards, and are made especially appealing by those who control

> **gender roles** The behaviours associated with widely shared expectations about how males and females are supposed to act.

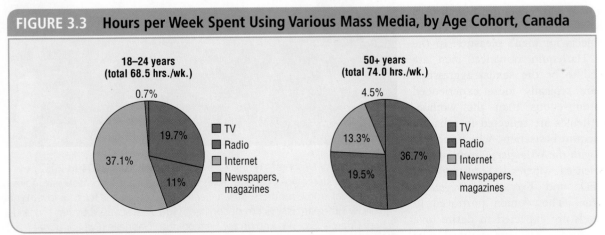

FIGURE 3.3 **Hours per Week Spent Using Various Mass Media, by Age Cohort, Canada**

18–24 years
(total 68.5 hrs./wk.)

0.7%
19.7%
37.1%
11%

- TV
- Radio
- Internet
- Newspapers, magazines

50+ years
(total 74.0 hrs./wk.)

4.5%
13.3%
36.7%
19.5%

- TV
- Radio
- Internet
- Newspapers, magazines

Source: Television Bureau of Canada, 2016. "Reach and Time Spent: Major Media Comparisons." Pp. 6, 13. http://www.tvb.ca/page_files/pdf/RTSA/RTS14.pdf (retrieved 5 July 2015).

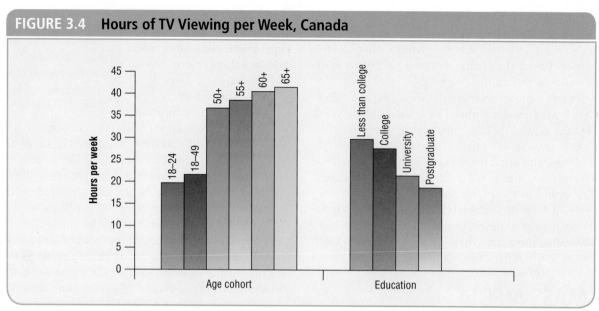

FIGURE 3.4   Hours of TV Viewing per Week, Canada

Source: Television Bureau of Canada, 2015, *Cross-Media Reach and Time Spent: Major Media Comparison.*

the mass media. We can illustrate this point by considering how feminist sociologists analyze gender roles.

Gender roles are of special interest to feminist sociologists, who claim that people are not born knowing how to express masculinity and femininity in conventional ways. Instead, say feminist sociologists, people *learn* gender roles, in part through the mass media.

The learning of gender roles through the mass media begins when small children see that only a kiss from Prince Charming will save Snow White from eternal sleep. Here is an early lesson about who can expect to be passive and who potent. The lesson continues in magazines, romance novels, television, advertisements, music, and the Internet. For example, a central theme in Harlequin romance novels (the world's top sellers in this genre) is the transformation of women's bodies into objects for men's pleasure. In the typical Harlequin romance, men are expected to be the sexual aggressors. They are typically more experienced and promiscuous than the women. These themes are reflected in a listing of Harlequin bestsellers, which include *In Bed with the Wrangler*; *Greek Tycoon*; *Inexperienced Mistress*; *Seduction and the CEO*; and *Executive's Pregnancy Ultimatum*. The women portrayed in the novels are expected to desire love before intimacy. They are assumed to be sexually passive, giving only subtle cues

to indicate their interest in male overtures. Supposedly lacking the urgent sex drive that preoccupies men, women are often held accountable for moral standards and contraception. Readers are assured that adopting this submissive posture ensures that things turn out for the best. As the eHarlequin.com website says, "Happily ever after

The TV show *Desperate Housewives*, which aired from 2004 to 2012, reinforced stereotypical gender roles by chronicling the domestic struggles of five stay-at-home mothers. Susan (Teri Hatcher) searches for true love. Lynette (Felicity Huffman) is a victim of constant high stress caused by her four kids. Bree (Marcia Cross) is known for her cooking. Gabrielle (Eva Longoria) used to be a model. Edie (Nicollette Sheridan) is a blonde bombshell and serial divorcée.

© ABC/Photofest

is always guaranteed with our books" (Grescoe, 1996; Harlequin, 2006; Jensen, 1984).

People do not passively accept messages about appropriate gender roles. They often interpret them in unique ways and sometimes resist them. For the most part, however, they try to develop skills that will help them perform gender roles in a conventional way (Eagley and Wood, 1999: 412–13). Of course, conventions change. What children learn about femininity and masculinity today is less sexist than what they learned just a generation or two ago. Comparing *Cinderella* and *Snow White* with *Tangled*, for example, we immediately see that children who watch Disney movies today are sometimes presented with more assertive and heroic female role models than the passive heroines of the 1930s and 1940s. Yet we must not exaggerate the degree of change. *Cinderella* and *Snow White* are still popular movies. Moreover, for every *Tangled*, there is a *Little Mermaid*, a movie that simply modernizes old themes about female passivity and male conquest.

As the learning of gender roles through the mass media suggests, not all media influences are created equal. We may be free to choose which media messages influence us. However, most people are inclined to choose the messages that are most widespread, most closely aligned with existing cultural standards, and made most enticing by the mass media. As feminist sociologists remind us, in the case of gender roles, these messages support conventional expectations about how males and females are supposed to act.

RESOCIALIZATION AND TOTAL INSTITUTIONS

In concluding our discussion of socialization agents, we must underline the importance of resocialization in the lifelong process of social learning. **Resocialization** takes place when powerful socializing agents deliberately cause rapid change in people's values, roles, and self-conception, sometimes against their will.

You can see resocialization at work in the ceremonies staged when someone joins a fraternity, a sorority, the Canadian Armed Forces, or a religious order. Such a ceremony, or **initiation rite**, signifies the transition of the individual from one group to another and ensures his or her loyalty to the new group. Initiation rites require new recruits to abandon old self-perceptions and assume new identities.

Often the rites comprise three stages: (1) separation from the person's old status and identity (ritual rejection); (2) degradation, disorientation, and stress (ritual death); and (3) acceptance of the new group culture and status (ritual rebirth).

Much resocialization takes place in what Erving Goffman (1961) called **total institutions**. Total institutions are settings in which people are isolated from the larger society and under the strict control and constant supervision of a specialized staff. Because of their "pressure cooker" atmosphere, resocialization in total institutions is often rapid and thorough, even in the absence of initiation rites. Asylums, prisons, drug and alcohol rehabilitation centres, and armies are examples of total institutions. Typically, drug or alcohol rehabilitation takes three to six

resocialization What occurs when powerful socializing agents deliberately cause rapid change in a person's values, roles, and self-conception, sometimes against that person's will.

initiation rite A ritual that signifies the transition of the individual from one group to another and helps to ensure his or her loyalty to the new group.

total institutions Settings in which people are isolated from the larger society and under the strict control and constant supervision of a specialized staff.

Getty Images/Digital Vision

Not all initiation rites or rites of passage involve resocialization; some rites of passage are normal parts of primary and secondary socialization and merely signify the transition from one status to another. Here, an Italian family celebrates the first communion of a young girl.

months in a highly structured, drug-free setting in a remote location. Basic training in the Canadian Forces takes three-and-a-half months at the Canadian Forces Leadership and Recruit School in Saint-Jean-sur-Richelieu, about 50 km outside Montreal.

A famous failed experiment illustrates the immense resocializing capacity of total institutions (Haney, Banks, and Zimbardo, 1973; Zimbardo, 1972). In the early 1970s, a group of researchers in Palo Alto, California, created their own mock prison. They paid about two dozen male volunteers to act as guards and inmates. The volunteers were mature, emotionally stable, intelligent, university students from middle-class American and Canadian homes. None had a criminal record. By the flip of a coin, half of the volunteers were designated prisoners and the other half guards. The guards made up their own rules for maintaining law and order in the mock prison. The prisoners were picked up by city police officers in a squad car, searched, handcuffed, fingerprinted, booked at the police station, and taken blindfolded to the mock prison. At the mock prison, each prisoner was stripped, deloused, put into a uniform, given a number, and placed in a cell with two other inmates.

To better understand what it means to be a prisoner or a prison guard, the researchers wanted to observe and record social interaction in the mock prison for two weeks. However, they were forced to end the experiment abruptly after only six days because what they witnessed frightened them. In less than a week, the prisoners and prison guards could no longer tell the difference between the roles they were playing and their "real" selves. Much of the socialization these young men had undergone over a period of about 20 years was quickly suspended.

About a third of the guards began to treat the prisoners like despicable animals, taking pleasure in cruelty. Even the guards who were regarded by the prisoners as tough but fair stopped short of interfering in the tyrannical and arbitrary use of power by the most sadistic guards.

All of the prisoners became servile and dehumanized, thinking only about survival, escape, and their growing hatred of the guards. Had they been thinking as university students, they could have walked out of the experiment at any time. Some of the prisoners did, in fact, beg for parole. However, by the fifth day of the experiment they were so programmed to think of themselves as prisoners that they returned docilely to their cells when their request for parole was denied.

The Palo Alto experiment suggests that your sense of self and the roles you play are not as fixed as you may

American Private Lynndie England became infamous when photographs were made public showing her and other American soldiers abusing Iraqi prisoners in obvious contravention of international law. "She's never been in trouble. She's not the person that the photographs point her out to be," said her childhood friend Destiny Gloin (quoted in "Woman Soldier," 2004). Ms. Gloin was undoubtedly right. Private England at Abu Ghraib prison was not the Lynndie England from high school. As in the Palo Alto prison experiment, she was transformed by a structure of power and a culture of intimidation that made the prisoners seem subhuman.

think. Radically alter your social setting and, like the university students in the experiment, your self-concept and patterned behaviour are also likely to change. Such change is most evident among people undergoing resocialization in total institutions. However, the sociological eye is able to observe the flexibility of the self in all social settings—a task made easier by the fact that the self has become more flexible over time. We now turn to an examination of the growing flexibility of the self.

LO³ SOCIALIZATION ACROSS THE LIFE COURSE
ADULT SOCIALIZATION AND THE FLEXIBLE SELF

The development of the self is a lifelong process (Mortimer and Simmons, 1978). When young adults enter a profession or get married, they must learn new occupational and family roles. Retirement and old age present an entirely new set of challenges. Giving up a job, seeing children leave home and start their own families, losing a spouse and close friends are all changes later in life that require people to think of themselves in new ways and to redefine who they are. Many new roles are predictable. To help us learn them, we often engage in <mark>anticipatory socialization</mark>, which involves beginning to take on the norms and behaviours of the roles to which we aspire. (Think of 12-year-old fans of *Pretty Little Liars* learning from the show what it might mean to be a young adult.) Other new roles are unpredictable. You might unexpectedly fall in love and marry someone from a different ethnic, racial, or religious group. You might experience a sudden and difficult transition from peace to war. If so, you will have to learn new roles and adopt new cultural values or at least modify old ones. Even in adulthood, then, the self remains flexible.

Today, people's identities change faster, more often, and more completely than they did just a few decades ago. One important factor contributing to the growing flexibility of the self is globalization. As we saw in Chapter 2, Culture, people are now less obliged to accept the culture into which they are born. Because of globalization, they are freer to combine elements of culture from a wide variety of historical periods and geographical settings.

A second factor increasing our freedom to design ourselves is our growing ability to fashion new bodies from old. People have always defined themselves partly in terms of their bodies; your self-conception is influenced by whether you're a man or a woman, tall or short, healthy or ill, conventionally attractive or plain. However, our bodies used to be fixed by nature. People could do nothing to change the fact that they were born with certain features and grew older at a certain rate.

Now, however, you can change your body, and therefore your self-conception, radically and virtually at will—if, that is, you can afford it. Bodybuilding, aerobic exercise, and weight reduction regimens are more popular than ever. Plastic surgery allows people to buy new breasts, noses, lips, eyelids, and hair—and to remove unwanted fat, skin, and hair from various parts of their bodies. In 2015, more than 1.7 million North Americans underwent cosmetic surgery, over five times more than in 1992. More than 14 million North Americans underwent collagen, Botox, and other "minimally invasive" procedures in 2015, 200 times more than in 1992 (American Society of Plastic Surgeons, 2016).

anticipatory socialization
Learning the norms and behaviours of the roles to which one aspires.

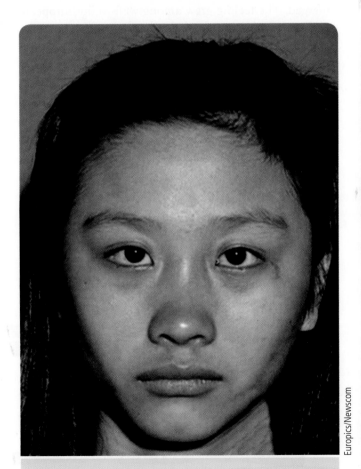

Before plastic surgery

Europics/Newscom

After plastic surgery

Europics/Newscom

virtual communities An association of people, scattered across the city or around the world, who communicate via computer about a subject of common interest.

Other body-altering procedures include sex-change operations and organ transplants. At any given time, more than 50 000 North Americans are waiting for a replacement organ. Brisk, illegal international trade in human hearts, lungs, kidneys, livers, and eyes enables well-to-do people to enhance and extend their lives (Rothman, 1998). As these examples illustrate, many new opportunities for changing one's body, and therefore one's self-conception, have been introduced in recent decades.

SELF-IDENTITY AND THE INTERNET

Further complicating the process of identity formation today is the growth of the Internet. In the 1980s and early 1990s, most observers believed that social interaction by means of computer would involve only the exchange of information between individuals. They were wrong. Computer-assisted social interaction profoundly affects how people think of themselves as they form social networks and virtual communities—associations of people, scattered across town or across the planet, who communicate via the Internet about subjects of common interest (Brym and Lenton, 2001; Haythornthwaite and Wellman, 2002).

Because social networks and virtual communities allow people to conceal their identities, they are free to assume new identities and discover parts of themselves they were formerly unaware of. Shy people can become bold, normally assertive people can become voyeurs, old people can become young, straight people can become gay, and women can become men (see Chapter 12, The Mass Media). Experience on the Internet reinforces our main point—that the self has become increasingly flexible in recent decades, and people are freer than ever to shape their selves as they choose.

However, as you'll now see, this freedom comes at a cost, particularly for young people. To appreciate the cost, we first consider what childhood and adolescence looked like a few centuries ago.

DILEMMAS OF CHILDHOOD AND ADOLESCENT SOCIALIZATION

In preindustrial societies, children were considered to be small adults. From a young age, they were expected to conform as much as possible to the norms of the adult world. That was largely because children were put to work

Child labour during the Industrial Revolution

as soon as they could contribute to the welfare of their families. Often, this contribution meant doing chores by the age of 5 and working full-time by the age of 10 or 12. Marriage, and thus the achievement of full adulthood, was common by the age of 15 or 16.

Beginning around 1600 in Europe and North America, the idea of childhood as a distinct stage of life emerged. The feeling grew among well-to-do Europeans and North Americans that boys should be allowed to play games and receive an education that would allow them to develop the emotional, physical, and intellectual skills they would need as adults. Until the nineteenth century, girls continued to be treated as "little women" (the title of Louisa May Alcott's famous 1868–69 novel). Most working-class boys didn't enjoy much of a childhood until the twentieth century. Only in the last century did the idea of childhood as a distinct and prolonged stage of life become universal in the West (Ariès, 1962 [1960]).

THE EMERGENCE OF CHILDHOOD AND ADOLESCENCE

The idea of childhood emerged when and where it did because of social necessity and social possibility. Prolonged childhood was *necessary* in societies that required better-educated adults to do increasingly complex work, because childhood gave young people a chance to prepare for adult life. Prolonged childhood was *possible* in societies where improved hygiene and nutrition allowed most people to live more than 35 years, the average lifespan in Europe in the early seventeenth century. In other words, before the late seventeenth century, most people did not live long enough to permit the luxury of childhood. Moreover, there was no social need for a period of extended training and development before the comparatively simple demands of adulthood were thrust on young people.

In general, wealthier and more complex societies whose populations enjoy a long average life expectancy stretch out the pre-adult period of life. For example, we saw that in Europe in the seventeenth century, most people reached mature adulthood by the age of about 16. In contrast, in such countries as Canada today, most people are considered to reach mature adulthood only around the age of 30, by which time they have completed their formal education, possibly gotten married, and "settled down." Once teenagers were relieved of adult responsibilities, a new term had to be coined to describe the teenage years: *adolescence*. Subsequently, the term *young adulthood* entered popular usage as an increasingly large number of people in their late teens, 20s, and early 30s delayed marriage to attend university (see the Sociology at the Movies feature in this chapter).

Although terms such as *adolescence* and *young adulthood* describing the stages of life were firmly entrenched in North America by the middle of the twentieth century, some of the categories of the population they were meant to describe began to change dramatically. Somewhat excitedly, some analysts began to write about the "disappearance" of childhood and adolescence (Friedenberg, 1959; Postman, 1982).

Although undoubtedly overstating their case, these social scientists did identify some of the social forces responsible for the changing character of childhood and adolescence in recent decades. We examine these social forces in the concluding section of this chapter.

SOCIOLOGY AT THE MOVIES

Ted and *Ted 2*

On the day after his eighth Christmas, John's two-part wish came true. First, his teddy bear, Ted, came to life. Much to the surprise of John and others, Ted could walk, talk, and even think for himself. Second, John and Ted became the best of friends.

Forward 27 years: John (played by Mark Wahlberg) is 35 and unmarried. He lives with Ted. He has a job but remains apathetic toward his work, and he is in a relationship with his girlfriend, Lori (Mila Kunis), to whom he is equally uncommitted. Sometimes John and Ted sit around eating cereal and getting high, so John shows up for work late. Sometimes John leaves work early. Sometimes he takes the entire day off so he can spend time with Ted.

Lori is upset that Ted takes up so much of John's life. She thinks John needs to grow up and move on. John is torn between his loyalty to Ted and his affection for Lori. He eventually gets Ted to move out of his apartment, but one evening, when John and Lori are attending a party at the home of Lori's boss, Ted phones. Ted happens to be throwing a party at his new apartment, and Sam Jones, the star of their favourite movie, *Flash Gordon*, is attending! John can't resist. He abandons Lori, goes over to Ted's place, gets drunk, and loses track of time. Furious, Lori dumps John.

John finally wakes up to his stupidity, telling Ted: "Lori was right. I should have stopped hanging out with you a long time ago. I'm never going to have a life with you around. I'm 35 years old and I'm going nowhere, all I do is smoke pot and watch movies with a teddy bear. Because of that I just lost the love of my life . . . I've got to be on my own, Ted, I can't see you anymore."

John's change of heart raises an important sociological issue posed by a host of recent movies. Like *Ted*, *The Wedding Crashers* (2005), *The 40-Year-Old Virgin* (2005), *Failure to Launch* (2006), and *Clerks II* (2006) all beg the question of how it came about that people old enough to be considered adults just a couple of generations ago now seem stuck between adolescence and adulthood. They aren't married. Some of them live with their parents. They may still be in school. Some of them lack steady, well-paying, full-time jobs. They represent a growing category of young adults who are often a big worry to their elders. Between 1981 and 2001, the percentage of Canadians between the ages of 25 and 34 living with their parents doubled—rising from 12 percent to 24 percent for the 25–29 age cohort and from 5 percent to 11 percent for the 30–34 age cohort (Beaupré, Turcotte, and Milan, 2007).

A principal reason for this phenomenon is economic. In the first few decades after World War II, housing and education costs were low, and the number of years one had to spend in school to get a steady, well-paying job was modest. Today, housing and education costs are high, and young people must typically spend more years in school before starting their careers.

(Continued)

As a result, many young people continue to live in their parents' home into their 20s and 30s as a matter of economic necessity. In *Ted*, John and Lori eventually get back together and Ted begins living a life of his own. In the real world, similar happy endings are often delayed by circumstances beyond the control of people who are no longer adolescents but not quite adults.

In *Ted 2*, John is divorced. Still, the sequel holds out hope—ironically, in the "person" of Ted. The teddy bear matures. He marries a real woman. His wife claims he's good at sex even though Hasbro didn't make him anatomically correct. The couple opt for a sperm donor, so one

night, Ted and John break into the home of Tom Brady, the football quarterback. As Brady sleeps, they try to extract the required specimen. Failure results in Ted winding up in court, where he succeeds in proving that he's a person, not a thing, and deserves the rights of all adults. Don't all people in their 20s and 30s deserve those rights, too?

Critical Thinking Questions

1. What are the criteria for "adulthood" in Canadian society?
2. How and why do the criteria for adulthood change as societies develop?

Ted and John discuss life problems over drinks.

© Universal Pictures/courtesy Everett Collection/The Canadian Press

LO⁴ PROBLEMS OF CHILDHOOD AND ADOLESCENT SOCIALIZATION TODAY

Declining adult supervision and guidance, increasing mass media and peer group influence, and increasing assumption of substantial adult responsibilities to the neglect of extracurricular activities have done much to change the socialization patterns of North American youth over the past half century. Let us consider each of these developments in turn.

DECLINING ADULT SUPERVISION AND GUIDANCE

In a six-year in-depth study of adolescence, Patricia Hersch wrote that "in all societies since the beginning of time, adolescents have learned to become adults by observing, imitating and interacting with grown-ups around them" (1998: 20). However, in contemporary North America, adults are increasingly absent from the lives of adolescents. Why? According to Hersch, "society has left its children behind as the cost of progress in the workplace" (1998: 19). What she means is that more adults are working longer hours than ever before. In Canada, adults in the paid labour force living with a spouse or a child spend about 20 percent less time in activities with family members during a typical workday than they did in

1986. The main reason? They are required to spend more time at work (Turcotte, 2007). Because adults have less time to spend with their children than they used to, young people are increasingly left alone to socialize themselves and build their own community.

This community sometimes revolves around high-risk behaviour (see Figure 3.5). It is therefore not coincidental that the peak hours for juvenile crime are between 3 p.m. and 6 p.m. on weekdays—that is, after school and before most parents return home from work (Hersch, 1998: 362). Girls are less likely to engage in juvenile crime than boys are, partly because parents tend to supervise and socialize their sons and daughters differently (Hagan, Simpson, and Gillis, 1987). These research findings suggest that many of the teenage behaviours commonly regarded as problematic result from declining adult guidance and supervision.

INCREASING MEDIA AND PEER GROUP INFLUENCE

Declining adult supervision and guidance also leave North American youth more susceptible to the influence of the mass media and peer groups. As one parent put it, "When they hit the teen years, it is as if they can't be children anymore. The outside world has invaded the school environment" (quoted in Hersch, 1998: 111). In an earlier era, family, school, church, and community usually taught young people more or less consistent beliefs and values. Now, however, the mass media and peer groups often pull young people in different directions from the school and the family, leaving them uncertain about what constitutes appropriate behaviour and making the job of growing up more stressful than it used to be (Arnett, 1995).

DECLINING EXTRACURRICULAR ACTIVITIES AND INCREASING ADULT RESPONSIBILITIES

As the chapter's anecdote about Robert Brym's involvement in high school drama illustrates, extracurricular activities are important for adolescent personality development. These activities provide opportunities for students to develop concrete skills and thereby make sense of the world and their place in it. In schools today, academic subjects are too often presented as disconnected bits of knowledge that lack relevance to the student's life. Drama, music, and athletics programs are often better at giving students a framework within which they can develop a strong sense of self, because they are concrete activities with clearly defined rules. By training and playing hard on a hockey team, mastering an instrument, or acting in plays, students can learn something about their physical, emotional, and social capabilities and limitations, about what they are made of, and about what they can and cannot do. These are just the sorts of activities adolescents require for healthy self-development.

If you're like most young Canadians today, you spend fewer hours per week on extracurricular activities associated with school than your parents did when they went to school. Many young Canadians are simply too busy with homework, household chores, child-care responsibilities, and part-time jobs to enjoy the benefits of school activities outside the classroom. Canadian teens average more than seven hours of paid and unpaid labour per day, spending nearly 50 hours a week on school work, homework, paid work, and housework—a 50-hour workweek. About half of Canadian teenagers work at jobs averaging 15 hours a week. Canadian teens work more than teens do in the United States, the United Kingdom, France, Australia, and other rich countries (Bibby, 2001: 35; Siad, 2007).

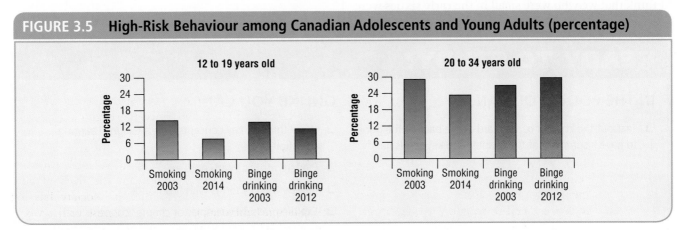

FIGURE 3.5 **High-Risk Behaviour among Canadian Adolescents and Young Adults (percentage)**

Note:
"Smoking" = Smoked daily or occasionally.
"Binge drinking" = Consumed at least 5 drinks per occasion at least 12 times in the past year.
Sources: Adapted from Statistics Canada. 2014b. "Table 051-0001. Estimates of Population, by Age Group and Sex for July 1, Canada, Provinces and Territories"; Statistics Canada. 2014c. http://www5.statcan.gc.ca/cansim/a26?lang=eng&id=510001 (retrieved 6 July 2015); "Table 105-0501. Health Indicator Profile, Annual Estimates, by Age Group and Sex, Canada, Provinces, Territories, Health Regions (2013 boundaries) and Peer Groups (year to date—(averages)."

Half of McDonald's employees are under the age of 18.

Justin Sullivan/Getty Images

"THE VANISHING ADOLESCENT"

Some analysts wonder whether the assumption of so many adult responsibilities, the lack of extracurricular activities, declining adult supervision and guidance, and increasing mass media and peer group influence are causing childhood and adolescence to disappear. As early as 1959, one sociologist spoke of "the vanishing adolescent" in North American society (Friedenberg, 1959). More recently, another commentator remarked, "I think that we who were small in the early sixties were perhaps the last generation who actually had a childhood, in the ... sense of ... a space distinct in roles and customs from the world of adults, oriented around children's own needs and culture rather than around the needs and culture of adults" (Wolf, 1997: 13). Childhood and adolescence became universal categories of social thought and experience in the twentieth century. Under the impact of the social forces discussed above, however, the experience and meaning of childhood and adolescence now seem to be changing radically.

READY TO STUDY?

IN THE BOOK, YOU CAN:

❑ Tear out the chapter review card at the back of the book to have a summary of the chapter and key terms handy.

ONLINE YOU CAN:

❑ Work through key concepts with a Guided Learning Question.

❑ Prepare for tests with quizzes.

❑ Review the key terms with flash cards.

❑ Explore practical examples of chapter concepts with Connect a Concept exercises.

GO TO NELSON.COM/STUDENT TO ACCESS THESE DIGITAL RESOURCES.

4

From Social Interaction to Social Organizations

© Tomas Loewy

LEARNING OBJECTIVES

In this chapter, you will learn to

LO¹ Define *social interaction* as people communicating face to face, acting and reacting in relation to one another.

LO² Identify how various aspects of social structure influence the texture of emotional life.

LO³ Recognize that in social interaction, nonverbal communication is as important as language is.

LO⁴ See how emotional and material resources flow through patterns of social relations called *social networks*.

LO⁵ Explain how social groups bind people together, impose conformity on them, and separate them from non–group members.

LO⁶ Appreciate that bureaucracies can often be made more efficient by adopting more democratic structures with fewer levels of authority.

LO¹ FEMINIST THEORY AND SOCIAL INTERACTION

A researcher and his assistants once eavesdropped on 1200 conversations of people laughing in public places, such as shopping malls (Provine, 2000). When they heard someone laughing, they recorded who laughed (the speaker, the listener, or both) and the gender of the speaker and the listener. To simplify things, they eavesdropped only on two-person groups.

They found that women laugh more than men do in everyday conversations. The biggest discrepancy in laughing occurred when the speaker was a woman and the listener was a man. In such cases, women laughed more than twice as often as men did. However, even when a man spoke and a woman listened, the woman was more likely to laugh than the man was.

Research also shows that men are more likely than women are to engage in long monologues and interrupt when others are talking (Tannen, 1994a, 1994b). They are also less likely to ask for help or directions because doing so would imply a reduction in their authority. Much male–female conflict results from these differences. A stereotypical case is the lost male driver and the helpful female passenger. The female passenger, seeing that the male driver is lost, suggests that they stop and ask for directions. The male driver does not want to ask for directions because he thinks that would make him look incompetent. If both parties remain firm in their positions, an argument is bound to result.

Social interaction involves communication among people acting and reacting to one another. Feminist sociologists are especially sensitive to gender differences in social interactions like those just described. They see that gender often structures interaction patterns.

Consider laughter. If we define *status* as a recognized social position, it is generally true that people with higher status (in this case, men) get more laughs, whereas people with lower status (in this case, women) laugh more. That is perhaps why class clowns are nearly always boys. Laughter in everyday life, it turns out,

> **social interaction** Involves people communicating face to face or via computer, acting and reacting in relation to other people. It is structured around norms, roles, and statuses.

Role conflict Occurs when two or more statuses held at the same time place contradictory role demands on a person.

Role strain Occurs when incompatible role demands are placed on a person in a single status.

is not as spontaneous as you may think. It is often a signal of who has higher or lower status. Social structure influences who laughs more.

Social statuses are just one of the three building blocks that structure all social interactions. The others are roles and norms. A *role* is a set of expected behaviours. Whereas people *occupy* a status, they *perform* a role. Students may learn to expect that when things get dull, the class clown will brighten their day. The class clown will rise to the occasion, knowing that his classmates expect him to do so. A *norm* is a generally accepted way of doing things. Classroom norms are imposed by instructors, who routinely punish class clowns for distracting their classmates from the task at hand (see Figure 4.1).

SOCIAL STRUCTURE AND EMOTIONS

Just as statuses, roles, and norms structure laughter, they influence other emotions, although their influence is often not apparent. In fact, most people think that emotions are a lot like the common cold. In both cases, an external disturbance causes a reaction that people presumably experience involuntarily. The external disturbance, for example, could be a grizzly bear attack that causes us to experience fear, or exposure to a virus that causes us to catch a cold. In either case, we can't control our body's patterned response. Emotions, like colds, just happen to us (Thoits, 1989: 319).

Feminists were among the first sociologists to note the flaw in the view that emotional responses are typically involuntary (Hochschild, 1979, 1983). Seeing how often women, as status subordinates, must *control* their emotions, they generalized the idea. Emotions don't just happen to us, they argued. We manage them. If a grizzly

---

FIGURE 4.1 Statuses and Roles

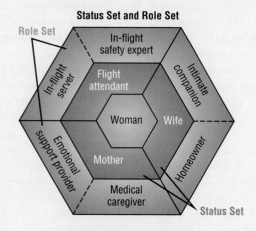

Status Set and Role Set

A person occupies several recognized positions or statuses at the same time—for example, mother, wife, and flight attendant. All of these statuses together form a *status set*. Each status is composed of several sets of expected behaviours or roles. A *role set* is a cluster of roles attached to a single status. For example, a wife is expected to act as an intimate companion to her husband and to assume certain legal responsibilities as co-owner of a home. In this figure, dashed lines separate roles and dark solid lines separate statuses.

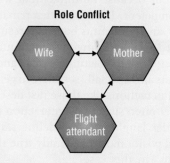

Role Conflict

Role conflict takes place when different role demands are placed on a person by two or more statuses held at the same time. How might a flight attendant experience role conflict because of the contradictory demands of the statuses diagrammed above?

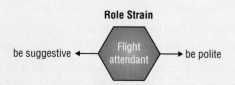

Role Strain

Role strain occurs when incompatible role demands are placed on a person in a single status. For instance, in the 1960s, when most air travellers were businessmen, flight attendants (or "stewardesses" as they were called at the time), were required by their employers to be slim and single and to appear to be sexually "available." This requirement caused role strain: Stewardesses had to be suggestive while also politely warding off unwanted, impolite, and even crude overtures.

bear attacks you in the woods, you can run as fast as possible or calm yourself, lie down, play dead, and silently pray for the best. You are more likely to survive the grizzly bear attack if you control your emotions and follow the second strategy. You will also temper your fear with a new emotion: hope (see Figure 4.2).

When people manage their emotions, they usually follow certain cultural "scripts," like the culturally transmitted knowledge that lying down and playing dead gives you a better chance of surviving a grizzly bear attack. We usually know the culturally designated emotional response to a particular external stimulus and we try to respond appropriately. If people don't succeed in achieving the culturally appropriate emotional response, they are likely to feel guilt, disappointment, or (as in the case of the bear attack) something much worse.

Sociologist Arlie Russell Hochschild is a leading figure in the study of **emotion management**. In fact, she coined the term. She argues that emotion management involves people obeying "feeling rules" and responding appropriately to the situations in which they find themselves (Hochschild, 1979, 1983). So, for example, people talk about the "right" to feel angry and they acknowledge that they "should" have mourned a relative's death more deeply. We have conventional expectations not only about what we should feel but also about how much we should feel, how long we should feel it, and with whom we should share those feelings. For example, we are expected to mourn the end of a love relationship. Shedding tears would be regarded as a completely natural reaction among Canadians today, but if you shot yourself—as was the fad among some European Romantics in the early nineteenth century—then you would be regarded as deranged. If you went on a date with someone new half an hour after breaking up with your long-time girlfriend or boyfriend, then most people would regard you as callous. Norms and rules govern our emotional life.

emotion management The act of obeying "feeling rules" and responding appropriately to situations.

emotional labour Emotion management that many people do as part of their job and for which they are paid.

EMOTIONAL LABOUR

Hochschild distinguishes emotion management (which everyone does in everyday life) from **emotional labour** (which many people do as part of their job and for which they are paid). We've all seen teachers deal with students who routinely hand in assignments late, pass notes, chatter during class, talk back, and act as class clowns. Those teachers do emotional labour. Sales clerks, nurses, and flight attendants must be experts in emotional labour. They spend a considerable part of their workday dealing with other people's misbehaviour, anger, rudeness, and unreasonable demands. They also do promotional and public relations work on behalf of the organizations that employ them. ("We hope you enjoyed your flight on Air Canada and that we can serve you again the next time you travel.") In all of these tasks, they carefully manage their own emotions while trying to keep their clientele happy and orderly.

Hochschild estimates that in the United States, nearly half of the jobs that women do and one-fifth of the jobs that men do involve substantial amounts of emotional labour.

FIGURE 4.2 How People Get Emotional

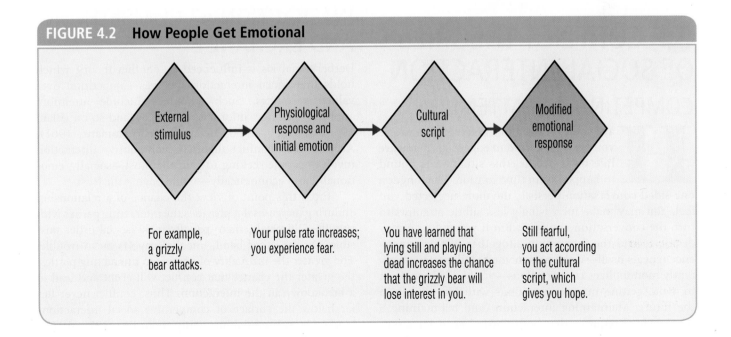

External stimulus	Physiological response and initial emotion	Cultural script	Modified emotional response
For example, a grizzly bear attacks.	Your pulse rate increases; you experience fear.	You have learned that lying still and playing dead increases the chance that the grizzly bear will lose interest in you.	Still fearful, you act according to the cultural script, which gives you hope.

More women than men do emotional labour because they are typically better socialized to undertake caring and nurturing roles.

Note, too, that as the focus of the economy shifts from the production of goods to the production of services, the market for emotional labour grows. More and more people are selected, trained, and paid for their skill in emotional labour. Consequently, business organizations increasingly govern the expression of feelings at work, which becomes less spontaneous and authentic over time. This process affects women more than it does men because women do more emotional labour than men do.

Our observations fly in the face of common sense. We typically think of our interactions as outcomes of our emotional states. We interact differently with people depending on whether they love us, make us angry, or make us laugh. We usually think our emotions are evoked involuntarily and result in uncontrollable action. However, emotions are not as unique, involuntary, and uncontrollable as people often believe. Underlying the turbulence of emotional life is a measure of order and predictability governed by sociological principles.

Just as building blocks need cement to hold them together, so norms, roles, and statuses require a sort of "social cement" to prevent them from falling apart and to turn them into a durable social structure. What is the nature of the cement that holds the building blocks of social life together? Asked differently, exactly how is social interaction maintained? This is the most fundamental sociological question we can ask, because it is really a question about how social structures, and society as a whole, are possible. It is the subject of the next two sections of this chapter.

LO² CONFLICT THEORIES OF SOCIAL INTERACTION
COMPETING FOR ATTENTION

Have you ever been in a conversation where you can't get a word in edgewise? If you are like most people, this situation is bound to happen from time to time. The longer a one-sided conversation persists, the more neglected you feel. You may make increasingly less subtle attempts to turn the conversation your way. But if you fail, you may decide to end the interaction altogether. If this experience repeats itself—if the person you're talking to consistently monopolizes conversations—you're likely to want to avoid getting into conversations with him or her in the future. Maintaining interaction (and maintaining a relationship) requires that both parties' need for attention is met.

Most people don't consistently try to monopolize conversations. If they did, there wouldn't be much talk in the world. In fact, taking turns is one of the basic norms that govern conversations; people literally take turns talking to make conversation possible. Nonetheless, a remarkably large part of all conversations involves a subtle competition for attention. Consider the following snippet of dinner conversation:

John: "I'm feeling really starved."
Mary: "Oh, I just ate."
John: "Well, I'm feeling really starved."
Mary: "When was the last time you ate?"

Sociologist Charles Derber recorded this conversation (Derber, 1979: 24). John starts by saying how hungry he is. The attention is on him. Mary replies that she's not hungry, and the attention shifts to her. John insists he's hungry, shifting attention back to him. Mary finally allows the conversation to focus on John by asking him when he last ate. John thus "wins" the competition for attention.

Derber (1979) recorded 1500 conversations in family homes, workplaces, restaurants, classrooms, dormitories, and therapy groups. He concluded that North Americans usually try to turn conversations toward themselves. They usually do so in ways that go unnoticed. Nonetheless, says Derber, the typical conversation is a covert competition for attention. Derber is careful to point out that conversations are not winner-take-all competitions. Unless both people in a two-person conversation receive some attention, the interaction is likely to cease. Therefore, conversation typically involves the exchange of attention.

INTERACTION AS COMPETITION AND EXCHANGE

Derber's analysis is influenced by conflict theory, which holds that social interaction involves competition over valued resources. Such resources include attention, approval, prestige, information, money, and so on (Blau, 1964; Coleman, 1990; Hechter, 1987; Homans, 1961). According to conflict theorists, competitive interaction involves people seeking to gain the most—socially, emotionally, and economically—while paying the least.

From this point of view, the chance of a relationship enduring increases if it provides the interacting parties with payoffs. Ultimately, then, payoffs make social order possible. On the other hand, unequal payoffs mean trouble. The greater the inequality of payoffs to interacting parties, the greater the chance that conflict will erupt and lead to a breakdown in the interaction. Thus, conflict never lies far below the surface of competitive social interactions marked by substantial inequality (Bourdieu, 1977 [1972]; Collins, 1982).

SYMBOLIC INTERACTION THEORY AND SOCIAL INTERACTION

Is social interaction *always* a competitive and conflict-prone struggle over valued resources, as conflict theorists suggest? A moment's reflection suggests otherwise. People frequently act in ways they consider fair or just, even if that does not maximize their personal gain (Gamson, Fireman, and Rytina, 1982). Some people even engage in altruistic or heroic acts from which they gain nothing and risk much. The plain fact is that social life is richer than conflict theorists would have us believe. Selfishness and conflict are not the only bases of social interaction.

When people behave fairly or altruistically, they are interacting with others based on *norms* they have learned. These norms say they should act justly and help people in need, even if it costs a lot to do so. How then do people learn norms (as well as roles and statuses)? The first step involves what George Herbert Mead called "taking the role of the other," that is, seeing yourself from the point of view of the people with whom you interact (see Chapter 3, Socialization). According to Mead, we interpret other people's words and nonverbal signals to understand how they see us, and we adjust our behaviour to fit their expectations about how we ought to behave. During such symbolic interaction, we learn norms and adopt roles and statuses.

Such social learning is different from studying a user manual or a textbook. It involves constantly negotiating and modifying the norms, roles, and statuses that we meet as we interact with others, shaping them to suit our preferences. People learn norms, roles, and statuses actively and creatively, not passively and mechanically (Berger and Luckmann, 1966; Blumer, 1969; Strauss, 1993). Let us explore this theme by considering the ingenious ways in which people manage the impressions they give to others during social interaction.

GOFFMAN'S DRAMATURGICAL ANALYSIS

One of the most popular variants of symbolic interactionism is **dramaturgical analysis**. As first developed by Erving Goffman (1959), dramaturgical analysis takes literally Shakespeare's line from *As You Like It:* "All the world's a stage, and all the men and women merely players."

From Goffman's point of view, people constantly engage in role-playing. This fact is most evident when we are "front stage" in public settings. Just as being front stage in a play requires the use of props, gestures, and memorized lines, so does acting in a public space. A server in a restaurant,

for example, must dress in a uniform, smile, and recite fixed lines ("How are you? My name is Sam and I'm your server today. May I get you a drink before you order your meal?"). When the server goes "backstage," he or she can relax from the front-stage performance and discuss it with co-workers ("Those kids at table six are driving me nuts!"). Thus, we often distinguish between our public roles and our "true" selves.

Note, however, that even backstage we engage in role-playing and impression management; it's just that we are less likely to be aware of it. For instance, in the kitchen, a server may try to present herself in the best possible light to impress another server so that she can eventually ask him out for a date. Thus, the implication of dramaturgical analysis is that there is no single self, just the ensemble of roles we play in various social contexts. Servers in restaurants play many roles off the job. They play on basketball teams, sing in church choirs, and hang out with friends at shopping malls. Each role is governed by norms about what kind of clothes to wear, what kind of conversation to engage in, and so on. Everyone plays on many front stages in everyday life.

They do not always do so enthusiastically. If a role is stressful, people may engage in role distancing. **Role distancing** involves giving the impression of just "going through the motions" but lacking serious commitment to a role. Thus, when people think a role they are playing is embarrassing or beneath them, they typically want to give their peers the impression that the role is not their "true" self. "My parents force me to sing in the church choir"; "I'm working at McDonald's just to earn a few extra dollars, but I'm going back to college next semester"; "This old car I'm driving is just a loaner." These are the kinds of rationalizations individuals offer when distancing themselves from a role.

Onstage, people typically try to place themselves in the best possible light; they engage in "impression management." For example, a study of McMaster University medical school in Hamilton, Ontario, found that when students enter medical school, they quickly adopt a new vocabulary and wear a white lab coat to set themselves apart from patients. They try to model their behaviour after the doctors who have authority over them. When dealing with patients, they may hide their ignorance under medical jargon to maintain their authority. They may ask questions they know the answer to so that they can impress their teachers. According to one third-year student: "The best way of impressing [advisers] with your competence is asking questions you

dramaturgical analysis
Views social interaction as a sort of play in which people present themselves so that they appear in the best possible light.

role distancing Involves giving the impression that we are just going through the motions and that we lack serious commitment to a role.

know the answer to. Because if they ever put it back on you, 'Well what do *you* think?' then you can tell them what you think and you'd give a very intelligent answer because you knew it. You didn't ask it to find out information. You ask it to impress people." Medical students don't take a course in how to act like a doctor, but they learn their new role in the course of impression management (Haas and Shaffir, 1987).

Let us now inquire briefly into the way people use words and nonverbal signals to communicate in face-to-face interaction. Having a conversation is actually a wonder of intricate complexity. As you will see, even today's most advanced supercomputer cannot conduct a natural-sounding conversation with a person (Kurzweil, 1999: 61, 91).

LO³ VERBAL AND NONVERBAL COMMUNICATION

In the 1950s, an article appeared in a British newspaper trumpeting the invention of an electronic translating device at the University of London. According to the article, "As fast as [a user] could type the words in, say, French, the equivalent in Hungarian or Russian would issue forth on the tape" (quoted in Silberman, 2000: 225). The report was an exaggeration, to put it mildly. It soon became a standing joke that if you asked a computer to translate "The spirit is willing, but the flesh is weak" (Matthew 26:41) into Russian, the output would read, "The vodka is good, but the steak is lousy." Today we are closer to high-quality machine translation than we were in the 1950s. However, a practical universal translator exists only on *Star Trek*.

The Social Context of Language

Why can people translate better than computers can? Because computer programs find it difficult to make sense of the *social and cultural context* in which language is used. The same words can mean different things in different settings, so computers, lacking contextual cues, routinely botch translations. That is why machine translation works best when applications are restricted to a single social context—say, weather forecasting or oil exploration. In such

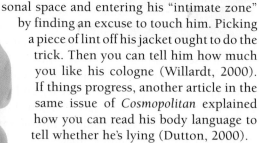

Like many hand gestures, the "fig" means different things in different times and places. You probably know it as a sign that adults make when they play with children and pretend "I've got your nose." But in ancient Rome, the fig was meant to convey good luck; in India it represents a threat; and in Russia, Turkey, and South Korea it means "Screw you." It signifies the letter "t" in the American Sign Language alphabet, but it had to be modified in the International Sign Language alphabet to avoid giving offence.

cases, specialized vocabularies and meanings specific to the context of interest are built into the program. Ambiguity is reduced and computers can "understand" the meaning of words well enough to translate them with reasonable accuracy. Similarly, humans must be able to reduce ambiguity and make sense of words to become good translators. They do so by learning the nuances of meaning in different cultural and social contexts over an extended time. *Nonverbal* cues assist them in that task.

Facial Expressions, Gestures, and Body Language

Cosmopolitan magazine once featured an article advising female readers on "how to reduce otherwise evolved men to drooling, panting fools." Basing his analysis on the work of several psychologists, the author of the article first urged readers to "delete the old-school seductress image (smoky eyes, red lips, brazen stare) from your consciousness." Then, he wrote, you must "upload a new inner temptress who's equal parts good girl and wild child." The article recommended invading a man's personal space and entering his "intimate zone" by finding an excuse to touch him. Picking a piece of lint off his jacket ought to do the trick. Then you can tell him how much you like his cologne (Willardt, 2000). If things progress, another article in the same issue of *Cosmopolitan* explained how you can read his body language to tell whether he's lying (Dutton, 2000).

Whatever we may think of the soundness of *Cosmopolitan*'s advice or the images of women and men it tries to reinforce, this example drives home the point that social interaction typically involves a complex mix of verbal and nonverbal messages. The face alone is capable of more than 1000 distinct expressions, reflecting the whole range of human emotion. Arm movements, hand gestures, posture, and other aspects of body language send many more messages to a person's audience (Wood, 1999).

Despite the wide variety of facial expressions in the human repertoire, most researchers believed until recently that the facial expressions of six emotions are similar across cultures. These six emotions are happiness, sadness, anger, disgust, fear, and surprise (Ekman, 1978). However, since the mid-1990s, some researchers have questioned whether a universally recognized set of facial

ID1974/Shutterstock.com

expressions reflects basic human emotions. Among other things, critics have argued that "facial expressions are not the readout of emotions but displays that serve social motives and are mostly determined by the presence of an audience" (Fernandez-Dols, Sanchez, Carrera, and Ruiz-Belda, 1997: 163). From this point of view, a smile will reflect pleasure if it serves a person's interest to present a smiling face to his or her audience. Conversely, a person may be motivated to conceal anxiety by smiling or to conceal pleasure by suppressing a smile.

At times, different cultural expectations can lead to colossal misunderstanding. Until recently, it was considered rude among educated Japanese to say "no." Disagreement was instead conveyed by discreetly changing the subject and smiling politely. Consequently, it was common for visiting North Americans to think that their Japanese hosts were saying "yes" because of the politeness, the smile, and the absence of a "no" when in fact they were saying "no."

Similarly, no gesture or body posture means the same thing in all societies and all cultures. In our society, people point with an outstretched hand and an extended finger. However, people raised in other cultures tip their head or use their chin or eyes to point out something. We nod our heads "yes" and shake "no," but others nod "no" and shake "yes."

Finally, we must note that people in all societies communicate by manipulating the space that separates them from others (Hall, 1959, 1966). This point is well illustrated in our *Cosmopolitan* example. Sociologists commonly distinguish four zones that surround us. The size of these zones varies from one society to the next. In North America, an intimate zone extends about 0.5 metre from the body. It is restricted to people with whom we want sustained, intimate physical contact. A personal zone extends from about 0.5 metre to 1.5 metres away. It is reserved for friends and acquaintances. We tolerate only a little physical intimacy from such people. The social zone is situated in the area roughly 1.5 metres to 3.5 metres away from us. Apart from a handshake, no physical contact is permitted from people we restrict to that zone. The public zone starts around 3.5 metres from our bodies. It is used to distinguish a performer or a speaker from an audience.

status cues Visual indicators of a person's social position.

stereotypes Rigid views of how members of various groups act, regardless of whether individual group members really behave that way.

Status Cues

Aside from facial expressions, gestures, and body language, nonverbal communication takes place by means of status cues, or visual indicators of other people's social position. Goffman (1959) observed that when individuals come into contact, they typically try to acquire information that will help them define the situation and make interaction easier. That goal is accomplished in part by attending to status cues.

Although status cues can be useful in helping people define the situation and thus greasing the wheels of social interaction, they also pose a danger; status cues can quickly degenerate into stereotypes, or rigid views of how members of various groups act, regardless of whether individual group members really behave that way. Stereotypes create social barriers that impair interaction or prevent it altogether.

For instance, every year in Toronto, police officers stop, question, and document hundreds of thousands of

Among other things, body language communicates the degree to which people conform to gender roles, or widely shared expectations about how males and females are supposed to act. In these photos, which postures suggest power and aggressiveness? Which suggest pleasant compliance? Which are "appropriate" to the sex of the person?

Courtesy of Robert Brym

people on foot, on bicycles, and in cars. They write down each person's name, phone number, date of birth, address, height, weight, race, and the names of that person's associates. This procedure is commonly called "carding." Reasons for carding include "general investigation," "loitering," "suspicious activity," "related to a radio call," or "as a result of a traffic stop." In the great majority of cases, no charge or arrest results. Less than a fifth of the people who are carded have had a criminal record in the preceding decade.

In Toronto's 72 police districts, black people are on average 3.2 times more likely than white people to be carded, although they represent just 8.4 percent of the city's population (City of Toronto, 2015; *Toronto Star*, 2015; see Figure 4.3). The people *least* likely to be stopped while driving are older, highly educated Asian females. The people *most* likely to be stopped while driving are young, highly educated black males (Wortley, Brownfield, and Hagan, 1996). Presumably, young black men who are highly educated drive relatively expensive cars because they earn relatively high incomes, so they are regarded with particular suspicion by the police! In this case, a social cue has become a stereotype that guides police policy. Many black people, the great majority of whom never commit an illegal act, view this police practice as harassment. Racial stereotyping therefore helps perpetuate the sometimes poor relations between the black community and law enforcement officials.

As our discussion shows, face-to-face interaction may at first glance appear to be straightforward and unproblematic. Most of the time, it is. However, underlying the surface of human communication is a wide range of cultural assumptions, unconscious understandings, and nonverbal cues that make interaction possible.

NETWORKS, GROUPS, AND ORGANIZATIONS

THE HOLOCAUST

In 1941, the large stone and glass train station was one of the proudest structures in Smolensk, a provincial capital of about 100 000 people on Russia's western border. Always bustling, it was especially busy on the morning of June 28. Besides the usual passengers and well-wishers, hundreds of Soviet Red Army soldiers were nervously talking, smoking, writing hurried letters to their loved ones, and sleeping fitfully on the station floor while waiting for their train. Nazi troops had invaded the nearby city of Minsk in Belarus a couple of days before. The Soviet soldiers were being positioned to defend Russia against the inevitable German onslaught.

Robert Brym's father, then in his 20s, had been standing in line for nearly two hours to buy food when he noticed flares arching over the station. Within seconds, Stuka bombers, the pride of the German air force, swept down, releasing their bombs just before pulling out of their dive. Inside the station, shards of glass, blocks of stone, and mounds of earth fell indiscriminately on sleeping soldiers and nursing mothers alike. Everyone panicked. People trampled over one another to get out. In minutes, the train station was rubble.

Nearly two years earlier, Robert's father had managed to escape Poland when the Nazis invaded his hometown near Warsaw. Now he was on the run again. By the time the Nazis occupied Smolensk a few weeks after their

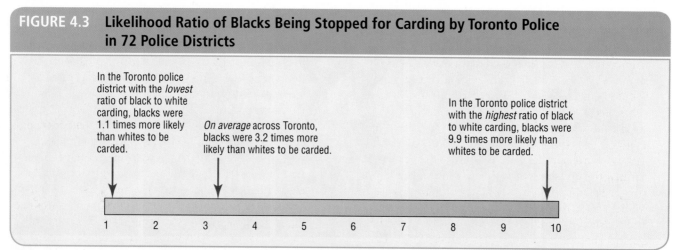

FIGURE 4.3   Likelihood Ratio of Blacks Being Stopped for Carding by Toronto Police in 72 Police Districts

In the Toronto police district with the *lowest* ratio of black to white carding, blacks were 1.1 times more likely than whites to be carded.

On average across Toronto, blacks were 3.2 times more likely than whites to be carded.

In the Toronto police district with the *highest* ratio of black to white carding, blacks were 9.9 times more likely than whites to be carded.

Note: Between 2008 and 2011, 788 050 Torontonians were carded. This figure shows how many times more likely carding was for blacks than for whites. For example, on average, blacks were 3.2 times more likely to be carded than whites were.

Source: *Toronto Star*. 2015. "Known to police." http://www.thestar.com/news/gta/knowntopolice.html (retrieved 22 July 2015).

dive-bombers destroyed its train station, Robert's father was deep in the Russian interior serving in a workers' battalion attached to the Soviet Red Army.

"My father was one of 300 000 Polish Jews who fled eastward into Russia before the Nazi genocide machine could reach them," says Robert. "The remaining 3 million Polish Jews were killed in various ways. Some died in battle. Many more, like my father's mother and younger siblings, were rounded up like diseased cattle and shot. However, most of Poland's Jews wound up in the concentration camps. Those deemed unfit were shipped to the gas chambers. Those declared able to work were turned into slaves until they could work no more. Then they, too, met their fate. A mere 9 percent of Poland's 3.3 million Jews survived World War II. The Nazi regime was responsible for the death of 6.1 million Jews in Europe.

"One question that always perplexed my father about the war was this: How was it possible for many thousands of ordinary Germans—products of what he regarded as the most advanced civilization on earth—to systematically murder millions of defenceless and innocent Jews, Romani ("Gypsies"), gays and lesbians, and people with mental disabilities in the death camps?" To answer this question adequately, we must use sociological concepts.

HOW SOCIAL GROUPS SHAPE OUR ACTIONS

The conventional, nonsociological answer to the question of how ordinary Germans could commit the crime of the twentieth century is that many Nazis were evil, sadistic, or deluded enough to think that Jews and other undesirables threatened the existence of the German people. Therefore, in the Nazi mind, the innocents had to be killed. This answer is given in the 1993 movie *Schindler's List* and in many other accounts. Yet it is far from the whole story. Sociologists emphasize three other factors:

1. *Norms of solidarity demand conformity.* When we form relationships with friends, lovers, spouses, teammates, and comrades-in-arms, we develop shared ideas, or *norms of solidarity*, about how we should behave toward them to sustain the relationships. Because these relationships are emotionally important to us, we sometimes pay more attention to norms of solidarity than to the morality of our actions. For example, a study of the Nazis who roamed the Polish countryside to shoot and kill Jews and other "enemies" of Nazi Germany found that the soldiers often did not hate the people they systematically slaughtered, but they did not have many qualms about their actions (Browning, 1992). They simply developed deep loyalty to one another. They felt they had to get their assigned job done or face letting down their comrades. Thus, they

committed atrocities partly because they just wanted to maintain group morale, solidarity, and loyalty. They committed evil deeds not because they were extraordinarily bad but because they were quite ordinary—ordinary in the sense that they acted to sustain their friendship ties and to serve their group, just like most people would.

The case of the Nazi regime may seem extreme, but other instances of going along with criminal behaviour uncover a similar dynamic at work. Why do people rarely report crimes committed by corporations? Employees may worry about being reprimanded or fired if they become whistle-blowers, but they also worry about letting down their co-workers. Why do gang members engage in criminal acts? They may seek financial gain, but they also regard crime as a way of maintaining a close social bond with the other gang members.

A study of the small number of Polish Christians who helped save Jews during World War II helps clarify why some people violate group norms (Tec, 1986). The heroism of these Polish Christians was not correlated with their educational attainment, political orientation, religious background, or even attitudes toward Jews. In fact, some Polish Christians who helped save Jews were quite anti-Semitic. Instead, these Christian heroes were for one reason or another estranged or cut off from mainstream norms. Because they were poorly socialized into the norms of their society, they were freer not to conform and instead to act in ways they believed were right. We could tell a roughly similar story about corporate whistle-blowers or people who turn in members of their gang. They are disloyal from an insider's point of view but heroic from an outsider's point of view, often because they have been poorly socialized into the group's norms (recall the Sociology at the Movies box about pedophilia in the Catholic Church in Chapter 2, Culture, on pages 31–32).

2. *Structures of authority tend to render people obedient.* Most people find it difficult to disobey authorities because they fear ridicule, ostracism, and punishment. This was strikingly demonstrated in an experiment conducted by social psychologist Stanley Milgram (1974). Milgram informed his experimental subjects that they were taking part in a study on punishment and learning. He brought each subject to a room where a man was strapped to a chair. An electrode was attached to the man's wrist. The experimental subject sat in front of a console. It contained 30 switches with labels ranging from "15 volts" to "450 volts" in 15-volt increments. Labels ranging from "Slight Shock" to "Danger: Severe Shock" were pasted below the switches. The experimental subjects were told to administer a 15-volt shock for the

bureaucracy A large, impersonal organization composed of many clearly defined positions arranged in a hierarchy.

man's first wrong answer and then increase the voltage each time he made an error. The man strapped in the chair was, in fact, an actor. He did not actually receive a shock. As the experimental subject apparently increased the current, however, the actor began to writhe, shouting for mercy and begging to be released. If the experimental subjects grew reluctant to administer more current, Milgram assured them the man strapped in the chair would be fine and insisted that the success of the experiment depended on the subject's obedience. The subjects were, however, free to abort the experiment at any time.

Remarkably, 71 percent of experimental subjects were prepared to administer shocks of 285 volts or more, even though the switches at that level were labelled "Intense Shock," "Extreme Intensity Shock," and "Danger: Severe Shock" and despite the fact that the actor appeared to be in great distress at this level of current (see Figure 4.4).

Milgram's experiment teaches us that as soon as we are introduced to a structure of authority, we are inclined to obey those in power. This is the case even if the authority structure is new and highly artificial, even if we are free to walk away

from it with no penalty, and even if we think that by remaining in its grip we are inflicting terrible pain on another human being. In this context, the actions and inactions of German citizens in World War II become more understandable if no more forgivable.

3. *Bureaucracies are highly effective structures of authority.* The Nazi genocide machine was also so effective because it was bureaucratically organized. As Max Weber (1964 [1947]) defined the term, a **bureaucracy** is a large, impersonal organization comprising many clearly defined positions arranged in a hierarchy. A bureaucracy has a permanent, salaried staff of qualified experts and written goals, rules, and procedures. Staff members always try to find ways of running their organization more efficiently. *Efficiency* means achieving the bureaucracy's goals at the least cost. The goal of the Nazi genocide machine was to kill Jews and other undesirables. To achieve that goal with maximum efficiency, the job was broken into many small tasks. Most officials performed only one function, such as checking train schedules, organizing entertainment for camp guards, maintaining supplies of Zyklon B gas, and removing ashes from the crematoria. The full horror of what was happening eluded many officials or at least could be conveniently ignored as they concentrated on their jobs, most of them far removed from the gas chambers and death camps in occupied Poland.

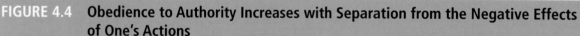

FIGURE 4.4   Obedience to Authority Increases with Separation from the Negative Effects of One's Actions

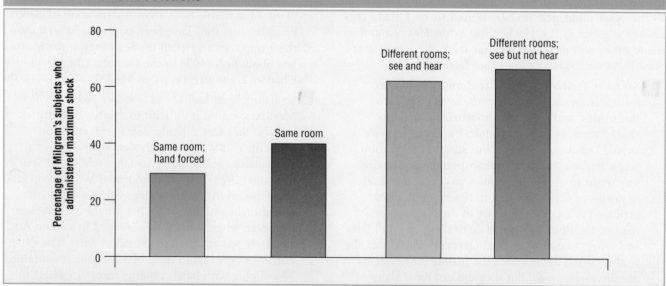

Milgram's experiment supports the view that separating people from the negative effects of their actions increases the likelihood of compliance.

Source: Adapted from "Closeness of the Victim" from *Obedience to Authority*. Chapter 4. Stanley Milgram. Copyright © 1994 by Stanley Milgram.

Many factors account for variations in Jewish victimization rates across Europe during World War II. One factor was bureaucratic organization. Not coincidentally, the proportion of Jews killed was highest not in the Nazi-controlled countries where the hatred of Jews was most intense (for example, Romania), but in countries where the Nazi bureaucracy was best organized (for example, Holland; Bauman, 1989; Sofsky, 1997 [1993]).

In short, the sociological reply to the question posed by Robert's father is that it was not just blind hatred but also the nature of groups and bureaucracies that made it possible for the Nazis to kill innocent people so ruthlessly.

LO⁴ SOCIAL NETWORKS

Suppose someone asked you to deliver a letter to a complete stranger on the other side of the country by using only acquaintances to pass the letter along. You give the letter to an acquaintance, who can give the letter to one of his or her acquaintances, and so on. Research shows that, on average, it would take no more than about six acquaintances to get the letter to the stranger. This fact suggests that in a fundamental sociological sense, we live in a small world. Just a few social ties separate us from everyone else.

Our world is small because we are enmeshed in overlapping sets of social relations, or social networks. Although any particular individual may know a small number of people, his or her family members, friends, co-workers, and others know many more people who extend far beyond that individual's personal network. So, for example, the authors of this textbook are likely to be complete strangers to you. Yet your professor may know one of us or at least know someone who knows one of us. Probably no more than two links separate us from you. Put differently, although our personal networks are small, they lead quickly to much larger networks. We live in a small world because our social networks connect us to the larger world.

Sociologists define a social network as a bounded set of units (individuals, organizations, countries, and so on) linked by the exchange of material or emotional resources, everything from money to friendship. The patterns of exchange determine the boundaries of the network. Network members exchange resources more frequently with each other than with non-members. Individuals in a network think of themselves as network members. Social networks may be formal (i.e., defined in writing) or informal (i.e., defined only in practice). The people you know personally form the boundaries of your personal network. However, each of your network members is linked to other people. This is what connects you to people you have never met, creating a "small world" that extends far beyond your personal network.

THE VALUE OF NETWORK ANALYSIS

The study of social networks is not restricted to ties among individuals (Wasserman and Faust, 1994; Wellman and Berkowitz, 1997 [1988]). The units of analysis (or *nodes*) in a network can be individuals, groups, organizations, and even countries. Thus, social network analysts have examined everything from intimate relationships between lovers to diplomatic relations among nations.

Unlike organizations, most networks lack names and offices. There is a Boy Scouts of Canada but no North American Trading Bloc. In a sense, networks lie beneath the more visible collectivities of social life, but that makes them no less real or important. Some analysts claim that we can gain only a partial sense of why certain things happen in the social world by focusing on highly visible collectivities. From their point of view, the whole story requires probing below the surface and examining the network level. The study of social networks clarifies a wide range of social phenomena, including how people find jobs and form communities (see the Sociology at the Movies feature in this chapter).

Finding a Job

Many people learn about important events, ideas, and opportunities from their social networks. Friends and acquaintances often introduce you to everything from an interesting university course or a great restaurant to a satisfying occupation or a future spouse. Social networks aren't the only source of information, but they are highly significant.

Consider how people find jobs. Do you look in the "Help Wanted" section of your local newspaper, scan the Internet, or walk around certain areas of town looking for "Employee Wanted" signs? Although these strategies are common, people often learn about employment opportunities from other people.

What kind of people? According to sociologist Mark Granovetter (1973), you may have strong or weak ties to another person. You have strong ties to people who are close to you, such as family members and friends. You have weak ties to mere acquaintances, such as people you meet at parties and friends of friends. In his research, Granovetter found that weak ties are more important than strong ties in finding a job, which is contrary to common sense. You might reasonably assume that a mere acquaintance wouldn't do much to help you find a job, whereas a close friend or relative would make a lot more effort in this regard. However, by focusing on the flow of information in personal networks, Granovetter found something

SOCIOLOGY AT THE MOVIES

The Social Network

Facebook is one of the world's most popular websites, with an estimated 1.65 billion active users as of the first quarter of 2016 (Statista, 2016). Its main source of revenue is selling information about its users to advertisers, which is why its default privacy settings have become less restrictive over time (McKeon, 2010). Mark Zuckerberg, its 26-year-old founder and principal shareholder, is the world's youngest self-made billionaire. He is now the sixth-richest person in the world, with a fortune that Forbes estimates at $51.7 billion (Forbes, 2016). *The Social Network* is the remarkable story of how Zuckerberg hatched Facebook in a Harvard dorm room in 2004 and cooked up a corporate omelet worth billions—necessarily breaking a few eggs in the process.

Mark Zuckerberg and Facebook co-founder Dustin Moskovitz in a scene from *The Social Network*

Sociologists have mined Facebook for data to test theories about relationships, identity, self-esteem, popularity, collective action, race, and political engagement (Rosenbloom, 2007). However, the movie pays no attention to this research. Instead, it asks whether Zuckerberg's success was due more to his genius, cunning, or greed. Aaron Sorkin, who wrote the crisp, witty, exhilarating screenplay, seems to think it was a little of all three.

If Sorkin had read more sociology, he might have concluded that social networks were also partly responsible for Facebook's stunning ascent. Think of the way Zuckerberg's personal network made available to him the resources needed to create Facebook. Zuckerberg was an undergraduate at Harvard, which regularly published a hard-copy *Facebook* containing photos and brief bios of Harvard students. Moreover, anyone familiar with the Internet in 2004—let alone a programming nerd like Zuckerberg—knew of the existence of popular dating and social networking sites operating on principles similar to those that Facebook would later adopt (Brym and Lenton, 2001).

Zuckerberg mobilized still more useful resources using strong and weak ties. Harvard upperclassmen Cameron and Tyler Winklevoss hired Zuckerberg to write code for a Harvard-based social networking site. Zuckerberg liked their idea so much that, while he was ostensibly working for them, he developed Facebook on his own. (The Winklevoss brothers later sued Zuckerberg, settling for $65 million.) For Facebook's startup costs, Zuckerberg borrowed $15 000 from his roommate, Eduardo Saverin, whom he later defrauded for his share in Facebook. (Saverin also successfully sued.) According to Zuckerberg, he even got the idea of extending Facebook beyond Harvard from Dustin Moskovitz, another roommate.

It may have taken a genius to see the enormous potential of a general Web-based social networking site and a combination of cunning and greed to "borrow" ideas and money from people in his personal network. But the raw materials for Facebook were in the air for anyone in Zuckerberg's position, and Zuckerberg's personal ties led him to them (*Bloomberg Game Changers*, 2010; Wright, 2010).

The irony at the centre of *The Social Network* is that Zuckerberg, who invents the world's most powerful friendship machine, had trouble keeping friends. In the opening scene, his girlfriend dumps him, and myriad other failed relationships litter the movie. The irony of the irony is that Zuckerberg had just enough of the right kind of friends—or at least access to useful nodes in his personal network—to make him what he is.

Critical Thinking Questions

1. Investigate the biography of a prominent national, provincial, or local businessperson. Which was more important in his or her achieving success—knowledge or networking?
2. In general, what do you think is more important in achieving business success? On what do you base your opinion?

different. Mere acquaintances are more likely to provide useful information about employment opportunities than friends or family members because people who are close to you typically share overlapping networks. Therefore, the information they can provide about job opportunities is often redundant.

In contrast, mere acquaintances are likely to be connected to *diverse* networks. They can therefore provide information about many different job openings and make introductions to many different potential employers. Moreover, because people typically have more weak ties than strong ties, the sum of weak ties holds more information about job opportunities than does the sum of strong ties. These features of personal networks allowed Granovetter to conclude that the "strength of weak ties" lies in their diversity and abundance.

Urban Networks

We rely on social networks for a lot more than job information. Consider everyday life in the big city. We often think of big cities as cold and alienating places where few people know one another. In this view, urban acquaintanceships tend to be few and functionally specific; we know someone fleetingly as a bank teller or a server in a restaurant but not as a whole person. Even dating can involve a series of brief encounters. In contrast, people often think of small towns as friendly, comfortable places where everyone knows everyone else (and everyone else's business). Indeed, some of the founders of sociology emphasized just this distinction. Notably, German sociologist Ferdinand Tönnies (1988 [1887]) contrasted *community* with *society*. According to Tönnies, a community is marked by intimate and emotionally intense social ties, whereas a society is marked by impersonal relationships held together largely by self-interest. A big city is a prime example of a society in Tönnies's judgment.

Tönnies's view prevailed until network analysts started studying big-city life in the 1970s. Where Tönnies saw only sparse, functionally specific ties, network analysts found elaborate social networks, some functionally specific and some not. For example, Barry Wellman and his colleagues studied personal networks in Toronto (Wellman, Carrington, and Hall, 1997 [1988]). They found that each Torontonian had an average of about 400 social ties, including immediate and extended kin, neighbours, friends, and co-workers. These ties provided everything from emotional aid (for example, visits after a personal tragedy) and financial support (small loans) to minor services (fixing a car) and information of the kind Granovetter studied.

Strong, enduring ties that last a long time are typically restricted to immediate family members, a few close relatives and friends, and a close co-worker or two. Beyond that, however, people rely on a wide array of ties for different purposes at different times. Downtown residents sitting on their front stoops on a summer evening, sipping beverages, and chatting with neighbours as the kids play road hockey may be less common than they were 50 years ago. However, the automobile, public transportation, the telephone, and the Internet help people stay in close touch with a wide range of contacts for a variety of purposes (Haythornthwaite and Wellman, 2002). Far from living in an impersonal and alienating world, the lives of today's city dwellers are network rich.

> **social group** A group composed of one or more networks of people who identify with one another and adhere to defined norms, roles, and statuses.
>
> **social category** A group composed of people who share similar status but do not identify with one another.

LO⁵ GROUPS

Social groups consist of one or more social networks, the members of which identify with one another, routinely interact, and adhere to defined norms, roles, and statuses. In contrast, social categories consist of people who share similar status but do not routinely interact or identify with one another. Coffee drinkers form a **social category**. Members of a family, sports team, or college form groups. Groups exert enormous influence on us.

GROUP CONFORMITY

The 2004 movie *Mean Girls* tells the story of 17-year-old Cady Heron (played by Lindsay Lohan), who was home-schooled in Africa by her archaeologist parents and is then plunked into a suburban American high school when the family moves back to the United States. The ways of the school bewilder her, so a friend prepares "Cady's Map to North Shore High School." It shows the layout of the cafeteria, with tables neatly labelled "Varsity Jocks," "J.V. Jocks," "Plastics," "Preps," "Fat Girls," "Thin Girls," "Black Hotties," "Asian Nerds," "Cool Asians," "Cheerleaders," "Burnouts," and so on.

If you drew a map of your high school cafeteria—for that matter, even your college or university cafeteria—the labels might be different, but chances are they would represent cliques that are just as segregated as North Shore High was. Everywhere, group members tend to dress and act alike, use the same slang, like and dislike the same kind of music, and demand loyalty, especially in the face of external threat. All groups demand conformity and, to

How are disconnected individuals turned into cohesive teams through social interaction and the sharing of symbols?

Photo and Co/Digital Vision/Getty Images

varying degrees, they get it, although, of course, group loyalties may change with changing social circumstances (see the Sociology on the Tube feature in this chapter).

The Asch Experiment

A famous experiment conducted by social psychologist Solomon Asch shows how group pressure creates conformity (Asch, 1955). Asch gathered seven men, one of whom was the experimental subject. The other six were Asch's confederates. Asch showed the seven men a card with a line drawn on it. He then showed them a second card with three lines of varying lengths drawn on it (see Figure 4.5). One by one, he asked the confederates to judge which line on card 2 was the same length as the line

Cady Heron (Lindsay Lohan) learns about group boundaries in *Mean Girls*.

Paramount/Photofest

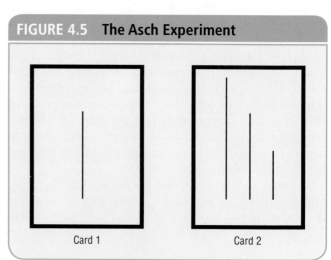

FIGURE 4.5   The Asch Experiment

Card 1   Card 2

Homeland and the Ambiguities of Group Membership

Ambiguities of group membership generate much of *Homeland*'s dramatic tension. Nicholas Brody is an American marine sergeant, captured and held prisoner by Al-Qaeda in Iraq from 2003 to 2011. After years of torture and deprivation, Al-Qaeda mastermind Abu Nazir "turns" Brody by treating him kindly, befriending him, converting him to Islam, and recruiting him to

Teakwood Lane Prod/Cherry Pie Prod/Keshet/FOX 21/ Showtime/The Kobal Collection at Art Resource, NY

tutor his youngest son, Issa, whom Brody comes to love. Then the American vice-president orders a drone attack. It kills many, including Issa. Abu Nazir convinces Brody to return to the United States and await instructions for avenging Issa's murder by assassinating the American vice-president.

Brody is welcomed as a war hero and soon wins a seat in the U.S. Congress. However, CIA agent Carrie Mathison has intelligence leading her to suspect that Brody is an Al-Qaeda agent. To get more information, she engineers an affair with Brody, who is married and has two children. They seem to fall in love.

Carrie eventually discovers evidence confirming Brody's affiliation with Abu Nazir. Confronted with the evidence, Brody is forced to become a CIA double agent charged with helping to bring down Abu Nazir. The operation is headed by Peter Quinn, whose boss, we discover, is not in the CIA. Quinn seems to have instructions to kill Brody after he disposes of Abu Nazir.

Is Brody loyal to the CIA or to Abu Nazir? Is he loyal to his wife or to Carrie? Is Carrie loyal to Brody or to the CIA? Is Quinn loyal to the CIA or to some other body? In the old days of TV, the good guys and the bad guys looked and talked differently and remained dedicated to their respective groups. Good drama on TV today is more realistic sociologically, recognizing that group loyalties can shift as circumstances change. In *Homeland*, we are even left wondering who the good guys and the bad guys are—the Americans, who suffer lethal terrorist attacks, or Abu Nazir, whose land was invaded by the Americans and whose innocent young son was killed by them. We are even asked to question our own group loyalties.

Critical Thinking Questions

1. Has your own group loyalty or that of a close friend or relative ever changed? If so, what were the social circumstances that that led to the shift?
2. How did members of the abandoned and newly joined groups react to the shift? Why?

---

on card 1. The answer was obvious. One line on card 2 was shorter than the line on card 1. One line was longer. One was exactly the same length. Yet, as instructed by Asch, all six confederates said that either the shorter or the longer line was the same length as the line on card 1. When it came time for the experimental subject to make his judgment, he typically overruled his own perception and agreed with the majority. Only 25 percent of Asch's experimental subjects consistently gave the right answer. Asch thus demonstrated how easily group pressure can overturn individual conviction and result in conformity.

Groupthink and Bystander Apathy

The power of groups to ensure conformity is often a valuable asset. Sports teams couldn't excel without the willingness of players to undergo personal sacrifice for the good of the group, nor could armies function. In fact, as sociologists have demonstrated and as high-ranking military officers have observed, group cohesion—not patriotism or bravery—is the main factor motivating soldiers to engage in combat (Marshall, 1947: 160–61; Stouffer et al., 1949). As one soldier says in the 2001 movie *Black Hawk Down*: "When I go home people will ask me: 'Hey, Hoot,

groupthink Group pressure to conform despite individual misgivings.

bystander apathy Occurs when people observe someone in an emergency but do not offer help because they feel no responsibility for the incident and justify their inaction by the fact that others are not responding to it.

reference group A group of people against whom an individual evaluates his or her situation or conduct.

why do you do it, man? What, you some kinda war junkie?' You know what I'll say? I won't say a goddamn word. Why? They won't understand. They won't understand why we do it. They won't understand that it's about the men next to you. And that's it. That's all it is."

However, being a "good team player" can have a downside, because group consensus can sometimes be misguided or dangerous. Dissent might save the group from making mistakes, but the pressure to conform despite individual misgivings—sometimes called **groupthink** (Janis, 1972)—can lead to disaster. For instance, groupthink was at work in high-level meetings preceding the space shuttle *Columbia* disaster in 2003. Transcripts of those meetings at the National Aeronautics and Space Administration (NASA) show that the official who ran shuttle management meetings, a non-engineer, believed from the outset that foam insulation debris could not damage the spacecraft. She dismissed the issue and cut off discussion when an engineer expressed his concerns. The others present quickly fell into line with the person running the meeting (Wald and Schwartz, 2003). A few days later, damage caused by foam insulation debris caused *Columbia* to break apart on reentry into Earth's atmosphere. Seven astronauts died.

The concept of **bystander apathy** is related to the idea of groupthink. Bystander apathy occurs when people observe someone in an emergency but do not offer help. One case that attracted worldwide attention in 2011 involved a two-year-old toddler in Foshan, China, who was seriously injured when she wandered into the path of a van. Surveillance footage showed that the driver did not stop. A second truck then drove over the child. Again, the driver did not stop. More than a dozen people turned a blind eye when they walked by the critically injured child. Finally, a trash collector pulled her off the road and managed to track down her mother. The child later died in hospital (to see the YouTube video of this incident, use the search term "tragic accident at Foshan").

Studies of bystander apathy suggest that, in general, as the number of bystanders increases, the likelihood of any one bystander helping a person in distress decreases because the greater the number of bystanders, the less responsibility any one individual feels. This behaviour shows that people usually take their cues for action from others and again demonstrates the power of groups over individuals.

Group Boundaries: Competition and Self-Esteem

The boundaries separating groups often seem unchangeable and even natural. They are not. In general, groups construct boundaries to assert their dominance, increase their self-esteem, or compete for scarce resources, such as jobs (Barth, 1969; Levine and Campbell, 1972; Tajfel, 1981).

The *Robbers Cave Study* is a classic experiment that illustrates the conditions leading to the crystallization of group boundaries (Sherif, Harvey, White, Hood, and Sherif, 1988 [1961]). Researchers brought two groups of 11-year-old boys to a summer camp at Robbers Cave State Park in Oklahoma. The boys were strangers to one another, and the two groups were kept apart for about a week. They swam, camped, and hiked. Each group chose a name for itself, and the boys printed their group's name on their caps and T-shirts. Then the two groups met. A series of athletic competitions was set up between them. Soon, each group became highly antagonistic toward the other. Each group came to hold the other in low esteem. The boys ransacked cabins, started food fights, and stole various items from members of the other group. Thus, under competitive conditions, the boys quickly drew sharp group boundaries.

The investigators next stopped the athletic competitions and created several apparent emergencies whose solution required cooperation between the two groups. One such emergency involved a leak in the pipe supplying water to the camp. The researchers assigned the boys to teams comprising members of *both* groups. Their job was to inspect the pipe and fix the leak. After engaging in several such cooperative ventures, the boys started playing together without fighting. Once cooperation replaced competition and the groups ceased to hold each other in low esteem, group boundaries melted away as quickly as they had formed. Significantly, the two groups were of equal status—the boys were all white, middle-class, and 11 years old—and their contact involved face-to-face interaction in a setting where norms established by the investigators promoted a reduction of group prejudice. Social scientists today recognize that such conditions must be in place before group boundaries fade (Sternberg, 1998: 512).

Reference Groups

So far, we have focused almost exclusively on face-to-face interaction in groups. However, people also interact with other group members in their imagination. Take reference groups, for example. A **reference group** is composed of people against whom an individual evaluates his or her situation or conduct. Put differently, members of a reference group function as "role models." Reference groups may influence us even though they represent a largely imaginary ideal.

For instance, the advertising industry promotes certain body ideals that many people try to emulate, although we know that hardly anyone looks like a runway model or a Barbie doll.

PRIMARY AND SECONDARY GROUPS

Many kinds of social groups exist. However, sociologists make a basic distinction between primary and secondary groups. In **primary groups**, norms, roles, and statuses are agreed on but are not put into writing. Social interaction creates strong emotional ties, extends over a long period, and involves a wide range of activities. It results in group members knowing one another well. The family is the most important primary group.

Secondary groups are larger and more impersonal than primary groups are. Compared with primary groups, social interaction in secondary groups creates weaker emotional ties. It extends over a shorter period and involves a narrow range of activities. It results in most group members having at most a passing acquaintance with one another. Your sociology class is an example of a secondary group.

Many secondary groups are **formal organizations**, or secondary groups designed to achieve explicit objectives. In complex societies like ours, the most common and influential formal organizations are bureaucracies. We now turn to an examination of these often frustrating but necessary organizational forms.

LO⁶ BUREAUCRACY

Earlier, we noted that Weber regarded bureaucracies as the most efficient type of secondary group. This runs against the grain of common knowledge. In everyday speech, when someone says "bureaucracy," people commonly think of bored clerks sitting in small cubicles spinning out endless trails of "red tape" that create needless waste and frustrate the goals of clients. The idea that bureaucracies are efficient may seem odd.

How can we square the reality of bureaucratic inefficiencies—even tragedies—with Weber's view that bureaucracies are the most efficient type of secondary group? The answer is twofold. First, we must recognize that when Weber wrote about the efficiency of bureaucracy, he was comparing it with older organizational forms. These had operated on the basis of either traditional practice ("We do it this way because we've always done it this way") or the charisma of their leaders ("We do it this way because our chief inspires us to do it this way"). Compared with such "traditional" and "charismatic" organizations, bureaucracies are generally more efficient.

Second, we must recognize that Weber thought bureaucracies could operate efficiently only in the ideal case. He wrote extensively about some of bureaucracy's less admirable aspects in the real world. In other words, he understood that reality is often messier than the ideal case. In reality, bureaucracies vary in efficiency. Therefore, rather than proclaiming bureaucracy efficient or inefficient, we need to find out what makes bureaucracies work well or poorly.

One factor underlying bureaucratic inefficiency is size. The larger the bureau-cracy, the more difficult it is for functionaries to communicate. Moreover, bigger bureaucracies make it easier for rivalries and coalitions to form.

A second factor underlying bureaucratic inefficiency is social structure. Figure 4.6 shows a typical bureaucratic structure: a hierarchy. The bureaucracy has a head, below which are three divisions, below which are six departments. As you move up the hierarchy, the power of

primary group A social group in which norms, roles, and statuses are agreed on but are not put into writing. Social interaction leads to strong emotional ties. It extends over a long period and involves a wide range of activities. It results in group members knowing one another well.

secondary group A social group that is larger and more impersonal than a primary group. Compared with primary groups, social interaction in secondary groups creates weaker emotional ties. It extends over a shorter period and it involves a narrow range of activities. It results in most group members having at most a passing acquaintance with one another.

formal organizations Secondary groups designed to achieve specific and explicit objectives.

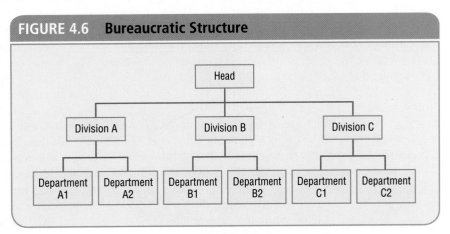

FIGURE 4.6 Bureaucratic Structure

the staff increases. Note also the red lines of communication that join the various bureaucratic units. Departments report only to their divisions. Divisions report only to the head.

Usually, the more levels in a bureaucratic structure, the more difficult communication becomes because people have to communicate indirectly, through department and division heads, rather than directly with one another. Information may be lost, blocked, reinterpreted, or distorted as it moves up the hierarchy, or an excess of information may cause top levels to become engulfed in a paperwork blizzard that prevents them from clearly seeing the needs of the organization and its clients. Bureaucratic heads may have only a vague and imprecise idea of what is happening "on the ground" (Wilensky, 1967).

Consider also what happens when the lines of communication directly joining departments or divisions are weak or nonexistent. As the lines joining units in Figure 4.6 suggest, Department A1 may have information that could help Department B1 do its job better, but A1 may have to communicate that information indirectly through the division level. At the division level, the information may be lost, blocked, reinterpreted, or distorted. Thus, just as people who have authority may lack information, people who have information may lack the authority to act on it directly (Crozier, 1964).

In the business world, large bureaucratic organizations are sometimes unable to compete against smaller, innovative firms, particularly in industries that are changing quickly (Burns and Stalker, 1961). This situation occurs partly because innovative firms tend to have more democratic organizational structures with fewer levels of authority, such as the network illustrated in Figure 4.7. Compare the network structure in Figure 4.7 with the traditional bureaucratic structure in Figure 4.6. Note that the network structure has fewer levels than the traditional bureaucratic structure. Moreover, in the network structure, lines of communication link all units. In the traditional bureaucratic structure, information flows only upward.

Much evidence suggests that bureaucracies with fewer levels of authority, decentralized decision making, and multiple lines of communication produce more satisfied workers, happier clients, and bigger profits (Kanter, 1989). Some of this evidence comes from Sweden and Japan. Beginning in the early 1970s, such corporations as Volvo and Toyota were at the forefront of bureaucratic innovation. They began eliminating middle-management positions. They allowed worker participation in a variety of tasks related to their main functions. They delegated authority to autonomous teams of a dozen or so workers that were allowed to make many decisions themselves. They formed "quality circles" of workers to monitor and correct defects in products and services. As a result, product quality, worker morale, and profitability improved. Today, these ideas have spread well beyond the Swedish and Japanese automobile industries and are evident in many large North American companies, both in the manufacturing and in the service sectors.

ORGANIZATIONAL CONSTRAINTS AND FREEDOM

In the second half of this chapter, we emphasized the capacity of networks, groups, and bureaucracies to constrain human behaviour. As we saw, such social collectivities can even encourage dangerously high levels of conformity, compel people to act against their better judgment, and dominate people in a vise of organizational rigidities.

We stressed the constraining aspect of social collectivities because we wanted to counter the commonsense view that motives alone determine the way people act. In conclusion, however, we should remember that people are often free to exercise two options other than bowing to the will of their social collectivities (Hirschman, 1970). In some circumstances, they can leave the social collectivities to which they belong. In other circumstances, they can struggle against the constraints their social collectivities seek to impose on them. After all, it is always possible to say no, even to the worst tyrant.

Less dramatically but no less importantly, knowledge, including sociological knowledge, can increase the ability of people to resist the constraints imposed on them. Recall the Milgram experiment we discussed earlier in this chapter, in which subjects administered what they thought were painful shocks to people just because the experimenters told them to. When the experiment was repeated years later, many of the subjects refused to go along with the demands of the experimenters. Some invoked the example of the Nazis to justify their refusal to comply. Others mentioned Milgram's original experiment. Their knowledge, some of it

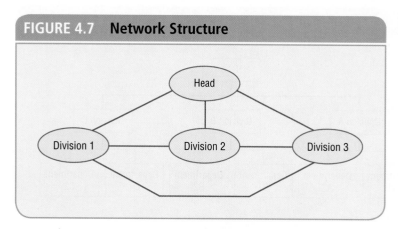

FIGURE 4.7 Network Structure

Head

Division 1 — Division 2 — Division 3

perhaps gained in sociology courses, enabled them to resist unreasonable demands (Gamson, Fireman, and Rytina, 1982).

Paradoxically, to succeed in challenging social collectivities, people must sometimes form a new social collectivity—a lobby, a union, a political party, a social movement (Lipset, Trow, and Coleman, 1956). People are always free to form new social collectivities that can counteract old ones. Embedded in social relations, we can use them for good or evil.

READY TO STUDY?

IN THE BOOK, YOU CAN:

❏ Tear out the chapter review card at the back of the book to have a summary of the chapter and key terms handy.

ONLINE YOU CAN:

❏ Work through key concepts with a Guided Learning Question.

❏ Prepare for tests with quizzes.

❏ Review the key terms with flash cards.

❏ Explore practical examples of chapter concepts with Connect a Concept exercises.

GO TO NELSON.COM/STUDENT TO ACCESS THESE DIGITAL RESOURCES.

Alex Milan Tracy/Sipa USA/AP Images

5
Deviance and Crime

LEARNING OBJECTIVES

In this chapter, you will learn to

LO¹ See how people define deviance and crime differently in different times and places.

LO² Interpret differences in crime rates over time and between different population categories.

LO³ Compare how deviance and crime were treated in the past with how they are treated today.

LO⁴ Explain how fear of crime is subject to manipulation by political and commercial groups that benefit from it.

LO⁵ Identify cost-effective and workable alternatives to some current methods of punishment.

LO¹ THE SOCIAL DEFINITION OF DEVIANCE AND CRIME

If you happen to come across members of the Tukano tribe in northern Brazil, don't be surprised if they greet you with a cheery "Have you bathed today?" You would probably find the question insulting, but think how you would feel if the Yanomamö people in Brazil's central highlands greeted you. An anthropologist reports that when he first encountered the Yanomamö, they rubbed mucus and tobacco juice into their palms, then inspected him by running their filthy hands over his body (Chagnon, 1992). He must have been relieved to return to urban Brazil and be greeted with a simple kiss on the cheek.

Rules for greeting people vary widely from one country to the next and among different cultural groups within one country. That is why a marketing company created an animated website showing business travellers how to greet their hosts in the 15 countries where the firm does business ("The Business of Touch," 2006). After all, violating local norms can cause great offence and result in the loss of a contract, a fact that one visitor to South Korea found out too late. He beckoned his host with an index finger, after which the host grew quiet. He discovered after he lost the deal that Koreans beckon only cats and dogs with an index finger. If you want to beckon someone politely in South Korea, you should do so with all four fingers facing down, much like Canadians wave goodbye.

Because norms vary widely, deviance is relative. What some people consider normal, others consider deviant, and vice versa. No act is deviant in and of itself. People commit deviant acts only when they break a norm and cause others to react negatively. From a sociological point of view, *everyone* is a deviant in one social context or another.

THE DIFFERENCE BETWEEN DEVIANCE AND CRIME

Deviance involves breaking a norm and evoking a negative reaction from others. Societies establish some norms as laws. **Crime** is

deviance Departure from a norm that evokes a negative reaction from others.

crime Deviance that is against the law.

law A norm stipulated and enforced by government bodies.

formal punishment Penalization by the judicial system for breaking a law.

informal punishment A mild sanction that is imposed during face-to-face interaction rather than by the judicial system.

stigmatization Process of negatively evaluating people because of a marker that distinguishes them from others.

deviance that breaks a **law**, which is a norm stipulated and enforced by government bodies.

Just as deviance is relative, so is crime. Consider that a list of famous people who have been labelled criminals would include Socrates, Jesus, Martin Luther, Louis Riel, Mahatma Ghandi, Martin Luther King, Jr., and Nelson Mandela. For many people today, these historical figures are heroes. In contrast, those who planned and participated in the extermination of Jews, Romani ("Gypsies"), leftists, and gays and lesbians in Nazi Germany were acting in a way that was defined as law-abiding at the time in Germany. You would probably consider the actions taken by the Nazis in Germany, rather than the actions of Jesus or Martin Luther, to be criminal. That is because norms and laws have changed dramatically. Today, anyone who advocates or promotes genocide commits a crime under Canadian law. We conclude that what is considered a crime in some times and places is considered perfectly normal in other times and places.

SANCTIONS

Many otherwise deviant acts go unnoticed or are considered too trivial to warrant negative *sanctions*, or actions indicating disapproval. People who are observed committing more serious acts of deviance are typically punished, either informally or formally.

Formal punishment results from people breaking laws. For example, criminals are usually formally punished by having to serve time in prison, pay a fine, or perform community service. Informal punishment is mild. It may involve raised eyebrows, a harsh stare, an ironic smile, gossip, ostracism, "shaming," or stigmatization (Braithwaite, 1989). When people are stigmatized, they are negatively evaluated because of visible characteristics that distinguish them from others (Goffman, 1963). For example, a study of newspaper portrayals of prostitutes in Victoria, British Columbia, shows that, in the 1980s, prostitutes were stigmatized as fallen women who spread disease and crime in public places and were themselves to blame for their moral failings. In the 1990s and 2000s, the stigmatization of prostitutes changed, as prostitutes were increasingly characterized as victims of ruthless pimps, violent clients, and the global sex trade.

The content of the stigma changed, but in both periods, negative and sensationalistic evaluations largely prevented serious discussion of how prostitution could be regulated to decrease risk to sex workers and their clients (Hallgrimsdottir, Phillips, and Benoit, 2006).

Types of deviance and crime vary in terms of the *severity of the social response*, which ranges from mild disapproval to capital punishment (Hagan, 1994). They vary also in terms of the *perceived harmfulness* of the deviant or criminal act. Note that actual harmfulness is not the only issue here—*perceived* harmfulness is involved too. Coca-Cola got its name because, in the early part of the last century, it contained a derivative of cocaine. Now cocaine is an illegal drug because people's perceptions of its harmfulness changed.

Finally, deviance and crime vary in terms of the *degree of public agreement* about whether an act should be considered deviant. Even the social definition of murder varies over time and across cultures and societies. For example, at the beginning of the twentieth century, Inuit communities sometimes deliberately allowed newborns to freeze to death. This was not considered to be a punishable offence if community members agreed that investing scarce resources in keeping the newborn alive could endanger everyone's well-being. Similarly, whether we classify the death of a miner as accidental or a case of manslaughter depends on the kind of worker safety legislation in existence. Some societies have more stringent worker safety rules than others, and deaths considered accidental in some societies are classified as criminal offences in others (McCormick, 1999). So we see that, even when it comes to serious crimes, social definitions are variable.

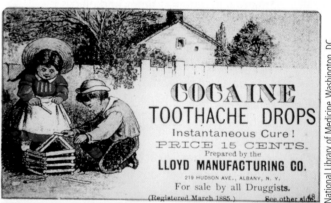

One of the determinants of the seriousness of a deviant act is its perceived harmfulness. Perceptions vary historically, however. For instance, until the early part of the twentieth century, cocaine was considered a medicine. It was an ingredient in cold formulas and toothache drops, and in these forms it was commonly given to children.

LO² MEASURING CRIME

Some crimes are more common than others are, and rates of crime vary over place and time and across different social groups. We now describe some of these variations and then we'll review the main sociological explanations of crime and deviance.

First, a word about crime statistics. Information on crime collected by the police is our main source of crime statistics. Since 1962, the Canadian Centre for Justice Statistics (CCJS), in co-operation with the policing community, has collected police-reported crime statistics through the *Uniform Crime Reporting* (UCR) *Survey*. UCR data reflect reported crime that has been substantiated by police. Information collected by the survey includes the number of criminal incidents, the clearance status of those incidents, and persons-charged information. The UCR Survey produces a continuous historical record of crime and traffic statistics reported by every police agency in Canada.

These statistics have two main shortcomings. First, much crime is not reported to the police. This is particularly true of so-called **victimless crimes**, which involve violations of the law in which no victim steps forward and is identified. Communicating for the purposes of prostitution, illegal gambling, and the use of illegal drugs are all victimless crimes. In addition, many common or "Level 1" assaults go unreported because the assailant is a friend or relative of the victim. Many victims of sexual assault are also reluctant to report the crime because they are afraid they will be humiliated or not believed and stigmatized by making the crime public.

The second main shortcoming of official crime statistics is that authorities and the wider public decide which criminal acts to report and which to ignore. If, for instance, the authorities decide to crack down on drugs, more drug-related crimes will be counted, not because more drug-related crimes are committed, but because more drug criminals are apprehended. Changes in legislation, which either create new offences or amend existing offences, also influence the number of recorded offences. Recognizing these difficulties, students of crime often supplement official crime statistics with other sources of information.

Self-report surveys are especially useful. In such surveys, respondents are asked to report their involvement in criminal activities, either as perpetrators or as victims. Self-report data compensate for many of the problems associated with official statistics. In general, self-report surveys report approximately the same rate of serious crime as official statistics do, but find two or three times the rate of less-serious crimes.

Self-report surveys tell us that a majority of Canadians have engaged in some type of criminal activity and that about a quarter of the population in any given year believes that they have been the victim of crime. These large proportions remind us that committing an act in violation of the law does not automatically result in being officially labelled a criminal. The process of criminal labelling can be likened to a funnel, wide at one end and narrow at the other. To be officially identified as a criminal, an individual's law-violating behaviour must first be observed and felt to justify action. The behaviour must be reported to the police who, in turn, must respond to the incident, decide that it warrants further investigation, file a report, and make an arrest. Next, the accused person must appear at a preliminary hearing (an arraignment) and a trial. If the person does not plead guilty, the possibility always exists that he or she will not be convicted because guilt has not been proven "beyond a reasonable doubt."

In **victimization surveys**, people are asked whether they have been victims of crime. Although these types of surveys date back to the mid-1960s in the United States, no national victimization survey was conducted in Canada until 1988 (Fattah, 1991). The latest such survey was conducted in 2014. It examined householders' experience with crime, including the impact of victimization and perceptions of personal safety (Perreault, 2015). It found that Canadians reported just 31 percent of victimization incidents to the police, with property crimes more likely to be reported than were crimes against persons. In part, this tendency reflects the requirement by insurance companies that individuals seeking compensation for property stolen or damaged as the result of a criminal act file a police report. With the exception of vandalism, all major categories of victimization were down since 1999. Although victimization surveys provide detailed information about crime victims, they provide less reliable data about offenders.

Bearing these caveats in mind, what does the official record show? Most Canadians would be understandably alarmed to hear that, in 2013, 1.8 million Criminal Code incidents were reported to police agencies (Boyce, Cotter, and Perreault, 2014). They might assume that each of these incidents mirrored the violent, dramatic, and lurid offences that daily media reports bring to our attention. But that is not the case. In 2013, fully 79 percent of Criminal Code incidents involved no violence at all (see Figure 5.1). True, the 2013 Canadian crime rate was about twice as high as it was in 1962. However, the long crime wave that began its upswing in the early 1960s peaked in 1992 (when it was about four times the 1962 level) and has been falling ever since. In 2013, the crime rate was at its lowest level since 1969 (Statistics Canada, 2015a). How do we explain the fall?

> **victimless crimes** Violations of the law in which no victim has stepped forward and been identified.
>
> **self-report surveys** Surveys in which respondents are asked to report their involvement in criminal activities, either as perpetrators or as victims.
>
> **victimization surveys** Surveys in which people are asked whether they have been victims of crime.

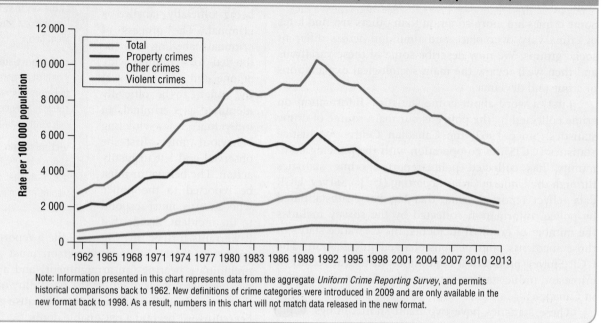

Note: Information presented in this chart represents data from the aggregate *Uniform Crime Reporting Survey*, and permits historical comparisons back to 1962. New definitions of crime categories were introduced in 2009 and are only available in the new format back to 1998. As a result, numbers in this chart will not match data released in the new format.

Source: Statistics Canada. 2015a. "Police officers, by province and territory." http://www.statcan.gc.ca/tables-tableaux/sum-som/l01/cst01/legal05a-eng.htm (retrieved 23 July 2015).

First, a growing number of well-trained troops are fighting crime. Today, there are about 69 000 police officers in Canada (Statistics Canada, 2015b). Recent declines in Canada's crime rate may reflect the introduction of community policing initiatives, enforcement efforts that target specific types of crime, the refinement of case management methods, improvements in the field of forensics, and crime prevention efforts (Logan, 2001: 3).

Second, the people most prone to street crime are young men, but Canada is aging and the number of young people in the population has declined in recent decades.

Third, the unemployment rate has followed a downward trend since 1992 (it stood at 12.1 percent in November 1992 and 7.0 percent in August 2015). Economic conditions have favoured a decrease in crime because the variable most strongly correlated with the crime rate is the male unemployment rate (John Howard Society, 1999: 3).

Finally, and more controversially, some researchers argue that declining crime rates may be linked to the legalization of abortion (Donahue and Levitt, 2001). They observe that the crime rate started to decline 19 years after abortion was legalized, suggesting that the decline occurred because, with the legalization of abortion, proportionately fewer unwanted children were in the population. They argue that unwanted children are more prone to criminal behaviour than wanted children are because they tend to receive less parental supervision and guidance.

Note that we have not claimed that putting more people in prison and imposing tougher penalties for crime help to account for lower crime rates. We will explain why these actions generally do not result in lower crime rates when we discuss *social control* (methods of ensuring conformity) and punishment. We will also probe one of the most fascinating questions raised by official statistics: If crime rates have been falling since 1992, what accounts for the increased enthusiasm of many Canadians (including members of the former Conservative government that was power from 2006 to 2015) for get-tough policies, our growing prison population, and our widespread fear of crime?

CRIMINAL PROFILES

Age and Gender

Men account for more than three-quarters of Canadian criminal court cases. However, with almost every passing year, women compose a slightly higher percentage of arrests (Mahony, 2013). This change is partly due to the fact that, in the course of socialization, traditional social controls and definitions of femininity are less often being imposed on women (see Chapter 8, Sexualities and Genders).

Most crime is committed by people who have not reached middle age. The 15- to 24-year-old age cohort is the most prone to criminal behaviour, with 18-year-olds having the highest crime rate. The percentage of 15- to 24-year-olds who are charged with a *violent* crime is about twice as high as the percentage of 15- to 24-year-olds in the population. For *property* crimes, the percentage is about three times higher (Brennan, 2013; Savoie, 2002: 3).

Race

Analysis of official statistics reveals that race is also a factor in who is arrested. Although Aboriginal people represent about 4 percent of Canada's population, they account for nearly a quarter of the federal inmate population. The overrepresentation of Aboriginal people in Canada's prisons is particularly marked in the Prairie provinces and the northern territories, where they form a relatively large part of the population. For example, at Saskatchewan Penitentiary, nearly two-thirds of inmates are Aboriginal (Office of the Correctional Investigator, 2013).

There are five reasons for the overrepresentation of Aboriginal people in Canada's prisons (Hartnagel, 2000). First, a disproportionately large number of Aboriginal people are poor. Although the great majority of poor people are law-abiding, poverty and its handicaps are associated with elevated crime rates. Second, the Aboriginal population is younger than the rest of the population and, as we have seen, young people are most crime-prone. Third, Aboriginal people tend to commit so-called **street crimes**—breaking and entering, robbery, assault, and the like—that are more detectable than **white-collar crimes** such as embezzlement, fraud, copyright infringement, false advertising, and so on. Fourth, the police, the courts, and other institutions may discriminate against Aboriginal people. As a result, Aboriginal people may be more likely to be apprehended, prosecuted, and convicted. Fifth, contact with Western culture has disrupted social life in many Aboriginal communities (see Chapter 7, Race and Ethnicity). This disruption has led to a weakening of social control over community members. Some people think that certain "races" are *inherently* more law-abiding than others, but they are able to hold such an opinion only by ignoring the powerful *social* forces that cause so many Aboriginal peoples to be incarcerated in Canada (Roberts and Gabor, 1990).

Most of the factors listed above also account for the above-average incarceration rate among black Canadians. Occupying a relatively low class position, engaging mainly in street crime as opposed to white-collar crime, and facing a discriminatory criminal justice system, black people are more likely than are whites to be motivated to commit criminal acts, to be detected and apprehended, and to be prosecuted, convicted, and jailed.

The claim that the criminal justice system engages in discriminatory practices based on race may be difficult for some Canadians to accept, but research suggests that the claim is credible. A Toronto survey on who gets stopped for police checks found that older and better-educated whites and Asians with no criminal record are significantly less likely to be stopped for police searches than are younger and less well-educated whites and Asians with a criminal record. In contrast, age, education, and lack of a criminal record do not insulate blacks from searches. In fact, better-educated and well-to-do blacks are *more* likely to be stopped and searched by police than are less well-educated and poorer blacks. These findings suggest that Toronto police keep a closer eye on blacks than they do on whites and Asians, and are particularly suspicious of blacks with education and money (Wortley and Tanner, 2008).

> **street crimes** Crimes including arson, break and enter, assault, and other illegal acts disproportionately committed by people from lower classes.
>
> **white-collar crimes** Illegal acts committed by respectable, high-status people in the course of work.

EXPLAINING DEVIANCE AND CRIME

> Lep: "I remember your li'l ass used to ride dirt bikes and skateboards, actin' crazy an' shit. Now you want to be a gangster, huh? You wanna hang with real muthaf—and tear shit up, huh? Stand up, get your li'l ass up. How old is you now anyway?"
>
> Kody: "Eleven, but I'll be twelve in November."
>
> —Sanyika Shakur (1993: 8)

Kody "Monster" Scott eagerly joined the notorious gang, the Crips, in South Central Los Angeles in 1975 when he was in Grade 6. He was released from Folsom Prison on parole in 1988, at the age of 24. Until about three years before his release, he was one of the most ruthless gang leaders in Los Angeles and the California prison system. In 1985, however, he decided to reform. He adopted the name Sanyika Shakur, became a black nationalist, and began a crusade against gangs. Few people in his position have chosen that path. In Scott's heyday, about 30 000 gang members roamed Los Angeles County. Today, there are more than 150 000.

What makes engaging in crime an attractive prospect for so many people? In general, why do deviance and crime occur at all? Sociologists rely on symbolic interactionism, functionalism, conflict theories, and feminist theories for explanations.

SYMBOLIC INTERACTIONIST APPROACHES TO DEVIANCE AND CRIME

People may learn deviant and criminal behaviour when they interact with others. Identifying the social circumstances that promote the learning of deviant and criminal roles is a traditional focus of symbolic interactionists.

Learning Deviance

The idea that becoming a habitual deviant or criminal is a learning process that occurs in a social context was firmly established by Howard S. Becker's classic study of marijuana users (Becker, 1963: 41–58). In the 1940s, Becker financed his Ph.D. studies by playing piano in Chicago jazz bands. He used the opportunity to carefully observe 50 fellow musicians, informally interview them in depth, and write up detailed field notes after performances.

Becker found that jazz musicians had to pass through a three-stage learning process before becoming regular marijuana users. Failure to pass a stage meant failure to learn the deviant role and become a regular user. These are the three stages:

1. *Learning to smoke the drug in a way that produces real effects.* First-time marijuana smokers do not ordinarily get high. To do so, they must learn how to smoke the drug in a way that ensures a sufficient dosage to produce intoxicating effects (taking deep drags and holding their breath for a long time). This process takes practice, and some first-time users give up, typically claiming that marijuana has no effect on them and that people who claim otherwise are just fooling themselves. Others are more strongly encouraged by their peers to keep trying. If they persist, they are ready to advance to stage two.

2. *Learning to recognize the effects and connect them with drug use.* Those who learn the proper smoking technique may not recognize that they are high or they may not connect the symptoms of being high with smoking the drug. They may get hungry, laugh uncontrollably, play the same song for hours on end, and yet still fail to realize that these are symptoms of intoxication. If so, they will stop using the drug. Becker found, however, that his fellow musicians typically asked experienced users how they knew whether they were high. Experienced users identified the symptoms of marijuana use and helped novices make the connection between what they were experiencing and smoking the drug. Once they made that connection, novices were ready to advance to stage three.

3. *Learning to enjoy the perceived sensations.* Smoking marijuana is not inherently pleasurable. Some users experience a frightening loss of self-control (paranoia). Others feel dizzy, uncomfortably thirsty, itchy, forgetful, or dangerously impaired in their ability to judge time and distance. If these negative sensations persist, marijuana use will cease. However, Becker found that experienced users typically helped novices redefine negative sensations as pleasurable. They taught novices to laugh at their impaired judgment, take pleasure in quenching their deep thirst, and find deeper meaning in familiar music. If and only if novices learned to define the effects of smoking as pleasurable did they become habitual marijuana smokers.

Learning *any* deviant or criminal role requires a social context in which experienced deviants or criminals teach novices the tricks of the trade. It follows that more exposure to experienced deviants and criminals increases the chance that an individual will come to value a deviant or criminal lifestyle and consider it normal (Sutherland, 1939, 1949). Moreover, the type of deviant or criminal that predominates in one's social environment has a bearing on the type of deviant or criminal that a novice will become. For example, depending on the availability of different types of deviants and criminals in their neighbourhoods, delinquent youths will turn to different types of crime. In some areas, delinquent youths are recruited by organized crime, such as the Mafia. In areas that lack organized crime networks, delinquent youths are more likely to create gangs. Thus, the relative availability of different types of deviants and criminals influences the type of deviant or criminal role a delinquent youth learns (Cloward and Ohlin, 1960).

Labelling

One night in Saskatchewan, after a night of heavy drinking, two 20-year-old university students, Alex Ternowetsky and Steven Kummerfield, both white and middle class, picked up Pamela George, an Aboriginal single mother who occasionally worked as a prostitute, in downtown Regina. They drove the 28-year-old woman outside the city limits, had her perform oral sex without pay, and then savagely beat her to death. Although originally charged with first-degree murder, a jury later found them guilty of the lesser charge of manslaughter. Justice Ted Malone of the Saskatchewan Court of Queen's Bench instructed the jurors to consider that the two men had been drinking and that George was "indeed a prostitute." Members of the victim's family were appalled, Native leaders outraged. Tone Cote of the Yorkton Tribal Council said the sentence would send the message that "it's all right for little white boys to go out on the streets, get drunk and use that for an excuse to start hunting down our people."

A variant of symbolic interactionism, **labelling theory**, holds that deviance results not just from the actions of the deviant but also from the responses of others, who define some actions as deviant and other actions as normal. As the above example suggests, terms like *deviant* or *criminal* are not applied automatically when a person engages in rule-violating behaviour. Some people engage in "primary deviance" insofar as they commit a deviant act but are not labelled as deviant by authorities. Others, like Ternowetsky and Kummerfield, commit "secondary deviance" insofar as authorities label them as deviant (Winter, 1996). Note that authorities typically exercise considerable discretion in how seriously they treat a deviant act, as the example of Ternowetsky and Kummerfield suggests.

Note too that some people, such as Pamela George, who are the victims of such acts, may find themselves labelled as deviant by authorities (and the public) because they are members of a stigmatized group (Matsueda, 1988, 1992).

That labelling plays an important part in who is caught and charged with crime was demonstrated in the 1960s by Aaron Cicourel (1968). Cicourel examined the tendency to label rule-breaking adolescents as juvenile delinquents if they came from families in which the parents were divorced. He found that police officers tended to use their discretionary powers to arrest adolescents from divorced families more often than adolescents from intact families who committed similar delinquent acts. Judges, in turn, tended to give more severe sentences to adolescents from divorced families than to adolescents from intact families who were charged with similar delinquent acts. Sociologists and criminologists then collected data on the social characteristics of adolescents who were charged as juvenile delinquents, "proving" that children from divorced families were more likely to become juvenile delinquents. Their finding reinforced the beliefs of police officers and judges. Thus, the labelling process acted as a self-fulfilling prophecy.

FUNCTIONALIST EXPLANATIONS

If symbolic interactionists focus on the learning and labelling of deviant and criminal roles, functionalists direct their attention to the social dysfunctions that lead to deviant and criminal behaviour.

Émile Durkheim

Functionalist thinking on deviance and crime originated with Durkheim (1938 [1895]), who made the controversial claim that deviance and crime are beneficial for society. For one thing, he wrote, when someone breaks a rule, it provides others with a chance to condemn and punish the transgression, remind them of their common values, clarify the moral boundaries of the group to which they belong, and thus reinforce social solidarity (see the Sociology at the Movies feature in this chapter). For another, Durkheim claimed, deviance and crime help societies adapt to social change. Martin Luther King, Jr., was arrested in Alabama in February 1965 for taking part in a demonstration supporting the idea that blacks should be allowed to vote, but later that year the passage of the Voting Rights Acts made it a crime to *prevent* blacks from voting in the United States. King's crime (and similar crimes by other civil rights activists) brought about positive social change, demonstrating the validity of Durkheim's point about the potentially positive functions of some types of deviance and crime.

Robert Merton

Robert Merton (1938) further developed Durkheim's theory by emphasizing the *dysfunctions* of deviance and crime. Merton argued that cultures often teach people to value material success. Just as often, however, societies do not provide enough legitimate opportunities for everyone to succeed. In Merton's view, such a discrepancy between cultural ideals and structural realities is dysfunctional, producing what he called strain.

strain The result of a culture teaching people to value material success, but society failing to provide enough legitimate opportunities for everyone to succeed.

Most people who experience strain will nonetheless force themselves to adhere to social norms, Merton wrote. He called this option "conformity." The rest adapt by engaging in one of four types of action. Rejecting the society's goals and its institutionalized means of achieving them, they may drop out of conventional society ("retreatism"). Rejecting the goals of conventional society but continuing to follow them, they may engage in "ritualism." Accepting cultural goals and creating novel means of achieving them results in "innovation." Although some innovators are business geniuses like Henry Ford and Steve Jobs, some are criminals (see the Sociology on the Tube feature in this chapter). Finally, rejecting cultural goals and finding new means of achieving new goals involves "rebellion"—the hippies of the 1960s represent this last form of adaptation to strain (see Figure 5.2).

Criminal Subcultures

Not only individuals adapt to the strain caused by social dysfunction—some social groups adapt by forming criminal gangs. Gang members feel that the legitimate world has rejected them—and they have a point. Although black and Aboriginal Canadians constitute fewer than 7 percent of the country's population, 25 percent of Canadian youth gang members are black and 21 percent are Aboriginal (Public Safety Canada, 2012). Little wonder. Blacks and Aboriginals are the two groups that experience the highest

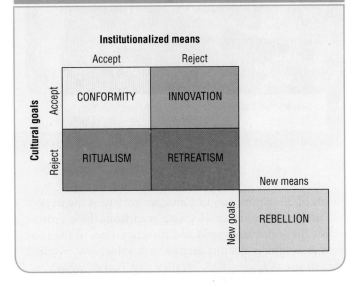

FIGURE 5.2 Merton's Strain Theory of Deviance

SOCIOLOGY AT THE MOVIES

Easy A

Olive Penderghast (Emma Stone) is embarrassed to admit she spent the weekend at home alone, so she tells her pushy high school friend, Rhi (Aly Michalka), she had a date with a college boy. On Monday, the following dialogue ensues:

Rhi: *"The whole weekend?"*

Olive: *"Yup."*

Rhi: *"Whoa, whoa. Wait a minute. You didn't have. . . ."*

Olive: *"No, no. Of course not."*

Rhi: *"You liar. . . ."*

Olive: *"Rhi, I'm not that kind of girl."*

Rhi: *"Oh really? The kind that does it or the kind that does it and doesn't have the lady balls to tell her best friend?"*

Scene from *Easy A*

Olive Bridge Ent/Adam Taylor/The Kobal Collection at Art Resource, NY

Rhi then drags Olive into a school restroom and insists on knowing the "truth." To shut her up, Olive finally "admits" she had sex with the mythical college boy. Big mistake. Marianne (Amanda Bynes) overhears the conversation. She is a self-righteous Christian enthusiast who promptly lets everyone in the school know that Olive is a fallen woman.

The school's norms are sexist and homophobic. They prohibit premarital sex for girls and encourage it for boys. They view only heterosexual sex as acceptable. So although Olive is seen as a slut, boys—outsiders and misfits in particular—see her as an opportunity. One boy who is gay, another who is obese, and a third who is a nerd get Olive to help them out by pretending she had sex with them. They become socially acceptable as Olive's reputation plummets.

Easy A is a well-written and funny movie, but what makes it sociologically interesting is the story it tells about the functions of norms and norm-breaking. Durkheim observed that norm-breakers like Olive reinforce group solidarity insofar as they encourage group members to publicly display outraged opposition to norm-breaking (Durkheim, 1938 [1895]). If Durkheim saw *Easy A*, he would immediately notice that everyone's gossiping and finger-pointing in reaction to Olive's alleged sexual transgression strengthened the norm that premarital sex for girls is unacceptable.

But *Easy A* also teaches us a sociological principle that Durkheim did not remark upon: Norm-breakers can provide outsiders with the opportunity to become insiders. In *Easy A*, the gay, obese, and nerdy boys become socially acceptable once they say they had sex with Olive. Olive the transgressor transforms them from outcasts to integral group members. In their functionalist interpretation of norms and norm-breaking, the writers of *Easy A* out-Durkheim Durkheim.

Critical Thinking Questions

1. Can you think of a situation in your own experience—at school; in your neighbourhood; during summer camp; in church, mosque, or synagogue—where norm-breaking reinforced group solidarity? Write a paragraph describing this situation.
2. Can you think of a situation where a norm-breaker gave outsiders an opportunity to become integrated into a group? Write a paragraph describing this situation.

---

levels of discrimination in Canadian society. A disproportionately large number of young men from these groups reject the legitimate world and turn to crime, in the process developing distinct norms and values—a criminal subculture (Cohen, 1955; Wortley and Tanner, 2008).

An important part of any gang subculture consists of the justifications its members spin for their criminal activities. These justifications make illegal activities appear morally acceptable and normal, at least to the gang members. Typically, criminals deny personal

Sons of Anarchy

All manner of deviant and criminal behaviour is common among members of the California motorcycle gang known as the Sons of Anarchy: beatings, gun running, narcotics consumption, influence peddling, pornography production, and killing. To symbolize their rule-breaking behaviour, gang members ride customized Harley-Davidsons and wear patches on their leather jackets proclaiming that they are "Men of Mayhem." However, although these mavericks operate

Prashant Gupta/© FX/courtesy Everett Collection/ The Canadian Press

The Sons of Anarchy demonstrate that even deviant and criminal groups obey internal laws that are often strict.

outside the law, they do not exist outside the laws of sociology. They adhere to clearly articulated statuses, roles, and norms.

Thus, the club has a president, vice-president, secretary, sergeant-at-arms, ordinary members, and probationary members. Each of these statuses has specific, role-related responsibilities. For instance, the secretary is responsible for keeping the club's records and accounts in order. The sergeant-at-arms is responsible for discipline. Regular meetings are held in the club's boardroom. Major decisions are decided by democratic vote.

Once statuses are assigned and group decisions are made, norm compliance is mandatory. Harsh sanctions follow noncompliance. In one particularly gruesome episode, a former club member returns with his club tattoo intact. This is strictly against club rules, so club members pin him down, strip off his shirt, and ask, "Fire or knife?" His choice of fire leads to a painful encounter between his tattoo and a blowtorch.

Sons of Anarchy is a highly glamourized version of biker gangs. Club members are well-groomed and enjoy sparkling white teeth. Still, the series illustrates an important point about social life. Deviant and criminal behaviour is typically socially structured. It is learned, organized, and shaped by the social environment in which it takes place. Anarchistic criminals can no more violate this social reality than law-abiding citizens can.

Critical Thinking Questions

1. Consider another TV series that focuses on deviance and crime, such as *Breaking Bad* or its prequel, *Better Call Saul*. How are deviance and crime socially structured in this series?
2. The term *organized crime* generally refers to crime enterprises such as the Mafia or any one of a number of Latin American drug cartels. But can there be any such thing as non-organized crime?

responsibility for their actions ("It wasn't my fault!") or deny the wrongfulness of the act ("I was just borrowing it."). They condemn those who pass judgment on them ("The cops are bigger crooks than anyone!"). They claim their victims get what they deserve ("She had it coming to her."). And they appeal to higher loyalties, particularly to friends and family ("I had to do it because he dissed my gang."). Such rationalizations enable criminals to clear their consciences and get on with the job (Sykes and Matza, 1957).

Although deviants may depart from mainstream culture in many ways, they are strict conformists when it comes to the norms of their own subculture. They tend to share the same beliefs, dress alike, eat similar food, and adopt the same mannerisms and speech patterns. Although most

members of the larger society consider gang subcultures deviant, gang members strongly discourage deviance *within* the subculture, which is governed by strict rules of obedience and hierarchy.

Functionalism and the Relationship between Crime and Class

One of the main problems with functionalist accounts is that they exaggerate the connection between crime and class. Many self-report surveys find, at most, a weak tendency for criminals to come disproportionately from lower classes. Some self-report surveys report no such tendency at all, especially among young people and for less serious types of crime (Weis, 1987). A stronger correlation exists between *serious street crimes* and class. Armed robbery and assault, for instance, are more common among people from lower classes. A stronger correlation also exists between *white-collar* crime and class. Middle- and upper-class people are most likely to commit fraud and embezzlement, for example. Thus, generalizations about the relationship between class and crime must be qualified by taking into account the severity and type of crime (Braithwaite, 1981).

Note also that official statistics usually exaggerate class differences because they are more accurate barometers of street crime than suite (white-collar) crime. More police surveillance occurs in lower-class neighbourhoods than in upper-class boardrooms, and widely cited police statistics do not record some white-collar crimes because they are handled by agencies other than the police. As we will now see, conflict theories help to overcome functionalism's inadequate explanation of the relationship between crime and class.

CONFLICT THEORIES

Conflict theorists maintain that rich and powerful members of society impose deviant and criminal labels on others, particularly those who challenge the existing social order. Meanwhile, the rich and powerful are usually able to use their money and influence to escape punishment for their own misdeeds.

Steven Spitzer (1980) summarizes this school of thought. He notes that capitalist societies are based on private ownership of property. Moreover, their smooth functioning depends on the availability of productive labour and respect for authority. When thieves steal, they challenge private property. Theft is therefore a crime. When so-called bag ladies and drug addicts drop out of conventional society, they are defined as deviant because their refusal to engage in productive labour undermines a pillar of capitalism. When young, politically volatile students demonstrate and militant trade unionists strike, they, too, represent a threat to the social order. Authorities may therefore define them as deviant.

Of course, Spitzer notes, the rich and powerful engage in deviant and criminal acts too. However, they are less likely to be reported, convicted, and prosecuted for criminal acts than other people are (Blumberg, 1989; Clinard and Yeager, 1980; Hagan, 1989; Sherrill, 1997; Snider, 1999; Sutherland, 1949). *Reporting* is less frequent because much white-collar crime takes place in private and is therefore difficult to detect. For instance, corporations may collude to fix prices and divide markets—both crimes—but executives may make such decisions in boardrooms, private clubs, and homes that are not generally subject to police surveillance. *Conviction* and *prosecution* are less frequent partly because wealthy white-collar criminals, including corporations, can

Former Canadian millionaire Conrad Black was convicted in 2007 of fraud and obstruction of justice. Sentenced to six and a half years in prison, he was released on bail after serving two and a half years, partly because some charges were dropped.

afford legal experts, public relations firms, and advertising agencies that advise their clients on how to bend laws, build up their corporate image in the public mind, and influence lawmakers to pass laws "without teeth."

In addition, the law is more lenient in meting out punishment for white-collar than for street crime. Compare the crime of break and enter with that of fraud. Fraud almost certainly costs society more than break and enter, but breaking and entering is a street crime committed mainly by lower-class people, while fraud is a white-collar crime committed mainly by middle- and upper-class people. Not surprisingly, prison sentences are nearly twice as likely in break and enter convictions as they are in fraud convictions (Thomas, 2002: 9).

Social Control

Conflict theorists argue that the rich and powerful exercise disproportionate control over the criminal justice system and are therefore able to engage in deviance and crime with relative impunity. One variant of conflict theory, **control theory**, generalizes this argument. According to control theorists, nearly everyone would like to have the fun, pleasure, excitement, and profit that deviance and crime promise. Moreover, they say, if we could get away with it, most of us would commit deviant and criminal acts to acquire more of those rewards. For control theorists, the reason most of us do not engage in deviance and crime is that we are prevented from doing so. In contrast, deviants and criminals break norms and laws because social controls imposed by various authorities are too weak to ensure conformity.

Travis Hirschi developed the control theory of crime (Gottfredson and Hirschi, 1990; Hirschi, 1969). He argued that adolescents are more prone to deviance and crime than adults are because they are incompletely socialized and therefore lack self-control. Adults and adolescents may both experience the impulse to break norms and laws, but adolescents are less likely to control that impulse. Hirschi went on to show that the adolescents who are most prone to delinquency are likely to lack four types of social control. They tend to have few social *attachments* to parents, teachers, and other respectable role models; few legitimate *opportunities* for education and a good job; few *involvements* in conventional institutions; and weak *beliefs* in traditional values and morality. Because of the lack of control stemming from these sources, these adolescents are relatively free to act on their deviant impulses. For similar reasons, boys are more likely to engage in juvenile delinquency than girls are, and people who experience job and marital instability are more likely than others are to engage in crime (Hagan, Simpson, and Gillis, 1987; Peters, 1994; Sampson and Laub, 1993). Tighter social control by authorities in all spheres of life decreases the frequency of deviant and criminal acts.

FEMINIST CONTRIBUTIONS

Although conflict theory shows how the distribution of power in society influences the definition, detection, and prosecution of deviance and criminality, it neglects the consequences of something you will learn about in detail in Chapter 8, Sexualities and Genders: On average, women are less powerful than men are in all social institutions. Feminist sociologists hold that gender-based power differences influence the framing of laws and therefore the definition and detection of crime and the prosecution of criminals.

To support their claim, feminists note that, until recently, many types of crime against women were largely ignored in Canada and most other parts of the world. This was true even when the crime involved non-consensual sexual intercourse, an act that was defined under Canadian criminal law as *rape* before 1983 and is now considered a form of *sexual assault*. Admittedly, the authorities sometimes severely punished rapes involving strangers. However, so-called date and acquaintance rape were rarely prosecuted, while Canadian law viewed marital rape as a contradiction in terms, as if it were logically impossible for a woman to be raped by her husband. Law professors, judges, police officers, rapists, and even victims did not think date rape was "real rape" (Estrich, 1987). Similarly, judges, lawyers, and social scientists rarely discussed physical violence against women and sexual harassment until the 1970s. Governments did not collect data on the topic, and few social scientists showed any interest in the subject. Relative powerlessness allowed many women to be victimized while the violence against them often went unnoticed by the larger society and their assailants went free.

It follows from the feminist argument that a shift in the distribution of power between women and men would alter this state of affairs. And in fact, that is precisely what happened after about 1970. A series of changes to Canadian criminal law since 1970 have emphasized that non-consensual sexual acts are sexual assaults. The new laws have helped raise people's awareness of date, acquaintance, and marital rape. Sexual assault is more often prosecuted now than it used to be. The same is true for other types of violence against women and for sexual harassment. These changes occurred because women's position in the economy, the family, and other social institutions has improved since 1970. Women now have more autonomy in the family, earn more, and enjoy more political influence. They also created a movement for women's rights that heightened concern about crimes disproportionately affecting them (MacKinnon, 1979). Social definitions of crimes against women changed as women became more powerful in Canadian society.

In the 1970s, some feminists expected that growing gender equality would also change the historical tendency for women to be far less crime-prone than men are. They reasoned that control over the activities of girls and women would weaken, thus allowing them to behave more like men. Widely publicized cases of violent crime by teenage girls add weight to such claims, and official data, although not dramatic, also support them. As Figure 5.3 shows, the ratio of female youth crime to male youth crime rose slowly but steadily between 1991 and 2010.

In sum, our overview shows that many theories contribute to understanding the social causes of deviance and crime (see Concept Summary 5.1). Each focuses on a different aspect of the phenomena, so familiarity with all of them allows us to develop a fully rounded appreciation of the complex processes surrounding the sociology of deviance and crime.

control theory Holds that the rewards of deviance and crime are ample. Therefore, nearly everyone would engage in deviance and crime if they could get away with it. The degree to which people are prevented from violating norms and laws accounts for variations in the level of deviance and crime.

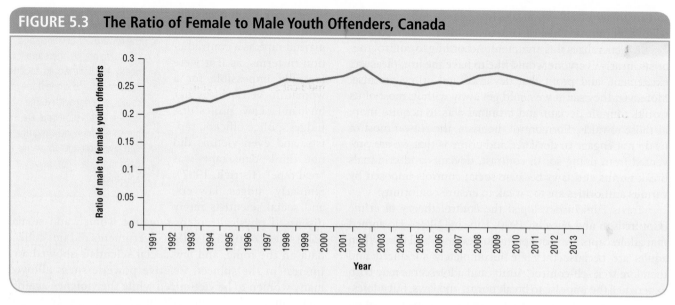

FIGURE 5.3   The Ratio of Female to Male Youth Offenders, Canada

Sources: Statistics Canada. 2012a "Youth courts, guilty cases by type of sentence, annually (number)." CANSIM Table 2520067. http://dc2.chass.utoronto.ca.myaccess.library.utoronto.ca/cgi-bin/cansimdim/c2_getArrayDim.pl (retrieved 24 September 2016).

CONCEPT SUMMARY 5.1	Major Theoretical Approaches to Deviance and Crime
Theory	**Summary**
Symbolic interactionism	Deviant and criminal roles must be learned in the course of social interaction if they are to become habitual activities. Moreover, deviance results not just from the actions of the deviant but also from the responses of others, who define some actions as deviant and other actions as normal.
Functionalism	Deviance and crime have positive functions for society insofar as they provide opportunities to clarify societal values, define moral boundaries, increase social solidarity, and allow useful social change. They also have dysfunctions. In particular, if societies do not provide enough legitimate opportunities for everyone to succeed, strain results, one reaction to which is to find alternative and illegitimate means of achieving one's goals.
Conflict theory	The rich and powerful are most likely to impose deviant and criminal labels on others, particularly those who challenge the existing social order. Meanwhile, the rich and powerful are often able to use their money and influence to escape punishment for their own misdeeds. Most people do not engage in deviance and crime because they are prevented from doing so by authorities. Deviants and criminals break norms and laws because social controls imposed by various authorities are too weak to ensure their conformity.
Feminist theory	Changes over time in the distribution of power between women and men influence the degree to which crimes against women are identified and prosecuted, and the degree to which women become criminals.

LO³ PUNISHMENT

All societies seek to ensure that their members obey norms and laws. All societies impose sanctions on rule breakers. However, the *degree* of social control varies over time and place. *Forms* of punishment also vary.

In many respects people are freer today than ever. We elect leaders, choose consumer products, change religions, and so forth. In other respects, however, social control has intensified over time. Much of the regimentation of modern life is tied to the growth of capitalism and the state. Factories require strict labour regimes, with workers arriving and leaving at fixed times and, while there, performing fixed tasks at a fixed pace. Institutions regulated by the state's armies, police forces, public schools, health care systems, and various other bureaucracies also demand strict work regimes, curricula, and procedures. These institutions existed on a much smaller scale in pre-industrial times or did not exist at all. Today, they penetrate our lives and sustain strong norms of belief and conduct (Foucault, 1977 [1975]).

Electronic technology makes it possible for authorities to exercise more effective social control than ever. With millions of cameras mounted in public places and workplaces, some sociologists say we now live in a "surveillance society" (Lyon and Zureik, 1996). Spy cameras enable observers to see deviance and crime that would otherwise go undetected and to take quick action to apprehend rule breakers. Moreover, when people are aware of the presence of surveillance cameras, they tend to alter their behaviour. For example, attentive shoplifters migrate to stores that lack electronic surveillance. On factory floors and in offices, workers display more conformity to management-imposed work norms when they're aware of surveillance cameras. On campuses, surveillance cameras inhibit at least some students from engaging in organized protests (Boal, 1998).

Among the most important recent developments in social control are the "medicalization of deviance" and the widespread use of prisons. Let us examine these reactions to deviance and crime in turn.

THE MEDICALIZATION OF DEVIANCE

Increasingly, we deal with deviance by medicalizing it. The **medicalization of deviance** refers to the fact that "medical definitions of deviant behaviour are becoming more prevalent in ... societies like our own" (Conrad and Schneider, 1992: 28–29). In an earlier era, much deviant behaviour was labelled evil. Deviants tended to be chastised, punished, and otherwise socially controlled by members of the clergy, neighbours, family members, and the criminal justice system. Today, however, a person prone to drinking sprees is more likely to be declared an alcoholic and treated in a detoxification centre. A person predisposed to violent rages is more likely to be medicated. A person inclined to overeating is more likely to seek therapy and, in extreme cases, surgery. A heroin addict is more likely to seek the help of a methadone program. As these examples illustrate, what used to be regarded as wilful deviance is now often regarded as involuntary deviance. Increasingly, what used to be defined as "badness" is defined as "sickness." As our definitions of deviance change, deviance is increasingly coming under the sway of the medical and psychiatric establishments (see Figure 5.4).

> **medicalization of deviance**
> The process of applying medical definitions to deviant behaviour, a practice that is becoming more prevalent.

FIGURE 5.4 **An Example of the Medicalization of Deviance**

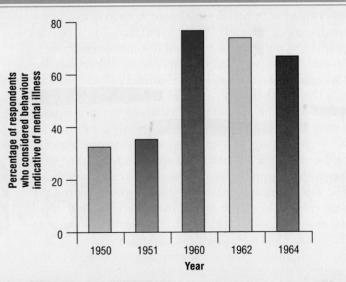

"Now here's a young woman in her twenties, let's call her Betty Smith . . . she has never had a job, and she doesn't seem to want to go out and look for one. She is a very quiet girl, she doesn't talk much to anyone—even her own family, and she acts like she is afraid of people, especially young men her own age. She won't go out with anyone, and whenever someone comes to visit her family, she stays in her own room until they leave. She just stays by herself and daydreams all the time and shows no interest in anything or anybody."

Five North American surveys conducted in the 1950s and 1960s presented respondents with the accompanying anecdote. The graph shows the percentage of respondents who considered the behaviour described in the anecdote to be evidence of mental illness. Notice the difference between the 1950s and the 1960s. (Nearly 100 percent of psychiatrists who evaluated the anecdote thought it illustrated "simple schizophrenia.")

Source: Material adapted from table "Results of Studies Using Vignettes in Defining Problem Behavior" from *Deviance and Medicalization: From Badness to Sickness*, by Peter Conrad and Joseph W. Schneider. Used by permission of Temple University Press. © 1992 by Temple University. All Rights Reserved.

The Spread of Mental Disorders

Some mental disorders have obvious organic causes, such as chemical imbalances in the brain. Researchers can often identify these problems precisely, treat them with drugs or other therapies, and conduct experiments to verify their existence and establish the effectiveness of one treatment or another. Little debate takes place over whether such ailments should be listed in the psychiatrist's "bible," the *Diagnostic and Statistical Manual of Mental Disorders* (DSM-5).

The organic basis for other ailments is unclear. In such cases, social values and political conflict can determine whether they are listed in the DSM-5. For instance, in the 1970s and 1980s, North American psychiatrists fiercely debated whether neurosis, posttraumatic stress disorder (PTSD), homosexuality, and self-defeating personality disorder were real mental disorders. In the end, homosexuality was dropped from an earlier version of the DSM-5, largely in response to the efforts of liberal-minded psychiatrists, as was self-defeating personality disorder, thanks to the efforts of feminists. Neurosis was retained at the insistence of Freudians. PTSD was added to an earlier version of the DSM-5 after a strenuous lobbying campaign by Vietnam War veterans and their supporters (Scott, 1990). These cases illustrate that the medicalization of deviance is in part a social and political process.

In the mid-nineteenth century there was just one officially recognized mental disorder: idiocy/insanity. The current edition of the DSM-5, published in 2013, lists 294. As the number of mental disorders has grown, so has the proportion of North Americans presumably affected by them. In the mid- nineteenth century, few people were defined as suffering from mental disorders, but one respected survey conducted in the early 1990s found that 48 percent of people will suffer from a mental disorder—very broadly defined, of course—during their lifetime (Blazer, Kessler, McGonagle, and Swartz, 1994; Shorter, 1997: 294).

The number and scope of mental disorders have grown partly because North Americans are now experiencing more stress than ever before, mainly because of the increased demands of work and a growing time crunch. At the same time, traditional institutions for dealing with mental health problems are less able to cope with them. The weakening authority of religious institutions and the weakening grip of the family over the individual leave the treatment of mental health problems more open to the medical and psychiatric establishments.

The cultural context also stimulates inflation in the number and scope of mental disorders. North Americans are inclined to turn their problems into medical and psychological issues, sometimes without inquiring deeply into the disadvantages of doing so. For example, in 1980, the term "attention deficit disorder" (ADD) was coined to label hyperactive and inattentive schoolchildren, mainly boys. By the mid-1990s, doctors were writing more than 6 million prescriptions a year for Ritalin, an amphetamine-like compound that controls ADD. Evidence shows that some children diagnosed with ADD have certain problems with their brain chemistry. Yet the diagnosis of ADD is typically conducted clinically, that is, by interviewing and observing children to see if they exhibit signs of serious inattention, hyperactivity, and impulsivity. This means that many children diagnosed with ADD may have no organic disorder at all. Some cases of ADD may be due to the school system failing to capture children's imagination. Some may involve children acting out because they are deprived of attention at home. Some may involve plain, old-fashioned youthful enthusiasm. (Doctors at Dalhousie University Medical School in Halifax made a plausible case that Winnie the Pooh suffered from ADD; see Shea, Gordon, Hawkins, Kawchuk, and Smith, 2000.) However, once hyperactivity and inattentiveness in school are defined as a medical and psychiatric condition, officials routinely prescribe drugs to control the problem and tend to ignore possible social causes.

Finally, we have witnessed inflation in the number and scope of mental disorders because various professional organizations have an interest in it. Consider PTSD. There is no doubt that PTSD is a real condition and that many veterans suffer from it. However, once the disorder was officially recognized in the 1970s, some therapists trivialized the term. By the mid-1990s some therapists were talking about PTSD "in children exposed to movies like *Batman*" (Shorter, 1997: 290). Some psychiatric social workers, psychologists, and psychiatrists may magnify the incidence of such mental disorders because doing so increases their stature and their patient load. Others may do so simply because the condition becomes trendy. Whatever the motive, overdiagnosis is the result.

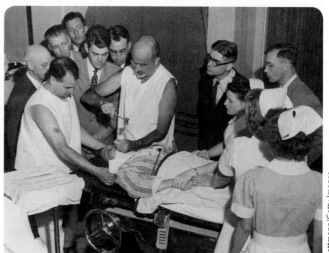

Dr. Walter Freeman performs a lobotomy in the 1930s using an instrument like an ice pick, which he invented for the procedure.

Bettmann/Getty Images

THE PRISON

In October 2001, a 63-year-old man with Parkinson's disease and addicted to cocaine was arrested in Ottawa. A passerby had noticed that the man had a firearm in his gym bag and had notified the police. The man, who was charged with possession of a weapon, did not resist arrest. He knew what awaited him. Roger Caron, dubbed "Mad Dog" Caron by the press, had first been sentenced to prison at the age of 16 for breaking and entering. He had spent most of his adult life as an inept robber, going in and out of eastern Canada's major prisons.

After having already spent almost 20 years in prison, Caron wrote a chilling account of his life behind bars. The book, *Go-Boy!*, describes in harrowing detail the harshness of the prison experience—the violence, the intense hatreds, the hard labour, the horrors of solitary confinement, the twisted, manipulative friendships, and the brutal use of corporal punishment (Caron, 1979: 59).

Go-Boy! was honoured with the Governor General's Literary Award and, in the years that followed, Caron wrote other books. However, he was unable to leave his past life behind. Following imprisonment for another botched robbery attempt, Caron was released from prison in 1998 and was still on parole at the time of his 2001 arrest for illegally possessing a firearm.

Regardless of the initial factors that caused Caron to turn to crime, it was his experiences in prison that turned him into a career criminal (CyberPress, 2001). His experience follows a pattern known to sociologists for a long time. Prisons are agents of socialization, and new inmates often become more serious offenders as they adapt to the culture of long-term prisoners (Wheeler, 1961).

Origins of Imprisonment

Because prison often turns criminals into worse criminals, it is worth pondering the institution's development and current dilemmas. As societies industrialized, imprisonment became one of the most important forms of punishment for criminal behaviour (Garland, 1990; Morris and Rothman, 1995). In pre-industrial societies, criminals were publicly humiliated, tortured, or put to death, depending on the severity of their transgressions. In the industrial era, depriving criminals of their freedom by putting them into prison seemed more civilized (Durkheim, 1973 [1899–1900]).

The Canadian Press/Fred Chartrand

Roger Caron, who was 16 years old when he was first sentenced to prison for breaking and entering, has spent much of his life behind bars. His acclaimed book, *Go-Boy!*, provides a chilling account of his life in almost all of the major prisons in eastern Canada.

New York Public Library

In pre-industrial societies, criminals who committed serious crimes were put to death, often in ways that seem cruel by today's standards. One method involved hanging them upside down, bound and alive, so that starving dogs could rip them apart.

moral panic Widespread fear that occurs when many people fervently believe that some form of deviance or crime poses a profound threat to society's well-being.

Goals of Incarceration

Some people still take a benign view of prisons, even seeing in them opportunities for *rehabilitation*. They believe that prisoners, while serving time, can be taught to become productive citizens on release. In Canada, this idea predominated from the 1950s to the early 1970s, when many prisons sought to reform criminals by offering them psychological counselling, drug therapy, skills training, education, and other programs that would help at least the less-violent offenders reintegrate into society (McMahon, 1992: xvii).

Today, however, many Canadians scoff at the idea that prisons can rehabilitate criminals. We have adopted a tougher line. Some politicians campaign on promises of a get-tough approach to crime and to criminals. Many people now see prison as a means of *deterrence*. In this view, people will be less inclined to commit crimes if they know they are likely to be caught and serve long and unpleasant prison terms. Others think of prisons as institutions of *revenge*. They believe that depriving criminals of their freedom and forcing them to live in poor conditions is fair retribution for their illegal acts. Still others see prisons as institutions of *incapacitation*. From this viewpoint, the chief function of the prison is to keep criminals out of society as long as possible to ensure they can do no more harm (Simon, 1993; Zimring and Hawkins, 1995).

There are more than 10.2 million prisoners in the world, about 45 percent of them in China, the United States, and Russia. Some 106 of every 100 000 Canadians are in prison (see Figure 5.5). Canada's incarceration rate is higher than that of some European countries, such as France and Germany, but it is below the world average and is only 15 percent of the rate of the United States, which is second in the world with 698 inmates per 100 000 people (first place goes to the tiny African island nation of Seychelles). Some 4.5 percent of the world's population lives in the United States—and 21.6 percent of the world's prisoners (International Centre for Prison Studies, 2015).

The size of the U.S. prison population has more than quadrupled since 1980, yet little evidence supports the view that throwing more people into jail lowers the crime rate in the United States, or anywhere else for that matter. In fact, many sociologists and criminologists believe that in some cases, prison has the opposite effect, turning small-time crooks into hardened criminals (Ore and Birgden, 2003). Why then has the U.S. prison population grown so quickly?

LO⁴ MORAL PANIC

Some analysts say that the United States has been gripped by **moral panic**, or widespread fear that crime poses a grave threat to society's well-being. Partly in response to lurid news stories and TV dramas that direct attention to the most notorious and atypical crimes, many members of the public incorrectly conclude that most crime is violent and predatory and that the current crime rate endangers just about everyone, even though it has been falling since the early 1990s (Cohen, 1972; Goode and Ben-Yehuda, 1994). Many sociologists agree that moral panic has seized the United States because powerful interests benefit from it. In particular:

1. The mass media benefit from moral panic because it allows them to earn hefty profits. They publicize every major crime because crime draws big audiences, and big audiences mean more revenue from advertisers. Fictional crime programs draw tens of millions of additional viewers to their TVs.

2. The crime prevention and punishment industry benefits from moral panic for much the same reason. Prison construction and maintenance firms and firearms manufacturers are big businesses that flourish in a climate of moral panic. Such industries want people to own more guns and imprison more people, so they lobby hard for relaxed gun laws and invigorated prison construction programs.

3. The criminal justice system is a huge bureaucracy with many employees. They benefit from moral panic because increased spending on crime prevention, control, and punishment secures their jobs and expands their turf.

FIGURE 5.5 Rate of Imprisonment, Selected Countries

Germany (76)
France (100)
Canada (106)
China (119)
England/Wales (148)
Russia (463)
United States (698)

| 0 | 100 | 200 | 300 | 400 | 500 | 600 | 700 | 800 |

Prisoners per 100 000 population

Source: International Centre for Prison Studies. 2015. http://www.prisonstudies.org/highest-to-lowest/prison-population-total?field_region_taxonomy_tid=All (retrieved 24 July 2015).

---

4. Perhaps most important, moral panic is useful politically. Since the early 1970s, many politicians have instilled fear of crime in the public, criticized opponents for being "soft on crime," and promised voters that endorsing a "get-tough" policy will bring them more security. Such arguments have formed the basis of entire political careers.

We recently witnessed a similar process in Canada. Over the objections of most Canadian criminologists, sociologists, and lawyers, and despite pleas from law enforcement officials as far away as Texas, where "get-tough" measures failed to curb crime, the former Conservative government (2006–15) passed a crime bill in 2012 that ratcheted up the moral panic in this country despite falling crime rates. Bill C-10 introduced new criminal offences, new and increased mandatory minimum sentences, longer waiting times before criminals could apply for pardons, harsher sentencing for young offenders, and plans to expand the prison system. As Figure 5.6 shows, the Canadian rate of incarceration has been increasing for decades and could have gone up even more if the Conservative government had not been defeated in 2015.

OTHER FORMS OF PUNISHMENT: TWO EXTREMES

Imprisonment is not the only form of punishment for criminal acts. In concluding this chapter, we consider two of the most hotly debated issues concerning other

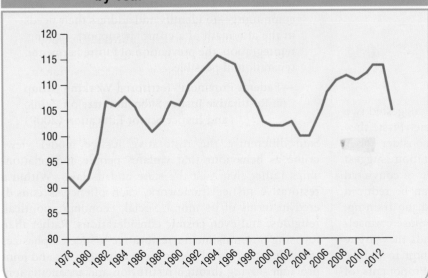

When in office, former Conservative prime minister Stephen Harper and former Minister of Public Safety Vic Toews championed efforts to "get tough on crime," supporting a mandate to build more prisons, although crime rates have been falling since the 1990s. Were their actions part of a moral panic?

The Canadian Press/John Woods

forms of punishment: (1) Should Canada reintroduce the death penalty for the most violent criminals? (2) Should we more often use strategies other than imprisonment for non-violent criminals?

Capital Punishment

Between 1859 and 1962, 710 Canadians were hanged by the state. Capital punishment has not been employed in Canada since 1962 and was formally abolished in 1976, but most Canadians favour its re-introduction. Approximately 6 in 10 Canadians favour punishing homicide with the death penalty, about the same proportion as Americans (Brennan, 2012; Jones, 2014).

Although the death penalty ranks high as a form of revenge, it is questionable whether it is much of a deterrent. First, murder is often committed in a rage, when the perpetrator is not thinking entirely rationally and is unlikely to consider the costs and consequences of his or her actions coolly. Second, the United States has capital punishment, but its homicide rate is much higher than that of Canada and Western European countries that do not practise capital punishment (Mooney, Knox, Schacht, and Nelson, 2001: 131).

We must also note that capital punishment is hardly a matter of blind justice. Research conducted in the United States reveals that, other things

FIGURE 5.6   Adult Prisoners per 100 000 Canadians by Year

Sources: Statistics Canada. 2014d. "Annual Estimates of Population for Canada, Provinces and Territories, from July 1, 1971 to July 1, 2014"; Statistics Canada. 2015c. CANSIM, Table 2510005 and Table 2510006. http://dc2.chass.utoronto.ca.myaccess.library.utoronto.ca/cgi-bin/cansimdim/c2_searchCansim.pl (retrieved 26 July 2015).

recidivism rate The proportion of convicted offenders who commit another crime.

restorative justice Focuses not on punishment but on rehabilitating offenders through reconciliation with victims and the larger community.

being equal, killers of white people are more likely to receive death sentences than are killers of black people, especially if the murderer is black (Culver, 1992). Social class is also a factor. A study conducted in Texas found that people represented by court-appointed lawyers were 28 percent more likely to be convicted than those who could afford to hire their own lawyers and, once convicted, 44 percent more likely to be sentenced to death (Vago and Nelson, 2003: 205). It is doubtful that we can view the death penalty as a justly administered punishment.

Sometimes people favour capital punishment because they think it saves money. They argue that killing someone costs less than keeping the person alive in prison for the rest of his or her life. However, the experience of the United States suggests otherwise. In that country, where an exhaustive system of judicial review is required before anyone is executed, trials of capital cases cost more than $2.6 million each on average—enough to keep a person in prison in Canada for almost 40 years (Costanzo, 1997).

Finally, in assessing capital punishment, it is important to remember that mistakes are common. Nearly 40 percent of death sentences in the United States since 1977 have been overturned because of new evidence or mistrial (Haines, 1996). In Canada, the wrongful convictions of Donald Marshall, Guy Paul Morin, David Milgaard, and many others for murders they did not commit should be sufficient to remind us that the wheels of justice do not always turn smoothly.

LO⁵ ALTERNATIVE STRATEGIES

In recent years, some analysts have suggested two main reforms to our prison regime. First, they have argued that we should reconsider rehabilitation. Advocates of rehabilitation suggest that the recidivism rate, or the proportion of convicted offenders who commit another crime, can be reduced through such programs as education and job training, individual and group therapy, substance abuse counselling, and behaviour modification. Second, they argue that, whenever possible, we should attempt to reduce the number of incarcerated offenders. Proponents of this idea say that at least part of the increase in crime in the past four decades is attributable to the introduction of new and broadened definitions of criminal conduct. They believe that charging and imprisoning more

Canadians, especially youth, are unlikely to help these individuals develop pro-social behaviour. Accordingly, they advise us to seek alternative methods that divert adults and juveniles from formal criminal justice system processing.

Although alternative procedures vary in each province and territory, their use generally arises after the police or Crown prosecutor recommends that an offender be considered suitable for "diversion." One example of an alternative measure is a victim–offender reconciliation program (VORP) in which victim and offender meet under controlled circumstances. Victims have the opportunity to describe the impact the crime has had on them, and offenders are usually required to apologize to their victims and compensate them financially. Alternative measures programs handle tens of thousands of youth cases every year. Most cases referred for diversion involve theft under $5000 (e.g., shoplifting), which is not surprising because to be recommended for diversion, the offence must be minor. To be considered candidates for diversion, offenders must first acknowledge that they are guilty of the act they have been accused of committing. Young offenders selected for inclusion in the program are usually more than 15 years old, and they generally complete the provisions of the agreements they make (Tufts, 2000).

Similarly, the Supreme Court of Canada has urged judges to "take into account the primary importance of restorative justice principles within Aboriginal conceptions of sentencing," especially for less-serious offences (Hendrick and Farmer, 2002: 11). **Restorative justice** is

> an approach to justice that focuses on addressing the harm caused by crime while holding the offender responsible for his or her actions, by providing an opportunity for the parties directly affected by crime—victim(s), offender and community—to identify and address their needs in the aftermath of a crime. It supports healing, reintegration, the prevention of future harm, and reparation, if possible.
>
> —Federal-Provincial-Territorial Working Group on Restorative Justice Subcommittee on Public and Justice Sector Education (2009)

Said differently, the restorative justice model views crime as behaviour that violates people and relationships rather than just the state and its laws. Within a restorative justice framework, each offence is considered in terms of its moral, social, economic, political, religious, and even cosmic considerations. Rather than focusing on punishment, restorative justice emphasizes individual and social healing, communication, and joint problem solving through restitution and reconciliation. Although the behaviour of the offender is condemned, the essential value of the individual is affirmed and the offender reassured that, through conformity, the stigma associated with a crime can be removed. In like fashion, proponents of decarceration recommend that such options as fines (the most commonly used penal sanction in Canada), probation, and community service become more widely used as alternatives to imprisonment.

A summary spanning 25 years of research on the subject allowed analysts to compare the effectiveness of restorative and nonrestorative justice programs in terms of victim satisfaction, offender satisfaction, restitution compliance, and reduction in recidivism (Latimer, Dowden, and Muise, 2007). In brief, the researchers found that participating in a restorative justice program resulted in higher victim satisfaction ratings, higher restitution compliance, and lower recidivism rates than participating in a nonrestorative justice program did. Analysis of the comparative effectiveness of restorative justice programs on offender satisfaction was inconclusive.

Despite such favourable findings, not everyone views such strategies as desirable. Some observers argue that the increased use of community programs does not reduce the numbers of people subject to formal social control. Rather, such strategies may simply "widen the net" through the creation of more intensive, intrusive, and prolonged control mechanisms (Lowman, Menzies, and Palys, 1987). Noting such objections, some analysts suggest that we go further still and lobby for legislative reform that would decriminalize certain categories of conduct currently prohibited under Canadian criminal law, such as marijuana possession. This last suggestion serves to remind us, yet again, that crime and deviance are social constructs.

Courtesy of Laura Beckman

Restorative justice focuses not on punishment but on rehabilitating offenders through reconciliation with victims and the larger community.

READY TO STUDY?

IN THE BOOK, YOU CAN:

❏ Tear out the chapter review card at the back of the book to have a summary of the chapter and key terms handy.

ONLINE YOU CAN:

❏ Work through key concepts with a Guided Learning Question.

❏ Prepare for tests with quizzes.

❏ Review the key terms with flash cards.

❏ Explore practical examples of chapter concepts with Connect a Concept exercises.

GO TO NELSON.COM/STUDENT TO ACCESS THESE DIGITAL RESOURCES.

6

Social Stratification: Canadian and Global Perspectives

Steve Raymer/Corbis Documentary/Getty Images

LEARNING OBJECTIVES

In this chapter, you will learn to

LO¹ Describe how wealth and income inequality in Canada have changed in recent decades.

LO² Compare competing explanations of income inequality.

LO³ Appreciate the social origins of poverty.

LO⁴ Understand why different sociologists argue that high levels of inequality are necessary, will inevitably disappear, or vary under identifiable conditions.

LO⁵ Identify the circumstances leading people to move up and down the structure of inequality.

LO⁶ Analyze change in the magnitude of inequality on a world scale.

LO⁷ Contrast competing explanations for the persistence of global inequality.

SOCIAL STRATIFICATION: SHIPWRECKS AND INEQUALITY

Writers and filmmakers sometimes tell stories about shipwrecks and their survivors to make a point about social inequality. They use the shipwreck as a literary device that allows them to sweep away all traces of privilege and social convention. What remains are human beings stripped to their essentials, guinea pigs in an imaginary laboratory for the study of wealth and poverty, power and powerlessness, esteem and disrespect.

The tradition began with Daniel Defoe's *Robinson Crusoe*, first published in 1719. Defoe tells the story of an Englishman marooned on a desert island. His strong will, hard work, and inventiveness turn the poor island into a thriving colony. Defoe was one of the first writers to portray capitalism favourably. He believed that people get rich if they possess the virtues of good businesspeople— and stay poor if they don't.

The 1975 Italian movie *Swept Away* tells almost exactly the opposite story. In the movie, a beautiful woman, one of the idle rich, boards her yacht for a cruise in the Mediterranean. She treats the hardworking deckhands in a condescending and abrupt way. The deckhands do their jobs but seethe with resentment. Then comes the storm. The yacht is shipwrecked. Only the beautiful woman and one handsome deckhand remain alive, marooned on a desert island. Now equals, the two survivors soon have passionate sex and fall in love.

All is well until the day of their rescue. As soon as they return to the mainland, the woman resumes her haughty ways. She turns her back on the deckhand, who is reduced again to the role of a common labourer. Thus, the movie sends the audience three harsh messages. First, it is possible to be rich without working hard, because a person can inherit wealth. Second, people can work hard without becoming rich. Third, something about the structure of society causes inequality, because inequality disappears only on the desert island, where there is no society as we know it.

Titanic is a more recent movie on the shipwreck-and-inequality theme. At one level, the movie shows that class differences are important. For example, in first class, living conditions are luxurious, whereas in third class, they are cramped. Indeed, on the *Titanic*, class differences spell

social stratification The way society is organized in layers or strata.

the difference between life and death. After the *Titanic* strikes the iceberg off the coast of Newfoundland and Labrador, the ship's crew prevents second- and third-class passengers from entering the few available lifeboats. They give priority to rescuing first-class passengers. Consequently, 75 percent of third-class passengers perished, compared with 39 percent of first-class passengers (see Table 6.1).

As the tragedy of the *Titanic* unfolds, however, another, contradictory theme emerges. Under some circumstances, we learn, class differences can be insignificant. In the movie, the sinking of the *Titanic* is the backdrop to a fictional love story about a wealthy young woman in first class and a working-class youth in the decks below. The sinking of the *Titanic* and the collapse of its elaborate class structure give the young lovers an opportunity to cross class lines and profess their devotion to each other. At one level, then, the movie *Titanic* is an optimistic tale that holds out hope for a society in which class differences matter little.

Robinson Crusoe, *Swept Away*, and *Titanic* raise many of the issues we address in this chapter. What are the sources of social inequality? Do determination, industry, and ingenuity shape the distribution of advantages and disadvantages in society, as the tale of *Robinson Crusoe* portrays? Or is *Swept Away* more accurate? Do certain patterns of social relations underlie and shape that distribution? Is *Titanic's* first message of social class differences still valid? Does social inequality still have big consequences for the way we live? What about *Titanic's* second message? Can people overcome or reduce inequality in society? If so, how?

To answer these questions, we first sketch patterns of social stratification in Canada and globally. We then critically review major theories of **social stratification**, the way society is organized in layers or strata. We also analyze the movement of individuals up and down the stratification system over time and their perceptions of the stratification system.

LO¹ PATTERNS OF SOCIAL INEQUALITY

WEALTH

Your wealth is what you own. For most adults, it includes a house (minus the mortgage), a car (minus the car loan), and some appliances, furniture, and savings (minus the credit card balance). Wealth is assets minus liabilities. Owning a nice house and a good car and having a substantial sum of money invested securely enhances your sense of well-being. You know you have a cushion to fall back on in difficult times, and you know you don't have to worry about paying for your children's postsecondary education or how you will make ends meet during retirement.

Wealth can also give you more political influence. Campaign contributions to political parties and donations to favourite political causes increase the chance that policies you favour will become law. Wealth even improves your health. Because you can afford to engage in leisure pursuits, turn off stress, consume high-quality food, and employ superior medical services, you are likely to live a healthier and longer life than someone who lacks these advantages.

In 2014, 89 Canadians enjoyed a net worth between $1.0 billion and $30.7 billion (Canada's Richest, 2015). These sums are so large that they are hard to imagine. You can begin to grasp them by considering that it would take you three years to spend $1 million at the rate of $1000 a day. How long would it take you to spend $1 billion? If you spent $1000 a day, you couldn't spend the entire sum in a lifetime. It would take nearly 3000 years to spend $1 billion at the rate of $1000 a day—assuming you didn't invest part to earn still more money (see the Sociology at the Movies feature in this chapter).

TABLE 6.1	Survivors of the 1912 Titanic Disaster by Class (percentage)			
	First Class	**Second Class**	**Third Class**	**Crew**
Children	100	100	34.2	n.a.
Women	97.2	86.0	46.1	n.a.
Men	32.6	8.3	16.2	21.7
Total	62.5	41.4	25.2	21.7

Adapted from: Anesi, Charles 1997. "The Titanic Casualty Figures." Based on British Parliamentary Papers, *Shipping Casualties* (*Loss of the Steamship* "Titanic"), 1912, cmd. 6352, Report of a Formal Investigation into the circumstances attending the foundering on the 15th April, 1912, of the British Steamship "Titanic," of Liverpool, after striking ice in or near Latitude 41° 46' N., Longitude 50° 14' W., North Atlantic Ocean, whereby loss of life ensued. (London: His Majesty's Stationery Office, 1912). http://www.anesi.com/titanic.htm (retrieved 11 March 2010).

SOCIOLOGY AT THE MOVIES

The Queen of Versailles

Jackie in front of her house in *The Queen of Versailles*

The Queen of Versailles is an award-winning documentary about David and Jackie Siegel, owners of the world's largest time-share company. It begins by describing the family's plan to build the largest single-family house in the United States. The house is modelled after the palace of Versailles in Paris. With its grand staircases, stained-glass domed roof, 30 bathrooms, 11 kitchens, 30-car garage, and indoor skating rink, the building is a monument to wealth and conspicuous consumption.

The construction of the 90 000-square-foot house halts as the business falters due to the 2008-09 economic crisis. The film then documents the struggles involved in trying to keep the business afloat, the stress in the household, and the lifestyle and character changes among family members.

Various sociological concepts are illustrated by *The Queen of Versailles*. The first centres on social mobility. Jackie Siegel comes from a modest, working-class background. She overcame a bad first marriage, became an engineer, and landed a job with IBM. After winning a beauty pageant, it became clear to her that it is often easier to achieve upward mobility through marriage than employment. She does so by marrying David, a billionaire 30 years her senior.

Preserving wealth in challenging economic times turns out to be a lot harder than earning it in good times (as David did) or marrying it (as Jackie did). The documentary shows David's mounting frustration, irritability, and disconnection as he fights downward mobility and retreats into isolation. It turns out that the way rich people cope with social problems is not so different from the way less privileged people do.

The documentary provides a glimpse of the lifestyles of the rich during good times. As their new home is under construction, the family has to make do in a 26 000- square-foot house, including a staff of 19, and an annual clothing budget of more than a million dollars. The parents and their seven children are pampered at every turn. Whenever her children don't amuse her, Jackie passes them along to a nanny. When dogs poop on the floor, maids are summoned to clean up. Exotic pets die because the children are too bored to feed them. Unused purchases are piled almost everywhere.

Change comes with the economic collapse and the arrival of hard times. Of course, "hard times" are relative. The Siegels are distraught at the thought of having to move their children from private school to public school. With the private plane and yacht gone, the family faces the exotic experience of flying commercial. In one revealing scene, Jackie at the Hertz car rental kiosk in an airport asks the attendant: "Where's my driver?"

While the documentary provides some entertaining insights into the extravagances of the elite, the most jarring scenes arise from the juxtaposition between the Siegels and those they employ. As the Siegels struggle to maintain their billionaire lifestyle, we see the challenges faced every day by their nanny and limo driver. Virginia, the nanny, displays unwavering commitment to the overly privileged children. Even though she has not seen her son in more than 20 years, she relentlessly cleans, cooks, and cares—all so she can send money home to her family in the Philippines. At the end of his full day of service, the limo driver borrows the Rolls-Royce to try to make a little bit of extra money to feed his family.

Like many successful businessmen, David sees himself as self-made; he attributes his success to himself and his ability to use power. As the documentary makes clear, however, his attribution of success to personal initiative is a delusion. Social and economic conditions always play an important role. In David's case, his success rests on a public policy that made cheap money easily available. When the policy changed, his fortunes collapsed. He blames "the system" for his "addiction" to cheap money. Suddenly, his fate is not his fault.

The Queen of Versailles is a revealing demonstration of how excessive wealth can insulate the privileged from the realities of ordinary people. Along the way, it clarifies how wealth can corrode people's character.

(Continued)

Critical Thinking Questions

1. How important are social and economic conditions versus individual initiative and hard work in determining financial success? To help answer this question, research the backgrounds of Canada's richest people to determine how many of them inherited family fortunes. The 30 richest Canadians in 2015 were David Thomson; Galen Weston; John, James, and Arthur Irving; James Pattison; Edward Rogers; Lino Saputo; Paul and André Desmarais; Hartley Richardson; Jeffrey Skoll; Carlo Fidani; Harrison McCain; J. Scott and Michael McCain; Daryl Katz; Bernard Sherman; Clay Riddell; Fred and Ron Mannix; Mark Scheinberg; Jean Coutu; Sharon, Naomi, and Danna Azrieli; Barry Zekelman; Paul Sobey; Frank Stronach; and David Cheriton.

2. Why do most people tend to explain their successes in terms of initiative and hard work, and their failures in terms of forces beyond their control?

A government study gives us insight into how net worth (defined as assets minus debt) changed between 1999 and 2005 (see Figure 6.1). Dividing Canadian families into the poorest fifth (or "quintile"), the second-poorest fifth, the middle fifth, the second-richest fifth, and the richest fifth, we see that over this 13-year period, the big winners were the richest families. Taking inflation into account, the net worth of the richest fifth increased by 81 percent; the net worth of the second fifth increased by 83 percent; and the net worth of the middle fifth increased by 79 percent. However, the net worth of the second-poorest fifth of Canadians increased by just 42 percent, while the net worth of the poorest fifth of Canadians *declined* by 15 percent. These figures lead us to conclude that, in terms of wealth, the rich became richer while the poor became poorer. In 2012, the top fifth of Canadians owned more than 67 percent of the country's net worth, while the bottom fifth had more debt than assets.

FIGURE 6.1   Median Net Worth of Families and Unattached Individuals, by Quintile, Canada, 1999–2012 (in 2012 dollars)

Quintile	2012 total net worth ($)	2012 share of net worth (%)
Top	5.44 trillion	67.4
4th	1.74 trillion	21.5
3rd	0.74 trillion	9.0
2nd	0.18 trillion	2.2
Bottom	−0.01 trillion	−0.1

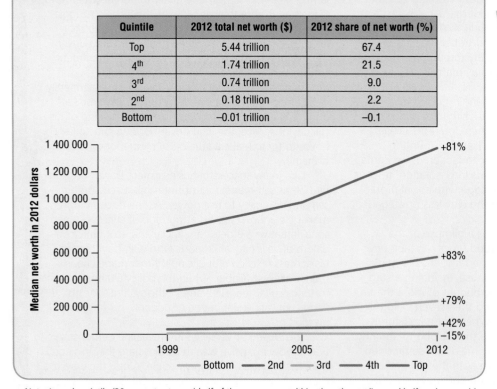

Note: In each quintile (20 percent category), half of the cases are wealthier than the median and half are less wealthy.

Source: Statistics Canada. 2015d. "Survey of Financial Security, 2012." http://www.statcan.gc.ca/daily-quotidien/140225/dq140225b-eng.htm (retrieved 27 July 2015).

INCOME

Income is the amount of money earned in a given period. Today, the average Canadian family earns over 21 times more than the average Canadian family did in 1950, but that is less impressive than it sounds. More than half the gain was due to inflation. After all, a soft drink that once cost a dime now costs a dollar. Moreover, the average number of earners per family increased as more women entered the paid labour force. As a result, more people are now generating the income of the average family than was the case in 1950. Even so, Canadian families earn considerably more now than they did 60 years ago, partly because they are more productive. That is, the average worker is more skilled and is using more sophisticated technology to produce more goods and services per hour of work.

How has the distribution of income changed over time? Is economic inequality growing or shrinking? To answer these questions, we again divide the population into fifths, but this time by income, not wealth: the top 20 percent of families and unattached individuals by income, the second 20 percent, the middle 20 percent, and so on. We can then determine what percentage of all income earned in Canada in a year is earned by each fifth. A completely unequal distribution would exist if the top quintile earned 100 percent of the country's income. A completely equal distribution would exist if each quintile earned 20 percent of the country's income.

Figure 6.2 shows that in 2011, the bottom quintile of families and unattached individuals earned just 4.8 percent of all income, while the top quintile earned 44.3 percent. This means that $4.43 of every $10 earned in Canada in 2011 was earned by the richest 20 percent of families. Moreover, the distribution of income has become more unequal since 1976. All quintiles earned a smaller share of total national income in 2011 than in 1976—except for the top quintile, which earned 3.3 percent more. This pattern mirrors the trend in most rich countries: Income gaps have been widening for more than three decades (Förster and Pellizzari, 2000; Fortin et al., 2012).

The incomes just reported represent the money that Canadians earn after paying income tax and receiving government benefits. Canada is a welfare state that collects taxes and redistributes them in the form of welfare payments, Employment Insurance payments, child tax credits, GST credits, and so on. The richest fifth of Canadians lose about a fifth of their income to income tax, while the poorest fifth of Canadians see their incomes increase by nearly two-thirds as a result of government transfers. If Canadians relied only on the market to distribute income, inequality would be much greater.

LO² EXPLANATIONS OF INCOME INEQUALITY

Why do some people fall into the highest quintile and others into the lowest? What explains the distribution of income? Obviously, a person's job has a significant influence. Bank managers are paid more than bank tellers, schoolteachers more than daycare workers. As well, people who work more earn more. But these are rather obvious factors that predict earnings. They can't be ignored, but are there more general factors that explain income inequality?

We know that some individuals earn high salaries because of their natural talent. Sidney Crosby (hockey), Andrew Wiggins (basketball), Ryan Gosling (acting), and Drake (rap music) are Canadians whose success on the world stage has provided them with substantial earnings. The principal reason for their excellence is a natural endowment in athletics, music, and so on. A genetic gift sets them apart. At the other end of the economic spectrum, some people suffer the genetic misfortune of Down syndrome, schizophrenia, or autism—conditions that usually prevent them from earning big salaries. Such people, at both ends of the spectrum, are exceptions, however. Sociologists believe that for the vast majority of people, genes play only a minor role in determining income.

Even for people with a natural talent in the performing arts or athletics, effort is essential. Practice and years of dedication to the basics of a profession are common to all who enjoy success. Effort is also significant for many Canadians who spend long hours at work—whether amassing billable hours in a law practice, doing the endless chores in a small business, or working overtime at a construction site. However, although diligence and perseverance might be necessary conditions for rewards, they are not sufficient. Effort alone does not result in high income (see Figure 6.3).

Raw talent needs to be sharpened. Training, coaching, schooling—these are crucial ways in which skills are developed and nurtured. Natural talent and effort are important ingredients in this process, to be sure, but education matters. Indeed, the importance of education as a determinant of occupation and income continues to increase (Baer, 1999; Statistics Canada, 2003a: 9).

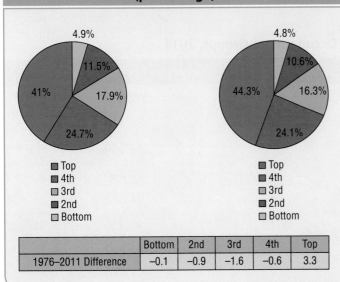

FIGURE 6.2 Share of Annual After-Tax Income, Canadian Families and Unattached Individuals, by Quintile, 1976 and 2011 (percentage)

	Bottom	2nd	3rd	4th	Top
1976–2011 Difference	−0.1	−0.9	−1.6	−0.6	3.3

Source: Statistics Canada. 2015e. "Market, total and after-tax income, by economic family type and income quintiles, 2011 constant dollars, annually." CANSIM Table 202 – 0701. http://dc2.chass.utoronto.ca.myaccess.library. utoronto.ca/cgi-bin/cansimdim/c2_getArrayDim.pl (retrieved 27 July 2015).

FIGURE 6.3 Explanations for Income Inequality

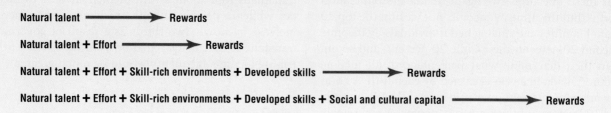

Natural talent ———————▶ Rewards

Natural talent + Effort ———————▶ Rewards

Natural talent + Effort + Skill-rich environments + Developed skills ———————▶ Rewards

Natural talent + Effort + Skill-rich environments + Developed skills + Social and cultural capital ———————▶ Rewards

human capital Investment in education and training. Just as productivity increases by upgrading manufacturing plants and introducing new technology, productivity gains can also result from investment in the skills and abilities of people.

social capital The networks or connections that individuals possess.

As the Canadian occupational structure moves farther away from its traditional resource-based foundation to a more mature knowledge-driven economy, the importance of education will continue to grow (see Table 6.2).

If physical capital is investment in industrial plants and equipment, **human capital** is investment in education and training. Just as productivity increases by upgrading manufacturing plants and introducing new technology, productivity gains can also result from investment in the skills and abilities of people. Jobs requiring advanced skills are increasingly numerous in Canada. Better-educated workers are more skilled and more productive in these jobs because they have made investments in acquiring the skills and knowledge essential to our economy (Betcherman and Lowe, 1997).

Much evidence supports a human capital interpretation of the link between schooling and incomes (Baer, 1999). However, it is not a complete explanation for why people earn what they earn. For example, in the legal profession, almost everyone makes the same human capital investment. Every lawyer acquires a law degree. Yet economic rewards vary even for people with the same experience and type of legal practice. Notably, female lawyers earn less on average than male lawyers do, even if they are matched in terms of experience and type of practice (Kay and Hagan, 1998).

Part of the reason that people with the same amount of human capital may receive different economic rewards is that they possess different amounts of social capital. **Social capital** refers to people's networks or connections. Individuals are more likely to succeed if they have strong bonds of trust, cooperation, mutual respect, and obligation with well-positioned individuals or families. Knowing the right people, and having strong links to them, helps in finding opportunities and taking advantage of them (Coleman, 1988).

TABLE 6.2 Average Annual Earnings by Selected Occupational Groups, 2011

Occupational Group	Average Annual Earnings
Managerial	$75 200
Natural and applied sciences	65 100
Health	54 500
Social science, education, government service, and religion	50 800
Trades, transport, and equipment operators	44 600
Processing, manufacturing, and utilities	40 300
Primary industry	39 500
Art, culture, recreation, and sport	31 100
Sales and service	26 600

Source: Statistics Canada. 2015f. "Earnings of Individuals, by Selected Characteristics and National Occupational Classification (NOC-S), 2011 Constant Dollars, Annually." CANSIM Table 2020106. dc2.chass.utoronto.ca.myaccess.library.utoronto.ca/cgi-bin/cansimdim/c2_arrays.pl (retrieved 27 July 2015).

A related version of this argument is captured in the notion of cultural capital (Bourdieu and Passeron, 1990). **Cultural capital** comprises the set of social skills people have: their ability to impress others, to use tasteful language and images effectively to influence and persuade people. Although the notion of social capital stresses your networks and connections with others, the idea of cultural capital emphasizes your impression management skills, your ability to influence others. In different ways, both concepts emphasize being part of the right "social club."

What the concepts of social and cultural capital also have in common is the idea that families higher in the social hierarchy enjoy more capital of all types. Connections and culture help you find a good job. The hiring of new recruits, then, depends on the talent, effort, and skills that people bring to the interview, but it also depends on the connections and culture that people have. Indeed, culture and connections often influence who gets an interview.

In summary, natural talent and effort are important, and for a few occupations very significant. For most Canadians, level of education (or developed skill) is a critical factor in finding continuous, well-paying employment. In addition, social and cultural capital are consequential for many people in achieving economic success. Explaining an individual's position in the income hierarchy depends on many factors, but the factors outlined in Figure 6.3 are crucial.

LO³ POVERTY

Defining Poverty

At the bottom of the income distribution are the homeless. In recent decades, the number of people with no fixed address has increased considerably. We do not know how many Canadians are homeless, but in cities across the country, people sleep under bridges, in back alleys, behind dumpsters, and in thickets in public parks. They do so night after night, month after month.

Homelessness is one manifestation of **poverty**. Exactly how many Canadians are poor is a matter of intense debate. Poverty lacks an agreed-on definition. A first disagreement occurs around whether poverty should be defined in absolute or relative terms. An absolute definition of poverty focuses on essentials, suggesting that poor families have inadequate resources to acquire the necessities of life (food, clothing, and shelter). Agreement on "essentials" depends on values and judgments (Sarlo, 2001). What is essential varies from time to time, place to place, and group to group. Many of our ancestors lived without indoor plumbing, and some Canadians still do, but most people would define indoor plumbing

as essential. A family could survive on a steady diet of cod and potatoes, but most would define such a family as poor.

A relative poverty line also has certain drawbacks. Two issues are central: relative to what, and how relative? Whether poverty ought to be defined narrowly in terms of economic measures (e.g., income) or more broadly with respect to community standards (e.g., safety of working conditions, environmental quality, type of housing) illustrates this second area of disagreement. Most definitions tend to be narrow, focusing primarily on income. But even if a relative poverty line is defined narrowly, how relative ought it to be? One-third of average income? One-half? Some other fraction?

Yet another disagreement plagues any definition. Should poverty be defined on the basis of income or consumption? Because "bare essentials" is a core idea in any definition of poverty, it makes good sense to think about, and measure, poverty as the cost of purchasing bare essentials. Deprivation occurs when a family cannot

cultural capital The widely shared, high-status cultural signals (attitudes, preferences, formal knowledge, behaviours, goals, and credentials) used for social and cultural inclusion and exclusion.

poverty Lacks an agreed-on definition. Analysts disagree whether poverty should be defined in absolute or relative terms and whether it should be based on income or consumption. Canada does not have an official poverty line. Statistics Canada reports a low-income cutoff that marks "the income level at which a family may be in straitened circumstances because it has to spend a greater proportion of its income on necessities than the average family of similar size."

Answers to the question of why some people are poor vary from individual-level to structural explanations.

Stone/Bushnell/Soifer/Getty Images

acquire the essentials, not necessarily when income is too low. Income and consumption are correlated, of course, but wealthy people can live off their savings even with low income.

In one sense, the definition of poverty means little to a homeless person sleeping on a hot air vent. The immediate experience of poverty by families in remote coastal communities, by single parents in the urban core, and by marginal Prairie farmers is unaffected by whether poverty is defined absolutely or relatively, narrowly or broadly, by income or by consumption. However, the definition of poverty is consequential for these people because social policies are enacted, or not enacted, based on levels and trends in poverty. Definitions matter.

Social policy has a profound impact on the distribution of opportunities and rewards in Canada. Politics can reshape the distribution of income and the system of inequality by changing laws governing people's right to own property. Politicians can also alter patterns of inequality by entitling people to various welfare benefits and by redistributing income through tax policies. When politicians de-emphasize poverty, legislative efforts to maintain or expand welfare benefits and redistribute income are less likely. A definition of poverty showing fewer poor Canadians implies little need for government action. Conversely, for politicians and political parties supporting the poor, a definition of poverty showing a growing proportion of poor people is beneficial to their cause.

Poverty definitions are also important for political reasons. A democratic society depends on the full participation of all citizens—everyone has the right to vote, anyone can run for political office, and everyone's voice should influence political choices. As the National Council of Welfare (1999a: 4) argues, the proportion of Canadians who are poor is "one measure of how well our democracy is working." Can someone without a permanent home or someone in a family with bare cupboards participate fully in our national affairs?

Unlike some other countries, such as the United States, Canada does not have an official definition of poverty. Statistics Canada argues that there is no internationally accepted definition of poverty and that any definition is arbitrary. Therefore, it does not attempt to estimate the number of Canadians who are poor (Fellegi, 2000: 124). Instead, Statistics Canada reports what it calls a "low-income cutoff." This cutoff conveys "the income level at which a family may be in straitened circumstances because it has to spend a greater proportion of its income on necessities than the average family of similar size" (Statistics Canada, 2000c: 122). The threshold is reported for seven different family sizes and for five sizes of community because "straitened circumstances" depend on the number of people in your family and where you live. Most advocates for the poor interpret these thresholds, shown for 2013 in Table 6.3, as poverty lines. For example, in Canada's largest

TABLE 6.3 Selected After-Tax Low-Income Cutoffs, 2013

Family Size	Population of Community	
	Rural	Urban over 500 000
1	$16 426	$23 861
4	30 523	44 340
7+	43 470	63 147

Source: Statistics Canada. 2014e. "Table 2 Low income cut-offs (1992 base) before tax." http://www.statcan.gc.ca/pub/75f0002m/2014003/tbl/tbl02-eng .htm (retrieved 28 July 2015).

cities, a family of four with after-tax income of less than $44 340 would be considered poor. In 2011, 12.9 percent of Canadians lived in poverty by this definition, nearly the same as in 1976 (Murphy, Zhang, and Dionne, 2012: 14; Statistics Canada, 2013e).

Myths about Poverty

The language we use to speak of the poor is often revealing. For example, referring to someone as "poor but honest" or "poor but virtuous" suggests that we view such combinations as unlikely and feel it necessary to single out those who possess both characteristics as exceptions to the rule. Popular mythology also depicts the poor—especially those who receive public assistance (i.e., welfare)—as lazy, irresponsible, and lacking in motivation, abilities, and moral values. These images are potent and contribute to stereotypes of the "deserving" and the "undeserving" poor (e.g., war veterans and children versus "welfare bums" and those "looking for a handout"). However, research conducted in the past few decades shows that many of the stereotypes about the poor are myths:

- *Myth 1: People are poor because they don't want to work.* The myth that poor people don't want to work ignores that many poor people cannot work because of a disability or because they must take care of their young children due to inadequate public child-care provisions in Canada. Moreover, it ignores that many poor people work full-time, and many more work part-time. However, having a job is no guarantee of escaping poverty because the minimum wage set by provincial and territorial governments is so low. In early 2015, the minimum wage varied from $10.20 (in Alberta and Sakatchewan) to $12.50 (in the Northwest Territories), with an unweighted provincial and territorial average of $10.69. Even if a person living in a large Canadian city worked 50 weeks at 40 hours a week for $10.69 an hour, he or she would earn only $21 380 a year—$2481 below the low-income cutoff (refer back to Table 6.3).

- *Myth 2:* *Most poor people are immigrants.* Actually, only recent immigrants experience poverty rates significantly higher than the Canadian-born, and recent immigrants are only a small fraction of all Canadian immigrants. Moreover, once they are established, immigrants have lower poverty rates than do people born in Canada (National Council of Welfare, 2004).

- *Myth 3:* *Most poor people are trapped in poverty.* In fact, more than 92 percent of people with low income in a given year escape poverty in less than two years; 80 percent escape in less than a year. Fewer than 8 percent are mired in poverty for more than two years (Statistics Canada, 2010a). We conclude that most people try to move out of difficult financial circumstances and most succeed, at least for a time.

Explaining Poverty

General explanations for the existence of poverty range from individual-level to structural explanations. Individual-level explanations focus on the attributes of people who are poor, asking how these people differ from people who are not poor. This type of explanation focuses on causes that lie within the person. Someone is poor, according to this logic, because of a personal attribute, such as low intelligence or a behavioural abnormality.

Some evidence suggests that individual attributes do explain a small amount of poverty. For example, we have noted that people with disabilities have a higher risk of living in poverty than do others. Not all people with disabilities live in poverty, however, and the vast majority of people living in poverty do not have a disability. On balance, this reminds us that poverty is, for the most part, not a consequence of individual attributes even though they are important in some cases.

A related explanation focuses more on the attitudes of individuals—not on attributes that are inherited, but on attributes or stigmas that are acquired. A social-psychological type of explanation emphasizes low self-esteem, lack of achievement motivation, and an inability to delay gratification. Poverty is perpetuated, on this logic, because poor families employ inadequate child-rearing practices that enhance bad attitudes. A related version of this argument stresses a "culture of poverty," a way of thinking and acting supposedly shared by poor families. This culture is said to reinforce and perpetuate itself through poor upbringing and ill-formed personalities.

Two objections undermine this type of explanation. First, descriptions of poverty stressing a culture of depression, lack of hope, and fatalism may be accurate, but these states of mind are typically *effects* of poverty, not its causes. Second, many people who are poor do work, are religious, don't smoke or drink, and so on. Therefore, evidence that supports explanations founded on these personal deficits is often lacking.

Another type of explanation has greater currency in sociology. It stresses the organization of the economy as the principal cause of poverty. Capitalist economies feature cyclical booms and busts, periods of low unemployment and high profits, followed by high unemployment and low profits. During recessions, many people lose their jobs and fall into poverty. Moreover, as we have seen, people with minimum-wage jobs don't earn enough to escape poverty. The lack of good jobs is thus a major cause of poverty.

Other analysts stress social policy as a factor affecting poverty levels. For example, as noted above, if you received the minimum hourly wage while working full-time year-round, you would still be poor, especially if you had children to support. In this sense, minimum-wage legislation is a social policy that creates a group of working poor.

The social world is not quite so simple, of course, and if minimum wages were to rise too much or too quickly, so too might the level of unemployment because some employers might not be able to afford a sudden big jump in wages. Debate over these issues continues, but the point is that our social policies affect people's well-being, and understanding the consequences of policies is critical.

The system of tax collection and tax allocation illustrates another way that social policies affect poverty. A *progressive* tax system is one in which a greater proportion of income is paid in tax as incomes rise. For example, those who earn $100 000 pay a larger percentage of their income as tax than do those who earn $50 000. In Canada, although our income tax system is progressive, the overall tax system is relatively neutral. Most Canadian families pay about the same percentage of their total income in tax. This occurs because two interrelated factors undermine the "Robin Hood" effect of progressive income taxes. First, other taxes, such as the GST and fuel taxes, are regressive. They are not based on the income of the taxpayer. Second, those who earn more are able to shelter much of their income from taxation in registered education savings plans and registered retirement savings plans, through capital gains tax exemptions, and so on. As a result, the tax system does little to erode poverty.

Finally, other sociologists stress ways of thinking, or ideological perspectives, as explanations for poverty. Negative images of various groups lead to an undervaluing of the ways of life of some people, such as Aboriginal people, recent immigrants, and members of visible minorities. Discrimination follows from this undervaluing. Discrimination causes poverty because it leads to less success in finding jobs and, when jobs are found, to more unsteady and low-paying work.

Is poverty an inevitable feature of society? It may be, at least to the extent that inequality is known to exist in all societies. However, the extent of poverty in Canada could be reduced if we chose to follow the example of western European nations. Many countries in western Europe have poverty rates well below Canada's because many European governments have established job-training and child-care programs that allow poor people to take jobs with livable wages and benefits. This is, however, clearly a political choice. Many Canadians argue that providing welfare benefits dampens the work ethic and actually perpetuates poverty. Although the western European evidence does not support that view, the political will does not currently exist in Canada to change our social policies and alleviate poverty.

The Feminization of Poverty

In the 1970s, feminist sociologists introduced the notion of the **feminization of poverty**, by which they meant that (1) women were more likely to be low-income earners than men were, and (2) the low-income gap between women and men was growing (Duffy and Mandell, 2011: 130–33).

The data suggest that while (1) is correct, (2) is not (Statistics Canada, 2012b; 2012c; 2013e). Thus, in 1976, 14.6 percent of women and 11.5 percent of men lived in poverty—a difference of 3.1 percent. By 2011, 13.5 percent of women and 12.3 percent of men lived in poverty—a difference of 1.2 percent. This trend contradicts the view that the low-income gap between women and men is growing.

Nonetheless, the gap between women and men living in poverty is real, and it is especially large among people in one-parent families and among the elderly. In 2011, 36.8 percent of women and 20.6 percent of men in one-parent families lived in poverty—a difference of 16.2 percent. In the same year, the gap between elderly women and elderly men was 7.0 percent (Statistics Canada, 2013e). Although enormous, these differences are an improvement over the situation in 1976, when the female–male poverty gap was 16.3 percent among the elderly and 30 percent among people in one-parent families.

The female–male poverty gap is largely a function of women's position in the labour market compared to that of men. Women typically spend fewer years working in the paid labour force than men do because they assume the bulk of domestic and child-rearing responsibilities in most families. This means that they usually accumulate smaller pensions and more modest savings than men do. When they are working in the paid labour force, women typically earn less than men do, again minimizing their savings and pensions. Moreover, relatively low wages for women means that the advantage of working for a wage as compared to collecting welfare is smaller for women than

© Picture Partners/Alamy

for men. Women are therefore more likely than men are to collect welfare payments and sink into poverty. Finally, women live an average of five years longer than men do, so their financial resources have more time to deplete.

Is inequality inevitable? That question has concerned sociologists since the mid-nineteenth century. We next review some classical answers to shed light on our prospects today.

IS STRATIFICATION INEVITABLE? THREE THEORIES

MARX'S CONFLICT THEORY

Karl Marx can fairly be regarded as the founder of conflict theory in sociology. It is ironic, therefore, that social stratification and the accompanying conflict between classes are *not inevitable* in Marx's view (Marx, 1904 [1859]; Marx and Engels, 1972 [1848]). He believed that capitalist growth would eventually produce a society without classes and therefore without class conflict.

In Marx's sense of the term, **class** is determined by a person's "relationship to the means of production" or the source of that person's income. The source of income is profit if the person owns a factory or a mine. It is a wage if he or she must work in a factory or a mine. Accordingly, Marx argued that capitalist societies have two main classes: the ownership class (or **bourgeoisie**, to use his term) and the working class (or what Marx termed the **proletariat**), distinguished from each other by whether they own productive property.

According to Marx, during the Industrial Revolution that began in Great Britain in the late eighteenth century, industrial owners were eager to adopt new tools, machines, and production methods so they could produce goods more efficiently and earn higher profits. Such innovations had unforeseen consequences. First, some owners were driven out of business by more efficient competitors. They were forced to become members of the working class. Together with former peasants pouring into the cities from the countryside to take factory jobs, this caused the working class to grow. Second, the drive for profits motivated owners to concentrate workers in increasingly larger factories, keep wages as low as possible, and invest as little as possible in improving working conditions. Thus, as the bourgeoisie grew richer and smaller, the proletariat grew larger and more impoverished.

Marx also believed that capitalism would experience increasingly severe economic crises of "overproduction" or "underconsumption" because the impoverished proletariat would be unable to afford all that industry could produce. During such crises, businesses would go bankrupt, unemployment would spread, and workers would become more aware of the severity of their exploitation. Their growing sense of *class consciousness* would encourage the growth of unions and workers' political parties which, according to Marx, would eventually try to create a new "communist" society in which there would be no private wealth. Instead, under communism, everyone would share wealth, said Marx.

Critical Evaluation of Marx's Conflict Theory

Things did not work out the way Marx had predicted for five reasons. First, industrial societies did not polarize into two opposed classes engaged in bitter conflict. Instead, a large and heterogeneous middle class of white-collar workers emerged. Some of them were nonmanual employees. Others were professionals. Many of them enjoyed higher income and status than manual workers did. With a bigger stake in capitalism than propertyless manual workers, nonmanual employees and professionals generally acted as a stabilizing force in society.

Second, although Marx correctly argued that investment in technology makes it possible for capitalists to earn high profits, he did not expect investment in technology also to make it possible for workers to earn higher wages and toil fewer hours under less oppressive conditions. Yet that is just what happened.

Third, many workers supported political parties that promoted improved state benefits, including employment insurance and health care, and they went on strike to demand higher wages from their employers. Their efforts won them improved living standards, which in turn tended to pacify them.

Fourth, communism took root not where industry was most highly developed, as Marx predicted, but in semi-industrialized countries, such as Russia in 1917 and China in 1949. Moreover, instead of evolving into classless and democratic societies, new forms of privilege and authoritarianism emerged under communism. According to a Russian quip from the 1970s, "under capitalism, one class exploits the other, but under communism it's the other way around." Many workers consequently became disillusioned with the promises of communism.

Fifth, businesspeople developed new ways to avert economic crises and prolong the life of capitalism by stimulating demand. To encourage people to buy more things, they began advertising, which created new "needs." To give people the means to buy new things they could not otherwise afford, businesspeople created easy credit. And to ensure that people frequently replaced the new things they bought, they started designing things to break down. Light bulbs with short 1000-hour lifespans, hosiery that develops runs after being worn just a few times, and inkjet printers containing a chip that makes them die after printing a set number of pages are among the abundant fruits of such "planned obsolescence."

class According to Marx, a grouping that is determined by a person's relationship to the means of production or the source of that person's income. In Weber's usage, class position is determined by a person's "market situation," including the possession of goods, opportunities for income, level of education, and level of technical skill.

bourgeoisie Owners of the means of production, including factories, tools, and land, according to Marx. They do not do any physical labour. Their income derives from profits.

proletariat The term Marx gave to the working class. Members of the proletariat perform physical labour but do not own means of production. They are thus in a position to earn wages.

THE FUNCTIONALIST THEORY OF DAVIS AND MOORE

In the mid-twentieth century, American sociologists Kingsley Davis and Wilbert Moore proposed a **functional theory of stratification** that, in contrast to Marx's theory, asserts the inevitability of social stratification (Davis and Moore, 1945). Davis and Moore observed that jobs differ in importance. A judge's work, for example, contributes more to society than does the work of a janitor. This presents a problem: How can people be motivated to undergo the long training they need to serve as judges, physicians, engineers, and so on? Higher education is expensive. You earn little money while training. Long and hard study rather than pleasure-seeking is essential. Clearly, an incentive is needed to motivate the most talented people to train for the most important jobs. The incentives, said Davis and Moore, are money and prestige. More precisely, social stratification is necessary (or "functional") because the prospect of high rewards motivates people to undergo the sacrifices needed to get a higher education. Without substantial inequality, they concluded, the most talented people would have no incentive to become judges, physicians, and so on.

Critical Evaluation of Functionalism

Although the functional theory of stratification may at first seem plausible, we can quickly uncover one of its chief flaws by imagining a society with just two classes of people—physicians and farmers. The farmers grow food. The physicians tend the ill. Then, one day, a rare and deadly virus strikes. The virus has the odd property of attacking only physicians. Within weeks, there are no more doctors in our imaginary society. As a result, the farmers are much worse off. Cures and treatments for their ailments are no longer available. Soon the average farmer lives fewer years than his or her predecessors. The society is less well off, although it survives.

Now imagine the reverse. Again, we have a society comprising only physicians and farmers. Again, a rare and lethal virus strikes. This time, however, the virus has the odd property of attacking only farmers. Within weeks, the physicians' stores of food are depleted. After a few more weeks, the physicians start dying of starvation. The physicians who try to become farmers catch the new virus and expire. Within months, the society has been wiped out. Who, then, does the more important work, physicians or farmers? Our thought experiment suggests that farmers do, for without them, society cannot exist.

> **functional theory of stratification** Argues that (1) some jobs are more important than others, (2) people must make sacrifices to train for important jobs, and (3) inequality is required to motivate people to undergo these sacrifices.

From a historical point of view, we can say that none of the jobs regarded by Davis and Moore as "important" would exist without the physical labour done by people in "less important" jobs. To sustain the witch doctor in a tribal society, hunters and gatherers had to produce enough for their own subsistence plus a surplus to feed, clothe, and house the witch doctor. To sustain the royal court in an agrarian society, peasants had to produce enough for their own subsistence plus a surplus to support the royal family. By using taxes, tithes, and force, government and religious authorities have taken surpluses from ordinary working people for thousands of years. Among other things, these surpluses were used to establish the first institutions of higher learning in the thirteenth century. Out of these, modern universities and colleges developed.

The question of which occupations are most important is not clear-cut. To be sure, physicians earn a lot more money than farmers today, and they also enjoy a lot more prestige. But it is not because their work is more important in any objective sense of the word.

Are farmers or physicians more important to society?

Sociologists have noted other problems with the functional theory of stratification (Tumin, 1953). First, it stresses how inequality helps society discover talent but it ignores the pool of talent lying undiscovered because of inequality. Bright and energetic adolescents may be forced to drop out of high school to help support themselves and their families. Capable and industrious high school graduates may be forced to forgo a postsecondary education because they can't afford it. Inequality may encourage the discovery of talent but only among those who can afford to take advantage of the opportunities available to them. For the rest, inequality prevents talent from being discovered.

Second, the functional theory of stratification fails to examine how advantages are passed from generation to generation. Like *Robinson Crusoe*, the functional theory correctly emphasizes that talent and hard work often result in material rewards. However, it is also the case that inheritance allows parents to transfer wealth to children, regardless of their talent. For example, more than one-quarter of Canada's billionaires inherited a substantial part of their fortunes and only one of them rose from rags to riches (Forbes.com, 2010).

WEBER'S COMPROMISE

Like the functionalists, Max Weber argued that the emergence of a classless society is highly unlikely. Like Marx, however, he recognized that under some circumstances people can act to lower the level of inequality in society.

Writing in the early twentieth century, Weber held that a person's class position is determined by his or her "market situation," including the possession of goods, opportunities for income, level of education, and level of technical skill. Accordingly, in Weber's view, four main classes exist in capitalist societies: large property owners, small property owners, propertyless but relatively highly educated and well-paid employees, and propertyless manual workers (Weber, 1946: 180–95).

Weber also recognized that two types of groups other than classes—status groups and parties—have a bearing on the way a society is stratified. **Status groups** differ from one another in the prestige or social honour they enjoy and in their lifestyle. Celebrities form an especially high-ranking status group in North America. Some enjoy prestige because they are rich or talented. Others enjoy prestige just because they attract a lot of attention. Consider Kim Kardashian. She first drew the attention of the mass media by hanging out with Paris Hilton. She received wider notice after the leak of a sex tape with her former boyfriend. She has no extraordinary talents and her family was not especially rich, although their reality TV show improved their economic status a lot. Nor did power catapult her into a high-status rank. She became well-known largely because of her "well-knownness" (Boorstin, 1992: 57). As such,

she illustrates how social honour alone can bestow rank on individuals.

In Weber's usage, **parties** are not just political groups but, more generally, organizations that seek to impose their will on others through the exercise of power (Weber, 1946: 152). Control over parties, especially large bureaucratic organizations, does not depend just on wealth. A person can head a military, scientific, political, or other bureaucracy without being rich, just as a person can be rich and still have to endure low prestige.

Weber argued that to draw an accurate picture of a society's stratification system, we must analyze classes, status groups, and parties as somewhat independent bases of social inequality. Each basis of stratification influences the others. For example, one political party may want to tax the rich and distribute benefits to the poor, thus increasing opportunities for upward mobility. Another political party may want to cut taxes to the rich and decrease benefits to the poor, thus decreasing opportunities for upward mobility. The class system will be affected in different ways depending on which party comes to power. From

status groups Groups that differ from one another in terms of the prestige or social honour they enjoy and in terms of their style of life.

parties In Weber's usage, organizations that seek to impose their will on others.

Everett Collection/Shutterstock.com

Kim Kardashian is famous for being famous.

this point of view, nothing is inevitable about the level of social stratification in society. We are neither headed inexorably toward classlessness nor are we bound to endure high levels of inequality. Instead, the level of social stratification depends on the complex interplay of class, status, and party, and their effect on **social mobility**, or movement up and down the stratification system. We devote the next section to exploring these themes.

LO⁵ SOCIAL MOBILITY

Mordecai Richler's *The Apprenticeship of Duddy Kravitz* (1959) is one of the classics of modern Canadian literature. Made into a 1974 film starring Richard Dreyfuss as Duddy, it is the story of a poor 18-year-old Jewish Montrealer in the mid-1940s who is desperately seeking to establish himself in the world. To that end, he waits on tables, smuggles drugs, drives a taxi, produces wedding and bar mitzvah films, and rents out pinball machines. He is an obnoxious charmer with relentless drive, a young man so fixed on making it that he is even willing to sacrifice his girlfriend and his only co-worker to achieve his goals. We cannot help but admire Duddy for his relentless ambition, even while we are shocked by his unprincipled guile.

Part of what makes *The Apprenticeship of Duddy Kravitz* universally appealing is that it could be a story about anyone. It is not just some immigrants and their children who may start out as pushy little people engaged in shady practices and unethical behaviour. As Richler reminds us repeatedly, many of the wealthiest establishment families in Canada and elsewhere started out in just this way. Duddy, then, is a universal symbol of "upward mobility"—and the compromises people must sometimes make to achieve it.

Much of our discussion to this point has focused on how we describe inequality and how we explain its persistence. Here we take up a different, although related, set of questions. To what extent are we trapped in a disadvantaged social position or assured of maintaining an advantaged position? At birth, do all people have the same freedom to gain wealth and fame? Are the opportunities we enjoy—our "life chances"—equally accessible to everyone?

Sociologists use the term *social mobility* to refer to the dynamics of the system of inequality and, in particular, to movement up and down the stratification system. If we think about inequality as either a hierarchy of more or less privileged positions or a set of higher and lower social classes, an important question is how much opportunity people have to change positions. Typically, change has been measured by using one of two benchmarks: your first position in the hierarchy (e.g., your first full-time job) and the position of your parents in the hierarchy. Comparing your first job with your current job is an examination of occupational or **intragenerational mobility**. Comparing the occupations of parents with their children's current occupation is an examination of the inheritance of social position or **intergenerational mobility**.

Whichever benchmark is used, social mobility analysts are interested in the openness or fluidity of society. Open or fluid societies have greater equality of access to all positions in the hierarchy of inequality, both the low and the high. Regardless of your social origins, in more open societies you are more likely to rise or fall to a position that reflects your capabilities. In contrast, in closed or rigid societies, your social origins have major consequences for where you are located in the hierarchy of inequality. In such societies, poverty begets poverty, wealth begets wealth. In feudal Europe or in the Indian caste system, your birth determines your fate—you are a peasant or a

Parents' socioeconomic status strongly influences children's educational attainment.

Arne Pastoor/Shutterstock.com

Roy Thomson, Canada's wealthiest man in 1976

Ken Thomson, Roy's son, Canada's wealthiest man in 1996

David Thomson, Roy's grandson, Canada's wealthiest man in 2016

lord, a member of an upper caste or a lower caste, based on the position of the family to which you are born.

In modern times, societies have become more open. The circumstances of your birth do not completely determine your fate. Think about the changes in Canadian society over the past century. A mainly agrarian, resource-based economy has transformed into a modern, advanced postindustrial nation. We have experienced substantial growth in well-paying occupations in finance, marketing, management, and the professions. To what extent have people from all walks of life, from all economic backgrounds, been able to benefit from this transformation?

In the 1950s and 1960s, proponents of the functional theory of stratification and human capital theory imagined that equality of opportunity would predominate. They argued that as more and more skilled jobs are created in the new economy, the best and the brightest must rise to the top to take those jobs and perform them diligently. We would then move from a society based on an **ascription-based stratification system** to one based on an **achievement-based stratification system**. In a system of inequality based on ascription, your family's station in life determines your own fortunes. In a system based on achievement, your own talents determine your lot in life. If you achieve good grades in school, your chance of acquiring a professional or managerial job rises.

Other sociologists, however, cautioned that this scenario of high individual social mobility might not follow from the transformation of the economy. They emphasized how advantaged families have long attempted to ensure that their offspring will inherit their advantages (Collins, 1979).

On the world stage, Blossfeld and Shavit (1993) demonstrated that in 11 of 13 advanced industrial countries, little evidence supports the view that greater equality of opportunity exists in societies with expanding education systems (Sweden and the Netherlands are the two exceptions). In most countries, the openness of the system of inequality did not increase over the last half of the twentieth century. Richard Wanner (1999) tested these ideas using Canadian data. He asked whether "Canada's investment in educational expansion reduced the amount of ascription in educational attainment" (Wanner, 1999: 409).

In other words, has the growth of education—more high schools, colleges, and universities—benefited people from all social backgrounds equally?

If in earlier decades the chances of children from poorer families going to university were small, then these chances should have increased in more recent decades if ascription were weakening. As measures of socioeconomic background, Wanner (1999) used mother's and father's education and father's occupation. He tested his central question by using detailed information from a sample of 31 500 Canadians. Wanner found that class-based ascription still operates strongly. Despite the fact that more Canadians are acquiring more years of schooling and more degrees than ever, the long arm of family socioeconomic background continues to exert a strong hold on educational attainment. The link between family advantage and children's educational achievement has not weakened.

Explanations for how and why this occurs remain a matter of controversy (Davies, 1999). One explanation focuses on the way the school system has become increasingly differentiated. New high school programs have proliferated. These include storefront schools for at-risk students in poorer neighbourhoods, language-immersion streams, private schools, and enriched learning tracks. These different types of schools tend to enroll students from different socioeconomic backgrounds. Students from lower socioeconomic backgrounds tend to take various routes through high school vocational programs and college diploma programs. Students from higher socioeconomic backgrounds typically continue on to university. That is how it is possible for Canadians to acquire more years of schooling and more degrees while the link between family background and educational achievement persists.

> **ascription-based stratification system** A system in which the allocation of rank depends on the features with which a person is born (ascribed characteristics).
>
> **achievement-based stratification system** A system in which the allocation of rank depends on a person's accomplishments.

Finally, we must note that young people are especially likely to experience limited upward mobility if they enter the job market during a recession, a period of declining economic activity (Harvey and Kalwa, 1983). During a recession, unemployment increases, making it harder to find a job. Young people who do find a job must often take work below the level for which they are trained. When the economic downturn ends and employment picks up, employers are inclined to hire not the young people who have been unemployed or underemployed for a few years, but a still more junior cohort of young people, who tend to be better trained and willing to work for lower wages. Thus, young people who enter the job market during a recession are likely to experience relatively low upward mobility over their entire careers. For example, the global recession of 2008–09 created a cohort of job market entrants, many of them with university and college degrees, who now realize that they may never achieve the economic successes of their parents' generation (Smith, 2012).

POLITICS AND THE PERCEPTION OF CLASS INEQUALITY

We expect you have had some strong reactions to our review of sociological theories and research on social stratification. You may therefore find it worthwhile to reflect more systematically on your own attitudes toward social inequality. Do you consider the family in which you grew up to have been lower class, working class, middle class, or upper class? Do you think the gaps between classes in Canadian society are big, moderate, or small? How strongly do you agree or disagree with the view that big gaps between classes are needed to motivate people to work hard and maintain national prosperity? How strongly do you agree or disagree with the view that inequality persists because it benefits the rich and powerful? How strongly do you agree or disagree with the view that inequality persists because ordinary people don't join together to get rid of it?

Answering these questions will help you to clarify the way you perceive and evaluate the Canadian class structure and your place in it. If you take note of your answers, you can compare them with the responses of representative samples of Canadians, which we review below.

Surveys show that few Canadians have trouble placing themselves in the class structure when asked to do so. Most Canadians consider themselves to be middle class or working class. They also think that the gaps between classes are relatively large. But do Canadians think that these big gaps between classes are needed to motivate people to work hard, thus increasing their own wealth and the wealth of the nation? Some Canadians think so, but most do not. A survey conducted in 18 countries, including Canada, asked more than 22 000 respondents if large differences in income are necessary for national prosperity. Canadians were among the most likely to disagree with that view (Pammett, 1997: 77).

So Canadians know that they live in a class-divided society. They also tend to think that deep class divisions are not necessary for national prosperity. Why then do Canadians think inequality continues to exist? The 18-nation survey sheds light on that issue. One of the survey questions asked respondents how strongly they agree or disagree with the view that "inequality continues because it benefits the rich and powerful." Most Canadians agreed with that statement. Only about a quarter of them disagreed with it in any way. Another question asked respondents how strongly they agree or disagree with the view that "inequality continues because ordinary people don't join together to get rid of it." Again, most Canadians agreed, with less than a third disagreeing in any way (Pammett, 1997: 77–78).

Despite widespread awareness of inequality and considerable dissatisfaction with it, most Canadians are opposed to the government playing an active role in reducing inequality. Most do not want governments to provide citizens with a basic income. They tend to oppose government job-creation programs. They even resist the idea that governments should reduce income differences through taxation (Pammett, 1997: 81). Most Canadians remain individualistic and self-reliant. On the whole, they persist in the belief that opportunities for mobility are abundant and that it is up to the individual to make something of those opportunities by means of talent and effort.

Significantly, however, all of the attitudes summarized above vary by class position. For example, discontent with the level of inequality in Canadian society is stronger at the bottom of the stratification system than at the top. The belief that Canadian society is full of opportunities for upward mobility is stronger at the top of the class hierarchy than at the bottom. We find considerably less opposition to the idea that government should reduce inequality as we move down the stratification system. This permits us to conclude that, if Canadians allow inequality to persist, it is because the balance of attitudes—and of the power that supports those attitudes—favours continuity over change.

LO⁶ GLOBAL INEQUALITY

LEVELS AND TRENDS IN GLOBAL INEQUALITY

Despite the existence of considerable social stratification in Canada, we live in one of the 20 or so richest countries in the world—an elite club that also includes the United States, Japan, Australia, Germany, France, the United Kingdom, and a dozen or so other western

A half-hour's drive from the centre of Manila, the capital of the Philippines, an estimated 70 000 Filipinos live on a 22-hectare mountain of rotting garbage 45 metres high. It is infested with flies, rats, dogs, and disease. On a lucky day, residents can earn up to $5 retrieving scraps of metal and other valuables. On a rainy day, the mountain of garbage is especially treacherous. In July 2000, an avalanche buried 300 people alive. People who live on the mountain of garbage call it "The Promised Land."

Time & Life Pictures/Getty Images

European countries. In contrast, the world's poor countries cover much of Africa and parts of South America and Asia. Inequality between rich and poor countries is staggering. In Manhattan, pet owners can treat their cats to US$100-a-plate birthday parties. In Cairo (Egypt) and Manila (the Philippines), garbage dumps are home to entire families who sustain themselves by picking through the refuse.

The average income of citizens in the highly industrialized countries far outstrips that of citizens in the developing societies. Nearly a third of Canadians—those who earn at least $68 000 a year—earn more than 40 times the world average income and rest in the world's top 1 percent of income earners ("How Rich Am I?," 2015; Statistics Canada, 2015g). About 800 million people in the world (more than 11 percent of the global population) are malnourished while the citizens of the 20 or so rich, highly industrialized countries spend more on pet food than it would take to provide basic education or water and sanitation or basic health and nutrition for everyone in the world (World Hunger Education Service, 2015; see Table 6.4 and the Sociology on the Tube feature in this chapter).

Has global inequality increased or decreased over time? Between 1975 and 2000, the annual income gap between the 20 or so richest countries and the rest of the world grew enormously. The share of world income going to the top 10 percent of individuals increased, and the share of world income going to the bottom 20 percent of individuals fell. On the slightly brighter side, the number of people in the world living on $1 a day or less peaked in 1950 and then started to decline gradually. However, if we consider only the less-developed countries, the number of people living on $1 a day or less *increased* by 20 million in the 1990s. Even by the most optimistic interpretation, these figures are little cause for joy. Nearly half of the world's population lives on $2 a day or less (Milanovic, 2005; Figure 6.5).

Statistics never speak for themselves. We need theories to explain them. Let us now outline and critically assess the two main theories that seek to explain the origins and persistence of global inequality.

> **modernization theory**
> Holds that global inequality results from various dysfunctional characteristics of poor societies: lack of investment capital, Western-style business techniques, stable Western-style governments, and a Western mentality.

LO7 MODERNIZATION THEORY: A FUNCTIONALIST APPROACH

Two main sociological theories claim to explain global inequality. The first, **modernization theory**, is a variant of functionalism. According to modernization theory, global inequality results from various dysfunctional characteristics of poor societies themselves. Specifically, modernization theorists say the citizens of poor societies lack sufficient *capital* to invest in Western-style agriculture and industry. They lack rational Western-style *business techniques* of marketing, accounting, sales, and finance. As a result, their productivity and profitability remain low. They lack stable Western-style *governments* that could provide a secure framework for investment. Finally, they lack a Western *mentality*: values that stress the need for savings, investment, innovation, education, high achievement, and self-control in having children (Inkeles and Smith, 1976; Rostow, 1960).

Societies characterized by these dysfunctions are poor. It follows that people living in rich countries can best help their poor cousins by transferring Western culture and capital to them and eliminating the dysfunctions. Only then will the poor countries be able to cap population growth, stimulate democracy, and invigorate agricultural and industrial production. Government-to-government foreign aid can accomplish some of this. Much work also needs to be done to encourage Western businesses to invest directly in poor countries and to increase trade between rich and poor countries.

The Amazing Race

The Amazing Race first aired in 2001 and is still going strong. It pits two-person teams against each other in races around the world using all manner of transportation from jet to hot air balloon to bus. Each race is divided into legs. At the end of each leg, the teams are given clues leading to the next destination. They must also perform a challenging task. The team coming in last on each leg is either eliminated or penalized with an impediment that makes the next leg more difficult. The team winning each leg receives a prize, typically a trip, a car, or money. Teams are eliminated until only one remains. The winning team receives a grand prize of a million dollars.

The challenge at the end of each leg emphasizes the exotic character of the location. In Season one, a leg ended at the Karni Mata Temple in Deshnoke, India, which is overrun with rats that are considered sacred by the locals. Contestants had to find their way through a labyrinth in the temple, avoiding as much as possible run-ins with the rodent hordes. A leg in Season 10 ended in China, where contestants had to eat a bowl of fish eyes, considered a delicacy in some parts of the country.

The producers of the show must walk a fine line between exoticism and the horrors of life in poor countries. Eating fish eyes is okay, but leper colonies, twelve-year-olds working sixteen hours a day weaving carpets, families living in huts made of cardboard and scrap tin, and mounds of noxious burning plastic (needed to get at the valuable metals in circuit boards shipped as garbage from Europe) are to be avoided at all cost. The show is meant to be fun, not a sociological lesson in underdevelopment.

We can find evidence of the fine line the producers tread by examining the gross domestic product per capita (GDPpc) of all 1148 non-U.S. locations the show visited from September 2001 to March 2014. (GDPpc is a measure of economic well-being—the dollar value of goods and services produced in a country in a year divided by the number of people in the country.) Using the classification system of the World Bank, the ten countries visited most frequently by *The Amazing Race* include eight high-income countries (Australia, Italy, Brazil, France, New Zealand, Germany, the United Kingdom, and Argentina), one upper-middle-income country (Thailand), one lower-middle-income country (India), and no low-income countries. While the world's poorest countries have a GDPpc that is around 2 percent of the GDP per capita of the United States, the average GDPpc of the 1148 *Amazing Race* locations is 43 percent of the GDPpc of the United States: poor enough to charm, not so poor as to shock.

Possibly not wanting audience members to get upset about even their limited glimpses into the difficult lives of people in less-developed countries, the producers alternate high-income with other locales both in the short-term and the long-term. Figure 6.4 arrays the 1148 non-U.S. locations of the show over time on the *x*-axis, from the first location on the left to the most recent location on the right. The *y*-axis shows GDPpc for the locations. Notice the rapid (short-term) jumps up and down between high-income and other locales. Notice also the long-term cycle between high-income and other locales. These patterns may be largely unintended, but it seems that the producers at least have it in the back of their minds not to allow viewers to focus for long on a less-developed country and thereby run the risk of dwelling on the causes, consequences, and extent of world poverty.

Could a more socially responsible reality TV show about the less-developed countries be produced? Possibly, but it is unlikely to succeed commercially. The BBC tried it in 2010. "Blood, Sweat, and Luxuries" took six British youth to poor countries to work with the people who produced the luxury goods the visitors craved. They mined sapphires in Madagascar, dug for gold in Ghana, worked abattoirs and tanneries in Ethiopia, and joined Filipino sweatshop workers making components for MP3 players. Working relentlessly in 40-degree heat, lacking flush toilets, and living near toxic slums proved too much for the young

The Amazing Race in Botswana

Joe LaBracio/© CBS/Courtesy: Everett Collection/The Canadian Press

FIGURE 6.4 **Location over Time by Gross Domestic Product per capita for Episodes of** *The Amazing Race*

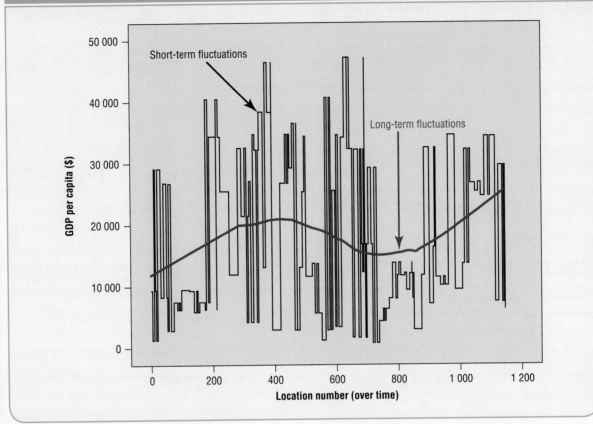

Source: Internet Movie Data Base. 2014. *"The Amazing Race* (2001—): Filming Locations."

Note: Data were collected from the Internet Movie Data Base (2014) and The World Bank (2014) by Tony Zhang. United States locations were not included because races start and end in the United States. GDPpc data are for 2009, except in two cases where the data closest to 2009 were used.

consumers—and apparently for their audience too. Despite good reviews from the critics, the show lasted only six episodes before it was axed.

Critical Thinking Questions

1. Can you think of a type of reality TV show that would simultaneously entertain and teach audiences about the causes, consequences, and extent of world poverty—a kind of "infotainment?" Or do reality and reality TV mix about as well as oil and water?

2. Why do audiences generally prefer reality TV to reality?

DEPENDENCY THEORY: A CONFLICT APPROACH

Proponents of **dependency theory**, a variant of conflict theory, have been quick to point out the chief flaw in modernization theory (Baran, 1957; Cardoso and Faletto, 1979; Wallerstein, 1974–89). For the past 500 years, the most powerful countries in the world have deliberately impoverished the less powerful countries. Focusing on internal characteristics blames the victim rather than the perpetrator of the crime. It follows that an adequate theory of global inequality should not focus on the internal characteristics of poor countries themselves. Instead, it should follow the principles of conflict theory and focus on patterns of domination and submission—specifically, in this

dependency theory Holds that global inequality is the result of patterns of domination and submission between rich and poor countries. From this point of view, rich countries have impoverished poor countries in order to enrich themselves.

TABLE 6.4 **Global Priorities (in US$ billions)**

Additional annual cost, basic education for everyone in the world[1]	6.3
Additional annual cost, water and sanitation for everyone in the world[1]	12.4
Annual dog and cat food sales, United States[2]	18.6
Additional, annual cost, reproductive health care for all women in the world[1]	18.6
Additional annual cost, basic health and nutrition for everyone in the world[1]	20.1
Annual global perfume sales[3]	27.5
Annual TV advertising, United States[3]	60.0
Annual global revenue, strip clubs[3]	75.0
Annual global revenue, cocaine sales[4]	88.0
Annual beer sales, United States[3]	96.0
Annual global arms sales[5]	1700.0

[1]Bureau of Labor Statistics. "CPI Inflation Calculator." http://data.bls.gov/cgi-bin/cpicalc.pl?cost1=1&year1=1998&year2=2011 (retrieved 28 December 2012); Negative Population Growth. "Total Midyear World Population, 1950–2050." http://www.npg.org/facts/world_pop_year.htm (retrieved 28 December 2012); United Nations. *World Development Report 1998* (New York: Oxford University Press): 37. United Nations data for 1998 are adjusted for world population increase, 1998–2011, and the U.S. consumer price index, 1998–2011.

[2]Pet Food Institute. 2012. "U.S. Pet Food Sales." http://www.petfoodinstitute.org/Index.cfm?Page=USPetFoodSales (retrieved 28 December 2012).

[3]Statistic Brain. 2012. http://www.statisticbrain.com/ (retrieved 28 December 2012).

[4]United Nations. 2012. "The global cocaine market." http://www.unodc.org/documents/wdr/WDR_2010/1.3_The_globa_cocaine_market.pdf (retrieved 28 December 2012).

[5]Global Issues. "World Military Expenditures." 2012. http://www.globalissues.org/article/75/world-military-spending#WorldMilitarySpending (retrieved 28 December 2012).

FIGURE 6.5 **World Poverty**

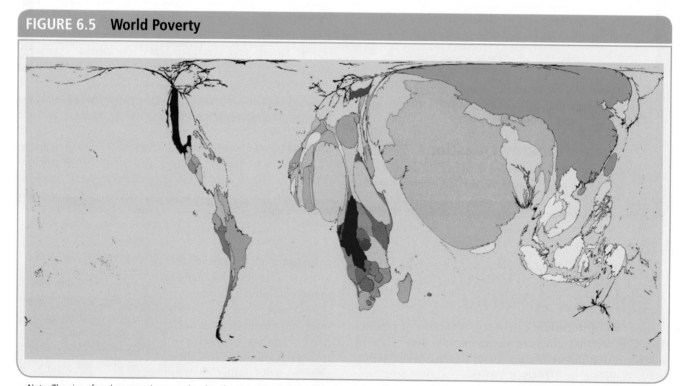

Note: The size of each country is proportional to the percentage of people in that country living on US$2 a day or less in purchasing power.

Source: University of Sheffield. 2006. "Absolute Poverty." http://www.worldmapper.org/posters/worldmapper_map180_ver5.pdf (retrieved 11 March 2010).
© Copyright 2006 SASI Group (University of Sheffield) and Mark Newman (University of Michigan).

case, on the relationship between rich and poor countries. That is just what dependency theory does.

According to dependency theorists, less global inequality existed in 1500 and even in 1750 than today. However, beginning around 1500, the armed forces of the world's most powerful countries subdued and then annexed or colonized most of the rest of the world. The Industrial Revolution began around 1780. It enabled the western European countries, Russia, Japan, and the United States to amass enormous wealth, which they used to extend their global reach. They forced their colonies to become a source of raw materials, cheap labour, investment opportunities, and markets for the conquering nations. The colonizers thereby prevented industrialization and locked the colonies into poverty.

In the decades following World War II, nearly all of the colonies in the world became politically independent. However, the dependency theorists say that exploitation by direct political control was soon replaced by new means of achieving the same end: substantial foreign investment, support for authoritarian governments, and mounting debt.

- *Substantial foreign investment.* Multinational corporations invested in the poor countries to siphon off wealth in the form of raw materials and profits. True, they created some low-paying jobs in the process, but they created many more high-paying jobs in the rich countries where the raw materials were used to produce manufactured goods. They also sold part of the manufactured goods back to the poor unindustrialized countries for additional profit.

- *Support for authoritarian governments.* According to dependency theorists, multinational corporations and rich countries continued their exploitation of the poor countries in the postcolonial period by giving economic and military support to local authoritarian governments. These governments managed to keep their populations subdued most of the time. When that was not possible, Western governments sent in troops and military advisers, engaging in what became known as "gunboat diplomacy." In the postcolonial period, the United States has been particularly active in using gunboat diplomacy in Central America. For example, in 1952 the democratic government of Guatemala began to redistribute land to impoverished peasants. Some of the land was owned by the United Fruit Company, a U.S. multinational corporation and the biggest landowner in Guatemala. Two years later, the CIA backed a right-wing coup in Guatemala, preventing land reform and allowing the United Fruit Company to continue its highly profitable business as usual (LaFeber, 1993).

- *Mounting debt.* The governments of the poor countries struggled to create transportation infrastructures (airports, roads, harbours, etc.), build their education systems, and deliver safe water and at least the most basic health care to their people. To accomplish these tasks,

they had to borrow money from Western banks and governments. Some rulers also squandered money on luxuries. So it came about that debt—and the interest payments that inevitably accompany debt—grew every year. Crushing interest payments leave governments of poor countries with too little money for development tasks. Foreign aid helps, but not much. Foreign aid to the world's developing countries is only one-seventh the amount that the developing countries pay to Western banks in loan interest (United Nations, 2004: 201).

> **core countries** Capitalist countries that are the world's major sources of capital and technology (the United States, Japan, and Germany).
>
> **peripheral countries** The world's major sources of raw materials and cheap labour (the former colonies).
>
> **semiperipheral countries** Former colonies that are making considerable headway in their attempt to become prosperous.

CORE, PERIPHERY, AND SEMIPERIPHERY

Although dependency theory provides a more realistic account of the sources of global inequality than modernization theory does, it leaves a big question unanswered: How have some countries managed to escape poverty and start rapid economic development? After all, the world does not consist of just **core countries** that are major sources of capital and technology (the United States, Japan, and Germany) and **peripheral countries** that are major sources of raw materials and cheap labour (the former colonies). In addition, a middle tier of **semiperipheral countries** consists of former colonies that are making considerable headway in their attempts to become prosperous (South Korea, Taiwan, and Israel, for example; Wallerstein, 1974–89). Comparing the poor peripheral countries with the more successful semiperipheral countries presents us with a useful natural experiment. The comparison suggests the circumstances that help some poor countries overcome the worst effects of colonialism.

The semiperipheral countries differ from the peripheral countries in four main ways, which we outline next (Kennedy, 1993: 193–227; Lie, 1998).

Type of Colonialism

Around the turn of the twentieth century, Taiwan and Korea became colonies of Japan. They remained so until 1945. However, in contrast to the European colonizers of Africa, Latin America, and other parts of Asia, the Japanese built up the economies of their colonies. They established transportation networks and communication systems.

In 1893, leaders of the British mission pose before taking over what became Rhodesia and is now Zimbabwe. To raise a volunteer army, every British trooper was offered about 23 square kilometres of native land and 20 gold claims. The Matabele and Mashona peoples were subdued in a three-month war. Nine hundred farms and 10 000 gold claims were granted to the troopers and about 100 000 cattle were looted, leaving the native survivors without a livelihood. Forced labour was subsequently introduced by the British so that the natives could pay a £2 a year tax.

They built steel, chemical, and hydroelectric power plants. After Japanese colonialism ended, Taiwan and South Korea were thus at an advantage compared with the former colonies of Britain and France. South Korea and Taiwan could use the Japanese-built infrastructure and Japanese-trained personnel as springboards to development.

Geopolitical Position

Although the United States was the leading economic and military power in the world by the end of World War II, it began to feel its supremacy threatened in the late 1940s by the Soviet Union and China. Fearing that South Korea and Taiwan might fall to the communists, the United States poured unprecedented aid into both countries in the 1960s. It also gave the countries large, low-interest loans and opened its domestic market to Taiwanese and South Korean products. Because the United States saw Israel as a crucially important ally in the Middle East, Israel also received special economic assistance. Other countries with less strategic importance to the United States received less help in their drive to industrialize.

State Policy

A third factor that accounts for the relative success of some countries in their efforts to industrialize and become prosperous concerns state policies. As a legacy of colonialism, the Taiwanese and South Korean states were developed on the Japanese model. They kept workers' wages low, restricted trade union growth, and maintained quasi-military discipline in factories. Moreover, by placing high taxes on consumer goods, limiting the import of foreign goods, and preventing their citizens from investing abroad, they encouraged their citizens to put much of their money in the bank. This situation created a large pool of capital for industrial expansion. The South Korean and Taiwanese states also gave subsidies, training grants, and tariff protection to export-based industries from the 1960s onward. (Tariffs are taxes on foreign goods.) These policies did much to stimulate industrial growth. Finally, the Taiwanese and South Korean states invested heavily in basic education, health care, roads, and other public goods. A healthy and well-educated labour force, combined with good transportation and communication systems, laid solid foundations for economic growth.

Social Structure

Taiwan and South Korea are socially cohesive countries, which makes it easy for them to generate consensus around development policies. It also allows them to get their citizens to work hard, save a lot of money, and devote their energies to scientific education.

Social solidarity in Taiwan and South Korea is based partly on the sweeping land reform they conducted in the late 1940s and early 1950s. By redistributing land to small farmers, both countries eliminated the class of large landowners, who usually oppose industrialization. Land redistribution got rid of a major potential source of social conflict. In contrast, many countries in Latin America and Africa have not undergone land reform. The United States often intervened militarily in Latin America to prevent land reform because U.S. commercial interests profited handsomely from the existence of large plantations (LaFeber, 1993).

Another factor underlying social solidarity in Taiwan and South Korea is that neither country suffered from internal conflicts like those that wrack Africa south of the Sahara desert. British, French, and other western European colonizers often drew the borders of African countries to keep antagonistic tribes in the same jurisdiction and often sought to stir up tribal conflict. Keeping tribal tensions alive made it possible to play one tribe against another, which made it easier for imperial powers to dominate. This policy led to much social and political conflict in postcolonial Africa. Today, the region suffers from frequent civil wars, coups, and uprisings. It is the most conflict-ridden area of the world. This high level of internal conflict acts as a barrier to economic development.

In sum, postcolonial countries that enjoy a solid industrial infrastructure, strategic geopolitical importance, strong states with strong development policies, and socially cohesive populations are in the best position to join the ranks of the rich countries in the coming decades. Countries that have some of these characteristics are likely to experience economic growth and an increase in the well-being of their populations. Such countries include China, India, Chile, Thailand, Indonesia, Mexico, Turkey, Russia, and Brazil. We conclude that, as is the case for social stratification within highly developed countries like Canada, the existing level of global inequality is not inevitable and can under some circumstances change for the better. We take up this theme again in the book's final chapter.

READY TO STUDY?

IN THE BOOK, YOU CAN:

❏ Tear out the chapter review card at the back of the book to have a summary of the chapter and key terms handy.

ONLINE YOU CAN:

❏ Work through key concepts with a Guided Learning Question.

❏ Prepare for tests with quizzes.

❏ Review the key terms with flash cards.

❏ Explore practical examples of chapter concepts with Connect a Concept exercises.

GO TO NELSON.COM/STUDENT TO ACCESS THESE DIGITAL RESOURCES.

7

Race and Ethnicity

LEARNING OBJECTIVES

In this chapter, you will learn to

LO¹ Recognize that race and ethnicity are socially constructed variables rather than biological or cultural constants.

LO² Analyze why racial and ethnic labels and identities change over time and place.

LO³ Appreciate that conquest and domination are among the most important forces leading to the crystallization of distinct ethnic and racial identities.

LO⁴ Describe the ways in which identifying with a racial or ethnic group can be economically, politically, and emotionally advantageous.

LO¹ DEFINING RACE AND INTELLIGENCE

WHAT IS RACE?

Race and Intelligence

In the 1920s, Peter Sandiford, a professor in the Department of Education at the University of Toronto, administered some IQ tests and concluded that Canada must adopt a policy of selective immigration to ensure that "misfits" and "defectives" are kept out of the country. He encouraged the immigration of Britons, Germans, and Danes, and discouraged the immigration of Poles, Italians, Greeks, and Asians. The latter groups scored low on his IQ tests, and he believed that their apparent intellectual inferiority was rooted in their biological makeup (McLaren, 1990). Around the same time in the United States, Jewish immigrants were scoring below non-Jews on IQ tests. Influential people used these results as an argument against Jewish immigration. In modern times, blacks have, on average, scored below European Americans on IQ tests. Some people say this justifies slashing budgets for schools where many black people live. Why invest good money in schooling, such people ask, if low IQ scores are rooted in biology and therefore fixed (Herrnstein and Murray, 1994)?

The people who argued against the immigration of certain groups and better education for blacks ignored two facts. First, IQ scores are remarkably flexible. The descendants of Sandiford's low-IQ Asians are among the stars of the Canadian system of higher education today. As Jews experienced upward mobility and could afford better education, their IQ scores rose to above-average levels. Enriched educational facilities routinely boost the IQ scores and achievements of poor black children (Campbell and Ramey, 1994; Frank Porter Graham Child Development Center, 1999; Gould, 1996; Hancock, 1994). We are obliged to conclude that the social setting in which a person is raised and educated has a big impact on IQ. The average IQ of members of racial and ethnic groups has nothing to do with biology (Cancio, Evans, and Maume, 1996; Fischer et al., 1996).

Race and Sports

Nonetheless, the view persists that races differ biologically. For instance, we commonly hear that, for biological reasons, black people are better than whites at sports. Is

prejudice An attitude that judges a person on his or her group's real or imagined characteristics.

discrimination Unfair treatment of people because of their group membership.

there any evidence to support that belief? At first glance, the evidence might seem strong. Aren't roughly two-thirds of NFL and NBA players black? Don't blacks of West African descent hold the 200 fastest 100-metre-dash times, all under 10 seconds? Don't North and East Africans regularly win 40 percent of the top international distance-running honours yet represent only a fraction of 1 percent of the world's population (Entine, 2000; Lapchick, 2004)? Although these facts are undeniable, the argument for the genetic basis of black athletic superiority begins to falter once we consider two additional points. First, nobody has ever identified genes linked to general athletic superiority. Second, black athletes do not perform unusually well in many sports, such as swimming, hockey, cycling, tennis, gymnastics, soccer, and equestrian events. The idea that black people are in general superior athletes is simply untrue.

Sociologists have identified certain social conditions that lead to high levels of participation in sports. These operate on all groups of people, whatever their race. Specifically, people who face widespread prejudice and discrimination often enter *professional* sports in disproportionately large numbers for lack of other ways to improve their social and economic standing. For such people, other avenues of upward mobility tend to be blocked. (**Prejudice** is an attitude that judges a person on his or her group's real or imagined characteristics. **Discrimination** is unfair treatment of people because of their group membership.) For example, it was not until the 1950s that prejudice and discrimination against North American Jews began to decline appreciably. Until then, Jews played a prominent role in some professional sports, such as boxing, baseball, and basketball. For example, when the New York Knicks played their first game on November 1, 1946, beating the Toronto Huskies 68–66, the starting lineup for New York consisted of Ossie Schechtman, Stan Stutz, Jake Weber, Ralph Kaplowitz, and Leo "Ace" Gottlieb—an all-Jewish squad ("Do You Know…?" n.d.). Similarly, Koreans in Japan today are subject to much prejudice and discrimination. They often pursue careers in professional sports. In contrast, Koreans in Canada face less prejudice and discrimination. Few become professional athletes.

The idea that black people are genetically superior to whites in athletic ability is the complement of the idea that they are genetically inferior to whites in intellectual ability. Both ideas have the effect of reinforcing black–white inequality. For although there are just a few thousand professional athletes in North America, there are millions of pharmacists, graphics designers, lawyers, systems analysts, police officers, nurses, and people in other interesting occupations that offer steady employment

Natursports/Shutterstock.com

and good pay. By promoting outstanding athletes such as LeBron James as role models for youth, the idea of "natural" black athletic superiority and intellectual inferiority in effect asks blacks to bet on a high-risk proposition—that they will make it in professional sports. At the same time, it deflects attention from a much safer bet—that they can achieve upward mobility through academic excellence (Guppy and Davies, 1998; Hoberman, 1997).

Racial Mixing

Another problem undermines the argument that genes determine the behaviour of racial groups: It is impossible to neatly distinguish races based on genetic differences. A high level of genetic mixing has taken place. In Canada in the eighteenth and nineteenth centuries, French settlers and Aboriginal people merged to form the Métis. In the United States in the same period, it was common for white male slave owners to rape black female slaves, who then gave birth to children of mixed race. We know from the census that racial intermarriage has been increasing in Canada since at least 1871. Usually, people who report multiple racial identities have parents of different racial origins (Kalbach and Kalbach, 1998). A growing number of North Americans are similar to Tiger Woods, who claims he is of "Cablinasian" ancestry—part Caucasian, part black, part Native American Indian, and part Asian. As these examples illustrate, the differences among black, white, Asian, and so forth are often anything but clear-cut.

Some respected scholars believe we all belong to one human race, which originated in Africa (Cavalli-Sforza, Menozzi, and Piazza, 1994). They argue that subsequent migration, geographical separation, and inbreeding led to the formation of more or less distinct races. However, particularly in modern times, humanity has experienced so much intermixing that race as a biological category has lost nearly all meaning. Some biologists and social scientists therefore suggest we drop the term *race* from the vocabulary of science.

A Sociological Definition of Race

Sociologists, however, continue to use the term *race*. They do so because perceptions of race continue to affect the lives of most people profoundly. Everything from your wealth to your health is influenced by whether others see you as black, white, brown, or something else. Race as a sociological concept is thus a valuable analytical tool to the degree that people who use the term remember that it refers to socially significant physical differences (e.g., skin colour) rather than to biological differences that shape behaviour patterns. Said differently, perceptions of racial difference are socially constructed and often arbitrary. The Irish and the Jews were once regarded as black by some people, and today many northern Italians still think of southern Italians from Sicily and Calabria as black (Gilman, 1991; Ignatiev, 1995; Roediger, 1991).

Finally, then, we can define race as a social construct used to distinguish people in terms of one or more physical markers. However, this definition raises an interesting question. If race is merely a social construct and not a useful biological term, why do we commonly use perceptions of physical difference to distinguish groups of people in the first place? Why, in other words, does race matter? Most sociologists believe that race matters because it allows social inequality to be created and perpetuated (see the Sociology at the Movies feature in this chapter). The English who colonized Ireland, the Americans who went to Africa looking for slaves, and the Germans who used the Jews as a scapegoat to explain their deep economic and political troubles after World War I, all created systems of racial domination. (A **scapegoat** is a disadvantaged person or category of people that others blame for their own problems.)

Once colonialism, slavery, and concentration camps were established, behavioural differences developed between

> **race** A social construct used to distinguish people in terms of one or more physical markers, usually with profound effects on their lives.
>
> **scapegoat** A disadvantaged person or category of people whom others blame for their own problems.

SOCIOLOGY AT THE MOVIES

Searching for Sugar Man

Apartheid was the brutal system of racial segregation that governed South Africa from 1948 to 1994—an extreme form of institutional racism. Nelson Mandela is known around the world as the black leader who heroically protested that racist system. He was imprisoned for 27 years for resisting apartheid but emerged to become the country's president.

Although apartheid privileged South African whites, many were disgusted by its social injustices. Those whites joined with blacks and, over the decades, protested and resisted the governing regime. During the same period, more than 15 000 km away, blacks and whites in the United States were protesting the system of segregation that denied people of colour their civil rights.

Protesting oppressive institutional arrangements is a grind. It requires focus, organization, and persistence. Those in power do not give up their privileges easily. Protest movements continually look for tools to inspire their members and keep them on task. Around the

Sixto Rodriguez

world, one important tool for rallying demonstrators is the protest song (Cullum, 2011).

Many protest singers participated in the American civil rights protests of the 1960s and 1970s. One of the most famous was Bob Dylan. But while Dylan was gaining international fame, record producers discovered a Latino singer–songwriter working in Detroit. They were confident he would be as big as Dylan. Sixto Rodriguez released two critically successful albums. However, they were commercial flops, and Rodriguez's

(Continued)

recording contract was promptly cancelled. He returned to a life of obscurity as a construction worker.

Rodriguez thought his musical career was done. But he was wrong. A bootlegged copy of his *Cold Play* album made its way to South Africa, where it reached an enthusiastic audience among apartheid protesters. Its songs became rallying cries for the opposition. Rodriguez won a cult-like following, reinforced by the false rumour of his on-stage suicide (Titlestad, 2013).

Searching for Sugar Man is a documentary of two South African protesters' journey in the late 1990s to determine the circumstances of Rodriguez's death. Much to their surprise, they find him living an anonymous life in Detroit. The documentary mixes archival footage and interviews to provide insights into how racial discrimination operates in South Africa and the United States. It reveals that although Rodriguez's albums sold more than 1 million copies worldwide, he has never received a penny in royalties (Frere-Jones, 2012).

Searching for Sugar Man won the best-documentary Academy Award in 2013. It is of sociological interest on several accounts. First, it reminds us of how racist and oppressive Western political institutions were only a few decades ago. Second, it provides a sense of the sustained effort required to overturn racially unjust institutional arrangements. Regime change is not for weak-willed romantics. Finally, we see an illustration of how interconnected the global village is. A neglected, black protest singer in the United States inspires white apartheid demonstrators halfway around the world. Their actions, in turn, reignite Rodriguez's late-in-life musical career.

Critical Thinking Questions

1. In recent decades, racial divisions and tensions have weakened in South Africa and the United States, but they have by no means disappeared. Why not?
2. Under what social conditions can racial divisions and tensions weaken further in these two countries?

---

ethnic group Comprises people whose perceived cultural markers are deemed socially significant. Ethnic groups differ from one another in terms of language, religion, customs, values, ancestors, and the like.

subordinates and their masters. For example, North American slaves and Jewish concentration camp inmates, with little motivating them to work hard except the ultimate threat of the master's whip, tended to do only the minimum work necessary to survive. Their masters noticed this and characterized their subordinates as inherently slow and unreliable workers (Collins, 1982: 66–9). In this way, racial stereotypes are born. The stereotypes then embed themselves in popular lore, journalism, literature, and political debate, reinforcing racial inequalities (see Figure 7.1). So we can see that race matters to the degree that it helps create and maintain systems of social inequality.

ETHNICITY, CULTURE, AND SOCIAL STRUCTURE

Race is to biology as ethnicity is to culture. A *race* is a socially defined category of people whose perceived *physical* markers are socially significant. An **ethnic group** comprises people whose perceived *cultural* markers are socially significant. Ethnic groups differ from one another in terms of language, religion, customs, values, ancestors, and the like. However, just as physical distinctions do not *cause* differences in the behaviour of various races, so cultural distinctions are often not by themselves the major source of differences in the behaviour of various ethnic groups. In other words, ethnic values and other elements of ethnic culture have less of an effect on the way people behave than we commonly believe. That is because *social-structural* differences frequently underlie cultural differences.

An example will help drive home the point. People often praise Koreans, Jews, and other economically successful groups for their cultural values, including an emphasis on education, family, and hard work. People less commonly notice, however, that Canada's immigration policy has been

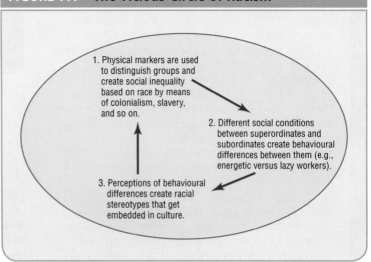

FIGURE 7.1   The Vicious Circle of Racism

1. Physical markers are used to distinguish groups and create social inequality based on race by means of colonialism, slavery, and so on.

2. Different social conditions between superordinates and subordinates create behavioural differences between them (e.g., energetic versus lazy workers).

3. Perceptions of behavioural differences create racial stereotypes that get embedded in culture.

Source: From BRYM/LIE. *Sociology*, 1E. © 2009 Nelson Education Ltd. Reproduced by permission.

Literate, urbanized, skilled immigrants with financial assets tend to be more upwardly mobile than other immigrants are.

RESOURCES AND OPPORTUNITIES

What matters most in determining the economic success of an ethnic or racial group are the *resources* that people possess (notably literacy, education, urbanity, and financial assets) and the *economic opportunities* open to them. To appreciate the latter point, compare Canada in the mid-twentieth century with Canada today.

In the 1950s, Canada was a society sharply stratified along ethnic and racial lines. The people with the most power and privilege were of British origin. WASPs (white Anglo-Saxon Protestants) controlled almost all of the big corporations in the country and dominated politics. Immigrants who arrived later enjoyed less power and privilege. Even among them, big economic differences were evident, with European immigrants enjoying higher status than immigrants of Asian ancestry, for example.

John Porter, one of the founders of modern Canadian sociology, called mid-twentieth-century Canada a **vertical mosaic**, a highly ethnically and racially stratified society. He thought that the retention of ethnic and racial culture was a big problem in Canada because it hampered the upward mobility of immigrants. In his view, the Canadian value system encouraged the retention of ethnic culture, making Canada a low-mobility society (Porter, 1965, 1979: 91).

By the 1970s, however, many Canadian sociologists, including Porter himself, had to reject or at least qualify the view that ethnic and racial culture determines economic success or failure. Events upset their earlier assumptions. The Canadian economy grew quickly in the decades after World War II. Many members of ethnic and racial-minority groups were economically successful despite ethnic and racial prejudice and discrimination. Economic differences among ethnic groups and, to a lesser degree, among racial groups, diminished. Among the wealthiest Canadians and among politicians at all levels of government, ethnic and racial diversity increased. Such diversity became even more evident among professional groups. For the most part, visible-minority status had little bearing on educational, occupational, and income attainment in Canada, especially among the Canadian-born (Guppy and Davies, 1998; Lautard and Guppy, 2008; Lian and Matthews, 1998; Pendakur and Pendakur, 1998). Aboriginal Canadians and black men born in Canada continued to face discrimination that significantly impeded their upward mobility. However,

highly selective. For the most part, the Koreans and Jews who arrived in Canada were literate, urbanized, and skilled. Some even came with financial assets (Brym, Shaffir, and Weinfeld, 2010; Li, 1995; Wong and Ng, 1998). They certainly confronted prejudice and discrimination, but far less than that reserved for the descendants of slaves or members of Canada's Aboriginal peoples. These social-structural conditions facilitated Jewish and Korean success. They gave members of these groups a firm basis on which to build and maintain a culture emphasizing education, family, and other middle-class virtues. In contrast, descendants of slaves and members of Canada's Aboriginal peoples were typically illiterate and unskilled, and they experienced more prejudice and discrimination than did other ethnic or racial groups in Canada. These social-structural disadvantages—not their culture—made them less economically successful on average than Koreans and Jews have been (compare Table 7.1).

TABLE 7.1	Percentage Low-Income by Selected Groups and Immigration Status, Canada

	White	Black	Chinese	Arab
Immigrants	13.6	28.5	25.1	36.7
Non-immigrants	11.7	30.8	17.9	34.7

Note: This table shows the percentage of people over the age of 15 below the low-income cutoff in each group. For the definition of "low-income cutoff," see Chapter 6. The percentages are probably low because of problems with the data source (Brym, 2014) but no evidence suggests that underestimates are higher in one group than in another.

Source: Statistics Canada. 2015h. *National Household Survey* (NHS) PUMF, 2011: individuals file. http://sda.chass.utoronto.ca.myaccess.library.utoronto.ca/cgi-bin/sdacensus/hsda?harcsda+nhs11i (retrieved 2 August 2015).

> **vertical mosaic** A highly ethnically and racially stratified society.

for the great majority of Canadians in the decades after World War II, ethnic and racial culture mattered less than the structure of mobility opportunities in determining a person's economic success.

From the 1990s to the 2010s, recent immigrants who were members of some visible-minority groups were significantly less successful economically than we would expect given their educational and other resources (refer back to Table 7.1). However, their cultural values had little to do with that. Canada experienced an unusually high rate of unemployment in the 1990s, hovering around 10 percent until late in the decade. That situation made it more difficult than in previous decades for recently arrived visible-minority immigrants to succeed economically. In addition, although many minority immigrants are selected to come to Canada because they are highly educated, their credentials are often not recognized by employers here. The mechanisms for receiving accreditation for foreign credentials are poorly developed in this country and need to be improved (Reitz, 2011).

Finally, labour force and housing discrimination are ongoing problems for visible-minority Canadians. Numerous studies conducted in Toronto, Montreal, and Vancouver document that job and housing applications are less likely to result in interviews if the applicant has a name that does not sound like that of a white person or if the applicant speaks on the phone with a non-Canadian accent (Hogan and Berry, 2011; Oreopoulos and Dechief, 2011). The relative lack of success of recent visible-minority immigrants thus reinforces our point. In addition to the resources a person possesses, it is the structure of opportunities for economic advancement that determines income and occupational and educational attainment. Ethnic or racial culture by itself plays at most a minor role.

In sum, we see that racial and ethnic inequality is more deeply rooted in social structure than in biology and culture. The biological and cultural aspects of race and ethnicity are secondary to their sociological character when it comes to explaining inequality. The interesting question from a sociological point of view is why social definitions of race and ethnicity change. We now consider that issue.

LO² SYMBOLIC INTERACTIONISM, RACE, AND ETHNIC RELATIONS
LABELS AND IDENTITY

John Lie moved with his family from South Korea to Japan when he was a baby. He moved from Japan to Hawaii when he was 10 years old, and again from Hawaii to the U.S. mainland when he started university. The move to Hawaii and the move to the U.S. mainland changed the way John thought of himself in ethnic terms.

In Japan, Koreans form a minority group. Before 1945, when Korea was a colony of Japan, some Koreans were brought to Japan to work as miners and unskilled labourers. The Japanese thought the Koreans who lived there were beneath and outside Japanese society (Lie, 2001). Not surprisingly, Korean children in Japan—including John—were often teased and occasionally beaten by their Japanese schoolmates. "The beatings hurt," says John, "but the psychological trauma resulting from being socially excluded by my classmates hurt more. In fact, although I initially thought I was Japanese like my classmates, my Korean identity was literally beaten into me.

"When my family immigrated to Hawaii, I was sure things would get worse. I expected Americans to be even meaner than the Japanese. (By Americans, I thought only of white European Americans.) Was I surprised when I discovered that most of my schoolmates were not white European Americans, but people of Asian and mixed ancestry! Suddenly I was a member of a numerical majority. I was no longer teased or bullied. In fact, I found that students of Asian and non-European origin often singled out white European Americans (called *haole* in Hawaiian) for abuse. We even had a 'beat up *haole* day' in school. Given my own experiences in Japan, I empathized somewhat with the white Americans. But I have to admit that I also felt a great sense of relief and an easing of the psychological trauma associated with being Korean in Japan.

"As the years passed, I finished public school in Hawaii. I then went to college in Massachusetts and got a job as a professor in Illinois and then in Michigan. I associated with, and befriended, people from various racial and ethnic groups. My Korean origin became an increasingly less important factor in the way people treated me. There was simply less prejudice and discrimination against Koreans during my adulthood in the United States than in my early years in Japan. I now think of myself less as Japanese or Korean than as American. My ethnic identity has changed over time in response to the significance others have attached to my Korean origin. I now understand what the French philosopher Jean-Paul Sartre meant when he wrote that 'the anti-Semite creates the Jew'" (Sartre, 1965 [1948]: 43).

The details of John Lie's life are unique. However, experiencing a shift in racial or ethnic identity is common. Social contexts, and in particular the nature of a person's relations with members of other racial and ethnic groups, shape and continuously reshape a person's racial and ethnic identity. Change your social context and your racial and ethnic self-conception eventually change too (Miles, 1989; Omi and Winant, 1986).

Consider Italian Canadians. Around 1900, Italian immigrants thought of themselves as people who came from a particular town or perhaps a particular province, such as

Since the 1960s, Indigenous North Americans have begun to vigorously assert themselves culturally and politically, asserting pride in their languages, art, and customs and making legal claims to the lands that were taken from them.

In time, however, an increasingly large number of Indigenous people began to reject the term *Indian*. White settlers and their governments took land from the Indigenous peoples, forced them onto reserves, and thus caused their resentment, anger, and solidarity to grow. Especially since the 1960s, Indigenous North Americans have begun to fight back culturally and politically, asserting pride in their languages, art, and customs and making legal claims to the lands that were taken from them. One aspect of their resistance involved questioning use of the term *Indian*. In Canada, many of them preferred instead to be called Native Canadians, Indigenous peoples, Aboriginal Canadians, or First Nations. These new terms are assertions of new-found pride. Today, many non-Indigenous North Americans accept these new terms out of respect for Indigenous North Americans and in recognition of their neglected rights. New, more or less stable ethnic identities have thus been negotiated as the power struggle between Indigenous peoples and more recent settlers continues. As the social context changed, the negotiation of ethnic identities proceeded apace.

CHOICE VERSUS IMPOSITION

The idea that race and ethnicity are socially constructed does not mean that everyone can always choose their racial or ethnic identity freely. Wide variations occur over time, between societies, and within societies in the degree to which people can exercise such freedom of choice.

The Canadians with the most freedom to choose their ethnic identity are whites whose ancestors arrived in Canada more than two generations ago. For example, identifying as an Irish Canadian no longer has the negative implications it did in, say, 1900. Then, the English Protestant majority typically

Sicily or Calabria. They did not usually think of themselves as Italians. Italy became a unified country only in 1861. A mere 30 years later, many Italian citizens still did not identify with their new Italian nationality. In both Canada and the United States, however, government officials and other residents identified the newcomers as Italians. The designation at first seemed odd to many of the new immigrants. However, over time it stuck. Immigrants from Italy started thinking of themselves as Italian Canadians because others defined them that way. A new ethnic identity was born (Yancey, Ericksen, and Leon, 1979).

As symbolic interactionists emphasize, the development of racial and ethnic labels, and ethnic and racial identities, is typically a process of negotiation. For example, members of a group may have a racial or an ethnic identity, but outsiders may impose a new label on them. Group members then reject, accept, or modify the label. The negotiation between outsiders and insiders eventually results in the crystallization of a new, more or less stable ethnic identity. If the social context changes again, the negotiation process begins anew.

One such case involves the labelling of the Indigenous peoples of North America by European settlers. When Christopher Columbus landed in North America in 1492, he assumed he had reached India. He called the Indigenous peoples "Indians" and the misnomer stuck—not only among European settlers but also among many Indigenous peoples themselves. Indigenous peoples still identified themselves in tribal terms—as Mi'kmaq or Mohawk or Haida—but they typically thought of themselves collectively and *in opposition to European settlers* as Indians. A new identity was thus grafted onto tribal identities because Indigenous peoples confronted a group that had the power to impose a name on them.

A St. Patrick's Day parade in Toronto

symbolic ethnicity A nostalgic allegiance to the culture of the immigrant generation, or that of the old country that is not usually incorporated into everyday behaviour.

racism The belief that a visible characteristic of a group, such as skin colour, indicates group inferiority and justifies discrimination.

institutional racism Bias that is inherent in social institutions and is often not noticed by members of the majority group.

colonialism Involves people from one country invading and taking political, cultural, and economic control over people from another country.

internal colonialism Involves one race or ethnic group subjugating another in the same country. It prevents assimilation by segregating the subordinate group in terms of jobs, housing, and social contacts.

expulsion The forcible removal of a population from a territory claimed by another population.

regarded working-class Irish Catholics as often drunk, inherently lazy, and born superstitious. This strong anti-Irish sentiment, which often erupted into conflict, meant that the Irish found it difficult to escape their ethnic identity even if they wanted to. Since then, however, Irish Canadians have followed the path taken by many other white European groups: They have achieved upward mobility and blended with the majority.

As a result, Irish Canadians no longer find their identity imposed on them. Instead, they can choose whether to march in a St. Patrick's Day parade, enjoy the remarkable contributions of Irish authors to English-language literature and drama, and take pride in the athleticism and artistry of Riverdance. For them, ethnicity is largely a symbolic matter, as it is for the other white European groups that have undergone similar social processes. Herbert Gans defines **symbolic ethnicity** as "a nostalgic allegiance to the culture of the immigrant generation, or that of the old country; a love for and a pride in a tradition that can be felt without having to be incorporated in everyday behaviour" (Gans, 1991: 436).

In contrast, most black Canadians lack the freedom to enjoy symbolic ethnicity. They may well take pride in their cultural heritage. However, their identity as black people is not optional because a considerable number of non-blacks are racists and impose it on them daily. **Racism** is the belief that a visible characteristic of a group, such as skin colour, indicates group inferiority and justifies discrimination. **Institutional racism** is bias that is inherent in social institutions and is often not noticed by members of the majority group (see the Sociology at the Movies feature earlier in this chapter). Surveys show that between 30 percent and 55 percent of Canadians (depending on the wording of the survey question) hold racist views (Henry et al., 2001: 147–51).

In his autobiography, the black militant Malcolm X poignantly noted how racial identity can be imposed on people. He described one of his black Ph.D. professors as "one of these ultra-proper-talking Negroes" who spoke and acted snobbishly. "Do you know what white racists call black Ph.D.s?" asked Malcolm X. "He said something like, 'I believe that I happen not to be aware of that. . . .' And I laid the word down on him, loud: 'Nigger!'" (X, 1965: 284). Malcolm X's point is that it doesn't matter to a racist whether a black person is a professor or a panhandler, a genius or a fool, a saint or a criminal. Where racism is common, racial identities are compulsory and at the forefront of a person's self-identity.

As the contrast between Irish Canadians and black Canadians suggests, then, relations among racial and ethnic groups can take different forms. We next examine how various forms of inequality promote conflict between racial and ethnic groups and thus help to sustain racial and ethnic distinctiveness.

LO³ CONFLICT THEORIES OF RACE AND ETHNIC RELATIONS

COLONIALISM AND INTERNAL COLONIALISM

Conflict theorists argue that one of the most important mechanisms promoting inequality and conflict between racial and ethnic groups is colonialism. **Colonialism** involves people from one country invading another. In the process, the invaders gain control over the native population and change or destroy their culture. The invaders develop the belief that the natives are inherently inferior and they confine them to unskilled jobs. All this serves to create and reinforce ideas about "inherent" racial and ethnic differences.

Once entrenched, colonizers may engage in **internal colonialism**, preventing the assimilation of subordinate racial or ethnic groups by segregating them residentially, occupationally, and in social contacts ranging from friendship to marriage (Blauner, 1972; Hechter, 1974). In Canada, the main victims of colonialism and internal colonialism are Aboriginal peoples, the Québécois, and black people.

CANADA'S ABORIGINAL PEOPLES

The single word that best describes the treatment of Canada's Aboriginal peoples by European immigrants is *expulsion*. **Expulsion** is the forcible removal of a population from a territory claimed by another population.

Expulsion is dramatically illustrated by the plight of the Beothuk, the Aboriginal inhabitants of what is

The Canadian policy of assimilation. In its annual report of 1904, the Department of Indian Affairs published these photographs of Thomas Moore of the Regina Industrial School, "before and after tuition." These images are "a cogent expression of what federal policy had been since Confederation and what it would remain for many decades. It was a policy of assimilation, designed to move Aboriginal communities from their 'savage' state to that of 'civilization' and thus to make in Canada but one community—a non-Aboriginal one" (Milloy, 1999).

today Newfoundland and Labrador. The Beothuk were Algonkian-speaking hunter–gatherers. In the sixteenth century, Europeans used Newfoundland and Labrador as a fishing port, returning to Europe each year after the fishing season. In the seventeenth century, year-round European settlement began. This caused a revolution in the life of the Beothuk because the Europeans viewed them as a nuisance. They offered incentives to Mi'kmaq Indians from Nova Scotia to kill off the Beothuk. The Beothuk population declined and gradually withdrew from European contact.

As European settlement grew in the eighteenth century, the Beothuk were squeezed into the interior. There they competed for scarce resources with fur traders. Eventually the Beothuk were reduced to a small refugee population living off the meagre resources of the Newfoundland and Labrador interior. The expulsion of the Beothuk from their traditional territories because of European colonization led to their eventual extinction. Today, all that remains of the Beothuk aside from their tragic history and a few artifacts

is a statue outside the Newfoundland and Labrador provincial legislature in St. John's.

The story of the Beothuk is an extreme case. However, *all* First Nations had broadly similar experiences. In the eighteenth and nineteenth centuries, as the European settlers' fur trade gave way to the harvesting of timber, minerals, oil, and gas, Aboriginal peoples were shunted aside so the Canadian economy could grow.

At the time, Europeans thought they were "assimilating" the Aboriginal peoples. The 1876 Indian Act underlined the importance of transforming a hunting–gathering people into an agricultural labour force (Menzies, 1999). Sir John A. Macdonald, Canada's first prime minister, spoke of the need "to do away with the tribal system and assimilate the Indian people in all respects with the inhabitants of the Dominion, as speedily as they are fit to change" (quoted in Montgomery, 1965: 13).

Many Aboriginal peoples understood the settlers' actions as an attempt to obliterate their heritage. No other conclusion seems warranted when one considers the collaboration

genocide The intentional extermination of an entire population defined as a race or a people.

between government and various churches in establishing Canada's 130 "residential schools." The government and the churches removed Aboriginal children from their families and forced them to study in boarding schools. There, they were prevented from speaking their languages and practising their religions, and were compelled to adopt the dominant, white European culture, often by means of physical abuse. Sexual abuse of children attending residential schools was also common. Little wonder that the government of Canada has been accused by some Aboriginal peoples of perpetuating cultural genocide (Cardinal, 1977). (**Genocide** is the intentional extermination of an entire population defined as a race or a people.) About a fifth of Aboriginal Canadians now living on reserves attended residential schools in their youth, and about 70 percent of them experienced physical abuse while enrolled (Reading and Wien, 2009: 22).

Adding insult to injury, early historical writing about Canada depicted the First Nations as either irrelevant or evil. Typically, in *The History of the Dominion of Canada*, a book widely used in Canadian schools at the turn of the twentieth century, only five pages were devoted to Aboriginal peoples (Clement, 1897). The book describes them as "cruel,"

"rude," "false," "crafty," "savages," and "ferocious villains" who plotted against the Europeans with "fiendish ingenuity." Canadian schoolbooks continued to portray Aboriginal peoples in pretty much this way until the mid-twentieth century.

Throughout North America, the confrontation with European culture undermined the way of life of the Aboriginal peoples. Because of internal colonialism and, in particular, expulsion from their traditional lands, Canada's First Nations were prevented from practising their traditional ways and from assimilating into the larger society. Most of them languished on reserves and, more recently, in urban slums. There they experienced extraordinarily high rates of unemployment, poverty, ill health, and violence (see Table 7.2).

It is a credit to Canada's First Nations that they have made significant progress in recent decades despite the many obstacles just listed. In 1950, only about 200 businesses were owned or operated by members of First Nations in Canada. Today, the figure is more than 30 000. British Columbia's first Aboriginal lawyer was called to the bar in 1962. Today, there are about 200 Aboriginal lawyers in the province. Nearly half of Aboriginal Canadians between the ages of 25 and 64 have a postsecondary qualification, and more than 13 percent of Aboriginal women between the ages of 25 and 44 have a university degree. While these figures are still significantly

TABLE 7.2 Relative Well-Being of Aboriginal Peoples in Canada and African Americans

Measure of Well-Being	Aboriginal Peoples in Canada	African Americans
Unemployment rate	14%	11%
Unemployment rate vs. the national rate	2.1 times	1.9 times
Median income	$22 344	$23 738
Median income vs. the national average	60%	74%
Incarceration rate (per 100 000 population)	1400	2207
Incarceration rate vs. the national rate	10 times	3 times
Homicide rate (per 100 000 population)	8.8	17.3
Homicide rate vs. the national rate	6.1 times	3.7 times
Infant mortality rate (per 1000 live births)	11.7	12.4
Infant mortality rate vs. the national rate	2.3 times	2 times
Life expectancy (in years)	72.8	74.9
Life expectancy vs. the national average	91%	95%
Dropout rate*	23%	8%
Dropout rate vs. the national average	2.7 times	1.1 times

*20- to 24-year-olds without a high school diploma, and not in school.

Source: From Scott Gilmore, "Out of sight, out of mind." http://www.macleans.ca/news/canada/out-of-sight-out-of-mind-2/ (retrieved 2 August, 2015). *Originally published in Maclean's™ magazine on Feb. 2, 2015. Used with permission of Rogers Media Inc. All rights reserved.*

below the comparable figures for non-Aboriginals, they have skyrocketed since 2001, especially for women; while there were just a few hundred Aboriginal Canadians in university in the 1970s, today there are about 30 000, two-thirds of them women. Moreover, while non-Aboriginal Canadians and Aboriginal men have seen their participation rate in the paid labour market decline since the 2008-09 recession, Aboriginal women have seen their participation rate increase.

Employment growth has been especially robust in high-paying, knowledge-based sectors including finance, education, and professional services. Successful Indigenous Canadians can now be found in all walks of life—among musicians (Susan Aglukark, Tanya Tagaq Gillis, A Tribe Called Red), jurists (Justice Murray Sinclair of Manitoba), athletes (Carey Price, star goalie of the Montreal Canadiens), writers (Joseph Boyden, Thomas King), filmmakers (Alanis Obomsawin), politicians (Leona Aglukkaq, Shelly Glover), and so on (Denis, 2016; Griner, 2013; The Law Society of British Columbia, 2015; Mendelson, 2006; Statistics Canada, 2013f; TD Economics, 2015).

Especially since the 1960s, Canada's First Nations have periodically demonstrated in protest against the conditions of their existence. The most recent of these protests, the "Idle No More" movement, erupted in late 2012, after the federal government, eager to see new oil and gas pipelines built from Alberta to the British Columbia coast, weakened the consultation and approval process for construction along Canada's waterways. Such pipeline construction increases the risk of serious environmental damage, and some of the affected territory is on Native reserves. First Nations demonstrations against the new legislation began in Saskatchewan, and protesters later began blocking rail lines in British Columbia, Ontario, and Quebec. The chief of a reserve in northern Ontario went on a hunger strike to force a meeting with the prime minister and publicize the plight of her people. The latest wave of Aboriginal protest raises once again the question of whether and in what form non-Aboriginal Canadians should take responsibility for past and current injustices.

> **conquest** The forcible capture of land and the economic and political domination of its inhabitants.

THE QUÉBÉCOIS

In Canada, colonialism and internal colonialism involved not just expulsion but also **conquest**, the forcible capture of land and the economic and political domination

Carey Price, star goalie of the Montreal Canadiens. His mother is former chief of the Ulkatcho First Nation in British Columbia.

Francois Lacasse/NHLI/Getty Images

of its inhabitants. For example, as part of their centuries-long struggle to control North America, the English conquered New France and its 60 000 Canadien settlers in 1759. They thereby created a system of ethnic stratification that remained in place for more than 200 years and became a major source of political conflict (McRoberts, 1988).

The British recognized that any attempt to impose their language, religion, laws, and institutions on the former French colony could result in unacceptably high levels of resistance and conflict. Therefore, they tried to accommodate farmers and the Catholic clergy by reinforcing their rights and privileges. The British believed this would win the allegiance of these two Canadien groups, who would in turn help to build loyalty to Britain among the population as a whole. In contrast, the British undermined the rights and privileges of Canadien merchants engaged mainly in the fur trade. They took over virtually all large-scale commerce. In this manner, big business became a British domain. Agriculture, religion, and politics remained the province of the French. This pattern of ethnic stratification remained intact for two centuries.

True, by 1950 most farmers had been transformed into urban industrial workers. Some Québécois had become physicians, lawyers, and members of the "new middle class" of administrators, technicians, scientists, and intellectuals. However, the upper reaches of the stratification system remained overwhelmingly populated by people of British origin. Social separation reinforced economic segregation. The French and the British tended to speak different languages, live in different towns and neighbourhoods, interact occasionally, befriend one another infrequently, and intermarry rarely. The novel that became emblematic of the social relations between French and English in Quebec is entitled *Two Solitudes* (MacLennan, 1945).

Apart from its rigid system of ethnic stratification, Quebec in the middle of the twentieth century was remarkable because of its undeveloped government services. Health, education, and welfare were largely controlled by the Catholic Church. Intervention of the government in economic matters was almost unknown. Because of this political backwardness, members of Quebec's new middle class, together with blue-collar workers, began campaigning to modernize the provincial political system in the late 1940s. They pressed for more liberal labour laws that would recognize the right of all workers to form unions and to strike. They wanted state control over education and a new curriculum that stressed the natural and social sciences rather than the classical languages and catechism. They desired a government that would supply a wide range of social services to the population. They demanded that the state provide better infrastructure for economic development and assist francophone entrepreneurs in expanding their businesses. The partial realization of these aims in the 1960s came to be known as the Quiet Revolution.

However, the modernization of the Quebec state failed to resolve four issues:

1. *The potential demographic decline of the Québécois.* By 1981, Québécois women were giving birth to fewer children on average than women in any other province. In fact, they were having fewer than the 2.1 children women must bear on average to ensure that the size of the population does not decline (Romaniuc, 1984: 14–18). Noticing this trend in the 1970s, many Québécois felt they were becoming an endangered species.

2. *The assimilation of immigrants into English culture.* Fears of demographic decline were reinforced by the preference of most new immigrants to have their children educated in English-language schools. Together with the falling birth rate, this development threatened to diminish the size—and therefore, potentially, the power—of Quebec's francophone population.

3. *Persistent ethnic stratification.* The Quiet Revolution helped create many thousands of jobs for highly educated francophones—but almost exclusively in the government bureaucracy, the educational system, and new Crown corporations, such as Hydro-Québec. It became apparent in the 1970s that management positions in the private sector remained the preserve of English-origin Canadians.

4. *The continued use of English as the language of private industry.* English remained the language of choice in the private sector because the largest and technologically most advanced businesses were controlled by

Réné Levesque (1922–87), the founder of the Parti Québécois and the twenty-third premier of Quebec

The Canadian Press/Doug Ball

English Canadians and Americans. This situation was felt particularly keenly when the expansion of the state sector, and therefore the upward mobility of the francophone new middle class, slowed in the 1970s.

Because of the issues just listed, many Québécois felt that the survival and prosperity of their community required active state intervention in non-francophone institutions. For example, many Québécois came to believe that most shares of banks, trust companies, and insurance firms should be held in Quebec and that these financial institutions should be obliged to reinvest their profits in the province. They argued that the state should increase its role as economic planner and initiator of development and should forbid foreign ownership of cultural enterprises. Finally, the Québécois increasingly demanded compulsory French-language education for the children of most immigrants, obligatory use of French among private-sector managers, and French-only signs in public places.

Most Québécois regarded these proposals as the only means by which their community could survive and attain equality with other groups. Moreover, because the Quebec state did not have the legal authority to enact some of the proposed changes, they felt that the province ought to negotiate broader constitutional powers with the federal government. A large minority of Québécois went a step further. They became convinced that Quebec ought to become a politically sovereign nation, albeit a nation economically associated with Canada.

The pro-independence Parti Québécois won the provincial election in 1976. In 1980, it held a referendum to see whether Quebecers favoured "sovereignty association." Nearly 60 percent voted "no." A second referendum was held in 1995. This time, the forces opposed to sovereignty association won by the narrowest of margins—about 1 percent. The sovereignty question then subsided, and the Parti Québécois lost provincial elections in 2003, 2007, and 2008. It promised yet another referendum but failed to deliver when it regained power from 2012–14. Thus, in the early twenty-first century, Canada's future is still uncertain because of the economic, social, and cultural segregation of the Québécois from English Canada that is a legacy of conquest.

BLACK CANADIANS

We have seen that colonialism and internal colonialism, whether accomplished by expulsion or conquest, create big barriers to assimilation that can endure for centuries. A third form of colonial action—slavery—creates similar barriers. **Slavery** is the ownership and control of people.

By about 1800, 24 million Africans had been captured and placed on slave ships headed to North, Central, and South America. Because of violence, disease, and shipwreck, fewer than half survived the passage. Black slaves were bought and sold in Canada until at least the 1820s. Only in 1833, when the British government banned slavery throughout the British Empire, did the practice become illegal in all of what is now Canada. Slavery was abolished in the United States 30 years later.

slavery The ownership and control of people.

It is true that the extent of slavery in Canada paled in comparison with its widespread use in the United States, where tobacco and cotton production depended entirely on the work of dirt-cheap black labour. It is also true that for decades Canada served as the terminus of the "underground railway," a network that smuggled escaped slaves out of the United States to freedom in Canada. As Martin Luther King, leader of the American civil rights movement in the 1950s and 1960s, said in Toronto in 1967:

Deep in our history of struggle for freedom Canada was the North Star. The Negro slave knew that far to the north a land existed where a fugitive slave, if he survived the horrors of the journey, could find freedom. The legendary underground railroad started in the south and ended in Canada. Our spirituals, now so widely admired around the world, were often codes. We sang of "heaven" that awaited us, and the slave masters listened in innocence, not realizing that we were not speaking of the hereafter. Heaven was the word for Canada and the Negro sang of the hope that his escape on the underground

TO BE SOLD,

A BLACK WOMAN, named PEGGY, aged about forty years ; and a Black boy her son, named JUPITER, aged about fifteen years, both of them the property of the Subscriber.

The Woman is a tolerable Cook and washer woman and perfectly understands making Soap and Candles.

The Boy is tall and strong of his age, and has been employed in Country business, but brought up principally as a House Servant—They are each of them Servants for life. The Price for the Woman is one hundred and fifty Dollars—for the Boy two hundred Dollars, payable in three years with Interest from the day of Sale and to be properly secured by Bond &c.—But one fourth less will be taken in ready Money.

PETER RUSSELL.

York, Feb. 10th 1806.

Upper Canada Gazette, February 10, 1806

Many distinguished people were slave owners, including Peter Russell, who held positions in the executive and legislative councils and became administrator of Upper Canada.

railroad would carry him there. One of our spirituals, "Follow the Drinking Gourd," in its disguised lyrics contained directions for escape. The gourd was the big dipper, and the North Star to which its handle pointed gave the celestial map that directed the flight to the Canadian border.

—Martin Luther King. 1967.*

What King neglected to mention is that after the American Civil War (1861–65), the Canadian government reversed its practice of allowing black settlement. Government policy required the rejection of most immigration applications by black people. This policy reflected

* Source: *Conscience for Change*. Toronto: CBC Learning Systems. Reprinted by arrangement with The Heirs to the Estate of Martin Luther King Jr., c/o Writers House as agent for the proprietor New York, NY. © 1967 Dr. Martin Luther King, Jr. © renewed 1995 Coretta Scott King.

Jacob Lawrence. The Migration of the Negro, Panel No. 57. 1940–1941. The Phillips Collection, Washington DC. © 2016 The Jacob and Gwendolyn Lawrence Foundation, Seattle / SODRAC 2016.

Jacob Lawrence's *The Great Migration* series of paintings illustrates the mass exodus of black Americans from the south to the north in search of a better life. Many former slaves came to Canada by the "underground railway," a network of blacks and whites who opposed slavery. The former slaves settled mainly in southern Ontario after Lieutenant Governor John Graves Simcoe signed the Upper Canadian Act Against Slavery in 1793.

a deeply felt prejudice on the part of the Canadian population that persisted throughout the twentieth century (Sissing, 1996). Moreover, social relations between black Canadians and the white European majority were anything but intimate and based on equality. Until the mid-twentieth century, blacks tended to do unskilled labour and be residentially and socially segregated—for example, in the Halifax community of Africville, established around 1850 by runaway American slaves (Clairmont and Magill, 1999).

Canadian immigration policy was liberalized in the 1960s. Racial and ethnic restrictions were removed. Immigrants were now admitted on the basis of their potential economic contribution to Canada, their close family ties with Canadians, or their refugee status (see Table 7.3). As a result, Canada became a much more racially and ethnically diverse society (see Figure 7.2). Today, about three-quarters of Canadian immigrants are members of visible-minority groups, most of them from Africa, Asia, and South and Central America. Among them, according to the 2011 *National Household Survey*, are 946 000 blacks. They form Canada's third-largest visible minority (after Chinese and East Indians), representing 2.9 percent of the population and nearly one-sixth of the visible-minority population (see Table 7.4).

With the influx of new immigrants in recent decades, the social standing of Canada's black community has improved significantly. Many new immigrants had completed postsecondary education before their arrival. Others attended colleges and universities in Canada. Nonetheless, black Canadians still tend to interact little with white Canadians of European descent, especially in their intimate relations, and they still tend to live in different neighbourhoods. Like the aftermath of expulsion and conquest, the aftermath of slavery—prejudice, discrimination, disadvantage, and segregation—continues to act as a barrier to assimilation (see the Sociology at the Movies feature earlier in this chapter).

TABLE 7.3	Immigrants by Category, Canada, 2013	
Category	**Number**	**Percentage**
Family class	79 684	30.8
Economic immigrants	148 181	57.2
Refugees	24 049	9.3
Other	7 039	2.7
Total	258 953	100.0

Source: Reproduced by permission of Citizenship and Immigration Canada, *Facts and Figures 2013—Immigration Overview: Permanent Residents.* http://www.cic.gc.ca/english/resources/statistics/facts2013/permanent/02.asp.

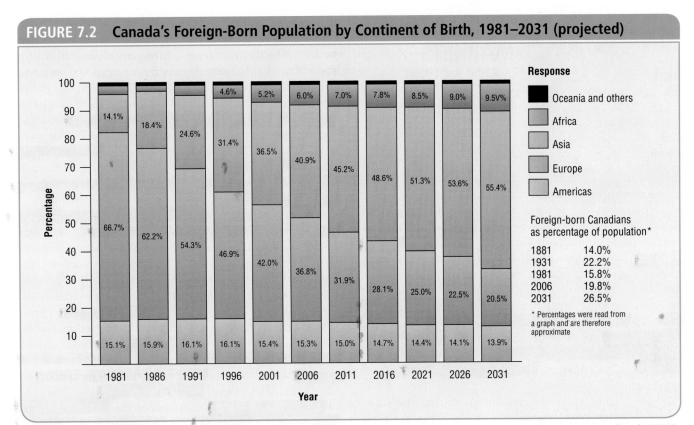

FIGURE 7.2 Canada's Foreign-Born Population by Continent of Birth, 1981–2031 (projected)

Source: Statistics Canada, 2010c. "Projections of the Diversity of the Canadian Population, 2006 to 2031," 91-551-XIE 2010001, 2006 to 2031. Released March 9, 2010.

TABLE 7.4 Population by Visible-Minority Group, Canada, 2006 and 2031 (projected)

Group	2006		2031	
	Thousands	Percentage	Thousands	Percentage
South Asian	1 320	4.1	3 640	8.7
Chinese	1 269	3.9	2 714	6.4
Black	815	2.5	1 809	4.3
Filipino	427	1.3	1 020	2.4
Latin American	317	1.0	733	1.7
Arab	276	0.8	930	2.2
Southeast Asian	250	0.8	449	1.1
West Asian	164	0.5	523	1.2
Korean	148	0.5	407	1.0
Japanese	85	0.3	142	0.3
Other	213	0.7	489	1.2
Subtotal	5 285	16.3	12 855	30.6
Rest of population	27 237	83.7	29 222	69.4
Total	32 522	100.0	42 078	100.0

Source: Statistics Canada, 2010c. "Projections of the Diversity of the Canadian Population, 2006 to 2031," 91-551-XIE 2010001, 2006 to 2031. Released March 9, 2010.

split labour market Exists where low-wage workers of one race and high-wage workers of another race compete for the same jobs. In that situation, high-wage workers are likely to resent the presence of low-wage competitors. Conflict is bound to result and racist attitudes to develop or become reinforced.

SPLIT LABOUR MARKETS AND ASIAN CANADIANS

We have seen how the theory of colonialism and internal colonialism explains the persistence of inequality and segregation among racial and ethnic groups. A second theory that focuses on the social-structural barriers to assimilation is the theory of the **split labour market**, first proposed by sociologist Edna Bonacich (1972). Bonacich's theory explains why racial identities are reinforced by certain labour market conditions. In brief, she argues that where low-wage workers of one race and high-wage workers of another race compete for the same jobs, high-wage workers are likely to resent the presence of low-wage competitors and conflict is bound to result. Consequently, racist attitudes develop or are reinforced.

Resentment certainly crystallized during the early years of Asian immigration in Canada. Chinese, then Japanese, and later Sikhs were allowed into Canada from about the 1850s to the early 1920s for one reason: to provide scarce services and cheap labour in the booming West. Chinese-owned restaurants, grocery stores, laundries, and import businesses dotted the West, especially British Columbia, by the early twentieth century (Li, 1998; Whitaker, 1987). Numerically more important, however, were the Asian labourers who worked in lumbering, mining, and railway construction. For example, 15 000 Chinese men were allowed into Canada to complete construction of the final and most difficult section of the Canadian Pacific Railway (CPR), which involved blasting tunnels and laying rail along dangerous Rocky Mountain passes. The Chinese were paid half the wages of white workers. It is said that they "worked like horses." It is also said that they "dropped like flies" because of exposure, disease, malnutrition, and explosions. Three Chinese workers died for every kilometre of track laid. Asian immigration in general was widely viewed as a threat to cherished British values and institutions, an evil to be endured only as long as absolutely necessary. Therefore, once the CPR was completed in 1885, the Chinese were no longer welcome in British Columbia. A prohibitively expensive "head tax" equal to two months' wages was placed on each Chinese immigrant. The tax was increased tenfold in 1903. In 1923, Chinese immigration was banned altogether. During the Great Depression, more than 28 000 Chinese were deported because of high unemployment. Asian immigration did not resume on a large scale until the 1960s, when racial criteria were finally removed from Canadian immigration regulations.

Underlying European Canadian animosity against Asian immigration was a split labour market. The fact that Asian immigrants were willing to work for much lower wages than European Canadians fuelled deep resentment among European Canadians, especially when the labour market was flooded with far too many job seekers. European Canadians formed "exclusion leagues" to pressure the government to restrict Asian immigration, and on occasion they even staged anti-Asian riots. Such actions solidified racial identities among both the rioters and the victims of the riots and made assimilation impossible.

In sum, the theory of split labour markets, like the theory of internal colonialism, emphasizes the social-structural roots of race and ethnicity. The groups that have had most trouble assimilating into the British values and institutions that dominate Canadian society are those that were subjected to expulsion from their native lands, conquest, slavery, and split labour markets. These circumstances have

Head Tax Certificate: In an example of legislated racism, immigrants from China were required by law to pay a "head tax" to enter Canada between 1885 and 1923. The tax began at $50 and rose as high as $500.

National Archives of Canada/C149236

left a legacy of racism that has created social-structural impediments to assimilation, such as forced segregation in low-status jobs and low-income neighbourhoods.

LO⁴ SOME ADVANTAGES OF ETHNICITY

Conflict theories emphasize how social forces outside a racial or an ethnic group create inequality and bind group members together, preventing their assimilation into the dominant values and institutions of society. They focus on the disadvantages of race and ethnicity. Moreover, they deal only with the most disadvantaged minorities. The theories have less to say about the internal conditions that promote group cohesion and in particular about the value of group membership. They do not help us understand why some European Canadians of Greek or German or Irish origin continue to participate in the life of their ethnic communities, even if their families have been in the country for more than two or three generations.

High levels of immigration renew racial and ethnic communities by providing them with new members who are familiar with ancestral languages and customs. Part of the reason that ethnic communities remain vibrant in Canada is that immigration continues at a rapid pace; only Australia and Israel have a larger percentage of immigrants than Canada does. However, as we have seen, little of Canada's current immigration is composed of white Europeans. Immigration levels do not explain the persistence of ethnic identity among members of some white ethnic groups of European origin.

Among white European groups, three main factors enhance the value of continued ethnic group membership:

1. *Ethnic group membership can have economic advantages.* The economic advantages of ethnicity are most apparent for immigrants, who often lack extensive social contacts and fluency in English or French. They commonly rely on members of their ethnic group to help them find jobs and housing. In this way, immigrant communities become tightly knit. However, some economic advantages extend into the third generation and beyond. For example, community solidarity is an important resource for "ethnic entrepreneurs." These are businesspeople who operate largely within their ethnic community. They draw on their community for customers, suppliers, employees, and credit, and they may be linked economically to the homeland as importers and exporters. They often pass on their businesses to their children, who in turn can pass the businesses on to the next generation. In this way, strong economic incentives encourage some people to remain ethnic group members, even beyond

the immigrant generation (Light, 1991; Portes and Manning, 1991).

2. *Ethnic group membership can be politically useful.* Consider, for instance, the way some Canadians reacted to the rise of separatism in Quebec in the 1960s. To bridge the growing divide between francophone Quebec and the rest of the country, the federal government under Pierre Trudeau's Liberals had promoted a policy of bilingualism. French and English were made official languages. This policy meant that federal government services would be made available in both languages and instruction in French would be encouraged in English schools.

Members of some ethnic groups, such as people of Ukrainian origin in western Canada, felt neglected by this turn of events. They saw no reason that the French should be accorded special status and wanted a share of the resources available for promoting ethnic languages and cultures. As a result, the Trudeau government proclaimed a new policy of multiculturalism in 1971. Federal funds became available for the promotion of Ukrainian and all other ethnic cultures in Canada. This entire episode of Canadian ethnic history bolstered western support for the Liberal Party and softened western opposition to bilingualism. Moreover, it helped to stimulate ethnic culture and ethnic identification throughout the country. We thus see that ethnicity can be a political tool for achieving increased access to resources.

3. *Ethnic group membership tends to persist because of the emotional support it provides.* Like economic benefits, the emotional advantages of ethnicity are most

Courtesy of the Pier 21 Society/Library and Archives Canada/PA-111579

Pier 21 is located at 1055 Marginal Road, Halifax, Nova Scotia. Many immigrants to Canada were processed there. It opened its doors in 1928. As the era of ocean travel was coming to an end in March 1971, the Immigration Service left Pier 21.

transnational communities Communities whose boundaries extend between or among countries.

pluralism The retention of racial and ethnic culture combined with equal access to basic social resources.

apparent in immigrant communities. Speaking the ethnic language and sharing other elements of one's native culture are valuable sources of comfort in an alien environment. Even beyond the second generation, however, ethnic group membership can perform significant emotional functions. For example, some ethnic groups have experienced unusually high levels of prejudice and discrimination involving expulsion or attempted genocide. For people who belong to such groups, the resulting trauma is so severe it can be transmitted for several generations. In such cases, ethnic group membership offers security in a world still seen as hostile long after the threat of territorial loss or annihilation has disappeared (Bar-On, 1999). Ethnic group membership also offers emotional support beyond the second generation by providing a sense of rootedness. Especially in a highly mobile, urbanized, technological, and bureaucratic society such as ours, ties to an ethnic community can be an important source of stability and security (Isajiw, 1978).

Retaining ethnic ties beyond the second generation has never been easier. Inexpensive international communication and travel allow ethnic group members to maintain strong ties to their ancestral homeland in a way that was impossible in earlier times. Immigration used to involve cutting all or most ties to a country of origin because of the high cost of travel and long-distance telephone calls. Lack of communication encouraged assimilation in people's newly adopted countries.

Today, however, ties to the ancestral communities are often maintained in ways that sustain ethnic culture. For example, about 25 000 Jews have immigrated from the former Soviet Union to Canada since the early 1970s, settling mainly in Toronto. They frequently visit relatives in the former Soviet Union and Israel, speak with them on the phone, and use the Internet to exchange e-mail with them. They also receive Russian-language radio and TV broadcasts, act as conduits for foreign investment, and send money to relatives abroad (Brym, 2001; Brym with Ryvkina, 1994; Markowitz, 1993). This sort of intimate and ongoing connection with the motherland is typical of most recent immigrant communities in North America. Thanks to inexpensive international travel and communication, some ethnic groups have become **transnational communities** whose boundaries extend between or among countries.

In sum, ethnicity remains a vibrant force in Canadian society for a variety of reasons. Even some white Canadians whose families settled in this country more than two generations ago have reason to identify with

their ethnic group. Bearing this in mind, what is the likely future of race and ethnic relations in Canada? We conclude by offering some tentative answers to that question.

LO⁵ THE FUTURE OF RACE AND ETHNICITY IN CANADA

The world comprises more than 200 countries and more than 5000 ethnic and racial groups. As a result, no country is ethnically and racially homogeneous and in many countries, including Canada, the largest ethnic group forms less than half of the population (see Figure 7.3 and Table 7.5). Canada's British roots remain important. Our parliamentary democracy is based on the British model. The Queen's representative, the governor general, is our head of state. We still celebrate Queen Victoria's birthday (May 24). English is the country's predominant language, with more than 56 percent of Canadians over the age of 14 claiming it as their mother tongue. Our French patrimony is also strong, especially of course in Quebec. Nationwide, 22 percent of Canadians claim French as their mother tongue (Statistics Canada, 2010b). Nonetheless, Canada is one of the most racially and ethnically heterogeneous societies, and it will become still more diverse in coming decades (Pendakur, 2000).

As racial and ethnic diversity has increased, Canadian ethnic and race relations have changed. Two hundred years ago, Canada was a society based on expulsion, conquest, slavery, and segregation. Today, we are a society based on segregation, **pluralism**, and assimilation—pluralism being understood as the retention of racial and ethnic culture combined with equal access to basic social resources. On a scale of tolerance, Canada has come a long way in the past 200 years (see Figure 7.4).

Canada is a tolerant land compared with other countries, too. In the late twentieth and early twenty-first centuries, racial and ethnic tensions in some parts of the world erupted into wars of secession and attempted genocide. In the 1990s, conflict among Croats, Serbs, and other ethnic groups tore Yugoslavia apart. Russia fought two bloody wars against its Chechen ethnic minority. In Rwanda, Hutu militia and soldiers massacred many thousands of Tutsi civilians. A few years later, Tutsi soldiers massacred many thousands of Hutu civilians. Comparing Canada with countries that are not rich, stable, and postindustrial may seem to stack the deck in favour of concluding that Canada is a relatively tolerant society. However, even when we compare Canada with other rich, stable, postindustrial countries, it seems relatively tolerant by most measures. For example, a survey of 44 countries found

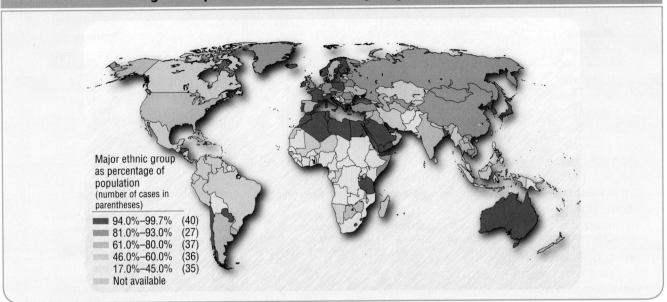

Major ethnic group as percentage of population (number of cases in parentheses)

94.0%–99.7%	(40)
81.0%–93.0%	(27)
61.0%–80.0%	(37)
46.0%–60.0%	(36)
17.0%–45.0%	(35)
Not available	

Sources: "Ethnic Groups in the World," *Scientific American*. Found at http://www.sciam.com/1998/0998issue/0998numbers.html (December 4, 2001). CIA *World Factbook 2001*. Found at http://www.cia.gov/cia/publications/factbook/ (January 10, 2002).

that "only in Canada does a strong majority of the population (77 percent) have a positive view of immigrants." Far behind in second place came the United States, at 49 percent (Pew Research Center, 2002).

Growing tolerance does not imply the absence of ethnic and racial discrimination and stratification (see the Sociology on the Tube feature in this chapter). Although Canada is becoming less ethnically and racially stratified

TABLE 7.5   Canada's 25 Largest Ethnic Groups, 2011

1	Canadian	10 563 805	14	Filipino	662 600
2	English	6 509 500	15	British Isles	576 030
3	French	5 065 690	16	Russian	550 520
4	Scottish	4 714 970	17	Welsh	458 705
5	Irish	4 544 870	18	Norwegian	452 705
6	German	3 203 330	19	Métis	447 655
7	Italian	1 488 425	20	Portuguese	429 850
8	Chinese	1 487 580	21	American	372 575
9	First Nations (North American Indian)	1 369 115	22	Spanish	368 305
10	Ukrainian	1 251 170	23	Swedish	341 845
11	East Indian	1 165 145	24	Hungarian	316 765
12	Dutch	1 067 245	25	Jewish	309 650
13	Polish	1 010 705			

Note: Respondents were allowed to select more than one ethnic identity, so the number of responses is larger than the number of Canadians.

Source: Statistics Canada. 2013g. "Ethnic Origin (264), Single and Multiple Ethnic Origin Responses (3), Generation Status (4), Age Groups (10) and Sex (3) for the Population in Private Households of Canada, Provinces, Territories, Census Metropolitan Areas and Census Agglomerations," *2011 National Household Survey*.

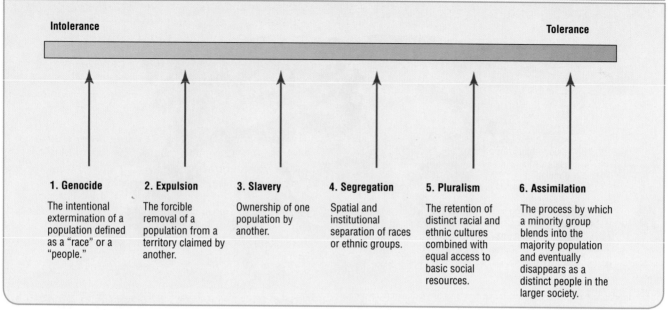

FIGURE 7.4   Six Degrees of Separation: Types of Ethnic and Racial Group Relations

Intolerance   Tolerance

1. Genocide

The intentional extermination of a population defined as a "race" or a "people."

2. Expulsion

The forcible removal of a population from a territory claimed by another.

3. Slavery

Ownership of one population by another.

4. Segregation

Spatial and institutional separation of races or ethnic groups.

5. Pluralism

The retention of distinct racial and ethnic cultures combined with equal access to basic social resources.

6. Assimilation

The process by which a minority group blends into the majority population and eventually disappears as a distinct people in the larger society.

Source: From KORNBLUM. *Sociology in a Changing World*, 4E. © 1997 South-Western, a part of Cengage Learning, Inc. Reproduced by permission. www.cengage.com/permissions

from one census to the next, serious problems remain (Lautard and Guppy, 2011). For one thing, Aboriginal Canadians are making insufficiently rapid progress in their efforts to raise their educational and economic standing. Most of them remain clustered at the bottom of Canada's socioeconomic hierarchy. For another, the upward mobility of immigrants, three-quarters of whom are members of visible-minority groups, has slowed since the early 1990s, as discussed earlier. Therefore, if present trends continue, Canada's mosaic will continue to be stratified, mainly along racial lines. Unless dramatic changes occur, a few groups will continue to enjoy less wealth, income, education, good housing, health care, and other social rewards than other Canadians do.

SOCIOLOGY ON THE TUBE

Little Mosque on the Prairie

Little Mosque on the Prairie, a Canadian comedy series that ran from 2007 to 2012, followed the everyday lives of people in the fictional town of Mercy, Saskatchewan. It challenged common misperceptions about Muslims and depicted them as essentially no different from anyone else.

Converts to any religion are sometimes more orthodox than those born into it. Highly motivated to convert in the first place, and sometimes feeling the need to prove their faith to their co-religionists by displays of zeal, converts can become, as the saying goes, "more papist than the Pope." In Season 1 of *Little Mosque on the Prairie*, we met such a convert, a young man by the name of Marlon. After converting, Marlon donned the *taqiya* (short round cap) and the *kurta* (long loose shirt). He questioned and denounced any Muslim who was not 100 percent committed to the most traditional and antiquated precept of the faith. Before long, he had established himself as a nuisance to the lifelong Muslims in Mercy. Fed up, they plotted ways to show Marlon how illiberal and annoying he had become. Through humour, the episode served to undermine the stereotype that most Muslims are extreme in their beliefs.

Throughout the series, relations between Muslims and non-Muslims in Mercy were, for the most part, harmonious. For instance, there was practically no response from Mercy's non-Muslim community when Marlon decided to convert. In the first season of *Little Mosque on the Prairie*, the mosque's *imam*, Amaar, became the best friend of Duncan, the town's Anglican minister.

Courtesy of WestWind Pictures

Some critics said that *Little Mosque on the Prairie* papered over serious problems in the lives of Canadian Muslims. They have a point. According to one survey, 37 percent of Canadians said they have a negative impression of Islam and 10 percent said they have neither a positive nor a negative impression (Trudeau Foundation, 2006). Canadian Muslims are mainly immigrants from Pakistan and the Middle East. They often experience lower rates of upward mobility than immigrants did between the end of World War II and the 1980s. Such issues were not raised in *Little Mosque on the Prairie*.

On the other hand, the situation is decidedly better in Canada than in other Western countries. Canadian Muslims form the most highly educated community of Muslims in the world. In France and in England, Muslim immigrants are on the whole much worse off economically and in terms of mobility prospects than they are in Canada. Especially in France, they are prevented from certain public displays of their religious heritage. In both European countries, Muslims have occasionally rioted to protest the conditions of their existence,

something that Canada has never seen. Not surprisingly in this context, Muslims in France and England more frequently adopt extremist attitudes than they do in Canada.

Similarly, in the United States, antipathy to Muslims is more widespread than it is in Canada. Some Americans have sought to prevent the construction of mosques, in at least one case even going so far as to set fire to a construction site. In 2011, the American television station TLC launched a reality show called *All-American Muslim* documenting the lives of Muslims outside Detroit. However, after a member of the Christian Florida Family Association objected that the show was pro-Muslim propaganda, the show lost sponsors (including Lowes, the home improvement chain). It was cancelled in its first season (Freedman, 2011).

Canadians' reception of *Little Mosque on the Prairie* was a lot warmer. It became one of the most popular Canadian comedy series ever aired. In 2007, it was nominated for a host of prizes by the Directors Guild of Canada, the Gemini Awards, and the Canadian Comedy Awards, and it won the Gemini's Canada Award for media representation of multiculturalism. So, despite ignoring unpleasant realities that require the attention of all Canadians, *Little Mosque on the Prairie* accurately reflected the fact that Muslims in Canada are on the whole better off and more respected than are their co-religionists in other Western countries.

Critical Thinking Question

How do you account for the different reception of *Little Mosque on the Prairie* in Canada and *All-American Muslim* in the United States? Consider the causes and consequences of different immigration and military policies in the two countries.

READY TO STUDY?

IN THE BOOK, YOU CAN:

❏ Tear out the chapter review card at the back of the book to have a summary of the chapter and key terms handy.

ONLINE YOU CAN:

❏ Work through key concepts with a Guided Learning Question.

❏ Prepare for tests with quizzes.

❏ Review the key terms with flash cards.

❏ Explore practical examples of chapter concepts with Connect a Concept exercises.

GO TO NELSON.COM/STUDENT TO ACCESS THESE DIGITAL RESOURCES.

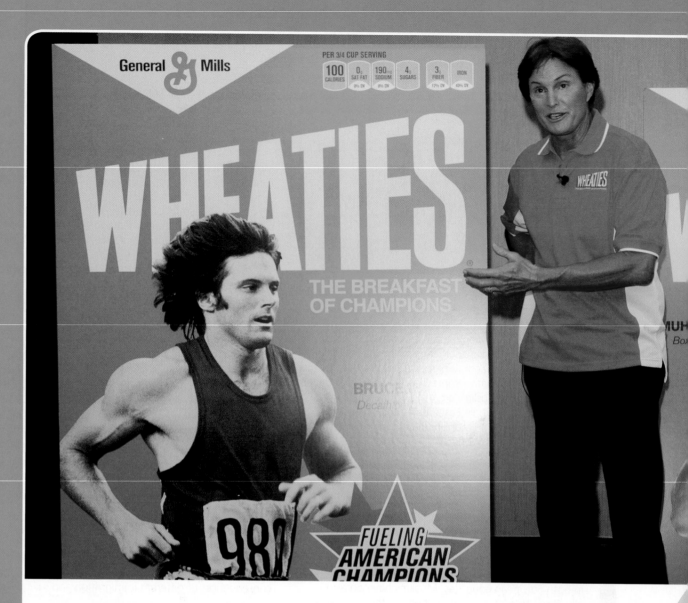

8
Sexualities and Genders

VANITY FAIR

"Call me Caitlyn"

By BUZZ BISSINGER *Photos by* ANNIE LEIBOVITZ

Bruce Jenner on cereal box: Suntzulynn for LE/Splash News/Newscom; Caitlyn Jenner on magazine cover: *Vanity Fair*/ZUMA Press/Newscom

LEARNING OBJECTIVES

In this chapter, you will learn to

LO 1 Distinguish biologically determined sex from socially determined gender.

LO 2 Appreciate that gender is shaped largely by the way parents raise children, teachers interact with pupils, and the mass media portray ideal body images.

LO 3 Identify the social forces pushing people toward heterosexuality.

LO 4 Recognize that the social distinction between men and women serves as an important basis of inequality in the family and the workplace.

LO 5 Explain how male aggression against women is rooted in gender inequality.

LO 6 Outline social policies that could lower the level of inequality between women and men.

LO 1 SEX, INTERSEX, GENDER, TRANSGENDER

SEX AND INTERSEX

At the 1976 Montreal Olympics, Bruce Jenner set a new world record in the decathlon, vaulting to fame as the world's greatest athlete. His picture appeared on a cereal box, and in the following decades he acted in a series of TV shows and became a successful race car driver. He got married for the first time in 1972, for the second time in 1981, and for the third time in 1991. His third wife was Kris Kardashian. Beginning in 2007, they appeared in the reality TV show, *Keeping Up with the Kardashians*.

Jenner and Kardashian legally divorced in March 2015. A month later, Jenner announced in a TV interview that, since he was a teenager, he had been upset with the sex and gender he had been assigned at birth. He said that, in the 80s, he had cross-dressed and taken hormone replacement therapy, stopping only when he became involved with Kris Kardashian. He also said that her inability to deal with the issue that lay at the core of his identity contributed to the dissolution of their marriage. Jenner now says he thinks of himself as a woman, which is why he changed his first name to Caitlyn. However, Caitlyn Jenner has never been attracted to men and has not undergone sex reassignment surgery, although she does not rule it out for the future. She considers herself asexual (Bissinger, 2015; Lee, 2015; Sawyer, 2015).

Caitlyn Jenner's story raises a host of issues concerning sexualities and genders, the subject of this chapter. What is the difference between sex and gender? How are sex and gender related? Are there just two sexes and genders? What makes a person more or less male or female? How do members of society deal with sexual diversity? These are among the questions we will touch on here.

We begin by noting that your **sex** depends fundamentally on your genetic makeup. The overwhelming majority of people are born with 23 pairs of chromosomes, one pair of which determines their sex. If a person's sex chromosome is of the XX variety, she

sex Your sex depends on your genetic makeup—specifically, on whether your sex chromosome is XX (female), XY (male) or X, XXY, XXYY, and so on, the latter sex chromosomes often resulting in a person who does not fit conventional male or female sex categories.

intersex Intersex people do not fit conventional male or female sex categories. Often, intersex people do not have a sex chromosome that is XX or XY, and their genitals, reproductive system, and secondary sexual characteristics (such as breasts and body hair) are not distinctly male or female in the conventional sense of the terms.

gender Your sense of being male or female and playing masculine and feminine roles in ways defined as appropriate by your culture and society.

gender identity A person's identification with, or sense of belonging to, a particular sex—biologically, psychologically, and socially.

transgender People who are uncomfortable with the gender assigned to them at birth or who do not fit neatly into conventional male or female gender categories.

essentialism A school of thought that views gender differences as a reflection of biological differences between women and men.

social constructionism A school of thought that views gender differences as a reflection of the different social positions occupied by women and men.

Gender identity is your identification with, or sense of belonging to, a particular sex—psychologically, socially, and usually biologically. When you behave according to widely shared expectations about how males or females are supposed to act, you adopt a *gender role.*

Caitlyn Jenner is not intersex. She is *apparently* a man sexually. However, her gender identity does not correspond with her sex. She is a woman in terms of gender identity. People like Jenner who are uncomfortable with the gender assigned to them at birth or who do not fit neatly into conventional male or female gender categories are considered **transgender**. There are no survey-based estimates of the percentage of Canadians who identify as transgender, but the best estimate from the United States is 0.3 percent (Gates, 2011).

will be a woman. If a person's sex chromosome is of the XY variety, he will be a man. However, other sex chromosome types occur naturally: X, XXY, XXYY, and so on. Such combinations often result in people who are **intersex,** that is, they do not fit the conventional male or female sex categories. Their genitals, reproductive system, and secondary sexual characteristics such as breasts and body hair may not be distinctly male or female in the conventional sense of the terms. It is estimated that 1.7 percent of people lie somewhere between male and female as conventionally understood (Fausto-Sterling, 2000; Hird, 2005).

GENDER AND TRANSGENDER

Being male or female involves not just biological characteristics but also certain "masculine" and "feminine" feelings, attitudes, and behaviours. Accordingly, sociologists distinguish biological sex from sociological **gender**. Your gender comprises the feelings, attitudes, and behaviours typically associated with being male or female.

Neither biologists nor social scientists have yet developed convincing explanations for why sex and gender identity may not correspond (Lips, 2014: 18). However, we do know that, unlike sex, gender is not determined solely by biology, a subject to which we now turn.

THE SOCIAL LEARNING OF GENDER

GENDER THEORIES

Most arguments about the origins of gender differences in human behaviour adopt one of two perspectives. Some analysts see gender differences as a reflection of naturally evolved tendencies and argue that society must reinforce those tendencies if it is to function smoothly. Sociologists call this perspective **essentialism** because it views gender as part of the nature or "essence" of one's biological and social makeup (Weeks, 1986). For example, functionalists typically view gender in essentialist terms.

Other analysts see gender differences mainly as a reflection of the different social positions occupied by women and men. Sociologists call this perspective **social constructionism** because it views gender as "constructed" by people's interaction with social structure and culture. Conflict, feminist, and symbolic interactionist theories focus on various aspects of the social construction of gender.

ESSENTIALISM

Sociobiologists and evolutionary psychologists have proposed one popular essentialist theory. They argue that humans instinctively try to ensure that their genes are passed on to future generations. However, they say, men and women develop different strategies for achieving that goal. A woman has a bigger investment than a man does in ensuring the survival of their offspring because she produces only a small number of eggs during her reproductive life. At most, she can give birth to about 20 children. It is therefore in a woman's best interest to maintain primary responsibility for her genetic children and to seek out the single mate who can best help support and protect them. In contrast, men can produce as many as a billion sperm per ejaculation and this feat can be replicated daily (Saxton, 1990: 94–5). To maximize their chance of passing on their genes to future generations, men must have many sexual partners.

According to sociobiologists and evolutionary psychologists, as men compete with other men for sexual access to many women, competitiveness and aggression emerge (DeSteno and Salovey, 2001). Women, says one evolutionary psychologist, are greedy for money, while men want casual sex with women, treat women's bodies

Many sociobiologists and evolutionary psychologists claim that male sexual jealousy leading to violence is part of a "reproductive strategy."

as their property, and react violently to women who incite male sexual jealousy. These are supposedly "universal features of our evolved selves" that contribute to the survival of the human species (Buss, 2000). Thus, from the point of view of sociobiology and evolutionary psychology, gender differences in behaviour are based on biological differences between women and men.

FUNCTIONALISM AND ESSENTIALISM

Functionalists reinforce the essentialist viewpoint when they claim that traditional gender roles help to integrate society (Parsons, 1942). In the family, wrote Talcott Parsons, women traditionally specialize in raising children and managing the household. Men traditionally work in the paid labour force. Each generation learns to perform these complementary roles by means of gender role socialization.

For boys, noted Parsons, the essence of masculinity is a series of "instrumental" traits, such as rationality, self-assuredness, and competitiveness. For girls, the essence of femininity is a series of "expressive" traits, such as nurturance and sensitivity to others. Boys and girls first learn their respective gender traits in the family as they see their parents going about their daily routines. The larger society also promotes gender role conformity. It instills in men the fear that they won't be attractive to women if they are too feminine, and it instills in women the fear that they won't be attractive to men if they are too masculine. In the

functionalist view, then, learning the essential features of femininity and masculinity integrates society and allows it to function properly.

A CRITIQUE OF ESSENTIALISM FROM THE CONFLICT AND FEMINIST PERSPECTIVES
Criticisms

Conflict and feminist theorists disagree sharply with the essentialist account. They have lodged four main criticisms against it:

1. *Essentialists ignore the historical and cultural variability of gender and sexuality.* Wide variations exist in what constitutes masculinity and femininity. Moreover, the level of gender inequality, the rate of male violence against women, the criteria used for mate selection, and other gender differences that appear universal to the essentialists vary widely too. This variation deflates the idea that there are essential and universal behavioural differences between women and men. Three examples help illustrate the point:
   - In societies with low levels of gender inequality, the tendency decreases for women to stress the good provider role in selecting male partners, as does the tendency for men to stress women's domestic skills (Eagley and Wood, 1999).
   - When women become corporate lawyers or police officers or take other jobs that involve competition or threat, their production of the hormone testosterone is stimulated, causing them to act more aggressively. Aggressiveness is partly role-related (Blum, 1997: 158–88).
   - Hundreds of studies conducted mainly in North America show that women are developing traits that were traditionally considered masculine. Women have become considerably more assertive, competitive, independent, and analytical since the early 1970s (Biegler, 1999; Nowell and Hedges, 1998).

   As these examples show, gender differences are not constants, and they are not inherent in men and women. They vary with social conditions.

2. *Essentialism tends to generalize from the average, ignoring variations within gender groups.* On average, women and men do differ in some respects. For example, one of the best-documented gender differences is that men are on average more verbally and physically aggressive than women are. However, when sociobiologists and evolutionary psychologists say men are inherently more aggressive than women are, they make it seem as if this is true of all men and all women. As Figure 8.1 shows, however, it is not. When trained researchers measure verbal or physical

FIGURE 8.1 The Distribution of Aggressiveness among Men and Women

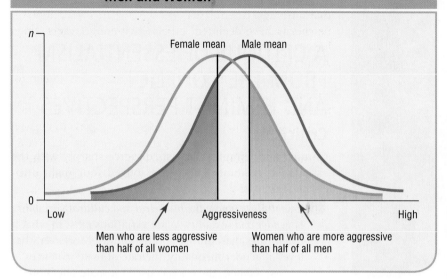

aggressiveness, scores vary widely within gender groups. Aggressiveness is distributed so that considerable overlap exists between women and men. Many women are more aggressive than the average man and many men are less aggressive than the average woman.

3. *No direct evidence directly supports the essentialists' major claims.* Sociobiologists and evolutionary psychologists have not identified any of the genes that, they claim, cause male jealousy, female nurturance, the unequal division of labour between men and women, and so forth.

4. *Essentialists' explanations for gender differences ignore the role of power.* Essentialists assume that existing behaviour patterns help ensure the survival of the species and the smooth functioning of society. However, as conflict and feminist theorists argue, this assumption overlooks the fact that men are usually in a position of greater power and authority than women are. This fact may account for many gender differences, as we will now see.

Conflict Theory

Conflict theorists dating back to Marx's collaborator, Friedrich Engels, locate the root of male domination in class inequality (Engels, 1970 [1884]). According to Engels, men gained substantial power over women when preliterate societies were first able to produce more than their members needed for their own subsistence. At that point, some men gained control over the economic surplus. They soon devised two means of ensuring that their offspring would inherit the surplus. First, they imposed the rule that only men could own property. Second, by means of socialization and force, they ensured that women remained sexually faithful to their husbands. As industrial capitalism developed, Engels wrote, male domination increased because industrial capitalism

made men still wealthier and more powerful while it relegated women to subordinate domestic roles.

Feminist Theory

Feminist theorists doubt that male domination is so closely linked to the development of industrial capitalism. For one thing, they note that gender inequality is greater in agrarian than in industrial capitalist societies. For another, male domination is evident in societies that call themselves socialist or communist. These observations lead many feminists to conclude that male domination is rooted less in industrial capitalism than in the patriarchal authority relations, family structures, and patterns of socialization and culture that exist in most societies (Lapidus, 1978: 7).

Despite this disagreement, conflict and feminist theorists concur that behavioural differences between women and men result less from any essential differences between them than from men being in a position to advance their interests over the interests of women. From the conflict and feminist viewpoints, functionalism, sociobiology, and evolutionary psychology can themselves be seen as examples of the exercise of male power, that is, as rationalizations for male domination and sexual aggression.

SOCIAL CONSTRUCTIONISM AND SYMBOLIC INTERACTIONISM

As we have seen, essentialism is the view that masculinity and femininity are inherent and universal traits of men and women, whether because of biological or social necessity or some combination of the two. In contrast, social constructionism is the view that *apparently* natural or innate features of life, such as gender, are actually sustained by *social* processes that vary historically and culturally. As such, conflict and feminist theories can be regarded as types of social constructionism. So can symbolic interactionism.

Symbolic interactionists, you will recall, focus on the way people attach meaning to things in the course of their everyday communication. One of the things to which people attach meaning is what it means to be a man or a woman. We illustrate the symbolic interactionist approach by first considering how boys and girls learn masculine and feminine roles in the family and at school. We then show how gender roles are maintained in the course of everyday social interaction and through advertising in the mass media.

GENDER SOCIALIZATION

Barbie dolls have been around since 1959. Based on the creation of a German cartoonist, Barbie is the first modern doll modelled after an adult. (Lili, the German original, became a life-sized pornographic doll.) Some industry experts predicted mothers would never buy their little girls a doll with breasts. Were *they* wrong. Mattel now sells about 10 million Barbies and 20 million accompanying outfits annually. According to Mattel, the average American girl between the ages of 3 and 11 owns 10 Barbie dolls; the average British or Italian girl owns 7, and the average French or German girl owns 5. The Barbie trademark is worth US$2 billion, making it the most valuable toy brand in the world ("Life in plastic," 2002).

What do girls learn when they play with Barbie? The author of a website devoted to Barbie undoubtedly speaks for many when she writes, "Barbie was more than a doll to me. She was a way of living: the Ideal Woman" (Elliott, 1995; see also Nicolaiedis, 1998; Turkel, 1998). One ideal that Barbie stimulates among many girls concerns body image. After all, Barbie is a scale model of a woman with a 40-18-32 figure (Hamilton, 1996: 197). Researchers who compared Barbie's gravity-defying body with the actual proportions of several representative groups of adult women concluded that the probability of this body shape was less than 1 in 100 000 (Norton, Olds, Olive, and Dank, 1996). (Ken's body shape is far more realistic at 1 in 50.) The closets of Barbie's pink house are jammed with outfits. Bathrooms, gyms, beauty parlours, and vanity sets feature prominently among the Barbie accessories available. Presumably, this quest for physical perfection is designed to attract Ken, Barbie's boyfriend. The message Barbie conveys to girls is that the ideal woman is defined primarily by her attractiveness to men.

A comparable story, with competition and aggression as its theme, could be told about how boys' toys, such as GI Joe, teach stereotypical male roles. True, a movement to market more gender-neutral toys arose in the 1960s and 1970s; there is now even a Presidential Barbie. However, a strong tendency remains to market toys based on gender. Typically, in the late 1990s, Mattel produced a pink, flowered Barbie computer for girls with fewer educational programs than its blue Hot Wheels computer for boys (Mooney, Schacht, Knox, and Nelson, 2003: 232).

Yet toys are only part of the story of gender socialization and hardly its first or final chapter. Research conducted in the early 1970s showed that from birth, infant boys and girls who are matched in length, weight, and general health are treated differently by parents—fathers in particular. Girls tend to be identified as delicate, weak, beautiful, and cute; boys as strong, alert, and well-coordinated (Rubin, Provenzano, and Lurra, 1974). One experiment found that when viewing a videotape of a nine-month-old infant, subjects tended to label its startled reaction to a stimulus as "anger" if the child had earlier been identified

by the experimenters as a boy, and as "fear" if it had earlier been identified as a girl, *regardless of the infant's actual sex* (Condry and Condry, 1976). More recent research shows that although parents' gender-stereotyped perceptions of newborns' have declined, especially among fathers, they have not disappeared (Fagot, Rodgers, and Leinbach, 2000; Gauvain, Fagot, Leve, and Kavanagh, 2002)

Parents, and especially fathers, are more likely to encourage their sons to engage in boisterous and competitive play and discourage their daughters from doing likewise. In general, parents tend to encourage girls to engage in cooperative, role-playing games (Fagot et al., 2000; Gauvain et al., 2002; Parke, 2001, 2002). These different play patterns lead to the heightened development of verbal and emotional skills among girls and to more concern with winning and the establishment of hierarchy among boys (Tannen, 1990). Boys are more likely than girls are to be praised for assertiveness. Girls are more likely than boys are to be rewarded for compliance (Kerig, Cowan, and Cowan, 1993). Given this early socialization, it seems perfectly "natural" that boys' toys stress aggression, competition, spatial manipulation, and outdoor activities, while girls' toys stress nurturing, physical attractiveness, and indoor activities (Hughes, 1995). Still, what seems natural must be continuously socially reinforced. Presented with a choice between playing with a tool set and a dish set, preschool boys are about as likely to choose one as the other—unless the dish set is presented as a girl's toy and they think their fathers would view playing with it as "bad." Then, they tend to pick the tool set (Raag and Rackliff, 1998).

Only someone who has spent very little time in the company of children would think they are passive objects of socialization. They are not. Parents, teachers, and other authority figures typically try to impose their ideas of appropriate gender behaviour on children, but children creatively interpret, negotiate, resist, and self-impose these ideas all the time. Gender, we might say, is something that is done, not just given (Messner, 2000; West and Zimmerman, 1987). This is nowhere more evident than in the way children play.

Gender Segregation and Interaction

Consider the Grade 4 and Grade 5 classroom that sociologist Barrie Thorne (1993) observed. The teacher periodically asked the children to choose their own desks. With the exception of one girl, they always segregated *themselves* by gender. Similarly, when children played chasing games in the schoolyard, groups often *spontaneously* crystallized along gender lines. The teacher often reaffirmed such gender boundaries by pitting the boys against the girls in spelling and math contests. These contests were marked by cross-gender antagonism and expression of within-gender solidarity.

However, Thorne also observed many cases of boys and girls playing together. She also noticed considerable "boundary crossing." Boundary crossing involves boys

gender ideology A set of ideas about what constitutes appropriate masculine and feminine roles and behaviour.

playing stereotypically girls' games and girls playing stereotypically boys' games. The most common form of boundary crossing involved girls who were skilled at specific sports that were central to the boys' world, such as soccer, baseball, and basketball. Boys and girls also interacted easily and without strong gender identities coming to the fore in activities requiring cooperation, such as a group project. Mixed-gender interaction was also more common in less public and crowded settings; boys and girls were more likely to play together and in a relaxed way in the relative privacy of their neighbourhoods. In contrast, in the schoolyard, where they were under the scrutiny of their peers, gender segregation and antagonism were more evident.

In sum, Thorne's research makes two important contributions to our understanding of gender socialization. First, children are actively engaged in the process of constructing gender roles. They are not just passive recipients of adult demands. Second, while schoolchildren tend to segregate themselves by gender, boundaries between boys and girls are sometimes fluid and sometimes rigid, depending on social circumstances. In other words, the content of children's gendered activities is by no means fixed.

This is not to suggest that adults have no gender demands and expectations. They do, and their demands and expectations contribute importantly to gender socialization. For instance, many schoolteachers and guidance counsellors still expect boys to do better in science and math and girls to achieve higher marks in English (Lips,

Mike Kemp/Jupiterimages

1999). Parents often reinforce these stereotypes in their evaluation of different activities (Eccles, Jacobs, and Harold, 1990). Although not all studies comparing mixed- and single-sex schools suggest that girls do much better in the latter (Bornholt, 2001; Jackson and Smith, 2000), most do.

In single-sex schools, girls experience faster cognitive development; higher occupational aspirations and attainment; greater self-esteem and self-confidence; and more teacher attention, respect, and encouragement in the classroom. They also develop more egalitarian attitudes toward the role of women in society. Why? Because such schools place more emphasis on academic excellence and less on physical attractiveness and heterosexual popularity. They provide more successful same-sex role models, and they eliminate sex bias in teacher–student and student–student interaction because there are no boys around (Hesse-Biber and Carter, 2000: 99–100).

Adolescents must usually start choosing courses in school by the age of 14 or 15. By then, their **gender ideologies** are well formed. Gender ideologies are sets of interrelated ideas about what constitutes appropriate masculine and feminine roles and behaviour. One aspect of gender ideology becomes especially important around Grades 9 and 10: adolescents' ideas about whether, as adults, they will focus mainly on the home, or on paid work outside the home, or on a combination of the two. Adolescents usually make course choices with gender ideologies in mind. Boys are strongly inclined to consider only their careers in making course choices. Most girls are inclined to consider both home responsibilities and careers, although a minority considers only home responsibilities and another minority considers only careers. Consequently, boys tend to choose career-oriented courses, particularly in math and science, more often than girls do. In college and university, the pattern is accentuated. Young women tend to choose easier courses that lead to lower-paying jobs because they expect to devote a large part of their lives to child-rearing and housework (Hochschild with Machung, 1989: 15–18). The top fields of study for university and college graduates clearly indicate the continuing impact of gender ideologies on Canadian men and women (Table 8.1). We examine the wage gap between women and men in the second half of this chapter.

THE MASS MEDIA AND BODY IMAGE

The social construction of gender does not stop at the school steps. Outside school, children, adolescents, and adults continue to negotiate gender roles as they interact with the mass media.

If you systematically observe the roles played by women and men on TV programs and in ads one evening, you will probably discover a pattern noted by sociologists since the 1970s. Women will more frequently be seen

TABLE 8.1 Major Field of Postsecondary Study Completed, Canada, by Gender

	Women		Men	
Business, management, & public administration	1 998 590	26.4	1 188 985	16.41
Health & related fields	1 667 565	22.1	393 035	5.42
Social & behavioural sciences & law	984 965	13.0	512 795	7.08
Education	833 695	11.0	275 765	3.81
Humanities	494 720	6.5	326 875	4.51
Personal, protective, & transportation services	428 305	5.7	471 705	6.51
Visual and performing arts & communication technologies	293 845	3.9	254 785	3.52
Architecture, engineering, & related technologies	264 030	3.5	2 929 940	40.43
Physical and life sciences & technologies	262 810	3.5	291 870	4.03
Mathematics, computer, & information sciences	221 505	2.9	380 195	5.25
Agriculture, natural resources, & conservation	105 840	1.4	220 390	3.04
Other	2 270	0.0	720	0.01
Total	7 558 140	100.0	7 247 060	100.0

Note: The data for this table came from the *2011 National Household Survey*.

Source: Newfoundland and Labrador Statistics Agency, Economics and Statistics Branch. n.d. "Major Field of Study by Age Group and Sex." http://www.stats.gov.nl.ca/Statistics/social/PDF/ED_Major%20Field%20of%20Study_AgeGroup_Sex.pdf (retrieved 27 August 2015).

cleaning house, taking care of children, modelling clothes, and acting as objects of male desire. Men will more frequently be seen in aggressive, action-oriented, and authoritative roles. The effect of these messages on viewers is to reinforce the normality of traditional gender roles.

Many people try to shape their body after the body images portrayed in the mass media. Survey data show that body dissatisfaction is widespread and the mass media play an important role in generating discomfort. One survey of North American university graduates showed that 56 percent of women and 43 percent of men were dissatisfied with their overall appearance (Garner, 1997). Only 3 percent of the dissatisfied women, but 22 percent of the dissatisfied men, wanted to gain weight. This difference reflects the greater desire of men for muscular, stereotypically male physiques. Most of the dissatisfied men, and even more of the dissatisfied women (89 percent), wanted to lose weight. This finding reflects the general societal push toward slimness and its greater effect on women.

Let's assume that *Playboy* "Playmate of the Month" centrefolds represent the North American ideal body type for women. From information in the magazine, it is possible to calculate the body mass index (BMI) of 609 centrefolds from December 1953 to January 2009 (see Figure 8.2). (The body mass index is equal to one's body mass in kilograms divided by the square of one's

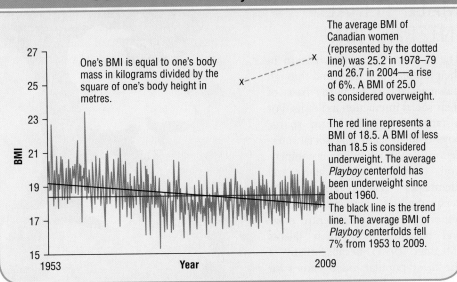

FIGURE 8.2 Body Mass Index (BMI) of 609 *Playboy* Centrefolds, December 1953–January 2009

One's BMI is equal to one's body mass in kilograms divided by the square of one's body height in metres.

The average BMI of Canadian women (represented by the dotted line) was 25.2 in 1978–79 and 26.7 in 2004—a rise of 6%. A BMI of 25.0 is considered overweight.

The red line represents a BMI of 18.5. A BMI of less than 18.5 is considered underweight. The average *Playboy* centerfold has been underweight since about 1960.

The black line is the trend line. The average BMI of *Playboy* centerfolds fell 7% from 1953 to 2009.

Sources: Tjepkema, Michael, n.d., "Measured Obesity: Adult Obesity in Canada: Measured Height and Weight," Statistics Canada, *Nutrition: Findings from the Canadian Community Health Survey*, Issue No. 1; Gammon, Katherine, 2009, "Infoporn: Today's Playmates Are More like Anime Figures than Real Humans," *Wired* 17, 2.

body weight in metres.) The BMI of *Playboy* centrefolds fell 7 percent from 1953 to 2009. According to the accepted standard, a BMI of less than 18.5 indicates an underweight woman. By this benchmark, the average *Playboy* centrefold has been underweight since about 1960. A BMI greater than 25.0 is the accepted standard for an overweight woman. From 1978–79 to 2004, the average BMI for Canadian women rose 6 percent, from 25.2 to 26.7. Here, then, is a recipe for rising anxiety about one's body: a body ideal that is growing slimmer and an average body type that is becoming bulkier.

Body dissatisfaction motivates many people to diet—in North America, more than 80 percent of women and more than 50 percent of men (Garner, 1997). A Canadian survey shows that Canadian women are far more likely than men are to attempt losing weight, even if they fall within the range of healthy weights (Health Canada, 1999b: 118). Some are willing to live dangerously. About a quarter of women and a sixth of men in North America say they would willingly trade more than three years of their life to achieve their weight goals. Half of female smokers and 30 percent of male smokers say they smoke to control their weight. Surveys suggest that between 1 percent and 5 percent of American women suffer from anorexia nervosa (characterized by weight loss, excessive exercise, food aversion, distorted body image, and an intense and irrational fear of body fat and weight gain). About the same percentage of American female college and university students suffer from bulimia, characterized by cycles of binge eating and purging through self-induced vomiting or the use of laxatives, purgatives, or diuretics. For college and university men, the prevalence of bulimia is between 0.2 percent and 1.5 percent (Averett and Korenman, 1996: 305–06).

Singer Taylor Swift was #1 on *Maxim* magazine's "Hot 100" list for 2015. What made her "hot"?

MALE–FEMALE INTERACTION

The gender roles children learn in their families, at school, and through the mass media form the basis of their social interaction as adults. For instance, by playing team sports, boys tend to learn that social interaction is most often about competition, conflict, self-sufficiency, and hierarchical relationships (leaders versus the led). They understand the importance of taking centre stage and boasting about their talents (Messner, 1995). Because many of the most popular video games for boys exclude female characters, use women as sex objects, or involve violence against women, they reinforce

Lipstick and Blood by Cuban artist José Gómez Fresquet (Frémez), circa 1970

some of the most unsavoury lessons of traditional gender socialization (Dietz, 1998). To cite just one example, in *Grand Theft Auto*, a player can have sex with a prostitute, beat her up, and steal his money back. On the other hand, by playing with dolls and baking sets, girls tend to learn that social interaction is most often about maintaining cordial relationships, avoiding conflict, and resolving differences of opinion through negotiation (Subrahmanyam and Greenfield, 1998). They understand the importance of giving advice and not promoting themselves or being bossy.

Because of these early socialization patterns, misunderstandings between men and women are common. A stereotypical example: Harold is driving around lost. However, he refuses to ask for directions because doing so would amount to an admission of inadequacy and therefore a loss of status. Meanwhile, it seems perfectly "natural" to Sybil to want to share information, so she urges Harold to ask for directions. The result: conflict between Harold and Sybil (Tannen, 1990: 62).

Gender-specific interaction styles have serious implications for who is heard and who gets credit at work. For instance, Deborah Tannen's research discovered the typical case of the female office manager who doesn't want to seem bossy or arrogant. Eager to preserve consensus among her co-workers, she spends much time soliciting their opinions before making an important decision. However, her boss perceives her approach as indecisive and incompetent. He wants to recruit leaders for upper-management positions, so he overlooks the woman and selects an assertive man for a senior job that just opened up (Tannen, 1994a: 132).

The contrasting interaction style between male and female managers can lead to women not getting credit for competent performance. That is why they sometimes complain about a glass ceiling, a social barrier that makes it difficult for them to rise to the top level of management. As we will see soon, factors other than interaction styles—such as outright discrimination and women's generally greater commitment to family responsibilities—also restrict women's upward mobility. But gender differences in interaction styles also play a role in constraining women's career progress.

LO³ HOMOSEXUALITY

The preceding discussion identifies powerful social forces that push us to define ourselves as conventionally masculine or feminine in behaviour and appearance. For most people, gender socialization by the family, the school, and the mass media is compelling and sustained by daily interactions. A minority of people, however, resist conventional gender roles.

Heterosexuals are people who desire sexual partners of the other sex, homosexuals are people who prefer sexual partners of the same sex, and bisexuals are people who enjoy sexual partners of either sex. People usually call homosexual men *gays* and homosexual women *lesbians*.

Because of widespread animosity toward homosexuals—even among celebrities (see Figure 8.3)—some people who engage or want to engage in same-sex acts do not identify themselves as gay, lesbian, or bisexual (Flowers and Buston, 2001; Herdt, 2001; Laumann et al., 1994: 299). However, sexuality has two dimensions apart from identity: desire and behaviour. Identity, desire, and behaviour are not perfectly correlated. For instance, one can express homosexual desire or have same-sex sexual partners without identifying as a homosexual (Michael et al., 1994: 174–79).

One survey of North American college students showed that homosexual experiences and desires are far more frequent than is homosexual identification. Men were 3.5 times more likely to say they had homosexual experiences and desires than they were to identify as gay. Women were 5.6 times more likely to say they had same-sex sexual experiences or desires than to identify as lesbians (Figure 8.4).

What might account for the male–female difference? One possibility is that many heterosexual men find sex between women exciting, so a considerable number of young women engage in sexual acts with other women for the benefit of men—a growing phenomenon according to analysts who have observed the party, bar, and club scenes in recent years (Rupp and Taylor, 2010).

SEXUAL ORIENTATION AND QUEER THEORY

Research not only confirms that sexuality is multidimensional but also calls into question whether the conventional characterization of people as heterosexual, bisexual, or gay/lesbian adequately captures the range of sexual orientations in human populations.

The provocatively labelled stream of thought known as queer theory denies the existence of stable sexual

glass ceiling A social barrier that makes it difficult for women to rise to the top level of management.

heterosexuals People who prefer members of the opposite sex as sexual partners.

homosexuals People who prefer sexual partners of the same sex. People usually call homosexual men *gays* and homosexual women *lesbians*.

bisexuals People who enjoy sexual partners of either sex.

queer theory Examines empirical mismatches among sex, gender, and sexual desire to debunk the notion that sex, gender, and sexuality are perfectly correlated and emphasize how fluid social contexts influence sexual identities and the performance of sexual acts.

FIGURE 8.3   Celebrities Insulting Gays and Lesbians

2006: Jessie James, celebrity motorcycle builder and former husband of Sandra Bullock, sent an e-mail calling co-workers "f*ggots."

Ethan Miller/Getty Images

2007: In a radio Interview, Rap star Beanie Sigel attacked the way Kanye West dresses, calling him a homosexual who should come out of the closet.

Johnny Nunez/WireImage/Getty Images

2009: Chef Gordon Ramsay called Australian TV personality Tracy Grimshaw a lesbian on *A Current Affair* and showed a visual depiction of her as a naked, subservient female pig.

Franco Origlia/Getty Images

2011: Basketball star Kobe Bryant was fined $100 000 by the NBA. After he was accused of a technical foul, he shouted at a referee, calling him a "f***ing f*ggot."

Cal Sport Media/Alamy

2011: During a performance of his comedy act, Tracy Morgan said he would stab his son if he told Morgan he was gay.

s_bukley/Shutterstock.com

2012: Toronto Blue Jays shortstop Yunel Escobar was suspended for three games after writing "Maricon," meaning "f*ggot" in Spanish, on his eye black.

Tom Szczerbowski/Stringer/Getty Images

Filipino boxer Manny Pacquiao was the second-highest paid athlete in the world in 2015. He has won world championships in eight different weight classes and since 2010 has been a member of the Philippine House of Representatives. In 2016 he proclaimed that gay people are "worse than animals."

Gene Blevins/ZUMA Press/Newscom

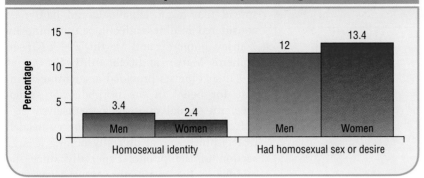

FIGURE 8.4 Homosexuality Indicators, North American University Students (percentage)

Source: Ellis, L., B. Robb, and D. Burke. 2005. "Sexual Orientation in United States and Canadian College Students." *Archives of Sexual Behavior* 34: 569–81.

orientations altogether (Green, 2007). From the queer theorist's point of view, when we apply labels like heterosexual, bisexual, gay, and lesbian to ourselves or others we are adopting official or at least socially accepted labels that fail to capture the fluidity and variability of people's actual identities and performances. Such labels impose social conventions on people, thus acting as forms of control and domination and deflecting attention from the uniqueness of each individual.

Supporting these assertions, researchers asked a sample of 1784 Americans, half women and half men, to choose one of seven labels to define their sexuality: heterosexual, mostly heterosexual, bisexual, mostly gay/lesbian, gay/lesbian, questioning/uncertain, and other (Vrangalova and Savin-Williams, 2012). Table 8.2 shows the distribution of women and men who responded positively to the first five categories.

To understand better the differences among the various sexual orientations, the researchers also asked respondents to situate themselves along two dimensions: sexual

TABLE 8.2 Self-Reported Sexual Orientation by Sex (percentage)

	Men	Women
Heterosexual	81	71
Mostly heterosexual	9	20
Bisexual	3	6
Mostly gay/lesbian	2	1
Gay/lesbian	5	2
Total	100	100

Source: Vrangalova, Zhana and Ritch C. Savin-Williams. 2012. "Mostly Heterosexual and Mostly Gay/Lesbian: Evidence for New Sexual Orientation Identities." *Archives of Sexual Behavior* 41: 85–101.

attraction to men and women, and number of male and female sexual partners. They measured sexual attraction by asking respondents to indicate on a scale of 1 to 5 how sexually attracted they are to men and to women. They measured number of sexual partners by asking respondents the total number of male and female partners with whom they have had a genital sexual experience. Figure 8.5 illustrates the results for women. It shows that, for *all five* sexual orientations, women are on average *simultaneously* attracted to same-sex and other-sex partners, albeit to varying degrees. For example, women who define themselves as heterosexual (signified by green squares) scored 4.86 out of 5 on other-sex attraction and 1.49 out of 5 on same-sex attraction. It also shows that, for all five sexual orientations, women have had on average more than one male *and* at least one female sexual partner. For example, heterosexual women had on average 10.2 other-sex partners and 1.7 same-sex partners. The pattern for men differs only in detail.

Our discussion demonstrates the existence of wide variation in attitudes toward sex, sexual identity, sexual orientation, and sexual conduct over time and place. It therefore helps to dispel myths about sexuality as natural or "fixed" and about men and women, and heterosexuals and homosexuals, as sexual "opposites."

HOMOSEXUALITY

Homosexuals were not identified as a distinct category of people until the 1860s, when the term *homosexuality* was coined. The term *lesbian* is of even more recent vintage. Nevertheless, homosexual behaviour has existed in every society. Some societies, such as ancient Greece, have encouraged it. More frequently, homosexual acts have been forbidden.

We do not yet understand well why some individuals develop homosexual orientations. Some scientists believe that the cause of homosexuality is mainly genetic, others think it is chiefly hormonal, while still others point to life experiences during early childhood as the most important factor. According to the American Psychological Association (1998), it "emerges for most people in early adolescence without any prior sexual experience…. [It] is not changeable."

In general, sociologists are less interested in the origins of homosexuality than in the way it is socially constructed, that is, in the wide variety of ways it is expressed and repressed (Foucault, 1990 [1978]; Plummer, 1995).

Homosexuality has become less of a stigma over the past century. Two factors are chiefly responsible for

FIGURE 8.5 Same/Other Sexual Attraction and Number of Same/Other Sex Partners for Women of Five Sexual Orientations

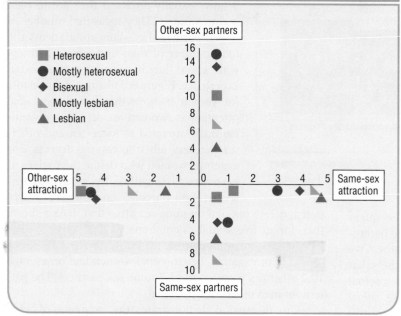

Source: Compiled from Vrangalova, Zhana and Ritch C. Savin-Williams. 2012. "Mostly Heterosexual and Mostly Gay/Lesbian: Evidence for New Sexual Orientation Identities." *Archives of Sexual Behavior* 41: 85–101.

his colleagues interviewed thousands of men and women. In the 1940s, they concluded that homosexual practices were sufficiently widespread that homosexuality could hardly be considered an illness affecting a tiny minority (Kinsey, Pomeroy, and Martin, 1948; Kinsey, Pomeroy, Martin, and Gebhard, 1953).

If sexologists provided a scientific rationale for belief in the normality of sexual diversity, sexual minorities themselves provided the social and political energy needed to legitimize sexual diversity among a large section of the public. Especially since the middle of the twentieth century, gays and lesbians have built large communities and subcultures, particularly in major urban areas (Greenhill, 2001; Ingram, 2001). They have gone public with their lifestyles (Owen, 2001). They have organized demonstrations, parades, and political-pressure groups to express their self-confidence and demand equal rights with the heterosexual majority (Goldie, 2001). These actions have done much to legitimize homosexuality and sexual diversity in general.

this, one scientific, the other political. In the twentieth century, sexologists—psychologists and physicians who study sexual practices scientifically—first recognized and stressed the wide diversity of existing sexual practices. Alfred Kinsey was among the pioneers in this field. He and

On April 1, 2001, the Netherlands became the first country to recognize full and equal marriage rights for homosexual couples. Within hours, Dutch citizens were taking advantage of the new law. The Dutch law is part of a worldwide trend to legally recognize long-term same-sex unions. On July 20, 2005, Canada became the fourth country to legalize homosexual marriage. As of July 2016, same-sex marriage was legal in 21 countries and some jurisdictions within countries.

REUTERS/Michael Kooren

Opposition to Homosexuality

Nonetheless, opposition to people who don't conform to conventional gender roles remains strong at all stages of the life cycle (see the Sociology at the Movies feature in this chapter). When you were a child, did you ever poke fun at a sturdily built girl who was good at sports by calling her a "dike"? As an adolescent or young adult, have you ever attempted to insult a man by calling him a "fag"? If so, your behaviour was not unusual. Many children and young adults continue to express the belief that heterosexuality is superior to homosexuality (Bibby, 2001). "That's gay!" is a common expression of disapproval among teenagers.

Among adults, opposition to people who don't conform to conventional gender roles is also strong. Do you happen to think that relations between adults of the same sex are always, or almost always, wrong? If so, you are not that unusual. In Canada, about 4 out of 10 adults hold that opinion. Rejection of homosexuality is correlated with age, gender, and region. Older adults, men, and residents of provinces other than Quebec and British Columbia are most inclined to reject homosexuality (Bibby, 2006: 21–22).

Antipathy to homosexuals is so strong among some people that they are prepared to back up their beliefs with force. A study of about 500 young adults in the San Francisco Bay area (one of the most sexually tolerant areas in North America) found that 1 in 10 admitted physically attacking or threatening people they believed were homosexuals. Twenty-four percent reported engaging in anti-gay name-calling. Among male respondents, 18 percent reported acting in a

Milk

Until he was 40, Harvey Milk worked in a large investment firm in New York and supported the Republican Party. However, he was a closet homosexual and was bored with his life, so he decided to do something

Focus Features/The Kobal Collection at Art Resource, NY

that one least expects from a member of the pinstripe crowd. He joined a hippie theatre troupe, fell in love with another man, came out of the closet, and opened a camera store in the Castro district, the centre of San Francisco's gay community. There Milk felt at home.

It was the mid-70s, however, and even in San Francisco the gay community was harassed and persecuted, not least by the San Francisco police. Anti-gay discrimination radicalized and politicized Milk. In 1977, he became the first openly gay man to hold public office in the United States when he brought together a gay–liberal–union–black–Latino alliance and was elected to the San Francisco Board of Supervisors.

Milk, starring the extraordinary Sean Penn in the title role, tells the inspiring story of Harvey Milk's political and romantic life from the time of his fateful decision to change his life at the age of 40 until he was murdered (along with San Francisco's mayor, George Moscone) in 1978 at the age of 48. The murderer was Dan White, another member of the Board of Supervisors, a married and deeply religious anti-gay activist who fought his own homosexual impulses and eventually became psychologically unstable under the strain.

Critical Thinking Questions

1. Harvey Milk and Dan White represent two reactions to the discovery of one's homosexuality. What sociological factors might account for these different reactions?
2. Do you think there is more, less, or the same level of hostility against gays and lesbians today than there was in the mid-1970s? What is the basis for your opinion?
3. What sociological factors might account for an increase or a decrease in the level of hostility against gays and lesbians over time?

---

violent or threatening way and 32 percent reported name-calling. In addition, a third of those who had *not* engaged in anti-gay aggression said they would do so if a homosexual flirted with or propositioned them (Franklin, 2000).

The consequences of **homophobia**, or fear of homosexuals, can be devastating. For example, when 14-year-old Christian Hernandez told his best friend that he was gay, the consequences proved disastrous. "He told me he couldn't accept it," recalls Hernandez. "And he began to spread it around." For two years, the Niagara Falls student

was teased and harassed almost daily. After school one day, a group of boys waited for him. Their leader

homophobia The fear of homosexuals.

told Hernandez that "he didn't accept faggots, that we brought AIDS into the world" and stabbed him in the neck with a knife. Hernandez required a week's hospitalization. When he told his parents what had happened, his father replied that he'd "rather have a dead son than a queer son" (Fisher, 1999).

Research suggests that some anti-gay crimes may result from repressed homosexual urges on the part of the aggressor (Adams, Wright, and Lohr, 1998). From this point of view, aggressors are homophobic because they cannot cope with their own, possibly subconscious, homosexual impulses. Their aggression is a way of acting out a denial of these impulses. Although this psychological explanation may account for some anti-gay violence, it seems inadequate when set alongside the finding that fully half of all young male adults admitted to some form of anti-gay aggression in the San Francisco study cited above. An analysis of the motivations of these San Franciscans showed that some of them did commit assaults to prove their toughness and heterosexuality. Others committed assaults just to alleviate boredom and have fun. Still others believed they were defending themselves from aggressive sexual propositions. A fourth group acted violently because they wanted to punish homosexuals for what they perceived as moral transgressions (Franklin, 1998). It seems clear, then, that anti-gay violence is not just a question of abnormal psychology but a broad cultural problem with several sources. Still, opposition to anti-gay violence is also growing and public opinion polls report increasing acceptance of homosexuality.

Opposition to Sexual Minorities in General

Opposition to homosexuals is part of a larger phenomenon. Like the Calgary bus driver who said he would quit his job if he was assigned to drive a bus wrapped in a rainbow flag during the city's 2015 Pride Week, some people oppose sexual minorities in general ("Calgary Transit," 2015).

Consider how most people react to babies who are born with an unusually large clitoris or small penis. Most parents and physicians believe that, in such cases, early surgery is required because children with these characteristics will have great difficulty adjusting to a society that, for the most part, finds it difficult to accept people with "ambiguous genitalia." They justify their belief with the research finding that, while babies first develop a vague sense of being a boy or a girl at about the age of one, they develop a full-blown sense of gender identity only between the ages of two and three (Blum, 1997). Accordingly, they hold that a child's sex and gender can be successfully reassigned before the age of 18 months by means of reconstructive surgery, socialization by family members, the instruction and influence of medical professionals and, beginning at puberty, hormone therapy (Creighton and Mihto, 2001; Lightfoot-Klein, Chase, Hammond, and Goldman, 2000).

Others hold that sex and gender reassignment is coercive and inhumane if conducted at an early age.

They hold that young children should not be forced to undergo sex reassignment surgery. Instead, they should be allowed to choose their sex and gender identity at puberty and, if they wish, undergo sex reassignment at that time. The problem, they contend, is not that children with "ambiguous genitalia" will have great difficulty adjusting to a society that can't tolerate them but that society is intolerant of sexual minorities. From this point of view, babies should not be mutilated because of widespread intolerance. Rather, rejection of sexual minorities should give way to greater tolerance so that people with "ambiguous genitalia" can choose their own sexual destiny once they are old enough to make responsible decisions.

In sum, strong social and cultural forces lead us to distinguish men from women and heterosexuals from homosexuals. We learn these distinctions throughout the socialization process, and we continuously construct them anew in our daily interactions. Most people use positive and negative sanctions to ensure that others conform to conventional heterosexual gender roles. Some people resort to violence to enforce conformity and punish deviance.

Our presentation also suggests that the social construction of conventional gender roles helps create and maintain social inequality between women and men. In the remainder of this chapter, we examine some of the present-day consequences of gender inequality.

LO⁴ GENDER INEQUALITY

THE EARNINGS GAP

The earnings gap between men and women is one of the most important expressions of gender inequality today. When Canadian data on female and male earnings were first collected in 1967, the ratio of female-to-male earnings for full-year, full-time workers stood at about 58 percent. This means that women were earning 58 cents for every dollar men earned. By 1980, the ratio was 64 percent and it rose fairly steadily to about 73 percent in 1993 (Statistics Canada, 2003c). Since then, however, the ratio has fluctuated between about 68 percent and 74 percent. In 2011, the most recent year for which data are available as of this writing, women earned 72.0 cents for every dollar men earned (see Figure 8.6). At the 1967–2011 rate of improvement, women will achieve earnings equality with men in 2089!

Table 8.3 shows the gender wage gap in the average earnings of people in the 10 broad occupational categories used by Statistics Canada. If the wage gap were due to universal gender differences, it would not vary across occupational categories. However, it does vary considerably,

FIGURE 8.6 **Ratio of Female-to-Male Earnings, Canada (in 2011 dollars)**

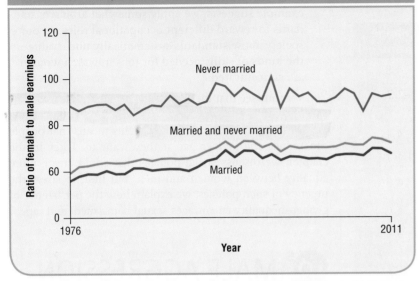

Source: Adapted from Statistics Canada, 2015i. "Female-to-Male Earnings Ratios, by Selected Characteristics, 2011 Constant Dollars, Annually (percentage)." CANSIM database, Table 2020104.

from 0.42 in primary industries (farming, fishing, and the like) to 0.84 in occupations in natural and applied science, suggesting that social conditions specific to given occupations account in part for the magnitude of the gender wage gap.

TABLE 8.3 Female–Male Earnings Ratio in Broad Occupational Categories, Canada

Occupational Category	Female–Male Earnings Ratio
Management	0.72
Business, finance, and administration	0.67
Natural and applied science	0.84
Health	0.47
Social science, education, government, and religion	0.69
Art, culture, recreation, and sport	0.76
Sales and service	0.55
Trades, transport, and equipment operation	0.55
Primary industry	0.42
Processing, manufacturing, and utilities	0.64

Note: The data in this table are for 2015.

Source: Adapted from Statistics Canada, 2015f. "Earnings of Individuals, by Selected Characteristics and National Occupational Classification (NOC-S), 2011 Constant Dollars, Annually." CANSIM database, Table 2020106.

Four main factors contribute to the gender gap in earnings (Bianchi and Spain, 1996; England, 1992):

1. *Gender discrimination.* In February 1985, when Microsoft already employed about 1000 people, it hired its first two female executives. According to a well-placed source involved in the hiring, both women got their jobs because Microsoft was trying to win a U.S. Air Force contract. Under government's guidelines, Microsoft didn't have enough women in top management positions to qualify. The source quotes then 29-year-old Bill Gates, president of Microsoft, as saying, "Well, let's hire two women because we can pay them half as much as we will have to pay a man, and we can give them all this other 'crap' work to do because they are women" (quoted in Wallace and Erickson, 1992: 291).

   This incident is a clear illustration of gender discrimination, rewarding women and men differently for the same work. Discrimination on the basis of sex is against the law in Canada. Yet progress is slow; as noted earlier, the female-to-male earnings ratio has barely budged since 1993.

2. *Women tend to be concentrated in low-wage occupations and industries.* The second factor leading to lower earnings for women is that the programs they select in high school and afterward tend to limit them to jobs in low-wage occupations and industries. The concentration of women in certain occupations and men in others is referred to as occupational sex segregation. Although women have made big strides since the 1970s in several fields, including management, business and financial professions, medicine, and law, they are still concentrated in lower-paying clerical and service occupations and the teaching profession, and underrepresented in higher-paying occupations (see Table 8.4). This pattern is particularly strong for women of colour, Aboriginal women, and women with disabilities (Chard, 2000: 229; Shain, 1995).

3. *Heavy domestic responsibilities reduce women's earnings.* In 2011, women who had never been married earned 92.8 cents for every dollar earned by men. The comparable figure for all women was 72.0 cents (refer back to Figure 8.6). Most of this

gender discrimination
Rewarding men and women differently for the same work.

occupational sex segregation The concentration of women in certain occupations and men in others.

TABLE 8.4 Percentage of Women by Occupational Category, Canada, 1987 and 2015

	1987	2015	Change (percentage)
Management	30.4	35.1	4.8
Business, finance & administration	70.6	68.3	−2.3
Natural & applied sciences	19.8	23.9	4.1
Health	78.1	79.9	1.7
Social science, education, government services & religion	56.3	70.8	14.6
Art, culture, recreation & sport	47.8	55.5	7.7
Sales & service	54.1	57.1	2.9

Source: Statistics Canada (2015j). "Labour force survey estimates (LFS), by National Occupational Classification for Statistics (NOC-S) and sex, annually." CANSIM database, Table 2820010.

acquaintance rape A sexual assault involving intercourse committed by a non-relative whom the victim knows.

20.8-cent gap represents the economic cost to women of getting married and assuming disproportionately heavy domestic responsibilities. Of course, raising children can be one of the most emotionally satisfying experiences. That should not, however, blind us to the fact it is also work that decreases the time available for education, training, and paid work. Because women are disproportionately involved in child-rearing, they suffer the brunt of this economic reality. They devote fewer hours to paid work than men do, experience more labour-force interruptions, and are more likely than men are to take part-time jobs, which pay less per hour and offer fewer benefits than full-time work does (Waldfogel, 1997). Women also do considerably more housework and eldercare than men do (Boyd, 1997: 55; Sauve, 2002). Even when they work full-time in the paid labour force, women continue to shoulder a disproportionate share of domestic responsibilities (Chapter 9, Families).

4. *Work done by women is commonly considered less valuable than work done by men, because it is viewed as involving fewer skills.* Women tend to earn less than men do because the skills involved in their work are often undervalued (Figart and Lapidus, 1996; Sorenson, 1994). For example, kindergarten teachers (nearly all of whom are women) earn less than office machine repair technicians (nearly all of whom are men). It is, however, questionable whether it takes

less training and skill to teach a young child the basics of counting and cooperation than it takes to get a photocopier to collate paper properly. As this example suggests, we apply somewhat arbitrary standards to reward different occupational roles. In our society, these standards systematically undervalue the kinds of skills needed for jobs in which women are concentrated.

We thus see that the gender gap in earnings is based on several *social* circumstances rather than on any inherent difference between women and men. This means that people can reduce the gender gap if they want to. Later in the chapter, we discuss social policies that could create more equality between women and men. But first, to stress the urgency of such policies, we explain how the persistence of gender inequality encourages sexual harassment and rape.

LO⁵ MALE AGGRESSION AGAINST WOMEN

Serious acts of aggression between men and women are common. The great majority are committed by men against women. For example, in recent years, about 25 000 sexual assaults have been reported to Canadian police annually. More than 8 out of 10 victims are women and nearly all of the accused perpetrators are men. Among young singles, the rate of sexual assault is higher than in the population as a whole (Statistics Canada, 2008b; see Figure 8.7).

Consider research on **acquaintance rape**—sexual assaults involving intercourse committed by a non-relative whom the victim knows (Meyer, 1984; Senn, Desmarais, Veryberg, and Wood, 2000). One Canadian study found that more than a fifth of female postsecondary students said they had given in to unwanted sexual intercourse because they had been overwhelmed by a man's continued arguments and pressure. Nearly 7 percent reported they had unwanted sexual intercourse because a man threatened or used some degree of physical force, and almost 14 percent claimed that a man had attempted unwanted sexual intercourse while they were either intoxicated or under the influence of drugs (DeKeseredy and Kelly, 1993).

Although Canadian law requires that people take "reasonable steps to ascertain consent" before engaging another in any sexual act, interpretations of what is "reasonable" vary. Moreover, the courts have failed to provide explicit norms for what "reasonable steps" should be. Indeed, the biggest category of cases in which men accused of sexual assault successfully argue "reasonable steps" and win acquittals are cases in which women have been deliberately drugged or are unconscious because of excessive alcohol use at the time of the assault (Sheehy, 2003: 579).

FIGURE 8.7 Percentage of University Students Who Severely Assaulted a Dating Partner in the Past Year, by Country (*n* = 6700)

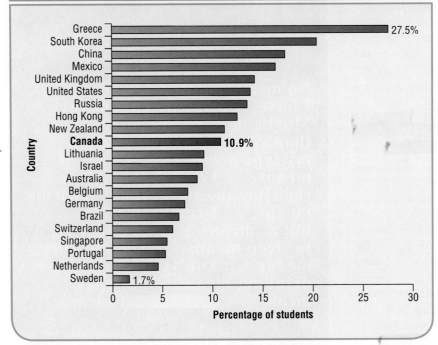

Note: Some of the U.S. data were collected in 1998. Data from other countries were collected between 2001 and 2005. "Severely assaulted" was defined as students who, in the year preceding the survey, used a knife or a gun on a partner, punched or hit a partner with something that could hurt, choked a partner, slammed a partner against a wall, beat up a partner, burned or scalded a partner, or kicked a partner.

Source: *International Dating Violence Study*. Tabulation courtesy of Murray A. Straus based on Douglas, Emily M. and Murray A. Straus, (2006) "Assault and injury of dating partners by university students in 19 nations and its relation to corporal punishment experienced as a child," *European Journal of Criminology* 3:293–318. Reprinted with permission by the authors.

Why do men commit more frequent (and more harmful) acts of aggression against women than women commit against men? It is not because men on average are physically more powerful than women are. Greater physical power is more likely to be used to commit acts of aggression only when norms justify male domination and men have much more *social* power than women have. When women and men are more equal socially, and norms justify gender equality, the rate of male aggression against women is lower. This point is evident if we consider sexual assault and sexual harassment (see also the discussion of wife abuse in Chapter 9, Families).

SEXUAL ASSAULT

Some people think rapists are men who suffer a psychological disorder that compels them to achieve immediate sexual gratification even if violence is required. Others think rape occurs because of flawed communication. They believe some victims give mixed signals to their assailants by, for example, wearing revealing clothes or flirting.

Such explanations are not completely invalid. Interviews with victims and perpetrators show that some offenders do suffer from psychological disorders. Others misinterpret signals in what they regard as sexually ambiguous situations (Hannon et al., 1995). But such cases account for only a small proportion of the total. Men who commit sexual assault rarely have a mental illness, and it is abundantly clear to most assailants that they are doing something their victims strongly oppose.

What then accounts for sexual assault being as common as it is? A sociological answer is suggested by the fact that sexual assault is sometimes not about sexual gratification at all. Some offenders cannot ejaculate or even achieve an erection. Significantly, however, all forms of sexual assault involve domination and humiliation as principal motives. It is not surprising, therefore, that some offenders were physically or sexually abused in their youth. They develop a deep need to feel powerful as psychological compensation for their early powerlessness. Others are men who, as children, saw their mothers as potentially hostile figures who needed to be controlled or as mere objects available for male gratification. They saw their fathers as emotionally cold and distant. Raised in such an atmosphere, rapists learn not to empathize with women. Instead, they learn to want to dominate them (Lisak, 1992).

Psychological factors aside, certain social situations also increase the rate of sexual aggression. One such situation is war. In war, conquering male soldiers often feel justified humiliating the vanquished, who are powerless to stop them. Rape is often used for this purpose, as was especially well documented in the ethnic wars that accompanied the breakup of Yugoslavia in the 1990s (Human Rights Watch, 1995).

The relationship between male dominance and sexual aggression is also evident in research on American fraternities. Many college and university fraternities tend to emphasize male dominance and aggression as a central part of their culture. Sociologists who have interviewed fraternity members have shown that most fraternities try to recruit members who can reinforce a macho image and avoid any suggestion of effeminacy and homosexuality. Research also shows that fraternity houses that are especially prone to sexual assault tend to sponsor parties that treat women in a particularly degrading way. By emphasizing a narrow and aggressive form of masculinity, some fraternities tend

quid pro quo sexual harassment Takes place when sexual threats or bribery are made a condition of employment decisions.

hostile environment sexual harassment Involves sexual jokes, touching, and comments that interfere with work or create an unfriendly work environment.

to facilitate sexual assault on campuses (Boswell and Spade, 1996).

Another social circumstance that increases the likelihood of sexual assault is participation in athletics. Of course, the overwhelming majority of athletes are not rapists. However, there are proportionately more rapists among men who participate in athletics than among non-athletes (Welch, 1997). That is because many sports embody a particular vision of masculinity in North American culture: competitive, aggressive, and domineering. By recruiting men who display these characteristics and by encouraging the development of these characteristics in athletes, sports can contribute to off-field aggression, including sexual aggression. Furthermore, among male athletes, there is a distinct hierarchy of sexual aggression. Male athletes who engage in contact sports are more prone to be rapists than other athletes. There are proportionately even more rapists among athletes involved in collision and combative sports, notably football (Welch, 1997).

Sexual assault, we conclude, involves the use of sex to establish dominance. Its incidence is highest in situations in which early socialization experiences predispose men to want to control women, where norms justify the domination of women, and where a big power imbalance exists between men and women.

SEXUAL HARASSMENT

Sexual harassment comes in two forms. **Quid pro quo sexual harassment** takes place when sexual threats or bribery are made a condition of employment decisions. (The Latin phrase *quid pro quo* means "one thing for another.") **Hostile environment sexual harassment** involves sexual jokes, touching, and comments that interfere with work or create a hostile work environment. Research suggests that relatively powerless women are the most likely to be sexually harassed. Specifically, women who are young, unmarried, and employed in nonprofessional jobs are most likely to become objects of sexual harassment, particularly if they are temporary workers, if the ratio of women to men in the workplace is low, and if the organizational culture of the workplace tolerates sexual harassment (Sev'er, 1999; Welsh, 1999).

Ultimately then, male aggression against women, including sexual harassment and sexual assault, is encouraged by a lesson most of us still learn at home, in school, at work, through much of organized religion,

No means **no**. Not now means **no**. I have a boy/girlfriend means **no**. Maybe later means **no**. No thanks means **no**. You're not my type means **no**. $#@!!! off means **no**. I'd rather be alone right now means **no**. Don't touch me means **no**. I really like you but ... means **no**. Let's just go to sleep means **no**. I'm not sure means **no**. You've/I've been drinking means **no**. Silence means **no**. ▭▭▭▭ means **no**.

DATE RAPE \dāt\ \'rāp\n: Not understanding **no**

Poster courtesy of the Canadian Federation of Students

In the 1990s, the Canadian Federation of Students introduced the slogan, "No means no" when it comes to sex. The problem is that some versions of "no," such as "not now" or "maybe later" are sufficiently ambiguous that they may be taken as consent. Therefore, in 2014, the State of California passed a law that sexual partners must consent by saying "yes" to sex. At Dalhousie, McGill, Concordia, and other Canadian universities, campaigns were soon initiated to publicize the higher level of consent now expected of sexual partners (Anderssen, 2014).

and in the mass media: It is natural and right for men to dominate women. To be sure, recent decades have witnessed important changes in the way women's and men's roles are defined. Nevertheless, in the world of paid work, in the household, in government, and in all other spheres of life, men still tend to command substantially more power and authority than women. Daily patterns of gender domination, viewed as legitimate by most people, are built into our courtship, sexual, family, and work norms. From this point of view, male aggression against women is simply an expression of male authority by other means.

These facts do not mean that all men endorse the principle of male dominance, much less that all men are inclined to engage in sexual assault or other acts of aggression against women. Indeed, scholars increasingly speak of *masculinities* in the plural, rather than the singular, to acknowledge differences among men and to emphasize that "masculinity" is neither innate nor a fixed entity (Messerschmidt, 1993). Many men favour gender equality, and most men never abuse a woman. Nevertheless, the fact remains that many aspects of our culture legitimize male dominance, making it seem valid or proper. For example, mainstream pornography, jokes about "dumb blondes," and leering might seem examples of harmless play. At a subtler, sociological level, however, they are assertions of the appropriateness of women's submission to men. Such frequent and routine reinforcements of male authority increase the likelihood that some men will consider it their right to assault women physically or sexually if the opportunity to do so exists or can be created. During 2013 frosh week at St. Mary's University in Halifax and the University of British Columbia in Vancouver, students chanted a cheer celebrating non-consensual sex with a minor. Some participants said the cheer was harmless fun, failing to recognize that "just kidding" has a cost. For instance, researchers have found that university men who enjoy sexist jokes are most likely to report engaging in acts of sexual aggression against women (Ryan and Kanjorski, 1998).

We thus see that male aggression against women and gender inequality are not separate issues. Gender inequality is the foundation of aggression against women. In concluding this chapter, we consider how gender equality can be increased in the coming decades. As we proceed, you should bear in mind that gender equality is not just a matter of justice. It is also a matter of safety.

GENDER RISK ACROSS 137 COUNTRIES

Women face dangers everywhere but the level of risk varies around the world. Combining data on rates of female homicide, rape, and domestic violence, we find that women are physically safest in southwestern Europe and parts of Scandinavia and at greatest risk in northern and eastern Africa, the Middle East, much of south Asia, and Peru. How can we explain this variation?

Research shows that three main factors contribute to female gender risk (Brym, 2015a: pp. 106–27). The most important factor is average national income. The richer the country, the less the female gender risk. Why? As economic development occurs, factories and offices grow while farming shrinks in importance. Demand for women's paid work increases, so women are drawn out of the home and into the system

of formal education and the paid labour force. There, men are paid more than women are for doing similar work. Domestic work, child care, and care of the elderly remain disproportionately the responsibility of women even after they start working full-time in the paid labour force. Women enter new social settings in which they may be exposed to violence. These and other issues encourage many women to demand the vote, run for office, and champion government policies that promise to correct the many problems they face. In short, economic development increases women's independence and power, leading many women to achieve movement toward greater gender equality and safety.

However, exceptions abound; even in some rich countries, female gender risk is relatively high. The biggest exceptions are Qatar, Kuwait, and the United Arab Emirates, all in the Persian Gulf region. All three of these countries are rich but in all three of them male authority predominates inside and outside the home. They illustrate a general pattern: in general, where patriarchy is most deeply entrenched, women are most likely to be killed, raped, and subjected to domestic violence.

However, even when we take wealth and patriarchy into account, we still find exceptions. Consider Tunisia, a Middle Eastern nation with a long history of patriarchy that the United Nations classifies as an upper-middle-income country in the same league economically as Argentina and Hungary (United Nations, 2014: 148). Women face less risk in Tunisia than one would expect, based on its historical level of patriarchy and its level of economic well-being. That is because Tunisian governments have been pushing to improve women's rights since the 1950s. Equality of women and men is affirmed in many Tunisian laws, and young women are as well educated as young men are. Tunisia is not Norway when it comes to female gender risk (Brym and Andersen, 2016), but it does illustrate a pattern that exists around the world: the more governments pass laws promoting equality between women and men, the lower the level of female homicide, rape, and domestic abuse.

LO⁶ TOWARD 2089

The twentieth century witnessed growing equality between women and men in many countries. In Canada, the decline of the family farm made children less economically useful and more costly to raise. As a result, women started having fewer children. The industrialization of Canada, and then the growth of the economy's service sector, increased demand for women in the paid labour force. In 1946, just 17.8 percent of adult women were in the paid labour force, compared to 87.2 of adult men. In 2010, the figure for women was 62.8 percent, compared to 72 percent for men. This demand gave women substantially more economic power and also encouraged them to have fewer children. The legalization and availability of contraception made it possible for women to exercise unprecedented control over their bodies. The women's movement fought for, and won, increased rights for women on a number of economic, political, and legal fronts. All of these forces brought about a massive cultural shift, a fundamental reorientation of thinking on the part of many Canadians about what women could and should do in society.

One indicator of the progress of women is the Gender Inequality Index, computed annually by the United Nations (United Nations Development Programme, 2015). It takes into account inequality between men and women in terms of health, participation in the paid labour force, and political influence. A score of zero indicates equality with men on these three dimensions, while a score of 1 indicates maximum inequality. Data for 2014 are available for 188 countries. As Figure 8.8 shows, nine of the ten most gender-egalitarian countries are in Northern and Eastern Europe, with Slovenia leading the pack. Women in these countries are close to equality with men. Canada ranked 23rd and the United States ranked 47th.

In general, more gender equality exists in rich than in poor countries. The top-ranked countries are all rich, suggesting that gender equality is a function of economic development. However, our analysis of the GII data suggests that political factors are important too. For example, in some of the former communist countries of Eastern Europe, gender equality is higher than we would expect, given their level of economic development. Meanwhile, in some of the Muslim-majority countries, gender inequality is lower than we would expect, given their level of economic development. These anomalies exist because the former communist countries tend to make gender equality a matter of public policy, while many Muslim-majority countries discriminate against women in the public sphere (Brym et al., 2005; Brym, 2014b: pp. 106–27).

The Gender Inequality Index figures suggest that Canadian women still have a long way to go before they achieve equality with men. We have also seen that the gender gap in earnings is shrinking but will not disappear until 2089—and then only if it continues to diminish at the same rate as it did from 1967 to 2011. That is a big "if," because progress is never automatic.

Socializing children at home and in school to understand that women and men are equally adept at all jobs is important in motivating them to excel in non-traditional

FIGURE 8.8   *Gender Inequality Index,* **Top 10 and Bottom 10 Countries, plus Canada and the United States**

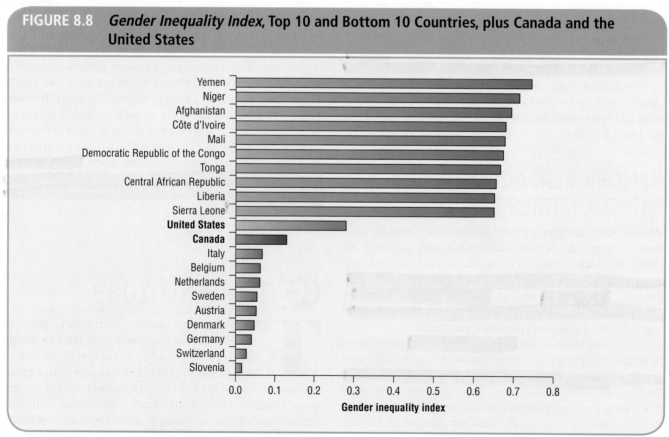

Source: United Nations Development Programme, 2015. "Table 5: Gender Inequality Index." *Human Development Report 2015.* http://hdr.undp.org/en/composite/GII (retrieved 30 April, 2016).

fields. Hiring more women to compensate for past discrimination in hiring, firing, promotion, and training is also important. However, without in any way minimizing the need for such initiatives, we should recognize that their impact will be muted if women continue to undertake disproportionate domestic responsibilities and if occupations with a high concentration of women continue to be undervalued in monetary terms.

Two main policy initiatives will probably be required in the coming decades to bridge the gender gap in earnings. One is the development of a better child-care system. The other is the development of a policy of pay equity. Let us briefly consider these issues.

CHILD CARE

High-quality, government-subsidized, affordable child care is widely available in most western European countries. Sixty percent of children in the United Kingdom are in regulated child care, as are 69 percent of children in France and 78 percent in Denmark. The comparable figure for Canada is less than 21 percent (Ferns and Friendly, 2014: 7). As a result, many Canadian women with small children are either unable to work outside the home or able to work outside the home only on a part-time basis.

A universal system of daycare was proposed in Canada as early as 1970 but little was done at the federal level or in most provinces and territories. Quebec is an exception. In 1997, Quebec introduced a comprehensive family policy that attempts to integrate family benefits, paid parental leave, child care, and kindergarten. Its child-care component heralded universally available, affordable child care. A rapid expansion in the number of spaces occurred, although waiting lists grew as well. About 62 percent of the regulated daycare spaces available in Canada are in Quebec (Ferns and Friendly, 2014: 9; Cleveland, 2016).

No new regulated daycare spaces have been added outside Quebec since 2006. The need exists. More than half of Canadian preschoolers received some kind of care outside of the home but only a quarter of them are enrolled in daycare programs. Relatives care for a growing number of young children (Statistics Canada, 2005b.)

In 2004, affordable, high-quality, regulated daycare was a central electoral promise of the victorious Liberal Party. By mid-2005, the beginnings of a national system began to take shape when the federal government reached child-care agreements with Saskatchewan, Manitoba, Ontario, and Newfoundland and Labrador. The system, had it taken root across the country, would have paid for itself. One study estimates that the annual cost of a high-quality, affordable, universal system of child care and early child-care education would be less than the dollar value of the increased employment of mothers and the improvement in child development (Cleveland and Krashinsky, 1998).

However, after his election in 2006, former prime minister Stephen Harper scrapped the agreements in favour of taxable benefits of $1200 for every child under six. The amount and the targeting were widely criticized as failing to address the burdens that women who work for pay needed to support their families. In 2007–08, government child-care funding ranged from $195 per child in Alberta to $1694 per child in Quebec, with 7 of Canada's 10 provinces contributing less than $400 per child (Beach, Friendly, Ferns, Prabhu, and Forer, 2009: 183, 186; see Figure 8.9).

> **pay equity** Equal pay for work of equal value, or the equal dollar value of different jobs. It is established in gender-neutral terms by comparing jobs in terms of the education and experience needed to do them and the stress, responsibility, and working conditions associated with them.

EQUAL PAY FOR WORK OF EQUAL VALUE

On paper, Canadian women have had the right to equal pay for the same jobs done by men since the 1950s. Unfortunately, although early laws proclaimed lofty goals, they failed to result in fair wages.

In the 1980s, researchers found that women earned less than men did, partly because jobs in which women were concentrated were valued less than jobs in which men were concentrated. They therefore tried to establish gender-neutral standards by which they could judge the dollar value of work. These standards included such factors as the education and experience required to do a particular job and the level of responsibility, amount of stress, and working conditions associated with it. Researchers felt that, by using these criteria to compare jobs in which women and men are concentrated, they could identify pay inequities. The underpaid could then be compensated accordingly. In other words, women and men would receive equal pay for work of equal value, even if they did different jobs.

During the mid-1980s, some governments amended the law to state that women should be paid equally for work of equal value. This amendment required employers to compare the rates of pay for women and men in dissimilar jobs that nevertheless involved the same level of skill, effort, and responsibility, and the same working conditions. In 1985, Manitoba became the first Canadian province to demand that its public sector implement plans for equal pay for work of equal value—or **pay equity**, as it came to be called. Today, pay equity laws cover public and private employees in the federal jurisdiction, Ontario, and Quebec; and provincial government employees in Manitoba, New Brunswick, Nova Scotia, and Prince Edward Island. Policy frameworks for negotiating

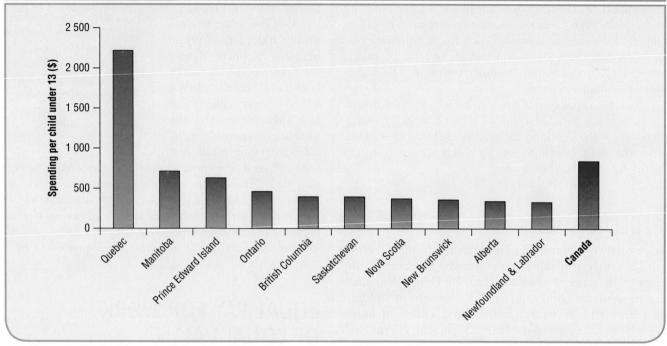

FIGURE 8.9   Spending on Child Care, Canada, by Province

Note: Figures are for 2012.

Source: Ferns, Carolyn and Martha Friendly. 2012. *The state of early childhood education and care in Canada 2012*, p.12.
http://childcarecanada.org/sites/default/files/StateofECEC2012.pdf (retrieved 29 August 2015).

pay equity with certain public sector employees exist in Saskatchewan, Newfoundland and Labrador, and British Columbia. Only Alberta has adopted no laws or policy frameworks for pay equity, either in the public or the private sector (Hay Group, 2014).

Legal and regulatory provisions vary widely. Enforcement mechanisms are meagre. Employers have found various ways to argue that unequal wages do not signify discrimination based on sex. Thus, although pay equity is undoubtedly a significant step toward achieving gender equality, inequity remains, as evidenced by the persistent wage gap between working men and women.

THE WOMEN'S MOVEMENT

Improved daycare and pay equity would do much to bridge the gender gap in earnings between women and men. However, improvements in the social standing of women do not depend on just the sympathy of government and business leaders. Progress on this front has always depended in part on the strength of the organized women's movement. That is likely to be true in the future, too. In concluding this chapter, it is therefore fitting to consider the state of the women's movement and its prospects.

The "first wave" of the women's movement emerged during the late nineteenth century and lasted into the early 1920s. The most important public achievements of this movement in Canada were the right to vote and the right to be considered persons under Canadian law (Nelson and Robinson, 2002). In 1916, women in Alberta, Manitoba, and Saskatchewan won the right to vote in provincial elections. Other provinces and territories followed: British Columbia (1917), Ontario (1917), Nova Scotia (1918), New Brunswick (1919), Yukon (1919), Prince Edward Island (1922), Newfoundland and Labrador (1925), Quebec (1940), and, finally, the Northwest Territories (1951). These rights were first granted to white women. Women from certain ethnic and racial groups did not receive the franchise until later (Nelson and Robinson, 2002).

In the mid-1960s, the "second wave" of the women's movement emerged. Second-wave feminists were inspired in part by the successes of the civil rights movement in the United States. They felt that women's concerns were largely ignored despite persistent and pervasive gender inequality. Like their counterparts more than a century earlier, they held demonstrations, lobbied politicians, and formed women's organizations to further their cause. They demanded equal rights with men in education and employment, the elimination of sexual violence, and women's control over reproduction.

Today, diversity exists in the feminist movement concerning ultimate goals. Three main streams may be distinguished (Tong, 1989):

1. *Liberal feminism* is the most popular current. Its advocates believe that the main sources of women's subordination are learned gender roles and the denial of opportunities to women. Liberal feminists advocate non-sexist methods of socialization and education, more sharing of domestic tasks between women and men, and extending to women all of the educational, employment, and political rights and privileges that men enjoy.

2. *Socialist feminists* regard women's relationship to the economy as the main source of women's disadvantages. They believe that the traditional nuclear family emerged along with inequalities of wealth. In their opinion, once men possessed wealth, they wanted to ensure that their property would be transmitted to their children, particularly their sons. They accomplished this in two ways. First, men exercised complete economic control over their property, thus ensuring it would not be squandered and would remain theirs and theirs alone. Second, they enforced female monogamy, thus ensuring that their property would be transmitted only to *their* offspring. Thus, according to socialist feminists, the economic and sexual oppression of women has its roots in capitalism.

    Socialist feminists also assert that the reforms proposed by liberal feminists are inadequate because they can do little to help working-class women, who are too poor to take advantage of equal educational and work opportunities. Socialist feminists conclude that only the elimination of private property and the creation of economic equality can bring about an end to the oppression of all women.

3. *Radical feminists* find the reforms proposed by liberals and the revolution proposed by socialists inadequate. Patriarchy—male domination and norms justifying that domination—is more deeply rooted than capitalism, say the radical feminists. After all, patriarchy predates capitalism. Moreover, it is just as evident in self-proclaimed communist societies as it is in capitalist societies. Radical feminists conclude that the very idea of gender must be changed to bring an end to male domination. Some radical feminists argue that new reproductive technologies, such as in vitro fertilization, are bound to be helpful in this regard because they can break the link between women's bodies and child-bearing (see Chapter 9, Families). However, the revolution envisaged by radical feminists goes beyond the realm of reproduction to include all aspects of male sexual dominance. From their point of

The "first wave" of the women's movement achieved its main goal—the right of women to vote—as a result of much demonstrating, lobbying, organizing, and persistent educational work.

view, mainstream pornography, sexual harassment, restrictive contraception, sexual assault, incest, sterilization, and physical assault must be eliminated so that women can reconstruct their sexuality on their own terms.

This thumbnail sketch by no means exhausts the variety of streams of the contemporary women's movement. Indeed, some observers say the movement entered its "third wave" in the mid-1980s, characterized by anti-racist and postmodernist feminists criticizing liberal, socialist, and radical feminists for generalizing from the experience of white women and for failing to understand

The "second wave" of the women's movement started to grow in the mid-1960s. Members of the movement advocated equal rights with men in education and employment, the elimination of sexual violence, and women's control over reproduction.

how women's lives are rooted in particular historical and racial experiences (Cassidy, Lord, and Mandell, 1998: 26; hooks, 1984). These new currents have done much to extend the relevance of feminism to previously marginalized groups.

Partly because of the political and intellectual vigour of the women's movement, some feminist ideas have gained widespread acceptance in Canadian society since the 1970s. Nonetheless, as this chapter documents, gender equality is still a remote goal.

SOCIOLOGY ON THE TUBE

Girls

Launched in 2012, *Girls* is a comedy that follows the adventures of four single women in their twenties living in New York City. The award-winning show is inevitably compared with *Sex and the City*, another hit show that centred on the lives of four single women in their thirties living in New York City. The choice of New York City in both cases is no accident: "The Big Apple" presents the perfect backdrop for the consumer-driven lifestyle and self-centred anguish of the characters in both shows.

In *Girls*, the show's creator, Lena Dunham, plays one of its central characters, Hannah Horvath. Hannah is an aspiring writer who has been informed by her parents that they are withdrawing their financial support. Now, she must make it on her own. She comes up with a desperate scheme to be compensated for her unpaid internship, but ends up without a job. For a while, the only job she can get is in a friend's coffee shop. Unlike *Sex and the City*, then, the characters in *Girls* are not just younger, but far less certain of themselves and of their future. For Hannah and her friends, the struggle to launch meaningful careers often ends in setback and failure. Moreover, their sex lives are unsatisfying, demeaning, and sometimes uncomfortable to watch. The women on *Sex and the City* bemoan the state of their sex lives too, but they do so as self-assured and financially independent career women. Their sexual exploits are presented humorously and with irony, so taboo subjects such as anal sex, masturbation, and abortion are open for discussion. What a difference a decade makes!

Aby Baker/Getty Images

Postmodern anguish in *Girls*

Despite the awards and accolades bestowed on the show, *Girls* has no shortage of detractors. One criticism has to do with its lack of diversity. The four young women are all white and from privileged backgrounds. Critics charge that this is a jarring oversight given that New York City is one of the most racially diverse cities in the world. Others criticize the show for its anti-feminist slant. For example, one television critic wonders what there is "to celebrate for feminism when a show depicts four entirely self-interested young women and a lead character having the most depressing, disempowered sexual relationships imaginable?" (Scott, 2012). Take, for example, Hannah's boyfriend, Adam. Beyond his sexual hang-ups, which include child rape fantasies, he is an immature, abusive, and self-absorbed jerk. Deep down, Hannah knows she deserves better but she can't make herself leave him.

Critical Thinking Questions

1. How vigorous is the feminist movement today compared to, say, the 1970s?
2. Has feminism become so much a part of our everyday lives that we often don't notice its influence?
3. Is the pull of feminism stronger for some categories of the population than for others? If so, which population categories find it least attractive? Which population categories find it most attractive?

READY TO STUDY?

IN THE BOOK, YOU CAN:

❏ Tear out the chapter review card at the back of the book to have a summary of the chapter and key terms handy.

ONLINE YOU CAN:

❏ Work through key concepts with a Guided Learning Question.

❏ Prepare for tests with quizzes.

❏ Review the key terms with flash cards.

❏ Explore practical examples of chapter concepts with Connect a Concept exercises.

GO TO NELSON.COM/STUDENT TO ACCESS THESE DIGITAL RESOURCES.

9

Families

Annette Shaff/Shutterstock.com

LEARNING OBJECTIVES

In this chapter, you will learn to

LO¹ Identify new family forms that have emerged in recent decades, making the traditional nuclear family less common than it used to be.

LO² Appreciate that the traditional nuclear family has been weakening since the 1800s, although it strengthened temporarily in the years immediately following World War II.

LO³ List the factors contributing to variation in patterns of mate selection, marital satisfaction, divorce, reproductive choice, housework and child care, and domestic violence.

LO⁴ Describe the characteristics of diverse family forms.

LO⁵ Explain how public policy can prevent the emergence of certain social problems that might otherwise result from the decline of the traditional nuclear family.

INTRODUCTION

CALGARY (July 5, 2015)—A Calgary man has been charged with second-degree murder in connection with the death of his wife who disappeared more than seven months ago.

Joshua Burgess, 29, was arrested Sunday, two days after Calgary police located the remains of Shannon Madill, 25.

Madill, a well-known performer in the Calgary area, was last seen by a family member on Nov. 27, 2014. She was scheduled to meet her brother at a Calgary theatre on November 30 but never turned up. Her family reported her missing the next day.

Police discovered Madill's body in the couple's home in the 1900 block of Spiller Road Southeast on Friday. Investigators were executing a search warrant at the residence. The search of the house continued Sunday. . . .

Police said that Burgess had been co-operative throughout the ordeal and there had been no previous calls to their residence.

"There was no history of domestic conflict (or) domestic violence whatsoever in that relationship," said Chisholm.

In December, Burgess stood alongside members of Madill's family as they made a passionate plea for information about her whereabouts.

At the time, Madill's family confirmed that the couple had separated but continued to live together in their Calgary home.*

For better or for worse, our most intense emotional experiences are bound up with our families. We love, hate, protect, hurt, express generosity toward, and envy nobody as much as our parents, siblings, children, and mates. Some families are islands of domestic bliss. A few, like the family described in the news story above, are sites of the most violent acts imaginable. In Canada, about 40 percent of homicides occur within family or intimate relationships (Statistics Canada, 2013a). Given the intensity of our emotional involvement with our families, should we be surprised that most people are passionately concerned with the rights and wrongs, the dos and don'ts, of family life? Should we be surprised that family issues lie close to the centre of political debate in this country?

*Source: *CTVNews*. "Husband charged in connection with death of actress wife in Calgary." 5 July 2015. http://www.ctvnews.ca/canada/husband-charged-in-connection-with-death-of-actress-wife-in-calgary-1.2454914 (retrieved 23 August 2015). Reproduced by permission of Bell Media Inc.

LO¹ IS "THE FAMILY" IN DECLINE?

Because families are emotional minefields, few subjects of sociological inquiry generate as much controversy. Much of the debate centres on a single question: Is the family in decline and, if so, what should be done about it? These questions are hardly new. John Laing, a Protestant minister in Ontario, wrote in 1878, "We may expect to see further disintegration until the family shall disappear. . . . In all things civil and sacred the tendency of the age is towards individualism . . . its plausible aphorisms and popular usages silently undermining the divine institution of the family" (quoted in Sager, 2000: vii). This alarm, or one much like it, is sounded whenever the family undergoes rapid change, and particularly when the divorce rate increases.

Today, when some people speak about the decline of the family, they are referring to the **nuclear family**. The nuclear family comprises a cohabiting man and woman who maintain a socially approved sexual relationship and have at least one child. Others are referring more narrowly to what we call the **traditional nuclear family**. The traditional nuclear family is a nuclear family in which the wife works in the home without pay while the husband works outside the home for money. This makes him the "primary provider and ultimate authority" (Popenoe, 1988: 1).

In the 1940s and 1950s, many sociologists and much of the Canadian public considered the traditional nuclear family to be the most widespread and ideal family form. However, for reasons we will examine below, fewer than 39 percent of Canadian families in 2011 were nuclear families, compared with almost 57 percent in 1981 (see Figure 9.1) and 69 percent in 1901. Moreover, because about 80 percent of mothers with school-aged children are in the paid labour force, only a small minority of Canadian adults live in traditional nuclear families today. New family forms, including single-parent families, common-law families, and gay and lesbian families, have become increasingly prevalent in recent decades (see Table 9.1).

Some sociologists, many of them functionalists, view the decreasing prevalence of the married-couple family and the rise of the "working mother" as an unmitigated disaster (Popenoe, 1996, 1998). In their view, rising rates of crime, illegal drug use, poverty, and welfare dependency (among other social ills) can be traced to the fact that so many children are not living in two-parent households with stay-at-home mothers. They call for various legal and cultural reforms to shore up the traditional nuclear family. For instance, they want to make it harder to get a divorce, and they want people to place less emphasis on individual happiness at the expense of family responsibility.

Other sociologists, influenced by conflict and feminist theories, disagree with the functionalist assessment (Coontz, 1992; Stacey, 1996). In the first place, they argue that it is inaccurate to talk about *the* family, as if this important social institution assumes or should assume only a single form. They emphasize that families have been structured in many ways and that the diversity of family forms is increasing as people accommodate the demands of new social pressures. Second, they argue that changing family forms do not necessarily represent deterioration in the quality of people's lives. In fact, such changes often represent *improvement* in the way people live. These sociologists believe that the decreasing prevalence of the traditional nuclear family and the proliferation of diverse family forms have benefited many men, women, and children and have not harmed other children as much as the functionalists think. They also believe that various economic and political reforms, such as the creation of an affordable nationwide daycare system, could eliminate most of the negative effects of single-parent households.

> **nuclear family** Consists of a cohabiting man and woman who maintain a socially approved sexual relationship and have at least one child.
>
> **traditional nuclear family** A nuclear family in which the husband works outside the home for money and the wife works without pay in the home.

FIGURE 9.1 Changing Canadian Families, Canada, 1981–2011 (percentage)

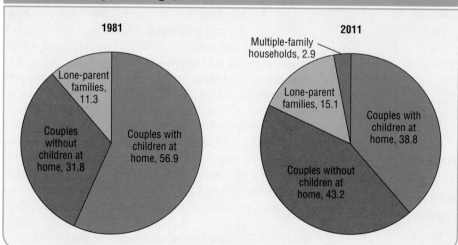

Sources: Statistics Canada, n.d., "Census Families Time Series, 1931–2001"; Statistics Canada, 2013, "Canadian Households in 2011: Type and Growth."

TABLE 9.1 The Traditional Nuclear Family and New Alternatives

Traditional Nuclear Family	New Alternatives
Legally married	Never-married singlehood, non-marital cohabitation
With children	Voluntary childlessness
Two-parent	Single-parent (never married or previously married)
Permanent	Divorce, remarriage (including binuclear family involving joint custody, stepfamily, or "blended" family)
Male primary provider, ultimate authority	Egalitarian marriage (including dual-career and commuter marriage)
Sexually exclusive	Extramarital relationships (including sexually open marriage, swinging, and intimate friendships)
Heterosexual	Same-sex intimate relationships or households
Two-adult household	Multi-adult households (including multiple spouses, communal living, affiliated families, and multigenerational families)

Source: Adapted from Macklin, Eleanor D. 1980. "Nontraditional Family Forms: A Decade of Research." *Journal of Marriage and the Family* 42: 906.

We first outline the functional theory of the family because the issues raised by functionalism are still a focus of sociological controversy (Mann, Grimes, Kemp, and Jenkins, 1997). Borrowing from the work of conflict theorists and feminists, we next show that the nuclear family has been in decline since the nineteenth century and is less prevalent than is often assumed. We then explain how change in the distribution of power between husbands and wives has affected mate selection, marital satisfaction, divorce, reproductive choice, domestic labour, and wife abuse. The discussion then turns to alternative family forms—how they are structured and how their frequency varies by class and sexual orientation. Finally, you will learn that although postindustrial families solve some problems, they are hardly an unqualified blessing. The chapter's concluding section considers the kinds of policies that might help alleviate some of the most serious concerns facing families today.

FUNCTIONALISM AND THE NUCLEAR IDEAL

FUNCTIONAL THEORY

For any society to survive, its members must cooperate economically. They must have babies. And they must raise offspring in an emotionally supportive environment so the offspring can learn the ways of the group and eventually operate as productive adults. Since the 1940s, functionalists have argued that the nuclear family is ideally suited to meet these challenges. In their view, the nuclear family provides a basis for five main functions: regulated sexual activity, economic cooperation, reproduction, socialization, and emotional support (Murdock, 1949: 1–22; Parsons, 1955).

Functionalists cite the pervasiveness of the nuclear family as evidence of its ability to perform these functions. To be sure, other family forms exist. **Polygamy** expands the nuclear unit "horizontally" by adding one or more spouses (almost always wives) to the household. Polygamy is still legally permitted in many less industrialized countries in Africa and Asia. However, the overwhelming majority of families are monogamous because they cannot afford to support several wives and many children (see Sociology on the Tube, *Sister Wives*).

polygamy Expands the nuclear family "horizontally" by adding one or more spouses (usually women) to the household.

The idealized North American family of the 1950s

Tim Bieber/The Image Bank/Getty Images

SOCIOLOGY ON THE TUBE 📺

Sister Wives

Kody Brown, an otherwise unexceptional 45-year-old advertising salesperson from Utah, has four wives and 18 children. Until 2014, he had been married to Meri for more than 20 years; he considers his other intimate relationships "commitments" or "spiritual unions." Meri and two of Kody's other wives were raised in polygamous families. The Browns are members of the Apostolic Union Brethren, a pro-polygamy group of fundamentalist Mormons. They have allowed their lives to be documented in *Sister Wives* since 2010 because they want to legitimize polygamy as a reasonable lifestyle choice.

Almost everyone's first question about polygamy is, "Doesn't it spawn intense jealousy?" We soon learn that it does. During *Sister Wives'* first season, Kody dates and becomes engaged to Robyn, his first new wife in 16 years. The arrival of the newcomer threatens the three older wives. Meri is especially jealous because Robyn is 31 while Meri is 41 and has been unable to have more than one child. As preparations for the wedding unfold, however, the four women become closer, and by the time the wedding day rolls around, Robyn has been accepted into the fold. In fact, in 2014 Meri divorced Kody voluntarily so that he and Robyn could legally adopt Robyn's children from her first marriage. In the resolution of various household issues that emerge, the audience learns that people can in fact lead pretty normal lives polygamously.

However, what is reasonable for certain individuals may not be reasonable for entire societies (Henrich, Boyd, and Richerson, 2012). Some 85 percent of human societies have permitted men to marry more than one woman, but monogamy tends to take root as societies develop economically and socially because it solves some big social problems. Societies in which polygamy is widespread experience intense competition for women because relatively few wealthy men marry a disproportionately large number of women, leaving relatively few women for all the non-wealthy men. Not surprisingly, the rate of rape tends to be high in such societies. So is the rate of murder, assault, robbery, and fraud, because non-wealthy men must engage in intense competition for resources that enable them to attract women.

Polygamous marriages are also characterized by relatively high levels of gender inequality and woman abuse. In contrast, when monogamy becomes institutionalized, gender inequality falls, as do crime rates and incidents of violent conflict within households, including incidents of child neglect and abuse. Polygamy may be a reasonable lifestyle choice for Kody Brown and his four wives, but little good can be said of it when entire societies allow it.

Critical Thinking Questions

1. Based on the evidence just presented, do you think the law should ban polygamy or allow it? Why?
2. As far as polygamy is concerned, could the law balance individual desires with the religious principles of some groups and the needs of society as a whole? How?

The **extended family** expands the nuclear family "vertically" by adding another generation—one or more of the spouses' parents—to the household. Extended families used to be common throughout the world. They still are in some places. However, according to the functionalists, the basic building block of the extended family (and of the polygamous family) is the nuclear unit.

George Murdock was a functionalist who conducted a famous study of 250 mainly preliterate societies in the 1940s. Murdock wrote, "Either as the sole prevailing form of the family or as the basic unit from which more complex familial forms are compounded, [the nuclear family] exists as a distinct and strongly functional group in every known society" (Murdock, 1949: 2). Moreover, the nuclear family, Murdock continued, is everywhere based on **marriage**. He defined marriage as a socially approved, presumably long-term, sexual and economic union between a man and a woman. It involves rights and obligations between spouses and between spouses and their children.

FUNCTIONS OF THE NUCLEAR FAMILY

Let us consider the five main functions of marriage and the nuclear family in more detail:

1. *Sexual regulation.* The nuclear family defines the boundaries within which legitimate sexual activity is permitted, thus making an orderly social life possible. Of course, sex is readily available outside marriage. Murdock found that only 22 percent of 250 mainly preliterate societies forbade or disapproved of premarital sex between non-relatives, and in more than half the societies, a married man could legitimately have an extramarital affair with one or more female relatives (Murdock, 1949: 5–6). It is hardly news that premarital and extramarital sex are common in postindustrial societies. So sex is not the primary motivation for marrying.

2. *Economic cooperation.* People marry also because "a man and a woman make an exceptionally efficient cooperating unit" (Murdock, 1949: 7). Historically, pregnancy and nursing have restricted women in their activities, whereas men possess superior strength. Therefore, women have traditionally performed lighter tasks close to home while men have specialized in lumbering, mining, quarrying, land clearing, house building, hunting, fishing, herding, and trade (Murdock, 1937). Thus, "marriage exists only when the economic and the sexual are united into one relationship, and this combination occurs only in marriage" (Murdock, 1949: 8).

3. *Reproduction.* Before the invention of modern contraception, sex often resulted in the birth of a baby. In pre-modern societies, children are an investment in the future. By the age of six or seven, children in such societies do some chores. Their economic value to the family increases as they mature. When children become adults, they often help support aging parents. So there is a big economic incentive to having children.

4. *Socialization.* The investment in children can be realized only if adults rear the young to maturity. This involves not only caring for them physically but also teaching them language, values, beliefs, skills, religion, and much else. Some functionalists regard socialization as the "basic and irreducible" function of the family (Parsons, 1955: 16).

5. *Emotional support.* Functionalists note that the nuclear family universally gives its members love, affection, and companionship. In the nuclear family, it is mainly the mother who is responsible for ensuring the family's emotional well-being. It falls on the father to take on the role of earning a living outside the family (Parsons, 1955: 23). The fact that he is the "primary provider" makes him the ultimate authority.

Does this functionalist account provide an accurate picture of family relations across history? To assess the adequacy of the theory, let us discuss the families in which the early functionalists themselves lived: families in urban and suburban middle-class North America in the 1950s.

LO² THE CANADIAN MIDDLE-CLASS FAMILY IN THE 1950s

As a description of family patterns in the 15 years after World War II, functionalism has its merits. During the Great Depression (1929–39) and World War II (1939–45), many Canadians were forced to postpone marriage because of widespread poverty, government-imposed austerity, and physical separation. After this long and dreadful ordeal, many Canadians just wanted to settle down, have children, and enjoy the peace, pleasure, and security that family life seemed to offer. Conditions could not have been better for doing just that. The immediate postwar era was one of unparalleled

> **extended family** Expands the nuclear family "vertically" by adding another generation—one or more of the spouses' parents—to the household.
>
> **marriage** Traditionally defined, is a socially approved, presumably long-term sexual and economic union between a man and a woman. It involves reciprocal rights and obligations between spouses and between parents and children.

crude divorce rate The number of divorces that occur in a year for every 1000 people in the population.

crude marriage rate The number of marriages that occur in a year for every 1000 people in the population.

total fertility rate The average number of children that would be born to a woman over her lifetime if she had the same number of children as do women in each age cohort in a given year.

optimism and prosperity. Real per capita income rose, as did the percentage of Canadians who owned their own homes. Laws passed during World War II to encourage women to join the paid labour force were cancelled. Things were now supposed to return to "normal," meaning that women were supposed to go back to being housewives and men to being bread-winners (Kingsbury and Scanzoni, 1993).

As a result of these conditions, Canadians experienced a marriage boom (see Figure 9.2). Increasingly, Canadians lived in married-couple families. The proportion of "never married" Canadians decreased and the average age at first marriage dropped for both women and men (McVey and Kalbach, 1995: 225; see Figure 9.3). As we might expect, the marriage boom soon gave way to a baby boom. The average Canadian family had four children; nearly all married women stayed home to raise their children (Nikiforuk, 1999). In 1951, 90 percent of married men but only 11.2 percent of married women worked in the paid labour force. Most women engaged in what has been called an "orgy of domesticity" in the postwar years, devoting increasing attention to child rearing and housework. They also became increasingly concerned with the emotional quality of family life as love and companionship became firmly established as the main motivations for marriage (Coontz, 1992: 23–41; Skolnick, 1991: 49–74).

The 1950s: An Historical Anomaly

What many functionalists fail to appreciate is that the immediate postwar period was in many respects an historical anomaly (Cherlin, 1992: 6–30). Trends in divorce, marriage, and child-bearing show a gradual *weakening* of the

nuclear family from the second half of the nineteenth century until the mid-1940s, and continued weakening after the 1950s. Specifically, throughout the nineteenth century, the divorce rate rose slowly. The **crude divorce rate** is the number of divorces that occur in a year for every 1000 people in the population. Meanwhile, the marriage rate fell. The **crude marriage rate** is the number of marriages that occur in a year for every 1000 people in the population. (Remarkably, data on these indicators have not been published by Statistics Canada for years after 2008.) The total fertility rate also fell (see Figure 9.4). The **total fertility rate** is the average number of children that would be born to a woman over her lifetime if she had the same number of children as do women in each age cohort in a given year.

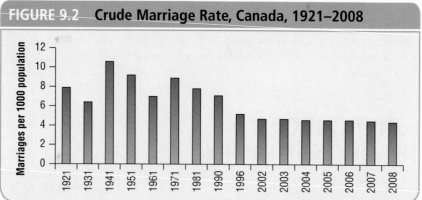

FIGURE 9.2 Crude Marriage Rate, Canada, 1921–2008

Sources: Adapted from the Statistics Canada products "Selected Marriage Statistics, 1921–1990," 1992a, Catalogue No. 82-552, and *The Daily*, Catalogue No. 11-001; Statistics Canada, 2007, "Table 101-1002: Mean Age and Median Age of Males and Females, by Type of Marriage and Marital Status, Canada, Provinces and Territories, Annual"; and Statistics Canada, 2013b, "Chart 6: Crude Marriage Rate and Crude Divorce Rate, Canada, 1926 to 2008."

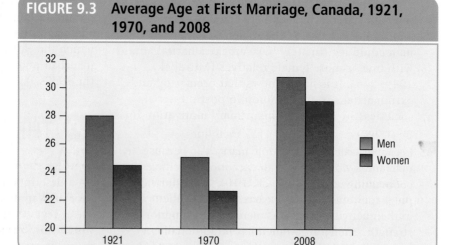

FIGURE 9.3 Average Age at First Marriage, Canada, 1921, 1970, and 2008

Sources: Statistics Canada. 2007, "Table 101-1002: Mean Age and Median Age of Males and Females, by Type of Marriage and Marital Status, Canada, Provinces and Territories, Annual"; Statistics Canada publications, "Marriage and Conjugal Life in Canada, 1991," 1992b, Catalogue 91-534, and *The Daily*, Catalogue 11-001, Monday, June 2, 2003d; and Statistics Canada, 2013c, "Mean Age and Median Age of Males and Females, by Marital Status, Canada, Provinces and Territories, 2005 to 2008." Special tabulation prepared by the Health Statistics Department.

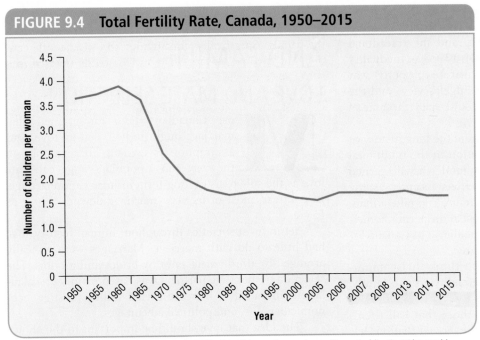

FIGURE 9.4 Total Fertility Rate, Canada, 1950–2015

Source: *CIA World Factbook*. 2015. "Total Fertility Rate." https://www.cia.gov/library/publications/the-world-factbook/fields/2127.html (retrieved 23 August 2015).

Canada's marriage rate started falling after 1946. The divorce rate started rising in the 1960s when the law was changed to make it easier to divorce. The total fertility rate started falling after 1961. Thus, by the early 1960s, the earlier trends had reasserted themselves. Only the peculiar historical circumstances of the postwar years, noted above, temporarily reversed them. The big picture from the nineteenth century until the present is that of a gradually weakening nuclear family. The early functionalists, it seems, generalized too hastily from the families they knew best—their own.

The Displacement of Family Functions

According to many modern-day functionalists, the nuclear family has become less prevalent since the nineteenth century because many of the traditional functions of the nuclear family have been eroded or partly taken over by other institutions. For example, the traditional division of labour, based on the physical capabilities and limitations of husband and wife, has weakened. That is because contraception and child-care services are now available, while demand for women to enter the paid labour force and pursue a higher education has increased. Women are no longer tied to the home in the way they once were. Children are not the economic asset they were in agricultural societies that lacked a social welfare system. Quite the opposite: It is now very expensive to raise children. Meanwhile, part of the task of socialization has been taken over by schools, the mass media, and peer groups, while reproduction outside the nuclear family is possible because of the introduction of in vitro fertilization

and other reproductive technologies. Thus, contemporary functionalists argue that the traditional nuclear family has been in decline for more than a century because other institutions perform many of the economic, reproductive, and socialization functions that were formerly reserved for the nuclear family.

Conflict and Feminist Theories

Other sociologists, influenced less by functionalism than by the conflict and feminist traditions, see the proliferation of non-nuclear families as a response to changes in power relations between women and men.

The idea that power relations between women and men explain the prevalence of different family forms was first suggested by Marx's close friend and co-author, Friedrich Engels. Engels argued that the traditional nuclear family emerged along with private property and inequalities of wealth.

According to Engels, little inequality existed in nomadic, hunting-and-gathering societies. Even in pastoral societies (which domesticated cattle and other animals) and horticultural societies (which used small hand tools for planting and harvesting), families did not own land. They considered land common property. A family might work a particular plot of land for some time, even generations, but if the plot fell into disuse, then another family had the right to use it. Substantial inequalities in wealth emerged only in early agricultural societies, when people attached large animals, such as oxen, to plows and it became possible to farm large tracts of land. That was when private property was legally recognized. That was when some families began to amass wealth. And that was when men came to enjoy legal control of property and the wealth it generated.

Once legal control of property was concentrated in the hands of a man, wrote Engels, he became concerned about how to transmit it to his children, particularly his sons. How could a man safely pass on an inheritance, asked Engels? Only by controlling his wife sexually and economically. Economic control ensured that the man's property would not be squandered and would remain his and his alone. Sexual control, in the form of enforced female monogamy, ensured that his property would be transmitted only to *his* offspring. Engels concluded that only the elimination of private property and the creation of economic equality—in a word, communism—could bring an end to gender inequality and the traditional nuclear family (Engels, 1970 [1884]: 138–39). Inequality deriving from men's control of private property was the basis of the nuclear family in Engels's view, and the elimination of private property would spell the end of the nuclear family.

Engels was of course right to note the long history of male economic and sexual domination in the traditional nuclear family. A century ago, any money a wife earned typically belonged to her husband. As recently as the 1950s, a Canadian wife could not rent a car, take a loan, or sign a contract without her husband's permission. It was only in the 1980s that it became illegal in Canada for a husband to rape his wife.

However, Engels was wrong to think that communism would eliminate gender inequality in the family. Gender inequality has been as common in societies that call themselves communist as in those that call themselves capitalist. For example, the Soviet Union left "intact the fundamental family structures, authority relations, and socialization patterns crucial to personality formation and sex-role differentiation. Only a genuine sexual revolution [or, as we prefer to call it, a *gender revolution*] could have shattered these patterns and made possible the real emancipation of women" (Lapidus, 1978: 7).

Because gender inequality exists in noncapitalist societies, most feminists believe something other than, or in addition to, capitalism accounts for gender inequality and the persistence of the traditional nuclear family. In their view, *patriarchy*—male dominance and norms justifying that dominance—is more deeply rooted in the economic, military, and cultural history of humankind than the classical Marxist account allows. For them, only a "genuine gender revolution" can alter this state of affairs.

Just such a revolution in family structures, authority relations, and socialization patterns picked up steam in Canada and other rich industrialized countries about half a century ago, although its roots extend back to the eighteenth century. As you will now see, the revolution is evident in the rise of romantic love and happiness as bases for marriage, the rising divorce rate, and women's increasing control over reproduction through their use of contraceptives, among other factors. We begin by considering the sociology of mate selection.

LO³ POWER AND FAMILIES

LOVE AND MATE SELECTION

Most Canadians take for granted that marriage ought to be based on love. Our assumption is evident, for example, in the way most popular songs celebrate love as the sole basis of long-term intimacy and marriage. In contrast, most of us view marriage devoid of love as tragic.

Yet in most societies throughout human history, love had little to do with marriage. Marriages were typically arranged by third parties, not by brides and grooms. The selection of marriage partners was based mainly on calculations intended to increase their families' prestige, economic benefits, and political advantages.

The idea that love should be important in the choice of a marriage partner first gained currency in eighteenth-century England with the rise of liberalism and individualism, philosophies that stressed the freedom of the individual over community welfare (Stone, 1977). The intimate linkage between love and marriage that we know today emerged only in the early twentieth century, when Hollywood and the advertising industry began to promote self-gratification on a grand scale. For these new spinners of fantasy and desire, an important aspect of self-gratification was heterosexual romance leading to marriage (Rapp and Ross, 1986).

Hollywood glamorized heterosexual romantic love and solidified the intimate linkage between love and marriage that we know today. Clark Gable and Vivien Leigh in *Gone with the Wind* (1939).

The Everett Collection / The Canadian Press

Today, wherever individualism is highly prized, love has come to be defined as the essential basis for marriage. A survey of college undergraduates in 11 countries asked, "If a man (woman) had all the qualities you desired, would you marry this person if you were not in love with him (her)?" In the five rich countries plus Brazil, between 3 percent and 8 percent of students said they would marry someone they were not in love with if that person possessed all the qualities they were looking for in a partner. In the five developing countries, the comparable percentage ranged from 10 percent to 50 percent (Levine et al., 1995; see Figure 9.5).

Still, it would be a mistake to think that love alone determines mate selection in our society—far from it. Three sets of social forces influence who you are likely to fall in love with and marry (Kalmijn, 1998: 398–404):

1. *Marriage resources.* Potential spouses bring certain resources with them to the "marriage market." They use these resources to attract mates and compete against rivals. These resources include financial assets, status, values, tastes, and knowledge. Most people want to maximize the financial assets and status they gain from marriage, and they want a mate who has similar values, tastes, and knowledge. As a result, the person with whom you fall in love and choose to marry is determined partly by the assets you and he or she bring to the marriage market.

2. *Third parties.* A marriage between people from two different groups can threaten the internal cohesion of one or both groups. Therefore, to varying degrees, families, neighbourhoods, communities, and religious institutions raise young people to identify with the groups they are members of and think of themselves as different from members of other groups. They may also apply sanctions to young people who threaten to marry outside the group. For example, although ethnic intermarriage has become increasingly common in Canada, parents often encourage their children to marry within their own ethnic group to preserve their unique culture (Kalbach, 2000; Kitano and Daniels, 1995). This is especially true among immigrants who come to Canada from cultures in which arranged marriage has been the tradition (Dugger, 1996). As a result, whom you fall in love with and choose to marry is determined partly by the influence of third parties.

3. *Demographic and compositional factors.* The probability of marrying inside your group increases with the group's size and geographical concentration. If you are a member of a small group or a group that is dispersed geographically, you stand a greater chance of having to choose an appropriate mate from outside your group. There may simply be too few prospects in your group from which to choose (Brym, Gillespie, and Gillis, 1985). In addition, the ratio of men to women in a group influences the degree to which members of each sex marry inside or outside the group. For instance, war and imprisonment can eliminate many male group members as potential marriage partners and encourage female group members to marry outside the group or forgo marriage altogether.

Finally, because people usually meet potential spouses in "local marriage markets"—schools, universities and colleges, places of work, neighbourhoods, bars, and clubs—the degree to which these settings are socially segregated influences mate selection. You are more likely to marry outside your group if local marriage markets are socially heterogeneous. As a result, the person you fall in love with and choose to marry is determined partly by the size, geographical dispersion, and sex ratio of the groups you belong to and the social composition of the local marriage markets you frequent.

Because of the operation of these three sets of social forces, the process of falling in love and choosing a mate is far from random. Most of us have selected or will select a partner of similar racial or ethnic background, age, and social class.

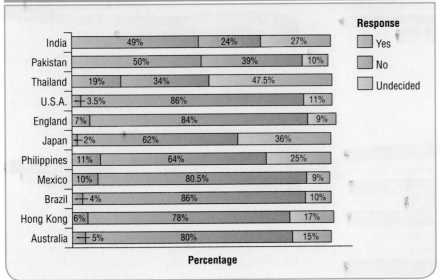

FIGURE 9.5 Responses to the question: "If a man (woman) had all of the other qualities you desired, would you marry this person if you were not in love with him (her)?"

Response
- Yes
- No
- Undecided

Country	Yes	No	Undecided
India	49%	24%	27%
Pakistan	50%	39%	10%
Thailand	19%	34%	47.5%
U.S.A.	3.5%	86%	11%
England	7%	84%	9%
Japan	2%	62%	36%
Philippines	11%	64%	25%
Mexico	10%	80.5%	9%
Brazil	4%	86%	10%
Hong Kong	6%	78%	17%
Australia	5%	80%	15%

Percentage

Note: Percentages may not add up to 100 because of rounding.

Source: Levine, R., Sato, S., Hashimoto, T., Verma, J. (1995). "Love and Marriage in Eleven Cultures." *Journal of Cross-Cultural Psychology* Vol. 26 (5) pp. 554–71. Copyright © 1995 by SAGE Publications, Inc. Reprinted by permission of SAGE Publications, Inc.

Mate Selection and the Internet

Armed with facts like those just listed, some websites, including eHarmony, PerfectMatch, GenePartner, and Chemistry, seek to turn the process of finding the love of your life into a science. By having clients reveal their personality characteristics and complete a checklist of likes and dislikes, they claim frequent success matching compatible partners.

It is in fact now commonplace for people to meet online and establish an intimate relationship. A study of a representative sample of more than 4000 adults found that 22 percent of the heterosexual respondents met their spouse or romantic partner online, making the Web the second most common way of meeting an intimate partner (Rosenfeld and Thomas, 2012). (Meeting through friends is still the most common method.)

Nonetheless, one should treat the inflated claims of matchmaking sites with skepticism. One analysis of 313 studies showed that personality traits and attitudes had no effect on the quality of long-term relationships. A study of 23 000 married couples showed that similarity of personalities accounted for only 0.5 percent of the variation in marital satisfaction (Finkel et al., 2012).

The reason that matchmaking websites routinely fail to predict what makes people suited for a satisfying, long-term relationship is that they cannot collect relevant data. Many important aspects of relationships emerge only after people have been together for a considerable time. How well do they communicate? How sexually compatible are they? How compatible are they in their methods of solving problems? How do they react to crises such as job loss, illness, and infertility? Websites such as eHarmony may have a good track record making matches, but they are much less successful in helping to create enduring and happy relationships because answers to questions like these can emerge only from time and experience together, not from responding to a questionnaire.

MARITAL SATISFACTION

Just as mate selection came to depend more on romantic love over the years, so marital stability came to depend more on having a happy rather than merely a useful marriage. This change occurred because women in Canada and many other societies have become more autonomous, especially over the past half century; one aspect of the gender revolution women are experiencing is that they are freer than ever to leave marriages in which they are unhappy.

One factor that contributed to women's autonomy was the legalization of birth control measures in Canada in 1969. The birth control pill made it easier for women to delay childbirth and have fewer children. A second factor that contributed to women's autonomy was their increased participation in the paid labour force. Once women enjoyed a source of income independent of their husbands, they gained the means to decide the course of their own lives to a greater extent than ever before. A married woman with a job outside the home is less tied to her marriage by economic necessity than is a woman who works only at home. If the woman who works outside the home is deeply dissatisfied with her marriage, she can more easily leave. In addition, beginning in the late 1960s, laws governing divorce were changed to make divorce easier.

The Social Roots of Marital Satisfaction

If marital stability now depends largely on marital satisfaction, what are the main factors underlying marital satisfaction? The sociological literature emphasizes five sets of forces (Collins and Coltrane, 1991: 394–406, 454–64):

1. *Economic forces.* Money issues are the most frequent subjects of family quarrels, and money issues loom larger when there isn't enough money to satisfy a family's needs and desires. Accordingly, marital satisfaction tends to fall and the divorce rate tends to rise as you move down the socioeconomic hierarchy. The lower the social class and the lower the educational level of the spouses, the more likely it is that financial pressures will make them unhappy and the marriage unstable. Marital dissatisfaction and divorce are also more common among groups with high poverty rates. In contrast, the marital satisfaction of wives and, even more, of husbands, generally increases when wives enter the paid labour force (Hughes, Galinsky, and Morris, 1992; Lupri and Frideres, 1988). This increase is due mainly to the beneficial financial effects. However, if either spouse spends so much time on the job that he or she neglects the family, marital satisfaction falls.

2. *Divorce laws.* Many surveys show that, on average, married people are happier than unmarried people are. Moreover, when people are free to end unhappy marriages and remarry, the average level of happiness increases among married people. Thus, the level of marital happiness has increased in Canada over the past few decades, especially for wives. That is partly because it has become easier to get a divorce and more acceptable to remarry and create a **blended family**, which includes the children of one or both spouses from a previous marriage. In countries where getting a divorce is more difficult (e.g., Italy and Spain), husbands and wives tend to be less happy than in countries where getting a divorce is easier (e.g., Canada and the United States; Stack and Eshleman, 1998).

3. *The family life cycle.* In Canada, the rate of divorce per 1000 population reaches a peak in the fifth year of marriage and then falls (Ambert, 1998: 5). For

marriages that last, marital satisfaction generally starts high, falls when children are born (especially for wives), reaches a low point when children are in their teenage years, and rises again when children reach adulthood (Glenn, 1990; Rollins and Cannon, 1974). Couples without children and parents whose children have left home (so-called *empty nesters*) enjoy the highest level of marital satisfaction. Parents who are just starting families or who have adult children living at home enjoy intermediate levels of marital satisfaction. Marital satisfaction is lowest during the "establishment" years, when children are attending school. Although most people get married at least partly to have children, it turns out that children, and especially teenagers, usually put big emotional and financial strains on families. These strains typically lower marital satisfaction.

4. *Housework and child care.* Marital happiness is higher among couples who perceive an equitable distribution of housework and child care (Rosenbluth, Steil, and Whitcomb, 1998). The farther couples are from an equitable sharing of domestic responsibilities, the more tension there is among all family members (Risman and Johnson-Sumerford, 1998). Research finds that equitable sharing tends to increase with education (Berk, 1985).

5. *Sex.* Having a good sex life is associated with marital satisfaction. Contrary to popular belief, surveys show that sex generally improves during a marriage. From these findings, some experts conclude that general marital happiness leads to sexual compatibility (Collins and Coltrane, 1991: 344). However, the reverse can also be true. Good sex can lead to a good marriage. After all, sexual preferences are deeply rooted in our psyches and our earliest experiences. We cannot easily alter them to suit our partners. If spouses are sexually incompatible, they may find it hard to change, even if they communicate well, argue little, and are generally happy on other grounds. However, if a husband and wife are sexually compatible, they may work hard to resolve other problems in the marriage for the sake of preserving their good sex life. Thus, the relationship between marital satisfaction and sexual compatibility is probably reciprocal. Each factor influences the other.

Let us now see what happens when low marital satisfaction leads to divorce.

DIVORCE

Before 1968, adultery was the only grounds for divorce in Canada, except in Nova Scotia, where cruelty was sufficient grounds even before Confederation (Morrison, 1987). The Divorce Act of 1968, the first federal divorce statute, expanded the grounds under which a divorce could be granted. The amendment of Canada's Divorce Act in 1985 allowed only one ground for divorce—marital breakdown, defined in three ways: (1) the spouses have lived apart for one year, (2) one of the spouses has committed an act of adultery, (3) one spouse has treated the other with mental or physical cruelty. Today, a spouse seeking divorce no longer has to prove grounds. Instead, a marriage is legally "dissolved" because the relationship is "irretrievably broken." Following these amendments, the divorce rate reached a historic high in 1987 but has since declined (Statistics Canada, 2000d). Some 38 percent of Canadian marriages now end in divorce.

Economic Effects

Women's income usually falls after divorce, while men's generally rises (Finnie, 1993). That is because husbands tend to earn more than wives do, children typically live with their mothers after divorce, and child-support payments are often inadequate.

In the past, Canadian laws regarding the division of marital assets on divorce and the awarding of alimony contributed to women's declining living standards after divorce. For example, in the early 1970s, Irene Murdock, a farm wife, claimed that her labours over 15 years had earned her a share in the family farm. However, the Supreme Court of Canada ruled that her work was simply that of an "ordinary farm wife" and did not entitle her to share in the property that she and her husband had accumulated during their marriage (Steel, 1987: 159).

Although all Canadian provinces and territories now have laws requiring spouses to share assets in the event of marital breakdown, the precise definition of what constitutes a family asset varies and creates inconsistencies across jurisdictions (Dranoff, 2001: 257). In addition, although the monetary value of tangible family assets (e.g., money in the bank, a house) can be calculated and shared, the valuable "new property" today is the earning

"Yes, this is a two career household. Unfortunately I have both careers."

Carol Simpson CartoonWork & Illustration

child support Money paid by the noncustodial parent to the custodial parent for the purpose of supporting the children of a separated marital, cohabiting, or sexual relationship.

power of a professional degree, highly paid employment, work experience, a skilled trade, or other "human capital" (Glendon, 1981). On divorce, the wife may receive an equal share of tangible property, but that does not usually result in her beginning post-divorce life on an equal footing with her former husband, especially if she retains physical custody of the couple's children and if she sacrificed her education and career so that he could earn a college or university degree.

Child support is money paid by the non-custodial parent to the custodial parent to support the children of a separated marital, cohabiting, or sexual relationship. Under the Divorce Act, either parent can be ordered to pay child support. However, because mothers retain custody in the great majority of cases—and because women are more likely to be economically disadvantaged in employment—those ordered to pay child support are usually fathers.

Every jurisdiction in Canada requires parents to support their children following separation or divorce. However, court orders do not guarantee that child support will be paid. In practice, orders for child and spousal support have often been difficult to enforce, and default rates have been high. All Canadian provinces and territories now have their own programs to protect against nonpayment of child support. Nonetheless, the problem of "deadbeat parents" (especially fathers) remains serious.

Some analysts argue that the main reason for nonpayment of child support is the unemployment or underemployment of the noncustodial parent (Meyer and Bartfield, 1996). If that is correct, "coercive child-support collection policies, such as automatic wage withholding, will have only limited success" and solving the problem "will be the old and unglamorous one, of solving un- and underemployment, both for the fathers and the mothers" (Braver, Fitzpatrick, and Bay, 1991: 184–85).

Emotional Effects

Although divorce enables spouses to leave unhappy marriages, questions have been raised about the emotional consequences of divorce for children, particularly in the long term. Some scholars claim that divorcing parents are simply trading the well-being of their children for their own happiness. What does research say about this issue?

Research shows that children of divorced parents tend to develop behavioural problems and do less well in school than do children in intact families (Demo, Fine, and Ganong, 2000). They are more likely to engage in delinquent acts and to abuse drugs and alcohol. They often experience an emotional crisis, particularly in the first two years after divorce. What is more, when children of divorced parents become adults, they are less likely than are children of nondivorced parents to be happy. They are more likely to suffer health problems, depend on welfare, earn low incomes, and experience divorce themselves. In one study, almost half the children of divorced parents entered adulthood as worried, underachieving, self-deprecating, and sometimes angry young men and women (Wallerstein, Lewis, and Blakeslee, 2000). Clearly, divorce can have serious, long-term, negative consequences for children.

However, much of the research that seems to establish a link between divorce and long-term negative consequences for children is based on families who seek psychological counselling. Such families are a small and unrepresentative minority of the population. By definition, they have more serious emotional problems than the large majority, who do not need psychological counselling after divorce. We must be careful not to generalize from such studies. Another problem with much of this research is that some analysts fail to ask whether factors other than divorce might be responsible for the long-term distress experienced by many children of divorced parents.

Factors Affecting the Well-Being of Children

Researchers who rely on representative samples and examine the separate effects of many factors on children's well-being provide the best evidence on the consequences of divorce for children. For example, a reanalysis of 92 relevant studies showed that, on average, the overall effect of divorce on children's well-being is not strong and is declining over time (Amato and Keith, 1991). This research also found that three factors account for much of the distress among children of divorce:

1. *A high level of parental conflict.* A high level of parental conflict creates long-term distress among children (Jekielek, 1998). Divorce without parental conflict does children much less harm. In fact, children in divorced families have a higher level of well-being on average than do children in high-conflict intact families. The effect of parental conflict on the long-term well-being of children is substantially greater than the effect of any other factor.

2. *A decline in living standards.* By itself, the economic disadvantage experienced by most children in divorced families exerts a small impact on their well-being. Nonetheless, it is clear that children of divorce who do not experience a decline in living standards suffer less harm.

3. *The absence of a parent.* Children of divorce often lose a parent as a role model and a source of emotional support, practical help, and supervision. By itself, this factor also has a small effect on children's well-being, even if the child has continued contact with the non-custodial parent (Resnick et al., 1997).

Subsequent studies confirm these generalizations and add an important observation. Many of the behavioural and adjustment problems experienced by children of divorce existed before the divorce took place. We cannot therefore attribute them to the divorce itself (Nielsen, 1999; Pasley and Minton, 2001; Stewart et al., 1997; Thompson and Amato, 1999).

In sum, claiming that divorcing parents selfishly trade the well-being of their children for their own happiness is an exaggeration. Although the heightened risk of poverty is real, high levels of parental conflict can also have serious negative consequences for children, even when they enter adulthood. In such high-conflict situations, divorce can benefit children. By itself, the absence of a parent has a small negative effect on children's well-being. However, this effect is becoming smaller over time, perhaps in part because divorce is so common that it is no longer a stigma.

REPRODUCTIVE CHOICE

We have seen that the power women gained from working in the paid labour force put them in a position to leave a marriage if it made them deeply unhappy. Another aspect of the gender revolution women are experiencing is that they are increasingly able to decide what happens in the marriage if they stay. For example, women now have more say over whether they will have children and, if so, when they will have them and how many they will have.

Children are increasingly expensive to raise. They no longer give the family economic benefits, as they did, say, on the family farm. Most women want to work in the paid labour force, many of them to pursue a career. As a result, most women decide to have fewer children, to have them farther apart, and to have them at an older age. Some decide to have none at all (Dalphonse, 1997).

Women's reproductive decisions are carried out by means of contraception and abortion. Abortion was declared a criminal offence in Canada in 1892. In the 1960s, an abortion reform movement spearheaded by Dr. Henry Morgentaler urged the repeal of abortion laws that, in his words, "compelled the unwilling to bear the unwanted" (quoted in Dranoff, 2001: 16). In 1969, the law was changed to permit "therapeutic abortion" if performed by a physician in an accredited hospital and if a three-member committee certified that the continuation of the pregnancy would likely endanger the health of the mother. In 1988, the Supreme Court of Canada struck down the law on abortion on the grounds that it contravened a woman's right to control her own reproductive life and, as such, contravened her constitutionally protected guarantees to security of her person. In 1989, the Supreme Court also unanimously determined that the civil law in Quebec, the Quebec Charter, and the common law do not protect fetal life or interests. In 1993, the Supreme Court of Canada struck down legislation that banned abortion clinics. Today, abortion clinics outside hospitals operate in most provinces and abortions are available in hospitals in all provinces and territories except Prince Edward Island.

In 2014, 81,897 Canadian women obtained abortions (Abortion Rights Coalition of Canada, 2016). On a global scale, the abortion rate in Canada is low, at about 15 per 1000 women between the ages of 15 and 44. The comparable rate is 21 in the United States, 45 in Russia, and 57 in Cuba (Sedgh et al., 2007: 219).

Attitudes toward abortion are mixed but polls suggest that the number of Canadians who do not want to reopen the abortion debate is twice as large as the number who believe that a new debate is overdue (Angus Reid Public Opinion, 2013). Attitudes toward abortion vary by age, with teens more likely than adults to approve of the availability of legal abortion for any reason.

Right-to-life versus pro-choice activists have been clashing since the 1970s. Right-to-life activists object to the decriminalization of abortion; pro-choice activists want the current situation preserved. Both groups have tried to influence public opinion and lawmakers to achieve their aims. A few extreme right-to-life activists (almost all men) have resorted to violence (Gegax and Clemetson, 1998).

As sociologists Randall Collins and Scott Coltrane (1995) note, it seems likely that the recriminalization of abortion would likely return us to the situation that existed in the 1960s. Many abortions took place then, but because they were illegal, they were expensive, hard to obtain, and posed dangers to women's health. If abortion laws were repealed, Collins and Coltrane predict that poor women and their unwanted children would suffer most. Taxpayers would wind up paying bigger bills for social assistance and medical care.

Elliott Landy / Redferns / Getty Images

HOUSEWORK AND CHILD CARE

As we have seen, women's increased participation in the paid labour force, their increased participation in the system of higher education, and their increased control over reproduction transformed several areas of family life. Despite this far-ranging gender revolution, however, one domain remains more resistant to change: housework, child care, and senior care. This fact was first documented in detail by sociologist Arlie Hochschild in the 1980s. She showed that even women who worked full-time in the paid labour force usually began a "second shift" when they returned home. There, they prepared meals, helped with homework, did laundry, and so on (Hochschild with Machung, 1989).

Today, men take a more active role in the day-to-day running of the household. Still, a 2000 study of household labour in 10 rich countries found that "women continue to be responsible for the majority of hours of unpaid labour" ranging from a low of 70 percent in Sweden to a high of 88 percent in Italy (Bittman and Wajcman, 2000: 173). In Canada, 20 percent of women—but only 8 percent of men—devoted 30 hours or more to unpaid household work according to the 2006 census. Men were almost twice as likely as women were to claim that they did not devote any time to such work (see Table 9.2).

Even these figures do not reveal the whole picture, however. Men tend to do low-stress chores that can often wait a day or a week. These jobs include mowing the lawn, repairing the car, and painting the fence. Although fathers of young children under the age of five are often happy to play with their children, they spend less time than mothers do providing more time-intensive forms of child care, such as feeding, washing, dressing, and medical care. In general, women tend to do the repetitive, higher stress chores that cannot wait. In short, the picture falls short of a revolution (Harvey, Marshall, and Frederick, 1991).

Two main factors shrink the gender gap in housework, child care, and senior care. First, the smaller the difference between the husband's and the wife's earnings, the more equal the division of household labour. Women who earn relatively high incomes use some of their money to pay outsiders to do domestic work. In addition, such women are able to translate earning power into domestic influence. Their increased financial status enables them to get their husbands to do more around the house.

Attitude is the second factor that shrinks the gender gap in domestic labour. The more the husband and wife agree that there *should* be equality in the household division of labour, the more equality there is. Seeing eye to eye on this issue is often linked to both spouses having a postsecondary education (Greenstein, 1996). Thus, if greater equality is going to exist between men and women in doing household chores, two things have to happen: (1) There must be greater equality between men and women in the paid labour force and (2) broader cultural acceptance of the need for gender equality must be achieved.

SPOUSAL VIOLENCE

About 12 percent of police-reported violent crime in Canada involves spousal violence, and 83 percent of victims of spousal violence are women. Women are three times as likely as men are to suffer an injury, five times as likely to require medical attention, and five times as likely to report that the violence they experienced caused them to fear for their lives. Compared with men, women are more likely to report being beaten, choked, or threatened with a gun or knife, or having these weapons used against them. Compared with women, men are more likely to report being slapped, having something thrown at them, or being kicked, bitten, or hit (Bunge, 2000; Statistics Canada, 2009b).

Three main types of spousal violence exist (Johnson and Ferraro, 2000):

1. *Common couple violence* occurs when partners have an argument and one partner lashes out physically at the other. For a couple that engages in this type of violence, violent acts are unlikely to occur often, escalate over time, or be severe. Both partners are about equally likely to engage in common couple violence, regardless of their gender.

2. *Intimate terrorism* is part of a general desire of one partner to control the other. Where one partner engages in intimate terrorism, violent acts are likely to occur often, escalate over time, and be severe. Among heterosexual couples, the aggressor is usually the man.

3. *Violent resistance* is the third main type of domestic violence. Among heterosexual couples, it typically involves a woman violently defending herself against a man who has engaged in intimate terrorism.

TABLE 9.2	Unpaid Housework in Canada for Women and Men over the Age of 14 (percentage)	
	Women	**Men**
No hours	7	12
Fewer than 5 hours	18	30
5 to 14 hours	31	34
15 to 29 hours	24	16
30 or more hours	20	8
Total	100	100

Note: These data are for 2006. The *2011 National Household Survey*, which replaced the long-form census, did not collect data on domestic labour.

Source: Statistics Canada. 2010f. "Unpaid Work (20), Age Groups (9) and Sex (3) for the Population 15 Years and Over of Canada, Provinces, Territories, Census Divisions and Census Sub-divisions, 2006 Census—20% Sample Data."

Gender Inequality and Spousal Violence

For heterosexual couples, spousal violence is associated with the level of gender equality in the family and in the larger society. The higher the level of gender inequality, the greater the frequency of spousal violence. Severe wife assault is therefore more common in lower-class, less highly educated families in which gender inequality tends to be high and men are likely to believe that male domination is justified. Severe wife abuse is also more common among couples who witnessed their mothers being abused and who were themselves abused when they were children, although research suggests that these socialization factors are considerably less influential than was once believed (Gelles, 1997; Simons, Wu, Johnson, and Conger, 1995; Smith, 1990). Still, male domination in both childhood socialization and current family organization increases the likelihood of severe wife assault.

In addition, Straus (1994) has shown that wife assault is associated with gender inequality in the larger society. Comparing measures of wife assault and gender inequality in each U.S. state, he found that as gender equality increases—as women and men become more equal in the larger society—wife assault declines. We conclude that for heterosexual couples, the incidence of domestic violence is highest where a big power imbalance between men and women exists, where norms justify the male domination of women, and, to a lesser extent, where early socialization experiences predispose men to behave aggressively toward women.

Summing up, we can say that conflict theorists and feminists have performed a valuable sociological service by emphasizing the importance of power relations in structuring family life. A substantial body of research shows that the gender revolution that started half a century ago has influenced the way we select mates, our reasons for being satisfied or dissatisfied with marriage, our propensity to divorce, the reproductive choices women make, the distribution of housework and child care, variations in the rate of spousal violence—in short, all aspects of family life. As you will now learn, the gender revolution has also created a much greater diversity of family forms.

LO4 FAMILY DIVERSITY

HETEROSEXUAL COHABITATION

About 90 percent of Canadians marry at least once, but marriage is becoming less important for some Canadians. Even in 1995, when asked, "In order for you to be happy in life, is it very important, important, not very important, or not at all important to be married?" just two-thirds of Canadian women rated marriage as important or very important. Younger Canadians were less likely than older Canadians to consider marriage important or very important. Those living in Quebec were markedly less likely to do so: 53 percent of women and 59 percent of men in Quebec considered marriage important or very important (Wu, 2000: 65–66). A new type of intimate relationship has emerged between strict singlehood and cohabitation. "Friends with benefits" have occasional sexual relations but without romance or commitment (see the Sociology at the Movies feature in this chapter). And although living in a common-law relationship may be a prelude to marriage for some people, for others it has become an alternative to marriage.

SOCIOLOGY AT THE MOVIES

Friends with Benefits

In most romantic comedies, the path to true love begins with a hint of romance. Not so with *Friends with Benefits*, which shows that the path to true love can begin with a booty call.

Jamie (Mila Kunis), a headhunter from New York, recruits Dylan (Justin Timberlake), an art director from Los Angeles, to take a new position at *GQ* magazine in New York. Unfamiliar with the city, Dylan begins to hang out with Jamie. They find they have much in common—including fear of emotional commitment. They wonder what it would be like to be in a relationship with no strings attached and no possibility of disappointment. After talking it over, the two decide to enter into a "friends with benefits" relationship. They'll have sex with one another but won't let themselves fall in love with one another.

However, after a while, Jamie wants a change. Taking a walk through Central Park, they encourage each other to try to pick someone up. Dylan starts talking to a woman who turns out to be married and uninterested. Jamie approaches a man and invites him on a date. Jamie falls hard for him. Feeling apprehensive and mindful of her past hurts, she tells him they

(Continued)

Mila Kunis and Justin Timberlake, the stars of *Friends with Benefits*.

won't have sex until after the fifth date. They enjoy five magical dates. As the night of the fifth date draws to a close, she asks him to spend the night. When she catches him sneaking out of her apartment the next morning, it becomes evident he is not her prince.

Jamie is heartbroken. She turns to Dylan for comfort. Dylan recommends that she accompany him back to Los Angeles for a weekend away at his family's place. There, Jamie meets Dylan's dad, sister, and nephew who take to her instantly. Over the course of the weekend, Jamie and Dylan appear to be rekindling their relationship. But the moment is short-lived—Jamie overhears Dylan telling his sister that Jamie doesn't mean anything to him. Feeling betrayed once again, Jamie abruptly leaves and flies home alone.

Dylan returns to New York, pondering what Jamie really means to him. It takes a heart-to-heart moment with his father to get him to face the truth. Dylan's father urges his son not to let the love of his life get away. If he does, Dylan will regret it. Dylan springs into action, employing all of his romantic impulses to sweep Jamie off of her feet and convince her that he is the one for her.

Even as *Friends with Benefits* decries the perils of modern love and reinforces the age-old message that, for each of us, one true love awaits, it suggests that a new type of relationship between strict singlehood and marriage is possible.

Critical Thinking Questions

1. Could a "friends with benefits" relationship exist on a long-term or even life-long basis? Why, or why not?
2. If a "friends with benefits" relationship could exist on a long-term or life-long basis, what would be its advantages and disadvantages compared to cohabitation and marriage?

Since the Canadian census first started collecting information on cohabitation in 1981, the number of cohabiting people 15 years of age and older has increased dramatically. The proportion of common-law families in Canada more than tripled between 1981 and 2011—from 5.6 percent to 16.9 percent of all families. In Quebec, the 2011 figure was 31.5 percent (Statistics Canada, 2009a, 2012e). Most Canadian women aged 18 to 49 approve of premarital sex and non-marital cohabitation when couples intend to marry at some point in the future. Some 55 percent of women outside Quebec and 73 percent of women in Quebec believe it is acceptable for couples to live together when they have no intention of making a long-term commitment and are simply sexually attracted to each other. In both cases, younger women and women in Quebec are particularly likely to voice such approval (Wu, 2000: 59).

SAME-SEX MARRIAGE AND CIVIL UNIONS

In 2001, the Netherlands became the first country to legalize same-sex marriage. By 2016, 16 countries (nation-wide or in some parts) had followed suit. Canada did so in 2005. In 2011, same-sex spouses formed nearly 65 000 Canadian families, 0.7 percent of the total number of families in the country (see Figure 9.6).

Many jurisdictions, especially in western Europe, allow homosexuals to register their partnerships under the law in so-called civil unions. Civil unions recognize the partnerships as having some or all of the legal rights of marriage. In the United States, more opposition to registered partnerships and same-sex marriages exists than in Europe and Canada. Yet, despite continuing opposition to same-sex

Kristina Nikishina/Epsilon/Getty Images

FIGURE 9.6 Same-Sex Unions in Canada, 2006 and 2011

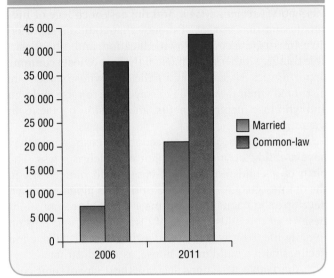

Sources: Statistics Canada, 2009d, "Same-Sex Couples by Type of Union (Married, Common-Law) and Sex, 2006 Census—20% Sample Data"; Statistics Canada, 2012d, "2011 Census of Population: Families, Households, Marital Status, Structural Type of Dwelling, Collectives."

The Canadian Press/Clement Allard

In 2002, in a precedent-setting move hailed by gay-rights activists as the first of its kind in the world, full parental rights were extended to same-sex couples in Quebec. In addition, same-sex couples were granted the same status and obligations as heterosexual married couples when they entered into a civil union. Here, lesbians react as the Quebec legislature passes the law.

marriage, the ultimate direction of change in many parts of the world is clear. Amid sharp controversy, the legal and social definition of "family" is being broadened to include cohabiting, same-sex partners in long-term relationships. This change reflects the fact that most homosexuals, like most heterosexuals, want a long-term, intimate relationship with one other adult (Chauncey, 2005). In fact, in Denmark, where homosexual couples can register partnerships under the law, the divorce rate for registered homosexual couples is lower than for heterosexual married couples (Ontario Consultants on Religious Tolerance, 2000).

Raising Children in Homosexual Families

Some same-sex couples raise children who (1) are the offspring of previous, heterosexual marriages, (2) are adopted, or (3) result from artificial insemination.

Many people believe that children brought up in homosexual families develop a confused sexual identity, exhibit a tendency to become homosexuals themselves, and suffer discrimination from children and adults in the "straight" community. A small but growing body of literature, mostly on lesbian families, suggests the contrary.

Children who grow up in homosexual families appear to be much like children who grow up in heterosexual families. For example, a 14-year study assessed 25 young adults who were the offspring of lesbian families and 21 young adults who were the offspring of heterosexual families (Tasker and Golombok, 1997). The researchers found that the two groups were equally well adjusted and displayed little difference in sexual orientation.

Homosexual and heterosexual families do differ in some respects, and those differences seem to favour children who grow up in homosexual families. For example, lesbian couples with children record higher satisfaction with their partnerships than do lesbian couples without children. In contrast, among heterosexual couples, it is the childless who record higher marital satisfaction (Koepke, Hare, and Moran, 1992). In addition, the partners of lesbian mothers spend more time caring for children than do the husbands of heterosexual mothers. Because children usually benefit from adult attention, we must consider this a plus.

Homosexual couples also tend to be more egalitarian than heterosexual couples are, sharing most decision making and household duties equally (Rosenbluth, 1997). That is because they tend to reject traditional marriage patterns. The fact that they tend to have similar gender socialization and earn about the same income also encourages equality (Kurdek, 1996; Reimann, 1997). In sum, available research suggests being raised in a lesbian family has no apparent negative consequences for the children and some benefits over and above being raised in a heterosexual family (Balkissoon, 2011; Foster, 2006; Wolpert, 2012).

LONE-PARENT FAMILIES

During the first half of the twentieth century, lone-parent families were generally the result of the death of one parent (Oderkirk and Lochhead, 1992). Today, solo parenting is usually the product of separation or divorce,

Sean Bolt/Shutterstock.com

after which child custody is typically granted to mothers. In 2011, more than 15 percent of Canadian families were headed by a lone parent and more than 80 percent of those families were headed by women. Poverty is far more prevalent among female-headed single-parent families than among any other type of family. The poverty rate in female-headed single-parent families is more than double the rate in male-headed single-parent families.

Low levels of social support, family dysfunction, and parental depression all have significant negative effects on children and are more common in low-income households (National Council of Welfare, 1999b). Child poverty is related to school failure, negative involvement with parents, stunted growth, reduced cognitive abilities, limited emotional development, and a high likelihood of dropping out of school (Duncan et al., 1998; Fields and Smith, 1998).

ZERO-CHILD FAMILIES

In Canada, what we prefer to call "zero-child families" are increasingly common. Our admittedly clumsy term seems necessary because the alternatives are so value-laden: a "childless family" implies that a family without children lacks something it should have, while the more recent "child-free family" suggests that a family without a child is unencumbered and that a child is therefore a burden. To maintain neutrality, we resort to clumsiness.

Roughly a fifth of women between the ages of 40 and 44 have never given birth (Lamanna and Riedmann, 2003: 369). To explain this fact we must first recognize that not having a child may be the result of circumstances beyond a couple's control. For example, one or both partners may be infertile, and some evidence suggests that infertility is a growing issue, perhaps because of chemical pollutants in the air and water. It seems that not having a child is more often a matter of choice, however, and the main reasons for the increasing prevalence of zero-child families are the rising cost of raising a child and the growth of attractive alternatives.

Just how expensive are children? In 2011, the best estimate of the average cost of raising a Canadian child up to the day before his or her nineteenth birthday was $243 660 (Cornell, 2011). Add the cost of college or university and that is a lot of money that could be spent on investments, the couple's own education, and other desirable things. Mothers bear most of the cost of lost economic opportunities. Usually, they are the ones whose careers are disrupted when they decide to stay home to raise children and who lose income, benefits, and pension payments in the process.

Couples also incur non-economic costs when they have a child, the most important of which is stress. The birth of a child requires that couples do more work in the home, give up free time and time alone together, develop an efficient daily routine, and divide responsibilities. All of this adds sources of disagreement and tension to daily life, so it is little wonder that marital satisfaction declines with a child in the house, as noted earlier.

Alternative attractions decrease the desire of some couples to have a child. People with high income, high education, and professional and managerial occupations are most likely to have zero-child families. Such people tend to place an especially high value on mobility, careers, and leisure-time pursuits. Usually, they are neither frustrated nor unhappy that they do not have a child. Despite their tendency to feel negatively stereotyped as "selfish," they tend to be more satisfied with their marriage than are couples with a child (Lamanna and Riedmann, 2003: 380).

LO⁵ FAMILY POLICY

Having discussed several aspects of the decline of the traditional nuclear family and the proliferation of diverse family forms, we can now return to the big question posed at the beginning of this chapter: Is the decline of the nuclear family a bad thing for society? Said differently, do two-parent families—particularly those with stay-at-home moms—provide the kind of discipline, role models, help, and middle-class lifestyle that children need to stay out of trouble with the law and grow up to become well-adjusted, productive members of society? Conversely, are family forms other than the traditional nuclear family the main source of teenage crime, poverty, welfare dependency, and other social ills?

The answer suggested by research is clear: yes and no (Houseknecht and Sastry, 1996; Popenoe, 1996; Sandqvist and Andersson, 1992). Yes, the decline of the traditional nuclear family can be a source of many social problems. No, it doesn't have to be that way.

The United States is a good example of how social problems can emerge from nuclear family decline. Sweden is a good example of how such problems can be averted. On almost all indicators of nuclear family decline, Sweden leads the United States. In Sweden, a smaller percentage of people get married. People usually get married at a later age than in the United States. The proportion of births outside of marriage is twice as high as in the United States. A much larger proportion of Swedish than American women with children under the age of three are in the paid labour force. Significantly, however, on almost all measures of children's well-being, Sweden also leads the United States. Thus, in Sweden, children enjoy higher average reading test scores than children in the United States do. The poverty rate in two-parent families is only one-tenth of the U.S. rate, while the poverty rate in single-parent families is only one-twelfth as high. The rate of infant abuse is one-eleventh of the U.S. rate. Overall, then, the decline of the traditional nuclear family has gone further in Sweden than in the United States, but children are much better off on average (Houseknecht and Sastry, 1996). How is this possible?

Painting class in a state-subsidized daycare facility in Stockholm, Sweden

Jonathan Blair/Corbis/Getty Images

One explanation is that Sweden has something the United States lacks: a substantial family support policy. When a child is born in Sweden, a parent is entitled to a year of parental leave at 80 percent of his or her salary and an additional 90 days at a flat rate. Fathers can take 10 days of leave with pay when the baby is born. Parents are entitled to free consultations at "well-baby clinics." Like all citizens of Sweden, they receive free health care from the state-run system. Temporary parental benefits are available for parents with a sick child under the age of 12. One parent can take up to 60 days off per sick child per year at 80 percent of salary. All parents can send their children to heavily government-subsidized, high-quality daycare. Finally, Sweden offers its citizens generous direct cash payments based on the number of children in each family.*

Among industrialized countries, the United States stands at the other extreme (see Sociology on the Tube, *Teen Mom* and *Teen Mom 2*). Since 1993, a parent has been entitled to 12 weeks of *unpaid* parental leave. Nearly 15 percent of Americans have no health care insurance. Health care is at a low standard for many millions more. There is no system of state daycare and no direct cash payments to families based on the number of children they have. The value of the dependant deduction on income

* We are grateful to Gregg Olsen, Department of Sociology, University of Manitoba, for some of this information.

tax has fallen nearly 50 percent in current dollars since the 1940s. Thus, when an unwed Swedish woman has a baby, she knows she can rely on state institutions to maintain her standard of living and help give her child an enriching social and educational environment. When an unwed American woman has a baby, she is pretty much on her own. She stands a good chance of sinking into poverty, with all of the negative consequences that has for her and her child.

In a study of 33 countries, Canada tied for fifth place in the number of weeks it allows new parents to take time off work, but stood in fifteenth place in terms of the generosity of its maternity leave payments (Smyth, 2003). There are enough regulated daycare spaces for only a fifth of Canadian children up to age 12, and on average, governments allocate $468 per year per child for child care. These averages are far below comparable figures for western European countries. Moreover, they are boosted by Quebec, where regulated daycare spaces are twice as plentiful as in the rest of the country, and government support for regulated daycare is more than three times as generous. Overall, Canada stands between the United States and Sweden. Much of the debate surrounding family policy in Canada concerns whether we should move in the direction of the American or the Swedish model.

In Canada, three criticisms are commonly raised against generous family support policies. First, some people say these policies encourage long-term dependence on welfare, illegitimate births, and the breakup of two-parent families. However, research shows that the divorce rate and the rate of births to unmarried mothers are not higher when welfare payments are more generous (Albelda and Tilly, 1997). Moreover, not all people who

SOCIOLOGY ON THE TUBE

Teen Mom and Teen Mom 2

Teen Mom and *Teen Mom 2* examine the lives of girls who got pregnant at about the age of 16, dropped out of school, kept their babies, and now struggle to raise a child. Some live with their parents and others with their young husbands, most of whom are unequipped to handle the responsibility of a child. Some of the girls work part-time in the paid labour force, others do only unpaid domestic work at home. Some take courses to learn a trade, others are beginning to date again.

seircell/Shutterstock.com

All of them love their babies. However, they confront a seemingly endless stream of dilemmas and trade-offs in an effort to balance the many demands placed on them. They want to be good mothers but they also want to develop job skills, get regular paid work, pursue a lasting relationship with a spouse, get along with their parents, and have just a little time alone every day to relax. They find it impossible to do all of these things. Hence their struggles, compromises, and frustrations.

The camera's candour is impressive. The viewer sees what appears to be an unvarnished depiction of the girls' daily life, including arguments and scenes of tender affection with husbands and parents, moments of loving intimacy and utter exhaustion between mothers and babies, and so on. Every episode of *Teen Mom* and *Teen Mom 2* gives audience members an opportunity to see the real-life choices the girls must make to survive and flourish. *Teen Mom* and *Teen Mom 2* are popular because they allow viewers to imagine how they might deal with similar circumstances.

Teenage pregnancy is common in some countries, such as the United States, where about 35 percent of girls between the ages of 15 and 19 have a child. Comparable figures for Canada and Sweden are, respectively, 12 percent and 6 percent (Organisation for Economic Co-operation and Development, 2014: 4). Moreover, unlike western European countries, which provide considerable state support to teenage mothers in the form of health care and child care, the United States government provides little such assistance. Consequently, teenaged mothers in the United States, who tend to be relatively poor and uneducated, are often unable to meet their children's basic needs. A minority of American teenagers who have a baby manage to raise happy and healthy children, get an education, maintain a stable marital relationship, and hold down a steady job. The majority of these teenagers do not. Child neglect and abuse are relatively common in the United States, especially among teenaged parents, and children born to teen mothers are especially prone to ill health and crime. *Teen Mom* and *Teen Mom 2* say nothing about such cases. Instead, it focuses on the relatively happy stories.

Critical Thinking Question

Teen Mom and *Teen Mom 2* tell viewers that teenage pregnancy is a common—indeed, normal—phenomenon, and that although it is a tough slog, determination, love, and good will typically allow couples and babies to emerge unscathed. To the degree that *Teen Mom* and *Teen Mom 2* ignore the mean reality that many teenaged couples and their babies face, does it play a cruel trick on viewers by distorting reality? Explain your answer.

prefer to work are able to find full-time, secure employment, and part-time jobs offer little in the way of job security, decent wages, or benefits.

Some provinces, such as Ontario, have incorporated "workfare" in their welfare systems. Workfare requires able-bodied people to do specific jobs as a condition of receiving welfare. However, it seems that most workfare jobs do not lead to steady, gainful employment (Kelly, 2013). Finally, it is surely absurd to believe that living on welfare represents a preferred lifestyle. For the overwhelming majority of welfare recipients, it indicates the loss of a job, spouse, or good health—personal tragedies to which none of us is immune (National Council of Welfare, 1999b: 68).

A second criticism of generous family support policies focuses on child care. Some critics say that non-family child care is bad for children under the age of three. In their view, only parents can provide the love, interaction, and intellectual stimulation that infants and toddlers need for proper social, cognitive, and moral development. However, when studies compare family care with daycare involving a strong curriculum, a stimulating environment, plenty of caregiver warmth, low turnover of well-trained staff, and a low ratio of caregivers to children, they find that daycare has no negative consequences and many positive consequences for children over the age of one or two (Clarke-Stewart, Gruber, and Fitzgerald, 1994; Cleveland, 2016; Harvey, 1999).

Research also shows that daycare has some benefits, notably enhancing a child's ability to make friends and improve cognitive performance. The benefits of high-quality daycare are especially evident in low-income families, which often cannot provide the kind of stimulating environment offered by high-quality daycare.

The third criticism lodged against generous family support policies is that they are expensive and have to be paid for by high taxes. That is true. Swedes are more highly taxed than the citizens of any other country. They have made the political decision to pay high taxes, partly to avoid the social problems and associated costs that sometimes emerge when the traditional nuclear family is replaced with other family forms and no institutions are available to help family members in need. The Swedish experience teaches us, then, that there is a clear trade-off between expensive family support policies and low taxes. It is impossible to have both, and the degree to which any country favours one or the other is a political choice.

READY TO STUDY?

IN THE BOOK, YOU CAN:

❏ Tear out the chapter review card at the back of the book to have a summary of the chapter and key terms handy.

ONLINE YOU CAN:

❏ Work through key concepts with a Guided Learning Question.

❏ Prepare for tests with quizzes.

❏ Review the key terms with flash cards.

❏ Explore practical examples of chapter concepts with Connect a Concept exercises.

GO TO NELSON.COM/STUDENT TO ACCESS THESE DIGITAL RESOURCES.

10
Religion and Education

LEARNING OBJECTIVES

In this chapter, you will learn to

LO¹ Distinguish the circumstances in which religion creates societal cohesion and reinforces social inequality from the circumstances in which religion promotes social conflict.

LO² Appreciate that religion governs fewer aspects of most people's lives than in the past, even though a religious revival has taken place in many parts of the world in recent decades.

LO³ List sociological factors associated with attending religious services.

LO⁴ See how functionalism, conflict theory, feminist theory, and symbolic interactionism help us understand how the educational system promotes upward mobility, creates social cohesion, and reinforces class, racial, and ethnic inequalities

LO⁵ Compare the quality of education in Canada to the quality of education in other countries.

RELIGION

In 1902, psychologist William James observed that religion is the common human response to the fact that we all stand at the edge of an abyss. It helps believers to cope with the terrifying fact that we all must die (James, 1976 [1902]: 116). It offers believers immortality, the promise of better times to come, and the security of benevolent spirits who watch over believers. It provides meaning and purpose in a world that might otherwise seem cruel and senseless.

The motivation for religion may be psychological, as James argued. However, the content and intensity of religious beliefs, and the form and frequency of religious practices, are influenced by the structure of society and a person's place in it. Why does one religion predominate here, another there? Why is religious belief stronger at one time than at another? Under what circumstances does religion act as a source of social stability, and under what circumstances does it act as a force for social change? Are people becoming more or less religious? These are all questions that have occupied sociologists of religion, and we will touch on all of them here. Note that we will not have anything to say about the truth of religion in general or the value of any religious belief or practice in particular. These are questions of faith, not science. They lie outside the province of sociology. As the *New Testament* says, "Faith is the substance of things hoped for, the evidence of things not seen" (Hebrews 11:1).

The cover of *Time* magazine once asked, "Is God dead?" As a sociological observation, the idea that God is dead is preposterous. Eight out of ten Canadians say they believe in God or a universal spirit (Davison, 2013). By this measure (and by other measures we will examine below), God is still very much alive in Canada. Nonetheless, as we will show, the scope of religious authority has declined in Canada and in other parts of the world. That is, religion governs fewer aspects of life than it used to. Some Canadians still look to religion to deal with all of life's problems, but increasingly more Canadians expect that religion can help them deal with only a restricted range of spiritual issues. Other institutions—medicine, psychiatry, criminal justice, education, and so forth—have grown in importance as the scope of religious authority has declined.

Foremost among these other institutions is the system of education. Organized religion used to be the main purveyor of formal knowledge and the most important agent

collective conscience The common sentiments and values that people share as a result of living together.

of socialization apart from the family. Today, the education system is the main purveyor of formal knowledge and the most important agent of socialization apart from the family. It is the partial displacement of religion by the educational system that justifies our analyzing religion and education side by side in a single chapter.

Although Canadians hold a strong belief in the importance of education, we have only a moderate level of confidence in our public education system. In one poll, nearly half of adult Canadians gave public schools a grade of "A" or "B" and a third gave them a "C" grade (Canadian Education Association, 2007: 9). Our chief concerns include low academic performance and equality of opportunity (Bricker and Greenspon, 2001: 162–5). We will address these issues in this chapter, paying particular attention to the way they are related to the larger problem of social inequality.

By taking this approach, we follow tradition. Sociologists of education have long been interested in the relationship between education and inequality. Some say that education promotes upward mobility. Others argue that education reproduces inequality generation after generation. As you will see, the evidence offers stronger support for the second argument. Before tackling these issues, however, we first examine the influence of society on religion and the influence of religion on society.

LO¹ CLASSICAL APPROACHES IN THE SOCIOLOGY OF RELIGION

DURKHEIM'S FUNCTIONALIST THEORY

More than one person has said that hockey is Canada's "national religion." Do you agree with that opinion? Before deciding, consider that 80 percent of Canadians tuned in to at least part of the gold medal men's hockey game between Canada and the United States at the 2010 Vancouver Winter Olympics, making them the largest TV audience in Canadian history ("Gold Medal," 2010). As when Canada's men's hockey team came from behind to defeat the Soviets in 1972, the nation virtually came to a standstill.

Few events attract the attention and enthusiasm of Canadians as much as the annual Stanley Cup finals. Apart from drawing a huge audience, the Stanley Cup playoffs generate a sense of what Durkheim would have called "collective effervescence." That is, the Stanley Cup finals excite us by making us feel part of something larger than us: the Montreal Canadiens, the Edmonton Oilers, the Toronto Maple Leafs, the Vancouver Canucks, the Calgary Flames, the Ottawa Senators, the institution of Canadian hockey, the spirit of Canada itself. As celebrated Canadian writer Roch Carrier (1979: 77) wrote in his famous short story, "The Hockey Sweater," "School was . . . a quiet place where we could prepare for the next hockey game, lay out our next strategies. As for church . . . there we forgot school and dreamed about the next hockey game. Through our daydreams it might happen that we would recite a prayer: We would ask God to help us play as well as Maurice Richard." For many hours each year, hockey enthusiasts transcend their everyday lives and experience intense enjoyment by sharing the sentiments and values of a larger collectivity. In their fervour, they banish thoughts of their own mortality. They gain a glimpse of eternity as they immerse themselves in institutions that will outlast them and athletic feats that people will remember for generations to come.

So, do you think the Stanley Cup playoffs are a religious event? There is no god of the Stanley Cup (although the nickname of Canadian hockey legend Wayne Gretzky—The Great One—certainly suggests that he transcended the status of a mere mortal). Nonetheless, the Stanley Cup playoffs may meet Durkheim's definition of a religious experience.

Durkheim said that when people live together, they come to share common sentiments and values. These common sentiments and values form a **collective conscience** that is larger than any individual is. On occasion, we experience the collective conscience directly. This causes us to distinguish the secular everyday world

Sergei Bachlakov/Shutterstock.com

Are the Stanley Cup playoffs a religious event?

Religious rituals are set practices that help unite people into a moral community.

RELIGION, FEMINIST THEORY, AND CONFLICT THEORY

Durkheim's theory of religion is a functionalist account. It offers useful insights into the role of religion in society. Yet conflict and feminist theorists lodge two main criticisms against it. First, it over-emphasizes religion's role in maintaining social cohesion. In reality, religion often incites social conflict. Second, it ignores the fact that when religion does increase social cohesion, it often reinforces social inequality.

Religion and Social Inequality

Consider first the role of world religions and social inequality. (Following convention, we regard the world religions as those that have the largest number of adherents and are widely dispersed geographically—Christianity, Islam, Hinduism, and Buddhism—plus Judaism, which has exerted disproportionate influence historically and globally; see Figure 10.1 and Table 10.1. Two large religious groupings do not meet these criteria. Chinese traditional religion, with about 400 million adherents, has many local variants and is a blend of Buddhism, Confucianism, and Taoism. Sikhism has about 23 million adherents, roughly 80 percent of them living in the state of Punjab, India.)

Little historical evidence helps us understand the social conditions that gave rise to the first world religions, Judaism and Hinduism, 3800 to 4000 years ago. But we know enough about the rise of Buddhism, Christianity, and Islam between 2700 and 1500 years ago to say that the impulse to find a better world is often encouraged by adversity in this one. We also know that Moses, Jesus, Muhammad, and Buddha all promoted a message of equality and freedom. Finally, we know that over generations, the charismatic leadership of

of the **profane** from the religious, transcendent world of the **sacred**. We designate certain objects as symbolizing the sacred. Durkheim called these objects **totems**. We invent set practices to connect us with the sacred. Durkheim referred to these practices as **rituals**.

The effect (or function) of rituals and of religion as a whole is to reinforce social solidarity, said Durkheim. The ritual heightens our experience of group belonging, increases our respect for the group's institutions, and strengthens our belief in the validity of the group's culture. So, in Durkheim's terms, the Stanley Cup playoffs share certain features with religious rituals. They cement society in the way Durkheim said all religious rituals do (Durkheim, 1976 [1915/1912]).

Durkheim would have found support for his theory in research showing that, in the United States, the suicide rate dips during the two days preceding Super Bowl Sunday and on Super Bowl Sunday itself, just as it does for the last day of the World Series, Christmas Day, and other collective celebrations (Curtis, Loy, and Karnilowicz, 1986). He would have found additional support in the finding that in Quebec, the suicide rate among young men is higher when the Montreal Canadiens are not in the Stanley Cup playoffs than when they are (Trovato, 1998). These patterns are consistent with Durkheim's theory of suicide, which predicts a lower suicide rate when social solidarity increases (see Chapter 1, Introducing Sociology).

profane Refers to the secular, everyday world.

sacred Refers to the religious, transcendent world.

totems Objects that symbolize the sacred.

rituals Set practices designed to connect people to the sacred.

FIGURE 10.1   The World's Predominant Religions

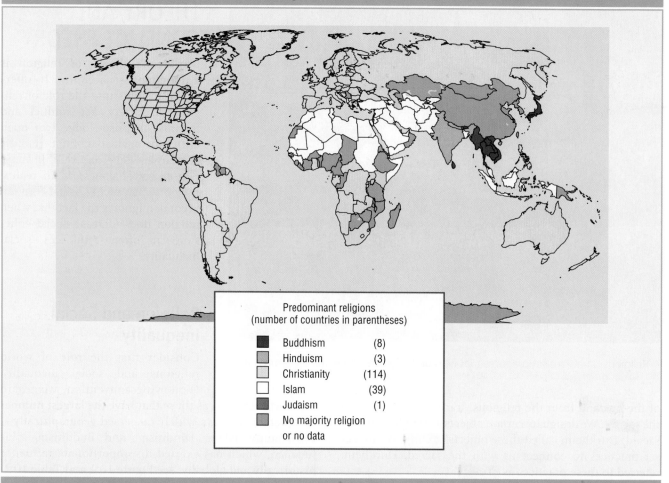

This map shows the predominant religion in each of the world's countries, defined as the religion to which more than 50 percent of a country's population adheres.

Source: Adherents.com (2001).

routinization of charisma
Weber's term for the transformation of divine enlightenment into a permanent feature of everyday life. It involves turning religious inspiration into a stable social institution with defined roles (interpreters of the divine message, teachers, dues-paying laypeople, and so on).

the world religions became "routinized." The **routinization of charisma** is Weber's term for the transformation of divine enlightenment into a permanent feature of everyday life. It involves turning religious inspiration into a stable social institution—a church—with defined roles, such as interpreters of the divine message, teachers, duespaying laypeople, and so forth. The routinization of charisma typically makes religion less responsive to the needs of ordinary people, and it often supports social inequalities and injustices, as you will now see.

Religion and the Subordination of Women

Marx first stressed how religion often tranquilizes the underprivileged into accepting their lot in life. He called religion "the opium of the people" (Marx, 1970 [1843]: 131).

We can draw evidence for Marx's interpretation from many times, places, and institutions. For example, the major world religions have traditionally placed women in a subordinate position. Catholic priests and Muslim mullahs must be men. Women have been allowed to serve as Protestant ministers only since the mid-nineteenth century and as rabbis in the more liberal branches of Judaism since the 1970s. Many scriptures that emphasize the subordination of women continue to inform practice to a degree. For example:

- Corinthians in the *New Testament* emphasizes that "women should keep silence in the churches. For they are not permitted to speak, but should be subordinate,

TABLE 10.1   Five World Religions: Origins, Beliefs, and Divisions

Religion	Origins	Beliefs	Divisions
Judaism	Judaism originated about 4000 years ago in what is now Iraq, when Abraham first asserted the existence of just one God. About 800 years later, Moses led the Jews out of Egyptian bondage. The emancipation of the Jews from slavery was a defining moment in the history of Judaism.	The central teachings rest on belief in one God (Yahweh) and on the idea that God sanctions freedom and equality. The 613 divine commandments (mitzvot) mentioned in the Five Books of Moses (Torah) form the core of orthodox Jewish practice. The mitzvot include prescriptions for justice, righteousness, and observance: Rest and pray on the Sabbath, honour the old and the wise, do not wrong a stranger in buying or selling, do not seek revenge or hold a grudge, etc. The Torah forms part of the Old Testament.	In seventeenth-century Eastern Europe, ecstatic Chasidic sects broke away from the bookish Judaism of the time. In nineteenth-century Germany, the Reform movement allowed prayer in German, the integration of women in worship, etc. Orthodox Judaism was a reaction against the liberalizing tendencies of Reform and involved a return to traditional observance. Conservative Judaism crystallized in Britain and the United States in the nineteenth century to reconcile what its practitioners regarded as the positive elements in Orthodoxy with the dynamism of Reform. Reconstructionism is a liberal twentieth-century movement known for its social activism and gender egalitarianism.
Christianity	Christianity originated about 35 CE in what is now Israel. Jesus, a poor Jew, criticized the Judaism of his time for its external conformity to tradition and ritual at the expense of developing a true relationship to God as demanded by the prophets.	Believe in God and love him; love your neighbour—these are the two main lessons of Jesus. These teachings were novel because they demanded that people match outward performance with inner conviction. It was not enough not to murder. One could not even hate. Nor was it enough not to commit adultery. One could not even lust after a neighbour's wife (Matthew 5: 21–30). These teachings made Jesus anti-authoritarian and even revolutionary. Admonishing people to love their neighbours impressed on them the need to emancipate slaves and women. Christians retained the Jewish Bible as the Old Testament, adding the gospels and letters of the apostles as the New Testament.	In 312 CE, the Roman Emperor converted to Christianity and turned Christianity into a state religion, after which the Church became the dominant institution in Europe. In the sixteenth century, Martin Luther, a German priest, challenged the Christian establishment by seeking to establish a more personal relationship between the faithful and God. His ideas quickly captured the imagination of half of Europe and led to the split of Christianity into Catholicism and Protestantism. In the Middle Ages, Christianity had split into Western and Eastern halves, the former centred in Rome, the latter in Constantinople (now Istanbul, Turkey). Various Orthodox churches today derive from the Eastern tradition. Protestantism has been especially prone to splintering because it emphasizes the individual's relationship to God rather than a central authority. Today, there are hundreds of different Protestant churches.

(Continued)

Religion	Origins	Beliefs	Divisions
Islam	Islam originated about 600 CE in what is now Saudi Arabia. The powerful merchants of Mecca had become greedy and corrupt, impoverishing and enslaving many people. Also, fear grew that the Persian and Roman Empires might soon fall, bringing the end of the world. Into this crisis stepped Muhammad, who claimed to have visions from God.	People who profess Islam have five duties. At least once in their life they must recite the Muslim creed aloud, correctly, with full understanding, and with heartfelt belief. (The creed is "There is no god but Allah and Muhammad is his prophet.") Five times a day, they must worship in a religious service. They must fast from sunrise to sunset every day during the ninth month of the lunar calendar (Ramadan). They must give charity to the poor. And at least once in their life, they must make a pilgrimage to the holy city of Mecca. Muhammad's teachings were written down in the Koran.	A dispute broke out over how the followers of Muhammad could identify his successor. The Sunni argued that the successor should be an elected member of a certain Meccan tribe. The Shi'a claimed that the successor should be Muhammad's direct descendant. Today, about 85 percent of Muslims are Sunni. The Shi'a are concentrated in Iran, Bahrain, and southern Iraq. Islam spread rapidly in the Middle East, Africa, and parts of Europe. From the eighth century to the eleventh century it initiated a great cultural flowering and encouraged considerable religious tolerance. Wahabbism, a Sunni fundamentalist movement, originated in the eighteenth century and became the state religion of what is now Saudi Arabia.
Hinduism	Hinduism originated about 2000 BCE in India in unknown circumstances. It had no single founder.	Hinduism has many gods, all of them thought to be aspects of the one true God. The major texts are epic poems such as the Bhagavad Gita. Only the body dies in Hindu belief. The soul returns in a new form after death. The form in which it returns depends on how one lives one's life. Hindus believe that people who live in a way that is appropriate to their position in society will live better future lives. One may reach a state of spiritual perfection (nirvana) that allows the soul to escape the cycle of birth and rebirth, and reunite with God. But people who do not live in a way that is appropriate to their position in society supposedly live an inferior life when they are reincarnated. These ideas made upward social mobility nearly impossible because, according to Hindu belief, striving to move out of one's station in life ensures reincarnation in a lower form.	Unlike the Western religions, Hinduism assimilates rather than excludes other religious beliefs and practices. Traditionally, Western religions rejected non-believers unless they converted. God tells Moses on Mount Sinai, "You shall have no other gods before me." In contrast, in the Bhagavad Gita, Krishna says that "whatever god a man worships, it is I who answer the prayer." This attitude of acceptance helped Hinduism absorb many of the ancient religions of the peoples on the Indian subcontinent. It also explains why there are such wide regional and class variations in Hindu beliefs and practices. Hinduism as it is practised bears the stamp of many other religions.

TABLE 10.1	Five World Religions: Origins, Beliefs, and Divisions (*Continued*)		
Religion	**Origins**	**Beliefs**	**Divisions**
Buddhism	Sometime around 450 BCE, Gautama Buddha objected to the stale ritualism of Hinduism and sought to achieve a direct relationship with God. He rejected Hindu ideas of caste and reincarnation, and offered a new way for everyone to achieve spiritual enlightenment, promising salvation to everyone.	Buddha promoted the "Four Noble Truths": (1) Life is suffering. Moments of joy are overshadowed by sorrow. (2) All suffering derives from desire. We suffer when we fail to achieve what we want. (3) Suffering ceases by training ourselves to eliminate desire. (4) We can eliminate desire by behaving morally, focusing intently on our feelings and thoughts, meditating, and achieving wisdom. Buddhism does not presume the existence of one true God. Rather, it holds out the possibility of everyone becoming a god of sorts. Similarly, it does not have a central church or text such as the Bible.	Buddhism is notable for the diversity of its beliefs and practices. Buddhism spread rapidly across Asia after India's ruler adopted it as his own religion in the third century BCE. He sent missionaries to convert people in Tibet, Cambodia (Kampuchea), Nepal, Sri Lanka (formerly Ceylon), Myanmar (formerly Burma), China, Korea, and Japan. The influence of Buddhism in the land of its birth started to die out after the fifth century CE and is negligible in India today. One of the reasons for the popularity of Buddhism in East and Southeast Asia is that Buddhism is able to coexist with local religious practices. Unlike Western religions, Buddhism does not insist on holding a monopoly on religious truth.

Sources: Brown (1996); Flood (1996); Gombrich (1996); Gottwald (1979); Hodgson (1974); Lapidus (2002 [1988]); Lopez (2001); McManners (1990); Robinson and Johnson, 1997[1982]); Rodinson (1996); Roth (1961); Schwartz (2003).

as even the law says. If there is anything they desire to know, let them ask their husbands at home. For it is shameful for a woman to speak in church."

- The *Sidur*, the Jewish prayer book, includes this prayer, which is recited by Orthodox and ultra-Orthodox men every morning: "Blessed are you, Lord our God, King of the Universe, who did not make me a woman."
- The *Koran*, the holy book of Islam, contains a Book of Women in which it is written that "righteous women are devoutly obedient.... As to those women on whose part you fear disloyalty and ill-conduct, admonish them, refuse to share their beds, beat them."

Religious feminists have unchallenged such ideas. For example, Muslim feminists have established that what many religious clerics present as divine Islamic law regarding women is actually based on interpretations that were authored by men over the centuries (Zakaria, 2014). Moreover, they contend that Islamic legal principles such as that of the "public interest" contradict and override principles that deny women equality with men. Meanwhile, Catholic and Orthodox Jewish feminists have been struggling for the ordination of women as priests and rabbis and the progressive reinterpretation of their own holy texts (Manson, 2014; Sigal, 2014).

Religion and Inequality of Sexual Orientation and Class

Most established religions have also for the most part supported inequality of sexual orientation. Thus, while homosexuality is quite widely tolerated in Buddhism, it is unacceptable in Islam, Hinduism and, except in their more liberal denominations, in Christianity and Judaism (Mackay, 2000: 73).

After becoming routinized, religions also typically support class inequality. They often emphasize charity, too—but not so much charity as to change the basic structure of inequality in society. Thus, in medieval and early modern Europe, Christianity, while collecting alms for the poor, promoted the view that the Almighty ordains class inequality, promising rewards to the lowly in the afterlife ("the meek shall inherit the earth"). As an Anglican hymn put it:

> All things bright and beautiful,
> The Lord God made them all.
> The rich man in his castle,
> The poor man at his gate,
> God made them high and lowly
> And ordered their estate.

(This verse was removed from the Anglican hymnal in 1920.) Similarly, the Hindu scriptures say that the highest caste sprang from the lips of the supreme creator, the next highest caste from his shoulders, the next highest from his thighs, and the lowest, "polluted" caste from his feet. They warn that if people attempt to achieve upward mobility, they will be reincarnated as animals. And the Koran says that social inequality is due to the will of Allah (Ossowski, 1963: 19–20).

Religion and Social Conflict

In the sociological sense of the term, a **church** is any bureaucratic religious organization that has accommodated itself to mainstream society and culture. As we have seen, church authorities often support various forms of inequality. However, religiously inspired protest against inequality often erupts from below.

A famous example of such protest involves the role of black churches in spearheading the American civil rights movement during the 1950s and 1960s (Morris, 1984). The impact was both organizational and inspirational. Organizationally, black churches supplied the ministers who formed the civil rights movement's leadership and the congregations whose members marched, boycotted, and engaged in other forms of protest. Additionally, Christian doctrine inspired the protesters. Perhaps their most powerful religious idea was that blacks, like the Jews in Egypt, were slaves who would be freed. (It was, after all, Michael—regarded by Christians as the patron saint of the Jews—who rowed the boat ashore.) Some white segregationists reacted strongly against efforts at integration, often meeting the peaceful protesters with deadly violence. However, the American South was never the same again. Religion had helped promote the conflict needed to make the South a more egalitarian and racially integrated place.

Closer to home, it is worth remembering the important role played in the creation of Canada's health care system and our social welfare network by the radical Christianity of the early twentieth-century Social Gospel movement. The Social Gospel movement became a strong political force in the depths of the Great Depression (1929–39). It emphasized that Christians should be as concerned with improving the here and now as with life in the hereafter. The efforts of Tommy Douglas, a Baptist minister, the leader of the Co-operative Commonwealth Federation (precursor of the New Democratic Party), and the father of socialized medicine in Canada, exemplify the Social Gospel concern with social justice. In Canada, too, then, religion has sometimes promoted conflict and change.

In sum, religion can maintain social order under some circumstances, as Durkheim said. When it does so, however, it often reinforces social inequality. Moreover, under other circumstances, religion can promote social conflict.

> **church** A bureaucratic religious organization that has accommodated itself to mainstream society and culture.

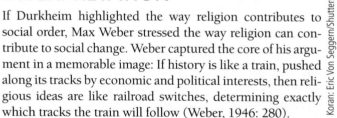

Sidur: Keith Levit/Shutterstock.com

Koran: Eric Von Seggern/Shutterstock.com

HOLY BIBLE

tatniz/shutterstock.com

WEBER AND THE PROBLEM OF SOCIAL CHANGE: A SYMBOLIC INTERACTIONIST INTERPRETATION

If Durkheim highlighted the way religion contributes to social order, Max Weber stressed the way religion can contribute to social change. Weber captured the core of his argument in a memorable image: If history is like a train, pushed along its tracks by economic and political interests, then religious ideas are like railroad switches, determining exactly which tracks the train will follow (Weber, 1946: 280).

Weber's most famous illustration of his thesis is his short book, *The Protestant Ethic and Spirit of Capitalism*. Like Marx, Weber was interested in explaining the rise of modern capitalism. Again like Marx, he was prepared to recognize the "fundamental importance of the economic factor" in his explanation (Weber, 1958 [1904–05]: 26). But Weber was also bent on proving the one-sidedness of any exclusively economic interpretation. He did so by offering what we would today call a symbolic interactionist interpretation of religion. True, the term *symbolic interactionism* was not introduced into sociology until more than half a century after Weber wrote *The Protestant Ethic*. Yet Weber's focus on the worldly significance of the *meanings* people attach to religious ideas makes him a forerunner of the symbolic interactionist tradition.

For specifically religious reasons, wrote Weber, followers of the Protestant theologian John Calvin stressed the need to engage in intense worldly activity and to display industry, punctuality, and frugality in their everyday life. In the view of such men as John Wesley and Benjamin Franklin, people could reduce their religious doubts and ensure a state of grace by working diligently and living simply. Many Protestants took up this idea. Weber called it the Protestant ethic (Weber, 1958 [1904–05]: 183). According to Weber, the Protestant ethic had wholly unexpected economic consequences. Where it took root, and where economic conditions were favourable, early capitalist enterprise grew most robustly.

Subsequent research showed that the correlation between the Protestant ethic and the strength of capitalist development is weaker than Weber thought. In some places, Catholicism has coexisted with vigorous capitalist growth and Protestantism with relative economic stagnation (Samuelsson, 1961 [1957]). Nonetheless, Weber's treatment of the religious factor underlying social change is a useful corrective to Durkheim's emphasis on religion as a source of social stability. Along with Durkheim's work, Weber's contribution stands as one of the most important insights into the influence of religion on society.

LO² THE RISE, DECLINE, AND PARTIAL REVIVAL OF RELIGION

SECULARIZATION

In 1651, British political philosopher Thomas Hobbes described life as "poore, nasty, brutish, and short" (Hobbes, 1968 [1651]: 150). The standard of living in medieval and early modern Europe was abysmally low. On average, a person lived only about 35 years. The forces of nature and human affairs seemed entirely unpredictable. In this context, magic was popular. It offered easy answers to mysterious, painful, and capricious events.

As material conditions improved, popular belief in magic, astrology, and witchcraft gradually lost ground (Thomas, 1971). Christianity substantially replaced them. The better and more predictable times made Europeans more open to the teachings of organized religion. In addition, the Church campaigned vigorously to stamp out opposing belief systems and practices. The persecution of witches in this era was partly an effort to eliminate competition and establish a Christian monopoly over spiritual life.

The Church succeeded in its efforts. In medieval and early modern Europe, Christianity became a powerful presence in religious affairs, music, art, architecture, literature, and philosophy. Popes and saints were the rock stars and movie celebrities of their day. The Church was the centre of life in both its spiritual and its worldly dimensions. Church authority was supreme in marriage, education, morality, economic affairs, politics, and so on. European countries proclaimed official state religions. They persecuted members of religious minorities, including Jews and, beginning in the sixteenth century, Protestants.

In contrast, a few hundred years later, Max Weber remarked on how the world had become thoroughly "disenchanted." By the turn of the twentieth century, he said, scientific and other forms of rationalism were replacing religious authority. His observations formed the basis of what came to be known as the **secularization thesis**, undoubtedly the most widely accepted argument in the sociology of religion until the 1990s. According to the secularization thesis, religious institutions, actions, and consciousness are unlikely to disappear, but they are certainly on the decline worldwide (Tschannen, 1991).

secularization thesis
Theory that religious institutions, actions, and consciousness are on the decline worldwide.

Secularization

Courtesy of Robert J. Brym

RELIGIOUS REVIVAL AND RELIGIOUS FUNDAMENTALISM

Despite the consensus about secularization that was evident in the 1980s, many sociologists modified their judgments in the 1990s. One reason for the change was that accumulated survey evidence showed that religion was not in an advanced state of decay. Actually, in many places, it was in robust health (see Figure 10.2). In 2011, 82 percent of Canadians said they believed in God and 76 percent said they had a religious affiliation. Eighteen percent of Canadians said they attended religious services at least once a week and another 28 percent said they attend religious services at least a few times a year (Wilkins-Laflamme, 2014).

> **fundamentalists** People who interpret their scriptures literally; seek to establish a direct, personal relationship with the higher being(s) they worship; and are relatively intolerant of non-fundamentalists.

The second reason many sociologists have modified their views about secularization is that an intensification of religious belief and practice has taken place among some people in recent decades. For example, since the 1960s, fundamentalist religious organizations have increased their membership. In North America, this tendency has been especially pronounced among Protestants (Finke and Starke, 1992). **Fundamentalists** interpret their scriptures literally; seek to establish a direct, personal relationship with the higher being(s) they worship; and are relatively intolerant of non-fundamentalists (Hunter, 1991). Fundamentalists often support conservative social and political issues (Bruce, 1988) and have been known to disapprove of some books and movies, including the *Harry Potter* series (see the Sociology at the Movies feature in this chapter).

During the same period, religious movements became dominant forces in many other countries. Hindu nationalists formed the government in India from 1998 to 2004. Jewish fundamentalists were always important players in Israeli political life, often holding the balance of power in Israeli governments, but they have become even more influential in recent years (Kimmerling, 2001: 173–207). A revival of Muslim fundamentalism began in Iran in the 1970s. Muslim fundamentalism then swept much of the Middle East, Africa, and parts of Asia. In Iran, Afghanistan, and Sudan, Muslim fundamentalists took power. Other predominantly Muslim countries' governments introduced elements of Islamic religious law (*shari'a*), either from conviction or as a precaution against restive populations (Lewis, 2002: 106).

Religious fundamentalism has thus become a worldwide political phenomenon. In not a few cases, it has taken extreme forms and involved violence as a means of establishing fundamentalist ideas and institutions (Juergensmeyer, 2000). At the same time, the Catholic Church played a critically important role in undermining communism in Poland, and Catholic "liberation theology" animated the successful fight against right-wing governments in Latin America (Kepel, 1994 [1991]; Smith, 1991). All of these developments amount to a religious revival that was unexpected in, say, 1970.

FIGURE 10.2 Percentage of People Who Think Religion Is Very Important, 44 Countries

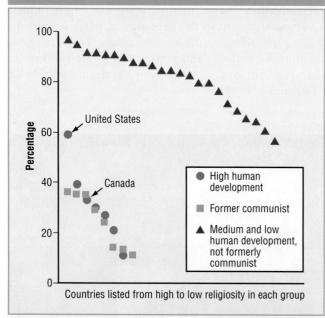

Countries listed from high to low religiosity in each group

This figure is derived from a 2002 survey of 38 000 people in 44 countries. (Poland is a former communist country and the United Nations ranks it 37th in its list of 53 countries in the "high human development" group. It is classified here as a former communist country.)

Sources: Pew Research Center, 2002, *The Pew Global Attitudes Project: How Global Publics View Their Lives, Their Countries, the World, America*; United Nations, 2002, *Human Development Report 2002*, New York: Oxford University Press.

THE SOCIAL AND POLITICAL CONTEXT OF MUSLIM FUNDAMENTALISM

In 1972, Robert Brym was finishing his B.A. at the Hebrew University of Jerusalem. One May morning he switched on the radio to discover that a massacre had taken place at Lod (now Ben Gurion) International Airport, just 42 kilometres from his apartment. Three Japanese men in business suits had arrived on Air France Flight 132 from Paris. They were members of the Japanese Red Army, a

SOCIOLOGY AT THE MOVIES

Harry Potter and the Deathly Hallows: Part I and Part II

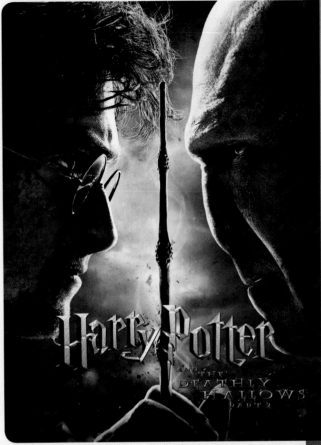

Harry Potter and the Deathly Hallows: Part I and *Part II* are the seventh and eighth movies in the highly popular series about a magical world of witches and wizards. In the first episode, we learned that the hero, Harry Potter (Daniel Radcliffe) was orphaned at the age of one when the most evil wizard of all, Lord Voldemort, murdered Harry's parents and tried to kill Harry. Harry went to live with his unwelcoming relatives, the Dursleys, who housed him in a closet under their stairs.

Shortly before his eleventh birthday, Harry's life is turned upside down. He learns that his dead parents were wizards, and so is he. A blizzard of letters summons him to Hogwarts School of Witchcraft and Wizardry. The school, housed in a thousand-year-old castle and headed by the renowned Professor Dumbledore, offers select students a seven-year program of instruction.

Harry Potter and the Deathly Hallows: Part I follows the story of Harry and his friends Hermione Granger (Emma Watson) and Ron Weasley (Rupert Grint) into maturity. The movie opens with the horrifying Lord Voldemort (Ralph Fiennes) and his Death Eaters plotting the destruction of Harry and his friends. When Harry and his friends get wind of the plot, they fly off to mysterious and remote locations so they can hide from Lord Voldemort while simultaneously searching for clues to the whereabouts of missing bits of Voldemort's soul. Presumably, if they can make his soul whole again, he will end his evil ways. The final showdown takes place in the last movie of the series. Voldemort succeeds in destroying Hogwarts, and the students who survive must choose between the hero and the villain.

All entries in the *Harry Potter* series have been enormously successful at the box office. Children are prominent in the lineups, many of them outfitted as though for Halloween. Some of them go to the movies on organized school field trips after studying the *Harry Potter* books at school.

Although most people view the *Harry Potter* series as harmless, others see things differently. They denounce it as "demonic." Many of them are conservative Protestants who claim that the books glorify witchcraft, make "evil look innocent," and subtly draw "children into an unhealthy interest in a darker world that is occultic and dangerous to physical, psychological and spiritual well-being" (Shaw, 2001). Two years before he became Pope Benedict XVI, Cardinal Ratzinger wrote a letter of support to a Bavarian sociologist who had written a book critical of the Potter phenomenon. The future pope told her, "It is good that you are throwing light on *Harry Potter*, because these are subtle seductions that work imperceptibly, and because of that deeply, and erode Christianity in the soul before it can even grow properly" (Associated Press, 2005).

The controversy about the Potter series eased somewhat as some conservative Christian commentators claimed to find Christian themes in the movies and the books ("Finding God," 2005). However, the controversy was great enough to make the *Harry Potter* books among the most frequently banned or challenged books in Canada and the United States (American Library Association, 2013; Freedomtoread .ca, 2015.)

(Continued)

Warner Bros. Pictures/Photofest

small, shadowy terrorist group with links to the General Command of the Popular Front for the Liberation of Palestine. Both groups wanted to help wrest Israel from Jewish rule.

After they picked up their bags, the three men pulled out automatic rifles and started firing indiscriminately. Before pausing to slip in fresh clips, they lobbed hand grenades into the crowd at the ticket counters. One man ran onto the tarmac, shot some disembarking passengers, and then blew himself up. This was the first suicide attack in modern Middle East history. Security guards shot a second terrorist and arrested the third, Kozo Okamoto. When the firing stopped, 26 people lay dead. Half were non-Jews. In addition to the two terrorists, 11 Catholics were murdered. They were Puerto Rican tourists who had just arrived on a pilgrimage to the Holy Land.

Both the Japanese Red Army and the General Command of the Popular Front for the Liberation of Palestine were strictly non-religious organizations. Yet something unexpected happened to Kozo Okamoto, the sole surviving terrorist of the Lod massacre. Israel sentenced him to life in prison but freed him in 1985 in a prisoner exchange with Palestinian forces. Okamoto wound up living in Lebanon's Beka'a Valley, the main base of the Iranian-backed Hezbollah fundamentalist organization. A revival of Islamic fundamentalism was sweeping the Middle East, and in 2000, he converted to Islam.

Kozo Okamoto's life tells us something important and not at all obvious about religious fundamentalism and politics in the Middle East and elsewhere. Okamoto was involved in extremist politics first and came to religion later. Religious fundamentalism became a useful way for him to articulate and implement his political views. This is not unusual. Religious fundamentalism often provides a convenient vehicle for framing political extremism, enhancing its appeal, legitimizing it, and providing a foundation for the solidarity of political groups (Pape, 2003; Sherkat and Ellison, 1999: 370).

Many people regard Islamic fundamentalism as a cause and extremist politics as an effect. In this view, some people happen to become religious fanatics, and then their fanaticism commands them to go out and kill their opponents. But Islamic fundamentalism has political sources (Brym, 2008). For example, Al-Qaeda is strongly antagonistic to American foreign policy in the Middle East. It despises U.S. support for repressive and non-democratic Arab governments like those of Kuwait and Saudi Arabia, which fail to distribute the benefits of oil wealth to the largely impoverished Arab people. It is also strongly opposed to the American position on the Israeli–Palestinian conflict, which it regards as too pro-Israeli and insufficiently supportive of Palestinian interests (to put it mildly). These political complaints are the breeding ground of support for Al-Qaeda in the Arab world. Thus, public opinion polls show that Arabs in the Middle East hold largely favourable attitudes toward American culture, democracy, and the American people, but extremely negative attitudes toward precisely those elements of American Middle East policy that Al-Qaeda opposes (Zogby International, 2001).

Al-Qaeda and other extremist organizations in the Middle East gain in strength to the degree that these political issues are not addressed in a meaningful way. As Zbigniew Brzezinski, national security adviser to former President Jimmy Carter, wrote, "To win the war on terrorism, one must . . . set two goals: first, to destroy the terrorists and, second, to begin a political effort that focuses on the conditions that brought about their emergence" (Brzezinski, 2002; Hunter, 1998). These are wise words. They are based on the sociological understanding that fundamentalism, like other forms of religion, is powerfully influenced by the social and political context in which it emerges.

THE REVISED SECULARIZATION THESIS

The spread of fundamentalist religion and the resilience and relative importance of religion in some highly developed countries led some sociologists to revise the secularization thesis in the 1990s. The revisionists acknowledge that religion has become increasingly influential in the lives of some individuals and groups over the past 30 years. They insist, however, that the scope of religious authority has continued to decline in most people's lives. That is, for most people, religion has less and less to say about education, family issues, politics, and economic affairs, even though it may continue to be an important source of spiritual belief and practice. In this sense, secularization continues (Chaves, 1994; Yamane, 1997).

According to the **revised secularization thesis**, in most countries, worldly institutions have broken off (or "differentiated") from the institution of religion over time. One such worldly institution is the education system. Religious bodies used to run schools and institutions of higher learning that are now run almost exclusively by non-religious authorities. Moreover, like other specialized institutions that separated from the institution of religion, the education system is generally concerned with worldly affairs rather than spiritual matters.

The overall effect of the differentiation of secular institutions has been to make religion applicable only to the spiritual part of most people's lives. Because the scope of religious authority has been restricted, people look to religion for moral guidance in everyday life less often than they used to. Moreover, most people have turned religion into a personal and private matter rather than one imposed by a powerful, authoritative institution. Said differently, people feel increasingly free to combine beliefs and practices from various sources and traditions to suit their own tastes.

THE MARKET MODEL

Another way to understand how a religious revival can take place in the midst of an overall decline in religious participation is to think of religion as a market. In this view, religious organizations are suppliers of services such as counselling, pastoral care, youth activities, men's and women's groups, performance groups, lectures, and discussions. These services are demanded by people who desire religious activities. Religious denominations are similar to product brands offering different "flavours" of religious experience (Barna, 2002; Bibby, 2002, 2004).

The market model raises the question of what motivates people to participate in religion. Some sociologists highlight the role of other-worldly or supernatural rewards (Stark and Bainbridge, 1987, 1997). They argue that religion promises such rewards in exchange for particular types of behaviour. It follows that religion is particularly appealing to poor people because the wealthy enjoy material benefits and therefore have less need and desire for supernatural promises.

However, some sociologists question whether supernatural rewards interest only the poor, noting historical examples of people who gave up their wealth to live a simple, spiritual life. They also argue that religions offer worldly benefits that attract the well-to-do (Collins, 1993). For instance, religious organizations regularly bestow public recognition on the wealthiest and most powerful people in society, as the name of Toronto's Timothy Eaton Memorial Church, among others, testifies. For such reasons, religion may appeal to the rich just as much as it appeals to the poor.

The market model usefully clarifies the social bases of heterogeneity and change in religious life by emphasizing that religious observance in North America is a highly decentralized, largely unregulated "industry" in which innovation and competition flourish. The market model also draws attention to the potential advantages of diversification. People often assume that an official or state religion, such as Christianity in the Roman Empire or Islam in contemporary Iran, is the best guarantee of religiosity. However, the market model emphasizes that religious diversity can also be a source of strength because it allows individuals to shop around for a religious organization that corresponds to their particular tastes. This may help explain why the United States, which has long banned state support for religion, has an exceptionally high rate of religious participation for a highly industrialized country (refer back to Figure 10.2; see the Sociology on the Tube feature in this chapter). In contrast, some regions in which state and religion remained entwined until quite recently, such as Quebec, have experienced some of the sharpest drop-offs in participation in religious organizations.

> **revised secularization thesis** Theory that worldly institutions break off from the institution of religion over time. As a result, religion governs an ever-smaller part of most people's lives and has become largely a matter of personal choice.

World meeting of religious leaders

Francois Lochon/The LIFE Images Collection/Getty Images

From *Duck Dynasty* to *The Good Wife*

Afraid of offending audiences and advertisers, television shows generally shy away from characters that are overtly religious. When religious characters are featured, they tend to be depicted stereotypically. One such example is born-again Christian Ned Flanders on *The Simpsons*. Ned's overly pious nature habitually annoys his neighbour, Homer Simpson, and even exasperates his pastor, Reverend Lovejoy.

More recently, reality TV shows have taken to broadcasting the extreme lifestyles of some religious groups. *Sister Wives* reveals the complicated lives of a polygamous family that belongs to an offshoot of the Church of Latter Day Saints. *Duck Dynasty* showcases

the outrageous antics of the eccentric but religiously devout Robertson family. Affiliated with the Church of Christ, the family ends each episode with a prayer.

There are exceptions to the stereotypical and sensationalist depictions of religious characters on television. For example, the Canadian sitcom *Little Mosque on the Prairie* employed both humor and sensitivity in showing Muslims and Christians sharing their church building in rural Saskatchewan. Another exception is the American drama, *The Good Wife*. The main character, Alicia Florrick, played by Julianna Margulies, relaunches her career as a lawyer when her husband, Peter, who works for the state attorney's office, is sent to jail for misusing public funds to pay for prostitutes. As Alicia contemplates and then attempts to repair her marriage, other characters develop their own storylines. One of these subplots involves the conversion of Peter and Alicia's teen-aged daughter, Grace, to Christianity. Their daughter's religiosity puzzles her parents, neither of whom can understand what prompted their daughter's spiritual turn.

A few episodes later, Alicia is asked by a news reporter whether she believes in God. It's a loaded question because her husband is running for office. In the United States, politicians and their families who don't profess belief in God are considered unelectable. Nonetheless, Alicia responds truthfully. She tells the reporter that she is an atheist. Peter's campaign team is aghast. Has she sabotaged her husband's aspiration to become governor? Apparently not. Her response elicits no change in her husband's approval ratings. Perhaps, the show implies, society has become more accepting of religious diversity.

Critical Thinking Questions

1. Is it realistic to expect that an American running for high office could identify himself or herself as an atheist and still hope to be elected? Why, or why not?
2. Is it realistic to expect that a Canadian running for high office could identify himself or herself as an atheist and still hope to be elected? Why, or why not?

Alicia Florrick and her daughter, Grace

David M. Russell/CBS/Getty Images

RELIGION IN CANADA
CHURCH, SECT, AND CULT

Sociologists generally divide religious groups into just three types: churches, sects, and cults (Troeltsch, 1931 [1923]; Stark and Bainbridge, 1979; see Table 10.2). As noted earlier, a *church* is a bureaucratic religious organization that has accommodated itself to mainstream society and culture. Because of this accommodation, it may endure for many hundreds, if not thousands, of years. The bureaucratic nature of a church is evident in the formal training of its leaders, its strict hierarchy of roles, and its clearly drawn rules and regulations. Its integration into mainstream society is evident in its teachings, which are generally abstract and do not challenge worldly authority. In addition, churches integrate themselves into the mainstream by recruiting members from all classes of society.

TABLE 10.2 **Church, Sect, and Cult Compared**

	Church	Sect	Cult
Integration into society	High	Medium	Low
Bureaucratization	High	Low	Low
Longevity	High	Low	Low
Leaders	Formally trained	Charismatic	Charismatic
Class base	Mixed	Low	Various but segregated

Source: From BRYM/LIE. *Sociology*, 1E. © 2009 Nelson Education Ltd. Reproduced by permission. www.cengage.com/permissions.

Churches take two main forms. First are **ecclesia**, or state-supported churches. For example, Christianity became the state religion in the Roman Empire in the fourth century, and Islam is the state religion in Iran and Sudan today. State religions impose advantages on members and disadvantages on non-members. Tolerance of other religions is low in societies with ecclesia.

Churches can also be pluralistic, allowing diversity within the church and expressing tolerance of non-members. Pluralism allows churches to increase their appeal by allowing various streams of belief and practice to coexist under their overarching authority. These subgroups are called **denominations**. For example, United Church, Anglican, Baptist, Lutheran, and Presbyterian are the major Protestant denominations in Canada today.

Sects typically form by breaking away from churches because of disagreement about church doctrine. Sometimes, sect members choose to separate themselves geographically, as the Hutterites do in their some 200 colonies, mostly in the western provinces. However, even in urban settings, strictly enforced rules concerning dress, diet, prayer, and intimate contact with outsiders can separate sect members from the larger society. Chasidic Jews in Toronto and Montreal prove the viability of this isolation strategy. Sects are less integrated into society and less bureaucratized than churches are. They are often led by **charismatic leaders**, men and women who claim to be inspired by supernatural powers and whose followers believe them to be so inspired. These leaders tend to be relatively intolerant of religious opinions other than their own. They tend to recruit like-minded members mainly from lower classes and marginal groups. Worship in sects tends to be highly emotional and based less on abstract principles than immediate personal experience (Stark, 1985: 314). Usually, sect-like groups appeal to the less affluent and churchlike groups to the more affluent. Many sects are short-lived, but those that do persist tend

to bureaucratize and turn into churches. If religious organizations are to enjoy a long life, they require rules, regulations, and a clearly defined hierarchy of roles.

Although major Muslim subgroups are sometimes called denominations by non-Muslims, they are in some respects more appropriately seen as sects. That is because they sometimes do not recognize one another as Muslim and sometimes come into violent conflict with one another, like the Sunni and Shi'a in Iraq today.

Cults are small groups of people deeply committed to a religious vision that rejects mainstream culture and society. Cults are generally led by charismatic individuals. They tend to be class-segregated groups, recruiting members from only one segment of the stratification system: high, middle, or low. For example, many North American cults today recruit nearly all their members from among the university-educated. Some of these cults seek converts almost exclusively on university and college campuses (Kosmin, 1991).

Because they propose a radically new way of life, cults tend to recruit few members and soon disappear. There are, however, exceptions—and some extremely important ones at that. Jesus and Muhammad were both charismatic

ecclesia State-supported churches.

denominations The various streams of belief and practice that some churches allow to coexist under their overarching authority.

sects Groups that usually form by breaking away from churches because of disagreement about church doctrine. Sects are less integrated into society and less bureaucratized than churches are. They are often led by charismatic leaders, who tend to be relatively intolerant of religious opinions other than their own.

charismatic leaders Religious leaders who claim to be inspired by supernatural powers and whose followers believe them to be so inspired.

cults Small groups of people deeply committed to a religious vision that rejects mainstream culture and society.

Uriel Sinai/Getty Images

TABLE 10.3	Religious Groups, Canada, 2011
Group	Percentage
Catholic	40.6
Roman	38.7
Orthodox	1.7
Other	0.2
Protestant	26.6
United Church	6.1
Anglican	5.0
Baptist	1.9
Lutheran	1.5
Pentecostal	1.5
Presbyterian	1.4
Other	9.2
Muslim	3.2
Hindu	1.5
Sikh	1.4
Buddhist	1.1
Jewish	1.0
Other	0.6
No religion	23.9
Total	**99.9**

Note: Total does not equal 100 percent because of rounding.

Source: Statistics Canada. 2013i. "Religion (108), Immigrant Status and Period of Immigration (11), Age Groups (10) and Sex (3) for the Population in Private Households of Canada, Provinces, Territories, Census Metropolitan Areas and Census Agglomerations," *2011 National Household Survey.*

LO³ RELIGIOSITY

It is now time to consider some social factors that determine how important religion is to people, that is, their **religiosity**. We can measure religiosity in various ways. Strength of belief, emotional attachment to a religion, knowledge about a religion, frequency of performing rituals, and frequency of applying religious principles in daily life all indicate how religious a person is (Glock, 1962). Ideally, we ought to examine many measures to get a fully rounded and reliable picture of the social distribution of religiosity. For simplicity's sake, however, we focus on just one measure here. In a Canada-wide survey, respondents were asked to indicate whether their level of involvement in religious activities at various points in their lives was "high," "moderate," "low," or "none." Figure 10.4 summarizes the results.

Some fascinating patterns emerge from the data. First, the people most heavily involved in religious activities are preteens and seniors. As a result, involvement forms a U-shaped curve, falling among teenagers and young adults and then beginning to rise steadily after the age of about 24.

How can we explain this pattern? Preteens have little say over whether they attend Sunday school, Hebrew school, confirmation classes, and the like. For many preteens, religious involvement is high because it is required of them, even if their parents do not always follow suit. Seniors sometimes have more time and more need for religion. Because they are not usually in school, employed in the paid labour force, or busy raising a family, they have more opportunity than young people do to attend religious services. Moreover, because seniors are generally closer to illness and death than

> **religiosity** The degree to which religion is important to people.

leaders of cults. They were so compelling that they and their teachings were able to inspire a large number of followers, including rulers of states. Their cults were thus transformed into churches.

Canada's changing immigration patterns have resulted in large gains for some religious groups. Notably, the number of Muslims more than doubled between 1991 and 2011 and reached an estimated 1.4 million or 3.2 percent of the population in 2011. Hindus, Sikhs, Buddhists, and Jews each represent just over 1 percent of the population. Yet Catholics and Protestants still compose more than two-thirds of Canada's population, and about two-thirds of recent immigrants are Christian, while an estimated 23.9 percent of Canadians had no religious affiliation in 2011 (see Table 10.3 and Figure 10.3).

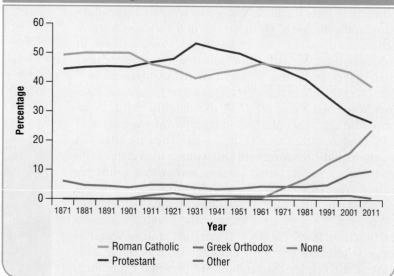

FIGURE 10.3 Religious Affiliations, Canada, 1871–2011

Sources: 1871–1971 from Statistics Canada, 1983, "Historical Statistics of Canada," Catalogue No. 11516XWE; 1981 from Ontario Consultants on Religious Tolerance, 2005, Information about Religion in Canada; 1991 and 2001 from Statistics Canada, 2003b, "Religions in Canada," Catalogue No. 96F0030XIE.

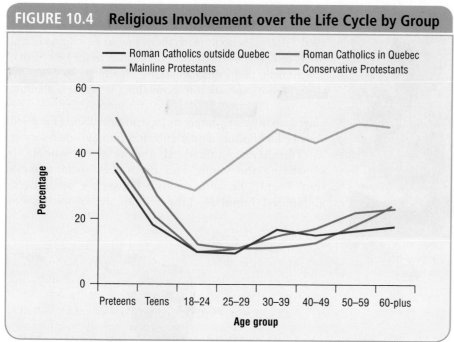

FIGURE 10.4 Religious Involvement over the Life Cycle by Group

— Roman Catholics outside Quebec   — Roman Catholics in Quebec
— Mainline Protestants   — Conservative Protestants

Source: Bibby, Reginald W, 2001. *Canada's Teens: Today, Yesterday, and Tomorrow*. Toronto: Stoddart. Reproduced by permission of the author.

are young people, they are more likely to require the solace of religion. To a degree, then, involvement in religious activities is a life-cycle issue. That is, children are relatively actively involved in religious activities because they are required to be and seniors are relatively actively involved because they feel greater need for religious involvement and are in a position to act on that need.

Another issue is at stake here, too. Different age groups live through different times, and today's seniors reached maturity when religion was a more authoritative force in society. A person's current religious involvement depends partly on whether he or she grew up in more religious times. So, although young people are likely to become more religiously involved as they age, they are unlikely ever to become as involved as seniors are today.

Second, the region of the country in which you live also correlates with the likelihood that you will attend religious services weekly. Newfoundland and Labrador, Prince Edward Island, and New Brunswick have the highest rates of monthly attendance; Quebec, Alberta, and British Columbia have the lowest.

Third, respondents whose parents attended religious services frequently are more likely to do so themselves (Jones, 2000). Religiosity is partly a learned behaviour. Whether parents give a child a religious upbringing is likely to have a lasting impact on the child.

This is by no means an exhaustive list of the factors that influence the frequency of attending religious services. For example, research also indicates that social inequality can promote religiosity, so rich countries with the lowest levels of social inequality, such as Denmark, tend to have the lowest levels of church attendance. Rich countries with high levels of social inequality, such as the United States, tend to have the high levels of church attendance. However, even this brief overview suggests that religiosity depends partly on obligation, opportunity, need, and learning. The people who attend religious services most frequently are those who must; those who were taught to be religious as children; those who need organized religion most; and those who have the most time to go to services.

THE FUTURE OF RELIGION

Secularization and religious revival are two of the dominant influences on religion worldwide. We can detect secularization in survey data that track religious attitudes and practices over time and also in the growing percentage of people who indicate in succeeding censuses that they have no religious affiliation (refer back to Figure 10.3). We also know that various secular institutions are taking over some of the functions formerly performed by religion, thus robbing it of its once pervasive authority over all aspects of life. It is an exaggeration to claim, as Max Weber did, that the whole world is gradually becoming "disenchanted." However, part of it certainly is.

At the same time, we know that even as secularization grips many people, many others have been caught up in a religious revival of vast proportions. Religious belief and practice are intensifying for these people, partly because religion serves as a useful vehicle for political expression. The fact that this revival was unexpected just a few decades ago should warn us not to be overly bold in our forecasts. It seems to us, however, that the two contradictory social processes of secularization and revival are likely to persist for some time to come, resulting in a world that is neither more religious nor more secular, but one that is certainly more polarized.

LO⁴ EDUCATION

Despite the continuing significance of religion for people around the world, the revised secularization thesis is right to claim that religion does not dominate life and thought as it did even a century ago. For example, education, not religion, dominates socialization outside the family in most rich countries. Almost everyone in Canada goes to school, a large minority goes to college or university, and many

Religiosity is partly a learned behaviour. Whether parents give a child a religious upbringing is likely to have a lasting impact on the child.

postmodern society. A third function of the education system involves the socialization of the young (Durkheim, 1956, 1961 [1925]). Schools teach the young to view Canada with pride, respect the law, think of democracy as the best form of government, and value capitalism. Finally, schools transmit culture from generation to generation, fostering a common identity and social cohesion in the process. Schools have played a particularly important role in assimilating the disadvantaged, minorities, and immigrants into Canadian society.

Durkheim emphasized the role of schools in socializing the young and promoting social integration. People, he said, are torn between egoistic needs and moral impulses. Like religion in an earlier era,

people continue their education in middle age. Beyond its importance as an agent of socialization, education is also a central determinant of opportunities for upward mobility. We care deeply about education not just because it shapes us but also because it influences how well we do.

MACROSOCIOLOGICAL PROCESSES

THE FUNCTIONS OF EDUCATION

Many Canadians believe that we enjoy equal access to basic schooling. They think schools identify and sort students based on merit and effort. They regard the education system as an avenue of upward mobility. From their standpoint, the brightest students are bound to succeed, whatever their economic, ethnic, racial, or religious background. In their view, **educational attainment** is largely an outcome of individual talent and hard work. *Educational attainment* refers to number of years of school completed. (In contrast, **educational achievement** refers to how much students actually learn.)

The view that the Canadian education system is responsible for sorting students based on talent and effort is a central component of the functional theory of education. The functional theory also stresses the training role of schools. That is, in schools, most people learn how to read, write, count, calculate, and perform other tasks essential to the workings of

educational attainment
The number of years of school that students complete.

educational achievement
How much students actually learn.

Apart from being rich and famous, what do Jon Bon Jovi, Bono, Snoop Dogg, Mark Zuckerberg, Samuel L. Jackson, Ron Howard, and Jeff Daniels have in common? They all married women they first dated in high school or college or university, exemplifying how educational institutions act as marriage markets. LeBron James, has been with his high school sweetheart, Savannah Brinson, since high school, and they have three children together. They married in September 2013.

educational institutions must ensure that the moral side predominates. By instilling a sense of authority, discipline, and morality in children, schools make society cohesive (Durkheim, 1956, 1961 [1925]).

Sorting, training, socializing, and transmitting culture are *manifest* functions, or positive goals that schools accomplish intentionally. However, schools also perform certain *latent*, or unintended, functions. For example, schools encourage the development of a separate youth culture that often conflicts with parents' values (Coleman, Campbell, and Hobson, 1966). Especially at the college and university levels, educational institutions bring potential mates together, thus serving as a "marriage market." Schools perform a useful custodial service by keeping children under surveillance for much of the day and freeing parents to work in the paid labour force. By keeping millions of young people temporarily out of the full-time paid labour force, colleges and universities restrict job competition and support wage levels (Bowles and Gintis, 1976). Finally, because they can encourage critical, independent thinking, educational institutions sometimes become "schools of dissent" that challenge authoritarian regimes and promote social change (Brower, 1975; Freire, 1972).

THE EFFECT OF ECONOMIC INEQUALITY FROM THE CONFLICT PERSPECTIVE

From the conflict perspective, the chief problem with the functionalist view is that it exaggerates the degree to which schools sort students by ability and thereby ensure that the most talented students eventually get the most rewarding jobs. Conflict theorists argue that, in fact, schools distribute the benefits of education unequally, allocating most of the benefits to children from upper classes and higher-status racial and ethnic groups. Amount and type of formal education are strongly correlated with earning power. As Figure 10.5 shows, two-thirds of the top 10 percent of income earners in Canada have a university degree compared to fewer than 18 percent of the remaining Canadians. Schools tend to reproduce the stratification system generation after generation (Jencks et al., 1972; Lucas, 1999).

Exactly how does class exert this influence? At least five social mechanisms operate in conjunction with the school system to reproduce inequality.

First is *financial constraint.* Some people do not attend university or college because they feel they can't afford it, even if they work part-time and take advantage of student loans. More than twice as many 19-year-olds from low-income families feel this way, compared with 19-year-olds from high-income families (see the yellow columns in Figure 10.6).

Second is the increase in *one-parent households.* Low-income parents are more likely than are high-income parents to experience the kinds of financial problems that can make marriage difficult and contribute to divorce. In turn, children from one-parent households are often unable to rely on adults for tutoring, emotional support and encouragement, supervision, and role modelling to the same degree as children from two-parent households can. This puts children from one-parent households at a disadvantage. Significantly, the red columns in Figure 10.6 show that 19-year-olds from low-income families are six times as likely as 19-year-olds from high-income families to have been raised in a one-parent household.

The third mechanism linking class to educational outcomes involves *lack of cultural capital.* High-income parents are two-and-a-half times as likely as low-income parents to have earned undergraduate degrees (see the blue columns in Figure 10.6). This fact is important because university education gives people **cultural capital** that they can transmit to their children, thus improving their chance of financial success. Cultural capital refers to "widely shared, high-status cultural signals (attitudes, preferences, formal knowledge, behaviours, goals, and credentials) used for social and cultural exclusion" (Lamont and Lareau, 1988: 156). If you possess a lot of cultural capital, you are more likely to have "highbrow" tastes in literature, music, art, dance, and sports—and to behave according to established rules of etiquette. You are more likely to create a household environment that promotes refined taste, provides formal lessons to help instill

cultural capital The widely shared, high-status cultural signals (attitudes, preferences, formal knowledge, behaviours, goals, and credentials) used for social and cultural exclusion.

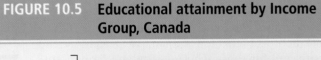

FIGURE 10.5 **Educational attainment by Income Group, Canada**

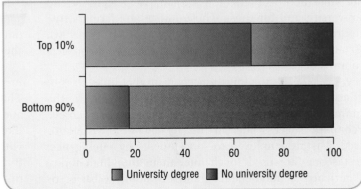

Source: Statistics Canada. 2013j. "Distribution of persons by income group and highest level of education attainment." https://www12.statcan.gc.ca/nhs-enm/2011/as-sa/99 -014-x/2011003/c-g/desc/longdesc01_2-eng.cfm (retrieved 8 August 2015).

FIGURE 10.6 **The Effects of Parents' Social Class on the Education of 19-Year-Old Canadians**

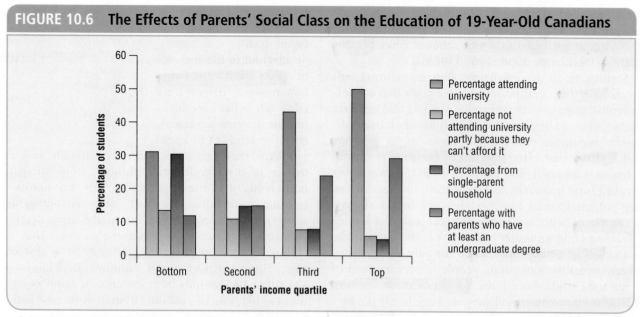

Source: Frenette, Marc. 2007. "Why Are Youth from Lower-Income Families Less Likely to Attend University? Evidence from Academic Abilities, Parental Influences, and Financial Constraints." Statistics Canada. Catalogue No. 11F0019MIE, No. 295. http://www.statcan.ca/english/research/11F0019MIE/ 11F0019MIE2007295.pdf (retrieved 26 April 2007).

such taste in your children, and thus increase their chance of success in school and, eventually, in the paid labour force (Bourdieu and Passeron, 1990; DiMaggio, 1982; Kingston, 2001).

Much evidence supports the conflict perspective. For instance, the green columns in Figure 10.6 show that Canadians from high-income families are 61 percent more likely than are those from low-income families to be enrolled in university at the age of 19. (Here, "high-income" families are those in the top 25 percent of family income and "low-income" families are those in the bottom 25 percent.) Research also shows that about 60 percent of 25- to 34-year-old Canadians whose fathers are professionals or managers attend university. The figure falls to 35 percent for those whose fathers are supervisory workers and to less than 30 percent for those whose fathers are skilled workers. Among those whose fathers are unskilled workers, fewer than 20 percent attend university, and for those whose fathers are farmers, the figure is around 10 percent (Guppy and Davies, 1998). Clearly, class strongly influences whether a person gets to university.

Streaming is the fourth mechanism that links class to educational outcomes. The more intelligent you are, the more likely you are to do well in school and to achieve economic success later in life. IQ and other standardized tests are employed to sort students by intelligence; test scores are used to channel them into high-ability ("enriched"), middle-ability, and low-ability ("basic" or "special education") classrooms. The trouble is that IQ and other standardized tests can measure only acquired proficiency in a given cultural system. The quantity and

quality of a person's exposure to whatever is counted as proper or correct plays a large role here. Even the most able Anglo-Canadian children would perform abysmally if tested in Mongolian.

The results of IQ and other standardized tests therefore depend on two factors: (1) how effectively an individual absorbs what his or her environment offers, and (2) how closely his or her environment reflects what the test includes. Consequently, members of underprivileged groups tend to score low on IQ and other standardized tests—not because they are on average less intelligent than members of privileged groups are, but because they do not have the training and the cultural background needed to achieve higher scores (Fischer et al., 1996). Nonetheless, educators persist in using IQ and other standardized tests to sort students into different types of classes (Samuda, Crawford, Philip, and Tinglen, 1980). The result: Streaming reproduces class differences, determines who goes to university and who doesn't, and influences who enters which social class in the larger society.

Finally, computers help to turn class inequality into inequality of educational attainment and achievement. The Internet is an increasingly important source of ideas and information, and people with high income are more likely to have access to the Internet at home than are people with low income. While the access gap is shrinking over time, a recent computer-related development is helping to ensure that class differences in educational attainment and achievement persist. Higher-education systems are increasingly turning to the Internet to offer distance education courses and MOOCs (massive open online courses), while some high schools are turning to largely unsupervised, computerized instructional systems.

Although such innovations sometimes enhance the quality of education, more often than not they are used to provide inferior instruction to students who are less well off. For instance, because of tight school budgets, tens of thousands of students in the United States are already taking entire courses in "virtual classrooms," which have computers loaded with educational software but no teachers at all (Herrera, 2011). Students in the private school system will never have to worry about such "innovations" in education. Similarly, online college and university courses are much less expensive to run on a per-student basis than are on-campus courses that enable students to write essays, take labs, debate their classmates in seminars, and enjoy close supervision by inspiring and caring instructors. However, because tuition for courses of the latter type is high, they are out of reach for most students from low-income families.

FUNCTIONALIST VERSUS CONFLICT THEORIES OF THE COMMUNITY COLLEGE

We can more fully illustrate how sociologists of education use functionalist and conflict theories by applying them to the case of the community college system, with its more than 400 000 full-time students in Canada. Aside from Canada's general population increase, two social forces contributed most heavily to the rise of the community college system. First, the country needed skilled workers in industry and services. Second, the belief grew that higher education would contribute to upward mobility and greater equality. The accuracy of that belief has become a point of contention among sociologists.

Functionalists examine the social composition of the student body in community colleges and find a disproportionate number of students from lower socioeconomic strata and minority ethnic groups. Many community colleges are located close to the neighbourhoods of disadvantaged students, allowing them to live at home while studying. College tuition fees are generally lower than university fees. Graduates of community colleges are usually able to find relatively good jobs and steady employment. These facts seem to confirm the functionalist view that the community college system creates new opportunities for disadvantaged youth who might otherwise have less rewarding jobs.

Conflict theorists deny that the growth of community colleges increases upward mobility and equality. In the long run, they argue, it is the entire stratification system that is upwardly mobile. That is, the quality of nearly all jobs improves but the relative position of community college graduates versus university graduates remains the same. In fact, conflict theorists argue that community colleges reinforce prevailing patterns of social and class inequality by directing students from disadvantaged backgrounds away from universities and thus decreasing the probability that they will earn a four-year degree and a high-status position in society (Karabel, 1986: 18).

GENDER AND EDUCATION: THE FEMINIST CONTRIBUTION

In some respects, women are doing better than men are in the Canadian education system. Women in colleges and universities have higher grade point averages than men do and they complete their degrees faster. The number of women enrolled as college and university undergraduates has exceeded the number of men for decades, and more women than men are enrolled in some graduate and professional programs, such as medicine and law. The enrollment gap between women and men is growing—not just in Canada but also in the United States, the United Kingdom, France, Germany, and Australia (Berliner, 2004). Men receive fewer than 40 percent of the quarter of a million degrees granted by Canadian colleges and universities annually.

The facts just listed represent considerable improvement over time in the position of women in the education system. Yet feminists who have looked closely at the situation have established that women are still at a disadvantage. Consider level of education and field of study. Although women receive more degrees than men do, the gap narrows considerably at the master's level and reverses at the Ph.D. level, where men receive about 56 percent of degrees (see Table 10.4).

Moreover, a disproportionately large number of men earn Ph.D.s and professional degrees in engineering, computer science, dentistry, and specialized areas of medicine—all relatively high-paying fields, most requiring a strong math and science background. A disproportionately large number of women earn Ph.D.s and professional degrees

TABLE 10.4	Degrees Granted, Canadian Universities, by Degree and Gender		
	Bachelor's	Master's	Doctorate
Men	38.9	45.4	55.8
Women	61.1	54.6	44.2
Total	100.0	100.0	100.0

Source: Statistics Canada. 2013k. "University degrees, diplomas and certificates granted, by program level, Classification of Instructional Programs, Primary Grouping (CIP_PG) and sex, annually (Number)." CANSIM Table 4770014.

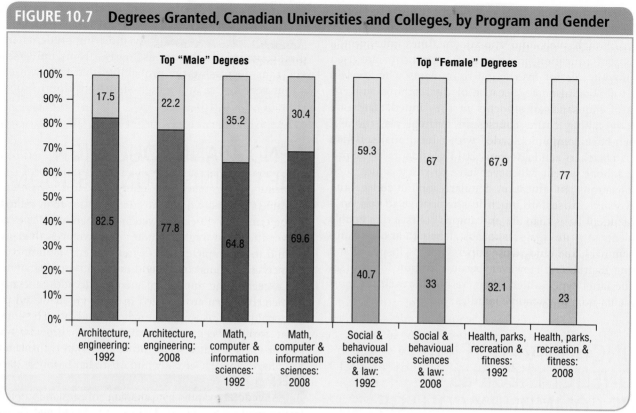

Note: Female percentages are depicted by light colours and male percentages by dark colours.

Source: Statistics Canada. 2013k. "University degrees, diplomas and certificates granted, by program level, Classification of Instructional Programs, Primary Grouping (CIP_PG) and sex, annually (Number)." CANSIM Table 4770014.

in education, English, foreign languages, and other relatively low-paying fields requiring little background in math and science. Figure 10.7 compares change over time in the two fields in which men are most predominant ("top 'male' degrees") and the two fields in which women are most predominant ("top 'female' degrees"). Female percentages are depicted by light colours and male percentages by dark colours.

The fields where women predominate are becoming more feminized over time. For example, among people who received degrees in the social and behavioural sciences and law, the percentage of women increased nearly 7 percent between 1992 and 2008. However, in fields where men predominate, change is slower and more mixed. For example, in architecture and engineering, the proportion of women rose by less than 5 percent between 1992 and 2008. In math, computer, and information sciences, the proportion of women *fell* by nearly 5 percent in this 16-year period.

Parents and teachers are partly responsible for these choices because they tend to direct boys and girls toward what they regard as masculine and feminine fields of study. Gender segregation in the labour market also influences choice of field of study. University students know women are more likely to get jobs in certain fields than in others and they make career choices accordingly

(Spade, 2001). Like class, gender structures the educational experience and its consequences.

MICROSOCIOLOGICAL PROCESSES

THE STEREOTYPE THREAT: A SYMBOLIC INTERACTIONIST VIEW

Macrosociological issues, such as the functions of education and the influence of class and gender on educational achievement, do not exhaust the interests of sociologists of education. They have also contributed much to our understanding of the face-to-face interaction processes that influence the educational process. Consider this finding from American research: When black and white children begin school, their achievement test scores are similar. Yet the longer they stay in school, the more black students fall behind. By Grade 6, blacks in many school districts are two full grades behind whites in achievement.

Clearly, something happens in school to increase the gap between black and white students. Symbolic interactionists suggest that this something is the self-fulfilling prophecy, an expectation that helps to bring about what it predicts.

We encountered examples of self-fulfilling prophecies in educational settings in Chapter 4, From Social Interaction to Social Organizations. For instance, we discussed one famous experiment in which, at the beginning of a school year, researchers randomly identified students as high or low achievers to their teachers. At the end of the school year, they found that the students arbitrarily singled out as high achievers scored higher on an IQ test than those arbitrarily singled out as low achievers. The researchers concluded that teachers' expectations influenced students' performance (Rosenthal and Jacobson, 1968; Weinstein, 2002).

Many teachers expect members of lower classes and some visible-minority groups to do poorly in school. Rather than being treated as young people with good prospects, such students are often under suspicion of intellectual inferiority and often feel rejected by teachers, white middle-class classmates, and the curriculum. This expectation, sometimes called a **stereotype threat,** has a negative impact on the school performance of disadvantaged groups (Massey, Charles, Lundy, and Fischer, 2003; Steele, 1997).

Minority-group students often cluster together because they feel alienated from dominant groups in their school or perhaps even from the institution itself. Too often, such alienation turns into resentment and defiance of authority. Many students from minority groups reject academic achievement as a goal because they see it as a value of the dominant culture. Discipline problems, ranging from apathy to disruptive and illegal behaviour, can result.

The corollary of identifying your race or ethnicity with poor academic performance is thinking of good academic performance as "selling out" to the dominant culture (Ogbu, 2003; Willis, 1984). Consistent with this argument, Aboriginal and black students in Canada have higher-than-average school dropout rates (Livingstone, 1999: 743; Toronto Board of Education, 1993). In contrast, research shows that challenging lower-class and minority students, giving them emotional support and encouragement, giving greater recognition in the curriculum to the accomplishments of the groups from which they originate, creating an environment in which they can relax and achieve—all of these strategies explode the self-fulfilling prophecy and improve academic performance (Steele, 1992).

Anecdotal evidence supporting this argument can be found in the compelling 1988 movie *Stand and Deliver*, based on the true-life story of high school math teacher Jaime Escalante. Escalante refused to write off his failing East Los Angeles Chicano pupils as "losers" and inspired them to remarkable achievements as they registered the best performance in the Advanced Placement Calculus Exam in the southern California school system.

In sum, the stereotype threat at the microsociological level combines with the macrosociological processes described earlier to help reproduce the stratification system. These social mechanisms increase the chance that those who are socially marginal and already disadvantaged will earn low grades and wind up with jobs closer to the bottom than to the top of the occupational structure.

> **stereotype threat** The impact of negative stereotypes on the school performance of disadvantaged groups.

LO⁵ CANADIAN EDUCATION IN AN INTERNATIONAL PERSPECTIVE

In Europe 300 years ago, the nobility and the wealthy usually hired personal tutors to teach their children to read and write; learn basic history, geography, and foreign languages; and study how to dress properly, conduct themselves in public, greet status superiors, and so on. Few people went to college.

Although the composition of Canada's student population is becoming increasingly multicultural, this is less true of Canada's teachers. An ongoing debate in Canada is whether students at all levels would be better served by a faculty whose composition reflects the diversity of our population and who offer a more inclusive curriculum.

@ iStockphoto.com/Christopher Futcher

Recent surveys suggest that Canadians have only a moderate level of confidence in the job being done by the public education sector.

Winnipeg Free Press/Marc Gallant/The Canadian Press

Only a few professions, such as theology and law, required extensive schooling. The great majority of Europeans were illiterate. As late as the 1860s, more than 80 percent of Spaniards and more than 30 percent of the French could not read (Vincent, 2000). Even as recently as a century ago, most people in the world had never attended even a day of school. As late as 1950, only about 10 percent of the world's countries boasted systems of compulsory mass education (Meyer, Ramirez, and Soysal, 1992).

Today, the situation is vastly different. Compulsory mass education became a universal feature of European and North American life by the early twentieth century, and nearly universal literacy was achieved by the middle of the twentieth century (Curtis, 1988; Vincent, 2000). Every country in the world now has a system of mass schooling. Still, universal literacy is a remote goal. Eighteen percent of the world's adults are illiterate, nearly two-thirds of them women. In sub-Saharan Africa, 40 percent of primary school-aged children do not attend school (United Nations Educational, Scientific, and Cultural Organization, 2008: 58). In contrast, 52 percent of Canadians between the ages of 25 and 64 had a college or university education in 2011, higher than the comparable percentage for any other country (Statistics Canada, 2012e).

Nonetheless, many Canadians believe that our public school system has turned soft if not rotten. They argue that the youth of Japan and South Korea spend long hours concentrating on the basics of math, science, and language, while Canadian students spend fewer hours in school and study more non-basic subjects (e.g., art, music, drama, physical education) that are of little practical value. If students do not spend more school time on subjects that "really" matter, they warn, Canada will suffer declining economic competitiveness in the twenty-first century. Many Canadians—8 in 10 according to one poll—want province-wide standardized tests for students and teachers because they presumably allow school performance to be objectively assessed (Bricker and Greenspon, 2001: 165–66).

Partly because of the perceived decline in school standards, a growing number of Canadian children do not attend public schools. About 1 percent of Canadian children are home-schooled and about 7 percent attend private schools (Boyer, 2012). In relatively affluent cities, such as Toronto, the latter figure is roughly 10 percent.

Private schools offer specialized programs, small classes, contact with the "right" people, and facilities that students in public schools can only dream of. For example, for the academic year 2015–16, the family of a new Canadian student entering Upper Canada College in Toronto in Grade 12 and boarding at the school would have to pay $8700 in application and registration fees, $33 550 for tuition, and $23 960 for boarding fees: a total of $66 210 for the year (Upper Canada College, 2015). Among other amenities, the college has its own indoor, regulation-sized hockey rink. At Toronto's Bishop Strachan School, the family of an equivalent student would pay to pay $63 270 for the year (Bishop Strachan School, 2015). There, among many other amenities, a personal trainer is available for consultations in the gym. To put such fees in perspective, it is useful to know that the annual median income for Canadian individuals would pay for about one semester of such fees at either of these schools (Statistics Canada, 2015k).

International comparisons show that Canadians perform relatively well in standardized math, science, and literacy tests. According to the most comprehensive and widely respected international study of 15-year-old student performance, Canada's school system ranks seventh in the world (see Table 10.5). Moreover, Canada is among the top six countries in terms of providing a good education to students from all socioeconomic classes (the others are Finland, Iceland, Japan, South Korea, and Sweden; Sokoloff, 2001). None of this is cause for complacency. We still need to do a lot to improve the quality of Canadian education, particularly for students from disadvantaged families. However, the public's fears about poor and declining educational standards are likely overdrawn.

TABLE 10.5 The World's Top 10 School Systems

Rank	Reading	Science	Math	Overall
1	Singapore	Singapore	Singapore	Singapore
2	Japan	Japan	South Korea	Japan
3	South Korea	Finland	Japan	South Korea
4	Finland	Estonia	Liechtenstein	Finland
5	**Canada**, Ireland	South Korea	Switzerland	Estonia
6		Viet Nam	Netherlands	Liechtenstein
7	Poland	Poland	Estonia	**Canada**
8	Estonia, Liechtenstein	**Canada**, Liechtenstein	Finland	Poland
9			**Canada**, Poland	Switzerland
10	Australia, New Zealand	Germany		Netherlands

Source: PISA. 2014. "PISA 2012 Results in Focus." http://www.oecd.org/pisa/keyfindings/pisa-2012-results-overview.pdf (retrieved 8 August 2015).

READY TO STUDY?

IN THE BOOK, YOU CAN:

❏ Tear out the chapter review card at the back of the book to have a summary of the chapter and key terms handy.

ONLINE YOU CAN:

❏ Work through key concepts with a Guided Learning Question.

❏ Prepare for tests with quizzes.

❏ Review the key terms with flash cards.

❏ Explore practical examples of chapter concepts with Connect a Concept exercises.

GO TO NELSON.COM/STUDENT TO ACCESS THESE DIGITAL RESOURCES.

11

Health and Medicine

Tetra Images/Getty Images

LEARNING OBJECTIVES

In this chapter, you will learn to

LO¹ Recognize that health risks are unevenly distributed by class, gender, race, and country of residence.

LO² Explain why many low-income and moderate-income Canadians have limited access to health services.

LO³ Identify the ways in which the social organization of health care systems influences people's health.

LO⁴ Describe how the rise of medical science is linked to (1) successful treatments and (2) the way doctors excluded competitors and established control over their profession and their clients.

LO⁵ Appreciate the benefits and dangers of alternative medical treatments.

THE BLACK DEATH

In 1346, rumours reached Europe of a plague sweeping the East. Originating in Asia, the epidemic spread along trade routes to China and Russia. A year later, 12 galleys sailed from southern Russia to Italy. Diseased sailors were onboard. Their lymph nodes were terribly swollen and eventually burst, causing painful death. Anyone who came in contact with the sailors was soon infected. As a result, the ships were driven out of several Italian and French ports. Yet the disease spread relentlessly, again moving along trade routes to Spain, Portugal, and England. Within two years, the Black Death, as it came to be known, killed a third of Europe's population. More than 650 years later, the plague still ranks as the most devastating catastrophe in human history (Herlihy, 1998; McNeill, 1976; Zinsser, 1935).

Today we know that the cause of the plague was a bacillus that spread from fleas to rats to people. It spread so efficiently because many people lived close together in unsanitary conditions. However, in the middle of the fourteenth century nobody knew anything about germs. Therefore, Pope Clement VI sent a delegation to Europe's leading medical school in Paris to discover the cause of the plague. The learned professors studied the problem. They reported that a particularly unfortunate conjunction of Saturn, Jupiter, and Mars in the sign of Aquarius had occurred in 1345. The resulting hot, humid conditions caused the earth to emit poisonous vapours. To prevent the plague, they said, people should refrain from eating poultry, waterfowl, pork, beef, fish, and olive oil. They should not sleep during the daytime or engage in excessive exercise. Nothing should be cooked in rainwater. Bathing should be avoided at all costs.

We do not know whether the Pope followed the professors' advice. We do know he made a practice of sitting between two large fires to breathe pure air. Because the plague bacillus is destroyed by heat, this may have saved his life. Other people were less fortunate. Some rang church bells and fired cannons to drive the plague away. Others burned incense, wore charms, and cast spells. But other than the Pope, the only people to have much luck in avoiding the plague were the well-to-do (who could afford to flee the densely populated cities for remote areas in the countryside) and the Jews (whose religion required that they wash their hands before meals, bathe once a week, and conduct burials soon after death).

Some of the main themes of the sociology of health and medicine are embedded in the story of the Black Death, or

The Black Death

life expectancy The average age at death of the members of a population.

fact suggests that health is not just a medical issue but also a sociological one. The first task we set ourselves here is to examine the sociological factors that account for the uneven distribution of health in society.

Second, the story of the Black Death suggests that health problems change over time. Epidemics of various types still break out, but there can be no Black Death where sanitation and hygiene prevent the spread of disease. Today we are also able to treat many infectious diseases, such as tuberculosis and pneumonia, with antibiotics. Twentieth-century medical science developed these wonder drugs and many other life-saving therapies.

Medical successes allow people to live longer than they used to. **Life expectancy** is the average age at death of the members of a population. Life expectancy in Canada in 1831 was approximately 40 years for men and 42 years for women (Lavoie and Oderkirk, 2000: 3). In contrast, a Canadian girl born between 2009 and 2011 can hope to live 83.6 years, a boy 79.3 years (Statistics Canada, 2013m). Yet, because of increased life expectancy, degenerative conditions, such as cancer and heart disease, have an opportunity to develop in a way that was not possible a century ago (see Table 11.1). Other factors, notably galloping weight gains, contribute to disease burden (see Figure 11.1).

The story of the Black Death raises a third issue, too. One cannot help being struck by the superstition and ignorance surrounding the treatment of the ill in medieval times. Remedies were often herbal but also included earthworms, urine, and animal excrement. People believed it was possible to maintain good health by keeping body fluids in balance. Therefore, cures that released body fluids were common. These cures included hot baths, laxatives, and diuretics, which increase the flow of urine.

at least implied by it. First, recall that some groups were more likely to die of the plague than others were. This is a common pattern. Health risks are always unevenly distributed. Women and men, upper and lower classes, rich and poor countries, and privileged and disadvantaged members of racial and ethnic groups are exposed to health risks to varying degrees. This

TABLE 11.1	Ten Leading Causes of Death, Canada, 1901 and 2011			
Percentage of Deaths				
1901			**2011**	
1.	Tuberculosis	12.0	1. Cancer	29.9
2.	Bronchitis and pneumonia	10.0	2. Heart disease	19.7
3.	Infections of the intestines	9.1	3. Stroke	5.5
4.	Senile debility	7.4	4. Chronic lower respiratory diseases	4.6
5.	Congenital debility	7.0	5. Accidents	4.4
6.	Diseases of the heart	5.6	6. Diabetes	3.0
7.	Apoplexy and paralysis	4.4	7. Alzheimer's disease	2.6
8.	Diphtheria and croup	3.9	8. Influenza and pneumonia	2.4
9.	Accidents	3.4	9. Suicide	1.5
10.	Cancer	2.8	10. Kidney disease	1.4
	Other	34.4	Other	25.0
	Total	100.0	Total	100.0

Sources: Dawson, S.E. 1906; Statistics Canada. 2015m, "Ten Leading Causes of Death, 2011." http://www.statcan.gc.ca/pub/82-625-x/2014001/article/11896-eng.htm (retrieved 7 August 2015).

FIGURE 11.1 Overweight and Obesity, Selected Countries

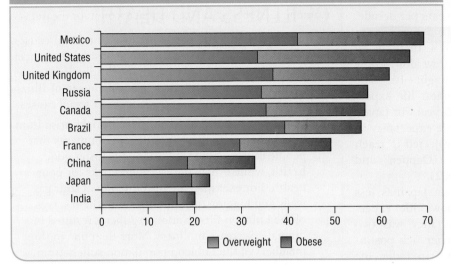

Note: Data are for 2013. Body mass index (BMI) is equal to body mass in kilograms divided by the square of body height in metres. A BMI of 25 is considered overweight and a BMI of 30 is considered obese.

Source: Martinez, R. 2015 "Prevalence of Overweight and Obesity Visualization." *Health Intelligence.* http://healthintelligence.drupalgardens.com/content/prevalence-overweight-and-obesity (retrieved 7 August 2015).

If these treatments didn't work, bloodletting was often prescribed. No special qualifications were required to administer medical treatment. Barbers doubled as doctors.

However, the backwardness of medieval medical practice and the advantages of modern scientific medicine can be exaggerated. For example, medieval doctors stressed the importance of prevention, exercise, a balanced diet, and a congenial environment in maintaining good health. We now know this is sound advice. Conversely, one of the great shortcomings of modern medicine is its emphasis on high-tech cures rather than on preventive and environmental measures. Therefore, in the final section of this chapter, we investigate how the medical professions gained substantial control over health issues and promoted their own approach to well-being, and how those professions have been challenged in recent years.

LO¹ HEALTH AND INEQUALITY

DEFINING AND MEASURING HEALTH

According to the World Health Organization (WHO, 2010b), **health** is

. . . a state of complete physical, social and mental well-being, and not merely the absence of disease or infirmity. Health is a resource for everyday life, not the object of living. It is a positive concept emphasizing social and personal resources as well as physical capabilities.

The WHO definition lists in broad terms the main factors that promote good health. However, when it comes to *measuring* the health of a population, sociologists typically examine the negative: rates of illness and death. They reason that healthy populations experience less illness and longer life than unhealthy populations. We follow that approach here.

Assuming ideal conditions, how long can a person live? To date, the record is held by Jeanne Louise Calment, a French woman who died in 1997 at the age of 122. (Other people claim to be older, but they lack authenticated birth certificates.) Calment was an extraordinary individual. She took up fencing at age 85, rode a bicycle until she was 100, gave up smoking at 120, and released a rap CD at 121 (Matalon, 1997). Only 1 in 100 people in the world's rich countries now lives to be 100. Since 1840, life expectancy in the world's rich

health According to the WHO, "A state of complete physical, social and mental well-being, and not merely the absence of disease or infirmity."

In the twenty-first century, the maximum lifespan may increase because of medical advances. So far, the record is held by Jeanne Louise Calment, a French woman who died in 1997 at the age of 122.

environmental racism The tendency to heap environmental dangers on the disadvantaged.

public health system Comprises government-run programs that ensure access to clean drinking water, basic sewage and sanitation services, and inoculation against infectious diseases.

countries has increased at a fairly steady rate of about 2.5 years per decade. Further increases seem likely, and if there is an upper limit, we don't know what it might be. The world's highest life expectancy is 83 years in Japan. By 2050, life expectancy in Japan is projected to reach 92 years (Oeppen and Vaupel, 2002).

Unfortunately, life expectancy outside Japan is less than 83 years today. Figure 11.2 shows life expectancy in selected countries. Life expectancy was two years shorter in Canada and in most other rich postindustrial countries than it was in Japan. In India, life expectancy was only 65 years. People in Lesotho, an impoverished African country south of the Sahara desert, have the world's shortest life expectancy at 44 years, only 11 years more than life expectancy in Europe in 1600. More than half a billion people in 32 countries—most in sub-Saharan Africa—have a life expectancy of less than 50 years (Geohive.com, 2005; Population Reference Bureau, 2014).

If the maximum observed life expectancy in a population is now 83 years, then Canadians are being deprived of about two years of life because of avoidable social causes (83 − 81 = 2). Avoidable social causes deprive the citizens of Lesotho of 39 years of life (83 − 44 = 39). Clearly, social causes have a big—and variable—impact on illness and death. We must therefore discuss them in detail.

THE SOCIAL CAUSES OF ILLNESS AND DEATH

People get sick and die partly because of natural causes. One person may have a genetic predisposition to cancer. Another may come in contact with the deadly Ebola virus. However, over and above such natural causes of illness and death, we can single out three types of *social* causes:

1. *Human-environmental factors.* Health risks arise from how human activity shapes the environments that people inhabit. Some environments foster good health, while others impose added risks for poor health. For example, the introduction of sour gas wells and logging operations around the reserves of the Lubicon First Nation in Alberta resulted in a dramatic increase in illness. More than one in three members of the Lubicon population suffers from such health problems as tuberculosis, respiratory difficulties, and cancer at rates far above the national average (Barlow and May, 2000: 183).

   Environmental racism, the tendency for hazardous waste sites and polluting industries to be located near First Nations communities or areas populated by the poor, the politically marginalized, or certain visible-minority groups, also contributes to lower levels of health. For example, in the 1980s, the pulp-and-paper industry's mercury poisoning of the English-Wabigoon river system in western Ontario near the Manitoba border led to the virtual destruction of the Grassy Narrows First Nation's way of life and means of livelihood (Shkilnyk, 1985). More recently, "patterns of atmospheric cycling have made the North a dumping ground for industrial chemicals that . . . [are] never used there. The chemicals bioaccumulate, delivering a higher level of toxic concentration to each level up the food chain. As a result, the breast milk of Inuit mothers is 10 times as contaminated as that of southern Canadian women" (Barlow and May, 2000: 184). This situation provides a striking illustration of how human-caused environmental conditions can cause illness and death (see Chapter 13, Technology, the Environment, and Social Movements).

2. Factors related to the public health and health care systems. The state of a nation's health depends partly on public and private efforts to improve people's well-being and treat their illnesses. The public health system comprises government-run

---

FIGURE 11.2   Life Expectancy, Selected Countries and Years

Sources: Population Reference Bureau. 2014. "2014 World Population Data Sheet." http://www.prb.org/pdf14/2014-world-population-data-sheet_eng.pdf (retrieved 7 August 2015); Tuljapurkar, Li, and Boe (2000). Tuljapurkar, Shripad, Nan Li, and Carl Boe. 2000. "A Universal Pattern of Mortality Decline in the G7 Countries." *Nature* 405: 789–92.

A health worker at Nazareth House in Cape Town, South Africa, lavishes care and attention on some of the 41 HIV/AIDS infected children in her care. Nearly 18 percent of South Africa's adult population is infected with HIV/AIDS.

programs that ensure access to clean drinking water, basic sewage and sanitation services, and inoculation against infectious diseases. The absence of a public health system is associated with high rates of disease and low life expectancy. The **health care system** comprises a nation's clinics, hospitals, and other facilities for ensuring health and treating illness. The absence of a system that ensures its citizens access to a minimum standard of health care is also associated with high rates of disease and shorter life expectancy. The 2014 Ebola outbreak killed 11 298 people as of August 6, 2015. It originated in West Africa and spread to Italy, Spain, the United Kingdom, and the United States. The total death toll from Ebola in these rich, Western countries: 1. The total death toll in the poor West African countries of Liberia, Sierra Leone, and Guinea, which lack what we would consider even rudimentary public health and health care systems: 11 283 (Centers for Disease Control and Prevention, 2015).

3. *Lifestyle factors.* Smoking, excessive use of alcohol and drugs, poor diet, lack of exercise, and social isolation are among the chief lifestyle factors associated with poor health and premature death. For example, smoking is associated with lung cancer, cardiovascular disease, strokes, emphysema, spontaneous abortion, premature birth, and neonatal death. In Canada, about 50 000 deaths a year are caused by smoking and other uses of tobacco products. About a fifth of all deaths can be attributed to tobacco use (Makomaski, Illing, and Kaiserman, 2004). Social isolation, too, affects a person's chance of becoming ill and dying prematurely. Thus, unmarried people have a greater chance of dying prematurely than do married people. At any age, the death of a spouse increases a person's chance of dying, while remarrying decreases the chance of dying (Helsing, Szklo, and Comstock, 1981). Social isolation is a particularly big problem among older people who retire, lose a spouse and friends, and cannot rely on family members or state institutions for social support. Such people are prone to fall into a state of depression, which contributes to ill health.

> **health care system**
> Composed of a nation's clinics, hospitals, and other facilities for ensuring health and treating illness.

People often think of lifestyle factors like smoking as matters of individual choice. However, like human environmental factors and factors related to the public health and health care systems, they are associated with social background factors, including country of residence, class, race, and gender. We now consider the impact of these social background factors, beginning with country of residence (see also the Sociology at the Movies feature and the Sociology on the Tube feature in this chapter).

Country of Residence

HIV/AIDS is the leading cause of death in the poverty-stricken part of Africa south of the Sahara desert. Figure 11.3

FIGURE 11.3	People Living with HIV/AIDS, All Ages (adult prevalence in parentheses)

North America
1.3 million (0.5%)

Western &
Central Europe
860 000 (0.2%)

Eastern Europe
& Central Asia
1.3 million (0.7%)

East Asia
880 000 (0.1%)

Caribbean
250 000 (1.0%)

Middle East &
North Africa
260 000 (0.1%)

South &
Southeast Asia
3.9 million (0.3%)

Latin America
1.5 million (0.4%)

Sub-Saharan Africa
25.0 million (4.7%)

Oceania
51 000 (0.2%)

Total: 35.3 million (0.8%)

Source: UNAIDS 2014. *Global Report: UNAIDS Report on the Global AIDS Epidemic 2013*, pp. A3–A15. http://www.unaids.org/sites/default/files/media_asset/UNAIDS_Global_Report_2013_en_1.pdf (retrieved 7 August 2015).

SOCIOLOGY AT THE MOVIES

Silver Linings Playbook

Released from a mental health institution where he has spent the past eight months, Pat Solatano (played by Bradley Cooper) has one thing on his mind. He wants to find his wife, Nikki, and get back together with her. It doesn't matter that Nikki has a restraining order against him. It doesn't even matter that the reason he was institutionalized was because he beat up a colleague whom he caught in the shower with his wife. Trapped in a delusion generated by bipolar disorder, Pat is convinced that his wife still loves him and wants him back.

His re-entry into normal life is rocky. Pat lives with his parents, whom he manages to upset with his bizarre behaviour. Moreover, Pat is convinced he doesn't need medication. It doesn't make him feel good. Besides, he has adopted a new philosophy. Summed up in the word "excelsior," Pat believes that if he chooses to see the good in everything—the silver linings—life will turn out well.

His friends, looking for a way to help Pat to move on with his life, invite him over for dinner to meet Tiffany Maxwell (played by Jennifer Lawrence, whose performance won her an Oscar for Best Actress). Tiffany is a recent widow struggling to get over sex addiction and depression. They take to one another right away. They reject social convention, asking each other inappropriate questions and happily exchanging information on the unpleasant side effects of their medication in front of their hosts.

It turns out that Tiffany knows Nikki, so Pat and Tiffany strike an odd bargain. Tiffany promises to deliver Pat's love letters to Nikki in violation of the restraining order. In exchange, Pat agrees to be Tiffany's dance partner in an upcoming competition. Over the next weeks, the couple practises hard. They grow close and fall in love. Pat's illusions about Nikki fall away as he reaches for his silver lining.

Silver Linings Playbook takes a stridently individualistic approach to mental illness. It portrays Pat's resolve to find the silver lining as the singular force that helps him overcome his delusions. In doing so, the film ignores the social background causes of many forms of mental illness. For example, people who live unusually stressful lives because they are often demeaned, humiliated, and subordinated in their interactions with others are prone to

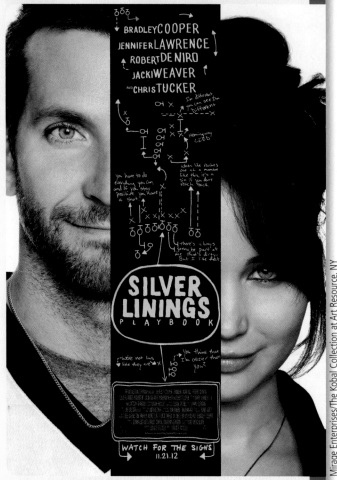

Pat and Tiffany in *Silver Linings Playbook*

schizophrenia. People diagnosed with schizophrenia are therefore found disproportionately among immigrants, minority groups that experience high levels of discrimination, and poor and homeless people (Link, Dohrenwend, and Skodol, 1986; Luhrmann, 2007; Selten and Cantor-Graae, 2005). *Silver Linings Playbook* is a nice story, but more often than not, resolve to find the silver lining cannot overcome the stressfulness of repeated social defeat.

Critical Thinking Questions

1. Can medication play a useful role in the treatment of mental illnesses that are associated with social background factors, or does medication mask the fundamental causes of such mental illnesses?
2. If some mental illnesses are associated with social background factors, what kinds of social policies are needed to treat these forms of mental illness?

SOCIOLOGY ON THE TUBE

Big Bang Theory

Sheldon Cooper, the quirky character played by Jim Parsons, is a theoretical physicist on the popular TV show, *Big Bang Theory*. The show follows the lives of Sheldon, his roommate, Leonard Hofstadter, an experimental physicist, and their socially awkward but scientifically inclined friends, Howard and Raj.

Sheldon Cooper

© CBS/Courtesy: Everett Collection/The Canadian Press

While Leonard is smitten with Penny, an aspiring actress who works as a waitress and lives in the apartment across the hall, Sheldon is more interested in advancing his career and lording his intellectual superiority over others. He is, however, oblivious to his social deficits. Sheldon often interprets language literally, so most jokes confuse him. His emotionally flat demeanour amuses and frustrates his friends. He is so afraid of germs that he makes Leonard sign an agreement to keep their apartment antiseptic. He follows strict routines that only he understands, such as knocking on a friend's door precisely three times and then uttering the person's name. On the many occasions others question his sanity, Sheldon's invariable response is that he couldn't be insane because his mother had him tested.

These unusual behaviours have led many people to speculate that Sheldon may have Asperger's Disorder, a mental illness that affects a small but growing proportion of the population. Although the show's creators dispute that Sheldon has Asperger's, Jim Parsons himself acknowledges that his inspiration for the role comes from reading and learning about the disorder.

Ironically, the question as to whether Sheldon has Asperger's may soon be moot. The latest edition of the *Diagnostic and Statistical Manual of Mental Disorders* (DSM-5), the psychiatrist's diagnostic "bible," no longer lists Asperger's as a separate disorder. Instead, Asperger's is combined with other diagnoses into a single mental illness called *autism spectrum disorder*. The change raises a number of interesting issues for sociologists.

Critical Thinking Questions

1. Some people previously diagnosed with Asperger's proudly identify themselves as "Aspies." What might happen to their identity now that the label has been officially discarded?
2. Insurance companies base payments on diagnostic criteria in DSM-5 but autism spectrum disorder is defined more narrowly than Asperger's was. Will people who received help in the past be barred from future treatment because they no longer fit the criteria in DSM-5?
3. More generally, how important are officially recognized medical labels in providing people with a sense of identity and the ability to receive treatment?

---

shows that by the end of 2012, 25 million sub-Saharan Africans were living with HIV/AIDS. Among adults, the prevalence of HIV/AIDS was 4.7 percent. In contrast, 0.5 percent of North American adults and 0.2 percent of western and central European adults were living with HIV/AIDS. Yet spending on research and treatment is concentrated overwhelmingly in the rich countries of North America and western Europe. As the case of HIV/AIDS illustrates, global inequality influences the exposure of people to different health risks.

infant mortality The number of deaths before the age of one for every 1000 live births in a population in one year.

You might think that prosperity increases health through biomedical advances, such as new medicines and diagnostic tools. If so, you are only partly correct. Biomedical advances do increase life expectancy. For example, vaccines against infectious diseases have done much to improve health and ensure longer life. However, the creation of a sound public health system is even more important in this regard. If a country can provide its citizens with clean water and a sewage system, epidemics decline in frequency and severity. Life expectancy soars.

The industrialized countries started developing public health systems in the mid-nineteenth century. Social reformers, concerned citizens, scientists, and doctors joined industrialists and politicians in urging governments to develop health policies that would help create a healthier labour force and citizenry (Bricker and Greenspon, 2001: 178–83; Goubert, 1989 [1986]; McNeill, 1976). But what was possible in North America and western Europe 150 years ago is not possible in many developing countries today. Most of us take clean water for granted, but more than a sixth of the world's people do not have access to a sanitary water supply (de Villiers, 1999).

Table 11.2 displays other indicators of health inequality for selected countries. We see that, in general, there is a positive association between national wealth and good health. Canada, the United States, and Japan are rich countries. They spend thousands of dollars per person on health care every year. More than 2 physicians serve every 1000 members of the population. **Infant mortality** (the annual number of deaths before the age of one for every 1000 live births) is low. India, which is poorer than Canada, the United States, and Japan, spends only a few hundred

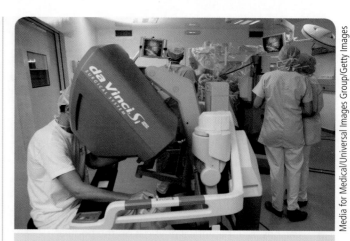

Biomedical advances increase life expectancy, but the creation of a sound public health system has even more dramatic benefits.

dollars per person per year on health care. Accordingly, its population is less healthy in many respects. The sub-Saharan country of Lesotho is one of the poorest countries in the world. It spends little on health care, has few medical personnel, and suffers from a high rate of infant mortality.

LO² CLASS INEQUALITIES AND HEALTH CARE

In Canada, despite our system of universal health care, socioeconomic status is related to numerous aspects of health and illness (Raphael, 2004). On average, people with low income die at a younger

TABLE 11.2 **Health Indicators, Selected Countries**

Country	Per capita total expenditure on health*	Physicians per 1000 population*	Infant mortality per 1000 live births	Percentage of population with access to improved drinking water**
Canada	4759	2.1	4.6	99
Lesotho	297	0.067	73.0	77
United States	9146	2.4	5.9	98
India	215	0.7	41.4	91
Japan	3741	2.3	2.1	100

*Purchasing power in U.S. dollars.

**Piped water into dwelling, plot or yard; public tap/stand pipe; tube well/borehole; protected dug well; protected spring; rainwater collection.

Note: Data are circa 2013 except the figure for physicians per 1000 population in Lesotho, which pertains to 2006.

Sources: Mokete, 'Musi. 2006. "Forty Years of Health Services Development in Lesotho (Successes, Failures and Challenges), 1966–2006." http://unpan1.un.org/intradoc/groups/public/documents/AAPAM/UNPAN025645.pdf (retrieved 7 August 2015); World Bank. 2015. "Physicians (per 1,000 people)." http://data.worldbank.org/indicator/SH.MED.PHYS.ZS (retrieved 7 August 2015); World Health Organization (WHO). 2015. Global Health Observatory Data Repository." http://apps.who.int/gho/data/?theme=home (retrieved 7 August 2015).

age than do people with high income. Canadians enjoy a lower rate of illness and longer life expectancy at each step up the income ladder. Poverty is associated with high rates of tobacco and alcohol consumption, obesity, physical inactivity, and violence (Health Canada, 1999a, 1999b).

Why does health deteriorate as we move down the class hierarchy? Sociologists propose several explanations:

- *High stress and the inability to cope with it.* People in lower classes experience relatively high stress levels because of their difficult living conditions (Kessler et al., 1994). Stress is associated with a variety of physical and mental health problems, including high blood pressure, cancer, chronic fatigue, violence, and substance abuse. Moreover, people higher up in the class structure are often able to turn stress off. They can, for instance, more easily take a few days off work or go on vacation. Many problems are more burdensome when such resources as money and influence are not available to address them. Upper-class people can pay others to fix their cars or their offspring's legal mishaps. Lower-class families may have to go into debt or simply accept some bad outcomes as unavoidable (Cockerham, 1998; Epstein, 1998; Evans, 1999; Wilkinson and Marmot, 2003). Mishaps aside, lower-class families must endure greater crowding; poorer dwelling quality; working conditions that are more noxious, dangerous, and unpleasant; and longer hours of work to make ends meet.

- *Differences in the earliest stages of development that have lifelong consequences.* Inequalities at the start of life have strong health consequences for a lifetime (Forrest and Riley, 2004). Poor nutrition during pregnancy, stress, maternal smoking and misuse of drugs and alcohol, insufficient exercise, and inadequate prenatal care typically lead to suboptimal fetal development (Wilkinson and Marmot, 2003: 14). Mothers with low income are more likely to provide such unfavourable starts to life.

- *Lack of knowledge.* People who are less educated and who have less exposure to educated advisers tend to have less knowledge about healthy lifestyles. For example, they are less likely to know what constitutes a nutritious diet. This, too, contributes to their propensity to illness. Illness, in turn, makes it more difficult for poor people to escape poverty (Abraham, 1993).

- *Unequal access to health resources.* A disproportionately large number of poor Canadians live in areas that have inferior medical services. For example, there are fewer hospitals, physicians, and nurses per capita in rural areas than in urban areas. As well, the quality of preventive, diagnostic, and treatment facilities is generally superior in urban areas. Moreover, many low- and middle-income Canadians have limited or no access to eye care, dentistry, mental health counselling, and prescription drugs (Boychuk, 2002; Health Canada, 1999a).

- *Environmental exposure.* As we saw earlier, poor people are more likely than rich people are to be exposed to environmental risks that have a negative impact on their health. There is a striking lack of incinerators, pulp and paper mills, oil refineries, dumpsites, factories, and mines in Westmount (Montreal), Tuxedo (Winnipeg), Rosedale (Toronto), and other wealthy Canadian neighbourhoods (see Chapter 13, Technology, the Environment, and Social Movements).

RACIAL INEQUALITIES IN HEALTH CARE

Racial disparities in health status are also large. For example, the life expectancy of First Nations people is about seven years less than that of other Canadians ("Our Voices," 2009). Despite the health risks to both the mother and the developing fetus, more than half of First Nations women and three-quarters of Inuit women smoke during pregnancy, compared with about 20 percent for all women in Canada (Canadian Centre on Substance Abuse, 1999).

Such health disparities are partly due to economic differences among racial groups. In addition, researchers have begun to emphasize how racially marginalized groups are subject to negative health outcomes because of the

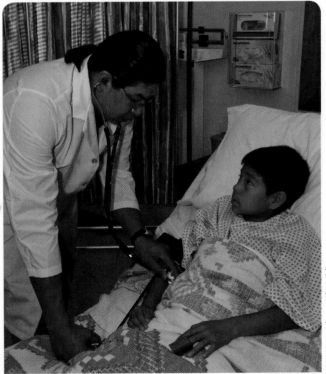

Why is the average health status of First Nations people relatively low?

morbidity Acute and chronic illness.

cumulative effects of social exclusion based on race. Researchers have observed these effects for First Nations people in Canada, African Americans, and other groups (Galabuzi, 2004; Wilkinson and Marmot, 2003).

How does social exclusion influence health apart from the obvious fact that excluded groups experience a higher poverty rate? In brief, labour market segregation, high unemployment, low occupation status, substandard housing, dangerous or distressed neighbourhoods, homelessness, dangerous worksites, extended work hours, multiple jobs, and experience with everyday forms of racism lead to unequal health service utilization and differential health status (Galabuzi, 2004: 3). Even when members of socially excluded groups are employed, they are more likely to continue living in inferior areas because of racial discrimination in housing, and such areas typically suffer from reduced access to medical services. Those who nevertheless seek medical services often encounter racially based misunderstanding or even hostility. The cumulative result of these factors is considerable. The rate of heart disease is 1.5 times higher among First Nations than among the Canadian population as a whole, type 2 diabetes is 3 to 5 times higher, tuberculosis infection is 8 to 10 times higher, and the percentage of those reporting poor or fair health is more than twice as high (Canadian Institute for Health Information, 2004: 81; Health Canada, 2014b).

Gender Inequalities in Health Care: The Feminist Contribution

Feminist scholars have brought health inequalities based on gender to the attention of the sociological community. In a review of the relevant literature, one researcher concluded that such inequalities are substantial (Haas, 1998):

- Gender bias exists in medical research. Public health systems have been slower to address and more likely to neglect women's health issues than men's health issues. So, until recently, more research focused on "men's diseases," such as cardiac arrest, than on "women's diseases," such as breast cancer. Similarly, women have been excluded from participating in many major health research studies (Johnson and Fee, 1997). Medical research is just beginning to explore the fact that women may react differently from men to some illnesses and may require different treatment regimes.

- Gender bias also exists in medical treatment. For example, women undergo fewer kidney transplants, cardiac procedures, and other treatments than men do.

- Because women live longer than men do on average, they experience greater lifetime risk of functional disability and chronic illness, and greater need for long-term care. The low status of women in

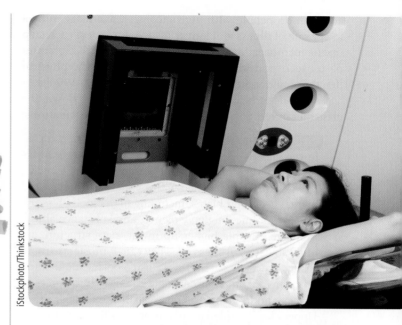

iStockphoto/Thinkstock

many less-developed countries results in their being nutritionally deprived and having less access to medical care than men do. As a result, women in developing countries suffer high rates of mortality and **morbidity** (acute and chronic illness) because of high rates of complication associated with pregnancy and childbirth. Fully 99 percent of all deaths attributable to pregnancy-related complications occur in less-developed countries (World Health Organization, 2012b).

- Canadian women face a higher risk than men do of poverty after divorce or widowhood. Because poverty contributes to ill health, we would expect improvements in women's economic standing to be reflected in improved health status for women.

In sum, although on average women live longer than men do, gender inequalities have a negative impact on women's health. Women's health is negatively affected by differences between women and men in access to gender-appropriate medical research and treatment, as well as the economic resources needed to secure adequate health care.

LO³ COMPARATIVE HEALTH CARE FROM A CONFLICT PERSPECTIVE

Health Care in the United States

We noted earlier that because rich countries spend more on health care than poor countries do, their populations enjoy longer life expectancy. This does not mean that money always buys good health. The United States spends 91 percent more per person on health care than Canada does, and 144 percent more than Japan does. It also has 14 percent more doctors per 1000 people than Canada does and 4 percent more than Japan does (refer back to Table 11.2). Yet the United States has a higher rate of infant mortality and shorter life expectancy than Canada and Japan do. Clearly, spending more money on health care does not always improve the health of a nation.

What accounts for the American anomaly? Why do Americans spend more on health care than any other country, yet wind up with a population that, on average, is less healthy than the population of other rich countries?

One reason for the anomaly is that the gap between rich and poor is greater in the United States than in Canada, Japan, and other rich countries. In general, the higher the level of inequality in a country, the less healthy its population is (Wilkinson, 1996). Because the United States contains a higher percentage of poor people than other rich countries do, its average level of health is lower. Moreover, because income inequality has widened in the United States since the early 1970s, health disparities among income groups have grown (Williams and Collins, 1995).

A second reason for the American anomaly is that physicians, hospitals, pharmaceutical companies, and other providers of health care are able to charge substantially higher prices in the United States than elsewhere (Anderson et al., 2003: 89). To understand why, we must examine the American health care system from a comparative conflict perspective.

You will recall that conflict theory is concerned mainly with the question of how privileged groups seek to maintain their advantages and subordinate groups seek to increase theirs. As such, conflict theory is an illuminating approach to analyzing the American health care system. We can usefully see health care in the United States as a system of privilege for some and disadvantage for others. It thus contributes to the poor health of less well-to-do Americans.

Consider, for example, that the United States, unlike all other rich countries, lacks a universal health care system. This means that it does not guarantee access to health care as a right of citizenship. Only elderly people, some of the poor, armed forces personnel, and some veterans receive medical benefits from the government under the Medicare, Medicaid, and military health care programs.

All told, the American government pays 53 percent of all medical costs out of taxes. In the United Kingdom, Sweden, and Denmark, the comparable figure is between 81 and 85 percent; in Japan and Germany, it is between 77 and 83 percent; and in France, Canada, and Italy, it is between 71 and 78 percent. Coverage in Germany, Italy, Belgium, Denmark, Finland, Greece, Iceland, Luxembourg, Norway, and Spain includes drugs, eyeglasses, dental care, and prostheses (Anderson et al., 2003; "Health Care Systems," 2001; Rogers, 2012; Schoen et al., 2004; Starr, 1994).

In 2010, the United States became the last of the world's rich countries to ensure that its population (or at least 95 percent of it) would at least be covered by health insurance. Before the new law was passed, about 15 percent of Americans lacked health insurance and another 15 percent lacked adequate coverage (Anderson et al., 2003; "Health Care Systems," 2001; Schoen et al., 2004; Starr, 1994). However, even after the new law was fully implemented in 2016, the distinctive feature of the American health care system—substantial private provision—persisted. It is an expensive mechanism that leaves many people poorly served. The relatively privileged obtain health services at high prices while the less well-off are effectively priced out.

The High Cost of Prescription Drugs

Americans also pay more for prescription drugs than anyone else in the world does—in 2011, 98 percent more than Canadians did (Patented Medicine Prices Review Board, 2011: 25). In recent decades, the price of prescription drugs in the United States has increased at more than twice the rate of inflation and more than any other item in the nation's health care budget. In Canada, the rise in the cost of prescription drugs has been below the rate of inflation almost every year since 1988 (Patented Medicine Prices Review Board, 2011: 19).

Rich countries other than the United States keep prescription drug prices down through some form of government regulation. For example, since 1987, Canadian drug companies have not been allowed to increase prices of brand-name prescription drugs above the inflation rate. New brand-name prescription drugs cannot exceed the highest Canadian price of comparable drugs used to treat the same disease. For new brand-name prescription drugs that are unique and have no competitors, the price must be no higher than the median price for that drug in the United Kingdom, France, Italy, Germany, Sweden, Switzerland, and the United States. If a company breaks the rules, the government requires a price adjustment. If the government deems that a company has deliberately flouted the law, it imposes a fine. Not surprisingly, more than a million Americans now regularly buy their brand-name prescription drugs directly from Canadian pharmacies.

American drug manufacturers justify their high prices by claiming they need the money for research and development (R&D). The American public benefits from R&D, they say, while lower prescription drug prices impair R&D in other countries. In fact, in the eight countries whose prescription drug prices and policies are monitored by the Canadian government, the correlation between drug prices and investment in R&D is precisely zero (calculated from data in Patented Medicine Prices Review Board, 2011: 25, 36). High prescription drug prices do not result in more R&D, and low prescription drug prices do not impair R&D.

socialized medicine In countries with socialized medicine, the government (1) directly controls the financing and organization of health services, (2) directly pays providers, (3) guarantees equal access to health care, and (4) allows some private care for individuals who are willing to pay for their medical expenses.

What we can say with confidence is that the pharmaceutical industry is the most profitable industry in the United States by far. We also know that drug companies spend about half as much on advertising and promotions as they do on R&D, driving up prescription drug prices. Finally, we know that the pharmaceutical industry spends more on lobbying and political campaign contributions than any other United States industry does. Most of the lobbying effort is aimed at influencing members of Congress to maintain a free market in prescription drug prices (Barry, 2002a, 2002b, 2002c).

The Canadian Health Care System

Regulation of prescription drug prices is not the only feature of Canadian health care that differs from health care in the United States. In contrast to the United States, Canada also has a national health insurance system that is sometimes loosely described as **socialized medicine**. Despite differences in how socialized medicine works in different countries, common to all such systems is the fact that the government directly controls the financing and organization of health services, directly pays providers, guarantees equal access to health care, and allows some private care for individuals who are willing to pay for it (Cockerham, 1998). Canada does not have a true system of socialized medicine, however, because the government does not employ Canadian doctors. Most of Canada's doctors are independent practitioners who are paid on a fee-for-service basis and submit claims directly to the provincial or territorial health insurance plan for payment.

Tommy Douglas is widely credited with being Canada's "father of medicare." He led the Co-operative Commonwealth Federation (CCF) to political victory in Saskatchewan in 1944, making it the first socialist party to win a North American election. (Later, Douglas helped turn the CCF into the New Democratic Party.) He served as premier of Saskatchewan from 1944 to 1961, introducing many social reforms including universal medical care. His government's actions stirred up sharp opposition, including a province-wide physicians' strike, but Saskatchewan's medicare ultimately succeeded. In 1968 it became a model for the whole country.

Although Canada's health care system is often lauded as among the best in the world, problems exist. One source of concern is waiting times for non-emergency services. Although our health care system is based on the premise that "all citizens will have access to the care they need within a reasonable time period" (Health Canada, 1999a),

Tommy Douglas (1904–86), leader of the Co-operative Commonwealth Federation (the precursor of the NDP) and the father of socialized medicine in Canada.

most people agree that some waits are too long, especially for emergency care. Nova Scotia and Prince Edward Island have long wait times for more procedures than other provinces do, while Saskatchewan, Ontario, and Newfoundland and Labrador are making substantial progress in this regard (Wait Time Alliance, 2014).

Still, about two-thirds of Canadians view their health care system positively. In contrast, only about one-third of Americans see their health care system in a positive light (Angus Reid Global Monitor, 2009). Most of the Canadians who hold negative opinions prefer a more American, two-tiered system that would allow people who can afford superior care to buy it. Most Americans who hold negative opinions prefer a Canadian-type system with greater government regulation. In both countries, therefore, health care remains a subject of political conflict.

LO⁴ THE PROFESSIONALIZATION OF MEDICINE

Earlier, we noted that from the conflict perspective the health system can usefully be viewed as a system of privilege and disadvantage. We now extend that argument by showing how physicians became such a privileged part of the health care system.

Barry Philp/GetStock.com

In the early nineteenth century, the practice of medicine was in a chaotic state. Herbalists, faith healers, midwives, druggists, and medical doctors vied to meet the health needs of the public. A century later, the dust had settled. Medical science was victorious. Its first series of breakthroughs involved identifying the bacteria and viruses responsible for various diseases and then developing effective procedures and vaccines to combat them. These and subsequent triumphs in diagnosis and treatment convinced most people of the superiority of medical science over other approaches to health. Medical science worked, or at least it seemed to work more effectively and more often than did other therapies.

It would be wrong, however, to think that scientific medicine came to dominate health care only because it produced results. A second, sociological reason for the rise to dominance of scientific medicine is that doctors were able to professionalize. A **profession** is an occupation that requires extensive formal education. Professionals regulate their own training and practice. They restrict competition within the profession, mainly by limiting the recruitment of practitioners. They minimize competition with other professions, partly by laying exclusive claim to a field of expertise. Professionals are usually self-employed. They exercise considerable authority over their clients. And they profess to be motivated mainly by the desire to serve their community even though they earn a lot of money in the process. Professionalization, then, is the process by which people gain control and authority over their occupation and their clients. It results in professionals enjoying high occupational prestige and income, and considerable social and political power (Freidson, 1986; Johnson, 1972; Starr, 1982).

The professional organization of Canadian doctors is the Canadian Medical Association (CMA), founded in 1867 by 167 doctors in Quebec City. It quickly set about broadcasting the successes of medical science and criticizing alternative approaches to health as quackery and charlatanism. The CMA was able to have laws passed to restrict medical licences to graduates of approved schools and to ensure that only graduates of those schools could train the next generation of doctors. By restricting entry into the profession and by specifying what "paramedical" practitioners could and could not do, members of the medical establishment ensured their own status, prestige, and high incomes. For example, midwifery was originally included in the work of the Victorian Order of Nurses, founded in 1897 by the National Council of Women to assist rural women who otherwise lacked access to health care. However, "the opposition of the medical establishment in Canada was so great to what it saw as an infringement of its prerogatives that the idea was allowed to die" (Mitchinson, 1993: 396). When medicine became a profession, it also became a monopoly.

The modern hospital is the institutional manifestation of the medical doctor's professional dominance.

Until the twentieth century, most doctors operated small clinics and visited patients in their homes. However, the rise of the modern hospital was guaranteed by medicine's scientific turn in the mid-nineteenth century. Expensive equipment for diagnosis and treatment had to be shared by many physicians. This required the centralization of medical facilities in large, bureaucratically run institutions that strongly resist deviations from professional conduct. Practically nonexistent in 1850, hospitals are now widespread. Yet despite their undoubted benefits, economic as well as health-related, hospitals and the medicine practised in them are not an unqualified blessing, as you are about to learn.

> **profession** An occupation that requires extensive formal education and whose practitioners regulate their own training and practice, restrict competition, and exercise considerable authority over their clients.

LO⁵ THE SOCIAL LIMITS OF MODERN MEDICINE

In early February 2003, a 64-year-old professor of medicine from Guangzhou, the capital of Guangdong Province in southern China, came down with an unidentified respiratory ailment. It did not bother him enough to cancel a planned trip to Hong Kong, so on February 12 he checked into that city's Metropole Hotel. Ironically, as it turned out, the desk clerk assigned him Room 911. Other ninth-floor guests included an older couple from Toronto and three young women from Singapore. All of these people, along with a local resident who visited the hotel during this period, fell ill between February 15 and 27 with the same medical problem as the professor. The professor died on March 4. The Canadian couple returned to Toronto on February 23 and the woman died at her home on March 5. The eventual diagnosis: severe acute respiratory syndrome, or SARS, a new (and in 9 percent of cases, deadly) pneumonia-like illness for which there is no vaccine and no cure.

By June 12, 8445 cases of SARS had been identified in 29 countries, and 790 people had died of the disease. Quickly and efficiently, global travel had spread HIV/AIDS, West Nile virus, and now SARS from remote and isolated locales to the world's capitals. As one of the world's most multicultural cities, Toronto has a large Chinese population, mainly from Hong Kong. It is therefore not surprising that, outside of China, Hong Kong, and Taiwan, Toronto became the world's number one SARS hot spot (Abraham, 2003; World Health Organization, 2003).

Once identified as a potential SARS case, a person was quarantined at home for 10 days. However, if people

Hong Kong during the 2003 SARS outbreak

Getty 16381015

exhibited symptoms of the disease, they were directed to a poorly ventilated institution—a hospital—where the air was maintained at a constant warm temperature that was ideal for the multiplication of germs. In hospitals, many young and older people with weakened immune systems congregated. A steady stream of germs poured in around the clock. Staff members often failed to follow elementary principles of good hygiene. Most of the 238 people in Toronto who had SARS caught it while in hospital before stringent isolation and disinfection procedures were imposed.

Our characterization of hospitals as ideal environments for the spread of germs may seem harsh. It is not. Hospitals have become dangerous places in North America. In Canada, about 80 percent of hospitals fall seriously short in preventing patients from getting hospital infections. Some 250 000 patients experience hospital infections every year. According to one medical researcher, if the government classified hospital infections as a cause of death, it would be the fourth-leading cause of death in the country (Zoutman et al., 2003).

The situation has deteriorated largely because we invest disproportionately in expensive, high-tech, cutting-edge diagnostic equipment and treatment while we skimp on simple, labour-intensive, time-consuming hygiene. Cleaning staffs are too small and insufficiently trained. Nurses are too few. According to research by the Harvard School of Public Health, these are the kinds of factors correlated with hospital-acquired infections. As one registered nurse says, "When you have less time to save lives, do you take 30 seconds to wash your hands? When you're speeding up you have to cut corners. We don't always wash our hands. I'm not saying it's right, but you've got to deal with reality" (quoted in Berens, 2002).

It was not always the reality. Until the 1940s, North American hospital workers were obsessed with cleanliness. They had to be. In the era before the widespread use of antibiotics, infection often meant death. In the 1950s, however, the prevention of infections in hospitals became less of a priority because antibiotics became widely available. It was less expensive to wait until a patient got sick and then respond to symptoms by prescribing drugs than to prevent the sickness in the first place. On the basis of this logic, doctors and nurses grew lax about hygiene. One American report cites a dozen health care studies showing that about half of doctors and nurses do not disinfect their hands between patients (Berens, 2002). One hospital north of Montreal cut serious infections by 80 percent simply by improving hygiene (CBC, 2004).

Using penicillin and antibiotics indiscriminately has other costs too. When living organisms encounter a deadly threat, only the few mutations that are strong enough to resist the threat survive and go on to reproduce. Accordingly, if you use a lot of antibiotics, "super germs" that are resistant to these drugs multiply. This is just what has happened. (It hasn't helped that antibiotics are routinely added to cattle feed to prevent disease and thereby lower beef production costs. This practice builds up resistance to antibiotics in humans.)

Penicillin could kill nearly all staphylococcus germs in the 1940s, but by 1982 it was effective in fewer than 10 percent of cases. In the 1970s, doctors turned to the more powerful methicillin, which in 1974 could kill 98 percent of staphylococcus germs. By the mid-1990s, it could kill only about 50 percent of them. Various strains of drug-resistant germs now cause pneumonia, blood poisoning, tuberculosis, and other infectious diseases. Drug-resistant germs that could formerly survive only in the friendly hospital environment have now adapted to the harsher environment outside the hospital walls. Some pharmaceutical companies are developing new antibiotics to fight drug-resistant bugs. However, their efforts lack energy because antibiotics are prescribed for only short periods and are therefore not big money makers (Groopman, 2008).

The epidemic of infectious diseases caused by slack hospital hygiene and the overuse of antibiotics suggests that market forces constrain the success of modern medicine. It is difficult to see how we can solve these problems without enforcing strict rules regarding hospital disinfection and getting governments to provide the incentive necessary to spur pharmaceutical companies to invest more in developing new antibiotics.

Meanwhile, many people are growing skeptical of the claims of modern medicine. They are beginning to challenge traditional medicine and explore alternatives that rely less on high technology and drugs and are more sensitive to the need for maintaining balance between humans and their environment in the pursuit of good health. In concluding this chapter, we explore some of these challenges and alternatives.

CHALLENGES TO TRADITIONAL MEDICAL SCIENCE

Patient Activism

By the mid-twentieth century, the dominance of medical science in Canada was virtually complete. Any departure from the dictates of scientific medicine was considered deviant. So when sociologist Talcott Parsons defined the sick role in 1951, he pointed out that illness suspends routine responsibilities and is not deliberate. He stressed that people playing the sick role must want to be well and must seek competent help, cooperating with health care practitioners at all times (Parsons, 1951: 428 ff.). Must they? According to Parsons's definition, a competent person suffering from a terminal illness cannot reasonably demand that doctors refrain from using heroic measures to prolong his or her life. And by his definition, a patient cannot reasonably question doctors' orders, no matter how well-educated the patient and how debatable the effect of the prescribed treatment. Although Parsons's definition of the sick role may sound plausible to many people born before the middle of the twentieth century, it probably sounds authoritarian and foreign to most other people today.

That is because things have changed. The public is more highly educated now than it was in the 1950s. Many people now have the knowledge, vocabulary, self-confidence, and political organization to participate in their own health care rather than passively accepting whatever experts tell them. Only about a third of Canadians say they follow a doctor's advice uncritically (Bricker and Greenspon, 2001: 221). Increasingly, patients are taught to perform simple, routine medical procedures themselves. Many people now use WebMD and other websites to find information about various illnesses and treatments. Increasingly, they are uncomfortable with doctors acting as authoritarian parents and patients acting as dutiful children.

Surveys reveal that 90 percent of Canadians now prefer that their doctor offer several treatment options rather than a single course of action, 86 percent say they usually ask their doctor many questions about procedures, 76 percent say they are more likely to question their doctor now than they were in the past, and 70 percent claim to always ask their doctor about medicines that are prescribed (Bricker and Greenspon, 2001: 119–20). Doctors now routinely seek patients' informed consent for some procedures rather than deciding what to do on their own. Similarly, most hospitals have established ethics committees, which were unheard of in the 1960s (Rothman, 1991). Clearly, patients want to play a more active role in their own care.

Some recent challenges to the authority of medical science are organized and political. For example, in the early 1980s, AIDS activists started challenging the stereotype of AIDS as a "gay disease." They demanded more research funding to help find a cure and helped to change research and treatment priorities in a way that could never have happened earlier (Epstein, 1996). Even before that, feminists had started supporting the reintroduction of midwifery and argued against medical intervention in routine child births, thereby challenging the wisdom of established medical practice. The previously male-dominated profession of medicine considered the male body the norm and paid relatively little attention to "women's diseases," such as breast cancer, and "women's issues," such as reproduction. This, too, is now changing thanks to feminist intervention (Boston Women's Health Book Collective, 1998; Rothman, 1982, 1989; Schiebinger, 1993). And although doctors and the larger society traditionally treated people with disabilities as incompetent children, various movements now seek to empower them (Charlton, 1998; Zola, 1982). As a result, attitudes toward people with disabilities are changing.

> **sick role** Playing the sick role, according to Talcott Parsons, involves the non-deliberate suspension of routine responsibilities, wanting to be well, seeking competent help, and cooperating with health care practitioners at all times.

Alternative Medicine

Other challenges to the authority of medical science are less organized and less political than those just mentioned. Consider, for example, alternative medicine. About 10 percent of Canadian men and 18 percent of Canadian women over the age of 12 use some form of alternative medicine, with the percentage rising from east to west (see Table 11.3). The most widely used health alternative is chiropractic services. Those with chronic disorders, including back problems and multiple chemical sensitivities, are more likely to consult an alternative health service provider. Use of alternative medicine increases with income and education (Park, 2005).

Despite its growing popularity, many medical doctors were hostile to alternative medicine until recently. They lumped all alternative therapies together and dismissed them as unscientific (Campion, 1993). By the late 1990s, however, a more tolerant attitude was evident in many quarters. For some kinds of ailments, physicians began to recognize the benefits of at least the most popular forms of alternative medicine. Thus, a 1998 editorial in the respected *New England Journal of Medicine* admitted that the beneficial effect of chiropractic on low back pain is "no longer in dispute" (Shekelle, 1998). This change in attitude was due in part to scientific evidence from Canada showing that spinal manipulation is a relatively effective and inexpensive treatment for low back pain (Manga, Angus, and Swan, 1993). At the same time, however, alternative forms of medicine should not be assumed to be entirely risk-free. For example, to date, the majority of Canadian lawsuits against chiropractors have involved

placebo effect The positive influence on healing of a strong belief in the effectiveness of a cure.

holistic medicine Medical practice that emphasizes disease prevention. Holistic practitioners treat disease by taking into account the relationship between mind and body and between the individual and his or her social and physical environment.

claims of muscular skeletal dysfunction, strains and sprains, and rib fractures. In other cases, however, more serious injury has occurred, including ruptured vertebral arteries and death (Cohen, 1999: 50).

The medical profession's grudging acceptance of chiropractic in the treatment of low back pain indicates what we can expect in the uneasy relationship between scientific and alternative medicine in coming decades. Doctors will for the most part remain skeptical about alternative therapies unless properly conducted experiments demonstrate their beneficial effects. Most people agree with this cautious approach—but not all.

For example, Catherine Zeta-Jones, Jane Fonda, Pamela Anderson, Tina Turner, Cher, Cindy Crawford, Whoopi Goldberg, Olivia Newton-John, former tennis star Martina Navratilova, Queen Elizabeth II, and former British prime minister Tony Blair have all used homeopathic medicine, as have many other less famous people. In homeopathy, a substance such as salt, arsenic, duck liver, or human mucous is diluted with alcohol or distilled water. The dilution may be as strong as one part per 100 and as weak as one part per trillion or more, but usually it is so weak that no molecules of the original substance can be detected in it. Consumption of the preparation is alleged to alleviate ailments ranging from flu to cancer.

According to the American Medical Association, the National Health Service of the United Kingdom, and other highly respected scientific bodies, no scientific evidence supports the claim that homeopathic treatments have any effect aside from a **placebo effect**, the positive influence on healing of a strong belief in the effectiveness of a cure. Insofar as some homeopaths steer patients away from the use of vaccines and delay their pursuit of proper medical treatment, they cause harm. Yet a substantial number of people are apparently influenced to turn to homeopathic medicine when their celebrity idols do (Ernst and Pittler, 2006).

Holistic Medicine

Medical doctors understand that a positive frame of mind often helps in the treatment of disease. For example, research verifies the existence of a placebo effect for some medical conditions; strong belief in the effectiveness of a cure can by itself improve the condition of about one-third of people suffering from chronic pain or fatigue (Campion, 1993). Doctors also understand that conditions in the human environment affect people's health. However, despite their appreciation of the effect of mind and environment on the human body, traditional scientific medicine tends to respond to illness by treating disease symptoms as a largely physical and individual problem. Moreover, scientific medicine continues to subdivide into more specialized areas of practice that rely more and more heavily on drugs and high-tech machinery. Most doctors are less concerned with maintaining and improving health by understanding the larger mental and social context within which people become ill.

Traditional Indian and Chinese medicine takes a different approach. India's Ayurvedic medical tradition views individuals in terms of the flow of vital fluids or "humours" and their health in the context of their environment. In this view, maintaining good health requires not only balancing fluids in individuals but also balancing the relationship between individuals and the world around them (Zimmermann, 1987 [1982]).

Despite significant differences, the fundamental outlook is similar in traditional Chinese medicine. Chinese medicine and its remedies, ranging from acupuncture to herbs, seek to restore individuals' internal balance, as well as their relationship to the outside world (Unschuld, 1985). Contemporary **holistic medicine**, the third and final challenge to traditional scientific medicine we will consider, takes an approach similar to these "ethno-medical" traditions. Practitioners of holistic medicine argue that good health requires maintaining a balance between mind and body, and between the individual and the environment.

TABLE 11.3	Percentage of Canadians Who Consulted an Alternative Health Care Provider, Top Seven Therapies	
	In Respondent's Lifetime	**In 12 Months Preceding the Survey**
Chiropractic	40	15
Massage therapy	35	19
Relaxation techniques	20	14
Prayer/spiritual practice	18	16
Acupuncture	17	4
Yoga	16	9
Herbal therapies	15	10

Note: Data are for 2006.

Source: Esmail, Nadeem. 2007. "Complementary and Alternative Medicine in Canada: Trends in Use and Public Attitudes, 1997-2006." Public Policy Sources 87. https://www.fraserinstitute.org/sites/default/files/ComplementaryAlternativeMedicine.pdf (retrieved 7 August 2015). Reproduced by permission of The Fraser Institute.

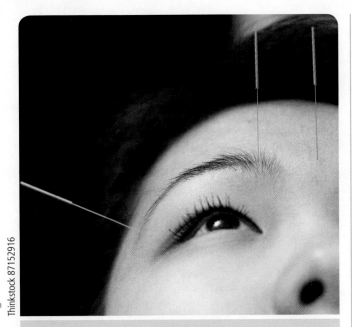

Acupuncture is one of the more widely accepted forms of alternative medicine.

Thinkstock 87152916

Most holistic practitioners do not reject scientific medicine. However, they emphasize disease *prevention*. Holistic practitioners seek to establish close ties with their patients and treat them in their homes or other relaxed settings. Rather than expecting patients to react to illness by passively allowing a doctor to treat them, they expect patients to take an active role in maintaining their good health. And, recognizing that industrial pollution, work-related stress, poverty, racial and gender inequality, and other social factors contribute heavily to disease, holistic practitioners sometimes become political activists (Hastings, Fadiman, and Gordon, 1980).

In sum, patient activism, alternative medicine, and holistic medicine represent the three biggest challenges to traditional scientific medicine today. Few people think of these challenges as potential replacements for scientific medicine. However, many people believe that, together with traditional scientific approaches, these challenges will help improve the health status of people in Canada and throughout the world in the twenty-first century.

READY TO STUDY?

IN THE BOOK, YOU CAN:

❏ Tear out the chapter review card at the back of the book to have a summary of the chapter and key terms handy.

ONLINE YOU CAN:

❏ Work through key concepts with a Guided Learning Question.

❏ Prepare for tests with quizzes.

❏ Review the key terms with flash cards.

❏ Explore practical examples of chapter concepts with Connect a Concept exercises.

GO TO NELSON.COM/STUDENT TO ACCESS THESE DIGITAL RESOURCES.

12
The Mass Media

LEARNING OBJECTIVES

In this chapter, you will learn to

LO¹ Appreciate that, although the most popular mass media are products of the twentieth century, their growth is rooted in the rise of Protestantism, democracy, and capitalism.

LO² Identify the ways in which the mass media make society more cohesive.

LO³ Identify the ways in which the mass media foster social inequality.

LO⁴ Describe how audiences filter, interpret, resist, and even reject media messages if the messages are inconsistent with audience beliefs and experiences.

LO⁵ Analyze how the mass media misrepresent women and members of racial minorities.

LO⁶ Recognize that the Internet and social media offer users more freedom than other mass media do.

THE SIGNIFICANCE OF THE MASS MEDIA

ILLUSION BECOMES REALITY

In *Oblivion* (2013), Jack and Victoria, played by Tom Cruise and Andrea Riseborough, live in, and work from, a pod mounted on a pole hundreds of metres above the surface of the earth. It is 2070. The planet is nearly dead. Years earlier, an alien race started a war that humans won but left the earth a nuclear wasteland. Most of the human survivors live in a giant space vehicle called Tet, which circles the earth and will soon evacuate the remains of humanity to Titan, Saturn's largest moon. Jack and Victoria remain on earth to repair drones that hunt down the remaining aliens and guard the nuclear reactors that suck up water and send power to Tet.

Jack and Victoria have had their memories wiped so they won't reveal strategic information if the aliens capture them. They get their orders from Sally (Melissa Leo) via video transmission from Tet. In fact, Sally provides Jack and Victoria with their entire definition of reality: the whole story of the tragedy that befell earth and what Tet is comes from the screen on which Sally regularly and frequently appears. Then Jack starts having flashbacks. Could this all be an illusion? Did the aliens actually win the war? Are Jack and Victoria mopping up the remaining humans? These are the questions that begin slowly to surface as the movie unfolds.

Oblivion may be an allegory for the fantasy worlds that the mass media create for us. Certainly, the realities we know best—the illusions created by the mass media—are every bit as pervasive and influential as religion was 500 or 600 years ago. If you think this is an exaggeration, consider that the average 18- to 24-year-old Canadian spends 2.8 hours a day watching television, 1.6 hours a day listening to the radio, and 5.3 hours on the Internet (Television Bureau of Canada, 2015). Add to this the time we spend going to the movies, listening to music downloads, and playing video games, and it becomes clear that about 40 percent of our time is spent interacting with the mass media—more than we spend sleeping, working, or going to school. We are so accustomed to interacting with the mass media that we find it increasingly difficult to be alone with our thoughts; a recent experiment found that two-thirds of men and about a quarter of women chose electric shocks over their own company (Wilson et al., 2014). You might want to keep a tally of your activities for a couple of days to find out how you fit into this pattern of activity.

Canadian media guru Marshall McLuhan said the media are extensions of the human body and mind.

Bettmann/Getty Images

Ask yourself, too, what you get out of your interactions with the mass media. Where do you get your ideas about how to dress, how to style your hair, and what music to listen to? Where do your hopes, aspirations, and dreams come from? If you're like most people, much of your reality is media-generated. Canadian media guru Marshall McLuhan, who coined the term *global village* in the early 1960s, said the media are extensions of the human body and mind (McLuhan, 1964). More than half a century later, it is perhaps equally valid to claim that the human body and mind are extensions of the mass media (Baudrillard, 1983, 1988; Bourdieu, 1998).

WHAT ARE THE MASS MEDIA?

The term **mass media** refers to print, radio, television, and other communication technologies that reach many people. Often, *mass media* and *mass communication* are used interchangeably to refer to the transmission of information from one person or group to another. The word *mass* implies that the media reach many people. The word *media* signifies that communication does not take place directly through face-to-face interaction. Instead, technology intervenes or mediates in transmitting messages from senders to receivers. Furthermore, communication via the mass media is usually one-way, or at least one-sided. There are

mass media Print, radio, television, and other communication technologies that reach many people.

few senders (or producers) and many receivers (or audience members). So most newspapers print a few readers' letters in each edition, but journalists and advertisers write virtually everything else. Ordinary people may appear on the *Dr. Phil* show or even delight in a slice of fame on *Survivor*, but producers choose the guests and create the program content. Similarly, a handful of people may visit your personal website, but over a billion people visit Facebook daily.

Usually, then, members of the audience cannot exert much influence on the mass media. They can choose only to tune in or tune out. And even tuning out is difficult because it excludes us from the styles, news, gossip, and entertainment most people depend on to grease the wheels of social interaction. Few people want to be cultural misfits. However, this does not mean that people are always passive consumers of the mass media. As we detail later, we filter, interpret, and resist what we see and hear if it contradicts our experiences and beliefs. Even so, in the interaction between audiences and media sources, the media sources usually dominate.

To appreciate fully the impact of the mass media on life today, we need to trace their historical development. That is the first task we set ourselves in the following discussion. We then critically review theories of the mass media's effects on social life. As you will see, each of these theories contributes to our appreciation of media effects. Finally, we assess developments on the media frontier formed by the Internet, television, and other mass media. We show that, to a degree, the new media frontier blurs the distinction between producer and consumer and has the potential to make the mass media somewhat more democratic for those who can afford access.

THE RISE OF THE MASS MEDIA

It may be difficult for you to imagine a world without the mass media. Yet, as Table 12.1 shows, most of the mass

The new media frontier blurs the distinction between producer and consumer and has the potential to make the mass media somewhat more democratic for those who can afford access.

Alvaro Canovas/*Paris Match*/Getty Images

TABLE 12.1 The Development of the Mass Media

Year	Media Development
1450	Movable metal type used in Germany, leading to the Gutenberg Bible
1702	First daily newspaper, London's *Daily Courant*
1833	First mass-circulation newspaper, *The New York Sun*
1837	Louis Daguerre invented a practical method of photography in France
1844	Samuel Morse sent the first telegraph message between Washington and Baltimore
1875	Alexander Graham Bell sent the first telephone message
1877	Thomas Edison developed the first phonograph
1895	Motion pictures were invented
1901	Italian inventor Guglielmo Marconi transmitted the first transatlantic wireless message from England to St. John's, Newfoundland
1906	First radio voice transmission
1920	First regularly scheduled radio broadcast, Pittsburgh
1928	First commercial TV broadcast in United States; Canada followed in 1931
1949	Network TV began in the United States
1952	VCR invented
1961	First cable television, San Diego
1969	First four nodes of the United States Department of Defense's ARPANET (precursor of the Internet) set up at Stanford University; University of California, Los Angeles; University of California, Santa Barbara; and the University of Utah
1975	First microcomputer marketed
1976	First satellite TV broadcast
1983	Cellphone invented
1989	World Wide Web conceived by Tim Berners-Lee at the European Laboratory for Particle Physics in Switzerland
1990	Windows 3.0 released (first mass-marketed graphical operating system)
1991	The World Wide Web became publicly accessible
1999	Wi-Fi (wireless Internet) became publicly available
2001	First iPod released Digital satellite radio introduced
2003	Camera phone invented First BlackBerry smartphone released in Waterloo, Ontario
2005	Facebook.com became public YouTube founded
2007	First iPhone released
2010	E Ink (Pearl display) invented, making e-readers like Kindle widely available

Sources: Berners-Lee, 1999; Croteau and Hoynes, 1997: 9–10; "The Silent Boom," 1997.

media are recent inventions. The first developed systems of writing appeared only about 5500 years ago in Egypt and Mesopotamia (now southern Iraq). The print media became truly a mass phenomenon only in the nineteenth century. The inexpensive daily newspaper, costing a penny, first appeared in the United States in the 1830s. At that time, long-distance communication required physical transportation. To spread the news, you needed a horse, a railroad, or a ship. The slow speed of communication was costly. For instance, the last military engagement between Britain and the United States in the War of 1812–14 was the Battle of New Orleans. It took place 15 days after a peace treaty was signed. The good news did not reach the troops near the mouth of the Mississippi until they had suffered 2100 casualties, including 320 dead.

The newspaper was the dominant mass medium even as late as 1950 (Schudson, 1991; Smith, 1980). However, change was in the air in 1844, when Samuel Morse sent the first telegraphic signal (Pred, 1973). From that time on, long-distance communication no longer required physical transportation. The transformative power of the new medium was soon evident. For example, until 1883, hundreds of local time zones existed in North America. The correct time was determined by local solar time and was typically maintained by a clock in a church steeple or a respected jeweller's shop window. Virtually instant communication by telegraph made it possible to coordinate time and establish just six time zones in Canada. Railroad companies spearheaded the move to standardize time. A Canadian civil and railway engineer, Sir Sandford Fleming, was the driving force behind the worldwide adoption of standard time (Blaise, 2001).

Most of the electronic media are creatures of the twentieth century. The first commercial television broadcasts date from the 1920s. The U.S. Department of Defense established ARPANET in 1969. It was designed as a system of communication between computers that would automatically find alternative transmission routes if one or more nodes in the network broke down because of, say, nuclear attack. ARPANET begat the Internet, which in turn begat the hyperlinked system of texts, images, and sounds known as the World Wide Web in 1991. By October 2016, nearly 3.5 billion people worldwide used the Web. It was a quick trip—a mere 140 years separate the Pony Express from the home videoconference.

LO¹ CAUSES OF MEDIA GROWTH

The rise of the mass media can be explained by three main factors—one religious, one political, and one economic:

1. *The Protestant Reformation.* In the early sixteenth century, Catholics relied on priests to tell them what was in the Bible. In 1517, however, Martin Luther protested certain practices of the Church. Among other things, he wanted people to develop a more personal relationship with the Bible. Within

40 years, Luther's new form of Christianity, known as Protestantism, was established in half of Europe. Suddenly, millions of people were being encouraged to read. The Bible became the first mass media product in the West and by far the best-selling book.

Technological improvements in papermaking and printing made the diffusion of the Bible and other books possible (Febvre and Martin, 1976 [1958]). The most significant landmark was Johann Gutenberg's invention of the printing press. In the 50 years after Gutenberg produced his monumental Bible in 1455, more books were produced than in the previous 1000 years. The printed book enabled the widespread diffusion and exchange of ideas. It contributed to the Renaissance (a scholarly and artistic revival that began in Italy around 1300 and spread to all of Europe by 1600) and to the rise of modern science (Johns, 1998).

A remarkable feature of the book is its durability. Many electronic storage media became obsolete just a few years after being introduced. For instance, eight-track tapes are icons of the 1970s and 5.25-inch floppy disks are icons of the early 1980s. They are barely remembered today. In contrast, books are still being published today, 560 years after Gutenberg published his Bible. Book publishing in Canada is a $2 billion a year industry, with tens of thousands of new titles published every year (Canadian Heritage, 2013).

In the 50 years after Johann Gutenberg invented the printing press, more books were produced than in the previous 1000 years.

2. *Democratic movements.* A second force that promoted the growth of the mass media was political democracy. From the eighteenth century on, the citizens of France, the United States, and other countries demanded and achieved representation in government. At the same time, they wanted to become literate and gain access to previously restricted centres of learning. Democratic governments, in turn, depended on an informed citizenry and therefore encouraged popular literacy and the growth of a free press (Habermas, 1989).

Today, the mass media, and especially TV, mould our entire outlook on politics. TV's influence first became evident in the 1960 U.S. presidential election. That was the year of the first televised presidential debate—between John F. Kennedy and Richard Nixon. One of the four reporters who asked questions during the debate later recalled: "The people who watched the debate on their television sets apparently thought Kennedy came off better than Nixon. Those who heard the debate on radio thought Nixon was superior to Kennedy" (quoted in "Candidates Debate," 1998). Kennedy smiled. Nixon perspired. Kennedy relaxed. Nixon fidgeted. The election was close, and most analysts believe that Kennedy got the edge simply because 70 million viewers thought he looked better on TV. Television was thus beginning to redefine the very nature of politics.

Soon, Canadian politicians were hiring "image consultants." Often, image manipulation used techniques honed in the United States. Often, the media consultants' advice influenced the results. This included much maligned "negative advertising" techniques. While voters claim they do not approve of negative advertising, it is effective sometimes (Kinsella, 2007). For example, in 2011, the Conservative Party branded Liberal Party leader Michael Ignatieff disloyal and power-hungry. The campaign was widely held to be partly responsible for undermining Liberal support in that year's federal election. On the other hand, four years later, the Conservatives framed Liberal Party leader Justin Trudeau as "just not ready" to lead the country. The campaign backfired and the Liberals won the election handily.

It is commonly claimed that television and other mass media have oversimplified politics. Some analysts say that politics has been reduced to a series of more or less well-managed images, catchy slogans, and ever-shorter uninterrupted comments or "sound bites." From this point of view, candidates are marketed for high office like Kellogg's sells breakfast cereal, and a politician's stage presence is more important than his or her policies in determining success at the polls.

National Archives of Canada/The Canadian Press

One of the most famous photographs in Canadian history is the driving of the last spike of the Canadian Pacific Railway (CPR) on November 7, 1885, at Craigellachie, British Columbia. The man holding the hammer is Donald Smith, who financed much of the construction of the CPR. The taller man standing behind him to his right in the stovepipe hat is Sir Sandford Fleming, the mastermind behind standard time. The railroads spearheaded the introduction of standard time, which could be coordinated thanks to the introduction of the telegraph.

3. *Capitalist industrialization.* The third major force stimulating the growth of the mass media was capitalist industrialization. Modern industries required a literate and numerate workforce. They also needed rapid means of communication to do business efficiently. Moreover, the mass media turned out to be a major source of profit in their own right.

We thus see that the sources of the mass media are deeply embedded in the religious, political, and economic needs of our society. Moreover, the mass media are among the most important institutions in our society today. How, then, do sociologists explain the effects of the mass media on society? To answer this question, we now summarize the relevant sociological theories.

THEORIES OF MEDIA EFFECTS
FUNCTIONALISM

As societies develop, they become larger and more complex. The number of institutions and roles proliferate. Because of the sheer scale of society, face-to-face interaction becomes less viable as a means of communication. As a result, the need increases for new means of coordinating the operation of the various parts of society. For example, people in New Brunswick must have at least a general sense of what is happening in Alberta, and they need to share certain basic values with Albertans if they are going to feel that they are citizens of the same country. The mass media do an important job in this regard. The nineteenth-century German philosopher Georg Hegel once said that the daily ritual of reading the newspaper unites the secular world, just as the ritual of daily prayer once united the Christian world. Stated more generally, his point is valid. The nationwide distribution of newspapers, magazines, movies, television, and the Internet cements the large, socially diverse, and geographically far-flung population of Canada. In a fundamental sense, the nation is an imagined community, and the mass media make it possible for us to imagine it (Anderson, 1991).

Thus, the mass media perform an important function by coordinating the operation of industrial and postindustrial societies. But, according to functionalist theorists, their significance does not stop there (Wright, 1975). In addition, the mass media are also important agents of socialization. Families have relinquished their former nearly exclusive right to transmit norms, values, and culture. The mass media have stepped into the breach, reinforcing shared ideals of democracy, competition, justice, and so on (see Chapter 3, Socialization).

A third function of the mass media involves social control; the mass media help ensure conformity. For example, news broadcasts, TV dramas, and "reality TV" programs pay much attention to crime, and they regularly sing the praises of heroes who apprehend and convict criminals. By exposing deviants and showcasing law enforcement officials and model citizens, the mass media reinforce ideas about what kinds of people deserve punishment and what kinds of people deserve rewards. In this way, they reproduce the moral order. Some people think *The Jerry Springer Show* is outlandish, and in a way it is. From a sociological point of view, however, it is also a deeply conservative program, for when television audiences become upset about marital infidelities and other outrages, they are reinforcing some of the most traditional norms and thus serving as agents of social control. As Nobel Prize–winning author Saul Bellow wrote, "a scandal [is] after all a sort of service to the community" (Bellow, 1964: 18).

The mass media's fourth and final function is to provide entertainment. Television, movies, magazines, and so on, give us pleasure, relaxation, and momentary escape from the tension and tedium of everyday life. How often have you come home after a long and frustrating day at school or work, picked up the remote control, channel-surfed, concluded that there's nothing really worth watching, but settled for a sitcom or some

From a sociological point of view, *The Jerry Springer Show* is a deeply conservative program that reinforces some of the most traditional norms and therefore serves as an agent of social control.

other form of easily digestible entertainment? How about checking out the latest YouTube postings? It is precisely because some products of the mass media require little effort on the part of the audience that they are important. They relieve stress. Moreover, they do so in a way that doesn't threaten the social order. Without such escapes, who knows how our daily tensions and frustrations might express themselves?

LO³ CONFLICT THEORY

Clearly, functionalism offers valuable insights into the operation of the mass media. However, conflict theorists have criticized the functional approach for paying insufficient attention to the social inequality fostered by the mass media. Specifically, conflict theorists say functionalism exaggerates the degree to which the mass media serve the interests of the entire society. They contend that some people benefit from the mass media more than others do. In particular, the mass media favour the interests of dominant classes and political groups (Gitlin, 1983; Herman and Chomsky, 1988; Horkheimer and Adorno, 1986 [1944]; Iyengar, 1991).

Conflict theorists maintain that there are two ways in which dominant classes and political groups benefit disproportionately from the mass media. First, the mass media broadcast beliefs, values, and ideas that create widespread acceptance of the basic structure of society, including its injustices and inequalities. Second, ownership of the mass media is highly concentrated in the hands of a small number of people and is highly profitable for them. Thus, the mass media are a source of economic inequality. Let us consider these issues in more detail.

Media Ownership

For decades, most of the Canadian mass media have been owned by fewer than a dozen families: the Siftons, the Thomsons, the Bassetts, the Southams, the Irvings, the Honderiches, the Blacks, and, more recently, the Shaws, the Rogerses, and the Péladeaus. There are just five multimedia giants in the country. In order of size (as measured by annual revenue), they are as follows:

1. *BCE*. Controls the CTV television network, *The Globe and Mail*, CFCF (the largest English-language television station in Montreal), CKY (Manitoba's largest TV station), *Report on Business* TV, TSN (The Sports Network), national CHUM radio, and so on. Approximate annual revenue: $20.9 billion.

2. *Rogers*. The Rogers family is a major shareholder. Rogers is one of the country's largest cable TV and broadband Internet service providers. It controls the Shopping Channel, CFMT (a multicultural television station in Toronto), Sportsnet, the Toronto Blue Jays, dozens of radio stations, scores of consumer and business magazines (including *Maclean's*, *Flare*, and *Canadian Business*), and so on. Approximate annual revenue: $12.7 billion.

3. *Shaw*. Controlled by the Shaw family of Calgary, Shaw Communications is another of the country's largest cable TV and broadband Internet service providers. It also owns 49 radio stations, Global Television, and television specialty stations, including The Food Network, History Television, and Showcase. Approximate annual revenue: $5.1 billion.

4. Quebecor. Controlled by the Péladeau family of Montreal, Quebecor publishes 28 daily newspapers including *Le journal de Montréal, Le journal de Québec, Ottawa Sun, Toronto Sun, The London Free Press, Winnipeg Sun, Edmonton Sun, Calgary Sun, and The Kingston Whig-Standard*. It also owns the largest cable TV provider in Quebec, Quebec's largest private TV network (TVA), Canoe.ca, and so on. Approximate annual revenue: $4.3 billion.

5. *CBC/Radio-Canada*. The fifth-largest multimedia giant in Canada is the only one that is publicly owned. Its most important assets are an English-language television network, a French-language television network, and four commercial-free radio networks. Approximate annual revenue: $1.9 billion, 57 percent of which is a federal government grant and the balance of which comes from advertising, program sales, and so on (CBC, 2014; *Financial Post*, 2014).

In the 1930s, it was not at all obvious that more than 90 percent of the Canadian mass media would be privately owned and controlled. Here is what Prime Minister R.B. Bennett had to say on the subject in 1932:

> The use of the air . . . that lies over the . . . land of Canada is a natural resource over which we have complete jurisdiction. . . . I cannot think that any government would be warranted in leaving the air to private exploitation and not reserving it for . . . the use of the people. Without [complete government control of broadcasting from Canadian sources, radio] can never become the agency by which national consciousness may be fostered and national unity . . . strengthened.
>
> —Quoted in Competition Bureau, 2002; House of Commons Debates, May 18, 1932

What was self-evident to Prime Minister Bennett in 1932 is a matter of controversy today. Some Canadians, like Bennett, still argue for strict government control of the mass media. Like Bennett, they believe that the mass media should be used to strengthen Canadian culture. Others want a more or less free market in which the great bulk of programming is American in origin or, failing that, American in style.

The Canadian Radio-television and Telecommunications Commission (CRTC) was established by an act of Parliament in 1968 as an independent agency responsible for regulating Canada's broadcasting and telecommunications systems. Its self-described mandate is to promote Canadian culture and economic competitiveness ("CRTC's Mandate," 2002). In practice, promoting Canadian culture means ensuring that 35 percent of the popular music played on English-language commercial radio stations between 6 a.m. and 6 p.m., Monday through Friday, is Canadian. Regulations for "ethnic" and French-language stations are somewhat different. Privately owned television stations must achieve a yearly Canadian content level of 60 percent between 6 a.m. and midnight and 50 percent between 6 p.m. and midnight. Canadian content rules for the CBC are slightly more demanding. "Canadian" means that the producer of the program is Canadian, key creative personnel are Canadian, and 75 percent of service costs and postproduction lab costs are paid to Canadians.

As a result of these regulations, about half of TV broadcasts in English Canada and 65 percent of popular music broadcasts are American. Moreover, many American TV and radio stations are widely available in Canada via cable, satellite, or the airwaves. (Over 90 percent of Canadian households subscribe to cable or use satellite services: Canadian Media Research, 2006). It seems reasonable to conclude that at least three-quarters of the TV and popular music to which Canadians have access is American.

Bearing the above facts in mind, do you think the Canadian government does enough or too much to ensure the preservation and enrichment of Canadian culture through the broadcast industry? Should the government be in the business of protecting Canadian culture at all? Or should it allow free-market forces to shape the structure and content of Canadian broadcasting? Would a free-market approach to broadcasting enable Canadians to get what they really want, or would it allow powerful American broadcasters to completely dominate the marketplace and virtually eliminate Canadian content?

Over time, concentration of the privately owned media has increased. That is, fewer and fewer people control Canada's mass media with every passing decade. Moreover, it is not just the degree of media concentration that has changed. The form of media concentration began to shift in the 1990s, too. Until the 1990s, media concentration involved mainly "horizontal integration." A small number of firms tried to control as much production as possible in their particular fields (newspapers, radio, television, etc.). In the 1990s, however, "vertical integration" became much more widespread. Media firms sought to control production and distribution in many fields. They became media "conglomerates." Today, a media conglomerate may own any combination of television networks, stations, and production facilities; magazines, newspapers, and book publishers; cable channels and cable systems; sports teams; Web portals; and software companies. A media conglomerate can create content and deliver it in a variety of forms. For instance, Rogers Communications Inc. owns the Toronto Blue Jays, creates sports entertainment, broadcasts it on its television stations, carries the signal to viewers' homes via its cable system, and spins off Blue Jays merchandise that it can sell in its stores.

Media Bias

Does the concentration of the mass media in fewer and fewer hands deprive the public of independent sources of information, limit the diversity of opinion, and encourage the public to accept their society as it is? Conflict theorists think so. They argue that when a few conglomerates dominate the production of news in particular, they shut out alternative points of view.

Occasionally, corporate attempts to control the news are blatant, as in 2011, when Quebecor Media launched a 24-hour television news network (*Sun News*) with an unapologetically right-wing, conservative slant. However, according to Edward Herman and Noam Chomsky (1988), more subtle mechanisms help to bias the news in a way that supports powerful corporate interests and political groups (see the Sociology on the Tube feature in this chapter). These biasing mechanisms include advertising, sourcing, and flak:

- *Advertising.* Most of the revenue earned by television stations, radio stations, newspapers, and magazines comes from advertising by large corporations. According to Herman and Chomsky, these corporations routinely seek to influence the news so it

will reflect well on them. In one American survey, 93 percent of newspaper editors said advertisers have tried to influence their news reports. Thirty-seven percent of newspaper editors admitted to being influenced by advertisers (Bagdikian, 1997). In addition, big advertisers may influence the news even without overtly trying to influence news carriers. For fear of losing business, news carriers may soften stories that big advertisers might find offensive.

- *Sourcing.* Studies of news-gathering show that most news agencies rely heavily for information on press releases, news conferences, and interviews organized by large corporations and government agencies. These sources routinely slant information to reflect favourably on their policies and preferences. Unofficial news sources are consulted less often. Moreover, unofficial sources tend to be used only to provide reactions and minority viewpoints that are secondary to the official story.

- *Flak.* Governments and big corporations routinely attack journalists who depart from official and corporate points of view. For example, Brian Ross, the leading investigative reporter for *20/20*, prepared a segment about Disney World in 1998. Ross claimed that Disney was so lax in doing background checks on employees that it had hired pedophiles. ABC killed the story before airtime. ABC is owned by Disney (McChesney, 1999). Similarly, tobacco companies systematically tried to discredit media reports that cigarettes cause cancer. In a notorious case, the respected public affairs show *60 Minutes* refused to broadcast a damaging interview with a former Philip Morris executive because CBS was threatened with legal action by the tobacco company. (This incident is the subject of the Oscar-nominated movie *The Insider*, released in 1999.)

On the whole, the conflict theorists' arguments are compelling. We do not, however, find them completely convincing (Gans, 1979). *Sun News* was unpopular and stopped broadcasting in 2015. And if it is true that 37 percent of newspaper editors have been influenced by advertisers, 63 percent have not. News agencies may rely heavily on government and corporate sources, but this does not stop them from routinely biting the hand that offers to feed them and evading flak shot their way. The daily newspaper is full of examples of mainstream journalistic opposition to government and corporate viewpoints. Even mainstream news sources, although owned by media conglomerates, do not always act like the lap dogs of the powerful (Hall, 1980).

Still, conflict theorists make a valid point if they restrict their argument to how the mass media support core societal values. In their defence of core values, the mass media are virtually unanimous (see the Sociology at the Movies feature in this chapter). For example, the mass

The Newsroom

The Newsroom takes place behind the scenes of the fictional Atlantis Cable News network (ACN). At first, ACN is a news organization like any other. It seeks to turn a profit, and if that means it has to shade

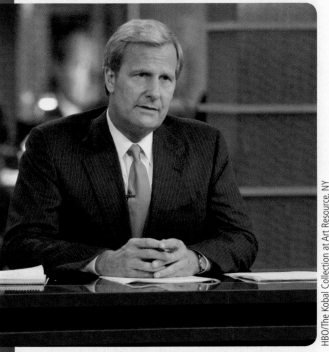

Will McAvoy of *The Newsroom*

HBO/The Kobal Collection at Art Resource, NY

the truth, appeal to the lowest common denominator, and avoid offending corporate interests and political authorities, then it is only trying to survive a tough competitive environment. Enter news anchor and former attorney, Will McAvoy (played by Jeff Daniels). Mad as hell and unwilling to take it anymore, McAvoy convinces his immediate boss that the network's flagship program, "News Night," must speak truth to power. From now on, ACN alone will decide what is aired and how it is presented. As McAvoy announces to his television audience in an early episode, "network newscasts . . . [are] in the exact same business as the producers of Jersey Shore. And that business was good to us, but 'News Night' is quitting that business right now."

"News Night" faces a powerful opponent in Leona Lansing (Jane Fonda), CEO of Atlantis World Media, the parent company of ACN. When McAvoy interviews Republican members of Congress, he humiliates them, infuriating Lansing. She reminds McAvoy's boss that members of Congress and the corporate interests they represent are ACN's bread and butter. If McAvoy continues his errant ways, advertisers will bolt and members of Congress will refuse to appear on air. She insists that McAvoy stop his crusade or be fired.

McAvoy refuses to bend. Then, on the verge of defeat, McAvoy and his boss get hold of information proving that Lansing's son was involved in a massive business fraud. They blackmail her. If she fires McAvoy, they will go public with the incriminating information. Lansing relents, and the first season of *The Newsroom* ends with Will McAvoy continuing to lead the charge against corporate and political authority. It is, of course, a fairy tale ending.

Critical Thinking Questions

1. In what sense does Season 1 of *The Newsroom* have a fairy tale ending?
2. Which Canadian television programs come closest to reflecting the ideals for which Will McAvoy stands? Why are these programs unusual?

media enthusiastically support democracy and capitalism. We cannot think of a single instance of a major Canadian news outlet advocating a fascist government or a socialist economy in Canada. Moreover, when conservative media critics complain of liberal bias in the media, they routinely use the CBC as their example. If the CBC is the best example of left-wing bias, the range of mass media opinion is narrow indeed.

Similarly, the mass media virtually unanimously endorse consumerism as a way of life. As discussed in

Chapter 2, Culture, consumerism is the tendency to define ourselves in terms of the goods and services we purchase. Endorsement of consumerism is evident in the fact that advertising fills the mass media and is its lifeblood. Estimated expenditures for Canadian Internet, TV, radio, newspaper, magazine, and billboard advertising are more than $11 billion a year, nearly as much as the federal government spends on children's benefits and more than half the amount it spends on national defence (Department of Finance Canada, 2014; Houpt, 2014). We

SOCIOLOGY AT THE MOVIES

Redacted

War is an ugly business, and this creates a problem for elected governments that decide to wage war. If the electorate is fully informed about the facts of war, they are less likely to support it. To manage this issue, governments use the mass media to provide the public with a selective view of a war's causes, conditions, and consequences.

The United States invasion of Iraq in 2003 was initiated by questionable motives. Declarations that Iraq was noncompliant with United Nations resolutions were questionable; the veracity of assertions that the regime had weapons of mass destruction was never demonstrated; Iraq's Al-Qaeda connections to the 9/11 tragedy were nonexistent. President Bush's administration had good reason to think that public support of "Operation Iraqi Freedom" was soft. Accordingly, they launched an expensive mass media campaign to "sell the war" through advertising.

To express his opposition to the Iraq War, director Brian De Palma produced *Redacted*, a fictional film based on real events. The main characters are a group of U.S. soldiers who control a surveillance checkpoint. The central real event is the rape of a teenaged girl who ends up murdered, along with the rest of her family.

In the film, the director shows that the realities of war are often brutal and always multi-sided. In one scene, for instance, a car speeds through a U.S.-controlled checkpoint. From the soldiers' viewpoint, the driver received clear warnings to stop for inspection. Because they were ignored, the soldiers fire repeatedly and kill a woman in the passenger seat. It turns out, however, that the driver was a young Iraqi man hurriedly driving his pregnant sister to the hospital to deliver her baby. He entered the checkpoint and saw the U.S. soldiers waving him through. He couldn't understand why they began firing. The two different versions of these events were reported to the American and Iraqi publics.

This movie's main point is that the mass media inevitably present a selective version of events. Their version of "truth" aims at shaping the views of their audience toward particular goals. This use of the mass

Scene from *Redacted*

media becomes especially evident when reporting events like wars that are full of ambiguity, contradiction, and harshness. Redaction, the deliberate censoring and obscuring of actual events, is central to the power of all mass media.

Like De Palma's 1989 film about the Vietnam War (*Casualties of War*), *Redacted* sensitizes viewers to how mass media presentations bias their understanding of events. The fact that De Palma is making the same point about U.S. foreign wars two decades after his first attempt is disheartening. However, during those two decades, the mass media experienced encouraging democratization. Digitization allows a wide range of audiences to record and broadcast alternative views of reality.

New social media have changed the mass media. The director exploits this change by blending all manner of social media accounts into *Redacted*. The multi-dimensional portrait of Iraqi reality includes a collage of cellphone photos, surveillance camera footage, video segments, and documentary excerpts. Effective war propaganda relies on audiences receiving a uniform message. De Palma's film suggests that social media may provide an effective challenge to such a monopoly of interpretation and encourage independent assessments about the worthiness of war.

Critical Thinking Question

To what degree do social media change the mass media's control of interpretations of reality? Give recent examples to support your opinion.

are exposed to a staggering number of ads each day; in fact, some estimates place the number in the thousands. Companies pay filmmakers to use their brand-name products conspicuously in their movies. In some magazines, ads figure so prominently a reader must search for the articles.

It is only when the mass media deal with news stories that touch on less central values that we can witness a diversity of media opinion. Specific government and corporate policies are often the subject of heated debate in the mass media. Thus, despite the indisputable concentration of media ownership, the mass media are diverse and often contentious on specific issues that do not touch on core values.

LO⁴ INTERPRETIVE APPROACHES

The view that the mass media powerfully influence a passive public is common among both functionalists and conflict theorists. Many people believe that violence on TV causes violence in real life, pornography on the magazine stands or online leads to immoral sexual behaviour, and adolescents are more likely to start smoking cigarettes when they see popular movie stars lighting up.

Functionalists and conflict theorists share this top–down, deterministic view; members of both schools of thought stress how the mass media bridge social differences and reinforce society's core values. True, the two schools of thought differ in that functionalists regard core values as serving everyone's interests, while conflict theorists regard them as favouring the interests of the rich and powerful. By focusing so tightly on core values, however, both approaches understate the degree to which audience members interpret media messages in different ways. The signal contribution of symbolic interactionist and related approaches is that they highlight the importance of such interpretive acts.

Just how much influence do the mass media actually exert over audiences? The question is mired in controversy, but it seems that the top–down, deterministic view is one-sided. You may recall our discussion of media violence in Chapter 1, Introducing Sociology. There we found that most experimental research on the subject is plagued by a validity problem. Simply stated, experiments on media violence may not be measuring what they say they are measuring. The sociological consensus seems to be that TV violence influences only a small percentage of viewers to commit acts of violence in the real world.

There are other reasons for questioning the strength of media effects. For instance, researchers have known since the 1950s that people do not change their attitudes and behaviours just because the media tell them to do so. That is because the link between persuasive media messages and actual behaviour is indirect. A **two-step flow**

Dan Porges/Photolibrary/Getty Images

of communication takes place (Katz, 1957; Schiller, 1989; Schudson, 1991). In Step 1, respected people of high status evaluate media messages. They are the opinion leaders of a neighbourhood or a community, people who are usually more highly educated, well-to-do, or politically powerful than others in their circle are. Because of their high status, they exercise considerable independence of judgment.

In Step 2, opinion leaders may influence the attitudes and behaviours of others. In this way, opinion leaders filter media messages. The two-step flow of communication limits media effects. If people are influenced to vote for certain candidates, buy certain products, or smoke cigarettes, it is less because the media tell them to and more because opinion leaders suggest they should.

Yet another persuasive argument that leads us to question the effects of mass media comes from interpretive sociologists, such as symbolic interactionists and interdisciplinary **cultural studies** experts. They use in-depth interviewing and participant observation to study how people interpret media messages.

British sociologist Stuart Hall (1980), one of the foremost proponents of this approach, emphasizes that people are not empty vessels into which the mass media pour a defined assortment of

two-step flow of communication Occurs between mass media and audience members and involves (1) respected people of high status and independent judgment evaluating media messages and (2) other members of the community being influenced to varying degrees by these opinion leaders.

cultural studies Focus not just on the cultural meanings that producers try to transmit but also on the way audiences filter and interpret mass media messages in the context of their own interests, experiences, and values.

beliefs, values, and ideas. Rather, audience members take an active role in consuming the products of the mass media. They filter and interpret mass media messages in the context of their own interests, experiences, and values. Thus, in Hall's view, any adequate analysis of the mass media needs to take into account both the production and the consumption of media products. First, he says, we need to study the meanings intended by the producers. Then we need to study how audiences consume or evaluate media products. Intended and received meanings may diverge; audience members may interpret media messages in ways other than those intended by the producers (Hall, 1980; Seiter, 1999).

Here is a personal example of the way audiences might interpret media messages in unexpected ways: When John Lie's parents were preparing to emigrate to the United States in the late 1960s, his mother watched many American movies and television shows. One of her favourite TV programs was *My Three Sons*, a sitcom about three boys living with their father and grandfather. From the show, she learned that boys wash dishes and vacuum the house in the United States. When the Lie family emigrated to Hawaii, John and his brother—but not his sister—had to wash dishes every night. When John complained, his mother reassured him that "in America, only boys wash dishes."

Even children's television viewing turns out to be complex when viewed through an interpretive lens. Research shows that young children distinguish "make-believe" media violence from real-life violence (Hodge and Tripp, 1986). That is one reason that watching *South Park* has not produced a nation of *South Park* clones. Similarly, research shows differences in the way working-class and middle-class women relate to TV. Working-class women tend to evaluate TV programs in terms of how realistic they are more than middle-class women do. This critical attitude reduces their ability to identify strongly with many characters, personalities, and storylines. For instance, working-class women know from their own experience that families often don't work the way they are shown on TV. They view the idealized, middle-class nuclear family depicted in many television shows with a mixture of nostalgia and skepticism (Press, 1991).

Age also affects how we relate to television. Senior viewers tend to be selective and focused in their television viewing. In contrast, people who grew up with cable TV and a remote control often engage in channel-surfing, conversation, eating, and housework, zoning in and out of programs in anything but an absorbed fashion (Press, 1991). The idea that such viewers are sponges, passively soaking up the values embedded in TV programs and then mechanically acting on them, is inaccurate.

LO⁵ FEMINIST APPROACHES

Finally, let us consider feminist approaches to the study of mass media effects. In the 1970s, feminist researchers focused on the representation—more accurately, the misrepresentation—of women in the mass media. They found that in TV dramas, women tended to be cast as homemakers, as secretaries, and in other subordinate roles, while men tended to be cast as professionals and authority figures. Women usually appeared in domestic settings, men in public settings. Advertising targeted women only as purchasers of household products and appliances. Furthermore, researchers discovered that the news rarely mentioned issues of importance for many women, such as wage discrimination in the paid labour force, sexual harassment and abuse, child-care problems, and so on. News reports sometimes trivialized or denounced the women's movement. Newsworthy issues (the economy, party politics, international affairs, and crime) were associated with men, and men were much more likely than women were to be used as news sources and to deliver the news (Watkins and Emerson, 2000: 152–53).

Most of this early feminist research assumed that audiences are passive. Analysts argued that the mass media portray women in stereotypical fashion, audience members recognize and accept the stereotypes as normal and even natural, and the mass media thereby reinforce existing gender inequalities. However, in the 1980s and 1990s, feminist researchers started criticizing this simple formula. Influenced by cultural studies, they realized that audience members selectively interpret media messages and sometimes even contest them.

A good example of this subtler and less deterministic approach is a study by Andrea Press and Elizabeth Cole (1999) of audience reaction to abortion as portrayed on TV shows. Over a four-year period, Press and Cole conducted 34 discussion groups involving 108 women. The women watched three TV programs focusing on abortion and then discussed their own attitudes and their reactions to the shows. The programs were pro-choice and dealt with women who chose abortion to avoid poverty.

Press and Cole found complex, ambivalent, and sometimes contradictory attitudes toward abortion among audience members. However, four distinct categories of opinion emerged:

1. *Pro-life women from all social classes* form the most homogeneous group. They think abortion is never justified. On principle, they reject the mass media's justifications for abortion.

2. *Pro-choice working-class women who think of themselves as members of the working class* adopt a pro-choice stand as a survival strategy, not on principle. They do not condone abortion, but they fear that laws restricting abortion would be applied prejudicially against women of their class. Therefore, they oppose any such restrictions. At the same time, they reject the TV message that financial hardship justifies abortion.

3. *Pro-choice working-class women who aspire to middle-class status* distance themselves from the "reckless" members of their own class who sought abortions

on the TV shows. They tolerate abortion for such people but they reject it for themselves and for other "responsible" women.

4. *Pro-choice middle-class women* believe that only an individual woman's feelings can determine whether abortion is right or wrong in her own case. Many pro-choice middle-class women have deep reservations about abortion, and many of them reject it as an option for themselves. However, they staunchly defend the right of all women, especially the kind of women portrayed in the TV shows they watched, to choose abortion.

One of the most striking aspects of Press and Cole's findings is that, for different reasons, three of the four categories of audience members (categories 1, 2, and 3) are highly skeptical of TV portrayals of the abortion issue. Their class position and attitudes act as filters influencing how they react to TV shows and how they view the abortion issue. Moreover, three of the four categories of audience members (categories 2, 3, and 4) reject the simple pro-choice versus pro-life dichotomy often portrayed by the mass media. Many pro-choice women express ambivalence about abortion and even reject it as an option for themselves. We must conclude that real women are typically more complicated than the stereotypes promoted in the mass media, and that women in the audience typically know that.

In recent years, some feminists have focused on the capacity of the mass media to reproduce and change the system of racial inequality in North American society. In the work of these scholars, the twin issues of female misrepresentation and active audience interpretation reappear, this time with a racial twist. On the one hand, they find that certain stereotypical images of women of colour recur in the mass media. Black women, for example, often appear in the role of the welfare mother, the highly sexualized Jezebel, and the mammy. On the other hand, they recognize that some mass media, especially independent filmmaking and popular music, have enabled women

© Splash News

Beyoncé

of colour to challenge these stereotypes. The music and videos of Erykah Badu, Missy Elliott, Lauryn Hill, Beyoncé Knowles, and Alicia Keys are especially noteworthy in this regard. These artists write and produce their own music. They often direct their own videos. Their work is a running critical commentary on real-world issues confronting young black women. Thus, in terms of both production and content, their work breaks down the established roles and images of black women in North America (Watkins and Emerson, 2000: 159–56).

Still, stereotypes persist. A 2009 study of North American primetime TV found men predominating in law enforcement, professional, and criminal roles. The shows portrayed men working in the paid labour force twice as often as women (Signorielli, 2009). Women's prime-time TV characters played "non-prestigious" roles 21 percent of the time, while only 13 percent of male characters were of this type (Figure 12.1). Moreover, the representation

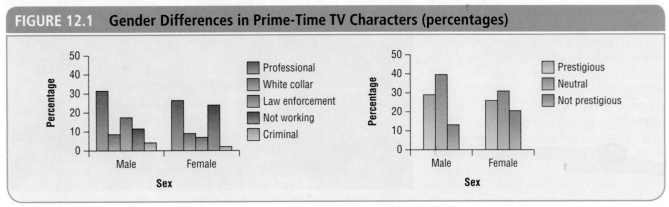

FIGURE 12.1 Gender Differences in Prime-Time TV Characters (percentages)

Note: Category selection results in percentages under 100.

Source: Adapted from Signorielli, N. 2009. "Race and Sex in Prime Time: A Look at Occupations and Occupational Prestige." *Mass Communication and Society* 12(3): 332–52.

of women in prime-time TV has stalled and even reversed slightly. In 2013–14, the percentage of women with speaking roles in prime-time TV fell more than 2 percentage points to 42 percent. Some 44 percent of prime-time programs employed four or fewer female actors.

The way in which the mass media treat women and members of various minority groups has for the most part improved over time. We have come a long way since the 1950s, when virtually the only blacks on TV were men who played butlers and buffoons. Research suggests that the mass media still have a long way to go before they cease reinforcing traditional stereotypes in North America (Signorielli, 2009). But research also suggests that audiences and artists are hardly passive vehicles of these stereotypes, instead struggling to diversify the way the mass media characterize them.

LO⁶ CENTRALIZED CONTROL AND RESISTANCE ON THE INTERNET

We have emphasized that the interaction between audiences and the traditional mass media (television, radio, and newspapers) is generally weighted in favour of the media. Audience members do not mindlessly absorb messages from these sources. However, they exercise little control over content.

In contrast, the Internet, especially its social media applications, offers more opportunity for audience influence than do the traditional mass media. True, the Internet provides fresh opportunities for media conglomerates to restrict access to paying customers and accumulate vast wealth. Simultaneously, however, the Internet gives consumers new creative capabilities, partially blurring the distinction between producer and consumer. In short, the Internet makes the mass media more democratic.

To develop this idea, we first consider the forces that restrict Internet access and augment the power of media conglomerates. We then discuss countertrends.

ACCESS

The Internet requires an expensive infrastructure of personal computers, servers, and routers; an elaborate network of fibre-optic, copper-twist, and coaxial cables; and many other components. This infrastructure has to be paid for, primarily by individual users. As a result, access is not open to everyone—far from it. In Canada, for example, households that are richer, better educated, urban, and younger are most likely to enjoy Internet access (Statistics Canada, 2010e).

Nor is Internet access evenly distributed globally. In the Scandinavian countries and the Netherlands, more than 90 percent of the population is connected. Canada, the United States, Singapore, and South Korea have penetration rates of around 80 percent. By contrast, many underdeveloped regions have rates in the single digits. Globally, the rate of Internet connectivity is much higher in rich countries than in poor countries (Internet World Stats, 2016).

CONTENT

According to some analysts, American domination is another striking feature of Internet content. The world's top search engines are Google, YouTube, and Facebook (Alexa, 2016). Some analysts say that American domination of the Web is an example of **media imperialism**, the control of a mass medium by a single national culture and the undermining of other national cultures.

MEDIA CONVERGENCE

Some researchers argue that the Internet not only restricts access and promotes American content, but also increases the power of media conglomerates. That is evident, for

Modern means of mass communication reach every corner of the earth.

Zhang Peng/LightRocket/Getty Images

example, in the realm of media convergence. **Media convergence** is the blending of the Internet, television, telephone, and other communications media into new hybrid media forms. The cellphone is the centrepiece of media convergence. It allows you to watch TV shows and videos, send and receive e-mails and text messages, browse the Web, and much else.

Media conglomerates like Bell and Rogers compete to offer the most appealing content at the fastest speeds, but they are united on industry-wide tactics to maximize profit. For instance, both companies strongly favour user-based billing (the more you use, the more you pay). Opponents argue that technology has lowered costs so much that user-based billing is just a money grab by some of the most profitable businesses in Canada—an unfair practice that restricts the poorest Canadians' access to the Internet and cellphones.

Efforts by huge media conglomerates to shape media convergence may seem like an old story. In some respects it is. Ownership of every mass medium has become more concentrated over time. Because entry costs are so high, only media giants can play the game. However, the Internet story comes with a twist. Media conglomerates can never fully dominate the Internet because it is the first mass medium that makes it relatively easy for consumers to become producers.

THE RISE OF SOCIAL MEDIA

Every minute, people upload 300 hours of digital video to YouTube (DMR, 2016). About 80 percent of laptops sport webcams and more than 80 percent of university and college students own laptops, so video chats through Skype or other services are commonplace ("Webcam Penetration Rates," 2011). In June 2015, Facebook boasted nearly 1.5 billion monthly active users. In late 2014, the average Facebook user had 338 "friends" (Facebook, 2011, 2013; Mazie, 2014; Statista, 2016). Meanwhile, there were 304 million monthly active Twitter users in June 2015. Some celebrities had tens of millions of followers (Katy Perry topped the list with 73.6 million followers; Canada's Justin Bieber was second with 66.1 million; Statista, 2015; Twitter Counter, 2015). Add to this the many millions of personal websites, public-access cameras, alternate reality and multiple-user gaming sites, and discussion groups devoted to every imaginable topic, and we must temper the image of the Internet as a medium that is subject to increasing domination by large conglomerates.

In many respects, the trend is the contrary: Individual users are making independent, creative contributions to Internet growth. And they react negatively if they lack access to computer-mediated communication. A recent experiment found that inability to answer a cellphone while completing word search puzzles causes anxiety, blood pressure, and heart rate to increase and cognitive performance to drop (Clayton, Leshner, and Almond, 2015).

Our use of social media affects our identity (how we see ourselves), our social relations (the patterned connections we form with others), and our social activism (the ways in which we seek to cause social change) (Bookman, 2014). Let us briefly consider each of these issues in turn:

- *Identity.* Social media offer people opportunities to manipulate the way they present themselves to others and explore aspects of their selves that they may suppress in embodied social interaction. Of course, people do not shift shapes, as it were, just because they can. The difference between self-presentation offline and online is typically modest. Nonetheless, differences exist, and they can change our self-conceptions in ways that are usually minor but sometimes major.

  Some users find that social media have taken over such a large slice of life that their online identity performances start to feel like their real selves (Turkle, 2011: 12). Some learn to become more assertive online than they are offline, and it is possible that once they learn to be bolder, they carry the lesson into real life to a degree. In some cases, people "in the closet" with respect to their sexual preferences use social media as a gateway to "coming out." In these and other ways, social media serve as "identity workshops" (Turkle, 1995).

© Inmagine Asia/Corbis

Social relations. In the 1990s, some analysts expected the Internet to isolate people, creating private worlds that would lead to the decline of family and community life. Others held the opposite opinion—that the Internet would create opportunities for people to form new communities based on common interests rather than geographical proximity or blood ties. Both scenarios contain an element of truth but both are problematic as assessments of the overall impact of the Internet in general, and social media in particular, on social relations. A few people do retire to the basement, keep the curtains on their windows tightly drawn, avoid face-to-face interaction, and spend their days in virtual worlds. Some people do form close and even intimate friendships online in communities of common interest, dropping nearly all real-world social relations. For most people, however, social media have not replaced real life—social media have become an integral part of their life (Wellman, 2014).

Thus, research shows that people tend to use social media to augment telephone and face-to-face communication, not to replace them. Most of the people we e-mail, message, and text are people we already know, and when we use social media to contact people we don't know, it is often to see whether we want to proceed to a phone call or a face-to-face meeting.

For most people, then, social media increase interaction and build community—but not community in the traditional sense. Traditional communities are fixed locations. To interact in them, you have to reside in them physically. You don't get to select community members. Everybody knows your business. In contrast, social media allow for the crystallization of communities that are multiplex (you can belong to many of them), variegated (you can decide how intimately you want to interact with different members of different communities), personalized (you can decide who to allow in and who to exclude), portable (you can take them with you), and ubiquitous (you can take them anywhere you please). Social media thus breed what sociologist Barry Wellman calls "networked individualism" (Wellman, 2014).

Nonetheless, some people spend so much time managing online profiles and relationships, and instantly responding to e-mails, tweets, and Facebook messages, that social media may be causing a decline in the depth and quality of face-to-face social interaction. Going on holiday with the family, having dinner with friends, and other traditional ways of enjoying the presence of others are now punctuated with social media interruptions and distractions that can have consequences for our well-being. In fact, a recent survey showed that the sense of well-being of people between the ages of 18 and 34 declined the more frequently they communicated with acquaintances and co-workers (as opposed to relatives and close friends) using a variety of platforms (mobile and landline phones; desktop and laptop computers).

In other words, frequent electronic communication with many acquaintances and co-workers on multiple platforms seems to burden younger people and make them less happy (Chan, 2014). Recent survey research also shows that the more often people use Facebook and the larger the size of their Facebook network, they more likely they are to be victimized by scam artists (Vishwanath, 2015). We thus see that an excess of networked individualism can have more than one downside.

Social activism. Finally, social media open up new ways of engaging in social change. People advocate and spread awareness of a wide variety of environmental, human rights, and other causes using blogs, Twitter, Facebook, and activist websites containing reports, news, videos, announcements, and Web links. People also use social media to mobilize others for demonstrations, petitions, meetings, support concerts, and fundraising. The most celebrated use of social media for these purposes occurred during the heyday of the Occupy movement and the Arab Spring in 2010–11 and the Idle No More movement in Canada in 2012. Many analysts expect that the role of social media in advocating and mobilizing for social and political change will grow in the coming years.

Other researchers are not so sure. They identify two counter-trends. First, they observe that in Syria, Egypt, Russia, China, and other non-democratic countries, authorities systematically monitor and analyze social media messages. Doing so allows them to identify, harass, and arrest anti-regime activists, including those who support democratization. Some observers worry about online surveillance in democratic countries, too, fearing that by monitoring social media, authorities in Canada and elsewhere will inhibit legitimate radical discourse.

A second counter-trend involves social media acting as a replacement for high-risk activism. By, say, allowing people to sign an online petition or contribute a dollar to a cause instead of engaging in an illegal strike or demonstration, social media may encourage "slacktivism" rather than activism (Brym et al., 2014; Gunitsky, 2015). Thus, in addition to facilitating advocacy and mobilization for social and political change, social media can have the opposite effect.

In sum, the Internet is a mass medium unlike any other in the sense that it provides unique opportunities for user autonomy and creativity. To be sure, it also increases opportunities for corporations and authorities to engage in the homogenization, surveillance, and possible control

Some people say that social media are causing a decline in the depth and quality of social interaction.

fashions, foods, and popular music, so we can see the Internet less as a site of American media imperialism than a site of globalization (Widyastuti, 2010). In 2016, the world's 25 most frequently visited websites included eight from China, two from Japan, two from Russia, one from Germany, and one from India (Alexa, 2016).

Of course, nobody knows exactly how the social forces we have outlined will play themselves out. In 1999, Napster emerged, enabling millions of people to share recorded music freely on the Web using a central server. Some analysts pointed to Napster as evidence of Internet democratization. Then the media conglomerates took Napster to court, forcing it to stop the giveaway on the grounds it was effectively stealing royalties from musicians and profits from music companies. Some analysts saw the court case as evidence of growing corporate control on the Web. However, a few years later, BitTorrent emerged, allowing people to share recorded music and videos without a central server, making it virtually impossible to shut it down.

of users, but at least on this mass medium, users enjoy many means of resistance (Lyon, 2007).

Even so-called American "media imperialism" seems to be less threatening than some analysts assume because of the decentralized nature of the Internet. Non-American influence is growing rapidly on the Web, while websites based in the United States adopt content liberally from Latin America, Asia, and elsewhere. Just as international influences are evident in today's hairstyles, clothing

Despite repeated legal actions to try to curb organizations like the Pirate Bay (a large torrent hub in Sweden), the dispersed locations of management, servers, developers, and users make litigation and enforcement extremely problematic. And so the tug-of-war between central control and democratization continues, with no end in sight. One thing is clear, however: The speed of technological innovation and the many possibilities for individual creativity on the Internet make this an exciting era to be involved in the mass media and to study it sociologically.

READY TO STUDY?

IN THE BOOK, YOU CAN:

❏ Tear out the chapter review card at the back of the book to have a summary of the chapter and key terms handy.

ONLINE YOU CAN:

❏ Work through key concepts with a Guided Learning Question.

❏ Prepare for tests with quizzes.

❏ Review the key terms with flash cards.

❏ Explore practical examples of chapter concepts with Connect a Concept exercises.

GO TO NELSON.COM/STUDENT TO ACCESS THESE DIGITAL RESOURCES.

13

Technology, the Environment, and Social Movements

© Matthew Chattle/Alamy Stock Photo

LEARNING OBJECTIVES

In this chapter, you will learn to

LO¹ See that although technology transforms society and history, social need shapes technological growth.

LO² Analyze the circumstances in which environmental issues are transformed into social problems.

LO³ Assess the unequal social distribution of environmental risks.

LO⁴ Summarize the role of market/technological and cooperative solutions to environmental problems.

LO⁵ Identify the social conditions that encourage people to rebel against the status quo.

LO⁶ Describe the social conditions that allow organized social movements to grow.

LO⁷ Recognize that the history of social movements is a struggle for the acquisition of constantly broadening citizenship rights—and opposition to those struggles.

TECHNOLOGY: SAVIOUR OR FRANKENSTEIN?

On August 6, 1945, the United States Air Force dropped an atomic bomb on Hiroshima. The bomb killed about 200 000 Japanese, almost all of them civilians. It hastened the end of World War II, making it unnecessary for American troops to suffer heavy losses in a land invasion of Japan.

Scholars interested in the relationship between technology and society recognize that Hiroshima divided the twentieth century into two distinct periods. We can call the period before Hiroshima the era of naive optimism. During that time, technology could do no wrong, or so it seemed to nearly all observers. **Technology** was widely defined as the application of scientific principles to the *improvement* of human life. It seemed to be driving humanity down a one-way street named progress, picking up speed with every passing year thanks to successively more powerful engines: steam, turbine, internal combustion, electric, jet, rocket, and nuclear. Technology produced tangible benefits. Its detailed workings rested on scientific principles that were mysterious to all but those with advanced science degrees. Therefore, most people regarded technologists with reverence and awe. They were viewed as a sort of priesthood whose objectivity allowed them to stand outside the everyday world and perform near-magical acts.

With Hiroshima, the blush was off the rose. Growing pessimism was, in fact, evident three weeks earlier, when the world's first nuclear bomb exploded at the Alamogordo Bombing Range in New Mexico. Dr. J. Robert Oppenheimer had been appointed scientific director of the top-secret Manhattan Project just 28 months earlier. After recruiting what General Leslie Groves called "the greatest collection of eggheads ever," including three past and seven future Nobel Prize winners, Oppenheimer organized the largest and most sophisticated technological project in human history up to that time. As an undergraduate at Harvard, Oppenheimer had studied Indian philosophy, among other subjects. On the morning of July 16, 1945, as the flash of intense white light faded and the purplish fireball rose, sucking desert sand and debris into a mushroom cloud more than 12 kilometres high, Oppenheimer quoted from Hindu scripture: "I am become Death, the shatterer of worlds" (quoted in Parshall, 1998).

> **technology** The practical application of scientific principles.

Dr. J. Robert Oppenheimer, the "father" of the atomic bomb

reactor at Chernobyl, Ukraine, exploded, releasing 30 to 40 times as much radioactivity as the blast at Hiroshima. It resulted in mass evacuations, more than 10 000 deaths, countless human and animal mutations, and hundreds of square kilometres of unusable cropland. In 1989, the *Exxon Valdez* ran aground in Prince William Sound, Alaska, spilling 42 million litres of crude oil, producing a dangerous slick more than 1600 kilometres long, causing billions of dollars of damage, and killing hundreds of thousands of animals.

By the mid-1980s, sociologist Charles Perrow was referring to such events as "normal accidents." The term **normal accident** recognizes that the very complexity of modern technologies ensures they will *inevitably* fail, although in unpredictable ways (Perrow, 1984). For example, a large computer program contains many thousands of conditional statements. They take the form if $x = y$, do z; if $a = b$, do c. When in use, the program activates many billions of *combinations* of conditional statements. As a result, complex programs cannot be tested for all possible eventualities. Therefore, when rare combinations of conditions occur, they may have unforeseen consequences that are usually minor, occasionally amusing, sometimes expensive, and too often dangerous. You experience normal accidents when your home computer crashes or hangs.

German sociologist Ulrich Beck also coined a term that stuck when he said we live in a risk society. A **risk society** is a society in which technology distributes danger among all categories of the population. Some categories, however, are more exposed to technological danger than others are. Moreover, in a risk society, danger does not result from **technological accidents** alone: Increased risk is due to mounting *environmental* threats that are

Overall, North Americans value science and technology highly. Still, in the postwar years, a growing number of people have come to share Oppenheimer's doubts about the bomb. Indeed, they have extended those doubts not just to the peaceful use of nuclear energy but also to technology in general (see the Sociology at the Movies box). Increasingly, people are beginning to think of technology as a monster run amok, a Frankenstein rather than a saviour.

In the 1970s and 1980s, a series of horrific disasters alerted many people (including some sociologists) to the fact that technological advance is not always beneficial, not even always benign. A gas leak at a poorly maintained Union Carbide pesticide plant in Bhopal, India, killed about 4000 people in 1984 and injured 30 000, a third of whom died excruciating deaths in the following years. In 1986, the No. 4

normal accident An accident that occurs inevitably although unpredictably because of the complexity of modern technologies.

risk society A society in which technology distributes environmental dangers among all categories of the population, although to varying degrees.

The public is now well aware of global warming and climate change. Their dangers are embedded in movies, TV shows, and even video games. Here we see a screen shot from *FUEL*, a video game in which race cars compete in extreme weather conditions caused by global warming.

Bettmann/Getty Images

Screenshot from *FUEL* videogame, courtesy of The Codemasters Software Company Limited.

SOCIOLOGY AT THE MOVIES

Scene from *Food, Inc.*

FOOD, INC.

In November 2010, Saputo Cheese closed a production line and recalled 150 000 kg of cheese after detecting *listeria* at its Montreal plant (*CBC News*, 2010). The company acted quickly to avoid repeating a 2008 tragedy, when a listeriosis outbreak at a Maple Leaf meat-processing plant in Toronto killed 23 people. In recent years, *E. coli* bacteria have also infected the Canadian food and water supply. The worst case occurred in 2000, when 2300 residents of Walkerton, Ontario, became ill and seven died from drinking tap water infected with *E. coli*.

Government inquiries into the causes of food and water contamination focus on the inadequacies of inspection agencies and procedures in an era of budget cuts. However, that is only part of the story. Highly profitable technologies for mass-producing food allow toxic bacteria to enter the food and water supply in the first place. *Food, Inc.*, an Academy Award nominee for best documentary, shows in sickening detail how the industrialization of food processing over the past few decades has allowed animal feces to be mixed in with meat in processing plants and to enter water supplies through farm runoff.

Food, Inc. also documents the cruel treatment to which high-tech agriculture subjects cattle, hogs, and chickens before they are slaughtered. For instance, the handful of big corporations that control chicken processing have figured out how farmers can raise chickens 40 percent faster and twice as big as the free-range variety. Unfortunately, the drugs required to accomplish this feat make the birds' bones so weak they can barely stand. Extreme crowding and total darkness in gigantic chicken coops containing scores of thousands of birds make it impossible for them to move around much anyway.

Meanwhile, much of the highly processed food produced by high-tech industry lacks nutritive value and contributes to a range of diseases. Highly processed food (fast food, snack food, luncheon meats, and so on) contains levels of salt, animal fat, and sugar that cause heart disease, diabetes, and cancer. Fruits and vegetables contain significantly fewer vitamins than they did a few decades ago.

Food, Inc. holds out some hope. Although exceptions exist, locally produced, organic food is typically more nutritious, less laden with chemicals, and produced with less cruelty to animals than is the technologically juiced variety (Weeks, 2009). That is why a growing number of people are turning to the low-tech alternative. Some people claim that locally produced, organic food is too expensive for most Canadians, but that assessment depends on how you calculate cost. When you take the health and environmental costs of high-tech food into account, it is uncertain which kind of food is more expensive. The great virtue of *Food, Inc.* is that it places food in a social context, enabling us to see who profits and who suffers from the application of industrial technologies to the production of high-tech food.

Critical Thinking Questions

1. What are the advantages and disadvantages of high-tech versus low-tech food?
2. Why are low-income earners often unable to purchase and consume locally produced, organic food? What policy changes might enable them to do so?

more widespread, chronic, and ambiguous than technological accidents—and therefore more stressful (Beck, 1992 [1986]; Freudenburg, 1997). New and frightening terms—climate change, global warming, acid rain, ozone depletion, endangered species—have entered our vocabulary. To many people, technology seems to be spinning out of control. From their point of view, it enables the production of ever more goods and services, but at the cost of breathable air, drinkable water, safe sunlight, plant and animal diversity, and normal weather patterns.

These considerations raise four tough questions. First, is technology *the* great driving force of historical and social change? This is the opinion of both cheerleaders and naysayers, those who view technology as our saviour and those who fear it is a Frankenstein. In contrast, we argue that technology is able to transform society only when it is coupled with a powerful social need. People control technology as much as technology transforms people.

Second, if some people do control technology, then exactly who are they? We argue against the view that scientific and engineering wizards are in control. The military and big corporations now decide the direction of most technological research and its application.

Third, what is the most dangerous spinoff of technology and how is risk distributed among various social groups? We focus on environmental degradation and, in particular, global warming, which is the main cause of widespread climate change. We show that although these dangers put all of humanity at risk, the degree of danger varies by class, race, and country. In brief, the socially and economically disadvantaged are most at risk.

Fourth, how can we overcome the dangers of environmental degradation and global warming? We argue that market and technological solutions are insufficient by themselves. In addition, much self-sacrifice, cooperation, and political activism will be required.

LO¹ TECHNOLOGY *AND* PEOPLE MAKE HISTORY

Russian economist Nikolai Kondratiev was the first social scientist to notice that technologies are invented in clusters. As Table 13.1 shows, a new group of major inventions has cropped up every 40 to 60 years since the Industrial Revolution. Kondratiev argued that these flurries of creativity cause major economic growth spurts, beginning 10 to 20 years later and lasting 25 to 35 years each. Thus, Kondratiev subscribed to a form of **technological determinism**, the belief that technology is the major force shaping human society and history (Ellul, 1964 [1954]).

Is it true that technology helps shape society and history? Of course it is. James Watt invented the steam engine in Britain in 1775. It was the main driving force in the mines, mills, factories, and railways of the Industrial Revolution. Gottlieb Daimler invented the internal combustion engine in Germany in 1883. It was the foundation stone of two of the world's biggest industries: automobiles and petroleum. John Atanasoff invented the first digital computer in 1939 at Iowa State College (now University). It utterly transformed the way we work, study, and entertain ourselves. It also put the spurs to one of the most sustained economic booms ever. We could easily cite other examples of how technology shapes history and transforms society.

However, if we probe a little deeper into almost any technology, we notice a pattern: They did not become engines of economic growth until *social* conditions allowed them to do so. The original steam engine, for instance, was invented by Hero of Alexandria in the first century CE. He used it as an amusing way of opening a door. People then promptly forgot the steam engine. Some 1700 years later, when the Industrial Revolution began, factories were first set up near rivers and streams, where water power was available. That was several years before Watt patented his steam engine. Watt's invention was all the rage once its potential became evident, but it did not cause the Industrial Revolution and it was adopted on a wide scale only after the social need for it emerged (Pool, 1997: 126–27).

TABLE 13.1	"Kondratiev Waves" of Modern Technological Innovation and Economic Growth			
Wave	**Invention Dates**	**New Technologies**	**Base**	**Economic Growth Spurt**
1	1760s–70s	Steam engine, textile manufacturing, chemistry, civil engineering	Britain	1780–1815
2	1820s	Railways, mechanical engineering	Britain, Continental western Europe	1840–70
3	1870s–80s	Chemistry, electricity, internal combustion engine	Germany, United States	1890–1914
4	1930s–40s	Electronics, aerospace, chemistry	United States	1945–70
5	1970s	Microelectronics, biotechnology	United States, Japan	1985–2007?*

*We speculate that the Great Recession of 2008–09 and the following period of slow economic growth marked the end of the latest Kondratiev wave.

Source: Adapted from Pacey (1983:32); Pacey, Arnold. 1983. *The Culture of Technology*. Cambridge, MA: MIT Press.

ORDVAC, an early computer developed at the University of Illinois, was delivered to the Ballistic Research Laboratory at the Aberdeen Proving Ground of the United States Army. Technology typically advances when it is coupled with an urgent social need.

U.S. Army Photos

Similarly, Atanasoff stopped work on the computer soon after the outbreak of World War II. However, once the military potential of the computer became evident, development resumed. The British computer, Colossus, helped decipher secret German codes in the last two years of the war and played an important role in the Allied victory. The University of Illinois delivered one of the earliest computers, ORDVAC, to the Ballistic Research Laboratory at the Aberdeen Proving Ground of the U.S. Army. Again, we see how a new technology becomes a major force in society and history only after it is coupled with an urgent social need. We conclude that technology and society influence each other. Scientific discoveries, once adopted on a wide scale, often transform societies. But scientific discoveries are turned into useful technologies only when social need demands it.

HOW HIGH TECH BECAME BIG TECH

Enjoying a technological advantage usually translates into big profits for businesses and military superiority for countries. In the nineteenth century, gaining technological advantage was still inexpensive. It took only modest capital investment, a little knowledge about the best way to organize work, and a handful of highly trained workers to build a shop to manufacture stirrups or even steam engines. In contrast, mass-producing cars, sending people to outer space, and performing other feats of twentieth- and twenty-first-century technology requires enormous

capital investment, detailed attention to the way work is organized, and legions of technical experts. Add to this the intensely competitive business and geopolitical environment of the twentieth and twenty-first centuries, and you can readily understand why ever larger sums have been invested in research and development over the past hundred years.

It was, in fact, already clear in the last quarter of the nineteenth century that turning scientific principles into technological innovations was going to require not just genius, but also substantial resources, especially money and organization. Thus, Thomas Edison established the first "invention factory" at Menlo Park, New Jersey, in the late 1870s. Historian of science Robert Pool (1997: 22) notes,

The most important factor in Edison's success—outside of his genius for invention—was the organization he had set up to assist him. By 1878, Edison had assembled at Menlo Park a staff of thirty scientists, metalworkers, glassblowers, draftsmen, and others working under his close direction and supervision. With such support, Edison boasted that he could turn out "a minor invention every ten days and a big thing every six months or so."

The phonograph and the electric light bulb were two such "big things." Edison inspired both. Both, however, were also expensive team efforts, motivated by vast commercial possibilities. (Edison founded General Electric, one of the largest companies in the world.)

At the beginning of the twentieth century, the scientific or engineering genius operating in isolation was only rarely able to contribute much to technological innovation. (Steve Wozniak inventing the first Apple computer in the 1970s is an exception.) By mid-century, most technological innovation was organized along industrial lines. Entire armies of experts and vast sums of capital were required to run the new invention factories. The prototype of today's invention factory was the Manhattan Project, which built the atomic bomb in the last years of World War II. By the time of Hiroshima, the manufacturing complex of the U.S. nuclear industry was about the same size as that of the U.S. automobile industry. The era of big science and big technology had arrived. Only governments and, increasingly, giant multinational corporations could afford to sustain the research effort of the second half of the twentieth century.

As the twentieth century ended, there seemed to be no limit to the amount that could be spent on research and development. During the twentieth century, the number of research scientists in North America increased a hundredfold. In the last 40 years of the century, research and development spending tripled, taking inflation into account. In that same period, industry's share of spending rose from one-third to two-thirds of the total while government's share dropped proportionately (Hobsbawm, 1994: 523; U.S. Department of Commerce, 1998: 609; Woodrow Federal Reserve Bank of Minneapolis, 2000; see Figure 13.1).

As a result of these developments, it should come as no surprise that military and profit-making considerations now govern the direction of most research and development. A reporter is supposed to have once asked bank robber Willie Sutton why he robbed banks. Sutton answered, "Because that's where the money is." Now taught as "Sutton's law" in some medical schools, money is hardly the only motivation prompting scientists and engineers to research particular topics. Personal interests, individual creativity, and the state of a field's intellectual development still influence the direction of inquiry. This is especially true for theoretical work done in universities, as opposed to applied research funded by governments and private industry. It would, however, be naive to think that practicality doesn't also enter the scientist's calculation of what he or she ought to study. Many researchers—even many of those who do theoretically driven research in universities—are pulled in particular directions by large research grants, well-paying jobs, access to expensive state-of-the-art equipment, and the possibility of winning patents and achieving commercial success.

Economic lures, increasingly provided by the military and big corporations, have generated moral and political qualms among some researchers. Some scientists and engineers wonder whether work on particular topics achieves optimum benefits for humanity. Certain researchers are troubled by the possibility that some scientific inquiries may be harmful to humankind. However, a growing number of scientists and engineers recognize that to do cutting-edge research, they must put aside residual misgivings, hop on the bandwagon, and adhere to military and industrial requirements and priorities. That, after all, is where the money is.

GLOBAL WARMING

The side effect of technology that has given people the most serious cause for concern is environmental degradation and, in particular, global warming. Since the Industrial Revolution, humans have been burning increasing quantities of fossil fuels (coal, oil, gasoline, natural gas, and so on) to drive their cars, furnaces, and factories. Burning these fuels releases carbon dioxide into the atmosphere. The accumulation of carbon dioxide allows more solar radiation to enter the atmosphere and less heat to escape. This process contributes to **global warming**, a gradual increase in the world's average surface temperature. Figure 13.2 graphs the world's annual average surface air temperature and the concentration of carbon dioxide in the atmosphere from 1880 to 2014. It shows a warming trend that mirrors the increased concentration of carbon dioxide in the atmosphere. It also shows that the concentration of carbon dioxide and global warming intensified in the 1950s.

From 1974 to 2014, surface air temperature rose at a rate of 2.05 degrees Celsius per century. This average may not seem like a big temperature change until you realize that the warming trend is much stronger in the northern hemisphere than in the southern hemisphere and that, at a certain temperature, even slight warming will turn ice to water. In recent years, many communities in Nunavut, including Arviat, Igloolik, Saniqiluaq, Repulse Bay, and Cape Dorset (the latter just 240 kilometres south of the Arctic Circle) have had to install refrigeration systems to keep the ice frozen in hockey arenas (Klein, 2013).

As temperatures rise, more water evaporates. More evaporation causes more rainfall and bigger storms, which lead to more soil erosion, which in turn destroys cultivable land. Warming melts ice, causing the sea level to rise and increasing the chance of flooding in heavily populated coastal regions in Egypt, Bangladesh, the United

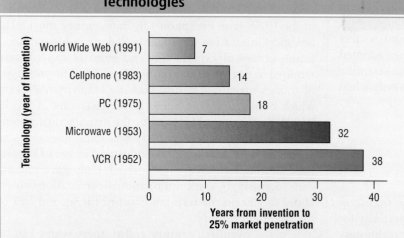

FIGURE 13.1 **Speed of Market Penetration for Selected Technologies**

Technology (year of invention) / Years from invention to 25% market penetration:

- World Wide Web (1991): 7
- Cellphone (1983): 14
- PC (1975): 18
- Microwave (1953): 32
- VCR (1952): 38

Because large multinational corporations now routinely invest astronomical sums in research and development to increase their chance of being the first to bring innovations to market, the time lag between new scientific discoveries and their technological application is continually shrinking.

Source: Based on data from "The Silent Boom," *Forbes*, July 7, 1997. Adapted by permission of ESR Research.

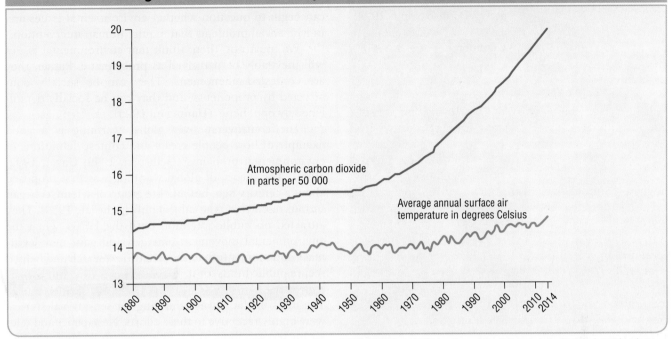

Sources: Etheridge, D.M. et al. 1998. Historical CO$_2$ Record from the Law Dome DE08, DE08-2, and DSS Ice Cores. http://cdiac.ornl.gov/ftp/trends/co2/lawdome
.combined.dat (retrieved 2 August 2015); National Oceanic and Atmospheric Administration, U.S. Department of Commerce. 2015. CO$_2$ Expressed as a Mole
Fraction in Dry Air, Micromol/Mol, abbreviated as Ppm. ftp://aftp.cmdl.noaa.gov/products/trends/co2/co2_mm_mlo.txt (retrieved 2 August 2015); Goddard
Institute for Space Studies, National Aeronautics and Space Administration, 2015, GLOBAL Land–Ocean Temperature Index in 0.01 Degrees Celsius Base
Period: 1951–1980. http://data.giss.nasa.gov/gistemp/tabledata_v3/GLB.Ts+dSST.txt (retrieved 2 August 2015).

States, and elsewhere. In the Far North, melting ice reveals tundra, areas of land above the tree line that are covered by grass, moss, and shrubs. Newly uncovered tundra contains rotting vegetation and animal remains, so it releases methane into the atmosphere, and methane is 21 times more effective in trapping heat than carbon dioxide is. The new water from melted ice reflects less heat than the ice did because it is darker than ice is, thus speeding up global warming. Higher levels of carbon dioxide in the air interact with bodies of water to produce carbonic acid, destroying plant and animal life in oceans and lakes.

In short, global warming causes widespread climate change, resulting in much suffering and death among all living things. One indication of this fact is provided by Figure 13.3, which graphs the worldwide dollar cost of damage because of "natural" disasters from 1970 to 2014. ("Natural" is in quotation marks because, as we have just seen, an increasingly large number of meteorological events are rendered extreme by human action.) Clearly, the damage caused by extreme meteorological events is on the upswing. Worldwide, the number of events that the insurance industry classifies as "natural catastrophes" increased steadily from 40 to 168 between 1970 and 2012 (Swiss Re, 2013: 2). (Some of these incidents are earthquakes, which do not have human causes, but the number of earthquakes shows no trend.)

FIGURE 13.3   Worldwide Insured losses Caused by Natural and Human Catastrophes, 1970–2014 (in 2005 $US billions)

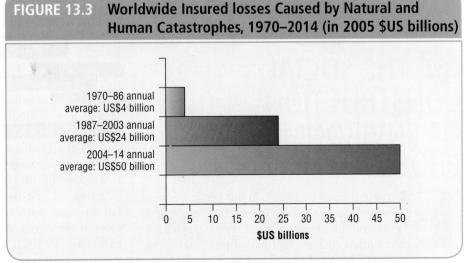

Sources: Department of Labor (2015), "CPI Inflation Calculator." http://data.bls.gov/cgi-bin/cpicalc.pl (retrieved 2 August 2015); Swiss Re. 2015. "Natural Catastrophes and Man-Made Disasters in 2014." http://media.swissre.com/documents/sigma2_2015_en_final.pdf (retrieved 2 August 2015).

Because of global warming, glaciers are melting, the sea level is rising, and extreme weather events are becoming more frequent.

Global warming threatens everyone. However, as you will now see, the degree to which it is perceived as threatening depends on certain social conditions being met. Moreover, the threat is not evenly distributed in society.

LO² THE SOCIAL CONSTRUCTION OF ENVIRONMENTAL PROBLEMS

Environmental problems do not become social issues spontaneously. Before they can enter the public consciousness, policy-oriented scientists, the environmental movement, the mass media, and respected organizations must discover and promote them. People have to connect real-life events to the information learned from these groups. Because some scientists, industrial interests, and politicians dispute the existence of environmental threats, the public can begin to question whether environmental issues are, in fact, social problems that require human intervention.

We must not, then, think that environmental issues will inevitably be perceived as problematic. Rather, they are contested phenomena. They can be socially constructed by proponents, and they can be socially demolished by opponents (Hannigan, 1995).

The controversy over global warming is a good example of how people create and contest definitions of environmental problems (Gelbspan, 1999; Ungar, 1992, 1999). The theory of global warming was first proposed about a century ago, but an elite group of scientists began serious research on the subject only in the late 1950s. They attracted no public attention until the 1970s, when the environmental movement emerged and gave new legitimacy and momentum to the scientific research and helped secure public funds for it. Respected and influential scientists now began to promote the issue of global warming. The mass media, always thirsting for sensational stories, were highly receptive to these efforts. Newspaper and television reports about the problem began to appear in the late 1970s and proliferated in the mid- to late 1980s.

The summer of 1988 brought the worst drought in half a century to North America. Respected organizations outside the scientific community, the mass media, and the environmental movement began expressing concern about the effects of global warming. By the early 1990s, public opinion polls showed that most North Americans with an opinion on the subject thought that using coal, oil, and gas contributes to global warming.

However, some industrialists, politicians, and scientists began to question whether global warming was, in fact, taking place. This group included Western coal and oil companies, the member states of the Organization of the Petroleum Exporting Countries (OPEC), other coal- and oil-exporting nations, and right-wing think-tanks, such as Canada's Fraser Institute in Vancouver, which is subsidized in part by major oil companies operating in Canada. "Bad scientific reporting, bad economics and bad judgement" is how the Fraser Institute summarized the analyses of those who regarded global warming as a serious issue requiring immediate action (Jones, 1997). Largely as a result of this onslaught, public concern about global warming began to falter.

Yet the evidence that global warming was substantial, dangerous, and caused by human activity continued to accumulate. In Canada, for example, ordinary people experienced first-hand ongoing drought on the Prairies, falling water levels in the Great Lakes, the melting of glaciers in the north, and the collapse of fish stocks on the east coast. In 2007, a large blue-ribbon panel of international climate experts, the Intergovernmental Panel on Climate Change (IPCC) issued a definitive report showing that global warming was real, dangerous, but stoppable

Ordinary people experienced first-hand the ongoing drought in Manitoba's Red River Valley.

through human intervention (Intergovernmental Panel on Climate Change, 2007). The public mood again shifted, and all of Canada's political parties adopted "green" platforms that promised swift and effective action. In 2009, the IPCC report was shown to contain a couple of errors, while scientists responsible for one of its data sets stupidly kept the data from public scrutiny. Again a furor erupted, although it was soon shown that the report's conclusions were accurate ("U.K. Panel," 2010). The ongoing debate clearly demonstrates that environmental issues become social problems only when social, political, and scientific circumstances allow them to be defined as such.

As you will now see, in addition to being socially defined, environmental problems are socially distributed. That is, environmental risks are greater for some groups than for others.

LO³ THE SOCIAL DISTRIBUTION OF RISK

You may have noticed that after a minor twister touches down on some unlucky community, TV reporters often rush to interview the surviving residents of trailer parks. The survivors stand amid the rubble that was their lives. They heroically remark on the generosity of their neighbours, their good fortune in still having their family intact, and our inability to fight nature's destructive forces. Why trailer parks? Small twisters aren't particularly attracted to them, but reporters are. That is because trailers are pretty flimsy in the face of even a small tornado. They often suffer a lot of damage from twisters and therefore make a more sensational story than the minor damage typically inflicted on upper-middle-class homes with firmly shingled roofs and solid foundations. This is a general pattern. Whenever disaster strikes, economically and politically disadvantaged people almost always suffer most. That is because their circumstances render them most vulnerable. In fact, the advantaged often consciously put the disadvantaged in harm's way to avoid risk themselves. This is what is known as **environmental racism**, the tendency to heap environmental dangers on the disadvantaged and especially on disadvantaged racial minorities.

> **environmental racism** The tendency to heap environmental dangers on the disadvantaged, and especially on disadvantaged racial minorities.

The Canadian Case

Environmental racism is evident in Canada. For example, the uranium used to construct the atom bombs that were dropped on Hiroshima and Nagasaki came from Port Radium in the Northwest Territories, the world's first uranium mine. More than 30 Dene hunters and trappers were recruited from the nearby village of Deline to haul and barge 45-kilogram burlap sacks of the raw ore

The first shipment of uranium being transported on Great Bear Lake in 1931. The American and Canadian governments knew about the dangers of uranium exposure, yet paid more than 30 Dene hunters $3 per day to haul uranium in burlap sacks along a 2100-kilometre route to Fort McMurray.

along a 2100 kilometre route to Fort McMurray, Alberta, for $3 a day. The American and Canadian governments had known about the dangers of exposure to uranium at least since 1931 (McClelland, 1931), yet they withheld this information from the workers, who were completely unprotected from the ore's deadly radiation. In the surrounding community, the Dene ate fish from contaminated dredging ponds and hunted and camped in contaminated areas. Dene children played with ore dust at docks and landings. Dene women sewed tents from used uranium sacks. Until recent decades, cancer was unknown in the community. Elders often lived into their 90s. By 1998, however, nearly half of the uranium workers had died of cancer while still in their 60s and 70s. Cancer and lung disease are alarmingly widespread in the community. Deline is known locally as "The Village of the Widows." Neither the workers nor their families have received any compensation from the government, not even an apology (Nikiforuk, 1998).

Broadly similar stories of environmental racism are legion. There is a disturbing association in Canada between level of contamination and the concentration of Aboriginal populations. Figure 13.4 illustrates this association. Using a broad measure of airborne pollution, it shows that where Aboriginal Canadians form a larger proportion of the population, the per capita weight of particulates in the air is heaviest.

Class also structures exposure to environmental risk in Canada. For example, Sydney, Nova Scotia, has one of the highest cancer rates of any city in Canada. The people who lived around Frederick Street, the poorest part of Sydney, had the highest neighbourhood cancer rate in town. Skin ailments, birth defects, respiratory problems, diseases of the nervous system, and other medical conditions were also unusually common around Frederick Street. The main reason? Sydney was home to a large steel mill for a century. Waste from the mill poured into the so-called tar ponds, a 50-hectare site polluted to a depth of 24 metres with cancer-causing chemicals. Frederick Street borders the tar ponds. Sludge oozed into people's basements, seeped into their vegetable gardens, and ran in open streams where children played. Billions of federal and provincial tax dollars were spent subsidizing the steel mill that was the source of the problem. Yet a serious cleanup effort began only in 2010, 30 years after elevated levels of toxins were first detected in Sydney Harbour and in local lobsters (Barlow and May, 2000: 144; see Figure 13.5).

The Less-Developed Countries

What is true for disadvantaged classes and racial groups in North America also holds for the less-developed countries—the underprivileged face more environmental dangers than do the privileged (Kennedy, 1993: 95–121). Mexico, Brazil, China, India, and other southern countries are industrializing rapidly. That puts tremendous strain on their natural resources. Rising demand for water, electricity, fossil fuels, and consumer products is creating more polluted rivers, dead lakes, and industrial waste sites. At a quickening pace, rainforests, grazing land, cropland, and wetlands are giving way to factories, roads, airports, and housing complexes. Smog-blanketed megacities continue to sprawl. Of the world's 21 largest cities, 18 are in less-developed countries, and 16 of the world's 20 most polluted cities are in China. Air quality in Beijing deteriorated beyond World Health Organization (WHO) safe limits every day in January 2013. In Beijing, official measurements of fine airborne particulates, which pose the greatest risk, are sometimes more than 40 times higher than WHO guidelines (*Bloomberg News*, 2013).

Given the picture sketched above, it should be unsurprising that, on average, people in less-developed countries are more concerned about the environment than people in rich countries are (Brechin and Kempton, 1994). However, the developing countries cannot afford much in the way of pollution control, so anti-pollution regulations are lax by North American, western European, and Japanese standards. This state of affairs is an incentive for some multinational corporations to place some of their foulest operations

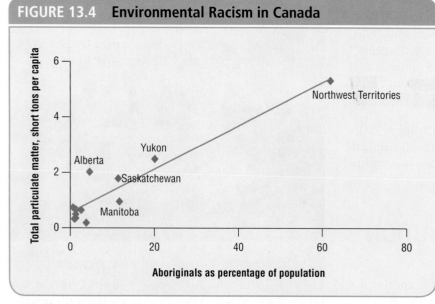

FIGURE 13.4 Environmental Racism in Canada

Note: The data are for 1995.

Sources: Statistics Canada, 2000a, "Population by Aboriginal Group, 1996 Census," "Household Environmental Practices"; U.S. Environmental Protection Agency, Office of Air Quality Planning and Standards, 2000, National Air Pollutant Emission Trends, 1900–1998.

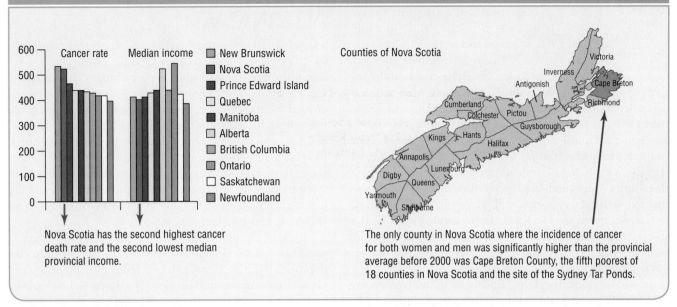

FIGURE 13.5   Class and Exposure to Environmental Risk: Nova Scotia

Cancer rate   Median income

☐ New Brunswick
☐ Nova Scotia
☐ Prince Edward Island
☐ Quebec
☐ Manitoba
☐ Alberta
☐ British Columbia
☐ Ontario
☐ Saskatchewan
☐ Newfoundland

Counties of Nova Scotia

Nova Scotia has the second highest cancer death rate and the second lowest median provincial income.

The only county in Nova Scotia where the incidence of cancer for both women and men was significantly higher than the provincial average before 2000 was Cape Breton County, the fifth poorest of 18 counties in Nova Scotia and the site of the Sydney Tar Ponds.

Sources: Cancer Care Nova Scotia, 2004, "Cancer Statistics in Nova Scotia"; Health Canada, 2003, "Canadian Cancer Statistics, 2003"; Province of Nova Scotia, 2010, "Counties of Nova Scotia"; Rural Communities Impact Policy Project, 2003, "Painting the Landscape of Rural Nova Scotia."

in the southern hemisphere. It is also the reason that the industrialization of the less-developed countries is proving so punishing to the environment. For example, car ownership is growing rapidly in China and India as the middle classes of those countries grow. When another 100 million Chinese upgrade from bicycles to Chery QQs at less than $4800 each, and an equal number of Indians upgrade from motor scooters to Tata Nanos at just over $3000, the result will be an even worse choking mess.

For the time being, however, the rich countries do most of the world's environmental damage. That is because their inhabitants earn and consume more than the inhabitants of less-developed countries. How much more? The richest fifth of humanity earns about 80 times as much as the poorest fifth (up from 30 times as much in 1950). In the past half-century, the richest fifth doubled its per capita consumption of energy, meat, timber, steel, and copper, and quadrupled its car ownership. In that same period, the per capita consumption of the poorest fifth hardly changed. The United States has only 4.5 percent of the world's population, but it uses about 25 percent of Earth's resources. And it produces more than 20 percent of global emissions of carbon dioxide, the pollutant responsible for about half of global warming. So the inhabitants of the northern hemisphere cause a disproportionately large share of the world's environmental problems, enjoy a disproportionate share of the benefits of technology, and live with fewer environmental risks than do people in the southern hemisphere.

In Tiananmen Square, Beijing, January 21, 2013

Visual China Group/Getty Images

WHAT IS TO BE DONE?
THE MARKET AND HIGH-TECH SOLUTIONS

Some people believe the environmental crisis will resolve itself. They think we already have two weapons that will work together to end the crisis: the market and high technology. The case of oil illustrates how these weapons can combine forces. If oil reserves drop or oil is withheld from the market for political reasons, the price of oil goes up. This makes it worthwhile for oil exploration companies to develop new technologies to recover more oil. When they

collective action Occurs when people act in unison to bring about or resist social, political, or economic change.

discover more oil and bring it to market, prices fall back to where they were. Generalizing this principle and projecting it into the future, optimists believe global warming and other forms of environmental degradation will be dealt with similarly. In their view, human inventiveness and the profit motive will combine to create the new technologies we need to survive and prosper.

Some evidence supports this optimistic scenario. For example, following the oil shocks of 1973 (when prices tripled) and 1978–79 (when prices tripled again), new discoveries were made and new efficiencies were implemented, so oil reserves grew and prices fell. In recent years, we have adopted new technologies to combat some of the worst excesses of environmental degradation. For example, we have replaced brain-damaging leaded gas with unleaded gas and developed environmentally friendly gases to replace ozone-destroying refrigerants. Efficient windmills and solar panels are now common. More factories are equipped with high-tech pollution-control devices, preventing dangerous chemicals from seeping into the air and water. We have introduced cost-effective ways to recycle metal, plastic, paper, and glass. New methods are being developed for eliminating carbon dioxide emissions from the burning of fossil fuels. We can now buy hybrid and electric cars.

However, three factors suggest market forces and technological fixes cannot solve environmental problems on their own:

1. *Imperfect price signals.* The prices of many commodities do not reflect their actual cost to society. In Canada, gasoline costs about $1.05 a litre at the time of this writing—inexpensive by world standards because we pay relatively low taxes on gas. However, the social cost of gas, including the cost of repairing the environmental damage caused by burning it, is two or three times that amount. Because of many such price distortions, the market often fails to send signals that might result in the speedy adoption of technological and policy fixes.

2. *The slow pace of change.* Our efforts so far to deal with global warming are just not good enough; global warming continues to accelerate. One widely respected group of climate scientists and statisticians calculated that if we continue to burn fossil fuels at current rates, then by 2024 it will be exceedingly difficult to avert disaster (Carbon Tracker Initiative, 2012).

3. *The importance of political pressure.* Political pressure exerted by environmental activists, community groups, and public opinion is often necessary to motivate corporate and government action on environmental issues. Without the efforts of such organizations, it is doubtful many environmental issues would be defined as social problems by corporations and governments.

LO⁴ THE COOPERATIVE ALTERNATIVE

The alternative to the market and high-tech approach involves people cooperating to reduce greatly their over-consumption of just about everything. This strategy includes investing heavily in energy-saving technologies, environmental cleanup, and subsidized, environmentally friendly industrialization in the developing countries. It would require renewed commitment to voluntary efforts, new laws and enforcement bodies to ensure compliance, increased environmentally related research and development by industry and government, more environmentally directed foreign aid, and new taxes to help pay for it all (Livernash and Rodenburg, 1998).

Is the solution realistic? Not in the short term. It would be political suicide for anyone in the rich countries to propose the drastic measures listed above. Not too many Canadian drivers would be happy paying $3 a litre for gas, for example. For the solution to be politically acceptable, the broad public in North America, western Europe, and Japan must be aware of the gravity of the environmental problem and be willing to make substantial economic sacrifices to get the job done.

Survey data suggest that nearly all Canadians are aware of the environmental problem and are doing something about it. For instance, in 2006, sorting and recycling programs for glass, cans, plastic, and paper were available to about 90 percent of Canadians, 95 percent of whom used them. However, it seems that we are in general prepared to act only when it doesn't inconvenience us much. When asked to indicate their main ways of getting to work, 81 percent of Canadians said they usually go by private motor vehicle and just 17 percent said they usually take public transit, cycle, or walk (Statistics Canada, 2006b: 52, 62).

Other surveys reveal much the same pattern. Many people know about the environmental crisis, say they want it dealt with, but are unwilling to be inconvenienced or pay much of the cost themselves. They regard environmental problems as too remote and abstract to justify making big personal sacrifices. It follows that more and bigger environmental catastrophes may have to occur before more people are willing to take massive remedial action.

SOCIAL MOVEMENTS

We noted above that governments and corporations are inclined to act on environmental issues only if they are pressured to do so by the public. But under what circumstances do many individuals engage in **collective action**, working in unison to bring about or resist social,

Protesting the effects of the Alberta tar sands

political, and economic change by means of demonstrations, strikes, riots, and the like? And under what circumstances is collective action turned into a **social movement**, an enduring collective attempt to change or resist change to part or all of society by establishing organizations, lobbies, unions, and political parties?

Answers to these questions are unclear, as Robert Brym learned in Grade 11: "One day in chemistry class I learned that water combined with sulphur dioxide produces sulphurous acid. The news shocked me. To understand why, you have to know that I lived in Saint John, New Brunswick, about 100 metres downwind of one of the largest pulp and paper mills in Canada. Waves of sulphur dioxide billowed from the mill's smokestacks day and night. The town's pervasive rotten-egg smell was a long-standing complaint in the area. But, for me, disgust turned to upset when I realized the fumes were toxic. Suddenly, it was clear why many people I knew—especially people living near the mill—woke up in the morning with a kind of 'smoker's cough.' Through the simple act of breathing, we were causing the gas to mix with the moisture in our bodies and form an acid that our lungs tried to expunge, with only partial success.

"Twenty years later, I read the results of a medical research report showing that area residents suffered from rates of lung disease, including emphysema and lung cancer, significantly above the North American average. But even in 1968, it was evident my hometown had a serious problem. I therefore hatched a plan. Our high school was about to hold its annual model parliament. The event was notoriously boring, partly because, year in year out, virtually everyone voted for the same party, the Conservatives. But here was an issue, I thought, that could turn things around. A local man, K.C. Irving, owned the pulp and paper mill. *Forbes* magazine ranked him as one of the richest men in the world. I figured that when I told the other students what I had discovered, they would

quickly demand the closure of the mill until Irving guaranteed a clean operation.

"Was *I* naive. As head of the tiny Liberal Party, I had to address the entire student body during assembly on election day to outline the party platform and rally votes. When I got to the part of my speech that explained why Irving was our enemy, the murmuring in the audience, which had been growing like the sound of a hungry animal about to pounce on its prey, erupted into loud boos. A couple of students rushed the stage. The principal suddenly appeared from the wings and commanded the student body to settle down. He then took me by the arm and informed me that, for my own safety, my speech was finished. So, I discovered on election day, was our high school's Liberal Party. And so, it emerged, was my high school political career.

"This incident troubled me for years, partly because of the embarrassment it caused, partly because of the puzzles it presented. Why didn't the other students rebel in the way I thought they would? Why did they continue to support an arrangement that was enriching one man at the cost of a community's health? Couldn't they see the injustice? I didn't know it at the time, but to answer such questions, it is necessary to turn to the literature on social movements."

LO⁵ BREAKDOWN THEORY: A FUNCTIONALIST ACCOUNT

Until about 1970, most sociologists believed that two conditions must be met for social movements to form:

1. *Social marginality.* The early leaders of social movements and their first recruits must be poorly integrated in society. Without such socially marginal people, social movements supposedly cannot form.

2. *Strain.* People's norms must be strained or disrupted. For example, one of the most popular variants of breakdown theory is **relative deprivation** theory. *Relative deprivation* refers to the growth of an intolerable gap between the social rewards people expect to receive and those they actually receive. (Social rewards are widely valued goods, such as money, education, security, prestige, and so forth.) Supposedly, people are

> **social movement** A collective attempt to change all or part of a political or social order by means of rioting, petitioning, striking, demonstrating, and/or establishing pressure groups, unions, and political parties.
>
> **relative deprivation** An intolerable gap between the social rewards people receive and the social rewards they expect to receive.

breakdown theory
Suggests that social movements emerge when traditional norms and patterns of social

solidarity theory Holds that social movements are social organizations that emerge when potential members can mobilize resources, take advantage of new political opportunities, and avoid high levels of social control by authorities.

resource mobilization The process by which social movements crystallize because of the increasing organizational, material, and other resources of movement members.

most likely to form social movements when the gap between rising expectations (brought on by, say, rapid economic growth and migration) and the receipt of social rewards (sometimes lowered by economic recession or war) becomes intolerable (Davies, 1969; Gurr, 1970; see Figure 13.6).

Following sociologist Charles Tilly and his associates, we can group these two conditions together as the **breakdown theory** of collective action. That is because both conditions assume that social movements result from the disruption or breakdown of previously integrative social structures and norms (Tilly, Tilly, and Tilly, 1975: 4–6). At a more abstract level, breakdown theory can be seen as a variant of functionalism because it regards collective action as a form of social imbalance that results from the improper functioning of social institutions.

Can breakdown theory adequately account for the crystallization of social movements? The short answer is no. Since 1970, sociologists have uncovered two main flaws in the theory. First, research shows that in most cases, leaders and early joiners of social movements are well-integrated members of their community, not socially marginal outsiders (Brym, 1980; Lipset, 1971). Second, researchers have found that high levels of relative deprivation are generally not associated with the crystallization

of social movements. That is because certain social conditions can prevent people from translating their discontent into an enduring social movement with a more or less stable membership, hired office personnel, a publicity bureau, a regularly published newsletter, and the like (McPhail, 1994; Tilly, Tilly, and Tilly, 1975; Torrance, 1986: 115–45). We now consider those social conditions.

SOLIDARITY THEORY: A CONFLICT APPROACH

Solidarity theory is a type of conflict theory that focuses on the social conditions that allow people to turn their discontent into a unified (or "solidary") political force. It identifies three such social conditions: adequate resource mobilization, sufficient political opportunities, and weak or inconsistent social control.

Resource Mobilization

Most collective action is part of a power struggle. The struggle usually intensifies as groups whose members feel disadvantaged become more powerful relative to other groups. How do disadvantaged groups become more powerful? By gaining new members, becoming better organized, and increasing their access to scarce resources, such as money, jobs, and means of communication (Bierstedt, 1974). **Resource mobilization** is the process by which groups engage in more collective action as their power increases because of their growing size and increasing organizational, material, and other resources (Jenkins, 1983; Zald and McCarthy, 1979).

Consider the effect of resource mobilization on the frequency of strikes in Canada. Research shows that in Canada between the mid-1940s and the mid-1970s, strike frequency was high when (1) unemployment was low, (2) union membership was high, and (3) governments were generous in their provision of social welfare benefits. *Low unemployment* indicates a strong economy. Workers are inclined to strike when business activity is robust because in such conditions they accumulate healthy strike funds, enjoy many alternative job opportunities, and know that employers and governments can afford to make concessions (employers make bigger profits and governments collect more taxes during economic booms). *A high level of unionization* is conducive to more strike activity because unions provide workers with leadership, strike funds, and coordination. Finally, *generous government benefits* give workers an economic buffer and thus increase their readiness to strike. So, as resource mobilization theory suggests, strong social ties among workers (as indicated by a high level of unionization) and access to jobs and money (as indicated by a booming economy and generous government benefits) increase challenges to authority (as indicated by strikes).

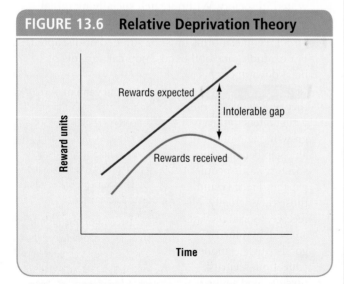

FIGURE 13.6 **Relative Deprivation Theory**

Reward units (vertical axis) / Time (horizontal axis)

Rewards expected

Intolerable gap

Rewards received

Source: From BRYM/LIE. *Sociology*, 1e. © 2009 Nelson Education Ltd. Reproduced by permission, www.cengage.com/permissions

Figure 13.7 shows the pattern of strike activity in Canada between 1946 and 2011. It adds substance to the resource mobilization approach. Until 1974, the trend in strike activity was upward. This was a period of growing prosperity, low unemployment, expanding state benefits, and increasing unionization. With access to increasing organizational and material resources, workers challenged authority increasingly more often in the three decades after World War II. In 1973, however, economic crisis struck. As a result of war and revolution in the Middle East, oil prices tripled, and then tripled again at the end of the decade. Inflation increased and unemployment rose. Soon, the government was strapped for funds and had to borrow heavily to maintain social welfare programs. Eventually, the debt burden was so heavy, the government felt obliged to cut various social welfare programs. At the same time, federal and provincial governments introduced laws and regulations limiting the right of some workers to strike and putting a cap on the wage gains that workers could demand.

The percentage of Canadian workers who belonged to unions began to decline. Strike action was made even more difficult when Canada signed free trade deals with the United States in 1988 and Mexico in 1994. It was now possible for employers to threaten to relocate in the United States or Mexico in the face of protracted strikes. Thus, in the post-1973 climate, the organizational and material resources of workers fell. As a result, strike activity plummeted. In 2011, the frequency of strikes per 100 000 Canadian non-agricultural workers was less than 25 percent that of 1974 (Brym, 2003; Brym, Birdsell-Bauer, and McIvor, 2013).

Political Opportunities

A second social condition that allows mass discontent to be translated into social movement formation involves the emergence of new **political opportunities** (McAdam, 1982; Piven and Cloward, 1977; Tarrow, 1994). Specifically, chances for protest and social movement formation emerge when influential allies offer support, when ruling political alignments become unstable, when elite groups are divided and come into conflict with one another, and when election campaigns provide a focus for discontent and a chance to put new representatives with new policies into positions of authority (Tarrow, 1994: 86–9; Useem, 1998). Said differently, collective action takes place and social movements crystallize not just when disadvantaged groups become more powerful

> **political opportunities**
> Chances for collective action and social movement growth that occur during election campaigns, when influential allies offer support to insurgents, when ruling political alignments become unstable, and when elite groups become divided and conflict with one another.

FIGURE 13.7 Weighted Frequency of Strikes, Canada, 1946–2011

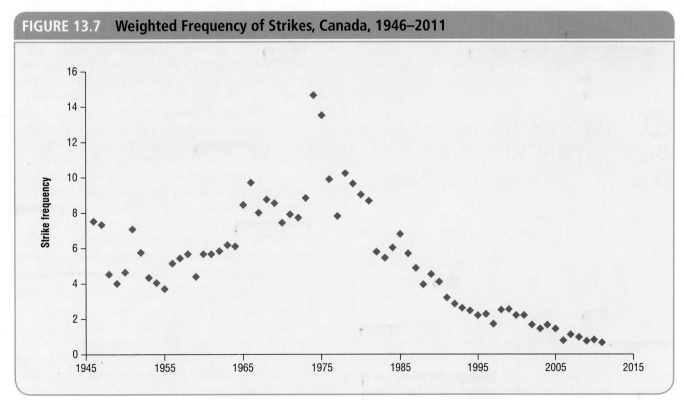

Note: Strike frequency = Number of strikes per 100 000 non-agricultural workers.

Source: Republished with permission of Blackwell Publishing, from Brym, Robert, Louise Birdsell-Bauer, and Mitch McIvor, "Is Industrial Unrest Reviving in Canada? Strike Duration in the Early 21st Century," *Canadian Review of Sociology* 50(2): pp. 227–38. © 2013 Canadian Sociological Association/La Société canadienne de sociologie; permission conveyed through Copyright Clearance Center, Inc.

frame alignment The process by which individual interests, beliefs, and values become congruent and complementary with the activities, goals, and ideology of a social movement.

but also when privileged groups and the institutions they control are divided and therefore become weaker. As economist John Kenneth Galbraith once said about the weakness of the Russian ruling class at the time of the 1917 revolution, if someone manages to kick in a rotting door, some credit has to be given to the door.

Social Control

The third main lesson of solidarity theory is that government reactions to protests influence subsequent protests. Specifically, governments can try to lower the frequency and intensity of protest by taking various *social control* measures (Oberschall, 1973: 242–83). These measures include making concessions to protesters, co-opting the most troublesome leaders (for example, by appointing them as advisers), and violently repressing collective action.

Note, however, that social control measures do not always have the desired effect. If grievances are very deeply felt, and yielding to protesters' demands greatly increases their hopes, resources, and political opportunities, government concessions may encourage protesters to press their claims further. And although the firm and decisive use of force usually stops protest, using force moderately or inconsistently often backfires. That is because unrest typically intensifies when protesters are led to believe that the government is weak or indecisive (Piven and Cloward, 1977: 27–36; Tilly, Tilly, and Tilly, 1975: 244).

LO⁶ FRAMING THEORY: THE CONTRIBUTION OF SYMBOLIC INTERACTIONISM

As we have seen, solidarity theory helps to overcome the flaws in breakdown theory. Still, the rise of a social movement sometimes takes strict solidarity theorists by surprise, as does the failure of an aggrieved group to press its claims by means of collective action. It seems, therefore, that something lies between (1) the capacity of disadvantaged people to mobilize resources for collective action, and (2) the recruitment of a substantial number of movement members. That "something" is **frame alignment** (Benford, 1997; Goffman, 1974; Snow, Rochford, Jr., Worden, and Benford, 1986). Frame alignment is the process by which social movement leaders make their activities, ideas, and goals congruent with the interests, beliefs, and values of potential new recruits to their movement—or fail to do so. Thanks to the efforts of scholars operating mainly in the symbolic interactionist

tradition, frame alignment has recently become the subject of sustained sociological investigation.

Types of Frame Alignment

Frame alignment can be encouraged in several ways:

- Social movement leaders can reach out to other organizations that, they believe, include people who may be sympathetic to their movement's cause. Thus, leaders of an anti-nuclear movement may use the mass media, telephone campaigns, and direct mail to appeal to feminist, anti-racist, and environmental organizations. In doing so, they assume that these organizations are likely to have members who would agree, at least in general terms, with the anti-nuclear platform.

- Movement activists can stress popular values that have so far not featured prominently in the thinking of potential recruits. They can also elevate the importance of positive beliefs about the movement and what it stands for. For instance, in trying to win new recruits, movement members might emphasize the seriousness of the social movement's purpose. They might analyze the causes of the problem the movement is trying to solve in a clear and convincing way. Or they might stress the likelihood of the movement's success. By doing so, they can increase the movement's appeal to potential recruits and perhaps win them over to the cause.

- Social movements can stretch their objectives and activities to win recruits who are not initially sympathetic to the movement's original aims. This may involve a watering down of the movement's ideals. Alternatively, movement leaders may decide to take action calculated to appeal to non-sympathizers on grounds that have little or nothing to do with the movement's purpose. When rock, punk, hip hop, or reggae bands play at nuclear disarmament rallies or gay liberation festivals, it is not necessarily because the music is relevant to the movement's goals, and bands do not play just because movement members want to be entertained. The purpose is also to attract non-members. Once attracted by the music, however, non-members may make friends and acquaintances in the movement and then be encouraged to attend a more serious-minded meeting.

As we see, then, there are many ways in which social movements can make their ideas more appealing to a larger number of people. However, movements must also confront the fact that their opponents routinely seek to do just the opposite. That is, while movements seek to align their goals, ideas, and activities with the way potential recruits frame issues, their adversaries seek to *disalign* the way issues are framed by movements and potential recruits.

The B.C. Forest Alliance provides a good illustration of this process (Doyle, Elliott, and Tindall, 1997). Launched in British Columbia in 1991, the B.C. Forest Alliance was created and bankrolled by a group of senior forest industry executives and guided by the world's largest public relations firm. Its goal was to counter the province's environmental movement. It did so in two main ways. First, in its TV and print ads, the alliance claimed it represented the "middle ground" in the debate between forest companies and environmentalists. In practice, the alliance rarely criticized forest companies, while it routinely characterized environmentalists as dope-smoking hippies with untenable ideas, such as shutting down the entire forest industry. Actually, very few environmentalists hold such extreme opinions, and research shows that the middle class in British Columbia broadly supports environmental groups.

The second way the alliance sought to counter the environmental movement was by arguing that more environmentalism means fewer jobs. This was a huge oversimplification. Job losses in the forest industry were also caused by the introduction of new technologies in some areas, aging equipment in others, First Nations land claims, and resource depletion because of overharvesting and inadequate reforestation. Muddying the waters in this way is typical of social movement opponents. Frame alignment should therefore be viewed as a conflict-ridden process in which social movement partisans and their opponents use all the resources at their disposal to compete for the way in which potential recruits and sympathizers view movement issues.

An Application of Frame Alignment Theory: Back to 1968

Frame alignment theory stresses the strategies employed by movement members to recruit non-members who are like-minded, apathetic, or even initially opposed to the movement's goals. Solidarity theory focuses on the broad social-structural conditions that facilitate the emergence of social movements. One theory usefully supplements the other.

The two theories certainly help clarify the 1968 high school incident described earlier in this chapter. In light of our discussion, it seems evident that two main factors prevented Robert Brym from influencing his classmates when he spoke to them about the dangers of industrial pollution from the local pulp and paper mill.

First, he lived in a poor and relatively unindustrialized region of Canada where people had few resources they could mobilize on their own behalf. Per capita income and the level of unionization were among the lowest of any province or state in North America. The unemployment rate was among the highest. In contrast, K.C. Irving, who owned the pulp and paper mill, was so powerful that most people in the region could not even conceive of the need to rebel against the conditions of life he created for them. He owned most of the industrial establishments in the province. Every daily newspaper, most of the weeklies, all of the TV stations, and most of the radio stations were his, too. Little wonder anyone rarely heard a critical word about his

operations. Many people believed that Irving could make or break local governments single-handedly. Should we therefore be surprised that mere high school students refused to take him on? In their reluctance, the students were only mimicking their parents, who, on the whole, were as powerless as Irving was mighty (Brym, 1979).

Second, many of Robert's classmates did not share his sense of injustice. Most of them regarded Irving as the great provider. They saw that his pulp and paper mill, as well as his myriad other industrial establishments, gave many people jobs. They regarded that fact as more important for their lives and the lives of their families than the pollution problem Robert raised. Frame alignment theory suggests Robert needed to figure out ways to build bridges between their understanding and his. He did not. Therefore, he received an unsympathetic hearing.

LO⁷ NEW SOCIAL MOVEMENTS

We can now turn to this chapter's final goal: sketching the history and prospects of social movements in broad, rapid strokes.

Around 1700, the modern state crystallized in Europe. Typically, each new state amalgamated several regions that might be distinguished from one another by ethnicity, language, or religion into a single entity with a central government, a national language, a unified army, and a flag and anthem. For the next 250 years, social movements responded to the new political structure they faced by extending their focus from local to national issues. They became larger and generally less violent. Often, they struggled to expand the rights of citizens, fighting at first for the right to free speech, freedom of religion, and justice before the law; next for the right to vote and run for office; and then, in the twentieth century, for the right to a certain minimum level of economic security and full participation in social life (Marshall, 1965; Tilly, 1979a, 1979b).

In the 1960s, political structures started to undergo massive changes once again under the forces of globalization. "New social movements" responded by setting even broader goals, attracting new kinds of participants, and becoming global in scope (Melucci, 1980, 1995). Let us consider each of these issues in turn.

Goals

Some new social movements promote the rights not of specific groups but of humanity as a whole to peace, security, and a clean environment. Such movements include the peace movement, the environmental movement, and the human rights movement. Other new social movements, such as the women's movement, the gay rights movement, and the Idle No More movement in Canada, seek to advance the rights of particular groups that have been excluded from full social participation. For example, gay rights groups have fought for laws that eliminate all forms of discrimination based on sexual orientation. They have also fought for the repeal of laws that discriminate on the basis of sexual orientation, such as anti-sodomy laws and laws that negatively affect parental custody of children (Adam, Duyvendak, and Krouwel, 1999).

Since the 1960s, the women's movement has succeeded in getting admission practices altered in professional schools, winning more freedom of reproductive choice for women, and opening up opportunities for women in the political, religious, military, educational, medical, and business systems (Adamson, Briskin, and McPhail, 1988). The Idle No More movement emerged in 2011 to promote land claims, environmental protection, and other issues of particular concern to Canada's First Nations. The emergence of such movements involves the extension of citizenship rights to all adult members of society and to society as a whole (Roche, 1995; Turner, 1986: 85–105).

Membership

New social movements are also novel in that they attract a disproportionately large number of highly educated, relatively well-to-do people from the social, educational, and cultural fields. Such people include teachers, professors, journalists, social workers, artists, actors, writers, and student apprentices to these occupations. For several reasons, people in these occupations are more likely to participate in new social movements than are people in other occupations. Their higher education exposes them to radical ideas and makes those ideas appealing. They tend to hold jobs outside the business community, which often opposes their values. And they often become personally involved in the problems of their clients and audiences, sometimes even becoming their advocates (Brint, 1984; Rootes, 1995).

Not coincidentally, the explosion of native activism that Canada has recently witnessed with the emergence of the Idle No More movement is largely the doing of university-educated Aboriginals. There were just a few hundred Aboriginal students in Canada's colleges and universities in the 1970s, but now there are more than 30 000. Two-thirds of them are women. They have high expectations about their careers, they are eager to achieve equality with the rest of the country, and they have given a loud, articulate voice to the aspirations of their community (Friesen, 2013).

The Idle No More movement is led mainly by university-educated First Nations women.

Globalization Potential

Finally, new social movements increase the scope of protest beyond the national level. For example, members of the peace movement viewed federal laws banning nuclear weapons as necessary. Environmentalists felt the same way about federal laws protecting the environment. However, environmentalists also recognized that the condition of the Brazilian rainforest affects climatic conditions worldwide. Similarly, peace activists understood that the spread of weapons of mass destruction could destroy all of humanity. Therefore, members of the peace and environmental movements pressed for *international* agreements binding all countries to protect the environment and stop the spread of nuclear weapons. Social movements went global.

Inexpensive international travel and communication facilitate the globalization of social movements. New technologies make it easier for people in various national movements to work with like-minded activists in other countries. In the age of CNN, inexpensive jet transportation, fax machines, websites, Skype, instant messaging, Facebook, and e-mail, it is possible not only to see the connection between apparently local problems and their global sources, but also to act both locally and globally.

Consider the Occupy movement, which spread quickly across the world in 2011, after Vancouver's anti-consumerist magazine, *Adbusters,* urged people to occupy Wall Street in protest against growing economic inequalities and the ravages of the Great Recession of 2008–09. Soon, scores of thousands of people in nearly a hundred cities in 82 countries took over parks and other public areas, holding demonstrations and setting up tent communities. They were mainly "millennials," people born after the early 1980s, who shared a deep sense of the injustice of growing economic inequality and recognized that only a mass movement could hold out the hope of real change (see the Sociology on the Tube feature in this chapter).

The remarkable spread of the Occupy Movement was facilitated by television stations with global reach, such as CNN, the BBC, and al Jazeera. Facebook, Twitter, Skype, and other Internet applications were widely used to coordinate protest activities. These media demonstrated the potential of new social movements to mobilize large numbers of people quickly and effectively in the era of instant, globalized communication.

Still, one must be careful not to exaggerate the role of the Internet in fostering the emergence and spread of

Mr. Robot

Elliot Alderson suffers from some kind of mental disorder. He snorts morphine to cope. And he hates the way the top 1 percent of the top 1 percent controls the planet and grows ever richer by conning people, stealing from them, and manipulating their "needs." In an early episode of *Mr. Robot*, someone says, "Give a man a gun and he'll rob a bank. Give a man a bank and he'll rob the world." It's an attitude that pervades the TV series and, presumably, mirrors the views of many of its fans.

Elliot works for a cybersecurity firm by day and hacks the computers of people he doesn't like by night. But given his precarious mental state, we have to wonder whether his unfolding drama is real or imagined. Is the head of a hacker group trying to recruit Elliot to delete records of most of the world's personal debt from E Corp computers, thus massively and almost instantly redistributing global wealth? Is E Corp trying to recruit Elliot to prevent hackers from wiping their servers clean? Could Elliot be working both sides at once?

Sam Esmail, the creator of *Mr. Robot*, has concocted a powerful formula for capturing his audience's attention: he draws a clear and rigid line between good and evil while injecting enough uncertainty into the boundary between reality and fantasy to keep us guessing. It helps that he cast the understated but intense Rami Malek as the hoodie-wearing Elliot, whose bulging eyes simultaneously suggest barely repressed rage over the world's injustices and the capacity to penetrate deeply into the working of people's minds, their computers, and their society.

At the same time, *Mr. Robot* raises important sociological questions.

Critical Thinking Questions

1. Based on what you have learned in this chapter, why might it not be possible for a small band of radical hackers to create enduring change at a global level? What other conditions would have to be in place to effect such change?
2. Even if a hacker group managed to delete the records of most of the world's personal debt, would that be enough to ensure a permanently lower level of economic equality in the world? What other changes would be needed to ensure a permanently lower level of economic equality?

Elliott Anderson meets Mr. Robot.

USA Network/Photofest

global social movements. For example, some analysts have referred to the democracy movement that swept the Middle East and North Africa in 2010–11 as a "Twitter Revolution" or a "Facebook Revolution" because these Internet applications were used as organizing tools during the uprising in Tunisia, Egypt, and elsewhere in the region. However, survey research conducted in Egypt during this period paints a more subtle picture. While using new electronic communications media was associated with being a demonstrator, other factors were more important in distinguishing demonstrators from mere sympathetic onlookers. Protesters tended to be people with strong grievances related to unemployment, poverty, and corruption. They were more available for protest activities than others were because they tended to be unmarried men living in cities. And they tended to have strong, pre-existing ties to various charitable, political, and other civic associations. The use of new electronic communications media was less important than were strong grievances, high availability, and dense social connections in distinguishing demonstrators from sympathetic onlookers (Brym et al., 2014).

The connection between computerized communication and the Egyptian uprising of 2011 is evident from this protester's demand for the overthrow of dictator Hosni Mubarak.

PATRICK BAZ/AFP/Getty Images

The globalization of social movements can be further illustrated by coming full circle and returning to the anecdote with which we began this chapter. In 1991, Robert Brym visited his hometown. He hadn't been back in years. As he entered the city, he vaguely sensed that something was different. "I wasn't able to identify the change until I reached the pulp and paper mill," says Robert. "Suddenly, it was obvious. The rotten-egg smell was now faint. I discovered that in the 1970s, a local woman whose son developed a serious case of asthma took legal action against the mill and eventually won. The mill owner was forced by law to install a 'scrubber' in the main smokestack to remove most of the sulphur dioxide emissions. Soon, the federal government was putting pressure on the mill owner to purify the polluted water that poured out of the plant and into the local river system."

Apparently, local citizens and the environmental movement had caused a deep change in the climate of opinion. This change influenced the government to force the mill owner to spend millions of dollars to clean up his operation. It took decades, but what was political heresy in 1968 became established practice by 1991. That is because environmental concerns had been amplified by the voice of a movement that had grown to global proportions. In general, as this case illustrates, globalization helps ensure that many new social movements transcend local and national boundaries and promote universalistic goals.

CONCLUSION

For many thousands of years, humans have done well on this planet. That is because we have created cultural practices, including technologies, that have allowed us to adapt to and thrive in our environment. Nonetheless, there have been some failures along the way. Many tribes and civilizations are extinct. And our success to date as a species is no warrant for the future. If we persist in using technologies that create an inhospitable environment, nature will deal with us in the same way it always deals with species that cannot adapt.

Broadly speaking, we have two survival strategies to cope with the challenges that lie ahead: competition and cooperation. Charles Darwin wrote famously about competition in *On the Origin of Species* (1859). He observed that members of each species struggle against one another and against other species in their struggle to survive. Most of the quickest, the strongest, the best camouflaged, and the smartest live long enough to bear offspring. Most of the rest are killed off. Thus, the traits passed on to offspring are those most valuable for survival. Ruthless competition, it turns out, is a key survival strategy of all species, including humans.

In *The Descent of Man*, Darwin mentioned our second important survival strategy: cooperation. In some species, mutual assistance is common. The species members that flourish are those that best learn to help one another (Darwin, 1871:163). The Russian geographer and naturalist Petr Kropotkin (1908 [1902]) elaborated on this idea. After spending five years studying animal life in Siberia, he concluded that "mutual aid" is at least as important a survival strategy as competition. Competition takes place when members of the same species compete for limited resources, said Kropotkin. Cooperation occurs when species members struggle against adverse environmental circumstances. According to Kropotkin, survival in the face of environmental threat is best assured if species members help one another. Kropotkin also showed that the most advanced species in any group—ants among insects, mammals among vertebrates, humans among mammals—are the most cooperative. Many evolutionary biologists now accept Kropotkin's ideas (Gould, 1988; Nowak, May, and Sigmund, 1995: 81).

As we have seen, a strictly competitive approach to dealing with the environmental crisis—relying on the market alone to solve our problems—now seems inadequate. Instead, it appears we require more cooperation and self-sacrifice. This involves pressuring governments and corporations, substantially reducing consumption, paying higher taxes for environmental cleanup and energy-efficient industrial processes, subsidizing the developing countries to industrialize in an environmentally friendly way, and so on. Previously, we outlined some grave consequences of relying too little on a cooperative survival strategy at this historical juncture. But which strategy you emphasize in your own life is, of course, your choice.

Similarly, throughout this book—when we discussed families, gender inequality, crime, race, population, and many other topics—we raised social issues lying at the intersection of history, social structure, and biography. We arrayed these issues on our sociological compass, set out alternative courses of action, and outlined their consequences. We thus followed our disciplinary mandate: helping people make informed choices based on sound sociological knowledge (Wilensky, 1997). In the context of the present chapter, however, we can make an even bolder claim for the discipline: Conceived at its broadest, sociology promises to help in the rational and equitable evolution of humankind.

Courtesy of Robert Brym

Sociology promises to help in the rational and equitable evolution of humankind.

READY TO STUDY?

IN THE BOOK, YOU CAN:

❏ Tear out the chapter review card at the back of the book to have a summary of the chapter and key terms handy.

ONLINE YOU CAN:

❏ Work through key concepts with a Guided Learning Question.

❏ Prepare for tests with quizzes.

❏ Review the key terms with flash cards.

❏ Explore practical examples of chapter concepts with Connect a Concept exercises.

GO TO NELSON.COM/STUDENT TO ACCESS THESE DIGITAL RESOURCES.

REFERENCES

Abortion Rights Coalition of Canada. 2016. *Statistics—Abortion in Canada*. Retrieved September 30, 2016 (http://www.arcc-cdac.ca/backrounders/statistics-abortion-in-canada.pdf).

Abraham, Carolyn. 2003. "Hong Kong Hotel Is Focus of Pneumonia Investigation." *Globe and Mail*, March 20. Retrieved June 16, 2003 (http://globeandmail.workopolis.com/servlet/Content/fasttrack/20030320/UBUGGN?section =Healthcare).

Abraham, Laurie Kaye. 1993. *Mama Might Be Better Off Dead: The Failure of Health Care in Urban America*. Chicago: University of Chicago Press.

Adam, Barry, Jan Willem Duyvendak, and Andre Krouwel. 1999. *The Global Emergence of Gay and Lesbian Politics*. Philadelphia: Temple University Press.

Adams, Henry E., Lester W. Wright, Jr., and Bethany A. Lohr. 1998. "Is Homophobia Associated with Homosexual Arousal?" *Journal of Abnormal Psychology* 105: 440–45.

Adams, Michael. 1997. *Sex in the Snow: Canadian Social Values at the End of the Millennium*. Toronto: Penguin.

Adamson, Nancy, Linda Briskin, and Margaret McPhail. 1988. *Feminist Organizing for Change: The Contemporary Women's Movement in Canada*. Toronto: Oxford University Press.

Adherents.com. 2001. *Religion Statistics: Predominant Religions*. Retrieved November 30, 2001 (http://www.adherents.com/adh_predom.html).

Adler, Patricia A., and Peter Adler. 1998. *Peer Power: Preadolescent Culture and Identity*. New Brunswick, NJ: Rutgers University Press.

Akwagyiram, Alexis. 2009. "Hip-Hop Comes of Age." *BBC News*. Retrieved October 12 (http://news.bbc.co.uk/2/hi/uk_news/magazine/8303041.stm).

Albas, Daniel, and Cheryl Albas. 1989. "Modern Magic: The Case of Examinations." *The Sociological Quarterly* 30: 603–13.

Albelda, Randy, and Chris Tilly. 1997. *Glass Ceilings and Bottomless Pits: Women's Work, Women's Poverty*. Boston: South End Press.

Alexa. 2016. *The top 500 sites on the Web*. Retrieved October 4, 2016 (http://www.alexa.com/topsites).

Amato, Paul R., and Bruce Keith. 1991. "Parental Divorce and the Well-Being of Children: A Meta-Analysis." *Psychological Bulletin* 110: 26–46.

Ambert, Anne-Marie. 1998. "Divorce: Facts, Figures and Consequences." Vanier Institute of the Family. Retrieved February 17, 2000 (http://www.vifamily.ca/cft/divorce/divorcer.htm).

American Library Association. 2013. Banned and Challenged Books. "Top 100 Banned/Challenged Books: 2000–2009." (Retrieved from http://www.ala.org/bbooks/top-100-bannedchallenged-books-2000-2009.)

American Psychiatric Association. n.d. *Obsessive Compulsive and Related Disorders*. Retrieved March 1, 2016 (http://www.dsm5.org/Documents/Obsessive%20Compulsive%20Disorders%20Fact%20Sheet.pdf).

American Psychological Association. 1998. "Answers to Your Questions about Sexual Orientation and Homosexuality." Retrieved June 14, 2000 (http://www.apa.org/pubinfo/orient.html).

American Society of Plastic Surgeons. 2012. "2011 Quick Facts." Retrieved November 6, 2012 (http://www.plasticsurgery.org/News-and-Resources/2011-Statistics-.html).

American Society of Plastic Surgeons. 2015. *Plastic Surgery Statistics Report*. Retrieved July 6, 2015 (http://www.plasticsurgery.org/Documents/news-resources/statistics/2014-statistics/plastic-surgery-statsitics-full-report.pdf).

_____. 2016. *2015 Plastic Surgery Report*. https://www.plasticsurgery.org/news/plastic-surgery-statistics.

American Sociological Association. 1999. *Code of Ethics and Policies and Procedures of the ASA Committee on Professional Ethics*. Washington, DC: Author.

Anderson, Benedict O. 1991. *The Imagined Community*, rev. ed. London, UK: Verso.

Anderson, Craig, and Brad J. Bushman. 2002. "The Effects of Media Violence on Society." *Science* 295, 5564: 2377–79.

Anderson, Gerald F., Uwe E. Reinhardt, Peter S. Hussey, and Varduhi Petrosyan. 2003. "It's the Prices, Stupid: Why the United States Is So Different from Other Countries." *Health Affairs* 22, 3: 89–105.

Anderson, Michael. 2003. "Reading Violence in Boys' Writing." *Language Arts* 80, 3: 223–31.

Anderssen, Erin. 2014. "Sex on campus: How no means no became yes means yes." *Globe and Mail* 14 November. Retrieved August 29, 2015 (http://www.theglobeandmail.com/life/relationships/sex-on-campus-how-no-means-no-became-yes-means-yes/article21598708/?page=all).

Anesi, Charles. 1997. *The Titanic Casualty Figures*. Based on *British Parliamentary Papers*, "Shipping Casualties (Loss of the Steamship 'Titanic')," 1912, cmd. 6352, "Report of a Formal Investigation into the circumstances attending the foundering on the 15th April, 1912, of the British Steamship 'Titanic,' of Liverpool, after striking ice in or near Latitude 41°46' N., Longitude 50°14' W., North Atlantic Ocean, whereby loss of life ensued." London, UK: His Majesty's Stationery Office, 1912. Retrieved March 11, 2010 (http://www.anesi.com/titanic.htm).

Angus Reid Global Monitor. 2009. "Views on Health Care Differ in Canada, U.S." Retrieved April 2, 2010 (http://www.angus-reid.com/polls/view/33946).

Angus Reid Global Monitor. 2010. "U.S., Britain and Canada Endorse Death Penalty." Retrieved March 8, 2010 (http://www.angus-reid.com/polls/view/us_britain_and_canada_endorse_death_penalty).

Angus Reid Public Opinion. 2013. "Canadians Have Mixed Feelings on Abortion, But Shun a New Debate." (Retrieved from http://www.angus-reid.com/polls/48613/canadians-have-mixed-feelings-on-abortion-but-shun-a-new-debate).

Ariès, Phillipe. 1962 [1960]. *Centuries of Childhood: A Social History of Family Life*, Robert Baldick, trans. New York: Knopf.

Arnett, Jeffrey Jensen. 1995. "Adolescents' Uses of Media for Self-Socialization." *Journal of Youth and Adolescence* 24: 519–33.

Asch, Solomon. 1955. "Opinion and Social Pressure." *Scientific American* July: 31–35.

Associated Press. 2005. "Writer: Pope Expressed Concern over Harry Potter Books." *USA Today*, 14 July. (Retrieved from http://usatoday30 .usatoday.com/news/world/2005-07 -14-pope-potter_x.htm.)

Averett, Susan, and Sanders Korenman. 1996. "The Economic Reality of The Beauty Myth." *Journal of Human Resources* 31: 304–30.

Baer, Doug. 1999. "Educational Credentials and the Changing Occupational Structure," pp. 92–106 in James Curtis, Edward Grabb, and Neil Guppy, eds., *Social Inequality in Canada: Patterns, Problems, Policies*, 3rd ed. Scarborough, ON: Prentice Hall Allyn and Bacon Canada.

Bagdikian, Ben H. 1997. *The Media Monopoly*, 5th ed. Boston: Beacon.

Balkissoon, Denise. 2011. "The Seven Habits of Highly Effective Lesbian Families." *Globe and Mail* 4 November. Retrieved February 2, 2013 (http:// www.theglobeandmail.com).

Baran, Paul A. 1957. *The Political Economy of Growth*. New York: Monthly Review Press.

Barlow, Maude, and Elizabeth May. 2000. *Frederick Street: Life and Death on Canada's Love Canal*. Toronto: HarperCollins.

Barna, G. 2002. *Grow Your Church from the Outside In: Understanding the Unchurched and How to Reach Them*. Ventura, CA: Regal Books.

Bar-On, Dan. 1999. *The Indescribable and the Undiscussable: Reconstructing Human Discourse after Trauma*. Ithaca, NY: Cornell University Press.

Barry, Patricia. 2002a. "Ads, Promotions Drive Up Drug Costs." AARP.

_____. 2002b. "Drug Industry Spends Huge Sums Guarding Prices." AARP.

_____. 2002c. "Drug Profits vs. Research." AARP.

Barth, Fredrik, ed. 1969. *Ethnic Groups and Boundaries: The Social Organization of Cultural Difference*. Boston: Little, Brown.

Baudrillard, Jean. 1983. *Simulations*. New York: Semiotext (e).

_____. 1988 [1986]. *America*, Chris Turner, trans. London, UK: Verso.

Bauer, Nancy. 2010. "Lady Power." *New York Times*, 20 June. (Retrieved from http://opinionator.blogs.nytimes .com/2010/06/20/lady-power/?_r=0).

Bauman, Zygmunt. 1989. *Modernity and the Holocaust*. Ithaca, NY: Cornell University Press.

Beach, Jane, Martha Friendly, Carolyn Ferns, Nina Prabhu, and Barry Forer. 2009. *Early Childhood Education and Care in Canada 2008*, 8th ed. Ottawa, ON: Childcare Resource and Research Unit.

Beaupré, Pascale, Pierre Turcotte, and Anne Milan. 2007. "When Is Junior Moving Out? Transitions from the Parental Home to Independence." *Canadian Social Trends* 82: 9–15. Statistics Canada. Catalogue No. 11-008-XPE. Retrieved March 26, 2007 (http://www.statcan.ca/english/ freepub/11-008-XIE/2006002/pdf/11 -008-XIE20060029274.pdf).

Beck, Ulrich. 1992 [1986]. *Risk Society: Towards a New Modernity*, Mark Ritter, trans. London, UK: Sage.

Becker, Howard S. 1963. *Outsiders: Studies in the Sociology of Deviance*. New York: Free Press.

Bell, Daniel. 1973. *The Coming of Post-Industrial Society: A Venture in Social Forecasting*. New York: Basic Books.

Bellow, Saul. 1964. *Herzog*. New York: Fawcett World Library.

Benford, Robert D. 1997. "An Insider's Critique of the Social Movement Framing Perspective." *Sociological Inquiry* 67: 409–39.

Berens, Michael J. 2002. "Infection Epidemic Carves Deadly Path." *Chicago Tribune*, 21 July. Retrieved June 16, 2003 (http://www .chicagotribune.com/news/specials/ chi-0207210272jul21.story).

Berger, Peter L., and Thomas Luckmann. 1966. *The Social Construction of Reality: A Treatise in the Sociology of Knowledge*. Garden City, NY: Doubleday.

Berk, Sarah Fenstermaker. 1985. *The Gender Factory: The Apportionment of Work in American Households*. New York: Plenum.

Berliner, Wendy. 2004. "Where Have All the Young Men Gone?" *Manchester Guardian* 18 May: 8.

Betcherman, Gordon, and Graham Lowe. 1997. *The Future of Work in Canada: A Synthesis Report*. Ottawa: Canadian Policy Research Networks Inc.

Bianchi, Suzanne M., and Daphne Spain. 1996. "Women, Work, and Family in America." *Population Bulletin* 51, 3: 2–48.

Bibby, Reginald W. 1987. *Fragmented Gods: The Poverty and Potential of Religion in Canada*. Toronto: Irwin.

_____. 2001. *Canada's Teens: Today, Yesterday, and Tomorrow*. Toronto: Stoddart.

_____. 2002. *Restless Gods: The Renaissance of Religion in Canada*. Toronto: Stoddart.

_____. 2004. *Restless Churches: How Canada's Churches Can Contribute to the Emerging Religious Renaissance*. Ottawa: Novalis.

_____. 2005. *Project Canada National Survey Series*. Lethbridge, AB: University of Lethbridge.

_____. 2006. *The Boomer Factor: What Canada's Most Famous Generation Is Leaving Behind*. Toronto: Bastian.

_____. 2011. "Religion," pp. 309–34 in Robert J. Brym, ed. *New Society*, 6th ed. Toronto: Nelson.

Bibby, Reginald, and Angus Reid, 2015. *Angus Reid Institute Religion Survey*.

Biegler, Rebecca S. 1999. "Psychological Interventions Designed to Counter Sexism in Children: Empirical Limitations and Theoretical Foundations," pp. 129–52 in William B. Swann, Jr., Judith H. Langlois, and Lucia A. Gilbert, eds., *Sexism and Stereotypes in Modern Society: The Gender Science of Janet Taylor Spence*. Washington, DC: American Psychological Association.

Bierstedt, Robert. 1963. *The Social Order: An Introduction to Sociology*. New York: McGraw-Hill.

_____. 1974. "An Analysis of Social Power," pp. 220–41 in *Power and Progress: Essays in Sociological Theory*. New York: McGraw-Hill.

Bishop Strachan School (The). 2015. *Tuition & Fees*. Retrieved August 8, 2015 (http://www.bss.on.ca/apply/ tuition-fees).

Bissinger, Buzz. "Caitlyn Jenner: The Full Story." *Vanity Fair*, July 2015. Retrieved August 28, 2015 (http:// www.vanityfair.com/hollywood/ 2015/06/caitlyn-jenner-bruce -cover-annie-leibovitz).

Bittman, Michael, and Judy Wajcman. 2000. "The Rush Hour: The Character of Leisure Time and Gender Equity." *Social Forces* 79: 165–89.

Blaise, Clark. 2001. *Time Lord: The Remarkable Canadian Who Missed His Train and Changed the World*. Toronto: Knopf Canada.

Blau, Peter M. 1964. *Exchange and Power in Social Life*. New York: Wiley.

Blauner, Robert. 1972. *Racial Oppression in America*. New York: Harper & Row.

Blazer, Dan G., Ronald C. Kessler, Katherine A. McGonagle, and Marvin S. Swartz. 1994. "The Prevalence and Distribution of Major Depression in a National Community Sample: The National Comorbidity Survey." *American Journal of Psychiatry* 151: 979–86.

Bloomberg Game Changers: Mark Zuckerberg. 2010 (Bloomberg video). Retrieved October 9, 2010 (http://www.bloomberg.com/video/63583008).

Bloomberg News. 2013. "Eye-Stinging Beijing Air Risks Lifelong Harm to Babies." *Bloomberg News*, 6 February. Retrieved February 6, 2013 (http://www.bloomberg.com/news/2013-02-06/eye-stinging-beijing-air-risks-lifelong-harm-to-babies.html).

Blossfeld, Hans-Peter, and Yossi Shavit, eds. 1993. *Persistent Inequality: Changing Educational Attainment in Thirteen Countries*. Boulder, CO: Westview Press.

Blum, Deborah. 1997. *Sex on the Brain: The Biological Differences between Men and Women*. New York: Penguin.

Blumberg, Paul. 1989. *The Predatory Society: Deception in the American Marketplace*. New York: Oxford University Press.

Blumer, Herbert. 1969. *Symbolic Interactionism: Perspective and Method*. Englewood Cliffs, NJ: Prentice-Hall.

Boal, Mark. 1998. "Spycam City." *The Village Voice*, 30 September–6 October. Retrieved March 26, 2001 (http://www.villagevoice.com/issues/9840/boal.shtml).

Böhm, Bettina, Hans Zollner, Jörg M. Fegert, and Hubert Liebhart. 2014. "Child Sexual Abuse in the Context of the Roman Catholic Church: A Review of the Literature from 1981–2013." *Journal of Child Sexual Abuse* 23: 635–56.

Bonacich, Edna. 1972. "A Theory of Ethnic Antagonism: The Split Labor Market." *American Sociological Review* 37: 547–59.

Bookman, Sonia. 2014. "Social Media: Implications for Social Life," pp. 64–74 in Robert Brym, ed., *Society in Question*, 7th ed. Toronto: Nelson.

Boorstin, Daniel J. 1992. *The Image: A Guide to Pseudoevents in America*. New York: Vintage.

Bornholt, Laurel. 2001. "Self-Concepts, Usefulness and Behavioural Intentions on the Social Context of Schooling." *Educational Psychology* 21, 1; March: 67–78.

Boroditsky, Lera. 2010. "Lost in Translation." *Wall Street Journal*, 23 July. (Retrieved from http://online.wsj.com/article/SB100014240527 48703467304575383131592767 868.html).

Boston Women's Health Book Collective, ed. 1998. *Our Bodies, Our Selves for the New Century: A Book by and for Women*. New York: Simon & Schuster.

Boswell, A. Ayres, and Joan Z. Spade. 1996. "Fraternities and Collegiate Rape Culture: Why Are Some Fraternities More Dangerous Places for Women?" *Gender and Society* 10: 133–47.

Bourdieu, Pierre. 1977 [1972]. *Outline of a Theory of Practice*, Richard Nice, trans. Cambridge, UK: Cambridge University Press.

_____. 1986. "The Forms of Capital," pp. 241–58 in John Richardson, ed., *Handbook of Theory and Research for the Sociology of Education*. New York: Greenwood.

_____. 1998. *Acts of Resistance: Against the Tyranny of the Market*, Richard Nice, trans. New York: New Press.

Bourdieu, Pierre, and Jean-Claude Passeron. 1990. *Reproduction in Education, Society and Culture*, 2nd ed., Richard Nice, trans. London, UK: Sage.

Bowles, Samuel, and Herbert Gintis. 1976. *Schooling in Capitalist America: Educational Reform and the Contradictions of Economic Life*. New York: Basic Books.

Boyce, Jillian, Adam Cotter, and Samuel Perreault. 2014. *Police-reported crime statistics in Canada, 2013*. Retrieved July 23, 2015 (http://www.statcan.gc.ca/pub/85-002-x/2014001/article/14040-eng.pdf).

Boychuk, Gerard W. 2002. "Federal Spending in Health: Why Here? Why Now?" pp. 121–36 in G. Bruce Doern, ed., *How Ottawa Spends 2002–2003: The Security Aftermath and National Priorities*. Toronto: Oxford University Press.

Boyd, Monica. 1997. "Feminizing Paid Work." *Current Sociology* 45, 2; April: 49–73.

Boyer, Dana. 2012. "Homeschooling 101." *Canadian Living*. Retrieved February 15, 2013 (http://www.canadianliving.com/moms/family _life/homeschooling_101.php).

Braithwaite, John. 1981. "The Myth of Social Class and Criminality Revisited." *American Sociological Review* 46: 36–57.

_____. 1989. *Crime, Shame and Reintegration*. New York: Cambridge University Press.

Braver, Sanford L., Pamela J. Fitzpatrick, and R. Curtis Bay. 1991. "Noncustodial Parent's Report of Child Support Payments." *Family Relations* 40, 2; April: 180–85.

Brechin, Steven R., and Willett Kempton. 1994. "Global Environmentalism: A Challenge to the Postmaterialism Thesis." *Social Science Quarterly* 75: 245–69.

Brennan, Richard J. 2012. "Majority of Canadians support return of death penalty." *Toronto Star* 8 February 2012. Retrieved July 26, 2015 http://www.thestar.com/news/canada/2012/02/08/majority_of _canadians_support_return_of _death_penalty_poll_finds.html).

Brennan, Shannon, and Mia Dauvergne. 2011. "Police-reported crime statistics in Canada, 2010." *Juristat* p. 22. Retrieved July 5, 2015 (http://www.statcan.gc.ca/pub/85-002-x/2011001/article/11523-eng.pdf).

Bricker, Darrell, and Edward Greenspon. 2001. *Searching for Certainty: Inside the New Canadian Mindset*. Toronto: Doubleday Canada.

Brint, Stephen. 1984. "New Class and Cumulative Trend Explanations of the Liberal Political Attitudes of Professionals." *American Journal of Sociology* 90: 30–71.

Brower, David. 1975. *Training the Nihilists: Education and Radicalism in Tsarist Russia*. Ithaca, NY: Cornell University Press.

Brown, Lyn Mikel, and Carol Gilligan. 1992. *Meeting at the Crossroads:*

Women's Psychology and Girls' Development. Cambridge, MA: Harvard University Press.

Brown, Peter. 1996. *The Rise of Western Christendom: Triumph and Diversity, A.D. 200–1000.* Oxford: Blackwell.

Browning, Christopher R. 1992. *Ordinary Men: Reserve Police Battalion 101 and the Final Solution in Poland.* New York: HarperCollins.

Bruce, Steve. 1988. *The Rise and Fall of the New Christian Right: Conservative Protestant Politics in America 1978–1988.* Oxford, UK: Clarendon Press.

Bryant, Marian E. 1999. "Sentencing Aboriginal Offenders." *Law Now,* October/November: 20–21.

Brym, Robert J. 1979. "Political Conservatism in Atlantic Canada," pp. 59–79 in Robert J. Brym and R. James Sacouman, eds., *Underdevelopment and Social Movements in Atlantic Canada.* Toronto: New Hogtown Press.

_____. 1980. *Intellectuals and Politics.* London, UK: George Allen and Unwin.

_____. 2001. "Jewish Immigrants from the Former Soviet Union in Canada, 1996." *East European Jewish Affairs* 31: 36–43.

_____. 2003. "Affluence, Strikes, and Power in Canada, 1973–2000," pp. 243–53 in James Curtis, Edward Grabb, and Neil Guppy, eds., *Social Inequality in Canada: Patterns, Problems, Policies,* 4th ed. Scarborough, ON: Prentice-Hall.

_____. 2006. "How High School Drama Helped Me to Become a Sociologist: An Essay in the Sociology of Autobiography." *Canadian Journal of Sociology* 31: 245–57.

_____. 2008. "Religion, Politics, and Suicide Bombing: An Interpretative Essay." *Canadian Journal of Sociology* 33: 89–108.

_____. 2014. *2011 Census Update: A Critical Interpretation.* Toronto: Nelson.

_____. 2015. *Sociology as a Life or Death Issue,* 3rd ed. Toronto: Nelson.

_____. 2015a. "Gender Risk," pp. 106–27 in Robert Brym, *Sociology as a Life or Death Issue,* 3rd Edition. Toronto: Nelson.

Brym, Robert, and Robert Andersen. 2016. "Democracy, Women's Rights, and Public Opinion in Tunisia." *International Sociology* 31: 1–15.

Brym, Robert, Louise Birdsell Bauer, and Mitch McIvor. 2013. "Is Industrial Unrest Reviving in Canada? Strike Duration in the Early 21st Century." *Canadian Review of Sociology* 50: 227–38.

Brym, Robert, Michael Gillespie, and A. Ron Gillis. 1985. "Anomie, Opportunity, and the Density of Ethnic Ties: Another View of Jewish Outmarriage in Canada." *Canadian Review of Sociology and Anthropology* 22: 102–12.

Brym, Robert, Melissa Godbout, Andreas Hoffbauer, Gabe Menard, and Tony Huiquan Zhang. 2014. "Social Media in the 2011 Egyptian Uprising." *British Journal of Sociology* 65: 266–92

Brym, Robert, and Rhonda Lenton. 2001. *Love Online: A Report on Digital Dating in Canada.* Toronto: MSN Canada. Retrieved November 28, 2012 (http://projects.chass.utoronto.ca/brym/loveonline.pdf).

Brym, Robert, and John Lie. 2009. *Sociology: The Points of the Compass.* Toronto: Nelson.

Brym, Robert John Lie, and Steven Rytina. 2010. *Sociology: Your Compass for a New World,* 3rd ed. Toronto: Nelson.

Brym, Robert J., with the assistance of Rozalina Ryvkina. 1994. *The Jews of Moscow, Kiev and Minsk: Identity, Antisemitism, Emigration.* New York: New York University Press.

Brym, Robert, Stephanie Chung, Sarah Dulmage, and Christian Farahat. 2005. "In Faint Praise of the World Bank's Gender Development Policy." *Canadian Journal of Sociology* 30: 95–111.

Brym, Robert, William Shaffir, and Morton Weinfeld, eds. 2010. *The Jews in Canada.* Toronto: Oxford University Press.

Brzezinski, Zbigniew. 2002. "Confronting Anti-American Grievances." *New York Times,* 1 September. (Retrieved from http://www.nytimes.com/2002/09/01/opinion/confronting-anti-american-grievances.html.)

Bunge, Valerie Pottie. 2000. "Spousal Violence," pp. 11–21 in Statistics Canada, *Family Violence in Canada: A Statistical Profile 2000.* Catalogue No. 85-224-XIE. Ottawa: Minister of Industry.

Bureau of Labor Statistics, United States Department of Labor. 2013. "CPI Inflation Calculator." Retrieved March 31, 2013 (http://www.bls.gov/data/inflation_calculator.htm).

Burling, Stacey. 2011. "Hoarding May Become an Official Disorder." Philly.com, 10 January. Retrieved October 23, 2012 (http://articles.philly.com/2011-01-10/news/27020216_1_generalized-anxiety-disorder-ocd-obsessive-compulsive-disorder).

Burns, Tom, and George M. Stalker. 1961. *The Management of Innovation.* London, UK: Tavistock.

"Business of Touch (The)." 2006. Retrieved April 7, 2006 (http://www.businessoftouch.com/index2.html).

Buss, David M. 2000. *Dangerous Passion: Why Jealousy Is As Necessary As Love and Sex.* New York: Free Press.

"Calgary Transit pride bus has driver threatening to quit." 2015. *CBC News* 28 August. Retrieved August 29, 2015 (http://www.cbc.ca/news/canada/calgary/calgary-transit-pride-bus-has-driver-threatening-to-quit-1.3207061).

Campbell, Donald, and Julian Stanley. 1963. *Experimental and Quasi-Experimental Designs for Research.* Chicago: Rand McNally.

Campbell, Frances A., and Craig T. Ramey. 1994. "Effects of Early Intervention on Intellectual and Academic Achievement: A Follow-up Study of Children from Low-Income Families." *Child Development* 65: 684–99.

Campion, Edward W. 1993. "Why Unconventional Medicine?" *New England Journal of Medicine* 328: 282.

"Canada's Richest People 2015: The Top 100 Richest Canadians." 2015. *Canadian Business* 15 January. Retrieved July 27, 2015 (http://www.canadianbusiness.com/lists-and-rankings/richest-people/top-100-richest-canadians-2015).

Canadian Centre on Substance Abuse. 1999. *Canadian Profile 1999: Alcohol, Tobacco and Other Drugs.* Ottawa: Centre on Substance Abuse and Centre for Addiction and Mental Health.

Canadian Council on Social Development. 2001. *The Progress of Canada's Children 2001—Highlights.* Retrieved February 17, 2002 (http://www.ccsd.ca/pubs/2-1/pcc2001.hl.htm).

Canadian Education Association. 2007. "Public Education in Canada: Facts, Trends, and Attitudes 2007." Retrieved August 8, 2015 (http://www.cea-ace.ca/sites/default/files/cea-2007-public-education-in-canada.pdf).

Canadian Heritage. 2013. "The Consumer Book Market in Canada." Retrieved August 5, 2015 (http://www.pch.gc.ca/eng/1290026005961/1290026005964).

Canadian Institute for Health Information. 2004. *Improving the Health of Canadians*. Ottawa: Author.

Canadian Marketing Association. 2007. "Canadian Ad Spend across All Media Signals Strong Growth to 2011: CMA." *Canada Newswire*, 12 November. Retrieved from http://www.newswire.ca/en/story/142367/canadian-ad-spend-across-all-media-signals-strong-growth-to-2011-cma.

Canadian Media Research. 2006. *How Many Canadians Subscribe to Cable TV or Satellite TV?* Prepared for the Canadian Radio-television and Telecommunications Commission. Retrieved October 20, 2011 (http://www.crtc.gc.ca/eng/publications/reports/radio/cmri.htm).

Canadian Radio-television and Telecommunications Commission. 2002. "CRTC's Mandate (The)." Retrieved May 15, 2003 (http://www.crtc.gc.ca/eng/BACKGRND/Brochures/B29903.htm).

Cancer Care Nova Scotia. 2004. "Cancer Statistics in Nova Scotia." Retrieved February 27, 2008 (http://cancercare.ns.ca/media/documents/CancerinNS_Overview.pdf).

Cancio, A. Silvia, T. David Evans, and David J. Maume. 1996. "Reconsidering the Declining Significance of Race: Racial Differences in Early Career Wages." *American Sociological Review* 61: 541–56.

"Candidates Debate (The)." 1998. *MSNBC News*. Retrieved May 2, 2000 (http://msnbc.com/onair/msnbc/TimeAndAgain/archive/ken-nix/Default.asp?cp1=1).

Carbon Tracker Initiative. 2012. "Unburnable Carbon—Are the World's Financial Markets Carrying a Carbon Bubble?" Retrieved March 31, 2013 (http://www.carbontracker.org/wp-content/uploads/downloads/2012/08/Unburnable-Carbon-Full1.pdf).

Cardinal, Harold. 1977. *The Rebirth of Canada's Indians*. Edmonton: Hurtig Publishers.

"Cardinal's departure (The)." 2002. *Boston Globe* 14 December. Retrieved December 21, 2015

(http://www.boston.com/globe/spotlight/abuse/stories3/121402_editorial.htm).

Cardoso, Fernando Henrique, and Enzo Faletto. 1979. *Dependency and Development in Latin America*, Marjory Mattingly Urquidi, trans. Berkeley, CA: University of California Press.

Cardozo, Andrew, and Ravi Pendakur. n.d. *Canada's Visible Minority Population: 1967–2017*. Retrieved March 16, 2012 (http://aix1.uottawa.ca/~pendakur/pdf%20docs/VisMin_1967-2017.pdf).

Carole, Melissa. 2011. "Mental Illness? Yes, But Also Homophobia." *Globe and Mail*, October 7: A21. (Retrieved from http://www.theglobeandmail.com.)

Caron, Roger. 1979. *Go-Boy! The True Story of a Life Behind Bars*. London, UK: Arrow Books.

Carrier, Roch. 1979. *The Hockey Sweater and Other Stories*, Sheila Fischman, trans. Toronto: Anansi.

Cassidy, Barbara, Robina Lord, and Nancy Mandell. 1998. "Silenced and Forgotten Women: Race, Poverty and Disability," pp. 26–54 in Nancy Mandell, ed., *Race, Class and Sexuality*, 2nd ed. Scarborough: Prentice-Hall Allyn and Bacon.

Cavalli-Sforza, L. Luca, Paola Menozzi, and Alberto Piazza. 1994. The *History and Geography of Human Genes*. Princeton, NJ: Princeton University Press.

CBC. 2014. "Annual Report 2013–2014." Retrieved August 5, 2015 (http://www.cbc.radio-canada.ca/site/annual-reports/2013-2014/index.html).

CBC News. 2004. *Hospital Hygiene Cuts Severe Infections by 80 Per Cent*. Retrieved July 27, 2005 (http://www.cbc.ca/story/science/national/2004/01/15/hand_washque04015.html?print).

Centers for Disease Control and Prevention. 2015. "2014 Ebola Outbreak in West Africa—Case Counts." Retrieved August 7, 2015 (http://www.cdc.gov/vhf/ebola/outbreaks/2014-west-africa/case-counts.html).

Central Intelligence Agency. 2010. The *World Factbook 2010*. Retrieved March 11, 2010 (https://www.cia.gov/library/publications/the-world-factbook).

Chagnon, Napoleon. 1992. *Yanomamö: The Last Days of Eden*. New York: Harcourt, Brace Yovanovich.

Chan, Michael. 2014. "Multimodal Connectedness and Quality of Life: Examining the Influences of Technology Adoption and Interpersonal Communication on Well-Being across the Life Span." *Journal of Computer-Mediated Communication* 20: 3–18.

Chard, Jennifer. 2000. "Women in a Visible Minority," pp. 219–44 in *Women in Canada, 2000: A Gender-Based Statistical Report*. Ottawa: Statistics Canada.

Charlton, James I. 1998. *Nothing about Us without Us: Disability Oppression and Empowerment*. Berkeley, CA: University of California Press.

Chauncey, George. 2005. *Why Marriage? The History Shaping Today's Debate over Gay Equality*. New York: Basic Books.

Chaves, Mark. 1994. "Secularization as Declining Religious Authority." *Social Forces* 72: 749–74.

Cherlin, Andrew J. 1992. *Marriage, Divorce, Remarriage*, revised and enlarged ed. Cambridge, MA: Harvard University Press.

CIA. *The World Factbook 2001*. Retrieved January 10, 2002 (http://www.cia.gov/cia/publications/factbook).

CIA. *The World Factbook 2015*. "Total Fertility Rate." Retrieved August 23, 2015 (https://www.cia.gov/library/publications/the-world-factbook/fields/2127.html).

Cicourel, Aaron. 1968. *The Social Organization of Juvenile Justice*. New York: Wiley.

Citizenship and Immigration Canada. 2015. "Facts and figures 2013—Immigration overview: Permanent residents." Retrieved June 26, 2015 (http://www.cic.gc.ca/english/resources/statistics/facts2013/permanent/10.asp).

City of Toronto. "Diversity." Retrieved July 22, 2015 (http://www1.toronto.ca/wps/portal/contentonly?vgnextoid=dbe867b42d853410VgnVCM10000071d60f89RCRD&vgnextchannel=57a12cc817453410VgnVCM10000071d60f89RCRD).

Clairmont, Donald H., and Dennis W. Magill. 1999. *Africville: The Life and Death of a Canadian Black Community*, 3rd ed. Toronto: Canadian Scholars' Press.

Clark, S.D. 1968. *The Developing Canadian Community*. Toronto: University of Toronto Press.

Clark, Warren. 2003. "Pockets of Belief: Religious Attendance Patterns in Canada." *Canadian Social Trends* 68 (Spring): 2–5. Statistics Canada Catalogue No. 11-008-XPE.

Clarke, Harold D., Jane Jenson, Lawrence LeDuc, and Jon H. Pammett. 1996. *Absolute Mandate: Canadian Electoral Politics in an Era of Restructuring*, 3rd ed. Toronto: Gage.

Clarke-Stewart, K. Alison, Christian P. Gruber, and Linda May Fitzgerald. 1994. *Children at Home and in Day Care*. Hillsdale, NJ: Lawrence Erlbaum.

Clayton, Russell B., Glenn Leshner, and Anthony Almond. 2015. "The Extended Self: The Impact of iPhone Separation on Cognition, Emotion, and Physiology." *Journal of Computer-Mediated Communication* 20, 2: 119–35.

Clement, Wallace H.P. 1897. *The History of the Dominion of Canada*. Toronto: William Briggs.

Cleveland, Gordon. 2016. "What Is the Role of Early Childhood Education and Care in an Equality Agenda?" In Robert Brym, ed. *Inequality and the Future of Canadian Society*. Oakville, ON: Rock's Mills Press, pp. 76–99.

Cleveland, Gordon, and Michael Krashinsky. 1998. *The Benefits and Costs of Good Child Care: The Economic Rationale for Public Investment in Young Children*. Toronto: University of Toronto.

Clinard, Marshall B., and Peter C. Yeager. 1980. *Corporate Crime*. New York: Free Press.

Cloward, Richard A., and Lloyd E. Ohlin. 1960. *Delinquency and Opportunity: A Theory of Delinquent Gangs*. New York: Free Press.

Cockerham, William C. 1998. *Medical Sociology*, 7th ed. Upper Saddle River, NJ: Prentice-Hall.

Cohen, Albert. 1955. *Delinquent Boys: The Subculture of a Gang*. New York: Free Press.

Cohen, Lynne. 1999. "Suing the Alternative Health-Care Provider." *Canadian Lawyer*, November/December: 47–51.

Cohen, Stanley. 1972. *Folk Devils and Moral Panics: The Creation of the Mods and Rockers*. London, UK: MacGibbon and Kee.

Colapinto, John. 1997. "The True Story of John/Joan." *Rolling Stone* 11 December: 54–73, 92–97.

_____. 2001. *As Nature Made Him: The Boy Who Was Raised as a Girl*. Toronto: HarperCollins.

Cole, Michael. 1995. *Cultural Psychology*. Cambridge, MA: Harvard University Press.

Coleman, James S. 1961. *The Adolescent Society*. New York: Free Press.

_____. 1988. "Social Capital in the Creation of Human Capital." *American Journal of Sociology* 94: 95–120.

_____. 1990. *Foundations of Social Theory*. Cambridge, MA: Harvard University Press.

Coleman, James S., Ernest Q. Campbell, and Carol J. Hobson. 1966. *Equality of Educational Opportunity*. Washington, DC: United States Department of Health, Education, and Welfare, Office of Education.

Collins, Randall. 1979. *The Credential Society: An Historical Sociology of Education*. New York: Academic Press.

_____. 1982. *Sociological Insight: An Introduction to Nonobvious Sociology*. New York: Oxford University Press.

_____. 1993. "Review of *A Theory of Religion* by Rodney Stark and William S. Bainbridge." *Journal for the Scientific Study of Religion* 32, 4: 402–04, 406.

Collins, Randall, and Scott Coltrane. 1991. *Sociology of Marriage and the Family: Gender, Love, and Property*, 3rd ed. Chicago: Nelson-Hall.

_____. 1995. *Sociology of Marriage and the Family*. Chicago: Nelson-Hall.

Competition Bureau. 2002. *Comments of the Commissioner of Competition to the Standing Committee on Canadian Heritage on the Study of the State of the Canadian Broadcasting System*. Ottawa: Government of Canada.

Comte, Auguste. 1975. *Auguste Comte: The Foundation of Sociology*, Kenneth Thompson, ed. New York: Wiley.

Condry, John, and Sandra Condry. 1976. "Sex Differences: A Study of The Eye of the Beholder." *Child Development* 47: 812–19.

Conrad, Peter, and Joseph W. Schneider. 1992. *Deviance and Medicalization: From Badness to Sickness*, expanded ed. Philadelphia: Temple University Press.

Converse, Jean M., and Stanley Presser. 1986. *Survey Questions: Handcrafting the Standardized Questionnaire*. Newbury Park, CA: Sage.

Cooley, Charles Horton. 1902. *Human Nature and the Social Order*. New York: Scribner's.

Coontz, Stephanie. 1992. *The Way We Never Were: American Families and the Nostalgia Trap*. New York: Basic Books.

Cornell, Camilla. 2011. "The Real Cost of Raising Kids." *MoneySense*. June.

Costanzo, Mark. 1997. *Just Revenge: Costs and Consequences of the Death Penalty*. New York: St. Martin's Press.

Creedon, Jeremiah. 1998. "God with a Million Faces." *Utne Reader* July–August: 42–48.

Creighton, Sarah, and Catherine Mihto. 2001. "Managing Intersex." *BMJ: British Medical Journal* 323, 7324; December: 1264–65.

Crozier, Michel. 1964. *The Bureaucratic Phenomenon*. Chicago: University of Chicago Press.

CTV News. "Husband charged in connection with death of actress wife in Calgary." 5 July 2015. Retrieved August 23, 2015 (http://www.ctvnews.ca/canada/husband-charged-in-connection-with-death-of-actress-wife-in-calgary-1.2454914).

Cullum, Brannon. 2011. "Music of the revolution: How songs of protest have rallied demonstrators." *Citizen Media, Sustaining Protest Movements*. Accessed April 9, 2014 (http://www.movements.org/blog/entry/music-of-the-revolution-how-songs-of-protest-have-rallied-demonstrators).

Culver, John H. 1992. "Capital Punishment, 1997–1998: Characteristics of the 143 Executed." *Sociology and Social Research* 76, 2 (January): 59–61.

Curtis, Bruce. 1988. *Building the Educational State: Canada West, 1836–1871*. London, ON: Althouse Press.

Curtis, James, John Loy, and Wally Karnilowicz. 1986. "A Comparison of Suicide-Dip Effects of Major Sport Events and Civil Holidays." *Sociology of Sport Journal* 3: 1–14.

CyberPress. 2001. "The Recidivist Roger Caron Stopped Once Again" (translated from the French), 14 October. Retrieved October 1, 2003 (http://216.239.37.120/transl).

Dalphonse, Sherri. 1997. "Childfree by Choice." *The Washingtonian* 32, 5: 48–57.

Damisch, L., B. Stoberock, and T. Mussweiler. 2010. "Keep Your Fingers Crossed! How Superstition Improves Performance." *Psychological Science* 21, 1014–20.

Darwin, Charles. 1859. *On the Origin of Species by Means of Natural Selection.* London, UK: John Murray.

_____. 1871. *The Descent of Man.* London, UK: John Murray.

Davies, James B. 1999. "Distribution of Wealth and Economic Inequality," pp. 138–50 in James Curtis, Edward Grabb, and Neil Guppy, eds., *Social Inequality in Canada: Patterns, Problems, Policies*, 3rd ed. Scarborough, ON: Prentice Hall Allyn and Bacon Canada.

Davies, James C. 1969. "Toward a Theory of Revolution," pp. 85–108 in Barry McLaughlin, ed. *Studies in Social Movements: A Social Psychological Perspective.* New York: Free Press.

Davies, Mark, and Denise B. Kandel. 1981. "Parental and Peer Influences on Adolescents' Educational Plans: Some Further Evidence." *American Journal of Sociology* 87: 363–87.

Davies, Scott. 2013. "Education," pp. 286–309 in Robert Brym, ed. *New Society*, 7th ed. Toronto: Nelson.

Davis, Fred. 1992. *Fashion, Culture, and Identity.* Chicago: University of Chicago Press.

Davis, Kingsley, and Wilbert E. Moore. 1945. "Some Principles of Stratification." *American Sociological Review* 10: 242–49.

Davis, Mike. 1990. *City of Quartz: Excavating the Future in Los Angeles.* New York: Verso.

Davison, Janet. 2013. "Are we living in post-religious times?" *CBC News* 20 March. Retrieved August 8, 2015 (http://www.cbc.ca/news/canada/ are-we-living-in-post-religious -times-1.1362828).

Dawson, S.E. 1906. "Principal Causes of Death." Table IV. *Fourth Census of Canada, 1901, Volume IV.* Ottawa: Library and Archives Canada.

DeKeseredy, Walter S., and Katherine Kelly. 1993. "The Incidence and Prevalence of Woman Abuse in Canadian University and College Dating Relationships." *Canadian Journal of Sociology* 18: 137–59.

Demo, David H., Mark A. Fine, and Lawrence H. Ganong. 2000. "Divorce as a Family Stressor," pp. 279–302 in P. C. McKenry and S. J. Price, eds. *Families & Change: Coping with Stressful Events and Transitions*, 2nd ed. Thousand Oaks, CA: Sage.

Denis, Jeff. 2016. "Sociology of Indigenous Peoples in Canada," in Robert Brym, ed. *New Society*, 8th ed. Toronto: Nelson.

Department of Finance Canada. 2014. "Your Tax Dollar." Retrieved August 5, 2015 (http://www.fin.gc.ca/ tax-impot/2014/2013-14-e.pdf).

Department of Labor. 2015. "CPI Inflation Calculator." Retrieved August 2, 2015 (http://data.bls.gov/ cgi-bin/cpicalc.pl).

Derber, Charles. 1979. *The Pursuit of Attention: Power and Individualism in Everyday Life.* New York: Oxford University Press.

Derrida, Jacques. 2004. *Positions*, Alan Bass, trans. London, UK: Continuum.

DeSteno, David, and Peter Salovey. 2001. "Evolutionary Origins of Sex Differences in Jealousy: Questioning the 'Fitness' of the Model," pp. 150–56 in W. Gerrod Parrott, ed., *Emotions in Social Psychology: Essential Readings.* Philadelphia: Psychology Press.

Deutscher, Guy. 2010. "Does Your Language Shape How You Think?" *New York Times*, August 26. Retrieved June 7, 2011 (http://www .nytimes.com).

de Villiers, Marq. 1999. *Water.* Toronto: Stoddart Publishing.

Dietz, Tracy L. 1998. "An Examination of Violence and Gender Role Portrayals in Video Games: Implications for Gender Socialization and Aggressive Behavior." *Sex Roles* 38: 425–42.

DiMaggio, Paul. 1982. "Cultural Capital and School Success: The Impact of Status Culture Participation on the Grades of U.S. High School Students." *American Sociological Review* 47: 189–201.

DMR. 2016. "145 Amazing YouTube Statistics (October 2016)." http:// expandedramblings.com/index.php/ youtube-statistics/ (retrieved 4 October 2016).

Donahue, John J., III, and Steven D. Levitt. 2001. "The Impact of Legalized Abortion on Crime." *Quarterly Journal of Economics* 116: 379–420.

Douglas, Emily M., and Murray A. Straus. 2006. "Assault and Injury of Dating Partners by University Students in 19 Nations and Its Relation to Corporal Punishment Experienced as a Child." *European Journal of Criminology* 3: 293–318.

Doyle, Aaron, Brian Elliott, and David Tindall. 1997. "Framing the Forests: Corporations, the B.C. Forest Alliance, and the Media," pp. 240–68 in William Carroll, ed. *Organizing Dissent: Contemporary Social Movements in Theory and Practice*, 2nd ed. Toronto: Garamond Press.

"Do You Know Who Scored The First Basket in the NBA?" *The First Basket: A Jewish Basketball Documentary*, n.d.

Dranoff, Linda Silver. 2001. *Everyone's Guide to the Law.* Toronto: HarperCollins.

Duffy, Ann, and Nancy Mandell. 2011. "Poverty in Canada," pp. 125–44 in Robert J. Brym, ed. *Society in Question*, 6th ed. Toronto: Nelson.

Dugger, Karen. 1996. "Social Location and Gender-Role Attitudes: A Comparison of Black and White Women," pp. 32–51 in Esther Ngan-Ling Chow, Doris Wilkinson, and Maxine Baca Zinn, eds., *Race, Class, and Gender.* Newbury Park, CA: Sage.

Duncan, Greg, W. Jean Yeung, Jeanne Brooks-Gunn, and Judith Smith. 1998. "How Much Does Childhood Poverty Affect the Life Chance of Children?" *American Sociological Review* 63: 402–23.

Durkheim, Émile. 1938 [1895]. *The Rules of Sociological Method*, G.E.G. Catlin, ed., S.A. Solovay and J. Mueller, trans. Chicago: University of Chicago Press.

_____. 1951 [1897]. *Suicide: A Study in Sociology*, G. Simpson, ed., J. Spaulding and G. Simpson, trans. New York: Free Press.

_____. 1956. *Education and Sociology*, Sherwood D. Fox, trans. New York: Free Press.

_____. 1961 [1925]. *Moral Education: A Study in the Theory and Application of the Sociology of Education*, Everett K. Wilson and Herman Schnurer, trans. New York: Free Press.

_____. 1973 [1899–1900]. "Two Laws of Penal Evolution." *Economy and Society* 2: 285–308.

_____. 1976 [1915/1912]. *The Elementary Forms of the Religious Life*, Joseph Ward Swain, trans. New York: Free Press.

_____. 1997 [1893]. *The Division of Labor in Society*. New York: Free Press.

Dutton, Judy. 2000. "Detect His Lies Every Time." *Cosmopolitan* April: 126.

Eagley, Alice H., and Wendy Wood. 1999. "The Origins of Sex Differences in Human Behaviour: Evolved Dispositions versus Social Roles." *American Psychologist* 54: 408–23.

Eccles, Jacquelynne S., Janis E. Jacobs, and Rena D. Harold. 1990. "Gender Role Stereotypes, Expectancy Effects and Parents' Socialization of Gender Differences." *Journal of Social Issues* 46: 183–201.

Edmundson, Mark. 2003. "How Teachers Can Stop Cheaters." *New York Times*, 9 September. Retrieved September 9, 2003 (http://www.nytimes.com).

Eichler, Margrit. 1987. *Nonsexist Research Methods*. Boston: Allen and Unwin.

_____. 1988. *Families in Canada Today*, 2nd ed. Toronto: Gage.

Ekman, Paul. 1978. *Facial Action Coding System*. New York: Consulting Psychologists Press.

Elections Canada. 2012. "Voter Turnout at Federal Elections and Referendums." (Retrieved from http://www.elections.ca.)

Elliott, H. L. 1995. "Living Vicariously through Barbie." Retrieved November 19, 1998 (http://ziris.syr.edu/path/public_html/barbie/main.html).

Ellis, L., B. Robb, and D. Burke. 2005. "Sexual Orientation in United States and Canadian College Students." *Archives of Sexual Behavior* 34: 569–81.

Ellul, Jacques. 1964 [1954]. *The Technological Society*, John Wilkinson, trans. New York: Vintage.

Engels, Frederick. 1970 [1884]. *The Origins of the Family, Private Property and the State*, Eleanor Burke Leacock, ed., Alec West, trans. New York: International Publishers.

England, Paula. 1992. *Comparable Worth: Theories and Evidence*. Hawthorne, NY: Aldine de Gruyter.

Entine, J. 2000. *Taboo: Why Black Athletes Dominate Sports and Why We Are Afraid to Talk about It*. New York: Public Affairs.

Epstein, Helen. 1998. "Life and Death on the Social Ladder." *New York Review of Books*, 45, 12; July 16: 26–30.

Epstein, Steven. 1996. *Impure Science: AIDS, Activism, and the Politics of Knowledge*. Berkeley, CA: University of California Press.

Ernst, Edzard, and Max H. Pittler. 2006. "Celebrity-Based Medicine." *Medical Journal of Australia* 185, 11/12: 680–81.

Esmail, Nadeem. 2007. "Complementary and Alternative Medicine in Canada: Trends in Use and Public Attitudes, 1997–2006." *Public Policy Sources* 87. Retrieved August 7, 2015 (http://www.fraserinstitute.org/uploadedFiles/fraser-ca/Content/research-news/research/publications/complementary-alternative-medicine-in-canada-2007.pdf).

Estrich, Susan. 1987. *Real Rape*. Cambridge, MA: Harvard University Press.

Etheridge, D.M. et al. 1998. *Historical CO_2 Record from the Law Dome DE08, DE08-2, and DSS Ice Cores*. Retrieved August 2, 2015 (http://cdiac.ornl.gov/ftp/trends/co2/lawdome.combined.dat).

"Ethnic Groups in the World." *Scientific American*. Retrieved December 4, 2001 (http://www.sciam.com/1998/0998issue/0998numbers.html).

Evans, Robert G. 1999. "Social Inequalities in Health." *Horizons* (Policy Research Secretariat, Government of Canada) 2, 3: 6–7.

Facebook. 2011. "Statistics." Retrieved September 20, 2011 (http://www.facebook.com/press/info.php?statistics).

Facebook. 2012. "Key Facts." Retrieved November 26, 2012 (http://newsroom.fb.com/Key-Facts).

Facebook. 2013. "Key Facts." Retrieved April 2, 2013 (http://newsroom.fb.com/Key-Facts).

Fagot, Beverly I., Carie S. Rodgers, and Mary D. Leinbach. 2000. "Theories of Gender Socialization," pp. 65–89 in Thomas Eckes, ed., *The Developmental Social Psychology of Gender*. Mahwah, NJ: Lawrence Erlbaum Associates.

Fattah, Ezzat A. 1991. *Understanding Criminal Victimization: An Introduction to Theoretical Victimology*. Scarborough, ON: Prentice Hall.

Fausto-Sterling, Anne. 2000. "The five sexes, revisited." *The Sciences* 40: 18–23.

Febvre, Lucien, and Henri-Jean Martin. 1976 [1958]. *The Coming of the Book: The Impact of Printing 1450–1800*, David Gerard, trans. London, UK: NLB.

Federal–Provincial–Territorial Working Group on Restorative Justice, Subcommittee on Public and Justice Sector Education. 2009. Correctional Service Canada 22 December. Retrieved July 26, 2015 (http://www.csc-scc.gc.ca/restorative-justice/003005-4005-eng.shtml).

Fellegi, Ivan. 2000. "On Poverty and Low Income." In Statistics Canada, *Income in Canada 1998*. Ottawa: Ministry of Industry.

Felson, Richard B. 1996. "Mass Media Effects on Violent Behavior." *Annual Review of Sociology* 22: 103–28.

Fernandez-Dols, Jose-Miguel, Flor Sanchez, Pilar Carrera, and Maria-Angeles Ruiz-Belda. 1997. "Are Spontaneous Expressions and Emotions Linked? An Experimental Test of Coherence." *Journal of Nonverbal Behavior* 21: 163–77.

Ferns, Carolyn, and Martha Friendly. 2012. "The state of early childhood education and care in Canada 2012." Retrieved August 29, 2015 (http://childcarecanada.org/sites/default/files/StateofECEC2012.pdf).

Fields, Jason, and Kristin Smith. 1998. "Poverty, Family Structure, and Child Well-Being." Washington, DC: U.S. Bureau of Census, Population Division.

Figart, Deborah M., and June Lapidus. 1996. "The Impact of Comparable Worth on Earnings Inequality." *Work and Occupations* 23: 297–318.

Financial Post. 2014. "FP500: 2014." Retrieved August 5, 2015 (http://www.financialpost.com/news/fp500/2014/index.html).

"Finding God in Harry Potter." 2005. *The Christian Post*, 16 July. Retrieved December 14, 2005 (http://www.christianpost.com/article/education/895/section/finding.god.in.harry.potter/1.htm).

Finke, Roger, and Rodney Starke. 1992. *The Churching of America, 1776–1990: Winners and Losers in Our Religious*

Economy. New Brunswick, NJ: Rutgers University Press.

Finkel, Eli J. et al. 2012. "Online Dating: A Critical Analysis from the Perspective of Psychological Science." *Psychological Science in the Public Interest* 13: 3066.

Finnie, Ross. 1993. "Women, Men and the Economic Consequences of Divorce: Evidence from Canadian Longitudinal Data." *Canadian Review of Sociology and Anthropology* 30, 2: 205–41.

First Nations and Inuit Health: Diseases and Health Conditions." Health Canada. Retrieved August 7, 2015 (http://www.hc-sc.gc.ca/fniah-spnia/diseases-maladies/index-eng.php).

Fischer, Claude S., Michael Hout, Martín Sánchez Jankowski, Samuel R. Lucas, Ann Swidler, and Kim Voss. 1996. *Inequality by Design: Cracking the Bell Curve Myth.* Princeton, NJ: Princeton University Press.

Fisher, John. 1999. *A Report on Lesbian, Gay and Bisexual Youth.* Ottawa: Égale.

Fleras, Augie, and Jean Leonard Elliott. (2002). *Engaging Diversity: Multiculturalism in Canada.* Toronto: Nelson.

Flood, Gavin D. 1996. *An Introduction to Hinduism.* Cambridge: Cambridge University Press.

Flowers, Paul, and Katie Buston. 2001. "'I Was Terrified of Being Different:' Exploring Gay Men's Accounts of Growing-Up in a Heterosexist Society." *Journal of Adolescence.* Special Issue: *Gay, Lesbian, and Bisexual Youth* 24: 51–65.

Forbes.com. 2010. "The World's Billionaires." Retrieved March 11, 2010 (http://www.forbes.com/lists/2010/10/billionaires-2010_The-Worlds-Billionaires_Rank.html).

Forbes (Kate Vinton). 2016. *Forbes Billionaires.* "Mark Zuckerberg Gains $4 Billion to Become World's Sixth Richest Person Ahead of Larry Ellison" (http://www.forbes.com/sites/katevinton/2016/04/27/mark-zuckerberg-gains-4-billion-to-become-worlds-sixth-richest-person-ahead-of-larry-ellison/#46befcd675be)

Forman, Murray. 2001. "It Ain't All about the Benjamins: Summit on Social Responsibility in the Hip-Hop Industry." *Journal of Popular Music Studies* 13: 117–23.

Forrest, C.B., and A.W. Riley. 2004. "Childhood Origins of Adult Health: A Basis for Life-Course Health Policy." *Health Affairs* 23, 5: 155–64.

Förster, Michael, and Michele Pellizzari. 2000. "Trends and Driving Factors in Income Distribution and Poverty in the OECD Area." *Labour Market and Social Policy Occasional Papers No. 42.* Paris: OECD.

Fortin, Nicole, David A. Green, Thomas Lemieux, Kevin Milligan, and W. Craig Riddell. 2012. "Canadian Inequality: Recent Development and Policy Options." *Canadian Public Policy* 38, 2: 121–45.

Forum Research Inc. 2015. "Instagram tops in user satisfaction." Retrieved July 6, 2015 (http://poll.forumresearch.com/data/Federal%20Social%20Media%20News%20Release%20%282015%2001%2006%29%20Forum%20Research.pdf).

Foster, Deborah. 2006. "Why Do Children Do So Well in Lesbian Households?" *Canadian Woman Studies* 24, 2, 3: 51–56.

Foucault, Michael. 1973. *The Birth of the Clinic: An Archaeology of Medical Perception,* A. M. Sheridan, trans. London UK: Routledge.

_____. 1977. *Discipline and Punish: The Birth of the Prison,* Alan Sheridan, trans. New York: Vintage.

_____. 1988. *Madness and Civilization: A History of Insanity in the Age of Reason,* Richard Howard, trans. New York: Random House.

_____. 1990 [1978]. *The History of Sexuality: An Introduction,* Vol. 1. Robert Hurley, trans. New York: Vintage.

Frank Porter Graham Child Development Center. 1999. "Early Learning, Later Success: The Abecedarian Study." Retrieved August 10, 2000 (http://www.fpg.unc.edu/~abc/abecedarian Web/index.htm).

Frank, Thomas, and Matt Weiland, eds. 1997. *Commodify Your Dissent: Salvos from the Baffler.* New York: W. W. Norton.

Franklin, Karen. 1998. *Psychosocial Motivations of Hate Crime Perpetrators.* Paper presented at the annual meeting of the American Psychological Association (San Francisco: August 16).

_____. 2000. "Antigay Behaviors Among Young Adults." *Journal of Interpersonal Violence* 15, 4: 339–62.

Freedman, Samuel G. 2011. "Waging a One-Man War on American Muslims." *New York Times,* December 16. Retrieved January 13, 2013 (http://www.nytimes.com).

Freedomtoread.ca. 2015. "Challenged Works List." Retrieved August 8, 2015 (http://www.freedomtoread.ca/censorship-in-canada/challenged-works-list).

Freeman, Sunny. 2012. "Canadians Stretched to Limit as Moody's Warns of Sky-High Debt Loads." *Globe and Mail,* September 6. (Retrieved from http://www.theglobeandmail.com.)

Freidson, Eliot. 1986. *Professional Powers: A Study of the Institutionalization of Formal Knowledge.* Chicago: University of Chicago Press.

Freire, Paolo. 1972. *The Pedagogy of the Oppressed.* New York: Herder and Herder.

Frenette, Marc. 2007. "Why Are Youth from Lower-Income Families Less Likely to Attend University? Evidence from Academic Abilities, Parental Influences, and Financial Constraints." Catalogue No. 11F0019MIE. Ottawa: Statistics Canada.

Frere-Jones, Sasha. 2012 "Cold Facts." *The New Yorker* 3 August. Retrieved April 11, 2014 (http://www.newyorker.com/online/blogs/sashafrerejones/2012/08/searching-for-sugar-man-malik-bendjellou.html).

Freud, Sigmund. 1962 [1930]. *Civilization and Its Discontents,* James Strachey, trans. New York: W. W. Norton.

_____. 1973 [1915–17]. *Introductory Lectures on Psychoanalysis,* James Strachey, trans., James Strachey and Angela Richards, eds. Harmondsworth, UK: Penguin.

Freudenburg, William R. 1997. "Contamination, Corrosion and the Social Order: An Overview." *Current Sociology* 45, 3: 19–39.

Friedenberg, Edgar Z. 1959. *The Vanishing Adolescent.* Boston: Beacon Press.

Friesen, Joe. 2013. "The Future Belongs to the Young." *Globe and Mail,* January 19: A4.

Galabuzi, G.-E. 2004. *Social Inclusion as a Determinant of Health.* Ottawa: Public Health Agency of Canada.

Galper, Joseph. 1998. "Schooling for Society." *American Demographics* 20, 3: 33–34.

Gammon, Katherine. 2009. "Infoporn: Today's Playmates Are More Like Anime Figures Than Real Humans." *Wired* 17, 2.

Gamson, William A., Bruce Fireman, and Steven Rytina. 1982. *Encounters with Unjust Authority*. Homewood, IL: Dorsey Press.

Gans, Herbert. 1979. *Deciding What's News: A Study of CBS Evening News, NBC Nightly News, Newsweek and Time*. New York: Pantheon.

_____. 1991. "Symbolic Ethnicity: The Future of Ethnic Groups and Cultures in America," pp. 430–43 in Norman R. Yetman, ed., *Majority and Minority: The Dynamics of Race and Ethnicity in American Life*, 5th ed. Boston, MA: Allyn and Bacon.

Ganss, G.E., ed. 1991. *Ignatius of Loyola: The Spiritual Exercises and Selected Works*. New York: Paulist Press.

Garland, David. 1990. *Punishment and Modern Society: A Study in Social Theory*. Chicago: University of Chicago Press.

Garner, David M. 1997. "The 1997 Body Image Survey Results." *Psychology Today* 30, 1: 30–44.

Gaskell, Jane, Arlene McLaren, and Myra Novogrodsky. 1995. "What's Worth Knowing? Defining the Feminist Curriculum," pp. 100–18 in Adie D. Nelson and Barrie W. Robinson, eds., *Gender in the 1990s: Images, Realities, and Issues*. Scarborough, ON: Nelson Canada.

Gates, Gary J. 2011. "How many people are lesbian, gay, bisexual, and transgender?" *The Williams Institute* April. Retrieved August 27, 2015 (http://williamsinstitute.law.ucla.edu/wp-content/uploads/Gates-How-Many-People-LGBT-Apr-2011.pdf).

Gauvain, Mary, Beverly I. Fagot, Craig Leve, and Kate Kavanagh. 2002. "Instruction by Mothers and Fathers During Problem Solving with Their Young Children." *Journal of Family Psychology* 6, 1; March: 81–90.

Gegax, T. Trent, and Lynette Clemetson. 1998. "The Abortion Wars Come Home." *Newsweek* 9 November: 34–35.

Gelbspan, Ross. 1999. "Trading Away Our Chances to End Global Warming." *Boston Globe*, May 19: E2.

Gelles, Richard J. 1997. *Intimate Violence in Families*, 3rd ed. Thousand Oaks, CA: Sage.

Geohive.com. 2005. "The Demographical Status of the World's Population." Retrieved June 26, 2005 (http://www.geohive.com/global/geo.php?xml=world&xsl=pop_data).

Ghalam, Nancy Z. 1997. "Attitudes Towards Women, Work and Family." *Canadian Social Trends* 46: 13–17. Statistics Canada Catalogue No. 11-008-XPE.

Ghosh, Bobby. 2011. "Rage, Rap and Revolution: Inside the Arab Youth Quake." *Time.com*, 17 February. Retrieved February 17, 2011 (http://www.time.com/time/world/article/0,8599,2049808,00.html).

Giddens, Anthony. 1987. *Sociology: A Brief but Critical Introduction*, 2nd ed. New York: Harcourt Brace Jovanovich.

_____. 1990. *The Consequences of Modernity*. Stanford, CA: Stanford University Press.

Gilman, Sander L. 1991. *The Jew's Body*. New York: Routledge.

Gilmore, Scott. 2015. "Canada's race problem? It's even worse than America's." *Maclean's* 22 January. Retrieved August 2, 2015 (http://www.macleans.ca/news/canada/out-of-sight-out-of-mind-2).

Gitlin, Todd. 1983. *Inside Prime Time*. New York: Pantheon.

Gleick, James. 2000. *Faster: The Acceleration of Just About Everything*. New York: Vintage.

Glendon, Mary Ann. 1981. *The New Family and the New Property*. Toronto: Butterworths.

Glenn, Norval D. 1990. "Quantitative Research on Marital Quality in the 1980s: A Critical Review." *Journal of Marriage and the Family* 52; November: 818–31.

Glock, Charles Y. 1962. "On the Study of Religious Commitment." *Religious Education* 62, 4: 98–110.

Goddard Institute for Space Studies, National Aeronautics and Space Administration. 2015. *GLOBAL Land-Ocean Temperature Index in 0.01 Degrees Celsius Base Period: 1951–1980*. Retrieved August 2, 2015 (http://data.giss.nasa.gov/gistemp/tabledata_v3/GLB.Ts+dSST.txt).

Goffman, Erving. 1959. *The Presentation of Self in Everyday Life*, reprinted ed. Garden City, NY: Anchor.

_____. 1961. *Asylums: Essays on the Social Situation of Mental Patients and Other Inmates*. Garden City, NY: Anchor Books.

_____. 1963. *Stigma: Notes on the Management of Spoiled Identity*. Englewood Cliffs, NJ: Prentice-Hall.

_____. 1974. *Frame Analysis*. Cambridge, MA: Harvard University Press.

Goldie, Terry. 2001. *In a Queer Country: Gay & Lesbian Studies in the Canadian Context*. Vancouver: Arsenal Pulp Press.

Gombrich, Richard Francis. 1996. *How Buddhism Began: The Conditioned Genesis of the Early Teachings*. London, UK: Athlone.

Goode, Erich, and Nachman Ben-Yehuda. 1994. *Moral Panics: The Social Construction of Deviance*. Cambridge, MA: Blackwell.

Gottfredson, Michael, and Travis Hirschi. 1990. *A General Theory of Crime*. Stanford, CA: Stanford University Press.

Gottwald, Norman K. 1979. *The Tribes of Yahweh: A Sociology of the Religion of Liberated Israel, 1250–1050 B.C.E.* Maryknoll, NY: Orbis.

Goubert, Jean-Pierre. 1989 [1986]. *The Conquest of Water*, Andrew Wilson, trans. Princeton, NJ: Princeton University Press.

Gould, Stephen J. 1988. "Kropotkin Was No Crackpot." *Natural History* 97, 7: 12–18.

_____. 1996. *The Mismeasure of Man*, rev. ed. New York: W. W. Norton.

Government of Canada. 2002. "Study Released on Firearms in Canada." Retrieved December 29, 2005 (http://www.cfc-ccaf.gc.ca/media/news_releases/2002/survey-08202002_e.asp).

Government of Canada. 2015. "Facts and Figures 2013—Immigration Overview: Permanent Residents," p. 5. Retrieved August 2, 2015 (http://www.cic.gc.ca/english/pdf/research-stats/facts2011.pdf/research-stats/facts2011.pdf).

Gramsci, Antonio. 1957. *The Modern Prince and Other Writings*. L Marks, trans. New York: International Publishers.

_____. 1971. *Selections from the Prison Notebooks*, Q. Hoare and G. Smith, eds. London, UK: Lawrence & Wishart.

Granovetter, Mark. 1973. "The Strength of Weak Ties." *American Sociological Review* 78: 1360–80.

Green, Adam Isaiah. 2007. "Queer Theory and Sociology: Locating the Subject and the Self in Sexuality Studies." *Sociological Theory* 25: 26–45.

Greenhill, Pauline. 2001. "Can You See the Difference: Queerying the Nation, Ethnicity, Festival, and Culture in Winnipeg," pp. 103–21 in Terry Goldie, ed., *In a Queer Country: Gay & Lesbian Studies in the Canadian Context*. Vancouver: Arsenal Pulp Press.

Greenstein, Theodore. 1996. "Husbands' Participation in Domestic Labor: Interactive Effects of Wives' and Husbands' Gender Ideologies." *Journal of Marriage and the Family* 58: 585–95.

Grescoe, P. (1996). *The Merchants of Venus: Inside Harlequin and the Empire of Romance*. Vancouver: Raincoast.

Griner, Allison. 2013. "Aboriginal lawyers stride in footsteps of legal pioneer." Thunderbird.ca, 25 March. Retrieved August 2, 2015 (http://thethunderbird.ca/2013/03/25/aboriginal-lawyers-stride-in-footsteps-of-legal-pioneer).

Groopman, Jerome. 2008. "Superbugs." *The New Yorker* 11 August 2008.

Guillén, Mauro F. 2001. "Is Globalization Civilizing, Destructive or Feeble? A Critique of Five Key Debates in the Social Science Literature." *Annual Review of Sociology* 27.

Gunitsky, Seva. 2015. "Corrupting the Cyber-Commons: Social Media as a Tool of Autocratic Stability." *Perspectives on Politics* 13: 42–54.

Guppy, Neil, and Scott Davies. 1998. *Education in Canada: Recent Trends and Future Challenges*. Ottawa: Ministry of Industry.

Gurr, Ted Robert. 1970. *Why Men Rebel*. Princeton, NJ: Princeton University Press.

Haas, Jack, and William Shaffir. 1987. *Becoming Doctors: The Adoption of a Cloak of Competence*. Greenwich, CT: JAI Press.

Haas, Jennifer. 1998. "The Cost of Being a Woman." *New England Journal of Medicine* 338: 1694–95.

Habermas, Jürgen. 1989. *The Structural Transformation of the Public Sphere*, Thomas Burger, trans. Cambridge, MA: MIT Press.

Hagan, John. 1989. *Structuralist Criminology*. New Brunswick, NJ: Rutgers University Press.

_____. 1994. *Crime and Disrepute*. Thousand Oaks, CA: Pine Forge Press.

Hagan, John, John Simpson, and A. R. Gillis. 1987. "Class in the Household: A Power-Control Theory of Gender and Delinquency."

American Journal of Sociology 92: 788–816.

Haines, Herbert H. 1996. *Against Capital Punishment: The Anti-Death Penalty Movement in America, 1972–1994*. New York: Oxford University Press.

Hall, Edward. 1959. *The Silent Language*. New York: Doubleday.

_____. 1966. *The Hidden Dimension*. New York: Doubleday.

Hall, Stuart. 1980. "Encoding/Decoding," pp. 128–38 in Stuart Hall, Dorothy Hobson, Andrew Lowe, and Paul Willis, eds., *Culture, Media, Language: Working Papers in Cultural Studies, 1972–79*. London, UK: Hutchinson.

Hallgrimsdottir, Helga Kristin, Rachel Phillips, and Cecilia Benoit. 2006. "Fallen Women and Rescued Girls: Social Stigma and Media Narratives of the Sex Industry in Victoria, B.C., from 1980 to 2005." *Canadian Review of Sociology and Anthropology* 43, 3: 265–80.

Halstead, Jason. 2010. "Husband Faces Charges in Wife's Death." *Edmonton Sun*. Retrieved March 22, 2010 (http://www.edmontonsun.com).

Hamachek, D. 1995. "Self-concept and School Achievement: Interaction Dynamics and a Tool for Assessing the Self-Concept Component." *Journal of Counseling and Development* 73: 419–25.

Hamilton, Roberta. 1996. *Gendering the Vertical Mosaic: Feminist Perspectives on Canadian Society*. Toronto: Copp-Clark.

Hancock, Lynnell. 1994. "In Defiance of Darwin: How a Public School in the Bronx Turns Dropouts into Scholars." *Newsweek* 24 October: 61.

Haney, Craig, W. Curtis Banks, and Philip G. Zimbardo. 1973. "Interpersonal Dynamics in a Simulated Prison." *International Journal of Criminology and Penology* 1: 69–97.

Hannigan, John. 1995. "The Postmodern City: A New Urbanization?" *Current Sociology* 43, 1: 151–217.

Hannon, Roseann, David S. Hall, Todd Kuntz, Van Laar, and Jennifer Williams. 1995. "Dating Characteristics Leading to Unwanted vs. Wanted Sexual Behavior." *Sex Roles* 33: 767–83.

Harding, David J., Cybelle Fox, and Jal D. Mehta. 2002. "Studying Rare Events through Qualitative Case Studies: Lessons from a Study

of Rampage School Shootings." *Sociological Methods and Research* 31, 2: 174–217.

Harlequin. 2006. "About eHarlequin.com." Retrieved August 24, 2007 (http://www.eharlequin.com/articlepage.html;jsessionid588F358D3D78BC869CC43E64EDA5987F8?articleId536&chapter50).

Harris, Marvin. 1974. *Cows, Pigs, Wars and Witches: The Riddles of Culture*. New York: Random House.

Harris, Peter. 2001. "How Much Money Are We Earning? The Average Canadian Wages Right Now." Workopolis.com, 6 February. Retrieved February 15, 2013 (http://www.workopolis.com/content/advice/article/1821-how-much-money-are-we-earning-the-average-canadian-wages-right-now).

Hartnagel, Timothy F. 2000. "Correlates of Criminal Behaviour," pp. 94–136 in Rick Linden, ed., *Criminology: A Canadian Perspective*, 4th ed. Toronto: Harcourt Canada.

Harvey, Andrew S., Katherine Marshall, and Judith A. Frederick. 1991. *Where Does the Time Go?* Ottawa: Statistics Canada.

Harvey, Edward B., and Richard Kalwa. 1983. "Occupational Status Attainment of University Graduates: Individual Attributes and Labour Market Effects Compared." *Canadian Review of Sociology and Anthropology* 20: 435–53.

Harvey, Elizabeth. 1999. "Short-Term and Long-Term Effects of Early Parental Employment on Children of the National Longitudinal Survey of Youth." *Developmental Psychology* 35: 445–49.

Hastings, Arthur C., James Fadiman, and James C. Gordon, eds. 1980. *Health for the Whole Person: The Complete Guide to Holistic Medicine*. Boulder, CO: Westview Press.

Hay Group. 2014. "Canadian pay equity requirements." Retrieved August 29, 2015 (http://www.haygroup.com/downloads/ca/Canadian%20pay%20equity%20requirements_update%20June%202014.pdf).

Haythornwaite, Caroline, and Barry Wellman. 2002. "The Internet in Everyday Life: An Introduction," pp. 3–41 in Caroline Haythornwaite and Barry Wellman, eds., *The Internet in Everyday Life*. Oxford: Blackwell.

Health Canada. 1999a. *Statistical Report on the Health of Canadians.* Retrieved December 25, 1999 (http://www.hc-sc.gc.ca/hppb/phdd/report/state/englover.html).

———. 1999b. *Toward a Healthy Future: Second Report on the Health of Canadians.* Prepared by the Federal, Provincial, and Territorial Advisory Committee on Population Health for the Meeting of Ministers of Health, Charlottetown, PEI, September. Retrieved April 4, 2000 (http://www.hc-sc.gc.ca).

———. 2003. "Canadian Cancer Statistics, 2003." Retrieved March 30, 2010 (http://www.cancer.ca/Canada-wide/About%20cancer/Cancer%20statistics/Canadian%20Cancer%20Statistics.aspx?sc_lang=en).

———. 2009. *Healthy Canadians: A Federal Report on Comparable Health Indicators 2008.* Retrieved April 2, 2010 (http://www.hc-sc.gc.ca/hcs-sss/pubs/system-regime/2008-fed-comp-indicat/index-eng.php).

———. 2014a. *Summary of Results of the Youth Smoking Survey, 2012–2013.* Retrieved July 5, 2015 (http://www.hc-sc.gc.ca/hc-ps/tobac-tabac/research-recherche/stat/survey-sondage2012-2013/result-eng.php).

———. 2014b. First Nations and Inuit Health: Diseases and Health Conditions." Retrieved August 7, 2015 (http://www.hc-sc.gc.ca/fniah-spnia/diseases-maladies/index-eng.php).

"Health Care Systems: An International Comparison." 2001. Ottawa: Strategic Policy and Research, Intergovernmental Affairs. Retrieved June 13, 2003 (http://www.pnrec.org/2001papers/DaigneaultLajoie.pdf).

Hechter, Michael. 1974. *Internal Colonialism: The Celtic Fringe in British National Development, 1536–1966.* Berkeley, CA: University of California Press.

———. 1987. *Principles of Group Solidarity.* Berkeley, CA: University of California Press.

Helsing, Knud J., Moyses Szklo, and George W. Comstock. 1981. "Factors Associated with Mortality after Widowhood." *American Journal of Public Health* 71: 802–09.

Hendrick, Dianne, and Lee Farmer. 2002. "Adult Correctional Services in Canada, 2000/01." *Juristat* 22, 10;

October. Catalogue No. 85-002-XPE. Ottawa: Canadian Centre for Justice Statistics and Statistics Canada.

Henrich, Joseph, Robert Boyd, and Peter J. Richerson. 2012. "The Puzzle of Monogamous Marriage." *Philosophical Transactions of the Royal Society: Biological Sciences* 367: 657–69.

Henry, Frances, Carol Tator, Winston Mattis, and Tim Rees. 2001. "The Victimization of Racial Minorities in Canada," pp. 145–60 in Robert J. Brym, ed., *Society in Question: Sociological Readings for the 21st Century,* 3rd ed. Toronto: Harcourt Canada.

Herdt, Gilbert. 2001. "Social Change, Sexual Diversity, and Tolerance for Bisexuality in the United States," pp. 267–83 in Anthony R. D'Augelli and Charlotte J. Patterson, eds., *Lesbian, Gay, and Bisexual Identities and Youth: Psychological Perspectives.* New York: Oxford University Press.

Herlihy, David. 1998. *The Black Death and the Transformation of the West.* Cambridge, MA: Harvard University Press.

Herman, Edward S., and Noam Chomsky. 1988. *Manufacturing Consent: The Political Economy of the Mass Media.* New York: Pantheon.

Herrera, Laura. 2011. "In Florida, Virtual Classrooms with No Teachers." *New York Times,* January 17. Retrieved May 24, 2011 (http://www.nytimes.com).

Herrnstein, Richard J., and Charles Murray. 1994. *The Bell Curve: Intelligence and Class Structure in American Life.* New York: Free Press.

Hersch, Patricia. 1998. *A Tribe Apart: A Journey into the Heart of American Adolescence.* New York: Ballantine Books.

Hesse-Biber, Sharlene, and Gregg Lee Carter. 2000. *Working Women in America: Split Dreams.* New York: Oxford University Press.

Higgins, Jenny. 2012. "Mount Cashel Orphanage Abuse Scandal Timeline." *Heritage: Newfoundland & Labrador.* Retrieved December 21, 2015 (http://www.heritage.nf.ca/articles/politics/wells-government-mount-cashel-timeline.php).

Hird, Myra J. 2005. *Sex, Gender and Science.* London, UK: Palgrave Macmillan.

Hirschi, Travis. 1969. *Causes of Delinquency.* Berkeley, CA: University of California Press.

Hirschman, Albert O. 1970. *Exit, Voice, and Loyalty: Responses to Decline in Firms, Organizations, and States.* Cambridge, MA: Harvard University Press.

Hobbes, Thomas. 1968 [1651]. *Leviathan.* Middlesex, UK: Penguin.

Hoberman, John. 1997. *Darwin's Athletes: How Sport Has Damaged Black America and Preserved the Myth of Race.* Boston: Houghton Mifflin.

Hobsbawm, Eric. 1994. *Age of Extremes: The Short Twentieth Century, 1914–1991.* London, UK: Abacus.

Hochschild, Arlie Russell. 1979. "Emotion Work, Feeling Rules, and Social Structure." *American Journal of Sociology* 85: 551–75.

———. 1983. *The Managed Heart: Commercialization of Human Feeling.* Berkeley, CA: University of California Press.

Hochschild, Arlie Russell, with Anne Machung. 1989. *The Second Shift: Working Parents and the Revolution at Home.* New York: Viking.

Hodge, Robert, and David Tripp. 1986. *Children and Television: A Semiotic Approach.* Cambridge, UK: Polity.

Hodgson, Marshall G. S. 1974. *The Venture of Islam: Conscience and History in a World Civilization,* 3 vols. Chicago: University of Chicago Press.

Hogan, Bernie, and Brent Berry. 2011. "Racial and Ethnic Biases in Rental Housing: An Audit Study of Online Apartment Listings." Oxford University, Oxford Internet Institute. Retrieved August 2, 2015 (http://people.oii.ox.ac.uk/hogan/wp-content/uploads/2011/06/Hogan-Berry_City_and_Community_Craigslist.pdf).

Homans, George Caspar. 1961. *Social Behavior: Its Elementary Forms.* New York: Harcourt, Brace and World.

hooks, bell. 1984. *Feminist Theory: From Margin to Center.* Boston: South End Press.

Horkheimer, Max, and Theodor W. Adorno. 1986 [1944]. *Dialectic of Enlightenment,* John Cumming, trans. London, UK: Verso.

Houpt, Simon. 2014. "Digital ad revenue tops other media categories for first time: report." *Globe and Mail* 17

September. Retrieved August 5, 2015 (http://www.theglobeandmail .com/report-on-business/industry -news/marketing/digital-ad-revenue -tops-other-media-categories-for -first-time-report/article20638694).

Houseknecht, Sharon K., and Jaya Sastry. 1996. "Family 'Decline' and Child Well-Being: A Comparative Assessment." *Journal of Marriage and the Family* 58: 726–39.

"How Rich Am I?" 2015. Retrieved July 28, 2015 (https://www .givingwhatwecan.org/get-involved/ how-rich-am-im).

Huesmann, L. Rowell, Jessica Moise-Titus, Cheryl-Lynn Podolski, and Leonard D. Eron. 2003. "Longitudinal Relations between Children's Exposure to TV Violence and Their Aggressive and Violent Behavior in Young Adulthood: 1977–1992." *Developmental Psychology* 39, 2: 201–21.

Hughes, Diane, Ellen Galinsky, and Anne Morris. 1992. "The Effects of Job Characteristics on Marital Quality: Specifying Linking Mechanisms." *Journal of Marriage and the Family* 54, 1; February: 31–42.

Hughes, Fergus P. 1995. *Children, Play and Development*, 2nd ed. Boston: Allyn and Bacon.

Human Rights Watch. 1995. *The Human Rights Watch Global Report on Women's Human Rights*. New York: Human Rights Watch.

Hunter, James Davison. 1991. *Culture Wars: The Struggle to Define America*. New York: Basic Books.

Hunter, Shireen T. 1998. *The Future of Islam and the West: Clash of Civilizations or Peaceful Coexistence?* Westport, CT: Praeger.

Ignatieff, Michael. 2000. *The Rights Revolution*. Toronto: Anansi.

Ignatiev, Noel. 1995. *How the Irish Became White*. New York: Routledge.

Ingram, Gordon Brent. 2001. "Redesigning Wreck: Beach Meets Forest as Location of Male Homoerotic Culture in Placemaking in Pacific Canada," pp. 188–208 in Terry Goldie, ed., *In a Queer Country: Gay & Lesbian Studies in the Canadian Context*. Vancouver: Arsenal Pulp Press.

Inkeles, Alex, and David H. Smith. 1976. *Becoming Modern: Individual Change in Six Developing Countries*. Cambridge, MA: Harvard University Press.

Intergovernmental Panel on Climate Change. 2007. Retrieved May 2, 2007 (http://www.ipcc.ch/).

International Centre for Prison Studies. 2015. Retrieved July 24, 2015 (http://www.prisonstudies.org/ highest-to-lowest/prison-population -total?field_region_taxonomy _tid=All).

International Dating Violence Study. Tabulation courtesy of Murray A. Straus, based on Douglas, Emily M., and Murray A. Straus, (2006), "Assault and Injury of Dating Partners by University Students in 19 Nations and Its Relation to Corporal Punishment Experienced as a Child." *European Journal of Criminology* 3:293–318. Reprinted with permission of the authors.

Internet Movie Data Base. 2014. "The Amazing Race (2001–): Filming Locations." Retrieved March 12, 2014 (http://www.imdb.com/title/ tt0285335/locations).

Internet World Stats. 2013. "Usage and Population Statistics." Retrieved April 4, 2013 (http://www .internetworldstats.com/stats .htm).

_____. 2015. "Internet Users in the World." Retrieved July 5, 2015 (http://www.internetworldstats.com/ stats.htm).

_____. 2016. http://www .internetworldstats.com/stats.htm.

Isajiw, Wsevolod W. 1978. "Olga in Wonderland: Ethnicity in a Technological Society," pp. 29–39 in L. Driedger, ed., *The Canadian Ethnic Mosaic: A Quest for Identity*. Toronto: McClelland & Stewart.

Isfeld, Gordon. 2016. "Canada's house-hold debt is now bigger than its GDP, for the first time." *National Post* 15 September. http://www.nationalpost .com/canada+household+debt +bigger+than+first+time/12195729/ story.html.

Iyengar, Shanto. 1991. *Is Anyone Responsible? How Television Frames Political Issues*. Chicago: University of Chicago Press.

Jackson, Carolyn, and Ian David Smith. 2000. "Poles Apart? An Exploration of Single-Sex and Mixed-Sex Educational Environments in Australia and England." *Educational Studies* 26, 4; December: 409–22.

James, Carl E. 2003. *Seeing Ourselves: Exploring Race, Ethnicity and Culture*, 3rd ed. Toronto: Thompson Educational Publishing.

James, William. 1976 [1902]. *The Varieties of Religious Experience: A Study in Human Nature*. New York: Collier Books.

Janis, Irving. 1972. *Victims of Groupthink*. Boston: Houghton Mifflin.

Jekielek, Susan M. 1998. "Parental Conflict, Marital Disruption and Children's Emotional Well-Being." *Social Forces* 76: 905–35.

Jencks, Christopher, Marshall Smith, Henry Acland, Mary Jo Bane, David Cohen, Herbert Gintis, Barbara Heyns, and Stephan Michelson. 1972. *Inequality: A Reassessment of the Effect of Family and Schooling in America*. New York: Basic Books.

Jenkins, J. Craig. 1983. "Resource Mobilization Theory and the Study of Social Movements." *Annual Review of Sociology* 9: 527–53.

Jensen, Margaret Ann. 1984. *Love's Sweet Return: The Harlequin Story*. Toronto: Women's Press.

John Howard Society. 1999. *Fact Sheet: Population Trends and Crime*. Toronto: John Howard Society of Ontario.

Johns, Adrian. 1998. *The Nature of the Book: Print and Knowledge in the Making*. Chicago: University of Chicago Press.

Johnson, Jeffrey G., Patricia Cohen, Elizabeth M. Smailes, Stephanie Kasen, and Judith S. Brook. 2002. "Television Viewing and Aggressive Behavior during Adolescence and Adulthood." *Science* 295, 5564: 2468–71.

Johnson, Michael P., and Kathleen J. Ferraro. 2000. "Research on Domestic Violence in the 1990s: Making Distinctions." *Journal of Marriage and the Family* 62: 948–63.

Johnson, Sara. 2004. "Adult Correctional Services in Canada, 2002/03." *Juristat* 24, 10: 16. Catalogue No. 85-002-XPE. Ottawa: Canadian Centre for Justice Statistics and Statistics Canada. Retrieved May 8, 2005 (http://www.statcan .ca/bsolc/english/bsolc?catno5 85-002-X20040108409).

Johnson, Terence J. 1972. *Professions and Power*. London, UK: Macmillan.

Johnson, Tracy L., and Elizabeth Fee. 1997. "Women's Health Research: An Introduction," pp. 3–26 in Florence P. Haseltine and Beverly

Greenberg Jacobson, eds., *Women's Health Research: A Medical and Policy Primer*. Washington, DC: Health Press International.

Jones, Frank. 2000. "Are Children Going to Religious Services?" pp. 202–25 in *Canadian Social Trends* 54 (Fall): 3–13. Catalogue No. 11-008-XPE.

Jones, Jeffrey M. 2014. "Americans' support for death penalty stable." *Gallup* 23 October. Retrieved July 26, 2015 (http://www.gallup.com/poll/178790/americans-support-death-penalty-stable.aspx).

Jones, Laura. 1997. "Global Warming Is All the Rage These Days … Which Enrages Many Doubting Scientists." The Fraser Institute. Retrieved May 5, 2002 (http://oldfraser.lexi.net/media/media_releases/1997/19971201a.html).

Josephson Institute. 2012. "The Ethics of American Youth: 2012." Retrieved September 9, 2013 (http://charactercounts.org/programs/reportcard/2012/index.html).

Juergensmeyer, Mark. 2000. *Terror in the Mind of God: The Global Rise of Religious Violence*. Berkeley, CA: University of California Press.

Kalbach, Madeline A. 2000. "Ethnicity and the Altar," pp. 111–21 in Madeline A. Kalbach and Warren E. Kalbach, eds., *Perspectives on Ethnicity in Canada: A Reader*. Toronto: Harcourt Canada.

Kalbach, Madeline A., and Warren E. Kalbach. 1998. "Becoming Canadian: Problems of an Emerging Identity." *Canadian Ethnic Studies* 31, 2: 1–17.

Kalmijn, Matthijs. 1998. "Intermarriage and Homogamy: Causes, Patterns, Trends." *Annual Review of Sociology* 24: 395–421.

Kanter, Rosabeth Moss. 1989. *When Giants Learn to Dance: Mastering the Challenges of Strategy, Management, and Careers in the 1990s*. New York: Simon and Schuster.

Karabel, Jerome. 1986. "Community Colleges and Social Stratification in the 1980s." In L. S. Zwerling, ed., *The Community College and Its Critics*. San Francisco: Jossey-Bass.

Katz, Elihu. 1957. "The Two-Step Flow of Communication: An Up-to-Date Report on an Hypothesis." *Public Opinion Quarterly* 21: 61–78.

Kay, Fiona, and John Hagan. 1998. "Raising the Bar: The Gender Stratification of Law Firm Capitalization." *American Sociological Review* 63: 728–43.

Kelly, Jesse M. 2013. "Does workfare work? Experts say no one really knows." *O.Canada.com* 1 April. Retrieved August 23, 2013 (http://o.canada.com/news/national/does-workfare-work-experts-say-no-one-really-knows).

Kennedy, Paul. 1993. *Preparing for the Twenty-First Century*. New York: HarperCollins.

Kepel, Gilles. 1994 [1991]. *The Revenge of God: The Resurgence of Islam, Christianity and Judaism in the Modern World*, Alan Braley, trans. University Park, PA: Pennsylvania State University Press.

Kerig, Patricia K., Philip A. Cowan, and Carolyn Pape Cowan. 1993. "Marital Quality and Gender Differences in Parent–Child Interaction." *Developmental Psychology* 29: 931–39.

Kessler, Ronald C., Katherine A. McGonagle, Shanyang Zhao, Christopher B. Nelson, Michael Hughes, Suzann Eshleman, Hans Ulrich Wittchen, and Kenneth S. Kendler. 1994. "Lifetime and 12-Month Prevalence of DSM-III-R Psychiatric Disorders in the United States." *Archives of General Psychiatry* 51: 8–19.

Kimmerling, Baruch. 2001. *The Invention and Decline of Israeliness: State, Society, and the Military*. Berkeley, CA: University of California Press.

King, Martin Luther. 1967. *Conscience for Change*. Toronto: CBC Learning Systems. Reprinted by arrangement with The Heirs to the Estate of Martin Luther King Jr., c/o Writers House as agent for the proprietor New York, NY Copyright © 1967 Dr. Martin Luther King Jr; copyright renewed 1991 Coretta Scott King.

Kingsbury, Nancy, and John Scanzoni. 1993. "Structural-Functionalism," pp. 195–217 in Pauline G. Boss, William J. Doherty, Ralph LaRossa, Walter R. Schumm, and Suzanne K. Steinmetz, eds., *Sourcebook of Family Theories and Methods: A Contextual Approach*. New York: Plenum.

Kingston, Paul W. 2001. "The Unfulfilled Promise of Cultural Capital Theory." *Sociology of Education* Supplement: 88–91.

Kinsella, Warren. 2007. *The War Room: Political Strategies for Business, NGOs, and Anyone Who Wants to Win*. Toronto: Dundurn.

Kinsey, Alfred C., Wardell B. Pomeroy, and Clyde E. Martin. 1948. *Sexual Behavior in the Human Male*. Philadelphia: W. B. Saunders.

Kinsey, Alfred, Wardell Pomeroy, Clyde Martin, and Paul Gebhard. 1953. *Sexual Behavior in the Human Female*. Philadelphia: W. B. Saunders.

Kitano, Harry, and Roger Daniels. 1995. *Asian Americans: Emerging Minorities*, 2nd ed. Englewood Cliffs, NJ: Prentice-Hall.

Klein, Jeff Z. 2013. "Rinks in Canada's Arctic Turn to Cooling Systems." *New York Times* 4 January. Retrieved January 4, 2013 (http://www.nytimes.com).

Kling, Kristen C., Janet Shibley Hyde, Carolin J. Showers, and Brenda N. Buswell. 1999. "Gender Differences in Self-Esteem: A Meta-Analysis." *Psychological Bulletin* 125, 4: 470–500.

Koepke, Leslie, Jan Hare, and Patricia B. Moran. 1992. "Relationship Quality in a Sample of Lesbian Couples with Children and Child-Free Lesbian Couples." *Family Relations* 41: 224–29.

Kohlberg, Lawrence. 1981. The *Psychology of Moral Development: The Nature and Validity of Moral Stages*. New York: Harper and Row.

Kornblum, William. 1997. *Sociology in a Changing World*, 4th ed. Fort Worth, TX: Harcourt Brace.

Kosmin, Barry A. 1991. *Research Report of the National Survey of Religious Identification*. New York: CUNY Graduate Center.

Kropotkin, Petr. 1908 [1902]. *Mutual Aid: A Factor of Evolution*, rev. ed. London, UK: W. Heinemann.

Kurdek, Lawrence A. 1996. "The Deterioration of Relationship Quality for Gay and Lesbian Cohabiting Couples: A Five-Year Prospective Longitudinal Study." *Personal Relationships* 3: 417–42.

Kurzweil, Ray. 1999. *The Age of Spiritual Machines: When Computers Exceed Human Intelligence*. New York: Viking Penguin.

LaFeber, Walter. 1993. *Inevitable Revolutions: The United States in Central America*, 2nd ed. New York: W. W. Norton.

Lamanna, Mary Ann, and Agnes Riedmann. 2003. *Marriages and*

Families: Making Choices in a Diverse Society, 8th ed. Belmont, CA: Wadsworth.

Lamont, Michele, and Annette Lareau. 1988. "Cultural Capital: Allusions, Gaps, and Glissandos in Recent Theoretical Developments." *Sociological Theory* 6: 153–68.

Lapchick, Richard. 2004. *2004 Racial and Gender Report Card*. Orlando, FL: University of Central Florida. Retrieved April 29, 2006 (http://www.bus.ucf.edu/sport/public/downloads/2004_Racial_Gender_Report_Card.pdf).

Lapidus, Gail Warshofsky. 1978. *Women in Soviet Society: Equality, Development, and Social Change*. Berkeley, CA: University of California Press.

Lapidus, Ira M. 2002. *A History of Islamic Societies*, 2nd ed. Cambridge: Cambridge University Press.

Latimer, Jeff, Craig Dowden, and Danielle Muise. 2007. "The Effectiveness of Restorative Justice Practices: A Meta-Analysis." Research and Statistics Division, Department of Justice Canada. Retrieved July 26, 2015 (http://www.justice.gc.ca/eng/rp-pr/csj-sjc/jsp-sjp/rp01_1-dr01_1/rp01_1.pdf).

Laumann, Edward O., John H. Gagnon, Robert T. Michael, and Stuart Michaels. 1994. *The Social Organization of Sexuality: Sexual Practices in the United States*. Chicago: University of Chicago Press.

Lautard, Hugh, and Neil Guppy. 2008. "Multiculturalism or Vertical Mosaic? Occupational Stratification among Canadian Ethnic Groups," pp. 120–29 in Robert J. Brym, ed., *Society in Question*, 5th ed. Toronto: Nelson.

_____. 2011. "Multiculturalism or Ethnic Mosaic? Occupational Stratification among Canadian Ethnic Groups," pp. 163–77 in Robert J. Brym, ed., *Society in Question*, 6th ed. Toronto: Nelson.

Lauzen, Martha M. 2014. "Boxed In: Employment of Behind-the-Scenes and On-Screen Women in 2013-14 Prime-time Television." San Diego CA: San Diego State University, Centre for the Study of Women in Television and Film. Retrieved August 5 2015 (http://womenintvfilm.sdsu.edu/files/2013-14_Boxed_In_Report.pdf).

Lavoie, Yolande, and Jillian Oderkirk. 2000. "Social Consequences of Demographic Change," pp. 2–5 in *Canadian Social Trends*, Volume 3. Toronto: Thompson Educational Publishing.

Law Society of British Columbia (The). 2015. "Quick Facts: About the Profession." Retrieved August 2, 2015 (https://www.lawsociety.bc.ca/page.cfm?cid=2189&t=About-the-Profession).

Lee, Esther. 2015. "Caitlyn Jenner Insists Kris Jenner Knew about Women's Clothing, Breast Growth, Hormone Use." *US Weekly*. 1 June. Retrieved August 26, 2015 (http://www.usmagazine.com/celebrity-news/news/caitlyn-jenner-insists-kris-knew-about-womens-clothes-hormone-use-201516).

Lenton, Rhonda L. 1989. "Homicide in Canada and the U.S.A." *Canadian Journal of Sociology* 14: 163–78.

Levine, R. A., and D. T. Campbell. 1972. *Ethnocentrism: Theories of Conflict, Ethnic Attitudes, and Group Behavior*. New York: Wiley.

Levine, Robert, Suguru Sato, Tsukasa Hashimoto, and Jyoti Verma. 1995. "Love and Marriage in Eleven Cultures." *Journal of Cross-Cultural Psychology* 26, 5: 554–71.

Lewis, Bernard. 2002. *What Went Wrong? Western Impact and Middle Eastern Response*. New York: Oxford University Press.

Li, Peter. 1995. "Racial Supremacism under Social Democracy." *Canadian Ethnic Studies* 27, 1: 1–17.

_____. 1998. *The Chinese in Canada*, 2nd ed. Toronto: Oxford University Press.

Lian, Jason Z., and David R. Matthews. 1998. "Does the Vertical Mosaic Still Exist? Ethnicity and Income in Canada, 1991." *Canadian Review of Sociology and Anthropology* 35: 461–81.

Lie, John. 1998. *Han Unbound: The Political Economy of South Korea*. Stanford, CA: Stanford University Press.

_____. 2001. *Multiethnic Japan*. Cambridge, MA: Harvard University Press.

LifeCanada. 2013. "Annual Abortion Rates." Retrieved February 2, 2013 (http://abortionincanada.ca/stats/annual-abortion-rates/).

"Life in plastic." 2002. *The Economist* 19 December. Retrieved August 29, 2015 (http://www.economist.com/node/1487595).

Light, Ivan. 1991. "Immigrant and Ethnic Enterprise in North America," pp. 307–18 in Norman R. Yetman, ed., *Majority and Minority: The Dynamics of Race and Ethnicity in American Life*, 5th ed. Boston: Allyn and Bacon.

Lightfoot-Klein, Hanny, Cheryl Chase, Tim Hammond, and Ronald Goldman. 2000. "Genital Surgery on Children Below the Age of Consent," pp. 440–79 in Lenore T. Szuchman and Frank Muscarella, eds., *Psychological Perspectives on Human Sexuality*. New York: Wiley.

Link, Bruce G., Bruce P. Dohrenwend & Andrew E. Skodol. 1986. "Socioeconomic Status and Schizophrenia: Noisome Occupational Characteristics as a Risk Factor." *American Sociological Review* 51: 242–58.

Lips, Hilary M., 1999. *A New Psychology of Women: Gender, Culture and Ethnicity*. Mountain View, CA: Mayfield.

_____. 2014. *Gender: The Basics*. London, UK: Routledge.

Lipset, Seymour Martin. 1963. "Value Differences, Absolute or Relative: The English-Speaking Democracies," pp. 248–73 in *The First New Nation: The United States in Historical Perspective*. New York: Basic Books.

_____. 1971. *Agrarian Socialism: The Cooperative Commonwealth Federation in Saskatchewan*, rev. ed. Berkeley, CA: University of California Press.

Lipset, Seymour Martin, Martin A. Trow, and James S. Coleman. 1956. *Union Democracy: The Internal Politics of the International Typographical Union*. Glencoe, IL: Free Press.

Lisak, David. 1992. "Sexual Aggression, Masculinity, and Fathers." *Signs* 16: 238–62.

Livernash, Robert, and Eric Rodenburg. 1998. "Population Change, Resources, and the Environment." *Population Bulletin* 53, 1. Retrieved August 25, 2000 (http://www.prb.org/pubs/population_bulletin/bu53-1.htm).

Livingstone, David W. 1999. *The Education–Jobs Gap: Underemployment or Economic Democracy*. Toronto: Garamond Press.

Lofland, John, and Lyn H. Lofland. 1995. *Analyzing Social Settings: A Guide to*

Qualitative Observation and Analysis, 3rd ed. Belmont, CA: Wadsworth.

Logan, Ron. 2001. "Crime Statistics in Canada, 2000." *Juristat* 21, 8. Catalogue No. 85-002-XPE. Ottawa: Canadian Centre for Justice Statistics and Statistics Canada.

Lopez, Donald S. 2001. *The Story of Buddhism: A Concise Guide to Its History and Teachings.* San Francisco: Harper.

Lowman, John, Robert T. Menzies, and Ted S. Palys. 1987. *Transcarceration: Essays in the Sociology of Social Control.* Aldershot, ON: Gower.

Lucas, Samuel Roundfield. 1999. *Tracking Inequality: Stratification and Mobility in American High Schools.* New York: Teachers College Press.

Lupri, Eugen, and James Frideres. 1988. "Marital Satisfaction over the Life Cycle," pp. 436–48 in Lorne Tepperman and James Curtis, eds., *Readings in Sociology: An Introduction.* Toronto: McGraw-Hill Ryerson.

Luhrmann, T. M. 2007. "Social defeat and the culture of chronicity: or, why schizophrenia does so well over there and so badly here." *Culture, Medicine and Psychiatry* 31: 135–72.

Lyon, David. 2007. *Surveillance Studies: An Overview* (Oxford, UK: Polity Press).

Lyon, David, and Elia Zureik, eds., 1996. *Computers, Surveillance, and Privacy.* Minneapolis, MN: University of Minnesota Press.

Mackay, Judith. 2000. *The Penguin Atlas of Human Sexual Behaviour.* New York: Penguin.

MacKinnon, Catharine A. 1979. *Sexual Harassment of Working Women.* New Haven, CT: Yale University Press.

Macklin, Eleanor D. 1980. "Nontraditional Family Forms: A Decade of Research." *Journal of Marriage and the Family* 42: 905–22.

MacLennan, Hugh. 1945. *Two Solitudes.* Toronto: Collins.

"Mad about Hockey: Superstitions." 2002. Retrieved June 20, 2002 (http://www.mcg.org/societe/hockey/pages/aasuperstitions_2.html).

Mahony, Tina Hotton. 2013. "Women and the criminal justice system." Retrieved July 23, 2015 (http://www.statcan.gc.ca/pub/89-503-x/2010001/article/11416-eng.htm)

Makomaski Illing, E. M., and M. J. Kaiserman. 2004. "Mortality Attributable to Tobacco Use in Canada and Its Regions, 1998." *Canadian Journal of Public Health* 95: 38–44.

Manga, Pran, Douglas E. Angus, and William R. Swan. 1993. "Effective Management of Low Back Pain: It's Time to Accept the Evidence." *Journal of the Canadian Chiropractic Association* 37: 221–29.

Mann, Susan A., Michael D. Grimes, Alice Abel Kemp, and Pamela J. Jenkins. 1997. "Paradigm Shifts in Family Sociology? Evidence from Three Decades of Family Textbooks." *Journal of Family Issues* 18: 315–49.

Manson, Jamie L. 2014. "Feminism in Faith: Sister Elizabeth Johnson's Challenge to the Vatican." Retrieved August 11, 2015 (http://www.buzzfeed.com/jamielmanson/feminism-in-faith-catholicism#.uu4gPgXOa).

Markowitz, Fran. 1993. *A Community in Spite of Itself: Soviet Jewish Émigrés in New York.* Washington, DC: Smithsonian Institute Press.

Marshall, S.L.A. 1947. *Men Against Fire: The Problem of Battle Command in Future War.* New York: Morrow.

Marshall, Thomas H. 1965. "Citizenship and Social Class," pp. 71–134 in Thomas H. Marshall, ed., *Class, Citizenship, and Social Development: Essays by T. H. Marshall.* Garden City, NY: Anchor.

Martineau, Harriet. 1985. *Harriet Martineau on Women,* Gayle Graham Yates, ed. New Brunswick, NJ: Rutgers University Press.

Martinez, R. 2015 "Prevalence of Overweight and Obesity visualization." Health Intelligence. Retrieved August 7, 2015 (http://healthintelligence.drupalgardens.com/content/prevalence-overweight-and-obesity).

Marx, Karl. 1904 [1859]. *A Contribution to the Critique of Political Economy,* N. Stone, trans. Chicago: Charles H. Kerr.

_____. 1967 [1867–94]. *Capital,* 3 vols. New York: International Publishers.

_____. 1970 [1843]. *Critique of Hegel's "Philosophy of Right,"* Annette Jolin and Joseph O'Malley, trans. Cambridge, MA: Harvard University Press.

Marx, Karl, and Friedrich Engels. 1972 [1848]. "Manifesto of the Communist Party," pp. 331–62 in R. Tucker, ed., *The Marx-Engels Reader.* New York: Norton.

Massey, Douglas S., Camille Z. Charles, Garvey F. Lundy, and Mary J. Fischer. 2003. *The Source of the River: The Social Origins of Freshmen at America's Selective Colleges and Universities.* Princeton, NJ: Princeton University Press.

Matalon, Jean-Marc. 1997. "Jeanne Calment, World's Oldest Person, Dead at 122." *The Shawnee News-Star,* August 5. Retrieved May 2, 2000 (http://www.news-star.com/stories/080597/life1.html).

Matsueda, Ross L. 1988. "The Current State of Differential Association Theory." *Crime and Delinquency* 34: 277–306.

_____. 1992. "Reflected Appraisals, Parental Labeling, and Delinquency: Specifying a Symbolic Interactionist Theory." *American Journal of Sociology* 97: 1577–1611.

Mazie, Steven. 2014. "Do You Have Too Many Facebook Friends?" Big Think. Retrieved August 5, 2015 (http://www.statista.com/statistics/264810/number-of-monthly-active-facebook-users-worldwide).

McAdam, Doug. 1982. *Political Process and the Development of Black Insurgency, 1930–1970.* Chicago: University of Chicago Press.

McChesney, Robert W. 1999. "Oligopoly: The Big Media Game Has Fewer and Fewer Players." *The Progressive,* November: 20–24.

McClelland, W. R. 1931. "Precautions for Workers in the Treating of Radium Ores." *Investigations in Ore Dressing and Metallurgy.* Ottawa: Bureau of Mines. Retrieved October 8, 2000 (http://www.ccnr.org/radium_warning.html).

McCormick, Chris, ed. 1999. *The Westray Chronicles: A Case Study in Corporate Crime.* Halifax: Fernwood.

McKeon, Matt. 2010. "The Evolution of Privacy on Facebook." Retrieved November 26, 2012 (http://mattmckeon.com/facebook-privacy/).

McLaren, Angus. 1990. *Our Own Master Race: Eugenics in Canada, 1885–1945.* Toronto: McClelland & Stewart.

McLuhan, Marshall. 1964. *Understanding Media: The Extensions of Man.* New York: McGraw-Hill.

McMahon, Maeve W. 1992. *The Persistent Prison? Rethinking Decarceration and Penal Reform.* Toronto: University of Toronto Press.

McManners, John, ed. 1990. *Oxford Illustrated History of Christianity.* Oxford: Oxford University Press.

McNeill, William H. 1976. *Plagues and Peoples.* Garden City, NY: Anchor Press.

McPhail, Clark. 1994. "The Dark Side of Purpose: Individual and Collective Violence in Riots." *Sociological Quarterly* 35: 1–32.

McRoberts, Kenneth. 1988. *Quebec: Social Change and Political Crisis,* 3rd ed. Toronto: McClelland & Stewart.

McVey, Wayne W., Jr., and Warren E. Kalbach. 1995. *Canadian Population.* Scarborough, ON: Nelson.

Mead, George H. 1934. *Mind, Self and Society.* Chicago: University of Chicago Press.

Melucci, Alberto. 1980. "The New Social Movements: A Theoretical Approach." *Social Science Information* 19: 199–226.

_____. 1995. "The New Social Movements Revisited: Reflections on a Sociological Misunderstanding," pp. 107–19 in Louis Maheu, ed. *Social Classes and Social Movements: The Future of Collective Action.* London, UK: Sage.

Mendelson, Michael. 2006. "Aboriginal Peoples and Postsecondary Education in Canada." Caledon Institute of Social Policy. Retrieved August 2, 2015 (http://www .caledoninst.org/Publications/ PDF/595ENG.pdf).

Menzies, C.R. 1999. "First Nations, Inequality and the Legacy of Colonialism," pp. 236–44 in J. Curtis, E. Grabb, and N. Guppy, eds., *Social Inequality in Canada,* 3rd ed. Scarborough, ON: Prentice Hall Allyn and Bacon Canada Inc.

Merton, Robert K. 1938. "Social Structure and Anomie." *American Sociological Review* 3: 672–82.

_____. 1968 [1949]. *Social Theory and Social Structure,* enlarged ed. New York: Free Press.

Messerschmidt, James W. 1993. *Masculinities and Crime: Critique and Reconceptualization of Theory.* Lanham, MD: Roman and Littlefield.

Messner, Michael. 1995. "Boyhood, Organized Sports, and the Construction of Masculinities," pp. 102–14 in Michael S. Kimmel and Michael A. Messner. *Men's Lives,* 3rd ed. Boston: Allyn and Bacon.

_____. 2000. "Barbie Girls versus Sea Monsters: Children Constructing Gender." *Gender & Society, Special Issue* 14, 6; December: 765–84.

Meyer, David R., and Judi Bartfield. 1996. "Compliance with Child Support Orders in Divorce Cases." *Journal of Marriage and the Family* 58, 1: 201–12.

Meyer, John W., Francisco O. Ramirez, and Yasemin Nuhoglu Soysal. 1992. "World Expansion of Mass Education, 1870–1980." *Sociology of Education* 65: 128–49.

Meyer, Thomas. 1984. "'Date Rape': A Serious Campus Problem that Few Talk About." *Chronicle of Higher Education* 5; December: 1, 12.

Michael, Robert T., John H. Gagnon, Edward O. Laumann, and Gina Kolata. 1994. *Sex in America: A Definitive Survey.* Boston: Little, Brown and Company.

Milanovic, Branko. 2005. *Worlds Apart: Measuring International and Global Inequality.* Princeton, NJ: Princeton University Press.

Milem, Jeffrey F. 1998. "Attitude Change in College Students: Examining the Effect of College Peer Groups and Faculty Normative Groups." *Journal of Higher Education* 69: 117–40.

Miles, Robert. 1989. *Racism.* London, UK: Routledge.

Milgram, Stanley. 1974. *Obedience to Authority: An Experimental View.* New York: Harper.

Miller, Ted R., and Mark A. Cohen. 1997. "Costs of Gunshot and Cut/ Stab Wounds in the United States, with Some Canadian Comparisons." *Accident Analysis and Prevention* 29: 329–41.

Milloy, John S. 1999. *A National Crime: The Canadian Government and the Residential School System, 1879 to 1986.* Winnipeg: University of Manitoba Press.

Mills, C. Wright. 1959. *The Sociological Imagination.* New York: Oxford University Press, pp. 3–4.

Mitchinson, Wendy. 1993. "The Medical Treatment of Women," pp. 391–421 in Sandra Burt, Lorraine Code, and Lindsay Dorney, eds., *Changing Patterns: Women in Canada,* 2nd ed. Toronto: McClelland & Stewart.

Mohr, Johann W., and Keith Spencer. 1999. "Crime," pp. 587–89 in James H. Marsh, ed., *The Canadian*

Encyclopedia, Year 2000 edition. Toronto: McClelland & Stewart.

Mokete, 'Musi. 2006. "Forty Years of Health Services Development in Lesotho (Successes, Failures and Challenges), 1966–2006." Retrieved August 7, 2015 (http://unpan1 .un.org/intradoc/groups/public/ documents/AAPAM/UNPAN025645 .pdf).

Montgomery, Malcolm. 1965. "The Six Nations and the Macdonald Franchise." *Ontario History* 57: 13.

Mooney, Linda A., David Knox, Caroline Schacht, and Adie Nelson. 2001. *Understanding Social Problems.* Toronto: Nelson Thomson Learning.

Mooney, Linda, Caroline Schacht, David Knox, and Adie Nelson. 2003. *Understanding Social Problems,* 2nd ed. Toronto: Nelson Thomson Learning.

Morris, Aldon D. 1984. *The Origins of the Civil Rights Movement: Black Communities Organizing for Change.* New York: Free Press.

Morris, Norval, and David J. Rothman, eds. 1995. *The Oxford History of the Prison: The Practice of Punishment in Western Society.* New York: Oxford University Press.

Morrison, Nancy. 1987. "Separation and Divorce," pp. 125–43 in M. J. Dymond, ed., *The Canadian Woman's Legal Guide.* Toronto: Doubleday.

Mortimer, Jeylan T., and Roberta G. Simmons. 1978. "Adult Socialization." *Annual Review of Sociology* 4: 421–54.

Moscovitch, Arlene. 1998. "Electronic Media and the Family." Vanier Institute of the Family. Retrieved May 14, 2003 (http://www.vifamily .ca/cft/media/media.htm).

Mundell, Helen. 1993. "How the Color Mafia Chooses Your Clothes." *American Demographics,* November. Retrieved May 2, 2000 (http://www .demographics.com/publications/ ad/93_ad/9311_ad/ad281.htm).

Murdock, George Peter. 1937. "Comparative Data on the Division of Labor by Sex." *Social Forces* 15: 551–53.

_____. 1949. *Social Structure.* New York: Macmillan.

Murphy, Brian, Xuelin Zhang, and Claude Dionne. 2012. "Low Income in Canada: a Multi-Line and Multi-Index Perspective." Statistics Canada. Income Research Paper

Series. Catalogue No. 75F0002M—No. 001. Retrieved December 25, 2012 (http://www.statcan.gc.ca/pub/75f0002m/75f0002m2012001-eng.pdf).

National Council of Welfare. 1999a. "A New Poverty Line: New, No or Maybe?" Retrieved April 9, 2000 (http://www.ncwcnbes.net/htm document/reportnewpovline/newpovline.html).

——. 1999b. *Children First: A Pre-Budget Report by the National Council of Welfare*. Retrieved April 9, 2000 (http://www.ncwcnbes.net/htmdocument/reportchildfirst.htm).

——. 2004. *Poverty Profile 2001*. Catalogue No. SD25-1/2001E. Ottawa: Minister of Public Works and Government Services Canada.

National Oceanic and Atmospheric Administration. 2010. *Use of NOAA ESRL Data*. Retrieved March 29, 2010 (ftp://ftp.cmdl.noaa.gov/ccg/co2/trends/co2_annmean_mlo.txt).

National Oceanic and Atmospheric Administration, U.S. Department of Commerce. 2013. *CO^2 Expressed as a Mole Fraction in Dry Air, Micromol/Mol, Abbreviated as Ppm*. Retrieved March 31, 2013 (ftp://ftp.cmdl.noaa.gov/ccg/co2/trends/co2_annmean_mlo.txt).

National Oceanic and Atmospheric Administration, U.S. Department of Commerce. 2015. *CO_2 Expressed as a Mole Fraction in Dry Air, Mcromol/Mol, Abbreviated as ppm*. Retrieved August 2, 2015 (ftp://aftp.cmdl.noaa.gov/products/trends/co2/co2_mm_mlo.txt).

National Opinion Research Center. 2006. *General Social Survey, 1972–2004*. Chicago: University of Chicago.

National Rifle Association. 2005. *Guns, Gun Ownership, & RTC at All-Time Highs, Less 'Gun Control,' and Violent Crime at 30-Year Low*. Retrieved December 29, 2005 (http://www.nraila.org/Issues/FactSheets/Read.aspx?ID5126).

Neal, Mark Anthony. 1999. *What the Music Said: Black Popular Music and Black Public Culture*. New York: Routledge.

Nelson, Adie, and Barrie W. Robinson. 2002. *Gender in Canada*, 2nd ed. Toronto: Prentice Hall.

Nelson, Dean, and Barney Henderson. 2009. "Slumdog Child Stars Miss Out on the Movie Millions."

Telegraph.co.uk, January 26. Retrieved January 2, 2010 (http://www.telegraph.co.uk/news/worldnews/asia/4347472/Poor-parents-of-Slumdog-millionaire-stars-say-children-were-exploited.html).

Newfoundland and Labrador Statistics Agency, Economics and Statistics Branch. n.d. "Major Field of Study by Age Group and Sex." Retrieved August 27, 2015 (http://www.stats.gov.nl.ca/Statistics/social/PDF/ED_Major%20Field%20of%20Study_AgeGroup_Sex.pdf).

Nicolaiedis, Nicos. 1998. "Pierre Marty's 'Doll' and Today's Barbies." *Revue française de psychanalyse, Special Issue: Psychosomatiqueet pulsionnalité* 62, 5; Nov./Dec.: 1579–81.

Nielsen, Linda. 1999. "College-Aged Students with Divorced Parents: Facts and Fiction." *College Student Journal* 33: 543–72.

Nikiforuk, Andrew. 1998. "Echoes of the Atomic Age: Cancer Kills Fourteen Aboriginal Uranium Workers." *Calgary Herald*, 14 March: A1, A4. Retrieved October 8, 2000 (http://www.ccnr.org/deline_deaths.html).

——. 1999. "A Question of Style." *Time* 31; May: 58–59.

Nisbett, Richard E., Kaiping Peng, Incheol Choi, and Ara Norenzayan. 2001. "Culture and Systems of Thought: Holistic versus Analytic Cognition." *Psychological Review* 108: 291–310.

Nolen, Stephanie. 1999. "Gender: The Third Way." *Globe and Mail*, September 25: D1, D4.

Northup, Solomon. 1855. *Twelve Years a Slave: Narrative of Solomon Northup, A Citizen of New York, Kidnapped in Washington City in 1841 and Rescued in 1853, From a Cotton Plantation Near the Red River, in Louisiana*. New York: Miller, Orton, and Mulligan.

Norton, Kevin I., Timothy S. Olds, Scott Olive, and Stephen Dank. 1996. "Ken and Barbie at Life Size." *Sex Roles* 34, 3–4; February: 287–94.

Nowak, Martin A., Robert M. May, and Karl Sigmund. 1995. "The Arithmetics of Mutual Help." *Scientific American* 272, 6: 76–81.

Nowell, Amy, and Larry V. Hedges. 1998. "Trends in Gender Differences in Academic Achievement from 1960 to 1994: An Analysis of Differences

in Mean, Variance, and Extreme Scores." *Sex Roles* 39: 21–43.

Oberschall, Anthony. 1973. *Social Conflict and Social Movements*. Englewood Cliffs, NJ: Prentice-Hall.

Oderkirk, Jillian, and Clarence Lochhead. 1992. "Lone Parenthood: Gender Differences." *Canadian Social Trends* 27; Spring: 16–19. Catalogue No. 11-008-XPE.

OECD. 2014. "SF2.4: Share of births out of wedlock and teenage births." Retrieved February 29, 2016 (http://www.oecd.org/els/family/SF2_4_Births_outside_marriage_and_teenage_births.pdf).

Oeppen, Jim, and James W. Vaupel. 2002. "Demography: Broken Limits to Life Expectancy." *Science* 296: 1029–31.

Office of the Correctional Investigator. 2013. "Aboriginal offenders—a critical situation." Retrieved July 23, 2015 (http://www.oci-bec.gc.ca/cnt/rpt/oth-aut/oth-aut20121022info-eng.aspx)

Ogbu, John U. 2003. *Black American Students in an Affluent Suburb: A Study of Academic Disengagement*. Mahwah, NJ: Erlbaum.

Omi, Michael, and Howard Winant. 1986. *Racial Formation in the United States*. New York: Routledge.

Ontario Consultants on Religious Tolerance. 2000. "Homosexual (Same-Sex) Marriages." Retrieved August 20, 2000 (http://www.religioustolerance.org/hom_marr.htm).

——. 2005. *Information about Religion in Canada*. Retrieved November 14, 2005 (http://www.religioustolerance.org/can_rel.htm).

Ore, Timothy, and Astrid Birgden. 2003. "Does Prison Work: A View from Criminology." *Policy* 19, 2. Retrieved March 8, 2010 (http://www.cis.org.au/policy/winter03/polwin03-9.pdf).

Oreopoulos, Philip, and Diane Dechief. 2011. "Why do some employers prefer to interview Matthew, but not Samir?" University of British Columbia, Metropolis British Columbia, Working Paper Series, No. 11–13. Retrieved August 2, 2015 (http://mbc.metropolis.net/assets/uploads/files/wp/2011/WP11-13.pdf).

Organisation for Economic Co-operation and Development (OECD). 2004. "Statistical Annex." *OECD Employment Outlook 2004*. Retrieved December 1, 2005

(http://www.oecd.org/
dataoecd/42/55/32494755.pdf).

_____. 2007. "PISA 2006 Science Competencies for Tomorrow's World." (Retrieved from http://www.oecd.org/pisa/pisaproducts/pisa2006/pisa2006results.htm.)

_____. 2012. "SF2.4: Share of Births Out of Wedlock and Teenage Births." Retrieved February 3, 2013 (http://www.oecd.org/els/familiesandchildren/SF2.4_Births%20outside%20marriage%20and%20teenage%20births%20-%20updated%20240212.pdf).

Ornstein, Michael D. 1998. "Survey Research." *Current Sociology* 46, 4: 1–87.

Ossowski, Stanislaw. 1963. *Class Structure in the Social Consciousness*, S. Patterson, trans. London, UK: Routledge and Kegan Paul.

Our Voices: First Nations, Métis, and Inuit Gender-Based Analysis. 2009. Retrieved March 15, 2013 (http://www.aboriginalgba.ca)

Owen, Michelle K. 2001. "'Family' as a Site of Contestation: Queering the Normal or Normalizing the Queer?" pp. 86–102 in Terry Goldie, ed., *In a Queer Country: Gay and Lesbian Studies in the Canadian Context*. Vancouver: Arsenal Pulp Press.

Pacey, Arnold. 1983. *The Culture of Technology*. Cambridge, MA: MIT Press.

Pammett, Jon H. 1997. "Getting Ahead Around the World," pp. 67–86 in Alan Frizzell and Jon H. Pammett, eds., *Social Inequality in Canada*. Ottawa: Carleton University Press.

Pape, Robert A. 2003. "The Strategic Logic of Suicide Terrorism." *American Political Science Review* 97: 343–61.

Park, Jungwee. 2005. "Use of Alternative Health Care." *Health Reports* 16, 2: 39–43.

Parke, Ross D. 2001. "Paternal Involvement in Infancy: The Role of Maternal and Paternal Attitudes." *Journal of Family Psychology* 15, 4; December: 555–58.

_____. 2002. "Parenting in the New Millennium: Prospects, Promises and Pitfalls," pp. 65–93 in James P. McHale and Wendy S. Grolnick, eds., *Retrospect and Prospect in the Psychological Study of Families*. Mahwah, NJ: Lawrence Erlbaum Associates, Inc.

Parshall, Gerald. 1998. "Brotherhood of the Bomb." *US News and World Report* 125, 7; 17–24 August: 64–68.

Parsons, Talcott. 1942. "Age and Sex in the Social Structure of the United States." *American Sociological Review* 7: 604–16.

_____. 1951. *The Social System*. New York: Free Press.

_____. 1955. "The American Family: Its Relation to Personality and to the Social Structure," pp. 3–33 in Talcott Parsons and Robert F. Bales, eds., *Family, Socialization and Interaction Process*. New York: Free Press.

Pasley, Kay, and Carmelle Minton. 2001. "Generative Fathering After Divorce and Remarriage: Beyond the 'Disappearing Dad,'" pp. 239–48 in Theodore F. Cohen, ed., *Men and Masculinity: A Text Reader*. Belmont, CA: Wadsworth.

Patented Medicine Prices Review Board. 2011. *Annual Report 2011*. Retrieved March 16, 2013 (http://www.pmprb-cepmb.gc.ca/CMFiles/Publications/Annual%20Reports/2011/2011-Annual-Report_EN_Final-for-Posting.pdf).

Pendakur, Krishna, and Ravi Pendakur. 1998. "The Colour of Money: Earnings Differentials among Ethnic Groups in Canada." *Canadian Journal of Economics* 31: 518–48.

Pendakur, R. 2000. *Immigrants and the Labour Force: Policy, Regulation and Impact*. Montreal: McGill-Queen's University Press.

Perreault, Samuel. 2015. "Criminal victimization in Canada, 2014." *Juristat* (Statistics Canada). Retrieved July 1, 2016 (http://www.statcan.gc.ca/pub/85-002-x/85-002-x2015001-eng.htm).

Perrow, Charles B. 1984. *Normal Accidents*. New York: Basic Books.

Peters, John F. 1994. "Gender Socialization of Adolescents in the Home: Research and Discussion." *Adolescence* 29: 913–34.

Pew Research Center. 2002. *The Pew Global Attitudes Project: How Global Publics View Their Lives, Their Countries, the World, America*. Reprinted by permission of The Pew Global Attitudes Project. Retrieved April 12, 2003 (http://www.people-press.org).

Piaget, Jean, and Bärbel Inhelder. 1969. *The Psychology of the Child*, Helen Weaver, trans. New York: Basic Books.

Piven, Frances Fox, and Richard A. Cloward. 1977. *Poor People's Movements: Why They Succeed, How They Fail*. New York: Vintage.

_____ and Richard A. Cloward. 1993. *Regulating the Poor: The Functions of Public Welfare*, updated ed. New York: Vintage.

PISA. 2014. "PISA 2012 Results in Focus." Retrieved August 8, 2015 (http://www.oecd.org/pisa/keyfindings/pisa-2012-results-overview.pdf)

Plummer, Kenneth. 1995. *Telling Sexual Stories: Power, Change and Social Worlds*. London, UK: Routledge.

Pool, Robert. 1997. *Beyond Engineering: How Society Shapes Technology*. New York: Oxford University Press.

Popenoe, David. 1988. *Disturbing the Nest: Family Change and Decline in Modern Societies*. New York: Aldine de Gruyter.

_____. 1996. *Life without Father: Compelling New Evidence that Fatherhood and Marriage Are Indispensable for the Good of Children and Society*. New York: Martin Kessler Books.

_____. 1998. "The Decline of Marriage and Fatherhood," pp. 312–19 in John J. Macionis and Nijole V. Benokraitis, eds., *Seeing Ourselves: Classic, Contemporary and Cross-Cultural Readings in Sociology*, 4th ed. Upper Saddle River, NJ: Prentice Hall.

Population Reference Bureau. 2012. *2012 World Population Data Sheet*. Retrieved April 1, 2010 (http://www.prb.org/pdf09/09wpds_eng.pdf).

_____. 2014. *2014 World Population Data Sheet*. Retrieved August 7, 2015 (http://www.prb.org/pdf14/2014-world-population-data-sheet_eng.pdf).

Porter, John. 1965. *The Vertical Mosaic: An Analysis of Social Class and Power in Canada*. Toronto: University of Toronto Press.

_____. 1979. *The Measure of Canadian Society: Education, Equality, and Opportunity*. Toronto: Gage.

Portes, Alejandro, and Robert D. Manning. 1991. "The Immigrant Enclave: Theory and Empirical Examples," pp. 319–32 in Norman R. Yetman, ed., *Majority and Minority: The Dynamics of Race and Ethnicity in American Life*, 5th ed. Boston: Allyn and Bacon.

Postman, Neil. 1982. *The Disappearance of Childhood*. New York: Delacorte.

Powers, Ann. 2009. "Frank Talk with Lady Gaga." *Los Angeles Times* 13 December.

Pred, Allan R. 1973. *Urban Growth and the Circulation of Information.* Cambridge, MA: Harvard University Press.

Press, Andrea L. 1991. *Women Watching Television: Gender, Class and Generation in the American Television Experience.* Philadelphia: University of Pennsylvania Press.

Press, Andrea L., and Elizabeth R. Cole. 1999. *Speaking of Abortion: Television and Authority in the Lives of Women.* Chicago: University of Chicago Press.

Province. 2010. "Gold Medal Men's Hockey Game Gets Record Canadian TV Audience." *The Province,* 1 March. Retrieved March 28, 2010 (http://www.theprovince.com/ entertainment/Gold+medal+hockey +game+gets+record+Canadian +audience/2628644/story.html).

Province of Nova Scotia. 2010. "Counties of Nova Scotia." Retrieved March 30, 2010 (http://www.gov.ns.ca/snsmr/ muns/info/mapping/counties.asp).

Provine, Robert R. 2000. *Laughter: A Scientific Investigation.* New York: Penguin.

Public Safety Canada. 2012. *Youth Gangs in Canada: What Do We Know?* Retrieved December 19, 2012 (http:// www.publicsafety.gc.ca/prg/cp/ bldngevd/2007-yg-1-eng.aspx).

Raag, Tarja, and Christine L. Rackliff. 1998. "Preschoolers' Awareness of Social Expectations of Gender: Relationships to Toy Choices." *Sex Roles* 38: 685–700.

Raphael, D. 2004. *Social Determinants of Health: Canadian Perspectives.* Toronto: Canadian Scholars' Press.

Rapp, Rayna, and Ellen Ross. 1986. "The 1920s: Feminism, Consumerism and Political Backlash in the United States," pp. 52–62 in J. Friedlander, B. Cook, A. Kessler-Harris, and C. Smith-Rosenberg, eds. *Women in Culture and Politics.* Bloomington, IN: Indiana University Press.

Reading, Charlotte Loppie, and Fred Wien. 2009. *Health Inequalities and Social Determinants of Aboriginal Peoples' Health.* National Collaborating Centre for Aboriginal Health.

Reimann, Renate. 1997. "Does Biology Matter? Lesbian Couples' Transition to Parenthood and Their Division of Labor." *Qualitative Sociology* 20, 2: 153–85.

Reisinger, Don. 2012. "YouTube Users Uploading 72 Hours of Video Each Minute." CNet.com. Retrieved April 4, 2013 (http://news.cnet .com/8301-1023_3-57438332-93/ youtube-users-uploading-72-hours -of-video-each-minute).

Reitz, Jeffrey G. 2011. "Tapping Immigrants' Skills," pp. 178–93 in Robert J. Brym, ed., *Society in Question,* 6th ed. Toronto: Nelson.

Report on Business Magazine. 2012. "Ranking Canada's Top 1,000 Companies by Profit." *Report on Business,* 28 June. Retrieved April 2, 2013 (http://www.theglobeandmail .com/report-on-business/rob -magazine/top-1000/2012 -rankings-of-canadas-top-1000 -public-companies-by-profit/ article4371923).

Resnick, Michael, Peter S. Bearman, Robert W. Blum, Karl E. Bauman, Kathleen M. Harris, Jo Jones, Joyce Tabor, Trish Beubring, Renee E. Sieving, Marcia Shew, Marjoie Ireland, Linda H. Beringer, and J. Richard Udry. 1997. "Protecting Adolescents from Harm." *Journal of the American Medical Association* 278: 823–32.

Richler, Mordecai. 1959. *The Apprenticeship of Duddy Kravitz.* Don Mills, ON: A. Deutsch.

Risman, Barbara J., and Danette Johnson-Sumerford. 1998. "Doing It Fairly: A Study of Postgender Marriages." *Journal of Marriage and the Family* 60: 23–40.

Roberts, Julian, and Thomas Gabor. 1990. "Race and Crime: A Critique." *Canadian Journal of Criminology* 92, 2; April: 291–313.

Robinson, Richard H., and Willard L. Johnson. 1997. *The Buddhist Religion: A Historical Introduction,* 4th ed. Belmont, CA: Wadsworth.

Roche, Maurice. 1995. "Rethinking Citizenship and Social Movements: Themes in Contemporary Sociology and Neoconservative Ideology," pp. 186–219 in Louis Maheu, ed., *Social Classes and Social Movements: The Future of Collective Action.* London, UK: Sage.

Rodinson, Maxime. 1996. *Muhammad,* 2nd ed. Anne Carter, trans. London, UK: Penguin.

Roediger, David R. 1991. *The Wages of Whiteness: Race and the Making of the American Working Class.* London, UK: Verso.

Rogers, Simon. 2012. "Healthcare spending around the world, country by country." *The Guardian* 30 June. Retrieved August 7, 2015 (http://www.theguardian .com/news/datablog/2012/jun/30/ healthcare-spending-world-country).

Rollins, Boyd C., and Kenneth L. Cannon. 1974. "Marital Satisfaction over the Family Life Cycle." *Journal of Marriage and the Family* 36: 271–84.

Romaniuc, Anatole. 1984. "Fertility in Canada: From Baby-Boom to Baby-Bust." *Current Demographic Analysis.* Ottawa: Statistics Canada.

Rootes, Chris. 1995. "A New Class? The Higher Educated and the New Politics," pp. 220–35 in Louis Maheu, ed., *Social Classes and Social Movements: The Future of Collective Action.* London, UK: Sage.

Rosenbloom, Stephanie. 2007. "On Facebook, Scholars Link up with Data." *New York Times,* December 17. Retrieved November 28, 2012 (http://www.nytimes.com).

Rosenbluth, Susan C. 1997. "Is Sexual Orientation a Matter of Choice?" *Psychology of Women Quarterly* 21: 595–610.

Rosenbluth, Susan C., Janice M. Steil, and Juliet H. Whitcomb. 1998. "Marital Equality: What Does It Mean?" *Journal of Family Issues* 19, 3: 227–44.

Rosenfeld, Michael J., and Reuben J. Thomas. 2012. "Searching for a Mate: The Rise of the Internet as a Social Intermediary." *American Sociological Review* 77: 523–47.

Rosenthal, Robert, and Lenore Jacobson. 1968. *Pygmalion in the Classroom: Teacher Expectation and Pupils' Intellectual Development.* New York: Holt, Rinehart, and Winston.

Rostow, Walt W. 1960. *The Stages of Economic Growth: A Non-Communist Manifesto.* New York: Cambridge University Press.

Roth, Cecil. 1961. *A History of the Jews.* New York: Schocken.

Rothman, Barbara Katz. 1982. *In Labor: Women and Power in the Birthplace.* New York: W. W. Norton.

_____. 1989. *Recreating Motherhood: Ideology and Technology in a Patriarchal Society.* New York: W. W. Norton.

Rothman, David J. 1991. *Strangers at the Bedside: A History of How Law and Bioethics Transformed Medical Decision Making*. New York: Basic Books.

_____. 1998. "The International Organ Traffic." *New York Review of Books* 45, 5: 14–17.

Rubin, Jeffrey Z., Frank J. Provenzano, and Zella Lurra. 1974. "The Eye of the Beholder: Parents' Views on Sex of Newborns." *American Journal of Orthopsychiatry* 44: 512–19.

Rupp, Leila J., and Verta Taylor. 2010. "Straight Girls Kissing." *Contexts* 9, 4: 28–32.

Rural Communities Impact Policy Project. 2003. "Painting the Landscape of Rural Nova Scotia." Retrieved March 30, 2010 (http://www.ruralnovascotia.ca/RCIP/PDF/RR_final_full.pdf).

Ryan, Kathryn M., and Jeanne Kanjorski. 1998. "The Enjoyment of Sexist Humor, Rape Attitudes, and Relationship Aggression in College Students." *Sex Roles* 38: 743–56.

Sager, Eric. 2000. "Canadian Families—A Historian's Perspective," pp. vii–xi in *Profiling Canada's Families II*. Nepean, ON: Vanier Institute for the Family.

Sampson, Robert, and John H. Laub. 1993. *Crime in the Making: Pathways and Turning Points through Life*. Cambridge, MA: Harvard University Press.

Samuda, R. J., D. Crawford, C. Philip, and W. Tinglen. 1980. *Testing, Assessment, and Counselling of Minority Students: Current Methods in Ontario*. Toronto: Ontario Ministry of Education.

Samuelsson, Kurt. 1961 [1957]. *Religion and Economic Action*, E. French, trans. Stockholm: Scandinavian University Books.

Sandqvist, Karin, and Bengt-Erik Andersson. 1992. "Thriving Families in the Swedish Welfare State." *Public Interest* 109: 114–16.

Sarlo, Christopher. 2001. *Measuring Poverty in Canada*. Vancouver, BC: The Fraser Institute.

Sartre, Jean-Paul. 1965 [1948]. *Anti-Semite and Jew*, George. J. Becker, trans. New York: Schocken.

Sauve, Roger. 2002. "Job, Family and Stress among Husbands, Wives and Lone-Parents 15–64 from 1990 to 2000." Retrieved March 3, 2003 (http://www.vifamily.ca/cft/connect.htm).

Savoie, Josée. 2002. "Crime Statistics in Canada, 2001." *Juristat* 22, 6. Catalogue No. 85-002-XPE. Ottawa: Canadian Centre for Justice Statistics and Statistics Canada.

Sawyer, Diane. 2015. "Bruce Jenner—The Interview." *20/20* 24 April. Retrieved August 26, 2015 http://abc.go.com/shows/2020/listing/2015-04/24-bruce-jenner-the-interview).

Saxton, Lloyd. 1990. *The Individual, Marriage, and the Family*, 9th ed. Belmont, CA: Wadsworth.

Schiebinger, Londa L. 1993. *Nature's Body: Gender in the Making of Modern Science*. Boston: Beacon Press.

Schiller, Herbert I. 1989. *Culture Inc.: The Corporate Takeover of Public Expression*. New York: Oxford University Press.

Schoen, Cathy, Robin Osborn, Phuong Trang Huynh, Michelle Doty, Karen Davis, Kinga Zapert, and Jordan Peugh. 2004. "Primary Care and Health System Performance: Adults' Experiences In Five Countries." *Health Affairs* (Web Exclusive) 4.487. Retrieved September 4, 2008 (http://content.healthaffairs.org/cgi/content/abstract/hlthaff.w4.487v1).

Schor, Juliet B. 1992. *The Overworked American: The Unexpected Decline of Leisure*. New York: Basic Books.

_____. 1999. *The Overspent American: Why We Want What We Don't Need*. New York: Harper.

Schudson, Michael. 1991. "National News Culture and the Rise of the Informational Citizen," pp. 265–82 in Alan Wolfe, ed., *America at Century's End*. Berkeley, CA: University of California Press.

Schwartz, Stephen. 2003. *The Two Faces of Islam: The House of Sa'ud from Tradition to Terror*. New York: Doubleday.

Scott, James C. 1998. *Seeing Like a State: How Certain Schemes to Improve the Human Condition Have Failed*. New Haven, CT: Yale University Press.

Scott, Wilbur J. 1990. "PTSD in DSM-III: A Case in the Politics of Diagnosis and Disease." *Social Problems* 37: 294–310.

Sedgh, Gilda, Stanley K.Henshaw, Susheela Singh, Akinrinola Bankole, and Joanna Drescher. 2007. "Legal Abortion Worldwide: Incidence and Recent Trends." *Perspectives on Sexual and Reproductive Health* 39, 4: 216–25.

Seiter, Ellen. 1999. *Television and New Media Audiences*. Oxford, UK: Clarendon Press.

Selten, Jean-Paul, and Elizabeth Cantor-Graae. 2005. "Social Defeat: Risk Factor for Schizophrenia." *British Journal of Psychiatry* 187: 101–02. Retrieved August 7, 2015 (http://bjp.rcpsych.org/content/bjprcpsych/187/2/101.full.pdf).

Senn, Charlene Y., Serge Desmarais, Norine Veryberg, and Eileen Wood. 2000. "Predicting Coercive Sexual Behavior Across the Lifespan in a Random Sample of Canadian Men." *Journal of Social and Personal Relationships* 17, 1; February: 95–113.

Sepinwall, Alan. 2012. *The Revolution Was Televised: The Cops, Crooks, Slingers and Slayers Who Changed TV Drama Forever*. Amazon: Self-published.

Seto, Michael. 2008. *Pedophilia and Sexual Offending Against Children*. Washington, DC: American Psychological Association.

Sev'er, Aysan. 1999. "Sexual Harassment: Where We Were, Where We Are and Prospects for the New Millennium." *Canadian Review of Sociology and Anthropology* 36, 4: 460–97.

Shain, A. 1995. "Employment of People with Disabilities." *Canadian Social Trends* 38: 8–13. Catalogue No. 11-008-XPE.

Shakur, Sanyika (a.k.a. Monster Kody Scott). 1993. *Monster: The Autobiography of an L.A. Gang Member*. New York: Penguin.

Shannon Brennan and Mia Dauvergne. 2011. "Police-reported crime statistics in Canada, 2010." *Juristat* p. 18. Retrieved July 5, 2015 (http://www.statcan.gc.ca/pub/85-002-x/2011001/article/11523-eng.pdf).

Shattuck, Roger. 1980. *The Forbidden Experiment: The Story of the Wild Boy of Aveyron*. New York: Farrar, Straus, and Giroux.

Shaw, Karen. 2001. "Harry Potter Books: My Concerns." Reachout Trust. Retrieved June 15, 2003 (http://www.reachouttrust.org/regulars/articles/occult/hpotter2.htm).

Shea, Sarah E., Kevin Gordon, Ann Hawkins, Janet Kawchuk, and Donna Smith. 2000. "Pathology in the Hundred-Acre Wood: A Neurodevelopmental Perspective on A. A. Milne." *Canadian Medical*

Association Journal 163, 12: 1557–59. Retrieved December 12, 2000 (http://www.cma.ca/cmaj/vol-163/issue-12/1557.htm).

Sheehy, Elizabeth. 2003. "From Women's Duty to Resist to Men's Duty to Ask: How Far Have We Come?" pp. 576–81 in T. Brettel Dawson, ed., *Women, Law and Social Change: Core Readings and Current Issues*, 4th ed. Concord, ON: Captus Press.

Shekelle, Paul G. 1998. "What Role for Chiropractic in Health Care?" *New England Journal of Medicine* 339: 1074–75.

Sherif, Muzafer, L. J. Harvey, B. Jack White, William R. Hood, and Carolyn W. Sherif. 1988 [1961]. *The Robber's Cave Experiment: Intergroup Conflict and Cooperation*, reprinted ed. Middletown, CT: Wesleyan University Press.

Sherkat, Darren E., and Christopher G. Ellison. 1999. "Recent Developments and Current Controversies in the Sociology of Religion." *Annual Review of Sociology* 25: 363–94.

Sherrill, Robert. 1997. "A Year in Corporate Crime." *The Nation* 7 April: 11–20.

Shkilnyk, Anastasia. 1985. *A Poison Stronger than Love: The Destruction of an Ojibway Community*. New Haven, CT: Yale University Press.

Shorter, Edward. 1997. *A History of Psychiatry: From the Era of the Asylum to the Age of Prozac*. New York: John Wiley and Sons.

Siad, Simona. 2007. "Canadian teens ranked the hardest working." *Toronto Star*, May 24. Retrieved November 6, 2012 (http://www.thestar.com/news/2007/05/24/canadian_teens_ranked_the_hardest_working.html).

Sigal, Samuel. 2014. "Feminism in Faith: Sara Hurwitz's Road to Becoming the First Ordained Orthodox Jewish Rabba." Retrieved August 11, 2015 (http://www.buzzfeed.com/sigalsamuel/feminism-in-faith-orthodox-judaism#.yb9jXNxnVz).

Signorielli, Nancy. 1998. "Reflections of Girls in the Media: A Content Analysis Across Six Media." Overview. Retrieved May 2, 2000 (http://childrennow.org/media/mc97/ReflectSummary.html).

_____. 2009. "Race and Sex in Prime Time: A Look at Occupations and Occupational Prestige." *Mass Communication and Society* 12, 3: 332–52.

Silberman, Steve. 2000. "Talking to Strangers." *Wired* 8, 5: 225–33, 288–96.

"Silent Boom (The)." 1997. *Forbes* 7 July: 170–71.

Simon, Jonathan. 1993. *Poor Discipline: Parole and the Social Control of the Underclass, 1890–1990*. Chicago: University of Chicago Press.

Simons, Ronald L., Chyi-In Wu, Christine Johnson, and Rand D. Conger. 1995. "A Test of Various Perspectives on the Intergenerational Transmission of Domestic Violence." *Criminology* 33: 141–60.

Sissing, T. W. 1996. "Some Missing Pages: The Black Community in the History of Québec and Canada." Retrieved June 14, 2002 (http://www.qesnrecit.qc.ca/mpages/title.htm).

Skolnick, Arlene. 1991. *Embattled Paradise: The American Family in an Age of Uncertainty*. New York: Basic Books.

Smith, Anthony. 1980. *Goodbye Gutenberg: The Newspaper Revolution of the 1980s*. New York: Oxford University Press.

Smith, Christian. 1991. *The Emergence of Liberation Theology: Radical Religion and Social Movement Theory*. Chicago: University of Chicago Press.

Smith, Elliot Blair. 2012. "American Dream Fades for Generation Y Professionals." Bloomberg.com, December 21. Retrieved December 30, 2012 (http://www.bloomberg.com/news/2012-12-21/american-dream-fades-for-generation-y-professionals.html).

Smith, Michael. 1990. "Patriarchal Ideology and Wife Beating: A Test of a Feminist Hypothesis." *Violence and Victims* 5: 257–73.

Smyth, Julie. 2003. "Sweden Ranked as Best Place to Have a Baby: Canada Places Fifth on Maternity Leave, 15th for Benefits." *National Post*, January 17. Retrieved June 27, 2004 (http://www.childcarecanada.org/ccin/2003/ccin1_17_03.html).

Snider, Laureen. 1999. "White-Collar Crime." P. 2504 in James H. Marsh, ed., *The Canadian Encyclopedia, Year 2000* edition. Toronto: McClelland & Stewart.

Snow, David A., E. Burke Rochford, Jr., Steven K. Worden, and Robert D. Benford. 1986. "Frame Alignment Processes, Micromobilization, and Movement Participation." *American Sociological Review* 51: 464–81.

Sofsky, Wolfgang. 1997 [1993]. *The Order of Terror: The Concentration Camp*, William Templer, trans. Princeton, NJ: Princeton University Press.

Sokoloff, Heather. 2001. "Wealth Affects Test Scores." *National Post*, December 5: A17. Retrieved January 22, 2004 (http://www.sgc.ca/Efact/emyths.htm).

Solicitor General Canada. 2002. "Factsheets." Retrieved January 22, 2004 (http://www.sgc.ca/Efact/emyths.htm).

Sorenson, Elaine. 1994. *Comparable Worth: Is It a Worthy Policy?* Princeton, NJ: Princeton University Press.

Spade, Joan Z. 2001. "Gender and Education in the United States," pp. 270–78 in Jeanne H. Ballantine and Joan Z. Spade, eds., *Schools and Society: A Sociological Approach to Education*. Belmont, CA: Wadsworth.

Spines, Christine. 2010. "Lady Gaga Wants You." *Cosmopolitan*, UK edition May: 50–54.

Spitz, René A. 1945. "Hospitalism: An Inquiry into the Genesis of Psychiatric Conditions in Early Childhood," pp. 53–74 in *The Psychoanalytic Study of the Child*, Vol. 1. New York: International Universities Press.

_____. 1962. "Autoerotism Re-Examined: The Role of Early Sexual Behavior Patterns in Personality Formation," pp. 283–315 in *The Psychoanalytic Study of the Child*, Vol. 17. New York: International Universities Press.

Spitzer, Steven. 1980. "Toward a Marxian Theory of Deviance," pp. 175–91 in Delos H. Kelly, ed. *Criminal Behavior: Readings in Criminology*. New York: St. Martin's Press.

Stacey, Judith. 1996. *Brave New Families: Stories of Domestic Upheaval in Late Twentieth Century America*. New York: Basic Books.

Stack, Stephen, and J. Ross Eshleman. 1998. "Marital Status and Happiness: A 17-Nation Study." *Journal of Marriage and the Family* 60: 527–36.

Stark, Rodney. 1985. *Sociology*. Belmont, CA: Wadsworth.

Stark, Rodney, and William Sims Bainbridge. 1979. "Of Churches, Sects, and Cults: Preliminary Concepts for a Theory of Religious

Movements." *Journal for the Scientific Study of Religion* 18: 117–31.

_____. 1987. *A Theory of Religion*. New York: P. Lang.

_____. 1997. *Religion, Deviance, and Social Control*. New York: Routledge.

Starr, Paul. 1982. *The Social Transformation of American Medicine*. New York: Basic Books.

_____. 1994. *The Logic of Health Care Reform: Why and How the President's Plan Will Work*, rev. ed. New York: Penguin.

Statista. 2015. "Number of monthly active Twitter users worldwide from 1st quarter 2010 to second quarter 2015 (in millions)." Retrieved August 5, 2015 (http://www.statista.com/statistics/282087/number-of-monthly-active-twitter-users).

Statista, 2016. "Number of monthly active Facebook users worldwide as of first quarter 2016)." Retrieved June 26, 2016 (http://www.statista.com/statistics/264810/number-of-monthly-active-facebook-users-worldwide).

Statistics Canada.1992a. "Selected Marriage Statistics, 1921–1990," Catalogue No. 82-552 http://publications.gc.ca/site/eng/9.812865/publication.html).

_____. 1992b. "Marriage and Conjugal Life in Canada, 1991," Catalogue 91-534.

_____. 1999. "National Longitudinal Survey of Children and Youth: Transition into Adolescence 1996/97." *The Daily*, July 6. Retrieved May 10, 2001 (http://www.statcan.ca/Daily/English/990706/d990706a.htm).

_____. 2000a. "Population by Aboriginal Group, 1996 Census." Retrieved October 7, 2000 (http://www.statcan.ca/english/Pgdb/People/Population/demo39a.htm).

_____. 2000b. "Household Environmental Practices." Retrieved October 7, 2000 (http://www.statcan.ca/english/Pgdb/Land/Environment/envir01a.htm).

_____. 2000c. *Income in Canada 1998*. Ottawa: Ministry of Industry.

_____. 2000d. "Divorces, 1998." *The Daily*, September 28. Retrieved May 10, 2001 (http://www.statcan.ca/Daily/English/000928/d000926.htm).

_____. 2001. "Television Viewing: Fall 1999." *The Daily*, January 25. Retrieved July 23, 2002 (http://www.statcan.ca/Daily/English/010125/d010125a.htm).

_____. 2003a. "Earnings of Canadians: Making a Living in the New Economy." Catalogue No. 96F0030 XIE2001014. Retrieved September 15, 2004 (http://www.statcan.ca/census01/products/analytic/companion/earn/contents.cfm).

_____. 2003b. "Religions in Canada." Catalogue No. 96F0030XIE2001015. Ottawa: Minister of Industry. Retrieved January 24, 2004 (http://www12.statcan.ca/english/census01/Products/Analytic/companion/rel/canada.cfm).

_____. 2003c. "Non-Wage Job Benefits, 2000." *The Daily*, May 21. Retrieved September 15, 2004 (http://www.statcan.ca/Daily/English/030521/d030521c.htm).

_____. 2003d. *The Daily*, Catalogue 11-001, Monday, June 2, 2003.

_____. 2005a. CANSIM database using CHASS (distributor). Version updated August 16, 2005 (http://dc1.chass.utoronto.ca.myaccess.library.utoronto.ca/census/mainmicro.html).

_____. 2005b. "Child Care, 1994/95 and 2000/01." *The Daily*, February 7. Retrieved March 14, 2006 (http://www.statcan.ca/Daily/English/050207/d050207b.htm).

_____. 2006a. "Access to Health Care Services in Canada, 2005." Retrieved April 2, 2010 (http://www.statcan.gc.ca/pub/82-575-x/82-575-x2006002-eng.htm).

_____. 2006b. "Households and the Environment 2006." Retrieved September 22, 2007 (http://www.statcan.ca/english/freepub/11-526-XIE/11-526-XIE2007001.pdf).

_____. 2007. "Table 101-1002: Mean Age and Median Age of Males and Females, by Type of Marriage and Marital Status, Canada, Provinces and Territories, Annual" (http://www5.statcan.gc.ca/cansim/a26?lang=eng&id=1011002).

_____. 2008a. "Screen Time among Canadian Adults: A Profile." *Health Reports* 19, 2: 31–43. Retrieved February 22, 2010 (http://www.statcan.gc.ca/pub/82-003-x/2008002/article/10600-eng.pdf).

_____. 2008b. "Sexual Assault in Canada, 2004 and 2007." Retrieved March 21, 2010 (http://www.statcan.gc.ca/pub/85f0033m/85f0033m2008019-eng.pdf).

_____. 2009a. "Couple Families by Presence of Children of all Ages in Private Households, 2006 Counts, for Canada, Provinces and Territories—20% Sample Data." Retrieved March 25, 2010 (http://www12.statcan.ca/census-recensement/2006/dp-pd/hlt/97-553/pages/page.cfm?Lang=E&Geo=PR&Code=01&Table=1&Data=Count&Age=1&StartRec=1&Sort=2&Display=Page).

_____. 2009b. "Family Violence in Canada: A Statistical Profile." Retrieved March 25, 2010 (http://www.phac-aspc.gc.ca/ncfv-cnivf/pdfs/fv-85-224-XWE-eng.pdf).

_____. 2009c. "Highest Level of Educational Attainment for the Population Aged 25 to 64, 2006 Counts for Both Sexes, for Canada, Provinces, and Territories—20% Sample Data." Retrieved February 21, 2010 (http://www12.statcan.ca/census-recensement/2006/dp-pd/hlt/97-560/pages/page.cfm?Lang=E&Geo=PR&Code=01&Table=1&Data=Count&Sex=1&StartRec=1&Sort=2&Display=Page).

_____. 2009d. "Same-Sex Couples by Type of Union (Married, Common-Law) and Sex, 2006 Census—20% Sample Data." Retrieved March 22, 2010 (http://www12.statcan.ca/census-recensement/2006/dp-pd/hlt/97-553/tables/Table4.cfm?Lang=E).

_____. 2010a. "Persistence of Low Income, by Selected Characteristics, Every 3 Years." CANSIM Table 202087.

_____. 2010b. "Population by Mother Tongue and Age Groups, 2006 Counts, for Canada, Provinces and Territories—20% Sample Data." Retrieved March 14, 2010 (http://www12.statcan.gc.ca/census-recensement/2006/dp-pd/hlt/97-555/T401-eng.cfm?Lang=E&T=401&GH=4&SC=1&S=99&O=A).

_____. 2010c. "Projections of the Diversity of the Canadian Population, 2006 to 2031." Catalogue No. 91-551-XIE 2010001, 2006 to 2031. Released March 9, 2010. Retrieved March 13, 2010 (http://www.statcan.gc.ca/pub/91-551-x/91-551-x2010001-eng.pdf).

_____. 2010d. "University Expenditures, by Type of Expenditure, Canada and Provinces, 1999/2000 and 2004/2005 to 2008/2009" (Table B.2.13).

_____. 2010e. "Canadian Internet Use Survey." Retrieved September 20, 2011 (http://www.statcan.gc.ca/daily-quotidien/110525/dq110525b-eng.htm).

_____. 2010f. "Unpaid Work (20), Age Groups (9) and Sex (3) for the Population 15 Years and Over of Canada, Provinces, Territories, Census Divisions and Census Sub-divisions, 2006 Census—20% Sample Data."

_____. 2012a. "Youth Courts, Guilty Cases by Type of Sentence, Annually (number)." CANSIM Table 2520067. Retrieved December 18, 2012 (http://dc2.chass.utoronto.ca.myaccess.library.utoronto.ca/cgi-bin/cansimdim/c2_getArrayDim.pl).

_____. 2012b. "Persons in Low Income by Economic Family Type, Annually." CANSIM Table 2020804.

_____. 2012c. "Persons in Low-Income Families, Annually." CANSIM Table 2020802.

_____. 2012d. "2011 Census of Population: Families, Households, Marital Status, Structural Type of Dwelling, Collectives." Retrieved January 29, 2013 (http://www.statcan.gc.ca/daily-quotidien/120919/dq120919a-eng.htm).

_____. 2012e. "Table D.6.3: Educational Attainment of the Population Aged 25 to 64, Off-Reserve Aboriginal, Non-Aboriginal, and Total Population, Canada, Provinces, and Territories, 2009, 2010 and 2011."

_____. 2013a. "Homicide Survey, Number of Solved Homicides, by Type of Accused-Victim Relationship, Canada, Annually (number)." CANSIM Table 2530006.

_____. 2013b. "Chart 6: Crude Marriage Rate and Crude Divorce Rate, Canada, 1926 to 2008." Retrieved January 28, 2013 (http://www.statcan.gc.ca/pub/89-503-x/2010001/article/11546/c-g/c-g006-eng.htm).

_____. 2013c. "Mean Age and Median Age of Males and Females, by Marital Status, Canada, Provinces and Territories, 2005 to 2008." Special tabulation prepared by the Health Statistics Department.

_____. 2013d. "Summary Elementary and Secondary School Indicators for Canada, the Provinces, and Territories, 2006/2007 to 2010/2011."

_____. 2013e. "Persons in low income before tax (in percent, 2007 to 2011)." Retrieved July 28, 2015 (http://www.statcan.gc.ca/tables-tableaux/sum-som/l01/cst01/famil41a-eng.htm?sdi=low%20income).

_____. 2013f. "Table 1. Proportion of Aboriginal people by selected levels of educational attainment, sex and age groups, Canada, 2011." Retrieved August 2, 2015 (http://www12.statcan.gc.ca/nhs-enm/2011/as-sa/99-012-x/2011003/tbl/tbl1-eng.cfm.

_____. 2013g. "Ethnic Origin (264), Single and Multiple Ethnic Origin Responses (3), Generation Status (4), Age Groups (10) and Sex (3) for the Population in Private Households of Canada, Provinces, Territories, Census Metropolitan Areas and Census Agglomerations," 2011 *National Household Survey.* Retrieved September 13, 2013 (http://www12.statcan.gc.ca/nhs-enm/2011/dp-pd/dt-td/Rp-eng.cfm?LANG=E&APATH=3&DETAIL=0&DIM=0&FL=A&FREE=0&GC=0&GID=0&GK=0&GRP=0&PID=105396&PRID=0&PTYPE=105277&S=0&SHOWALL=0&SUB=0&Temporal=2013&THEME=95&VID=0&VNAMEE=&VNAMEF=).

_____. 2013h. "Canadian Households in 2011: Type and Growth." (https://www12.statcan.gc.ca/census-recensement/2011/as-sa/98-312-x/98-312-x2011003_2-eng.cfm).

_____. 2013i. "Religion (108), Immigrant Status and Period of Immigration (11), Age Groups (10) and Sex (3) for the Population in Private Households of Canada, Provinces, Territories, Census Metropolitan Areas and Census Agglomerations, 2011 *National Household Survey.*" Retrieved September 19, 2013 http://www12.statcan.gc.ca/nhs-enm/2011/dp-pd/dt-td/Rp-eng.cfm?LANG=E&APATH=3&DETAIL=0&DIM=0&FL=A&FREE=0&GC=0&GID=0&GK=0&GRP=0&PID=105399&PRID=0&PTYPE=105277&S=0&SHOWALL=0&SUB=0&Temporal=2013&THEME=95&VID=0&VNAMEE=&VNAMEF=).

_____. 2013j. "Distribution of persons by income group and highest level of education attainment." Retrieved August 8, 2015 (https://www12.statcan.gc.ca/nhs-enm/2011/as-sa/99-014-x/2011003/c-g/desc/longdesc01_2-eng.cfm).

_____. 2013k. "University Degrees, Diplomas, and Certificates Granted, by Program Level, Classification of Instructional Programs, Primary Grouping (CIP_PG) and Sex, Annually (number)." CANSIM Table 4770014.

_____. 2013m. "Life Tables, Canada, Provinces and Territories 2009 to 2011." Retrieved August 7, 2015 (http://www.statcan.gc.ca/pub/84-537-x/84-537-x2013005-eng.htm).

_____. 2014a. Adapted from Summary Tables, "Suicides and suicide rate, by sex and age group," 2011. Retrieved June 23, 2015 (http://www.statcan.gc.ca/tables-tableaux/sum-som/l01/cst01/hlth66a-eng.htm).

_____. 2014b. Table 051-0001. "Estimates of Population, by Age Group and Sex for July 1, Canada, Provinces and Territories, Annual." Retrieved July 6, 2015 (http://www5.statcan.gc.ca/cansim/a26?lang=eng&id=510001).

_____. 2014c. Table 105-0501. "Health Indicator Profile, Annual Estimates, by Age Group and Sex, Canada, Provinces, Territories, Health Regions (2013 boundaries) and Peer Groups (year to date—(averages)." Retrieved July 6, 2015 (http://www5.statcan.gc.ca/cansim/a26?lang=eng&id=1050501#customizeTab).

_____. 2014d. "Annual Estimates of Population for Canada, Provinces, and Territories, from July 1, 1971 to July 1, 2014." Retrieved July 26, 2015 (http://www.stats.gov.nl.ca/statistics/population/PDF/Annual_Pop_Prov.PDF).

_____. 2014e. "Table 2: Low income cut-offs (1992 base) before tax." Retrieved July 28, 2015 (http://www.statcan.gc.ca/pub/75f0002m/2014003/tbl/tbl02-eng.htm).

_____. 2015a. "Canada's crime rate: Two decades of decline." Retrieved July 23, 2015 (http://www.statcan.gc.ca/pub/11-630-x/11-630-x2015001-eng.htm5).

_____. 2015b. "Police officers, by province and territory." Retrieved July 23, 2015 (http://www.statcan.gc.ca/tables-tableaux/sum-som/l01/cst01/legal05a-eng.htm).

_____. 2015c, CANSIM, Table 2510005 and Table 2510006. Retrieved July 26, 2015 (http://dc2.chass.utoronto.ca.myaccess.library.utoronto.ca/cgi-bin/cansimdim/c2_searchCansim.pl).

_____. 2015d. "Survey of Financial Security, 2012." Retrieved July 27, 2015 (http://www.statcan.gc.ca/daily-quotidien/140225/dq140225b-eng.htm).

_____. 2015e. "Market, total and after-tax income, by economic family type and income quintiles, 2011 constant dollars, annually." CANSIM, Table 202 – 0701. Retrieved July 27, 2015 (http://dc2.chass.utoronto.ca.myaccess.library.utoronto.ca/cgi-bin/cansimdim/c2_getArrayDim.pl).

_____. 2015f. "Earnings of Individuals, by Selected Characteristics and National Occupational Classification (NOC-S), 2011 Constant Dollars, Annually." CANSIM Table 2020106. (dc2.chass.utoronto.ca.myaccess.library.utoronto.ca/cgi-bin/cansimdim/c2_arrays.pl).

_____. 2015g. "Individuals by total income level, by province and territory (Canada)." Retrieved July 28, 2015 (http://www.statcan.gc.ca/tables-tableaux/sum-som/l01/cst01/famil105a-eng.htm).

_____. 2015h. *National Household Survey* (NHS) PUMF, 2011: individual's file. Retrieved August 2, 2015 (http://sda.chass.utoronto.ca.myaccess.library.utoronto.ca/cgi-bin/sdacensus/hsda?harcsda+nhs11).

_____. 2015i. "Female-to-Male Earnings Ratios, by Selected Characteristics, 2011 Constant Dollars, Annually (percentage)." CANSIM database, Table 2020104.

_____. 2015j. "Labour force survey estimates (LFS), by National Occupational Classification for Statistics (NOC-S) and sex, annually." CANSIM database, Table 2820010.

_____. 2015k. "Individuals by total income level, by province and territory." Retrieved August 8, 2015 (http://www.statcan.gc.ca/tables-tableaux/sum-som/l01/cst01/famil105a-eng.htm).

_____. 2015m. "Ten Leading Causes of Death, 2011." Retrieved August 7, 2015 (http://www.statcan.gc.ca/pub/82-625-x/2014001/article/11896-eng.htm).

_____. 2016. "Family characteristics by family type and age group, annually." CANSIM Table 110010. Retrieved July 8, 2016 (http://dc2.chass.utoronto.ca.myaccess.library.utoronto.ca/cgi-bin/cansimdim/c2_getArrayDim.pl).

Steel, Freda M. 1987. "Alimony and Maintenance Orders," pp. 155–67 in Sheilah L. Martin and Kathleen E. Mahoney, eds., *Equality and Judicial Neutrality*. Toronto: Carswell.

Steele, Claude M. 1992. "Race and the Schooling of Black Americans." *Atlantic Monthly*, April. Retrieved May 2, 2000 (http://www.theatlantic.com/unbound/flashbks/blacked/steele.htm).

_____. 1997. "A Threat in the Air: How Stereotypes Shape the Intellectual Identities and Performance of Women and African-Americans." *American Psychologist* 52: 613–29.

Sternberg, Robert J. 1998. *In Search of the Human Mind*, 2nd ed. Fort Worth, TX: Harcourt Brace.

Sternheimer, Karen. 2014. "Do Video Games Kill?" pp. 87–95 in Robert Brym, ed., *Society in Question*, 7th ed. Toronto: Nelson.

Stevenson, Wesley. 2014. "How many men are paedophiles?" *BBC News*. 30 July. Retrieved December 21, 2016 (http://www.bbc.com/news/magazine-28526106).

Stewart, Abigail, Anne P. Copeland, Nia Lane Chester, Janet E. Malley, and Nicole B. Barenbaum. 1997. *Separating Together: How Divorce Transforms Families*. New York: The Guilford Press.

Stone, Lawrence. 1977. *The Family, Sex and Marriage in England, 1500–1800*. New York: Harper and Row.

Stouffer, Samuel A. et al. 1949. *The American Soldier*, 4 vols. Princeton, NJ: Princeton University Press.

Straus, Murray A. 1994. *Beating the Devil Out of Them: Corporal Punishment in American Families*. New York: Lexington Books.

Strauss, Anselm L. 1993. *Continual Permutations of Action*. New York: Aldine de Gruyter.

Subrahmanyam, Kaveri, and Patricia M. Greenfield. 1998. "Computer Games for Girls: What Makes Them Play?" pp. 46–71 in Justine Cassell and Henry Jenkins, eds., *From Barbie to Mortal Kombat: Gender and Computer Games*. Cambridge, MA: MIT Press.

Sullivan, Mercer L. 2002. "Exploring Layers: Extended Case Method as a Tool for Multilevel Analysis of School Violence." *Sociological Methods and Research* 31, 2: 255–85.

Sumner, William Graham. 1940 [1907]. *Folkways*. Boston: Ginn.

Sutherland, Edwin H. 1939. *Principles of Criminology*. Philadelphia: Lippincott.

_____. 1949. *White Collar Crime*. New York: Dryden.

Swiss Re. 2005. "Natural Catastrophes and Man-Made Disasters in 2004." Retrieved March 2, 2005 (http://www.swissre.com).

_____. 2007. "Natural Catastrophes and Man-Made Disasters in 2006." April 30, 2007 (http://www.swissre.com/internet/pwswpspr.nsf/fmBookMarkFrameSet?ReadForm&BM5/vwAllbyIDKeyLu/mpdl-6z2krc?OpenDocument).

_____. 2008. "Natural Catastrophes and Man-Made Disasters in 2007." Retrieved March 29, 2010 (http://www.swissre.com/resources/678bb7004159bbdaa92ced3638166fb1-Sigma_1_2008_e.pdf).

_____. 2009. "Natural Catastrophes and Man-Made Disasters in 2008." Retrieved March 29, 2010 (http://www.swissre.com/resources/d6346004d4e9669ac76eecedd316cf3-sigma2_2009_e.pdf).

_____. 2010. "Natural Catastrophes and Man-Made Disasters in 2009." Retrieved March 29, 2010 (http://www.swissre.com/resources/6552260041b90e4aac79fc55ef9dd899-sigma1_2010_e_rev.pdf).

_____. 2013. "Natural Catastrophes and Man-Made Disasters in 2012." Retrieved March 31, 2013 (http://media.swissre.com/documents/sigma2_2013_en.pdf).

_____. 2015. "Natural Catastrophes and Man-Made Disasters in 2014." Retrieved August 2, 2015 (http://media.swissre.com/documents/sigma2_2015_en_final.pdf).

Sykes, Gresham, and David Matza. 1957. "Techniques of Neutralization: A Theory of Delinquency." *American Sociological Review* 22: 664–70.

Tajfel, Henri. 1981. *Human Groups and Social Categories: Studies in Social Psychology*. Cambridge, UK: Cambridge University Press.

Tannen, Deborah. 1990. *You Just Don't Understand Me: Women and Men in Conversation*. New York: William Morrow.

_____. 1994a. *Talking from 9 to 5: How Women's and Men's Conversational Styles Affect Who Gets Heard, Who Gets Credit, and What Gets Done at Work*. New York: William Morrow.

_____. 1994b. *Gender and Discourse*. New York: Oxford University Press.

Tarrow, Sidney. 1994. *Power in Movement: Social Movements, Collective Action and Politics*. Cambridge, UK: Cambridge University Press.

Tasker, Fiona L., and Susan Golombok. 1997. *Growing Up in a Lesbian Family: Effects on Child Development*. New York: The Guilford Press.

TD Economics. 2015. "Aboriginal women outperforming in labour markets." 6 July. Retrieved August 2, 2015 (https://www.td.com/document/PDF/economics/special/AboriginalWomen.pdf).

Tec, Nechama. 1986. *When Light Pierced the Darkness: Christian Rescue of Jews in Nazi-Occupied Poland*. New York: Oxford University Press.

Television Bureau of Canada. 2015. *Cross-Media Reach and Time Spent: Major Media Comparison*, pp. 6, 13. Retrieved July 5, 2015 (http://www.tvb.ca/pages/RTS).

Thoits, Peggy A. 1989. "The Sociology of Emotions." *Annual Review of Sociology* 15: 317–42.

Thomas, Keith. 1971. *Religion and the Decline of Magic*. London, UK: Weidenfeld and Nicolson.

Thomas, Mikhail. 2002. "Adult Criminal Court Statistics, 2000/01." *Juristat* 22, 2 (March). Catalogue No. 85-002-XPE. Ottawa: Canadian Centre for Justice Statistics and Statistics Canada.

_____. 2004. "Adult Criminal Court Statistics, 2003–04." *Juristat* 24, 12. Catalogue No. 85-002-XPE. Ottawa: Canadian Centre for Justice Statistics and Statistics Canada.

Thomas, William Isaac. 1966 [1931]. "The Relation of Research to the Social Process," pp. 289–305 in Morris Janowitz, ed., *W. I. Thomas on Social Organization and Social Personality*. Chicago: University of Chicago Press.

Thompson, Derek. 2016. "Who Are Donald Trump's Supporters, Really?" *The Atlantic* March.

Thompson, E.P. 1967. "Time, Work Discipline, and Industrial Capitalism." *Past and Present* 38: 59–67.

Thompson, Ross A., and Paul R. Amato. 1999. "The Postdivorce Family: An Introduction to the Issues," pp. xi–xxiii in Ross A. Thompson and Paul R. Amato, eds., *The Postdivorce Family: Children, Parenting and Society*. Thousand Oaks, CA: Sage Publications.

Thorne, Barrie. 1993. *Gender Play: Girls and Boys in School*. New Brunswick, NJ: Rutgers University Press.

Tilly, Charles. 1979a. "Collective Violence in European Perspective," pp. 83–118 in H. Graham and T. Gurr, eds., *Violence in America: Historical and Comparative Perspective*, 2nd ed. Beverly Hills, CA: Sage.

_____. 1979b. "Repertoires of Contention in America and Britain, 1750–1830," pp. 126–55 in Mayer N. Zald and John D. McCarthy, eds. *The Dynamics of Social Movements: Resource Mobilization, Social Control, and Tactics*. Cambridge, MA: Winthrop Publishers.

Tilly, Charles, Louise Tilly, and Richard Tilly. 1975. *The Rebellious Century, 1830–1930*. Cambridge, MA: Harvard University Press.

Titlestad, Michael 2013 "Searching for the Sugar-coated Man," *Safundi: The Journal of South African and American Studies* 14:4: 466–70.

Tjepkema, Michael. n.d. "Measured Obesity: Adult obesity in Canada: Measured height and weight." Statistics Canada. Retrieved January 14, 2013 (http://www.aboutmen.ca/application/www.aboutmen.ca/asset/upload/tiny_mce/page/link/Adult-Obesity-in-Canada.pdf).

Tkacik, Maureen. 2002. "The Return of Grunge." *Wall Street Journal*, December 11: B1, B10.

Toffler, Alvin. 1990. *Powershift: Knowledge, Wealth, and Violence at the Edge of the 21st Century*. New York: Bantam.

Tong, Rosemarie. 1989. *Feminist Thought: A Comprehensive Introduction*. Boulder, CO: Westview.

Tönnies, Ferdinand. 1988 [1887]. *Community and Society (Gemeinschaft und Gesselschaft)*. New Brunswick, NJ: Transaction.

Toronto Board of Education. 1993. *The 1991 Every Secondary Student Survey. Part II: Detailed Profiles of Toronto's Secondary School Students*. Toronto: Toronto Board of Education Research Services.

Toronto Star. 2015. "Known to police." Retrieved July 22, 2015 (http://www.thestar.com/news/gta/knowntopolice.html).

Torrance, Judy M. 1986. *Public Violence in Canada*. Toronto: University of Toronto Press.

Troeltsch, Ernst. 1931 [1923]. *The Social Teaching of the Christian Churches*, Olive Wyon, trans. 2 vols. London, UK: George Allen and Unwin.

Trovato, Frank. 1998. "The Stanley Cup of Hockey and Suicide in Quebec, 1951–1992." *Social Forces* 77: 105–27.

Trudeau Foundation. 2006. "Backgrounder: Environics Research Group Poll for the Trudeau Foundation." Retrieved January 13, 2013 (http://www.trudeaufoundation.ca/sites/default/files/resultats_en1.pdf).

Tschannen, Olivier. 1991. "The Secularization Paradigm: A Systematization." *Journal for the Scientific Study of Religion* 30: 395–415.

Tufts, Jennifer. 2000. "Public Attitudes Toward the Criminal Justice System." *Juristat* 20, 12 (December). Catalogue No. 85-002-XPE. Ottawa: Canadian Centre for Justice Statistics and Statistics Canada.

Tuljapurkar, Shripad, Nan Li, and Carl Boe. 2000. "A Universal Pattern of Mortality Decline in the G7 Countries." *Nature* 405: 789–92.

Tumin, M. 1953. "Some Principles of Stratification: A Critical Analysis." *American Sociological Review* 18: 387–94.

Turcotte, Martin. 2007. "Time Spent with Family During a Typical Workday, 1986 to 2005." *Canadian Social Trends* 82: 2–11. Catalogue No. 11-008-XPE. Retrieved March 26, 2007 (http://www.statcan.ca/english/freepub/11-008-XIE/2006007/pdf/11-008-XIE20060079574.pdf).

Turkel, Ann Ruth. 1998. "All about Barbie: Distortions of a Transitional Object." *Journal of the American Academy of Psychoanalysis* 26, 1; Spring: 165–77.

Turkle, Sherry. 1995. *Life on the Screen: Identity in the Age of the Internet*. New York: Simon & Schuster.

_____. 2011. *Alone Together: Why We Expect More from Technology and Less from Each Other*. New York: Basic Books.

Turner, Bryan S. 1986. *Citizenship and Capitalism: The Debate over Reformism*. London, UK: Allen and Unwin.

Twitaholic.com. 2013. "Top 100 Twitterholics Based on Followers." Retrieved April 2, 2013 (http://twitaholic.com/top100/followers/).

Twitter Counter. 2015. Retrieved August 5, 2015 (http://twittercounter.com/pages/100).

"U.K. Panel Calls Climate Data Valid." 2010. *New York Times*, March 30. Retrieved April 1, 2010 (http://www.nytimes.com).

UNAIDS. 2009. *2009 AIDS Epidemic Update*. Geneva. Retrieved April 1, 2010 (http://data.unaids.org/pub/Report/2009/JC1700_Epi_Update_2009_en.pdf).

UNAIDS. 2012. *Global Report: UNAIDS Report on the Global AIDS Epidemic*. Retrieved March 15, 2013 (http://www.unaids.org/en/media/unaids/contentassets/documents/epidemiology/2012/gr2012/20121120_UNAIDS_Global_Report_2012_with_annexes_en.pdf).

UNAIDS 2014. *Global Report: UNAIDS Report on the Global AIDS Epidemic 2013*. Retrieved August 7, 2015 (http://www.unaids.org/sites/default/files/media_asset/UNAIDS_Global_Report_2013_en_1.pdf).

Ungar, Sheldon. 1992. "The Rise and (Relative) Decline of Global Warming as a Social Problem." *Sociological Quarterly* 33: 483–501.

_____. 1999. "Is Strange Weather in the Air? A Study of U.S. National Network News Coverage of Extreme Weather Events." *Climatic Change* 41: 133–50.

United Nations Development Programme. 2015. *Human Development Report 2015*. "Table 5: Gender Inequality Index." Retrieved April 30, 2016 http://hdr.undp.org/en/composite/GII.

"United Nations Development Policy and Analysis Division. 2014. "Country Classification." Retrieved April 2, 2016 (http://www.un.org/en/development/desa/policy/wesp/wesp_current/2014wesp_country_classification.pdf).

United Nations Educational, Scientific, and Cultural Organization (UNESCO). 2008. "International Literacy Statistics: A Review of Concepts, Methodology and Current Data." Retrieved March 27, 2010

(http://www.uis.unesco.org/template/pdf/Literacy/LiteracyReport2008.pdf).

United Nations Statistics Division. 2013. "Total Fertility Rate." *The United Nations World Population Prospects: The 2010 Revision*.

Unschuld, Paul. 1985. *Medicine in China*. Berkeley, CA: University of California Press.

Upper Canada College. 2015. "Tuition & Fees." Retrieved August 8, 2015 (http://www.ucc.on.ca/admission/tuition-fees).

U.S. Department of Commerce. 1998. "Statistical Abstract of the United States: 1998." Retrieved October 8, 2000 (http://www.census.gov/prod/3/98pubs/98statab/sasec1.pdf).

U.S. Department of Labor. 2010. "CPI Inflation Calculator." Retrieved March 29, 2010 (http://www.bls.gov/data/inflation_calculator.htm).

U.S. Environmental Protection Agency, Office of Air Quality Planning and Standards. 2000. *National Air Pollutant Emission Trends, 1900–1998*. Retrieved August 3, 2000 (http://www.epa.gov/ttn/chief/trends98/emtrnd.html).

Useem, Bert. 1998. "Breakdown Theories of Collective Action." *Annual Review of Sociology* 24: 215–38.

Vago, Stephen, and Adie Nelson. 2003. *Law and Society*. Don Mills, ON: Pearson Educational Publishing.

Vincent, David. 2000. *The Rise of Mass Literacy: Reading and Writing in Modern Europe*. Cambridge, England: Polity Press.

Vishwanath, Arun. 2015. "Habitual Facebook Use and Its Impact on Getting Deceived on Social Media." *Journal of Computer-Mediated Communication* 20: 83–98.

Vrangalova, Zhana, and Ritch C. Savin-Williams. 2012. "Mostly Heterosexual and Mostly Gay/Lesbian: Evidence for New Sexual Orientation Identities." Archives of Sexual Behavior 41: 85–101.

Vygotsky, Lev S. 1987. *The Collected Works of L. S. Vygotsky*, Vol. 1, N. Minick, trans. New York: Plenum.

Wait Time Alliance. 2014. "Time to Close the Gap: Report Card on Wait Times in Canada." Retrieved August 7, 2014 (http://www.waittimealliance.ca/wp-content/uploads/2014/06/FINAL-EN-WTA-Report-Card.pdf).

Wald, Matthew L., and John Schwartz. 2003. "Alerts Were Lacking, NASA Shuttle Manager Says." *New York Times*, July 23. Retrieved July 23, 2003 (http://www.nytimes.com).

Waldfogel, Jane. 1997. "The Effect of Children on Women's Wages." *American Sociological Review* 62: 209–17.

Wallace, James, and Jim Erickson. 1992. *Hard Drive: Bill Gates and the Making of the Microsoft Empire*. New York: John Wiley.

Wallace, Marnie. 2009. "Police-Reported Crime Statistics in Canada, 2008." *Juristat* 29, 3. Retrieved October 14, 2010 (http://www.statcan.gc.ca/pub/85-002-x/2009003/article/10902-eng.htm).

Wallerstein, Immanuel. 1974–89. *The Modern World-System*, 3 vols. New York: Academic Press.

Wallerstein, Judith S., Julia Lewis, and Sandra Blakeslee. 2000. *The Unexpected Legacy of Divorce: The 25 Year Landmark Study*. New York: Hyperion.

Walmsley, Roy. 2012. *World Prison Population List*, 9th ed. London, UK: International Centre for Prison Studies. Retrieved December 18, 2012 (http://www.idcr.org.uk/wp-content/uploads/2010/09/WPPL-9-22.pdf).

Wanner, R. 1999. "Expansion and Ascription: Trends in Educational Opportunity in Canada, 1920–1994." *Canadian Review of Sociology and Anthropology* 36; August: 409–42.

Wasserman, Stanley, and Katherine Faust. 1994. *Social Network Analysis: Methods and Applications*. Cambridge: Cambridge University Press.

Watkins, S. Craig, and Rana A. Emerson. 2000. "Feminist Media Criticism and Feminist Media Practices." *Annals of the American Academy of Political and Social Science* 571: 151–66.

Webb, Eugene J., Donald T. Campbell, Richard D. Schwartz, and Lee Sechrest. 1966. *Unobtrusive Measures: Nonreactive Research in the Social Sciences*. Chicago: Rand McNally.

"Webcam Penetration Rates & Adoption." 2011. *Weareorganizedchaos.com*. Retrieved April 4, 2013 (http://weareorganizedchaos.com/index.php/tag/webcam-stats).

Weber, Max. 1946. *From Max Weber: Essays in Sociology*, rev. ed., H. Gerth and C. W. Mills, eds. and trans. New York: Oxford University Press.

_____. 1958 [1904–05]. *The Protestant Ethic and the Spirit of Capitalism.* New York: Scribner.

_____. 1964 [1947]. *The Theory of Social and Economic Organization*, T. Parsons, ed., A. M. Henderson and T. Parsons, trans. New York: Free Press.

_____. 1968 [1914]. *Economy and Society*, Guenther Roth and Claus Wittich, eds. Berkeley, CA: University of California Press.

Weeks, Carly. 2009. "The dark side of 'free-range' chickens." *Globe and Mail* 15 January. Retrieved August 3, 2015 (http://www.theglobeandmail.com/life/the-dark-side-of-free-range-chickens/article1146977).

Weeks, Jeffrey. 1986. *Sexuality*. London, UK: Routledge.

Weinreich, Max. 1945. "Der YIVO un di problemen fun unzer tzayt." [Yiddish: "YIVO and the problems of our time"] YIVO *bleter: shrift fun yidishn visenshaftlikhn institut* [YIVO Pages: Writing from the Yiddish Scientific Institute 25, 1:3–18.

Weinstein, Rhona S. 2002. *Reaching Higher: The Power of Expectations in Schooling*. Cambridge, MA: Harvard University Press.

Weis, Joseph G. 1987. "Class and Crime," pp. 71–90 in Michael Gottfredson and Travis Hirschi, eds. *Positive Criminology*. Beverly Hills, CA: Sage.

Welch, Michael. 1997. "Violence Against Women by Professional Football Players: A Gender Analysis of Hypermasculinity, Positional Status, Narcissism, and Entitlement." *Journal of Sport and Social Issues* 21: 392–411.

Wellman, Barry. 2014. "Connecting Communities On and Offline," pp. 54–63 in Robert Brym, ed., *Society in Question*, 7th ed. Toronto: Nelson.

Wellman, Barry, and Stephen Berkowitz, eds. 1997. *Social Structures: A Network Approach*, updated ed. Greenwich, CT: JAI Press.

Wellman, Barry, Peter J. Carrington, and Alan Hall. 1997 [1988]. "Networks as Personal Communities," pp. 130–84 in Barry Wellman and Stephen D. Berkowitz, eds., *Social Structures: A Network Approach*, updated ed. Greenwich, CT: JAI Press.

Welsh, Sandy. 1999. "Gender and Sexual Harassment." *Annual Review of Sociology* 25: 169–90.

West, Candace, and Don Zimmerman. 1987. "Doing Gender." *Gender and Society* 1: 125–51.

Wheeler, Stanton. 1961. "Socialization in Correctional Communities." *American Sociological Review* 26: 697–712.

Whitaker, Reg. 1987. *Double Standard.* Toronto: Lester and Orpen Dennys.

Whorf, Benjamin Lee. 1956. *Language, Thought, and Reality*, John B. Carroll, ed. Cambridge, MA: MIT Press.

Widyastuti, Adeline. 2010. *The Globalization of New Media Exposure: The Dependency on the Internet.* Saarbrücken, Germany: Lambert.

Wilensky, Harold L. 1967. *Organizational Intelligence: Knowledge and Policy in Government and Industry.* New York: Basic Books.

_____. 1997. "Social Science and the Public Agenda: Reflections on the Relation of Knowledge to Policy in the United States and Abroad." *Journal of Health Politics, Policy and Law* 22: 1241–65.

Wilkins-Laflamme, Sarah. 2014. "Report: Religion in Canada." Centre d'études ethniques des universités montréalaises (CEETUM). December. Retrieved August 8, 2014 (http://www.ceetum.umontreal.ca/documents/capsules/2014/wilk-en-2014.pdf).

Wilkinson, Richard G. 1996. *Unhealthy Societies: The Afflictions of Inequality.* London, UK: Routledge.

Wilkinson, Richard, and Michael Marmot, eds. 2003. *Social Determinants of Health: The Solid Facts.* Copenhagen: World Health Organization Regional Office for Europe.

Willardt, Kenneth. 2000. "The Gaze He'll Go Gaga For." *Cosmopolitan* April: 232–37.

Williams, David R., and Chiquita Collins. 1995. "U.S. Socioeconomic and Racial Differences in Health: Patterns and Explanations." *Annual Review of Sociology* 21: 349–86.

Williams, Eric. 1944. *Capitalism and Slavery.* Chapel Hill NC: University of North Carolina Press.

Willis, Paul. 1984. *Learning to Labour: How Working-Class Kids Get Working-Class Jobs*, reprinted ed. New York: Columbia University Press.

Wilson, T.D., Reinhard, D., Westgate, E.C., Gilbert, D.T., Ellerbeck, N., Hahn, C., Brown, C.L., & Shaked, A. (2014). "Just think: The challenges of the disengaged mind." *Science* 345, 75–77.

Wilson, William Julius. 1987. *The Truly Disadvantaged: The Inner City, the Underclass, and Public Policy.* Chicago: University of Chicago Press.

Winter, Michael F. 1996. "Societal Reaction, Labeling and Social Control: The Contribution of Edwin M. Lemert." *History of the Human Sciences* 9, 2: 53–77.

Wolf, Naomi. 1997. *Promiscuities: The Secret Struggle for Womanhood.* New York: Vintage.

Wolpert, Stuart. 2012. "Foster Kids Do Equally Well When Adopted by Gay, Lesbian or Heterosexual Parents." UCLA Newsroom, 18 October. Retrieved February 2, 2013 (http://newsroom.ucla.edu/portal/ucla/foster-children-adopted-by-gay-239748.aspx).

"Woman Soldier in Abuse Spotlight." 2004. *BBC News World Edition* 7 May. Retrieved March 3, 2005 (http://news.bbc.co.uk/2/hi/americas/3691753.stm).

Wong, Lloyd, and Michele Ng. 1998. "Chinese Immigrant Entrepreneurs in Vancouver: A Case Study of Ethnic Business Development." *Canadian Ethnic Studies* 30: 64–85.

Wood, Julia. 1999. *Everyday Encounters: An Introduction to Interpersonal Communication*, 2nd ed. Belmont, CA: Wadsworth.

Woodbury, Anthony. (2003). "Endangered Languages." *Linguistic Society of America.* Woodrow Federal Reserve Bank of Minneapolis.

Woodrow Federal Reserve Bank of Minneapolis. 2000. "What's a Dollar Worth?" Retrieved October 8, 2000 (http://woodrow.mpls.frb.fed.us/economy/calc/cpihome.html).

World Bank (The). 2014. "GDP per capita, PPP (constant 2005 international $)." Retrieved March 12, 2014 (http://data.worldbank.org/indicator/NY.GDP.PCAP.PP.KD).

World Bank (The). 2015. "Physicians (per 1000 people)." Retrieved August 7, 2015 (http://data.worldbank.org/indicator/SH.MED.PHYS.ZS).

World Health Organization. 2003. *Cumulative Number of Reported*

Probable Cases [SARS]. Retrieved June 16, 2003 (http://www.who.int/csr/sars/country/2003_06_16/en).

———. 2010a. "Suicide Rates per 100 000 by Country, Year and Sex." Retrieved February 16, 2010 (http://www.who.int/mental_health/prevention/suicide_rates/en/index.html).

———. 2010b. *WHO Statistical Information System (WHOSIS)*. Retrieved April 1, 2010 (http://www.who.int/whosis/en/index.html).

———. 2012a. *WHO Statistical Information System (WHOSIS)*. Retrieved March 15, 2013 (http://apps.who.int/whosis/data/).

———. 2012b. *Maternal mortality*. Retrieved March 15, 2013 (http://www.who.int/mediacentre/factsheets/fs348/en/index.html).

———. 2013. *Overweight and obesity*. Retrieved March 16, 2013(http://www.who.int/gho/ncd/risk_factors/overweight/en/index.html).

———. 2015. Global Health Observatory Data Repository." Retrieved August 7, 2015 (http://apps.who.int/gho/data/?theme=home).

World Hunger Education Service. 2015. "2015 World Hunger and Poverty Facts and Statistics." Retrieved July 28, 2015 (http://www.worldhunger.org/articles/Learn/world%20hunger%20facts%202002.htm).

World Values Survey. 2003. Machine readable data set. Retrieved May 1, 2004 (http://www.worldvaluessurvey.org).

World Values Survey. 2010. Retrieved October 20, 2010 (http://www.wvsevsdb.com/wvs/WVSAnalizeSample.jsp).

World Values Survey. 2012. Retrieved March 16, 2012 (http://www.wvsevsdb.com/wvs/WVSAnalize.jsp).

Wortley, Scot, David Brownfield, and John Hagan. 1996. *The Usual Suspects: Race, Age and Gender Differences in Police Contact*. Paper presented at the 48th Annual Conference of the American Society of Criminology, Chicago: November.

Wortley, Scot, and Julian Tanner. 2008. "Money, Respect and Defiance: Explaining Ethnic Differences in Gang Activity among Canadian Youth," pp. 181–210 in Frank van Gemert, Dana Peterson, and Inger-Lise Lien, eds., Youth Gangs, Migration and Ethnicity. London, U.K.: Willan Publishing.

Wortley, Scot, and Julian Tanner. 2011. "The Racial Profiling Debate: Data, Denials, and Confusion," pp. 295–302 in Robert J. Brym, ed. *Society in Question*. Toronto: Nelson.

Wright, Charles Robert. 1975. *Mass Communication: A Sociological Perspective*. New York: Random House.

Wright, Robert. 2010. "Zuckerberg: Non-Evil Non-Genius," *New York Times*, 5 October.

Wu, Zheng. 2000. *Cohabitation: An Alternative Form of Family Living*. Don Mills, ON: Oxford University Press.

X, Malcolm. 1965. *The Autobiography of Malcolm X*. New York: Grove.

Yamane, David. 1997. "Secularization on Trial: In Defense of a Neosecularization Paradigm." *Journal for the Scientific Study of Religion* 36: 109–22.

Yancey, William L., Eugene P. Ericksen, and George H. Leon. 1979. "Emergent Ethnicity: A Review and Reformulation." *American Sociological Review* 41: 391–403.

Zakaria, Rafia. 2014. "Feminism in Faith: Zainah Anwar's Quest to Reinterpret The Qur'an's Most Controversial Verse." Retrieved August 11, 2015 (http://www.buzzfeed.com/rafiazakaria/feminism-in-faith-islam-1#.mao3MLngoX).

Zald, Meyer N., and John D. McCarthy. 1979. *The Dynamics of Social Movements*. Cambridge, MA: Winthrop.

Zimbardo, Philip G. 1972. "Pathology of Imprisonment." *Society* 9, 6: 4–8.

Zimmermann, Francis. 1987 [1982]. *The Jungle and the Aroma of Meats: An Ecological Theme in Hindu Medicine*, Janet Lloyd, trans. Berkeley, CA: University of California Press.

Zimring, Franklin E., and Gordon Hawkins. 1995. *Incapacitation: Penal Confinement and the Restraint of Crime*. New York: Oxford University Press.

Zinsser, Hans. 1935. *Rats, Lice and History*. Boston: Little, Brown.

Zogby International. 2001. "Arab American Institute Polls Results: Arab Americans Are Strong Advocates of War Against Terrorism; Overwhelmingly Endorse President Bush's Actions; Significant Numbers Have Experienced Discrimination since Sept. 11." Retrieved December 21, 2002 (http://www.zogby.com/news/ReadNews.dbm?ID487).

Zola, Irving Kenneth. 1982. *Missing Pieces: A Chronicle of Living with a Disability*. Philadelphia: Temple University Press.

Zoutman, D. E., B. D. Ford, E. Bryce, M. Gourdeau, G. Hebert, E. Henderson, S. Paton, Canadian Hospital Epidemiology Committee, Canadian Nosocomial Infection Surveillance Program, Health Canada. 2003. "The State of Infection Surveillance and Control in Canadian Acute Care Hospitals." *American Journal of Infection Control* 31, 5: 266–73.

Zurbriggen, Eileen L. et al. 2010. "Report of the APA Task Force on the Sexualization of Girls." Washington, DC: American Psychological Association. Retrieved January 16, 2013 (http://www.apa.org/pi/women/programs/girls/report-full.pdf).

INDEX

Note: Page numbers in **boldface** indicate pages where a key term is defined.

crime (*continued*)
  types of, 92
  victimless crimes, **93**
  vs. deviance, 91–92
  white-collar crimes, 95, 100
criminal profiles, 94–95
criminal subcultures, 97–99
crude divorce rate, **188**
crude marriage rate, **188**
cults, 217–220, **219**
cultural capital, **117, 223**
cultural diversification, 34–41, 38
cultural fragmentation, 38
cultural hegemony, **13–14**
cultural relativism, **36**
cultural studies, **259**
culture, **27,** 138–140
  see also specific types of culture
  abstraction, 28, 31
  blending cultures, 39
  building blocks of, 31
  conflict analysis, 37–38
  as constraint, 33–34, 41–46
  cooperation, 28–29, 31
  countercultures, 45–46
  ethnicity, 138–139
  and ethnocentrism, 33–34
  as freedom, 33–34, 41
  functionalist analysis, 33–34
  origins and components of, 28–33
  postmodernism, 38, 39–41
  as problem solving, 27–28
  production, 30, 31, 34
  as restraint, 33–34
  and social class, 30–32
  subculture, 43, 45–46

date rape, 101
Davis, Kingsley, 122
death
  gunshot death rate, 23
  leading causes of, 232
  social causes of, 234–238
death penalty, 107–108
debt, 131
deferential Canadian culture, 41
democratic movements, 253
Democratic Revolution, **8–9**
denominations, **219**
dependency theory, **129–131**
dependent variable, **19**
Desperate Housewives, 60
detached observation, **21**
deterrence, 106
deviance, **91**
  conflict theory, 100–101
  explanations of, 95–102
  feminist explanations, 101–102
  functionalist explanations, 97–100
  labelling theory, 96–97

learning deviance, 96
medicalization of deviance, 103–104
sanctions, 92
social definition of, 91–92
symbolic interactionist approaches, 95–97
types of, 92
vs. crime, 91–92
Diagnostic and Statistical Manual of Mental Disorders (DSM-5), 44, 104
discrimination, 25, **136**
diversity, 38–39, 41
divorce, 55, 192, 193–195
dominant culture, 31–32
dramaturgical analysis, **75–76**
Duck Dynasty, 218
Durkheim, Émile, 9–10, 17, 97, 206–207
  see also functionalist theory
dysfunctions, **11,** 97

earnings gap, 170–172
Easy A, 98
ecclesia, **219**
economic cooperation, 187
economic inequality, 223–225
education, 221–222
  community college, 225
  economic inequality, 223–225
  feminist theory, 225–226
  functions of, 222–223
  and gender, 225–226
  hidden curriculum, 56
  international perspective, 227–229
  macrosociological processes, 222–226
  microsociological processes, 226–227
  postsecondary study, by gender, 163
  schools, 56
  stereotype threat, 226–227
educational achievement, **222**
educational attainment, **222**
ego, **52**
egoistic suicide, **10**
Eichler, Margrit, 17
emotion management, **73**
emotional labour, **73–74**
emotional support, 187
emotions, 72–73
empty nesters, 193
Engels, Friedrich, 160, 189–190
the environment
  cooperative alternative, 278
  global warming, 272–274
  social construction of environmental problems, 274–277
  social distribution of risk, 275–277
  solutions, market and high-tech, 277–278
environmental racism, **234, 275**–277
environmental risks, 275–277
equal pay for work of equal value, 177–178

equilibrium, 10
essentialism, **158–160**
ethics in research, 18–19
ethnic group, **138,** 153, 154
ethnicity
  advantages of, 151–152
  choice vs. imposition, 141–142
  conflict theory, 142–151
  and culture, 138–139
  future of, 152–155
  labelling, 140–141
  resources and opportunities, 139–140
  symbolic ethnicity, 142
  symbolic interactionism, 140–142
ethnocentrism, **33–34,** 36
exchange, 74
experimental group, **19**
experiment, **19**–21, 24
expulsion, **142–143**
extended family, **187**
extracurricular activities, 67
Extreme Makeover, 54

Facebook, 82
facial expressions, 76–77
families
  see also specific types of families
  changes, 184–185
  conflict theory, 184, 189–190
  displacement of family functions, 189
  family diversity, 197–200
  feminist theory, 184, 189–190
  functionalism and, 55–56, 184, 185–187
  functions of, 55–56
  power, 190–197
  during the 1950s, 188–189
family diversity, 197–200
family life cycle, 192–193
family policy, 200–203
feminism, 16, **16,** 17, 178–181
  see also feminist theory
feminist theory, 16
  crime and deviance, 101–102
  education, 225–226
  emotional responses, 72–73
  essentialism, 159–160
  family, 184, 189–190
  health care, 240
  mass media, 260–262
  religion, 207–212
  and social interaction, 71–74
  socialization, 55, 59–61
feminization of poverty, **120**
field research, **21**–22
First Nations. *See* Aboriginal peoples
flak, 256
flexible self, 62–64
folkway, **29**
Food, Inc., 269

foreign investment, 131
formal organizations, **87**
formal punishment, **92**
Foucault, Michel, 14, 17
founders of sociology, 9–16
frame alignment, **282**–283
framing theory, 282–283
freedom, 25, 33–34, 41
Freud, Sigmund, 51–52
Friends with Benefits, 197–198
functional theory of stratification, **122**–123
functionalism. *See* functionalist theory
functionalist theory, 10–11, 17
    breakdown theory, 279–280
    community college, 225
    crime and deviance, 97–100
    culture and ethnocentrism, 33–34
    Émile Durkheim, 9–10
    essentialism, 159
    family, 55–56, 184, 185–187
    global inequality, 127–129
    mass media, 253–254
    modernization theory, 127–129
    and the nuclear family, 185–190
    religion, 206–207
    schools, 56
    social stratification, 122–123
    and socialization, 55
fundamentalists, **214**

gender, **16, 158**
    and crime, 94
    and education, 225–226
    gender risk, 175
    postsecondary study, 163
    religion, and subjugation of women, 208–211
    segregation and interaction, 161–162
    social learning of, 158–165
gender differences, and socialization, 53
gender discrimination, **171**
gender identity, **158**
gender ideology, **162**
gender inequality, 170–172
    earnings gap, 170–172
    and feminist theory, 16
    future of, 175–178
    gender inequality index, 176
    health care, 240
    and spousal violence, 197
gender interaction, 161–162, 164–165
gender roles, **59**–61
gender socialization, 161–165
gender theories, 158
generalized other, **53**
genocide, **144**
geopolitical position, 132
gestures, 76–77
Gilligan, Carol, 53

Girls, 180–181
glass ceiling, **165**
global inequality, 126–133
global structures, **7**
global village, 39
global warming, **272**–274
globalization, **24,** 25, 38–39, 41, 63, 285
Goffman, Erving, 15, 17, 61, 75–76
The Good Wife, 218
Gramsci, Antonio, 13–14, 17
groups. *See* social groups
groupthink, **86**

hand gestures, 76
Harry Potter and the Death Hollows: Part I and Part II, 215–216
head tax, 150
health, **233**
    see also medicine
    and country of residence, 235–238
    defining health, 233–234
    health indicators, 238
    and inequality, 233–238
    measurement of, 233–234
    social causes of illness and death, 234–235
health care
    in Canada, 242
    and class inequalities, 238–239
    and gender inequalities, 240
    and racial inequalities, 239–240
    in the United States, 240–242
health care system, **235**
heterosexual cohabitation, 197–198
heterosexuals, **165**
hidden curriculum, **56**
high culture, **31**
Hinduism, 33–34, 210
hip-hop, 45–46
HIV/AIDS, 235–237
Hoarders, 44
holistic medicine, **246**–247
Holocaust, 78–79
Homeland, 85
homelessness, 23, 117
homophobia, **169**–170
homosexuality, 165–170
homosexuals, **165**
hostile environment sexual harassment, **174**
housework, 193, 196
human capital, **116**

I, **52,** 54
id, **52**
identity, 140–141, 263
Idle No More movement, 145
illness, social causes of, 234–238
immigrants and immigration, 35, 36, 139, 146, 148–149, 153

impression management, 75–76
imprisonment, 105–106
incarceration, 105–106
income inequality, 114–117
independent variable, **19,** 34
individualism, 41
Industrial Revolution, **9**
inequality
    class inequality, 126, 211, 238–240
    and conflict theory, 13
    economic inequality, 223–225
    gender inequality, 170–172, 197
    global inequality, 126–133
    growth of, 25
    and health, 233–238
    in health care, 238–240
    income inequality, 114–117
    social inequality, 112–115, 207–208
infant mortality, **238**
informal punishment, **92**
informed consent, 18
initiation rite, **61**
institutional racism, **142**
intelligence, 135
intergenerational mobility, **124**
internal colonialism, **142,** 145
Internet, 59
    access, 262
    centralized control and resistance, 262–265
    content, 262
    mate selection, 192
    media convergence, 262–263
    self-identity, 64
    social media, 59, 263–265
interpretive approaches to mass media, 259–260
intersex, **158**
intimate terrorism, 196
intragenerational mobility, **124**
IQ tests, 135, 224
Islam, 154–155, 210, 211, 219

job search, 81–82
Judaism, 209

King, Martin Luther Jr., 97, 147–148
Kondratiev Waves, 270

labelling theory, **96**–97
labels, 140–141
language, **32**
    body language, 76–77
    Sapir-Whorf thesis, 32–33
    social context of, 76
latent functions, **11,** 223
laughter, 71–72
law, **92**
less-developed countries, 276–277
liberal feminism, 179

life expectancy, **232**, 234, 239
Little Mosque on the Prairie, 154–155
lone-parent families, 199–200, 223
looking-glass self, **52**
love, and mate selection, 190–192

macro-level focus, 16
macro-level structures, 13
macrostructures, **7**
male-female interaction. *See* gender interaction
manifest functions, **11**, 223
market model of religion, 217
marriage, **187**
    marital satisfaction, 192–193
    mate selection, 190–192
    same-sex marriage, 198–199
Martineau, Harriet, 16, 17
Marx, Karl, 11–12, 17, 208
    see also conflict theory
masculinities, 175
mass communication, 250
mass culture, **31**
mass media, 59, 60, **250**
    and body image, 162–164
    causes of media growth, 252–253
    conflict theory, 254–259
    development of, 251
    and feminist approach to socialization, 59–61
    feminist theory, 260–262
    functionalist theory, 253–254
    gender roles, 59–61
    increasing influence, 67
    interpretive approaches, 259–260
    media bias, 256–259
    media effects, theories of, 253–262
    media ownership, 255–256
    and moral panic, 106
    rise of, 250–252
    significance of, 249–253
material culture, **30**
mate selection, 190–192
McLuhan, Marshall, 39, 250
me, **52**, 54
Mead, George Herbert, 15–16, 17, 52–53, 54
Mean Girls, 83
media bias, 256–259
media convergence, 262–**263**
media effects, 253–262
media imperialism, **262**, 265
media influence, 67
media ownership, 255–256
medicalization of deviance, **103**–104
medicine
    see also health
    alternative medicine, 245–246
    challenges to traditional medical science, 245–247

holistic medicine, 246–247
patient activism, 245
prescription drugs, 241–242
professionalization of medicine, 242–243
socialized medicine, 242
social limits of modern medicine, 243–245
mental disorders, 104
Merton, Robert, 10–11, 17
Merton's strain theory of deviance, 97
mesostructures, **7**
micro-level communication, 16
micro-level focus, 16
microsociological processes, 226–227
microstructures, **7**
middle-class family, 187–190
Milgram's obedience experiment, 79–80, 88–89
Milk, 169
Mills, C. Wright, 4, 6
modernization theory, **127**–129
modern medicine, 243–247
Moore, Wilbert, 122
moral panic, **106**–107
morbidity, **240**
more, **29**
Mount Cashel Orphanage, 29–30
Mr. Robot, 286
multiculturalism, 35–**36**
Multiculturalism Act, 36
Muslim. *See* Islam
Muslim fundamentalism, 214–216

National Household Survey, 148
Nazism, 40, 78–79, 92
the Netherlands, 168
network analysis, 81–82
networks. See social networks
new social movements, 283–287
The Newsroom, 257
nonverbal communication, 76–81
normal accident, **268**
norms, **29**
    creation of, 28–29
    and social interaction, 72, 74, 75
    of solidarity, 79
    types of, 29
    variations in, 91
nuclear family, **184**, 185–187, 200–203

obedience, 79–80
Oblivion, 249
occupational sex segregation, **171**
open-ended question, **21**
opportunity, 24–25, 139–140
overweight and obesity, 233

Palo-Alto experiment, 62
Parsons, Talcott, 10–11, 17

participant observation, **22**, 24
parties, **123**
patient activism, 245
patriarchy, **7**, 16, 179, 190
pay equity, **177**–178
pedophilia, 29
peer groups, 57–59, 67
peripheral countries, **131**
personal problems, 7
placebo effect, **246**
plagiarism, 18–19
plastic surgery, 63
pluralism, **152**
political opportunities, 281–282
politics, and class inequality, 126
polygamy, **185**
popular culture, **31**
population, 21
Porter, John, 15, 17, 139
Postindustrial Revolution, **24**
postmodernism, 38, **39**–41
poststructuralism, **14**
posttraumatic stress disorder (PTSD), 104
poverty, **117**–120
    defining poverty, 117–118
    explanations, 119–120
    feminization of poverty, 120
    low-income cutoff, 118
    myths about, 118–119
    world poverty, 130
power, 16, 190–197
prejudice, **136**
prescription drugs, 241–242
primary group, **87**
primary socialization, **55**
prisons, 105–106
privacy, 18
privilege, 13, 242
production, **30**, 31, 34
profane, **207**
profession, **243**
professionalization of medicine, 242–243
progressive tax system, 119
proletariat, **121**
prolonged childhood, 64–65
Protestant ethic, **14**, 212–213
Protestant Reformation, 252
public health system, **234**–235
punishment, 92, 102–106, 107–109
    alternative strategies, 108–109
    capital punishment, 107–108
    medicalization of deviance, 103–104
    prisons, 105–106

Québécois, 145–147
Quebecor, 255
The Queen of Versailles, 113–114
queer theory, **165**–167
quid pro quo sexual harassment, **174**
Quiet Revolution, 146

race, 137, **137**
    choice *vs.* imposition, 141–142
    conflict theory, 142–151
    and crime, 95
    defining race, 135–138
    future of, 152–155
    health care, racial inequalities in,
        239–240
    and intelligence, 135
    labelling, 140–141
    racial mixing, 136–137
    sociological definition, 137–138
    and sports, 35–136, 135–136
    symbolic interactionism, 140–142
racism, 6–7, 25, 138, **142**
    environmental racism, 234, 275–277
    institutional racism, 142
radical feminists, 179
randomization, **19**
rape, 101
    see also sexual assault
rate, **9**
rationalization, **42**
reactivity, **21**
recidivism rate, **108**, 109
Redacted, 258
reference group, **86**–87
rehabilitation, 106
relative deprivation, **279**–280
reliability, **20**
religion, 28, 39, 205–206
    in Canada, 218–220
    classical approaches, 206–213
    conflict theory, 207–212
    feminist theory, 207–212
    functionalist theory, 206–207
    future of, 221
    market model, 217
    Muslim fundamentalism, 214–216
    religious fundamentalism, 214
    religious revival, 214, 221
    revised secularization thesis, 217
    rise, decline, and partial revival of,
        213–217
    secularization, 213, 221
    and sexual orientation, 211
    social change, 212–213
    and social conflict, 212
    and social inequality, 207–208
    and subordination of women, 208–211
    symbolic interactionism, 212–213
    types of religious groups, 218–220
    world religions, 209–211
religiosity, **220**–221
religious revival, 214, 221
reproduction, 187
reproductive choices, 195
research, **17**
    data analysis, 18
    data collection, 18
    ethics in research, 18–19

research cycle, 17–19
research literature, 18
research methods. *See* research
    methods
research question, 17
research cycle, 17–19
research methods, 18, 19–24
    analysis of existing documents and
        official statistics, 22–24
    experiments, 19–21, 24
    field research, **21**–22
    participant observation, 22, 24
    strengths and weaknesses, 24
    surveys, 21, 24
resocialization, **61**–62
resource mobilization, **280**–281
resources, 139–140
restorative justice, **108**–109
retreatism, 97
revenge, 106
Revenge Body, 54
revised secularization thesis, **217**
rhesus monkeys, 50
Rhodesia, 132
rights revolution, **37**–38
risk, social distribution of, 275–277
risk society, **268**
rites of passage, **38,** 61
ritualism, 97
rituals, **207**
Robbers Cave Study, 86
Robinson Crusoe (Defoe), 111
Rogers, 255
role, **49,** 72, 74
role conflict, **72**
role distancing, **75**
role strain, **72**
routinization of charisma, **208**

sacred, **207**
safety, 18
same-sex marriage, 198–199
sample, **21**
sanctions, 92
Sanders, Bernie, 5
Sapir-Whorf thesis, **32**
scapegoat, **137**
Schindler's List, 79
schools, 56, 229
    see also education
Scientific Revolution, **8,** 9
scripts, 73
Searching for Sugar Man, 137–138
secondary group, **87**
secondary socialization, **56**
sects, 218–**219**
secularization thesis, **213**
self, **51**
    flexible self, 62–64
    looking-glass self, 52
    stages of development, 52–53

self-esteem, 86
self-fulfilling prophecy, **57,** 227
self-identity, 50–51, 64
self-report surveys, **93,** 99
semiperipheral countries, **131**
senior care, 196
severe acute respiratory syndrome
    (SARS), 243–244
sex, **157**–158, 193
sexual assault, 101, 172, 173–174
sexual harassment, 174–175
sexual minorities, 170
sexual orientation, 165–167, 211
sexual regulation, 187
shared values, 10
Shaw Communications, 255
shock TV, 5–6
sick role, **245**
significant others, **52**
Silver Linings Playbook, 236
Sister Wives, 186
six degrees of separation, 154
slavery, 6–7, **147**
social activism, 264
social capital, **116**
social category, **83**
social change, 212–213
social classes, **12**
    see also class
social collectivities
    organizational constraints and
        freedom, 88–89
    social groups. *See* social groups
    social networks, 64
social conflict, 212
social constructionism, **158,** 160
social control, 100–101, 102, 103, 282
social convention, 16
social deprivation, 50
social group, 79–81, **83**
    ambiguities of group membership, 85
    bystander apathy, 86
    conformity, 83–87
    group boundaries, 86
    groupthink, 86
    primary groups, 87
    reference group, 86–87
    secondary groups, 87
social inequality, 112–115, 207–208
    see also social stratification
social interaction, **71**
    as competition and exchange, 74
    conflict theories, 74–78
    and feminist theory, 71–74
    symbolic interactionism, 75–76
social isolation, 49–50
social marginality, 279
social media, 59, 263–265
social mobility, **124**–126
social movement, 40, 278–**279**
    breakdown theory, 279–280

INTRODUCING SOCIOLOGY

LO¹ DEFINE SOCIOLOGY

Sociology puts society under the microscope. It provides a way of moving beyond individual-level understandings of the world around us and invites us to think more broadly about ways of understanding social life. For example, deciding to have a child is perhaps the most personal decision a woman can make. However, at certain times in certain societies, the great majority of young women decide to have one or two children instead of six. Sociology helps us identify the social forces that cause many people to make such personal decisions almost simultaneously, even though they may not be aware of the social influences operating on them. Sociologists understand **sociology** to mean the systematic study of human behaviour in a social context. The challenge is to move beyond the taken-for-granted understandings of our world to an examination of the powerful influence of social forces on our day-to-day lives.

LO² IDENTIFY THE SOCIAL RELATIONS THAT SURROUND YOU, PERMEATE YOU, AND INFLUENCE YOUR BEHAVIOUR

Patterns of social relations affect your innermost thoughts and feelings, influence your actions, and help shape who you are. **Social structures** are stable patterns of social relations. American sociologist C. Wright Mills argued that sociologists must identify and explain the connection between people's personal troubles and the social structures in which they are embedded. The **sociological imagination** allows us to see the connection between personal troubles and social structures (Mills, 1959). To broaden your sociological awareness, you must recognize the four levels of social structure that surround and permeate us:

- **Microstructures:** Patterns of *intimate* social relations formed in face-to-face interaction (e.g., families).
- **Mesostructures:** Patterns of social relations in organizations between *acquaintances* who do not often interact at the face-to-face level (e.g., government bureaucracy).
- **Macrostructures:** Overarching patterns of social relations above and beyond mesostructures (e.g., patriarchy).

- **Global structures:** International social relations (e.g., economic trade agreements between nation-states).

The sociological imagination originated in three revolutions that gave people an entirely new way to think about society. The **Scientific Revolution** encouraged people to reach conclusions about the workings of the world based on *evidence*, not speculation. The **Democratic Revolution** encouraged people to take responsibility for organizing society and for intervening in social problems. The **Industrial Revolution** created large cities where people lived and worked together on massive scales for the first time. It created many social problems, such as extreme poverty, pollution, strikes, and revolutions.

LO³ SUMMARIZE THE FOUR MAIN SCHOOLS OF SOCIOLOGICAL THEORY

There are four major theoretical perspectives in sociology (see Concept Summary 1.1):

1. **Functionalism:** Focuses on macrostructures, emphasizes the interdependence of parts of society, and examines how each part contributes to the overall stability of society. Key terms: **dysfunctions**, equilibrium, **latent functions**, **manifest functions**, shared values, social stability, and **social structures**.
2. **Conflict theory:** Focuses on macrostructures, emphasizes how social inequality sometimes produces social stability and sometimes social instability, and promotes social equality. Key terms: **class conflict**, **class consciousness**, inequality, **cultural hegemony**, power, and **social class**.
3. **Symbolic interactionism:** Focuses on interpersonal communication in microstructures, emphasizes that social life is possible because people attach meanings to things, and stresses that people create social circumstances rather than merely react to them. Key terms: active agents, **Protestant ethic**, **symbols**, and subjective meaning.
4. **Feminism:** Focuses on male domination and female subordination in macrostructures and microstructures. Argues female subordination is a product of social convention, not biological necessity; thus it must be challenged. Key terms: **gender**, gender inequality, **patriarchy**, power, and social convention.

CONCEPT SUMMARY 1.1 Four Theoretical Traditions in Society

Theoretical Tradition	Main Levels of Analysis	Main Focus	Main Question	Major Theorists
Functionalist	Macro	Values	How do the institutions of society contribute to social stability and instability?	Émile Durkheim, Talcott Parsons, Robert Merton, S.D. Clark
Conflict	Macro	Inequality	How do privileged groups seek to maintain their advantages and subordinate groups seek to increase theirs, often causing social change in the process?	Karl Marx, Max Weber, Antonio Gramsci, Michel Foucault, John Porter
Symbolic interactionist	Micro	Meaning	How do individuals communicate to make their social settings meaningful?	George Herbert Mead, Max Weber, Erving Goffman
Feminist	Macro and micro	Patriarchy	Which social structures and interaction processes maintain male dominance and female subordination?	Harriet Martineau, Margrit Eichler

Source: From BRYM/LIE. *Sociology*, 1E. © 2009 Nelson Education Ltd. Reproduced by permission. www.cengage.com/permissions.

LO⁴ DESCRIBE HOW SOCIOLOGICAL RESEARCH SEEKS TO IMPROVE PEOPLE'S LIVES AND TEST IDEAS USING SCIENTIFIC METHODS

Research is the process of systematically observing reality to assess the validity of a theory. Sociological research can improve people's lives by providing insight into the relationship between personal troubles and social structures. For example, Durkheim's research on **altruistic suicide**, **egoistic suicide**, and **anomic suicide** illustrates the importance of moving beyond individual-level, psychologically based explanations of suicide; by examining suicide sociologically, we have a more comprehensive understanding of the issue.

Research is crucial to the development of sociological theories and ways of understanding our social world, leading to new understandings of our continually changing society. Research forces us to move beyond common sense understandings to systematic observation of the social world. Sociologists use research to test and revise their ideas about the social world. They do so by following a six-step *research cycle* that begins with formulating a research question and ends with the publishing of results.

LO⁵ DISTINGUISH THE FOUR MAIN METHODS OF COLLECTING SOCIOLOGICAL DATA

The four main methods of collecting sociological data vary across a number of dimensions, some of which include their ability to establish a causal **association**, their **reactivity**, and the **generalizability** of research findings. These four main methods are **experiment**, **survey**, **participant observation**, and **analysis of existing documents and official statistics** (see Concept Summary 1.2). A sociologist selects the methodological approach that is most appropriate for

CONCEPT SUMMARY 1.2 Strengths and Weaknesses of Four Research Methods

Method	Strengths	Weaknesses
Experiment	High reliability; excellent for establishing cause-and-effect relationships	Low validity for many sociological problems because of the unnaturalness of the experimental setting
Survey	Good reliability; useful for establishing cause-and-effect relationships	Validity problems exist unless researchers make strong efforts to deal with them
Participant observation	Allows researchers to develop a deep and sympathetic understanding of the way people see the world; especially useful in exploratory research	Low reliability and generalizability
Analysis of existing documents and official statistics	Often inexpensive and easy to obtain; provides good coverage; useful for historical analysis; nonreactive	Often contains biases reflecting the interests of their creators and not the interests of the researcher

Source: From BRYM/LIE. *Sociology*, 1E. © 2009 Nelson Education Ltd. Reproduced by permission. www.cengage.com/permissions.

answering the research question. These methods are used to gather and analyze data. The *research cycle* involves (1) formulating a research question, which must be stated so that it can be answered by systematically collecting and analyzing sociological data; (2) reviewing the existing literature on the subject of the research question so as to stimulate the researcher's sociological imagination and avoid duplication of effort; (3) selecting a research method that is appropriate to the problem at hand; (4) collecting data by observing subjects, interviewing them, reading documents produced by or about them, and so on; (5) analyzing the data; and (6) publishing the results of the research so that (a) it will be useful for the sociological community, the subjects of the research, and the broader public, and (b) other sociologists can scrutinize and criticize the research so that it can later be improved.

LO⁶ EXPLAIN HOW SOCIOLOGY CAN HELP US DEAL WITH MAJOR CHALLENGES THAT SOCIETY FACES TODAY

The **Postindustrial Revolution** and **globalization** have created more freedoms, but they have also created more constraints. On the one hand, people are afforded more freedom because traditional limits on social relationships are weakening. Today, we witness greater acceptance of sexual diversity and a variety of family forms, cities are more ethnically and racially diverse, communication is global and instantaneous, and people are migrating around the globe on a scale never seen before. On the other hand, postindustrialism and globalization create new limitations on freedom. Many high-paying jobs are being replaced by low-paying jobs, economic inequality has increased, bureaucracies are becoming more impersonal, economic development is profit-driven, technological advances have led to environmental disasters, and we live in a time marked by compulsory consumerism.

NOTES

1-4 Visit nelson.com/student for additional study tools!

NEL

CHAPTER 2 IN REVIEW

CULTURE

LEARNING OBJECTIVES

LO¹ DEFINE CULTURE AND ITS MAIN FUNCTIONS

Culture is everything that people think, do, have, and create to adapt to and thrive in their surrounding environment. Sociologists define *culture* broadly as all the ideas, practices, and material objects that people create to deal with real-life problems that exist in **society**.

LO² EXPLAIN HOW CULTURE HELPS HUMANS ADAPT AND THRIVE IN THEIR ENVIRONMENTS

Humans have thrived because we have three main tools in our cultural survival kit—abstraction, cooperation, and production (see Table 2.1):

1. **Symbols** allow us to classify our experiences and generalize from them. Symbols develop out of **abstraction** and have specific meanings, such as the alphabet, the word *spoon*, or language in general. According to the **Sapir-Whorf thesis**, we have an experience, conceptualize the experience, and then form **language** to express our concept of this experience. Language forces people to think in different ways. For example, speakers of Tzeltal relate to their environment geographically rather than egocentrically ("north" and "south" instead of "left" and "right").
2. **Cooperation** creates a complex social life by sharing resources and working together. It establishes **norms**

and **values**. Ranging from weakest to strongest, the three types of norms are **folkways**, **mores**, and **taboos**.

3. **Production:** Only humans can make and use tools that improve our ability to take what we want from nature. Sociologists call these tools and techniques **material culture**.

Different types of culture are consumed by different classes. While all classes consume **popular** or **mass culture**, upper classes tend to consume **high culture**. For example, all classes of people may listen to Nicki Minaj or Justin Bieber, but fewer people will pay for tickets to hear the latest violin prodigy play with a symphony orchestra at an expensive concert. Another way to understand how culture is connected to social class is to think of the effect of **dominant culture**, which allows wealthier categories of people to exercise some control over others.

LO³ RECOGNIZE HOW CULTURE CAN MAKE PEOPLE FREER

Culture can provide us with an opportunity to exercise our *freedom*. We create elements of culture in our everyday life to solve practical problems and express our needs, hopes, joys, and fears. Symbolic interactionists treat culture as an *independent variable*. People are not empty vessels into which society pours predetermined beliefs, symbols, and values; instead, we produce and interpret culture in a creative fashion to meet our diverse and changing needs. Diversity, globalization, and **postmodernism** are all aspects of the new freedom that culture allows us today.

| TABLE 2.1 | The Building Blocks of Culture |

The human capacity for ...	Abstraction	Cooperation	Production
Gives rise to these elements of culture ...	Ideas	Norms and values	Material culture
In medicine, for example ...	*Theories* are developed about how a certain drug might cure a disease.	*Experiments* are conducted to test whether the drug works as expected.	*Treatments* are developed on the basis of the experimental results.

Source: Adapted from Bierstedt, Robert, 1963, *The Social Order: An Introduction to Sociology*, New York: McGraw-Hill.

LO⁴ ANALYZE THE WAYS IN WHICH CULTURE IS BECOMING MORE DIVERSE, MULTICULTURAL, AND GLOBALIZED

Because we have a greater diversity of cultures to choose from than previous generations did, culture is becoming freer in contemporary societies. Advocates of **multiculturalism** argue that school curricula should present a more balanced picture of Canadian history, culture, and society to better mirror the country's ethnic and racial diversity in the past and growing ethnic and racial diversity today.

Some sociologists argue that multiculturalism leads to **cultural relativism**, which is the opposite of **ethnocentrism**. At its extreme, cultural relativism treats all cultural practices as if they are of equal value—an "anything goes; everything's equal" approach to cultural differences. Critics argue that cultural relativism validates inhumane practices that are contrary to the values of multiculturalism. For example, could a multicultural society exist if it tolerated the anti-democratic and racist values held by the South African apartheid regime (1948–1992)? Multiculturalists reply that the **rights revolution** does not need to be taken to such extremes. The Canadian Charter of Rights and Freedoms promotes moderate cultural relativism based on the values of tolerance and diversity. From a conflict theory perspective, socially excluded groups have struggled to win equal rights under the law, and these rights must be protected by the Canadian legal system.

Globalization has heightened cultural fragmentation. It is the process by which formerly separate economies, nation-states, and cultures are becoming tied together and interdependent. Previously isolated cultures are now characterized by an eclectic mix of elements from different times and places, an erosion of authority, and a decline of consensus around core values. In a postmodern culture, people are less obliged to accept the culture into which they are born and freer to combine elements of different cultures.

LO⁵ RECOGNIZE HOW CULTURE CAN PLACE LIMITS ON PEOPLE'S FREEDOM

The second face of culture is *constraint*. The raw materials of culture that we create consist of cultural elements that either existed before we were born or that other people have created since our birth. Many sociologists argue that existing culture places limitations on what we can think, do, and become.

Two constraining aspects of culture are **rationalization** and **consumerism**. Max Weber argued that rationalization is one of the most constraining aspects of modern culture, making life akin to living inside an "iron cage." Rationalization has made us into efficient producers, fitting people to the needs of institutions rather than the other way around. Weber argued that when rationality becomes too extreme, there are negative, unintended, and irrational consequences. For example, the clock was introduced as a *rational* means of regulating daily routines to obtain a given goal (more efficient workers that can maximize output), but it has led to an irrational end (contemporary lives are too hectic).

The cultural imperative of being "good consumers" encourages people to define themselves by the goods they purchase. *Consumerism* also acts as a social control mechanism that normally prevents countercultures from disrupting the social order. It transforms deviations from mainstream culture into means of making money and entices rebels to become entrepreneurs (Frank and Weiland, 1997). The fate of American hip-hop is testimony to the capacity of consumerism to change **countercultures** into mere **subcultures**, thus constraining dissent and rebellion.

2-2   Visit nelson.com/student for additional study tools!

NEL

SOCIALIZATION

LO¹ RECOGNIZE THAT HUMAN ABILITIES REMAIN UNDEVELOPED UNLESS SOCIAL INTERACTION UNLEASHES THEM

The examples of feral children and children growing up without social interaction point to the importance of **socialization** in learning culture and becoming fully human. Without socialization, our ability to learn culture and become human is only a potential. Sociologists do not believe that we are born with an innate self that develops naturally over time. Instead, sociologists believe that socialization is central to the development of our sense of **self**.

Socialization takes place throughout the life cycle. The main theories of how our sense of self develops through childhood are symbolic interactionist. Cooley's **looking-glass self** describes how our self-concept depends on how we see ourselves evaluated by others. Mead's work on the **I** and the **me** point to a subjective and objective aspect of the self. The objective aspect of the self—the me—develops according to culturally approved standards. According to Mead, our self develops across four stages of **role**-taking, from taking on the role of **significant others** to taking on the role of the **generalized other**. Socialization can vary depending on one's social location—as the learning of differing **gender roles** illustrates—or the structure of the society in which one lives.

LO² COMPARE CHANGE OVER THE PAST CENTURY IN THE SOCIALIZING INFLUENCE OF THE FAMILY, SCHOOLS, PEER GROUPS, AND THE MASS MEDIA

Agents of socialization include families, schools, **peer groups**, and the mass media. **Primary socialization** takes place in families, although families are less important to socialization than they once were. **Secondary socialization** happens outside of the family. Secondary socialization occurs in schools, peer groups, and, increasingly, the mass media. Sociologists researching secondary socialization in schools often focus on the **hidden curriculum**, which teaches students how to be good citizens once they leave school. The **self-fulfilling prophecy** is another way to understand the processes of secondary socialization in school settings. Teachers' expectations about students' performance can influence their performance.

Peer groups are instrumental in developing a sense of self. The importance of peer group influence grew in the twentieth century and is considered by many sociologists to be the dominant socializing agent for students in middle school and beyond. However, most agree that the mass media have become increasingly important socializing agents in the twenty-first century. Television and the Internet—two forms of mass media—are particularly strong influences. As demonstrated in Figure 3.3, exposure to media influence differs by age cohort.

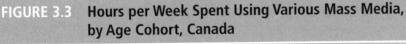

FIGURE 3.3 **Hours per Week Spent Using Various Mass Media, by Age Cohort, Canada**

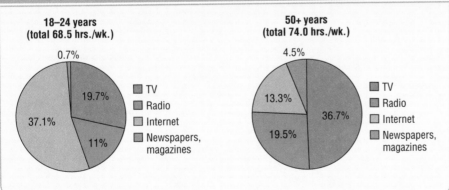

Source: Television Bureau of Canada, 2016. "Reach and Time Spent: Major Media Comparisons." Pp. 6, 13. http://www.tvb.ca/page_files/pdf/RTSA/RTS14.pdf (retrieved 5 July 2015).

LO³ APPRECIATE THAT PEOPLE'S IDENTITIES CHANGE FASTER, MORE OFTEN, AND MORE COMPLETELY THAN THEY DID JUST A COUPLE OF DECADES AGO

The example of childhood illustrates how people's identities are shaped by their social context. A distinct life stage called *childhood* emerged when individuals were required to prepare for increasingly complex work in adult life through extended learning in schools. It was also made possible by longer life expectancy rooted in improved hygiene and nutrition. And yet, some predict that the stages we call childhood and adolescence may disappear altogether; whether or not this comes to pass, we do know that social forces will continue to shape and re-shape the life course.

Globalization, the Internet, and body-altering surgeries are just some of the forces that enable identities to change faster, more often, and more completely than in previous decades. For example, the Internet provides the opportunity to become immersed in **virtual communities** where we are free to assume multiple identities and develop new dimensions of one's sense of self.

LO⁴ LIST THE FACTORS TRANSFORMING THE CHARACTER OF CHILDHOOD AND ADOLESCENCE TODAY

Several factors have transformed the character of childhood and adolescence in the past 40 to 50 years. Among them are *declining adult supervision and guidance, increasing media influence, declining extracurricular activities,* and *increasing adult responsibilities*. With many working adults spending less time engaged in family activities, young people are increasingly engaging in their own socialization, which sometimes immerses them in communities that revolve around high-risk behaviour like smoking and binge drinking.

Mass media have also emerged as an important influence in the face of declining adult supervision and guidance. Students' involvement in the kinds of extracurricular activities that can contribute to a strong sense of self—such as drama and athletics—has declined. For some students, this is because they have increasingly taken on adult responsibilities like paid work, household chores, and child-care responsibilities.

3-2   Visit nelson.com/student for additional study tools!

NEL

FROM SOCIAL INTERACTION TO SOCIAL ORGANIZATIONS

LEARNING OBJECTIVES

LO¹ DEFINE SOCIAL INTERACTION AS PEOPLE COMMUNICATING FACE TO FACE, ACTING AND REACTING IN RELATION TO ONE ANOTHER

Social interaction involves communication among people acting and reacting to one another. In everyday social interaction, people generally occupy a *status* (recognized social position), perform a *role* (set of expected behaviours), and follow social *norms* (generally accepted ways of doing things).

Every person occupies several statuses at the same time (e.g., student, daughter, sister, and restaurant server). Together, these statuses form a *status set*. Each status is composed of several sets of expected behaviours or roles. A *role set* is a cluster of roles attached to a single status. Sometimes people experience **role conflict** and **role strain** (see Figure 4.1 in Chapter 4).

Statuses, roles, and norms influence our emotions. Arlie Hochschild (1979, 1983) argued that emotions are not just involuntary outcomes of spontaneous emotional states, because humans actively engage in **emotion management**. People *control* their emotions by following "feeling rules" to respond appropriately to situations. In the service sector, many employees—predominantly female—are expected to engage in high levels of **emotional labour**.

LO² IDENTIFY HOW VARIOUS ASPECTS OF SOCIAL STRUCTURE INFLUENCE THE TEXTURE OF OUR EMOTIONAL LIFE

Conflict theorists view social interaction as competitive. Some argue that we compete for attention in our social interactions. Others hold that social interaction involves competition over valued resources while trying to minimize our costs. People will stay in a relationship as long as the rewards exceed the costs.

For *symbolic interactionists*, social interaction consists of more than competition between selfish individuals. Social interaction is a product of the norms, roles, and statuses we have learned. We constantly modify norms, roles, and statuses. Social interaction is active and creative, not passive and mechanistic. Erving Goffman's **dramaturgical analysis** is a variant of symbolic interactionism (1959). Social interaction is a sort of play where people engage in role-playing to appear in the best possible light; they engage in *impression management*. Each role is governed by norms. How well we act depends on our commitment to the role. If a role is stressful, people may engage in **role distancing**. According to Goffman, then, there is no single self but rather an ensemble of roles.

LO³ RECOGNIZE THAT IN SOCIAL INTERACTION, NONVERBAL COMMUNICATION IS AS IMPORTANT AS LANGUAGE IS

Social interaction typically involves a complex mix of verbal and nonverbal messages. Underlying the surface of human communication is a wide range of cultural assumptions, unconscious understandings, and nonverbal cues that make interaction possible. In different cultures and societies, facial expressions, gestures, body language, and **status cues** may mean different things. Status cues can quickly degenerate into **stereotypes**. Stereotypes create social barriers that impair interaction or prevent it altogether. A contemporary example involves racial stereotyping and police "carding" in Toronto and elsewhere (see Figure 4.3).

LO⁴ SEE HOW EMOTIONAL AND MATERIAL RESOURCES FLOW THROUGH PATTERNS OF SOCIAL RELATIONS CALLED SOCIAL NETWORKS

A **social network** is a bounded set of individuals linked by the exchange of material or emotional resources. People exchange more resources with people in their network than with non-members. We live in a "small world" because each member in our network is linked to people in other networks. Sociologists use social network analysis to examine such issues as how people search for jobs and how people interact in urban settings. Mark Granovetter (1973) discovered that people acquire more useful information through "weak ties" (acquaintances, former friends, friends-of-friends, etc.) than through "strong ties" (friends, family, roommates, etc.).

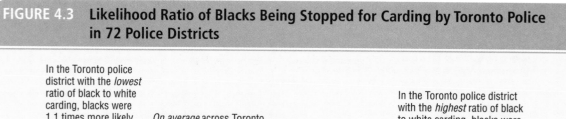

FIGURE 4.3 Likelihood Ratio of Blacks Being Stopped for Carding by Toronto Police in 72 Police Districts

In the Toronto police district with the *lowest* ratio of black to white carding, blacks were 1.1 times more likely than whites to be carded.

On average across Toronto, blacks were 3.2 times more likely than whites to be carded.

In the Toronto police district with the *highest* ratio of black to white carding, blacks were 9.9 times more likely than whites to be carded.

1   2   3   4   5   6   7   8   9   10

Note: Between 2008 and 2011, 788 050 Torontonians were carded. This figure shows how many times more likely carding was for blacks than for whites. For example, on average, blacks were 3.2 times more likely to be carded than whites were.

Source: *Toronto Star*. 2015. "Known to police." http://www.thestar.com/news/gta/knowntopolice.html (retrieved 22 July 2015).

LO⁵ EXPLAIN HOW SOCIAL GROUPS BIND PEOPLE TOGETHER, IMPOSE CONFORMITY ON THEM, AND SEPARATE THEM FROM NON–GROUP MEMBERS

Social groups consist of one or more social networks, the members of which identify with one another, routinely interact, and adhere to defined norms, roles, and statuses. In contrast, **social categories** consist of people who share similar status but do not routinely interact or identify with one another.

In **primary groups**, social interaction creates strong emotional ties, extends over a long period, and involves a wide range of activities. **Secondary groups** are larger and more impersonal than primary groups are. Compared with primary groups, social interaction in secondary groups creates weaker emotional ties, extends over a shorter period, and involves a narrow range of activities. Primary groups impose more conformity on members and draw stricter boundaries between insiders and outsiders.

The power of groups to ensure conformity is often a valuable asset. For example, sports teams are more successful when players sacrifice themselves for the team. Conformity can also have negative consequences. For example, the pressure to conform can lead to **groupthink** or **bystander apathy**. People can act in deplorable ways through the power of authority and norms of solidarity.

LO⁶ APPRECIATE THAT BUREAUCRACIES CAN OFTEN BE MADE MORE EFFICIENT BY ADOPTING MORE DEMOCRATIC STRUCTURES WITH FEWER LEVELS OF AUTHORITY

According to Max Weber (1964 [1947]), a **bureaucracy** is a large, impersonal, and **formal organization** composed of many clearly defined positions arranged in a hierarchy. A bureaucracy has a permanent, salaried staff of qualified experts, and written goals, rules, and procedures. Weber viewed bureaucracies as the most efficient kind of secondary group.

Other organizational sociologists argue that bureaucracies become inefficient when they are too large (Burns and Stalker, 1961). Large bureaucratic companies sometimes cannot compete with smaller, specialized, and flexible companies. Innovative firms have more democratic organizational structures with fewer levels of authority. Decentralized decision making enables direct lines of communication between all units. This enables them to adapt quickly to their environment. It also produces more satisfied workers, happier clients, and larger profits (Kanter, 1989).

4-2 Visit nelson.com/student for additional study tools!

NEL

DEVIANCE AND CRIME

LO¹ SEE HOW PEOPLE DEFINE DEVIANCE AND CRIME DIFFERENTLY IN DIFFERENT TIMES AND PLACES

Deviance and **crime** are socially defined. In other words, definitions of deviance and crime vary among cultures, across history, and from one social context to the next. This is because norms vary widely, and norms are at the root of deviance and crime. A **law** is a norm stipulated and enforced by government bodies. Sociologists see deviance and crime as relative and socially defined, rather than being a characteristic of an individual or a kind of action. This is because individual characteristics and actions are defined differently, depending on the time and place. Types of crime and deviance vary in terms of the severity of the social response, the perceived harmfulness of the act, and the degree of public agreement about whether an act should be considered deviant.

Many acts go unnoticed or are deemed too trivial to warrant a reaction indicating disapproval, also known as a *sanction*. Sanctions vary from mild, **informal punishment**, including **stigmatization**, to **formal punishment** through the judicial system.

LO² INTERPRET DIFFERENCES IN CRIME RATES OVER TIME AND BETWEEN DIFFERENT POPULATION CATEGORIES

Crime statistics collected by the police provide the main source of information on crime. This information is used by the government to publish annual reports on types of offences and characteristics of offenders. However, these statistics do not include **victimless crimes** and cannot include acts not reported or otherwise ignored. For this reason, **self-report surveys** and **victimization surveys** are often used to supplement official crime statistics. Together, these sources of information tell us that crime in Canada peaked in 1992 and has been steadily declining since. Males

---

CONCEPT SUMMARY 5.1 Major Theoretical Approaches to Deviance and Crime

Theory	Summary
Symbolic interactionism	Deviant and criminal roles must be learned in the course of social interaction if they are to become habitual activities. Moreover, deviance results not just from the actions of the deviant but also from the responses of others, who define some actions as deviant and other actions as normal.
Functionalism	Deviance and crime have positive functions for society insofar as they provide opportunities to clarify societal values, define moral boundaries, increase social solidarity, and allow useful social change. They also have dysfunctions. In particular, if societies do not provide enough legitimate opportunities for everyone to succeed, strain results, one reaction to which is to find alternatives and illegitimate means of achieving one's goals.
Conflict theory	The rich and powerful are most likely to impose deviant and criminal labels on others, particularly those who challenge the existing social order. Meanwhile, the rich and powerful are often able to use their money and influence to escape punishment for their own misdeeds. Most people do not engage in deviance and crime because they are prevented from doing so by authorities. Deviants and criminals break norms and laws because social controls imposed by various authorities are too weak to ensure their conformity.
Feminist theory	Changes over time in the distribution of power between women and men influence the degree to which crimes against women are identified and prosecuted, and the degree to which women become criminals.

constitute the majority of the accused in criminal court cases. The age cohort most prone to criminal behaviour is 15 to 24 years of age. Aboriginal people and blacks are overrepresented in Canada's prisons, which relates at least in part to their tendency to commit **street crime**, which is less detectable than **white collar crime**. Other factors responsible for the relatively high rate of imprisonment among Aboriginal people and blacks include widespread poverty within these communities, discrimination in the criminal justice system, and the disruption of social life in Aboriginal communities due to European settlement. Sociologists have a range of ways of understanding and explaining deviance and crime (see Concept Summary 5.1).

LO³ COMPARE HOW DEVIANCE AND CRIME WERE TREATED IN THE PAST WITH HOW THEY ARE TREATED TODAY

Forms of punishment also vary over time and place. Imprisonment became popular with industrialization. It deprived criminals of their freedom. Imprisonment is seen by many as an opportunity for *rehabilitation*, although many Canadians no longer hold this belief. Others see incarceration as a means of *deterrence*. Still others think of prisons as institutions of *revenge* and *incapacitation*.

Increasingly, we are witnessing the **medicalization of deviance**. An example is a heroin addict who is more likely to seek the support available through a methadone program than in previous decades, when these programs were not available. Changes made to the *Diagnostic and Statistical Manual of Mental Disorders* (DSM-5) represent another example of the medicalization of deviance.

LO⁴ EXPLAIN HOW FEAR OF CRIME IS SUBJECT TO MANIPULATION BY POLITICAL AND COMMERCIAL GROUPS THAT BENEFIT FROM IT

Many sociologists argue that **moral panics** often benefit the powerful. For example, the mass media benefit from moral panics because they increase their profits: Crime attracts large audiences, which translates into higher revenues from advertisers. Political groups also stand to benefit from fear of crime, such as Canada's Conservative government passing Bill C-10 in 2012 despite the objections of criminologists, sociologists, lawyers, and police officers who argued that "get tough" measures are ineffective. The incarceration rate in Canada has been increasing for decades (see Figure 5.6 in the chapter).

LO⁵ IDENTIFY COST-EFFECTIVE AND WORKABLE ALTERNATIVES TO SOME CURRENT METHODS OF PUNISHMENT

Cost-effective and workable alternatives to current methods of punishment for minor crimes, such as rehabilitation and restorative justice programs, have positive consequences, including lowered **recidivism rates** and higher victim satisfaction rates. Another alternative is to reduce the number of incarcerated offenders, especially youth, on the grounds that charging and imprisoning them for minor crimes is unlikely to help develop pro-social behaviour among them. They would be better diverted from criminal justice system processing to alternatives, such as a victim–offender reconciliation program.

5-2 Visit nelson.com/student for additional study tools!

NEL

SOCIAL STRATIFICATION: CANADIAN AND GLOBAL PERSPECTIVES

LO¹ DESCRIBE HOW WEALTH AND INCOME INEQUALITY IN CANADA HAVE CHANGED IN RECENT DECADES

The evidence lends support to the expression "the rich get richer while the poor get poorer." Between 1999 and 2005, the net worth (assets minus debt) of the richest quintile of Canadian families increased by 81 percent, while the members of the poorest quintile saw a decline of their net worth by 15 percent. In 2011, the richest quintile earned 44.3 percent of all income in Canada, while the poorest quintile earned just 4.8 percent.

LO² COMPARE COMPETING EXPLANATIONS OF INCOME INEQUALITY

Income inequality is to some degree a result of people having different natural endowments, such as intelligence and athletic ability. To some degree, it is the result of how hard people work. However, for most people, social factors are more important. These factors include investment in training and education (**human capital**), strong ties to high-status individuals (**social capital**), and the social and financial capacity to acquire high-status cultural signals (attitudes, preferences, formal knowledge, behaviours, goals, and credentials) used for social and cultural inclusion and exclusion (**cultural capital**). In other words, income depends on talent, effort, skills, connections, and culture.

LO³ APPRECIATE THE SOCIAL ORIGINS OF POVERTY

Canada does not have an official definition of **poverty**. Statistics Canada reports a low-income cutoff that marks "the income level at which a family may be in straitened circumstances because it has to spend a greater proportion of its income on necessities than the average family of similar size" (Statistics Canada, 2000c: 122). Due to the lack of an agreed-on definition, analysts disagree about how many Canadians are living in poverty. The disagreement centres on whether poverty must be defined in *absolute* or *relative* terms, and if the definition should be based on income or

consumption. How poverty is defined is critical for determining how social policies are formulated. These policies have important consequences for individuals and families.

People's perceptions about wealth and poverty are reflected in how they speak about these issues. Myths are often used to explain why people are poor: People are poor because they don't want to work, most poor people are immigrants, and most poor people are trapped in poverty.

General explanations for the existence of poverty range from individual-level to structural accounts. Individual-level explanations focus on the individual attributes of people. They focus on inherited attributes that are perceived to rest "within the person," such as intelligence. Social-psychological explanations focus on attributes that are acquired, such as low self-esteem or lack of motivation. Structural accounts focus on the organization of the economy, social policies, class inequalities, and ideologies.

Feminist sociologists focus on the **feminization of poverty**, by which they mean that (1) women are more likely to be low-income earners than men are, and (2) the low-income gap between women and men is growing (Duffy and Mandell, 2011: 130–33). Although (1) is correct, (2) is not (Statistics Canada, 2012b; 2012c). The female–male poverty gap is a product of women's position in the labour market compared to men.

LO⁴ UNDERSTAND WHY DIFFERENT SOCIOLOGISTS ARGUE THAT HIGH LEVELS OF INEQUALITY ARE NECESSARY, WILL INEVITABLY DISAPPEAR, OR VARY UNDER IDENTIFIABLE CONDITIONS

Some theories regard social inequality as inevitable, others argue it will disappear, and some claim that it will vary depending on the circumstances (see the table "Sociological Perspectives on Stratification").

LO⁵ IDENTIFY THE CIRCUMSTANCES LEADING PEOPLE TO MOVE UP AND DOWN THE STRUCTURE OF INEQUALITY

Social mobility refers to movement up and down the stratification system. **Intragenerational mobility** is mobility

Sociological Perspectives on Stratification

Theorists	Key Arguments
Marx	Capitalist industrialization creates two main **classes**: the **bourgeoisie** (owners of means of production) and the **proletariat** (propertyless workers of the means of production). As capitalist industrialization proceeds, the bourgeoisie becomes smaller and richer while the proletariat becomes larger and poorer. In highly developed capitalist societies, the proletariat eventually becomes **class conscious**, takes control of industry and the state, and creates a society in which people contribute what they can and receive what they need. Classlessness is therefore inevitable. (In fact, the proletarian revolution did not take place in highly developed capitalist economies because a large middle class emerged, workers successfully fought for better wages and working conditions, and companies and governments artificially stimulated demand for products and services.)
Davis and Moore	If a society wishes to prosper, the most talented people must be motivated to study and work hard. The prospect of earning high salaries motivates them to do so. Consequently, a high level of class inequality is inevitable. (In fact, the importance of given occupations is highly debatable; talent is often not discovered because inequality prevents many talented people from pursuing higher education; and much wealth is transmitted between generations regardless of how talented the younger generation is.)
Weber	A person's "market situation" (possession of goods, opportunities for income, level of education, and level of technical skill) determines a person's class position. Therefore, four main classes exist: large property owners, small property owners, propertyless but relatively highly educated and well-paid employees, and propertyless manual workers. Two types of groups other than economic classes are responsible for social inequality: **status groups** (each of which has a different level of honour or prestige) and **parties** (or organizations, each of which has a different level of power, or ability to impose its will on others). Thus, there are three dimensions of inequality in society (class, status, and power) and an individual's rank may be different on each dimension. Significantly, parties may enact policies that increase or decrease class inequality. Therefore, neither classlessness nor a high level of inequality are inevitable.

Sources: Marx, Karl. 1904 [1859]. A Contribution to the Critique of Political Economy, N. Stone, trans. Chicago: Charles H. Kerr.; Davis, Kingsley, and Wilbert E. Moore. 1945. "Some Principles of Stratification." American Sociological Review 10: 242–49; Weber, Max. 1946. From Max Weber: Essays in Sociology, rev. ed., H. Gerth and C. W. Mills, eds. and trans. New York: Oxford University Press.

within a generation (comparing first full-time job to current job). **Intergenerational mobility** is mobility between generations (comparing the occupations of parents with their children's occupations). There is more opportunity for people to change positions and life chances in *open* than in *closed* societies. In closed societies, social origins have strong effects on one's socioeconomic status.

Functional theorists of stratification and human capital believed that equality of opportunity would happen in the 1950s and 1960s. They believed we would move from a system of inequality based on **ascription** found in closed societies, to one based on **achievement** found in open societies. However, it is the combination of ascribed and achieved statuses that determines a person's access to opportunity and life chances, as evidenced by the correlation between family background and educational achievement.

LO⁶ ANALYZE CHANGE IN THE MAGNITUDE OF INEQUALITY ON A WORLD SCALE

Canada is a member of a privileged group of the 20 richest countries in the world. The average income of citizens in these countries far surpasses that of citizens in the developing world. Global inequality increased between 1975 and 2000, marked by a widening of the income gap between the 20 richest countries and the rest of the world.

LO⁷ CONTRAST COMPETING EXPLANATIONS FOR THE PERSISTENCE OF GLOBAL INEQUALITY

Two major sociological theories explaining global inequality are **modernization theory** and **dependency theory**. According to modernization theory, global inequalities arise from the dysfunctional characteristics of impoverished societies. They focus on the lack of Western values and business practices, stable governments, education, and birth control measures.

Dependency theory examines how global inequality results from patterns of domination and submission between rich and poor countries. Dependency theorists criticize modernization theorists for blaming the victims, rather than the perpetrators of global inequality. They also argue that there are two distinct periods of dependency:

6-2 Visit nelson.com/student for additional study tools!

NEL

the colonial period (which involved direct political control by colonial powers over colonies), and the post-World War II period of post-colonial control (which involved indirect control through substantial investment, support for authoritarian governments, and mounting debt).

Some sociologists divide the world into **core**, **peripheral**, and **semiperipheral countries** to explain how some countries have been able to escape poverty. The relative success of semiperipheral countries to industrialize and prosper depended on whether (1) the colonial power constructed a solid economist infrastructure in the colony; (2) the former colony was geopolitically important to the United States; (3) the former colony enacted policies that encouraged saving and domestic industrialization and discouraged foreign competition; and (4) the former colony had a highly socially cohesive population. South Korea, Brazil, and India are examples of semiperipheral countries.

6-4 Visit nelson.com/student for additional study tools!

NEL

RACE AND ETHNICITY

LEARNING OBJECTIVES

LO¹ RECOGNIZE THAT RACE AND ETHNICITY ARE SOCIALLY CONSTRUCTED VARIABLES RATHER THAN BIOLOGICAL OR CULTURAL CONSTANTS

Three main arguments undermine the notion that genes determine the behaviours of racial groups:

1. The social setting in which a person is raised and educated has a large impact on their intelligence.
2. Although it appears that certain races are more athletically inclined, sociologists have found that certain social conditions lead to high levels of sports participation. People facing widespread **prejudice** and **discrimination** often enter professional sports in disproportionately large numbers due to the existence of few alternative opportunities for social mobility.
3. It is impossible to neatly distinguish races based on genetic differences.

Some social scientists argue that we should delete "race" from the sociological vocabulary since race as a *biological category* has lost all meaning. Others argue that since race as a social construct continues to be used to distinguish people in terms of one or more physical markets, usually with profound effects on their lives, we should continue to use the term.

Sociologists distinguish between race and ethnicity. Race is to biology as ethnicity is to culture. A race is a socially defined category of people whose perceived physical markers are socially significant. An **ethnic group** comprises people whose perceived *cultural* markers are socially significant. Ethnic groups differ from one another in terms of language, religion, customs, values, ancestors, and the like. Ethnic values and other elements of ethnic culture have less of an effect on the way people behave than we commonly believe because *social-structural* differences frequently underlie cultural differences (see Table 7.1).

LO² ANALYZE WHY RACIAL AND ETHNIC LABELS AND IDENTITIES CHANGE OVER TIME AND PLACE

Racial and ethnic identities change according to time and place. According to symbolic interactionists, the development of racial and ethnic labels and/or identities is typically a process of negotiation. For example, members of a group may have a racial or ethnic identity, but outsiders may impose a new label on them (e.g., *Indian* instead of *Mi'kmaq*). Group members then reject, accept, or modify the label (e.g., *Indian* to *First Nation*). The negotiation between outsiders and insiders eventually results in the crystallization of a new more or less stable ethnic identity. If the social context changes again, the negotiation process begins anew.

The contrast between Irish Canadians and black Canadians demonstrates that relations among racial and ethnic groups can take different forms, producing variations in how labels are applied and identities are crystallized. Irish Canadians are freer to choose their identity and display a high level of **symbolic ethnicity**. In contrast, most black Canadians lack the freedom to enjoy symbolic ethnicity. Because **racism** and **institutional racism** are prevalent in Canada, racial identities are imposed on black Canadians.

TABLE 7.1	Percentage Low-Income by Selected Groups and Immigration Status, Canada			
	White	**Black**	**Chinese**	**Arab**
Immigrants	13.6	28.5	25.1	36.7
Non-immigrants	11.7	30.8	17.9	34.7

Note: This table shows the percentage of people over the age of 15 below the low-income cutoff in each group. For the definition of "low-income cutoff," see Chapter 6. The percentages are probably low because of problems with the data source (Brym, 2014) but no evidence suggests that underestimates are higher in one group than in another.

Source: Statistics Canada, 2015h. *National Household Survey* (NHS) PUMF, 2011: individuals file. http://sda.chass.utoronto.ca.myaccess.library.utoronto.ca/cgi-bin/sdacensus/hsda?harcsda+nhs11i (retrieved 2 August 2015).

LO³ APPRECIATE THAT CONQUEST AND DOMINATION ARE AMONG THE MOST IMPORTANT FORCES LEADING TO THE CRYSTALLIZATION OF DISTINCT ETHNIC AND RACIAL IDENTITIES

Conflict theorists argue that one of the most important mechanisms promoting inequality and conflict between racial and ethnic groups is colonialism. **Colonialism** involves people from one country invading and taking political, cultural, and economic control over people from another country. Once entrenched, colonizers may engage in **internal colonialism**, preventing the assimilation of subordinate racial or ethnic groups by segregating them residentially, occupationally, and in social contacts ranging from friendship to marriage.

In Canada, there were three main forms of internal colonialism: expulsion, conquest, and slavery. **Expulsion** is the forcible removal of a population from a territory claimed by another people. Some sociologists argue that this term best describes the treatment of Aboriginal peoples in Canada by European immigrants. Others argue that the government of Canada engaged in cultural **genocide**. Genocide is the intentional extermination of an entire population defined as a race or a people, whereas cultural genocide is extermination of a people's culture and heritage.

Conquest is the forcible capture of land and the economic and political domination of its inhabitants. Until the start of the Quiet Revolution in 1960, the Québécois were disadvantaged in an English-created system of ethnic stratification that remained in place for more than 200 years.

Slavery is the ownership and control of people. It was abolished in Canada in 1833 when the British government officially banned slavery throughout the British Empire.

These practices of internal colonialism have had lasting impacts on Aboriginal Canadians and black Canadians in particular; among these impacts are high incarceration rates, infant mortality rates, and school dropout rates (see Table 7.2 in the chapter).

Despite Canada's reputation as an open multicultural society, our immigration laws contained racial and ethnic restrictions until the 1960s. Even when immigration was encouraged, discrimination was widespread. For example, early Chinese immigrants were victims of a **split labour market**, where low-wage Chinese workers and high-wage white workers competed for the same jobs. High-wage workers resented the presence of low-wage competitors, so conflict resulted, and racist attitudes were reinforced.

LO⁴ DESCRIBE THE WAYS IN WHICH IDENTIFYING WITH A RACIAL OR ETHNIC GROUP CAN BE ECONOMICALLY, POLITICALLY, AND EMOTIONALLY ADVANTAGEOUS

For many white European groups, three main factors enhance the value of continued ethnic group membership. First, ethnic group membership can have economic advantages, such as business networks. Second, ethnic group membership can be politically useful because ethnicity can be used as a political tool to gain access to resources from government. Third, ethnic group membership tends to persist because of the emotional support it provides in an increasingly fast-paced technologically driven society.

In our era, retaining ethnic ties beyond the second generation is relatively easy. Inexpensive international travel and communication has helped some ethnic groups become **transnational communities** whose boundaries extend between or among countries.

Two hundred years ago, Canada was a society based on expulsion, conquest, slavery, and segregation. Today, Canada is a society based on segregation, **pluralism**, and assimilation.

No country is ethnically and racially homogeneous, and in many countries, including Canada, the largest ethnic group forms less than half the population. This has produced a certain level of tolerance. However, prejudice, discrimination, and stratification have not been eradicated. Many analysts argue that political initiatives—such as employment equity programs—are required to ameliorate the situation of Canada's most disadvantaged groups.

7-2   Visit nelson.com/student for additional study tools!

NEL

SEXUALITIES AND GENDERS

LEARNING OBJECTIVES

LO¹ DISTINGUISH BIOLOGICALLY DETERMINED SEX FROM SOCIALLY DETERMINED GENDER

Sex is determined by one's genetic makeup. **Intersex** people do not conform to conventional male and female sex categories. **Gender** refers to one's sense of being male or female and playing masculine or feminine roles as defined by one's culture. People who are uncomfortable with the gender assigned to them at birth or who do not fit comfortably into conventional male or female gender categories are considered **transgender**.

LO² APPRECIATE THAT GENDER IS SHAPED LARGELY BY THE WAY PARENTS RAISE CHILDREN, TEACHERS INTERACT WITH PUPILS, AND THE MASS MEDIA PORTRAY IDEAL BODY IMAGES

In contrast to **essentialism**—a functionalist understanding of gender based on biological differences—sociologists generally espouse a **social constructionist** perspective. According to this school of thought, gender differences are a product of the different social positions occupied by women and men, not biological differences. The fact that gender and sexuality have varied widely across time and cultures suggests that gender is a social construction. Social constructionists also take issue with essentialist claims that overgeneralize and ignore the role of power.

Conflict theorists, feminist theorists, and symbolic interactionists all focus on various aspects of gender as a social construction. Symbolic interactionists in particular regard socialization as key to understanding how boys and girls learn masculine and feminine roles. Gender socialization often happens through toys—like Barbie and GI Joe—as well as through the interactions children have with significant others. For example, experiments have shown that adults interpret infant behaviour differently depending on whether they have been told the child is a boy or a girl, regardless of the infant's actual sex.

Symbolic interactionists also consider how gender roles are maintained in everyday social interactions. For example, children actively construct gender roles in their play patterns. The mass media also influence the construction of gender, for example, through the display of ideal body images. By the time children reach adolescence, **gender ideologies** are well formed.

LO³ IDENTIFY THE SOCIAL FORCES PUSHING PEOPLE TOWARD HETEROSEXUALITY

Sexuality has three dimensions: identity, desire, and behaviour. Sociologists are less interested in the origins of homosexuality than in how homosexuality is socially constructed. **Queer theory** denies the existence of stable sexual orientations altogether. Tolerance toward homosexuality has increased because of scientific and political factors, yet widespread animosity is still evident. **Homophobia** sometimes gives rise to violence. Sexual minorities in general often experience opposition.

LO⁴ RECOGNIZE THAT THE SOCIAL DISTINCTION BETWEEN MEN AND WOMEN SERVES AS AN IMPORTANT BASIS OF INEQUALITY IN THE FAMILY AND THE WORKPLACE

One of the present-day consequences of the social distinction between men and women is the earnings gap. The most recent data (for 2011) tell us that women earned about 72.0 cents for every dollar men earned. As Table 8.3 shows, the female–male earnings ratio varies by occupational category. Variation across these categories suggests that social conditions specific to given occupations account in part for the magnitude of the gender wage gap. **Gender discrimination, occupational sex segregation**, women's domestic responsibilities, and how we value work done by women versus work done by men are among the factors sociologists point to as being responsible for the earnings gap between men and women.

TABLE 8.3	Female–Male Earnings Ratio in Broad Occupational Categories, Canada	
Occupational Category		**Female–Male Earnings Ratio**
Management		0.72
Business, finance, and administration		0.67
Natural and applied science		0.84
Health		0.47
Social science, education, government, and religion		0.69
Art, culture, recreation, and sport		0.76
Sales and service		0.55
Trades, transport, and equipment operation		0.55
Primary industry		0.42
Processing, manufacturing, and utilities		0.64

Note: The data in this table are for 2015.

Source: Adapted from Statistics Canada, 2015f. "Earnings of Individuals, by Selected Characteristics and National Occupational Classification (NOC-S), 2011 Constant Dollars, Annually." CANSIM database, Table 2020106.

LO⁵ EXPLAIN HOW MALE AGGRESSION AGAINST WOMEN IS ROOTED IN GENDER INEQUALITY

Male aggression and gender inequality go hand in hand. Aggression against women, in the form of sexual assault (including **acquaintance rape**), **quid pro quo sexual harassment**, and **hostile environment sexual harassment**, happens more often when men have much more social power than women. Although some psychological factors can contribute to sexual aggression and assault against females, sociologists are interested in how social circumstances, such as war, and the culture of certain fraternities, and sports, can facilitate heightened male dominance and female degradation. When women and men are more equal socially and norms justify gender equality, the rate of male aggression against women is lower.

LO⁶ OUTLINE SOCIAL POLICIES THAT COULD LOWER THE LEVEL OF INEQUALITY BETWEEN WOMEN AND MEN

Better child-care and **pay equity** policies are needed to bridge the gender gap in earnings. Achieving high-quality, government-subsidized child care and developing a comprehensive pay equity policy depends in part on the strength of the women's movement. The women's movement has significantly improved the social standing of women, including the right to vote ("first wave" feminism) and equal rights in education and employment ("second wave" feminism). Considerable ideological differences are present within the contemporary women's movement (the "third wave"), ushering in a new era of anti-racist and postmodernist feminists who extend the relevance of feminism to previously marginalized groups.

8-2 Visit nelson.com/student for additional study tools!

NEL

FAMILIES

LEARNING OBJECTIVES

LO¹ IDENTIFY NEW FAMILY FORMS THAT HAVE EMERGED IN RECENT DECADES, MAKING THE TRADITIONAL NUCLEAR FAMILY LESS COMMON THAN IT USED TO BE

The **traditional nuclear family** is less common than it used to be, as is the **nuclear family** (see Figure 9.1). At the core of these family forms is **marriage**. While some sociologists

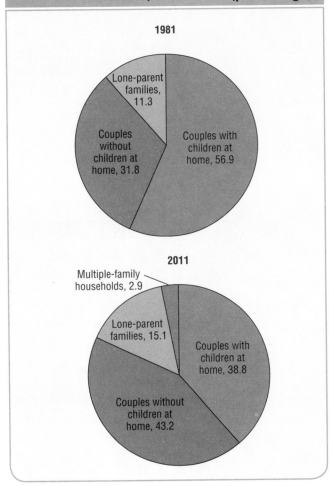

FIGURE 9.1 **Changing Canadian Families, Canada, 1981–2011 (percentage)**

1981

- Lone-parent families, 11.3
- Couples without children at home, 31.8
- Couples with children at home, 56.9

2011

- Multiple-family households, 2.9
- Lone-parent families, 15.1
- Couples without children at home, 43.2
- Couples with children at home, 38.8

Sources: Statistics Canada, n.d., "Census Families Time Series, 1931–2001"; Statistics Canada, 2013, "Canadian Households in 2011: Type and Growth."

express concern that the family is in decline, other sociologists believe that the nature of family is simply changing. Functionalists view this trend as negative. In the functionalist view, nuclear families have five main functions: regulated sexual activity, economic cooperation, reproduction, socialization, and emotional support. Other sociologists believe that families are structured in a multitude of ways and that sometimes these changes can represent improvement in people's lives.

LO² APPRECIATE THAT THE TRADITIONAL NUCLEAR FAMILY HAS BEEN WEAKENING SINCE THE 1800S, ALTHOUGH IT STRENGTHENED TEMPORARILY IN THE YEARS IMMEDIATELY FOLLOWING WORLD WAR II

Functionalist theory best fits the middle-class family in the 15 years after World War II, when there was a need and desire to return to a state of "normalcy"—men back in the workforce and women back at home. Yet examination of the **crude divorce rate**, the **crude marriage rate**, and the **total fertility rate** reveals that the nuclear family was weakening from the nineteenth century to the present day. The period after World War II was a time of unparalleled optimism and prosperity, leading to a marriage boom and a baby boom. It was an historical anomaly. By the early 1960s, earlier trends reasserted themselves.

LO³ LIST THE FACTORS CONTRIBUTING TO VARIATION IN PATTERNS OF MATE SELECTION, MARITAL SATISFACTION, DIVORCE, REPRODUCTIVE CHOICE, HOUSEWORK AND CHILD CARE, AND DOMESTIC VIOLENCE

The idea that love should be important to mate selection first gained currency in the eighteenth century. Sociologists identify three sets of social forces that influence whom you are likely to fall in love with: the resources that potential spouses possess, including financial assets and income, values, and knowledge; third parties, particularly in the case of individuals from different groups; and demographic and compositional factors, such as the sex ratio of the groups one belongs to and the social composition of the geographic region in which one lives.

Marital satisfaction tends to be higher among people with higher socioeconomic status, where divorce laws are liberal, in families where housework and child care are shared equally, and among spouses who enjoy satisfying sexual relations. Marital satisfaction also depends on the family's life cycle; couples without children and parents of adult children who have moved out enjoy the highest level of marital satisfaction. The economic effects of divorce are hardest on women and children. Women's income generally falls after divorce because women tend to earn less than men do, children tend to live with their mothers after divorce, and child support payments are often inadequate.

Women are still largely responsible for preparing meals, helping with homework, doing laundry, and so on, despite participating in the paid labour market. Men take a more active role in the household today than in previous decades, but men tend to do low-stress chores.

Greater gender equality in the family and the larger society has been shown to lead to a decline in domestic violence in heterosexual couples. For heterosexual couples, the incidence of domestic violence is highest where a significant power imbalance between men and women exists, where norms justify the male domination of women and where early socialization experiences predispose men to behave aggressively toward women.

LO⁴ DESCRIBE THE CHARACTERISTICS OF DIVERSE FAMILY FORMS

Many new alternatives to the traditional nuclear family exist (refer to Table 9.1). Cohabitation has become common because fewer people consider marriage very important. Same-sex marriage and civil unions have become more common than in previous decades. Given the costs of raising a Canadian child, many adults are choosing to forgo parenthood and instead are part of "zero-child families."

LO⁵ EXPLAIN HOW PUBLIC POLICY CAN PREVENT THE EMERGENCE OF CERTAIN SOCIAL PROBLEMS THAT MIGHT OTHERWISE RESULT FROM THE DECLINE OF THE TRADITIONAL NUCLEAR FAMILY

The decline of the traditional nuclear family is sometimes associated with a host of social problems. However, in some countries, such as Sweden, effective family support policies have been adopted for parental leave, health care benefits, and child care that reduce these problems. The United States, on the other hand, scores lower on measures of childhood well-being—such as poverty and infant abuse—than does Sweden and lacks the family-friendly policies like those of Sweden, suggesting that social problems can be averted by government policy and programs.

TABLE 9.1 The Traditional Nuclear Family and New Alternatives

Traditional Nuclear Family	New Alternatives
Legally married	Never-married singlehood, non-marital cohabitation
With children	Voluntary childlessness
Two-parent	Single-parent (never married or previously married)
Permanent	Divorce, remarriage (including binuclear family involving joint custody, stepfamily, or "blended" family)
Male primary provider, ultimate authority	Egalitarian marriage (including dual-career and commuter marriage)
Sexually exclusive	Extramarital relationships (including sexually open marriage, swinging, and intimate friendships)
Heterosexual	Same-sex intimate relationships or households
Two-adult household	Multi-adult households (including multiple spouses, communal living, affiliated families, and multigenerational families)

Source: Adapted from Macklin, Eleanor D. 1980. "Nontraditional Family Forms: A Decade of Research." *Journal of Marriage and the Family* 42: 906.

9-2 Visit nelson.com/student for additional study tools!

NEL

RELIGION AND EDUCATION

LEARNING OBJECTIVES

LO¹ DISTINGUISH THE CIRCUMSTANCES IN WHICH RELIGION CREATES SOCIETAL COHESION AND REINFORCES SOCIAL INEQUALITY FROM THE CIRCUMSTANCES IN WHICH RELIGION PROMOTES SOCIAL CONFLICT

Sociologists study how the structure of society and a person's place in it influence his or her religious beliefs and practices. The understanding of the role of religion in society is different depending on one's theoretical perspective. Functionalists believe religion reinforces social solidarity. By sharing a **collective conscience**, we come to distinguish the **sacred** from the **profane**. The practices and symbols connected to the sacred—**rituals** and **totems**—reinforce social solidarity.

Conflict and feminist theorists disagree with functionalism's emphasis on how religion can maintain social cohesion, arguing instead that religion can incite social conflict and maintain unequal relations. An example of this argument comes from Marx, who called religion the "opium of the people" because he believed that religion had the power to subdue people into accepting their lot in life. Sociologists also argue that the **routinization of charisma** can similarly support class inequality.

LO² APPRECIATE THAT RELIGION GOVERNS FEWER ASPECTS OF MOST PEOPLE'S LIVES THAN IN THE PAST, EVEN THOUGH A RELIGIOUS REVIVAL HAS TAKEN PLACE IN MANY PARTS OF THE WORLD IN RECENT DECADES

According to Weber's **secularization thesis**, religion and religious authority is declining worldwide, replaced by science and other forms of rationalism. However, research evidence indicates that this is an oversimplification. Among **fundamentalists**, **religiosity** has intensified. Religious movements are also enmeshed with many nations' governments. Some sociologists have proposed the **revised secularization thesis**, which holds that religion governs fewer aspects of people's lives and has become largely a matter of personal choice.

Still others adopt a *market model*, which conceives of religious organizations as suppliers of various services that are demanded by people who desire religious activities. Competitive religious markets (such as that of the United States) are effective in recruiting adherents because they cater well to diverse religious needs. Irrespective of theoretical approach, it is clear that religious polarization is growing; increasingly, many societies are witnessing a sharper division between a growing number of fundamentalists, a growing number of secularists, and a shrinking middle.

Sociologists generally divide religious groups into **churches**, **sects**, and **cults**. The primary differences between these three types of religious groups are the extent to which they are integrated into society, their level of bureaucracy, their longevity, who makes up the leadership, and the class base of their following. Churches can be further divided into **ecclesia** and **denominations**.

LO³ LIST SOCIOLOGICAL FACTORS ASSOCIATED WITH ATTENDING RELIGION SERVICES

Religiosity is influenced by a number of social factors, including age, region, family influence, and social inequality. For example, young people may be relatively active in religious activities because they are required to be by their parents and do not have work and other commitments that take them away from religious services. Generally speaking, those who attend religious services are those who must, those who were taught religion as children, those who need organized religion because of advanced age, and those who have the most time to go to services.

LO⁴ SEE HOW FUNCTIONALISM, CONFLICT THEORY, FEMINIST THEORY, AND SYMBOLIC INTERACTIONISM HELP US UNDERSTAND HOW THE EDUCATIONAL SYSTEM PROMOTES UPWARD MOBILITY, CREATES SOCIAL COHESION, AND REINFORCES CLASS, RACIAL, AND ETHNIC INEQUALITIES

Sociological Theories of Education

Theory	Key Question	Explanation
Functionalist	How do schools contribute to social equilibrium?	Schools have manifest functions, including sorting, training, socializing, and transmitting culture. They also have latent functions, including mate selection and the supervision of minors.
Conflict	How do schools reproduce social inequality?	Inequality in families' (1) economic resources, (2) ability to offer encouragement, emotional support, and tutoring to children, and (3) cultural capital lead children to different schools, streams, and extracurricular activities that, in turn, produce graduates suited to jobs higher or lower in the socioeconomic hierarchy.
Feminist	How does gender inequality influence educational outcomes?	Socialization in the family, in schools, and in the mass media tends to lead girls to specialize in subjects associated with relatively low-paying jobs.
Symbolic interactionist	How do students' and teachers' expectations influence educational outcomes?	The **stereotype threat** involves teachers having low expectations of students who are members of lower classes and/or belong to certain ethnic or racial groups. Students from lower classes and marginalized ethnic or racial groups tend to feel rejected. This has a negative impact on their performance. Some of them also come to regard high academic performance as "selling out." Poor academic performance generally leads to relatively low standing in the socioeconomic hierarchy.

LO⁵ COMPARE THE QUALITY OF EDUCATION IN CANADA TO THE QUALITY OF EDUCATION IN OTHER COUNTRIES

Like other countries, Canada has a system of mass schooling. Canadians are among the most highly educated people in the world. Nonetheless, many Canadians believe our education is of lower quality than other educational systems. In particular, the Japanese and South Korean practice of demanding long hours studying core subjects is seen by some as preferable to spending fewer hours in school and devoting time to art, music, and drama. In reality, international comparisons indicate that Canadians perform relatively well on standardized science, reading, and math tests.

10-2   Visit nelson.com/student for additional study tools!

NEL

HEALTH AND MEDICINE

LEARNING OBJECTIVES

LO¹ RECOGNIZE THAT HEALTH RISKS ARE UNEVENLY DISTRIBUTED BY CLASS, GENDER, RACE, AND COUNTRY OF RESIDENCE

Health is not only a medical issue but also a sociological one. **Life expectancy** and health risks are unevenly distributed in human populations. Women and men, upper and lower classes, rich and poor countries, and privileged and disadvantaged members of racial and ethnic groups are exposed to health risks to varying degrees.

Beyond natural causes, we know of three social causes of illness and death: human environmental factors (including **environmental racism**), factors related to the **public health system** and the **health care system** in a given country, and lifestyle factors like smoking and poor diet. The public health system—comprised of government-run programs ensuring access to clean drinking water, basic sewage and sanitation services, and inoculation against infectious disease—in particular is known to improve life expectancy and decrease disease rates. These social factors vary from country to country, resulting in varying rates of life expectancy, disease, and **infant mortality**.

LO² EXPLAIN WHY MANY LOW-INCOME AND MODERATE-INCOME CANADIANS HAVE LIMITED ACCESS TO HEALTH SERVICES

Despite Canada's health care system, many lower-income Canadians have limited access to health services, affecting life expectancy and rates of illness. As we move down the income ladder, health deteriorates. Sociologists point to differences in stress, early stages of development (such as poor nutrition during pregnancy), knowledge about what constitutes a healthy lifestyle, access to health resources such as diagnostic and treatment facilities, and environmental exposure. For these reasons, people with low income tend to die at a younger age than do people with high income. The health care system is also marked by racial and gender inequalities.

LO³ IDENTIFY THE WAYS IN WHICH THE SOCIAL ORGANIZATION OF HEALTH CARE SYSTEMS INFLUENCES PEOPLE'S HEALTH

Rich countries spend more on health care, but it does not necessarily mean that they have good health. For example, Americans spend more on health care than do people in any other country, but the average health status of Americans is lower than the average health status of Canadians. The level of social inequality is higher in the United States because of increased earnings gaps and health care providers charging higher prices than elsewhere. In general, the higher the level of inequality in a country, the less healthy its population is.

Americans also pay more for prescription drugs, in part because the American government does not regulate pricing. Therefore, the American health care system makes it difficult for many people to receive adequate care. The Canadian health care system, on the other hand, is often referred to as **socialized medicine**; the Canadian government directly controls many dimensions of the health care system, although it does not directly pay physicians. While many praise the Canadian health care system, many Canadians face long wait times for medical care.

LO⁴ DESCRIBE HOW THE RISE OF MEDICAL SCIENCE IS LINKED TO (1) SUCCESSFUL TREATMENTS AND (2) THE WAY DOCTORS EXCLUDED COMPETITORS AND ESTABLISHED CONTROL OVER THEIR PROFESSION AND THEIR CLIENTS

Physicians have not always been at the core of the practice of medicine. Rather, their privileged position in the health care system has been the result of the rise of medical science and the ability of physicians to form a **profession**. Their professionalization—along with identifying bacteria, viruses, and effective procedures and vaccines—resulted in the physicians' domination in health care. As professionals, physicians tightly regulate the training of doctors and the practice of medicine, and minimize competition by laying claim to their field of expertise. In Canada, the professional organization of Canadian doctors is the Canadian Medical Association (CMA); at its inception, the CMA set about publicizing the successes of medical science and criticizing alternative approaches, such as midwifery. Through professionalization, physicians are granted high occupational prestige, income, and social and political power.

LO⁵ APPRECIATE THE BENEFITS AND DANGERS OF ALTERNATIVE MEDICAL TREATMENTS

Many skeptics of modern medicine turn to alternative medical treatments that rely less on high technology and drugs and are more sensitive to the need to maintain a balance between humans and their environment in pursuit of good health. These alternatives include chiropractic services, homeopathy, and **holistic medicine**.

Alternative medical treatments are often subject to debate between alternative practitioners and those in the traditional practice of medicine. Some critics argue that users of alternative medical treatments experience a **placebo effect**, while others suggest the risks to these alternative paths to good health are too great. Holistic practitioners in particular do not reject traditional scientific medicine but instead emphasize disease prevention. Patients are encouraged to play an active role in maintaining good health in contrast to assuming the **sick role** first discussed by Talcott Parsons (Parsons, 1951). Despite the debates, many people believe that some alternatives to traditional medicine will ultimately help to improve the health of people in Canada and throughout the world.

11-2   Visit nelson.com/student for additional study tools!

NEL

THE MASS MEDIA

LO¹ APPRECIATE THAT, ALTHOUGH THE MOST POPULAR MASS MEDIA ARE PRODUCTS OF THE TWENTIETH CENTURY, THEIR GROWTH IS ROOTED IN THE RISE OF PROTESTANTISM, DEMOCRACY, AND CAPITALISM

The **mass media** are print, radio, television, and other communication technologies that reach many people. It is a mediated ("media") form of communication that transmits messages to many people ("mass"). Three main factors contributed to the rise of mass media:

1. *Religious*: The Protestant Reformation urged people to read the Bible in their own languages. The Bible became the first product of the mass media in the West.
2. *Political*: The democratic movement encouraged the growth of the free and independent press that presented a plurality of opinions.
3. *Economic*: Capitalist industrialization required a rapid means of communicating to conduct business efficiently and a literate workforce; business owners made substantial profits from the mass media.

LO² IDENTIFY THE WAYS IN WHICH THE MASS MEDIA MAKE SOCIETY MORE COHESIVE

The nationwide distribution of newspapers, magazines, movies, television, and Internet cements the large, socially diverse, and geographically far-flung population of Canada. Functionalists argue that the four main functions of the mass media are *coordination, socialization, social control,* and *entertainment*. First, the mass media help to coordinate information in a large society. Second, the mass media disseminate social norms and values, such as the value of competition that is reinforced in the news, business, editorial, and sports sections of newspapers. Third, the mass media help to promote social control by promoting conformity to societal norms and values. For example, newspapers, news broadcasts, and television shows vilify criminals and exalt law enforcement agents.

Fourth, the mass media provide entertainment that distracts people from daily frustrations and pressing concerns.

LO³ IDENTIFY THE WAYS IN WHICH THE MASS MEDIA FOSTER SOCIAL INEQUALITY

According to conflict theorists, functionalists exaggerate the degree to which the mass media represent the interests of the entire society, and pay no attention to how the mass media contribute to social inequality. Conflict theorists argue that the mass media serve the interests of dominant classes and political groups. There are two ways these groups benefit from the mass media. First, the beliefs, values, and ideas promoted by the mass media create widespread consent for the basic structure of society. Second, the mass media are highly profitable and are owned by a small number of people.

Media concentration in Canada has increased in recent decades. Until the 1990s, media conglomeration mainly involved *horizontal integration* (the process of acquiring or merging with other companies in the same industry for the purpose of gaining more control over the industry).

In the 1990s, *vertical integration* (the process of acquiring companies involved in the production and sale of various media products) became more widespread. For example, Rogers Communications Inc. owns the Toronto Blue Jays, broadcasts the team's games on its sports television station, analyzes the team on its sports radio station, owns the stadium where the Blue Jays play, carries signals to the viewer's homes via its cable system, and spins off team promotions at Rogers stores.

Conflict theorists argue that media concentration in Canada produces *media bias*. Edward Herman and Noam Chomsky (1988) argued that other, more subtle mechanisms also foster media biases in favour of dominant classes and political groups. They include advertising, sourcing, and flak. Critics argue that the mass media are not completely biased toward corporate interests. For example, mainstream journalists often report stories that are critical of corporate actions or points of views. However, considerable evidence supports the claim that the mass media promote the core society values that create widespread consent for the basic structures of society (democracy, capitalism, and consumerism).

LO⁴ DESCRIBE HOW AUDIENCES FILTER, INTERPRET, RESIST, AND EVEN REJECT MEDIA MESSAGES IF THE MESSAGES ARE INCONSISTENT WITH AUDIENCE BELIEFS AND EXPERIENCES

Symbolic interactionists provide an alternative perspective to the top–down, deterministic view of the mass media presented by functionalists and conflict theorists. Both approaches understate how audience members interpret media messages in different ways. However, there is only an indirect link between media messages and actual behaviour. There is a **two-step flow of communication** between the mass media and audience members because media messages are often filtered by opinion leaders.

Furthermore, **cultural studies** research on the mass media focuses not just on the cultural meanings that producers try to transmit but also on the way audiences filter and interpret mass media messages in the context of their own interests, experiences, and values. For example, even young children can distinguish between real-life violence and "make-believe" violence on television (Hodge and Tripp, 1986).

LO⁵ ANALYZE HOW THE MASS MEDIA MISREPRESENT WOMEN AND MEMBERS OF RACIAL MINORITIES

In the 1970s, feminists focused on how women were represented in the mass media. Women were usually depicted in subordinate roles and appeared in the domestic sphere, while men were usually depicted in dominant roles in public

settings (see Figure 12.1). Early feminist research assumed audiences passively accepted these images as normal. By the 1980s, feminist research on the mass media began to find that female audience members typically recognize that real women are more complicated than the stereotypical women portrayed by the mass media. Feminists also examined reoccurring stereotypical images of women of colour in the mass media. Recent research has identified that women's representation in prime-time TV has stalled or even reversed (Lauzen, 2014).

LO⁶ RECOGNIZE THAT THE INTERNET AND SOCIAL MEDIA OFFER USERS MORE FREEDOM THAN OTHER MASS MEDIA DO

Some social forces restrict Internet access. The Internet requires an expensive infrastructure. In the developed world, wealthier households have more access to the Internet. Globally, Internet connectivity is significantly higher in the richest countries. Some analysts argue that American domination of the Internet leads to **media imperialism**, the control of the mass medium by a single national culture and the undermining of other national cultures. However, they tend to ignore the degree to which other national cultures are making inroads on the Internet. **Media convergence**, the blending of the telephone, the World Wide Web, television, and other communications media as new, hybrid media forms, is increasing.

The Internet and social media offer more opportunity for audience influence than other forms of mass media do. The Internet makes mass media more democratic by partially blurring the distinction between producer and

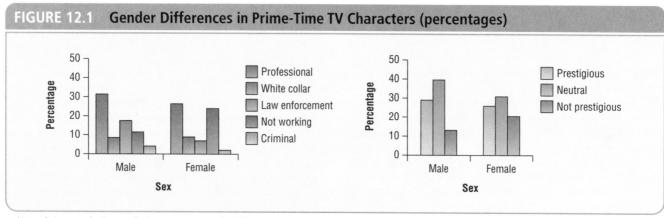

FIGURE 12.1 Gender Differences in Prime-Time TV Characters (percentages)

Note: Category selection results in percentages under 100.

Source: Adapted from Signorielli, N. 2009. "Race and Sex in Prime Time: A Look at Occupations and Occupational Prestige." *Mass Communication and Society* 12(3): 332–52.

12-2 Visit nelson.com/student for additional study tools!

NEL

consumer. For example, more than 300 million people express their opinions to many followers through their Twitter accounts.

Using social media affects our identity, social relations, and social activism. First, people have more freedom to manipulate how they present themselves to others through social media. Second, social media create opportunities for social connections between people who are geographically far from each other. Third, social media offer a variety of opportunities for social activism, such as promoting a political campaign over Twitter or Facebook. However, opportunities for social activism are limited by the monitoring and censorship of social media by authorities in undemocratic countries.

12-4 Visit nelson.com/student for additional study tools!

NEL

TECHNOLOGY, THE ENVIRONMENT, AND SOCIAL MOVEMENTS

LEARNING OBJECTIVES

LO¹ SEE THAT ALTHOUGH TECHNOLOGY TRANSFORMS SOCIETY AND HISTORY, SOCIAL NEED SHAPES TECHNOLOGICAL GROWTH

Prior to the atomic bombing of Hiroshima (August 6, 1945), humanity was naively optimistic about using **technology** to improve our lives. After multiple technological disasters, we have become more skeptical about the prospects of technology. Sociologists have coined different terms to describe the unintended consequences of technology. **Normal accident** refers to the fact that complex modern technologies will *inevitably* fail. Ulrich Beck (1992) claims that we live in a **risk society** where technology distributes environmental dangers among all categories of the population, albeit to varying degrees among different population categories.

Technological determinism is the belief that technology shapes human society and history. The creation of the steam engine, computers, and biotechnologies have profoundly reshaped the social landscape. However, technological developments become widespread only when there is *social demand* for them. By the mid-twentieth century, the era of big science and big technology had arrived. Only governments and large multinational corporations could afford to conduct extensive, cutting-edge research in technology and innovation, such as in the spacecraft industry.

LO² ANALYZE THE CIRCUMSTANCES IN WHICH ENVIRONMENTAL ISSUES ARE TRANSFORMED INTO SOCIAL PROBLEMS

The gradual increase in the world's average surface temperature, or **global warming**, resulted from the widespread burning of fossil fuels that began during the Industrial Revolution. Global warming eventually caused climate change. Global warming became a social problem only after the public began to respond to the lengthy campaign promoted by policy-oriented scientists, the environmental movement, the mass media, and respected organizations. Thus, global warming became a major social problem only after it was publicly defined as such.

LO³ ASSESS THE UNEQUAL SOCIAL DISTRIBUTION OF ENVIRONMENTAL RISKS

Environmental risks are unequally distributed. The economically and politically disadvantaged are more vulnerable and suffer more than privileged groups. The Dene people in the Northwest Territories, experienced **environmental racism** when the world's first uranium mine opened near their community. The working-class people living on Frederick Street in Sydney, Nova Scotia, experienced high cancer rates due to their proximity to industrial pollutants. People in the southern hemisphere are exposed to higher levels of pollution than people living in wealthy nations in the northern hemisphere.

LO⁴ SUMMARIZE THE ROLE OF MARKET/TECHNOLOGICAL AND COOPERATIVE SOLUTIONS TO ENVIRONMENTAL PROBLEMS

Some analysts argue that technology and the market can solve the environmental crisis because human creativity is motivated by profit. Many new technologies have been developed to combat environmental degradation. Others argue that, on their own, market forces and technology cannot solve the problem. That is because the price of many commodities, particularly petroleum products, do not reflect their actual cost to society; efforts to deal with the environmental crisis have not helped enough to date; and substantial political pressure is needed to motivate governments and corporations to act. Cooperation is an alternative to the market and high-tech approach that is likely to be more effective than a purely technology- and market-driven approach.

LO⁵ IDENTIFY THE SOCIAL CONDITIONS THAT ENCOURAGE PEOPLE TO REBEL AGAINST THE STATUS QUO

Some people take **collective action** and form a **social movement** by establishing organizations, lobbies, unions, and political parties. Prior to 1970, many sociologists believed that there were two preconditions behind social movements: *social marginality* and *strain*. These conditions formed the basis of the **breakdown theory**, a functionalist perspective on collective action. It suggests that social movements result from the disruption or breakdown of previously integrative structures and norms.

Critics of breakdown theory assert that leaders and early joiners of social movements are well integrated in their communities and that high levels of **relative deprivation** are, for the most part, not associated with the formation of movements. Many social movements are led by well-educated middle-class professionals; people living in extreme deprivation do not usually have the resources required to form a social movement.

Solidarity theory is an alternative way of understanding collective action. It originates in conflict theory. It focuses on the social-structural conditions that facilitate the emergence of social movements. Solidarity theorists focus on the social conditions that allow people to turn their discontent into a unified (or "solidary") political force. They hold that people are more likely to form a social movement when social control is weak or inconsistent, when adequate resources to protest are available (time, money, and other resources), and when **political opportunities** arise.

Resource mobilization is the process by which social movements crystallize because of the increasing organizational, material, and other resources of movement members. For example, in Canada, the percentage of non-agricultural workers who went out on strike increased from the mid-1940s to the mid-1970s because the rate of unionization increased, workers' wages increased, and government benefits were relatively generous. Since then, the rate of unionization has decreased, workers' wages have not increased significantly, and many government benefits have decreased. Strike frequency has fallen because workers have fewer strike resources.

LO⁶ DESCRIBE THE SOCIAL CONDITIONS THAT ALLOW ORGANIZED SOCIAL MOVEMENTS TO GROW

Symbolic interactionists argue that for social movements to grow, **frame alignment** must take place. Frame alignment theory focuses on strategies that movements use to recruit new members. Social movements must make their activities, ideas, and goals consistent with the interests, beliefs, and values of potential new recruits.

There are three main ways that frame alignment can be accomplished. First, social movements can appeal to other movements pursuing similar causes. An anti-tar sands organization, for example, could send e-mails to members of feminist, anti-racist, or labour organizations. Second, activists can elaborate on key values, causes, and the seriousness of the social problem that may not have occurred to potential recruits. For instance, an anti-tar sands organization could draw attention to the connection between environmental degradation, Aboriginal land claims, and long-term economic prosperity. Third, social movements can also stretch their objectives to appeal to a broader range of people. This move is often controversial because it sometimes leads to a "watering down" of the movement's message or purpose.

LO⁷ RECOGNIZE THAT THE HISTORY OF SOCIAL MOVEMENTS IS A STRUGGLE FOR THE ACQUISITION OF CONSTANTLY BROADENING CITIZENSHIP RIGHTS—AND OPPOSITION TO THOSE STRUGGLES

Around 1700, the modern state crystallized. For the next 250 years, social movements changed their focus from local to national issues. Under the impact of relatively inexpensive international travel and electronic communication, recent decades have witnessed the emergence of "new social movements," which have set themselves broader goals, attracted new kinds of members, and become global in scope (Melucci, 1980, 1995). They promote the rights of humanity as a whole, rather than the rights of specific groups. They mobilize many middle-class, well-educated people. Finally, they are internationally focused. Since coffee production, for example, is largely controlled by powerful transnational corporations, a campaign for fair-trade coffee must likewise be transnational. A campaign could lobby local governments in Nicaragua and Canada, consumers in Canada, and international law makers at the United Nations. These transnational social movements are broadening our understanding of citizenship and citizenship rights.

13-2   Visit nelson.com/student for additional study tools!

NEL